THE COLLECTED SPEECHES OF
MARGARET THATCHER

THE
COLLECTED SPEECHES
== OF ==
MARGARET THATCHER

EDITED BY

Robin Harris

HarperCollins*Publishers*

This book was originally published in Great Britain in 1997 by HarperCollins Publishers.

FIRST U.S. EDITION

Library of Congress Cataloging-in-Publication Data

Thatcher, Margaret.
    [Speeches]
    The collected speeches of Margaret Thatcher / Margaret Thatcher. — 1st ed.
        p.   cm.
    ISBN 0-06-018734-4
    1. Great Britain—Politics and government—1979–   . 2. Speeches, addresses, etc.,
English. I. Title.
DA591.T47A5 1998
941.085'8'092—dc21   96-47447

98 99 00 01 02 RRD 10 9 8 7 6 5 4 3 2 1

Contents

PART III – THE SECOND PARLIAMENT (1983–87)

PART IV – THE THIRD PARLIAMENT (1987–90)

CONTENTS

PART V – AFTER DOWNING STREET (1990–96)

Acknowledgements

IN COMPILING this collection of speeches I have incurred several obligations. I am grateful to Jason Tomes for the thoroughness of his research for the footnotes and to Debbie Fletcher for the good-humoured efficiency with which she typed and prepared the manuscript. But I am more than grateful to Lady Thatcher herself: without the political education she has given me over the last eleven years I would have lacked the insights necessary to put these speeches into context – and lacked much else besides.

Robin Harris

Introduction

This is not the first published collection of Margaret Thatcher's speeches;[1] but it is by far the most comprehensive. Inevitably, the process of selection reflects in some degree the editor's tastes and temperament. But, happily, many of the speeches are self-selecting. They have come to occupy a place in the unfolding of events that gives them undisputed historical importance. Indeed, some of them can, without running the risk of exaggeration, be said to have 'made history'. Each speech is preceded by a short introduction and accompanied by other factual notes which put it in context and draw out the more important, but sometimes less obvious, themes. Fuller discussion can often be found in the two volumes of Lady Thatcher's memoirs.[2]

Although the 1968 Conservative Political Centre speech is included, for its sketching out of proto-Thatcherism, as is the *Daily Telegraph* article from the 1975 party leadership campaign, the series only really begins with Mrs Thatcher becoming Leader of the Opposition in February 1975. Many of the ideas and themes in the Opposition speeches of 1975–79 would be developed almost (but never quite) out of recognition in the years ahead. Yet these early speeches are already notable for their consistency and breadth of principle. The speaker is clearly as much at ease discussing theology as monetary economics – which irritated her critics so much that they claimed (wrongly) that she confused the two. Domestic and foreign policy appear as parts of a seamless whole, in which the same truths are relevant and usually the same

---

[1] cf. *In Defence of Freedom: Speeches on Britain's Relations with the World 1976–1986*, compiled by Ronald Butt (London, Aurum, 1986); *The Revival of Britain: Speeches on Home and European Affairs 1975–1988*, compiled by Alistair B. Cooke (London, Aurum, 1988).
[2] Abbreviated in the text as I (*The Downing Street Years*) and II (*The Path to Power*).

enemies – in slightly different disguises – are present. There is a didactic quality about these speeches, which reflects the fact that the speaker is seeking to educate and persuade, not simply to seduce or beguile, the audience. There is also a note of urgency. Time seemed short to Mrs Thatcher – both for herself and for Britain.

Speech-making – and speech-writing – in Government, after 1979, were no less important. In power, explanation inevitably has to take second place to action, especially when the Government is confronted by a crisis such as that which engulfed Britain's economy in the first half of that first Parliament. But the words, though fewer, continued to flow, and gained force from the fact that they now clearly reflected the intentions and personality of the Prime Minister who uttered them, and who was so clearly 'not for turning'.

Paradoxically, given the long tradition of martial rhetoric, it is now-adays even more difficult to fashion the right phrases in a military crisis, of the sort represented by the Falklands War, than in an economic one. Margaret Thatcher did not seek to bring her personality into the nation's living rooms, as her hero Winston Churchill had done when she and her family sat round their wireless in Grantham listening to his stirring wartime oratory. It is significant that the Prime Minister's main speeches during the Falklands War were made in the House of Commons; and most of these are to be found in this volume – including many of the interruptions and replies, which alone can give an accurate impression of the atmosphere of half-spoken criticism, doubt and fear against which Margaret Thatcher justified the British Government's conduct in the conflict.

It is no secret that the Falklands War had a deep effect on Mrs Thatcher's approach to her political mission. She had arrived in Downing Street with certain clear views – her critics would have called them prejudices – about foreign and defence policy. But after the Falklands, she spoke with a new conviction as well as a new authority on those matters, which from then on would figure ever more prominently in her speeches. As in earlier years, Mrs Thatcher's distinctive approach was to demonstrate that the same fundamental principles – based on the same convictions – apply to internal and external affairs alike. Consistency and continuity with earlier Thatcher decisions are stressed time and again. And so the message that resolve pays – which had been formulated in overcoming the Labour Government's economic legacy, and then developed as a result of the Falklands – was reinforced in 1984 in the face of a violent miners' strike and then the IRA's attempt to murder the Prime Minister and the Cabinet in Brighton. The myth – which like many other myths conveyed a radical truth – of the 'Iron Lady' was thus burnished by traumatic but largely unconnected events.

Margaret Thatcher's final years as Prime Minister saw some further important developments in the content of her speeches. The emphasis shifted to non-economic themes – as it turned out, all too accurately reflecting a certain degree of inattention to economic essentials when Chancellor of the Exchequer Nigel Lawson embarked on his disastrous policy of shadowing the Deutschmark. In any case, the focus increasingly switched to social policy, on which the 1987 manifesto had proposed a range of far-reaching public sector reforms, and to the environment, on which Mrs Thatcher, with her scientific background, was heard with somewhat unlikely enthusiasm by the 'green' lobby. In foreign affairs, the attention in these years also increasingly moved away from the preoccupations of the Cold War to the threat of European federalism.

In the case of most politicians, indeed in the case of most former Prime Ministers, what they have to say after leaving office is of at best tangential importance. In spite of strenuous assertions by her critics that this dictum is of equal applicability in the case of Margaret Thatcher, the media and the general public have clearly concluded that it is not. Her speeches since leaving Downing Street, no longer constrained by collective responsibility, have not only restated but consciously developed the Thatcherite approach. Their impact has often been measured in domestic political terms by the degree of criticism they imply of her successor. But in fact their scope and purpose have been principally international. The dominant themes are the passing (or perhaps more accurately the stillbirth) of the 'new world order', the threat of trade protectionism, the tendency to appeasement of military aggression, short-sightedness in dealing with the ex-communist countries and, of course, the increasingly assertive drive towards a European super-state.

With the Keith Joseph Memorial Lecture in January 1996 we come full circle. The consistency, the applicability and the political potency of the Joseph/Thatcher prescription of limited government are demonstrated by the speaker – and confirmed by the furore with which the speech was received. The collection continues with three foreign policy speeches: one in Fulton, Missouri, fifty years on from Churchill's 'Iron Curtain' address; a speech to a conference dedicated to relaunching

Atlanticism, held in Prague; and a speech containing tactful but forceful messages to China's leaders, delivered in Beijing. All three point to new challenges facing the post-Cold War world and offer new as well as traditional prescriptions to deal with them. The collection ends with Lady Thatcher's Nicholas Ridley Lecture – her final major speech before the 1997 general election, and a crushing indictment of socialism in all its guises.

SPEECH-WRITING

[Speech-writing] often continued long into the night and can perhaps be described as fraught but fun. (I, p. 303)

Where discretion overflows into deviousness is, for most national politicians, a moot point. But for Margaret Thatcher there has never been any evident temptation – perhaps temperamentally there was never much possibility – of her believing one set of propositions and publicly subscribing to another. This makes her speeches of relatively greater importance for any understanding of her character and philosophy than would be the case for her predecessors or contemporaries (or successors).

Moreover, though polished presentation was important, it was never allowed to determine content. Quite the opposite, in fact. Speeches were primarily instruments of policy, not of propaganda – though the propagandist element was not neglected either. As Margaret Thatcher describes in her memoirs, the preparation of speeches was a means of analyzing, refining and (on occasion) formulating the Government's approach. And this was done by means of gathering and then dissecting huge quantities of information – quotations, statistics, cuttings – and arranging them around certain assertions of belief, which would themselves have to be restated from first principles.

An early insight into this frustrating but fruitful *modus operandi* is provided by the first speech in this volume. As the memoirs relate:

There is no better way to clarify your own thinking than to try to explain it clearly to someone else. I was conscious that there were great issues being discussed in politics at this time [the late 1960s]. Whatever else can be said of the sixties they were intellectually lively, even if too many of the ideas motivating change originated on the left. I took armfuls of books on philosophy, politics and history, White Papers, Hansard Society publications and speeches down to Lamberhurst [the Thatcher weekend home]. I had no one to guide or help me so I just plunged in. Like the proverbial iceberg, most of the work lay below the surface of the document I finally wrote. (II, p. 148)

It is possible to criticize such an approach to speech-writing for the time and effort it demanded. But this was the raw method that in later years would be given more sophisticated form when there were others 'to guide and help' the expression of Margaret Thatcher's ideas. It was, indeed, still apparent when the Leader's first (1975) Party Conference speech had to be written.

I told my speech-writers that I was not going to make just an economic speech. The economy had gone wrong because something else had gone wrong spiritually and philosophically. The economic crisis was a crisis of the spirit of the nation. But when I discussed the kind of draft I wanted with Chris Patten and others from the Research Department, I felt they were just not getting the message I wanted to despatch. So I sat down at home over the weekend and wrote out sixty pages of my large handwriting. I found no difficulty: it flowed and flowed. But was it a speech? (II, pp. 305–6)

In fact, fairly clearly it was not. Mrs Thatcher's material was integrated into other contributions and reworked by the playwright Ronnie Millar. But anyone who reads that first – and arguably best – Thatcher Party Conference speech will have no doubt that the ideas at the heart of it are not merely Mrs Thatcher's: the whole speech can even now be read as a succinct and undated definition of 'Thatcherism'.

There are two prevalent if contradictory myths about speech-writing. One is that politicians write all their own speeches. This, for leading figures at least, is almost impossible; and if they try to do so, they will fail to give the necessary time and energy to their other tasks. The other, opposing, myth is that it is the speech-writers who tell the politicians what to say and, presumably, think. With the exception of certain undistinguished and unintelligent political figures, this too is misleading. The speech-writer can always best do his work by formulating, perhaps more clearly, the thoughts of those who will deliver the words, not foisting on them his own thoughts. Certainly, with Margaret Thatcher speech-

writers may have on occasion to be mind-readers, but never ventrilo-
quists. And the Thatcher voice, however well modulated and tuned over
the years in Opposition, retained the same, distinctive *timbre* to be heard
in speeches twenty years later.

In Mrs Thatcher's case the process of speech-writing, as she herself
records, was a tense and troublesome – if, for those with thick skins and
strong nerves and views, satisfying – process, in which a wide array of
individual contributions were turned into the final text. As each draft
was reworked, the form and shape of the contents subtly changed to
become something different. What precisely did that final version represent? Certainly, in varying degrees it reflected the thoughts and phrases
of the speech-writers; certainly, too, it produced a text very different
from that which Mrs Thatcher herself might have sat down to write
without advice, argument or assistance; and yet undeniably the end
product was 'Thatcher'.

Referring to one of the final speeches in the 1983 general election
campaign, she recalls:

> On my return to No. 10 work began almost at once on the speech
> I was to deliver the next day at our Youth Rally at Wembley
> Conference Centre. My speech-writers and I worked late into the
> night, breaking for a hot meal which I served up in the kitchen
> from the capacious store of precooked frozen food I always kept
> there for such occasions. Shepherd's pie and a glass of wine can
> do a great deal to improve morale. Speech-writing was for me an
> important political activity. As one of my speech-writers said, 'No
> one writes speeches for Mrs Thatcher: they write speeches with Mrs
> Thatcher.' Every written word goes through the mincing machine of
> my criticism before it gets into a speech. These are occasions for
> thinking creatively and politically and for fashioning larger themes
> into which particular policies fit. I often found myself drawing on
> phrases and ideas from these sessions when I was speaking off the
> cuff, answering questions at Prime Minister's Question Time and
> for television interviews. This helped to preserve me from the occu-
> pational hazard of long-serving ministers; so I was never accused
> of thinking like a civil servant. (They had to think like me.) (I,
> pp. 302–3)

But if the basic approach to a Thatcher speech remained unchanged,
over the years the preparatory procedures became steadily more com-

plex. This particularly applied to the annual Party Conference speech, which Lady Thatcher soon recognized to be *sui generis*.

> The Leader's speech at a Party Conference is quite unlike the Conference speeches of other front-bench spokesmen. It has to cover a sufficiently wide number of subjects to avoid the criticism that one has 'left out' some burning issue. Yet each section of the speech has to have a thematic correspondence with all the other sections. Otherwise, you finish up with what I used to call a 'Christmas tree', on which pledges and achievements are hung and where each new topic is classically announced by the mind-numbing phrase 'I now turn to . . .'. A powerful speech of the sort required to inspire the Party faithful, as well as easing the worries of the doubters, is in some ways more like a piece of poetry than prose. Not that one should be tempted to use flowery language, but rather that it is the ideas, sentiments and mood below the surface which count. Material which could easily form a clear and persuasive article may be altogether inappropriate for a speech. And although one has to scrutinize a text to ensure the removal of dangerous ambiguities, an effective speech may afterwards read almost lamely in cold print. (II, p. 305)

Lady Thatcher has described in some detail the preparation of the 1986 Party Conference speech, especially important since that looked like being (and in fact turned out to be) the final Conference of the Parliament.

> Throughout the year I had collected in a file called 'ideas for speeches' articles, speeches and different briefing and policy items which came across my desk . . . During the summer recess I would have a meeting to discuss the general themes I should put across in my Conference speech. Speech contributions were commissioned from ministers, advisers, friendly journalists, and academics. On this occasion we began speech-writing with no fewer than twelve separate contributions and two and a half hefty files of background material. The weekend before the Conference different draft speech sections would be laid out and put together – literally – along the table in the Great Parlour at Chequers. Linking passages would be written and then the still disjointed and often repetitive first draft would be typed up. Everyone breathed a sigh of relief when they

knew that we at least had a speech of some sort; even though past experience suggested that this might bear little relationship to the final text. Then would come the long hours of refining and polishing until midnight (if we were lucky).

On the Friday morning I used to mark up the text with my own special code, noting pauses, stress and where to have my voice rise or fall. (I, pp. 567–8)

As the reader leafs through the speeches in this volume, he will certainly find some that are more elegant and profound than others. The tone and the occasion – even, unusually for politicians, the jokes – vary. But he will undoubtedly conclude that these are the words of a woman who knows her own mind and who has changed the minds of countless others.

A NOTE ON THE SOURCES

There are no significant textual difficulties in assembling a collection of speeches by a senior modern politician in an age when press releases and, increasingly, television provide a faithful account of what was said. (Hansard is, of course, the source for speeches in Parliament.) Where a press-released text contains an obvious misconstruction, the speech text has here been altered. Some punctuation changes have been made for the sake of clarity or consistency. In the case of several Party speeches the introductory banter which meant much to the audience but has no significance (or sometimes sense) now has also been omitted. Otherwise those speeches are reproduced 'warts and all'; though, all things considered, there are remarkably few warts.

I

OPPOSITION YEARS

Address to the Conservative Political Centre, Blackpool, 10 October 1968

The October 1968 Conservative Political Centre (CPC) Lecture was Mrs Thatcher's first public foray into 'Conservatism'. It was made at an important time for her and for the Tory Party. Enoch Powell's speech on immigration that April[1] and his criticisms of the collectivist economic management practised in the sixties by both Labour and Conservative administrations had produced much upheaval and some rethinking. Margaret Thatcher, though by October 1968 handling the Fuel and Power portfolio within the Shadow Cabinet, had cut her political teeth as Shadow Chancellor Iain Macleod's deputy, with special responsibility for exposing the absurdities of Labour's prices and incomes policy. Both Powellite – what would later be called 'monetarist' – influence and Mrs Thatcher's personal experience of dissecting socialist economic regulation are evident in the lecture. The underlying issue, which she does not fully tackle, though, is whether the causes of inflation – and so by implication the cures for it – are monetary or can be ascribed to the 'wage push' of trade unions. In her memoirs, Lady Thatcher notes of the speech that it 'summed up how far my understanding of these matters had gone – and how far it still needed to go'. (II, p. 149)

WHAT'S WRONG WITH POLITICS?

Criticism of politics is no new thing. Literature abounds with it.

In Shakespeare we find the comment of King Lear:

---

[1] Delivered in Birmingham on 20 April 1968, the speech called for an end to New Commonwealth immigration and for assisted voluntary repatriation. Tory Party Leader Edward Heath took exception to the language used and sacked Powell from the Shadow Cabinet.

'Get thee glass eyes;
And, like a scurvy politician, seem
To see the things thou dost not.'

Richard Sheridan,[1] reputed to have made one of the greatest speeches the House of Commons has ever heard (it lasted five hours and forty minutes), commented that 'conscience has more to do with gallantry than it has with politics.' Anatole France[2] was perhaps the most scathing: 'I am not so devoid of all talents as to occupy myself with politics.'

Nor have political leaders escaped criticism:

Disraeli[3] unites the maximum of Parliamentary cleverness with the minimum of statesmanlike capacity. No one ever dreams to have him lead. He belongs not to the bees but to the wasps and the butterflies of public life. He can sting and sparkle but he cannot work. His place in the arena is marked and ticketed for ever.

This from the Controller of the Stationery Office, in 1853, quoted in *The Statesman* by Henry Taylor. There is no need to remind you how utterly wrong that judgement was.

There are even some things that have improved over the years. Bribery and corruption, which have now gone, used to be rampant. The votes of electors were purchased at a high price. The famous Lord Shaftesbury,[4] when he was Lord Ashley, spent £15,600 on successfully winning Dorset in 1831. It is interesting to note that £12,000 of this went to public houses and inns for the refreshment of the people. And this when gin was a penny a glass! Some forty years before, Lord Penrhyn[5] spent £30,000 on his campaign – and then lost!

But we can't dismiss the present criticisms as easily as that. The

---

[1] Richard Brinsley Sheridan (1751–1816), Irish-born dramatist and politician. Foxite Whig MP 1780–1812; Under-Secretary for Foreign Affairs 1782; Secretary to the Treasury 1783; Treasurer of the Navy 1806–07. The speech in question called for the impeachment of Warren Hastings in 1787.
[2] Anatole France (1844–1924), French novelist, poet and critic.
[3] Benjamin Disraeli (1804–81), Earl of Beaconsfield 1876. English statesman and novelist. Conservative MP 1837–76; Chancellor of the Exchequer 1852, 1858–59, 1866–68; Leader of the Conservative Party 1868–81; Prime Minister 1868, 1874–80.
[4] Anthony Ashley Cooper (1801–85), 7th Earl of Shaftesbury 1851, social and industrial reformer, founder of the Ragged Schools Movement. Tory MP 1826–46; Lord of the Admiralty 1834–35.
[5] Richard Pennant (c.1737–1808), 1st Baron Penrhyn of Penrhyn 1783. Whig MP 1761–80, 1784–90.

dissatisfaction with politics runs too deep both here and abroad. People have come to doubt the future of the democratic system and its institutions. They distrust the politicians and have little faith in the future.

Why the Present Distrust?

Let us try to assess how and why we have reached this pass. What is the explanation? Broadly speaking, I think we have not yet assimilated many of the changes that have come about in the past thirty to forty years.

First, I don't think we realize sufficiently how new our present democratic system is. We still have comparatively little experience of the effect of the universal franchise, which didn't come until 1928. And the first election in this country which was fought on the principle of one person one vote was in 1950.[1] So we are still in the early stages of dealing with the problems and opportunities presented by everyone having a vote.

Secondly, this and other factors have led to a different party political structure. There is now little room for independent Members, and the controversies which formerly took place outside the parties on a large number of measures now have to take place inside. There is, and has to be, room for a variety of opinions on certain topics within the broad general principles on which each party is based.

Thirdly, from the party structure has risen the detailed programme which is placed before the electorate. Return to power on such a programme had led to a new doctrine that the party in power has a mandate to carry out everything in its manifesto. I myself doubt whether the voters really are endorsing each and every particular when they return a Government to power.

This modern practice of an election programme has, I believe, influenced the attitudes of some electors; all too often one is now asked, 'What are you going to do for me?', implying that the programme is a series of promises in return for votes. All this has led to a curious relationship between elector and elected. If the elector suspects the politician of making promises simply to get his vote, he despises him, but if the promises are not forthcoming he may reject him. I believe that

---

[1] The Equal Franchise Act 1928 lowered the voting age for women from thirty to twenty-one. The Representation of the People Act 1948 abolished business and university votes for Parliamentary elections.

parties and elections are about more than rival lists of miscellaneous promises – indeed, if they were not, democracy would scarcely be worth preserving.

Fourthly, the extensive and all-pervading development of the Welfare State is also comparatively new, not only here but in other countries as well. You will recollect that one of the four great freedoms in President Roosevelt's wartime declaration was 'freedom from want'.[1] Since then in the Western world there has been a series of measures designed to give greater security. I think it would be true to say that there is no longer a struggle to achieve a basic security. Further, we have a complete new generation whose whole life has been lived against the background of the Welfare State. These developments must have had a great effect on the outlook and approach of our people, even if we cannot yet assess it properly.

Fifthly, one of the effects of the rapid spread of higher education has been to equip people to criticize and question almost everything. Some of them seem to have stopped there, instead of going on to the next stage which is to arrive at new beliefs or to reaffirm old ones. You will perhaps remember seeing in the press the report that the student leader Daniel Cohn-Bendit[2] has been awarded a degree on the result of his past work. His examiners said that he had posed a series of most intelligent questions. Significant? I would have been happier had he also found a series of intelligent answers.

Sixthly, we have far more information about events than ever before; and since the advent of television, news is presented much more vividly. It is much more difficult to ignore situations which you have seen on film with your own eyes than if you have merely read about them, perhaps skimming the page rather hurriedly. Television is not merely one extra means of communication, it is a medium which because of the way it presents things is radically influencing the judgements we have to make about events and about people, including politicians.

Seventhly, our innate international idealism has received many nasty shocks. Many of our people long to believe that if representatives of all nations get together dispassionately to discuss burning international problems, providence and goodwill will guide them to wise and just

[1] Franklin Delano Roosevelt (1882–1945), 32nd President of the USA 1933–45 (Democrat), enunciated the Four Freedoms in an address to Congress on 6 January 1941.
[2] Daniel Cohn-Bendit (born 1945), Franco-German anarcho-communist, was a leader of the student revolt at the University of Paris in 1968.

conclusions, and peace and international law and order will thereby be secured. But in practice a number of nations vote not according to right or wrong even when it is a clear case to us, but according to their national expediencies. And some of the speeches and propaganda to explain blatant actions would make the angels weep as well as the electorate.

All of these things are a partial explanation of the disillusion and disbelief we encounter today. The changes have been tremendous and I am not surprised that the whole system is under cross-examination. I welcome healthy scepticism and questioning. It is our job continually to retest old assumptions and to seek new ideas. But we must not try to find one unalterable answer that will solve all our problems for none can exist.

You may know the story of the soldier of fortune who once asked the Sphinx to reveal the divine wisdom of the ages in one sentence, and the Sphinx said, 'Don't expect too much.'

In that spirit and against the background I have sketched, let us try to analyse what has gone wrong.

The Great Mistake – Too Much Government

I believe that the great mistake of the last few years has been for the Government to provide or to legislate for almost everything. Part of this policy has its roots in the plans for reconstruction in the post-war period when Governments assumed all kinds of new obligations. The policies may have been warranted at the time, but they have gone far further than was intended or is advisable.

During our own early and middle period of government we were concerned to set the framework in which people could achieve their own standards for themselves, subject always to a basic standard. But it has often seemed to me that from the early 1960s the emphasis in politics shifted. At about that time 'growth' became the key political word. If resources grew by X per cent per annum this would provide the extra money needed for the Government to make further provision. The doctrine found favour at the time and we had a bit of a contest between the parties about the highest possible growth rate. Four per cent or more. But the result was that for the time being the emphasis in political debate ceased to be about people and became about economics. Plans were made to achieve a 4 per cent growth rate.[1] Then came the present Government with a bigger plan and socialist ideas about its implementation – that is to say, if people didn't conform to the plan, they had to be compelled to. Hence compulsion on prices and incomes policy, and with it the totally unacceptable notion that the Government shall have the power to fix which wages and salaries should increase.[2] We started off with a wish on the part of the people for more Government intervention in certain spheres. This was met. But there came a time when the amount of intervention got so great that it could no longer be exercised in practice by Government but only by more and more officials or bureaucrats. Now, it is difficult if not impossible for people to get at the official making the decision and so, paradoxically, although the degree of intervention is greater, the Government has become more and more remote from the people. The present result of the democratic process has, therefore, been an increasing authoritarianism.

During July the *Daily Telegraph* published a rather interesting poll which showed how people were reacting against this rule of impersonal authority. The question was: 'In your opinion, do people like yourselves have enough say or not in the way the Government runs the country (68 per cent 'not enough'), the services provided by the nationalized industries (67 per cent 'not enough'), the way local authorities handle things (64 per cent 'not enough'). Note this rather high figure; people don't like remote local authorities any more than they like remote Governments.

Recently, more and more feature articles have been written and speeches made about involving people more closely with decisions of the Government and enabling them to participate in some of those decisions.

But the way to get personal involvement and participation is not for people to take part in more and more Government decisions but to make the Government reduce the area of decision over which it presides and consequently leave the private citizen to 'participate', if that be the fashionable word, by making more of his own decisions. What we need now is a far greater degree of personal responsibility and decision, far

[1] The 4 per cent growth target was proposed in 1962 by the National Economic Development Council.

[2] The National Plan, published in 1965, set out to secure 3.8 per cent economic growth per annum for the next five years. The Prices and Incomes Act 1966 gave the Government power to freeze wages and prices. By 1968 the National Plan had been abandoned.

more independence from the Government, and a comparative reduction in the role of Government.

These beliefs have important implications for policy.

Prices and Incomes

First, prices and incomes policy. The most effective prices policy has not come by controlling prices by the Government, through the Prices and Incomes Board,[1] but through the Conservative way of seeing that competition flourishes. There have been far more price cuts in the supermarkets than in the nationalized industries. This shows the difference between the Government doing the job itself and the Government creating the conditions under which prices will be kept down through effective competition.

On the incomes side, there seemed to be some confusion in the minds of the electorate about where the parties stood. This was not surprising in the early days because a number of speeches and documents from both sides of the House showed a certain similarity. For example, here are four separate quotations – two from the Labour Government and two from our period in office. They are almost indistinguishable.

1. 'Increases in the general level of wage rates must be related to increased productivity due to increased efficiency and effort.' (White Paper on Employment Policy, 1944)

2. 'It is essential, therefore, that there should be no further general increase in the level of personal incomes without at least a corresponding increase in the volume of production.' (Sir Stafford Cripps, 1948[2]

3. 'The Government's policy is to promote a faster rate of economic growth . . . But the policy will be put in jeopardy if money incomes rise faster than the volume of national production.' (Para. 1 of 'Incomes Policy, The Next Step', Cmmd 1626, February 1962)

[1] The National Board for Prices and Incomes was established in April 1965 and abolished in November 1970.
[2] Sir Stafford Cripps (1889–1952), Labour MP 1931–50; Lord Privy Seal 1942; Minister of Aircraft Production 1942–45; President of the Board of Trade 1945–47; Minister for Economic Affairs 1947; Chancellor of the Exchequer 1947–50.

4. '. . . the major objectives of national policy must be . . . to raise productivity and efficiency so that real national output can increase and so keep increases in wages, salaries and other forms of income in line with this increase.' (Schedule 2, Prices and Incomes Act 1966)

All of these quotes express general economic propositions, but the policies which flowed from those propositions were very different. We rejected from the outset the use of compulsion. This was absolutely right. The role of the Government is not to control each and every salary that is paid. It has no means of measuring the correct amount. Moreover, having to secure the state's approval before one increases the pay of an employee is repugnant to most of us.

There is another aspect of the way in which incomes policy is now operated to which I must draw attention. We now put so much emphasis on the control of incomes that we have too little regard for the essential role of Government, which is the control of money supply and management of demand. Greater attention to this role, and less to the outward detailed control, would have achieved more for the economy. It would mean, of course, that the Government had to exercise itself some of the disciplines on expenditure it is so anxious to impose on others. It would mean that expenditure in the vast public sector would not have to be greater than the amount which could be financed out of taxation plus genuine saving. For a number of years some expenditure has been financed by what amounts to printing the money. There is nothing *laissez-faire* or old-fashioned about the views I have expressed. It is a modern view of the role the Government should play now, arising from the mistakes of the past, the results of which we are experiencing today.

Tax and the Social Services

The second policy implication concerns taxation and the social services. It is no accident that the Conservative Party has been one which has reduced the rates of taxation. The decisions have not been a haphazard set of expedients, or merely economic decisions to meet the needs of the moment. They have stemmed from the real belief that Government intervention and control tend to reduce the role of the individual, his importance, and the desirability that he should be primarily responsible for his own future. When it comes to the development of the social services, the policy must mean that people should be encouraged, if necessary by taxation incentives, to make increasing provision for themselves out of their own resources. The basic standards through the state would remain as a foundation for extra private provision. Such a policy would have the advantage that the Government could concentrate on providing things which the citizen can't. Hospitals are one specific example.

The other day I came across a quotation which you will find difficult to place.

Such a plan as this was bound to be drastic and to express nothing less than a new pattern . . . [for the hospitals of this country] . . . Now that we have it, we must see that it lives. As I have said before, it is a plan which has hands and feet. It walks and it works. It is not a static conception stated once and for all, but something which is intended to live and to be dynamic . . . My Ministry will constantly be carrying this review forward so that there will always be ten years' work definitely projected ahead. (Hansard, 4 June 1962, Col 153)

No, it doesn't come from Harold Wilson.[1] It is not about our enormous overall plan, but a very limited plan in a small area in which the Government could make a distinctive contribution. It was Enoch Powell[2] introducing his ten-year hospital plan in the House of Commons on 4 June 1962.

Independence from the State

To return to the personal theme, if we accept the need for increasing responsibility for self and family it means that we must stop approaching things in an atmosphere of restriction. There is nothing wrong in people wanting larger incomes. It would seem a worthy objective for men and women to wish to raise the standard of living for their families and to give them greater opportunities than they themselves had. I wish more

[1] Harold Wilson (1916–95), Baron Wilson of Rievaulx 1983. Labour MP 1945–83; President of the Board of Trade 1947–51; Leader of the Labour Party 1963–76; Prime Minister 1964–70, 1974–76.
[2] Enoch Powell (born 1912), Conservative MP 1950–74; Ulster Unionist MP 1974–87; Financial Secretary to the Treasury 1957–58; Minister of Health 1960–63.

people would do it. We should then have fewer saying 'The state must do it.' What is wrong is that people should want more without giving anything in return. The condition precedent to high wages and high salaries is hard work. This is a quite different and much more stimulating approach than one of keeping down incomes.

Doubtless, there will be accusations that we are only interested in more money. This just is not so. Money is not an end in itself. It enables one to live the kind of life of one's own choosing. Some will prefer to put a large amount to raising material standards; others will pursue music, the arts, the cultures; others will use their money to help those here and overseas about whose needs they feel strongly – and do not let us underestimate the amount of hard-earned cash that this nation gives voluntarily to worthy causes. The point is that even the Good Samaritan had to have the money to help, otherwise he too would have had to pass by on the other side.

In choice of way of life, J.S. Mill's[1] views are as relevant as ever.

> The only freedom which deserves the name is that of pursuing our own good in our own way so long as we do not deprive others of theirs, or impede their efforts to obtain it . . . Mankind are greater gainers by suffering each other to live as seems good to themselves, than by compelling each to live as seems good to the rest.

These policies have one further important implication. Together they succeed at the same time in giving people a measure of independence from the state. And who wants a people dependent on the state and turning to the state for their every need? Also they succeed in drawing power away from Governments and diffusing it more widely among people and non-Governmental institutions.

The Problem of Size

The second mistake politics have made at present is in some ways related to the first one. We have become bewitched by the idea of size.

As a result, people no longer feel important in the scheme of things. They have the impression that everything has become so big, so organ-

---

[1] John Stuart Mill (1806–73), British philosopher and economist. Radical MP 1865–68. The quotation is from Chapter One of *On Liberty* (1859).

ized, so standardized and governmentalized that there is no room for the individual, his talents, his requirements or his wishes. He no longer counts.

It is not difficult to see how this feeling has come about. In industry the merits of size have been extolled for some years now and too little attention given to its demerits. Size brings great problems. One of the most important is the problem of making and communicating decisions. The task of decision tends to be concentrated at the top, and fewer people get used to weighing up a problem, taking a decision, sticking to it and carrying the consequences. The buck is passed. But even after a decision has been made, there is the problem of communicating it to those who have to carry it out in such a way that it is understood, and they are made to feel a part of the team. In a large-scale organization, whether Government, local government or industry, failure to do this can lead to large-scale mistakes, large-scale confusion and large-scale resentment. These problems can, and must, be overcome, but all too often they are not.

Government Agencies and the Public

The third mistake is that people feel they don't count when they try to get something done through Government agencies.

Consider our relations with Government departments. We start as a birth certificate; attract a maternity grant; give rise to a tax allowance and possibly a family allowance; receive a National Health number when registered with a doctor; go to one or more schools where educational records are kept; apply for an educational grant; get a job; start paying National Insurance and tax; take out a television and a driving licence; buy a house with a mortgage; pay rates; buy a few premium bonds; take out life assurance; purchase some shares; get married; start the whole thing over again; receive a pension and become a death certificate and death grant, and the subject of a file in the Estate Duty Office! Every one of these incidents will require a form or give rise to some questions, or be recorded in some local or national government office. The amount of information collected in the various departments must be fabulous. Small wonder that life really does seem like 'one damned form after another'.

A good deal of this form-filling will have to continue, but I think it time to reassert a right to privacy. Ministers will have to look at this aspect in deciding how to administer their policies. There is a tendency on the part of some politicians to suggest that with the advent of computers all this information should be centralized and stored on magnetic tape. They argue that this would be time-saving and more efficient. Possibly it would; but other and more important things would be at stake. There would be produced for the first time a personal dossier about each person, on which everything would be recorded. In my view, this would place far too much power in the hands of the state over the individual. In the USA, there is a Congressional Inquiry sitting on this very point because politicians there have recognized the far-reaching dangers of such a record.

Too Much Reliance on Statistics, Too Little on Judgement

Fourthly, I believe that there is too great a reliance on statistical forecasts; too little on judgement.

We all know the old one about lies, damned lies and statistics,[1] and I do not wish to condemn statistics out of hand. Those who prepare them are well aware of their limitations. Those who use them are not so scrupulous.

Recently, the economic forecasts have been far more optimistic than the events which happened. The balance of payments predictions have been wrong and wrong again. For example, in February this year the National Institute of Economic and Social Research forecast predicted a *surplus* of £100 million in the second half of this year. In August they predicted a *deficit* of £600 million for the whole of this year, but a surplus of £250 million *next* year. They commented, 'The balance of payments forecast taken year by year looks a lot worse than previously estimated, but the difference is largely one of timing – with the movement into surplus coming later, and with a still large rate of improvement.'

The truth is that statistical results do not displace the need for judgement, they increase it. The figures can be no better than the assumptions on which they are based, and these could vary greatly. In addition, the unknown factor which, by its very nature, is incapable of evaluation, may well be the determining one.

---

[1] 'There are three kinds of lies: lies, damned lies, and statistics' – a remark attributed to Benjamin Disraeli.

The Party Political System

Fifthly, we have not yet appreciated or used fully the virtues of our party political system. The essential characteristic of the British constitutional system is not that there is an alternative personality but that there is an alternative policy and a whole alternative Government ready to take office. As a result, we have always had an Opposition to act as a focus of criticism against the Government. We have, therefore, not suffered the fate of countries which have had a 'consensus' government, without an official opposition. This was one of the causes of trouble in Germany.[1] Nor do we have the American system, which as far as presidential campaigns go, appears to have become almost completely one of personalities.

There are dangers in consensus; it could be an attempt to satisfy people holding no particular views about anything. It seems more important to have a philosophy and policy which, because they are good, appeal to sufficient people to secure a majority.

A short time ago when I was speaking to a university audience and stressing the theme of personal responsibility and independence, a young undergraduate came to me and said, 'I had no idea there was such a clear alternative.' He found the idea challenging and infinitely more effective than one in which everyone virtually expects their MP or the Government to solve their problems.

The Conservative creed has never offered a life of ease without effort. Democracy is not for such people. Self-government is for those men and women who have learned to govern themselves. No great party can survive except on the basis of firm beliefs about what it wants to do. It is not enough to have reluctant support. We want people's enthusiasm as well.

---

[1] The reference is to disputes within the CDU-SPD 'Grand Coalition' Government of West Germany of 1966–69.

2

Article in the *Daily Telegraph*, 30 January 1975

Each of the three candidates in the first round of the Tory leadership election –
Margaret Thatcher, Edward Heath, Hugh Fraser – wrote articles for the main
Conservative newspaper, the Daily Telegraph. *Although Mrs Thatcher was still*
the rank outsider, she had already demonstrated her staying power by overcoming
personal campaigns launched against her – for allegedly 'hoarding' food at a time of
shortage, and for being too 'middle class'. Echoes of the second charge can be found
in the Telegraph *article. The attack was turned back on her opponents, who (the*
article implies) had lost the support of the traditional Conservative-voting middle
classes, and indeed of those who aspired to join the middle classes. The return to bedrock
Tory values and beliefs proved a popular theme among Conservative backbenchers:
in the first ballot on Tuesday 4 February Mrs Thatcher won 130 votes to Ted
Heath's 119.

MY KIND OF TORY PARTY

One of the most hackneyed of political quotations is Disraeli's dictum
that the Tory Party 'is a national party or it is nothing'. Yet it means
more than the obvious truths that Conservatives must put the interests
of the whole nation first and must seek their electoral support among
all classes and sections of the community. It means also that the Party
cannot long survive unless its policies are in tune with the deepest and
best instincts of the British people.

Two electoral defeats in a year do not represent total disaster;[1] but

[1] General election, 28 February 1974: Labour 301 seats, Conservatives 297, Liberals
14, Scottish Nationalists 7, Plaid Cymru 2, others 14. General election, 10 October
1974: Labour 319, Conservatives 277, Liberals 13, Scottish Nationalists 11, Plaid Cymru
3, others 12.

they could prove to be the beginning of a disastrous decline unless Conservatives have the courage and humility to examine the reasons for their defeat and ask themselves in what respects they have failed the British people.

To deny that we failed the people is futile, as well as arrogant. Successful Governments win elections. So do parties with broadly acceptable policies. We lost.

I was a member of the last Conservative Cabinet, from 1970 to 1974, with a share in the collective responsibility for its policies. It seems to me that this involves a further responsibility – to recognize the failures and to try to see that the mistakes are not repeated.

Probably no Chancellor, faced with the mass of conflicting advice that poured in during the early 1970s, could have got the balance between unemployment and inflation exactly right. The same problem faces Mr Healey[1] now – and it looks as if inflation is going to win again. Yet two lessons do emerge from our own experience. The first is that in the long run rapid inflation is the worst enemy and must at almost all costs be brought under control. The second is that we must never again allow a preoccupation with macro-economics and industrial growth to blind us to the day-to-day problems of ordinary people, in all walks of life.

Politicians should not be either professional efficiency experts or amateur industrial consultants. Their concern is with people, and they must look at every problem from the grassroots, not from the top looking down. International interest rates must be thought of in terms of the young couple's mortgage as well as of the balance of payments.

Politicians must be equally wary of political ideologies. It is not our business to plan the educational system as a sociological abstraction. Our job is to see that children and young people receive the education they need. 'Equality of opportunity' is a poor guide if it means the same mediocre schooling for all. The object is to provide a varied system which will give every child the best chance to develop individual intelligence and talents.

As Secretary of State, I encouraged the Direct Grant schools,[2] and tried to prevent the destruction of good maintained grammar schools, because they had provided a unique and irreplaceable educational ladder

[1] Denis Healey (born 1917), Baron Healey of Riddlesden 1992. Labour MP 1952–92; Defence Secretary 1964–70; Chancellor of the Exchequer 1974–79; Deputy Leader of the Labour Party 1980–83.

[2] Direct Grant schools, entry to which was often highly competitive, received direct funding from the Department of Education and Science and were outside local control.

for the bright children of poor parents. Socialist policies now will create a new class of deprived children.

I was attacked for fighting a rearguard action in defence of 'middle-class interests'. The same accusation is levelled at me now, when I am leading Conservative opposition to the socialist Capital Transfer Tax proposals.[1] Well, if 'middle class values' include the encouragement of variety and individual choice, the provision of fair incentives and rewards for skill and hard work, the maintenance of effective barriers against the excessive power of the state and a belief in the wide distribution of individual *private* property, then they are certainly what I am trying to defend.

This is not a fight for 'privilege'; it is a fight for freedom – freedom for *every* citizen.

The Capital Transfer Tax proposals could destroy – or nationalize – a medium-sized family business in two generations and a small farm in one. Industry and agriculture would increasingly become either state-controlled or concentrated into larger units. And experience has shown that neither process makes for long-term efficiency or good labour relations.

Worse still, if both saving and enterprise are penalized, those who can do most to increase the prosperity of the workers will simply take their money and their skills abroad.

Mr Healey makes no pretence that his proposals will redistribute wealth in favour of the poor – only in favour of the state. In the end they will destroy *all* wealth, to the detriment of all.

If a Tory does not believe that private property is one of the main bulwarks of individual freedom, then he had better become a socialist and have done with it. Indeed one of the reasons for our electoral failure is that people believe too many Conservatives *have* become socialists already. Britain's progress towards socialism has been an alternation of two steps forward with half a step back.

If every Labour Government is prepared to reverse every Tory measure, while Conservative Governments accept nearly all socialist measures as being 'the will of the people', the end result is only too plain. And why should anyone support a party that seems to have the courage of no convictions?

I cannot agree with those of my colleagues who attribute our loss of

---

[1] The Finance Act 1975 introduced a Capital Transfer Tax on gifts and bequests, starting at 10 per cent on transfers of £15,000 and rising to 75 per cent on transfers of over £2 million.

support in industrial areas to a 'middle-class image' and the provisions of the Industrial Relations Act,[1] urging us to pin our faith on 'industrial democracy' and 'co-partnership'. I do not believe these panaceas mean much to many workers. If management is bad and does not adequately consult its workers, it deserves to fail. Our job is to create conditions in which good management can succeed.

We lost because we did not appear to stand firmly for anything distinctive and positive. Sneering at 'middle-class values' is to insult the working class no less than the *bourgeois*. Do British workers have no deep feelings for freedom, for order, for the education of their children, for the right to work without disruption by political militants?

Of course they do. And if they are no more than cash-grabbing anarchists, then we must all bear some of the responsibility and try to show them the way back to sanity. But I do not believe they are.

Most of them want to do a fair day's work in a job that gives them satisfaction – and strongly resent what they regard as state subsidies to shirkers. Most of them deplore violence, truancy and indiscipline in schools, and cannot understand the complaisance of some of the middle-class intellectuals who run the schools.

Of course we must try to understand the *causes* of violence and protest, and try to remove them. But the violence itself must be checked, for it menaces the freedom and the rights of the majority.

My kind of Tory Party would make no secret of its belief in individual freedom and individual prosperity, in the maintenance of law and order, in the wide distribution of private property, in rewards for energy, skill and thrift, in diversity of choice, in the preservation of local rights in local communities.

Size is not all, any more than economic growth is all. Even efficiency is not enough. People come first – their needs, their hopes, their choice, their values and ideals. We have to understand these first – to be *seen* to be listening with sympathy and concern. It is important to be able to lead, certainly. But you cannot for long lead people where they do not want to go.

'Only connect'? Perhaps this is the first essential. It seems to me that our connections have come loose. I should like to do what I can to help repair them.

---

[1] The Industrial Relations Act 1971 created a new system of labour law, whereby collective bargaining agreements could be legally enforced by industrial courts. The trade unions obstructed its operation, and the Act was repealed in 1974.

3

Speech to the Conservative Central Council, Harrogate, 15 March 1975

Her address to the Conservative Central Council at Harrogate was the first major public speech Mrs Thatcher gave after becoming Party Leader (as a result of the outcome of the second ballot for the leadership on 11 February). This extract is significant because it already sets out the new Leader's priorities in a distinctive way. It is essentially a statement of belief – both in the virtues of liberty and (another future Thatcher theme) in the special, historic vocation of the British people to freedom.

Last October we were defeated – but not routed. The principles for which we stand, our banners in the political conflict, are still flying. We bear them proudly, confident that they represent what is best and most distinctive in the character of the British people, the qualities which always have been and still are the contribution which this nation has made to the world.

First among them I place a profound belief – indeed a fervent faith – in the virtues of self-reliance and personal independence. On these is founded the whole case for the free society, for the assertion that human progress is best achieved by offering the freest possible scope for the development of individual talents, qualified only by a respect for the qualities and the freedom of others.

In the old Roman world, the word 'liberty' meant a privilege. It was the British people who took the lead in asserting it as a fundamental human right, and who devised political institutions to protect and to promote it. We have planted that doctrine and those institutions in every quarter of the globe.

How ironic that both should be under attack in the very country where they were previously so strongly nourished. Make no mistake about it. This is the truth about the present situation in Britain. For many years there has been a subtle erosion of the essential virtues of the free society.

Self-reliance has been sneered at as if it were an absurd suburban pretention. Thrift has been denigrated as if it were greed. The desire of parents to choose and to struggle for what they themselves regarded as the best possible education for their children has been scorned.

In the name of equality, that decent, honourable ambition of many thousands of people is to be deliberately frustrated by the state. And now Direct Grant schools are to be attacked.[1] Also in the name of equality, another decent and honourable ambition, to save and to acquire a modest capital or property, is savagely penalized by taxation.

Trade unionism, which was encouraged by Conservative Governments in the past as a bulwark of economic independence, is now being distorted and the genuine interests of the individual worker are subordinated to the political purposes of a minority.

The small business – the seed corn of our future prosperity – is being strangled by vindictive taxes.

More than two thousand years ago, the great Athenian Pericles, in a speech which has survived through the ages, extolled the merits of the society in which free and intelligent obedience was accorded to a fair and reasonable code of laws. Now, defiance of fair and reasonable laws enacted constitutionally by a freely elected Parliament has been deliberately encouraged.

Do not believe, however, in spite of all this, that the people of this country have abandoned their faith in the qualities and characteristics which made them a great people. All that has happened is that we have temporarily lost confidence in our own strength. We have lost sight of the banners. The trumpets have given an uncertain sound.

It is our duty, our purpose, to raise those banners high, so that all can see them; to sound the trumpets clearly and boldly, so that all can hear them. Then we shall not have to convert people to our principles. They will simply rally to those which truly are their own.

We are fighting as we have always fought – for great and good causes.

---

[1] It was announced on 27 January 1975 that Direct Grant schools would be phased out from the next academic year.

For the rights of the weak as well as the strong. For the right of the little man as well as the big man.

We are fighting to defend them against the power and might of those who rise up to challenge them. And we will never stop fighting.

4

Speech to a Meeting of the Chelsea Constituency Association, 26 July 1975

The Chelsea Conservative Association speech of July 1975 was Margaret Thatcher's first – and highly controversial – speech on foreign policy as Leader of the Conservative Party. It was made against the background of preparations for the imminent Helsinki Summit – the high point, if that is the correct expression, of the era of détente between the two superpowers. Mrs Thatcher questioned whether the Soviet Union understood détente in the sense used by its Western proponents. Indeed, reviewing the evidence of Soviet global aggression and its defence build-up, she concluded – with Solzhenitsyn – that the West was in the process of losing the Cold War.

In her memoirs, Lady Thatcher notes that the Helsinki process, initiated by the 1975 Summit, did turn out to have its uses. It provided a programme for which human rights activists behind the Iron Curtain could fight, and one which gave the West a formal right to make representations on their behalf. But '[the dissidents'] bravery would have been of little account ... without the subsequent Western, particularly American, renewal of resolve and defence build-up ... Without that, Helsinki would have been just one more step on the road to defeat.' (II, p. 353)

Already this year, we have seen remarkable changes in world affairs. Here in Britain the question of our membership of the European Community has been clearly and dramatically settled.[1] The policies we have pursued over the past years have been overwhelmingly supported by the British people. Membership is no longer an issue. The argument is over and we are established as full partners, accepting the comradeship of our fellow Europeans. Now it is up to us to make our contribution to the new Europe.

But it is a dangerous world that we live in. Freedom has taken a

---

[1] In a referendum on 5 June 1975, 64.5 per cent of votes cast were in favour of continued British membership of the European Community (on a 64.5 per cent turnout).

major battering over the last few months. Close to home, in Portugal the first faint flickers of democracy are being snuffed out by communist reaction. Further east, the island of Cyprus is torn by communal strife. Next door, Middle Eastern neighbours struggle to achieve a just and lasting settlement.

Meanwhile, the world's most formidable navy – not America's, not Britain's, but Russia's – relentlessly extends it power from the Mediterranean to the Indian Ocean. Only this spring, the Soviet fleets displayed their awesome new potential to strike at the world's shipping lanes in the largest naval manoeuvres ever staged. Yet this is the moment the Labour Government has chosen to start pulling the Royal Navy out of the Mediterranean. And to ditch the Simonstown Agreement.[1] In South-East Asia, the loss of South Vietnam and Cambodia was a major setback for the free world. Who can tell where it will end?

To remain free we must stay strong and alert. In purely economic terms, a united Western Europe is as powerful as the Soviet Union. But in military terms we are much weaker. The Soviet Union now spends 20 per cent more each year than the United States on military research and development. Twenty-five per cent more on weapons and equipment. Sixty per cent more on strategic nuclear forces.

Then there is the Soviet navy, now a global force. It has more nuclear submarines than the rest of the world's navies put together. It has more surface ships than could possibly be needed to protect the Soviet Union's own coast and merchant shipping. Can anyone truly describe this as a defensive weapon?

In the light of these facts, it is clear that the safety of Europe can only be secured within the Western Alliance. America remains by far the most powerful element in that alliance. Only two months ago, President Ford specially visited Europe to emphasize that America's interest in our security is undiminished.[2] Perhaps this was the most important declaration of recent months. He renewed American pledges that United States troops would not be reduced in Europe, except in response to real concessions by the Warsaw Pact. Nothing could be more important, and nothing will curb Russian opportunism more surely, than the knowledge that America stands at Europe's side. Together we can preserve freedom for us all.

[1] The 1955 Simonstown Agreement, whereby the Royal Navy had the right to use the South African naval base, was ended by the British government on 16 June 1975.
[2] Gerald Ford (born 1913), 38th President of the USA 1974–77 (Republican), addressed the North Atlantic Council in Brussels on 29 May 1975.

But during the past few months freedom has come under heavy attack. Those who protested against American involvement in Vietnam and Cambodia have since overlooked and even managed to ignore the open savagery of the Khmer Rouge.[1] Where are the protest marchers now? These events are tragic for the peoples of Vietnam and Cambodia.

There was a feeling here in Europe, as in Asia, that the parties and people of the United States might be falling into a mood of isolationism. Many feared a withdrawal of the most powerful democracy from the centre of world affairs. Fortunately, this has not happened; but the less willing and able we Europeans become to carry our share of the common burden, the less willing the Americans will be to man the defences with us. An isolationist Britain would encourage an isolationist America.

The Conservative Party rejects any such course. We took Britain into Europe – Conservatives more than anyone else kept Britain in Europe during the referendum. In joining as full partners in the European Community we did not, and we shall not, turn our back on the Atlantic world. It was one of the greatest Conservative leaders – Winston Churchill – who cemented our alliance with America. It is just as much our duty to help keep America in Europe as it is to help Europe maintain its close links with America.

The Atlantic Alliance is the formal expression of the common interest of the nations of free Europe and North America. NATO, as part of it, was formed and is maintained to counter any threat of Soviet expansion.

Of course, we want a world in which our relations with the Soviet Union are based upon peace and trust – as they ought to be with every country. But if we have not yet got that world – and plainly we have not – then merely saying so, merely pretending that we have, is as foolish as it is dangerous.

This is the background to the Summit Conference on European Security and Co-operation which meets at Helsinki next week.

Détente sounds a fine word. And, to the extent that there really has been a relaxation in international tension, it is a fine thing. But the fact remains that throughout this decade of détente, the armed forces of the Soviet Union have increased, are increasing, and show no signs of diminishing.

Mr Brezhnev,[2] in a speech in June 1972, made a statement on détente

---

[1] When the Khmer Rouge captured Phnom Penh on 17 April 1975, the entire population of 2 million was expelled with appalling brutality.

[2] Leonid Brezhnev (1906–82), Soviet leader. First Secretary of the Communist Party 1964–66; General Secretary of the Communist Party 1966–82; President of the Presidium of the Supreme Soviet 1960–64, 1977–82.

25

which is quoted in virtually every Soviet speech or article on the subject. He said that peaceful co-existence 'in no way implies the possibility of relaxing the ideological struggle. On the contrary, we must be prepared for this struggle to be intensified and become an even sharper form of confrontation between the systems.' Within the last month the two Soviet leaders specially concerned with communism in the West, Messrs Suslov and Ponomarev,[1] have reasserted the same point, if anything even more strongly. There can be little doubt that if a leading Western statesman made an equivalent statement he would be bitterly condemned by the Soviets as an enemy of détente in Europe.

On our side we long for a *real* détente. We demand only that it is a *reality* – a reality which Russia supports in actions as well as words.

We in this country allow full and free expression for the point of view of the Soviet Union and its supporters here. But they have ruthlessly trampled on the ideals of the West in every country where it is in their power to do so.

Czechoslovakia in 1968 showed that the Soviets are prepared not only to destroy liberty, but also to crush systematically any brand of communism which differs from their own.[2] They are in principle arrayed against everything for which we stand.

So when the Soviet leaders jail a writer, or a priest, or a doctor, or a worker, for the crime of speaking freely, it is not only for humanitarian reasons that we should be concerned. For these acts reveal a country that is afraid of truth and liberty; it dare not allow its people to enjoy the freedoms we take for granted; and a nation that denies those freedoms to its own people will have a few scruples in denying them to others.

If détente is to progress then it ought to mean that the Soviet authorities relax their ruthless opposition to all forms and expressions of dissent. And as we talk of these things, we naturally think of Alexander Solzhenitsyn[3] and the other writers, thinkers and scientists who have fearlessly expressed their belief in freedom. They are not politicians or diplomats.

[1] Mikhail Suslov (1902–82), Soviet politician and ideologist. Member of the Politburo 1952–53, 1955–82; leader of Soviet delegations to congresses of foreign communist parties. Boris Ponomarev (born 1905), Soviet politician. Head of the International Department of the Central Committee of the Communist Party 1955–85.

[2] Soviet and Warsaw Pact forces invaded Czechoslovakia on 20 August 1968 to put a stop to reforms initiated by Alexander Dubcek (1921–92), First Secretary of the Czechoslovak Communist Party 1968–69.

[3] Alexander Solzhenitsyn (born 1919), Russian novelist and Nobel Prize-winner, whose works include *One Day in the Life of Ivan Denisovich* (1962) and *The Gulag Archipelago* (1973). He was expelled from the USSR in 1974.

But they have gained a deep understanding of the real attitudes and intentions of the Soviet ruling clique. And that understanding has taught them that the only way to obtain real concessions is by standing firm. Indeed, the whole history of negotiation with the Soviet Union teaches us that if you do something they want without insisting on something in return, the Soviets do not regard it as a kindness to be reciprocated, but as a weakness to be exploited.

There is a lot of fashionable nonsense talked about how we misunderstand communism, misrepresent communism, see communists under every bed. An attempt is being made, it seems, to create an atmosphere where truth and commonsense on these matters is actively discouraged. I believe the people of this country understand better the truth of the matter than those who try to mislead them.

We must work for a real relaxation of tension, but in our negotiations with the Eastern bloc we must not accept words or gestures as a substitute for genuine détente. No flood of words emanating from a summit conference will mean anything unless it is accompanied by some positive action by which the Soviet leaders show that their ingrained attitudes are really beginning to change.

That is why we so strongly support all those European and American spokesmen who have insisted that no serious advance towards a stable peace can be made unless some progress at least is seen in the free movement of people and of ideas. We in Europe have always been specially concerned that an accord with the Soviets should involve some progress in this direction. We would like them to read our books and newspapers, just as we can read theirs. We would like them to visit our countries, just as we can go to theirs. We will be alert not to miss the moment when the Soviets turn to genuine détente. But until that is achieved we must quietly determine to maintain Western military strength at a level adequate to deter any aggression.

At this very moment, we are all watching with apprehension the events in Portugal where a communist clique is trying to manoeuvre its way to power. Indeed, recent press reports suggest that the Portuguese Communist Party, which seems to regard 12 per cent of the popular vote as an entitlement to absolute power, is being subsidized by the Soviet Union. We must hope and work for the triumph of those moderate elements which yet survive in Portuguese politics. A democracy in which only left-wing parties are allowed is not a democracy at all.

How then should we approach the urgent need to relax tension in the world?

27

We must be firm in our desire for real détente – provided it is real. We must work hard for disarmament – provided it is genuine and balanced. But let us accept no proposals which would tip the balance of power still further against the West. The power of NATO is already at its lowest safe limit. And it is worth drawing the attention of some of our more gullible disarmers to the fact that if we reduce our conventional forces further, then should hostilities break out there would be no effective middle course between surrender or the early use of nuclear weapons.

We should, of course, be prepared to give and take, but not to give something for nothing. We want neither confrontation nor unilateral concessions. Serious and solid negotiation is the only way to real détente and lasting peace. In this dangerous world we must never allow the momentum of reconciliation to slacken.

Let us recognize that we in the West have a common interest and a common purpose: the pursuit and preservation of liberty. That is the basis of our unity and determination. Without that unity we should be weak; with it we can be strong. Strong to preserve a peace that will endure.

5

Speech to the Conservative Party Conference, Blackpool, 10 October 1975

As she records in her memoirs (see above, p. xv), Mrs Thatcher had her own definite ideas about her first Party Conference speech as Leader. She was not content merely to criticize the Labour Government's economic policies and performance – no mean self-denying ordinance at a time when inflation had risen to 26 per cent. She wanted to begin persuading the nation that Britain's economic decline had more deep-seated causes than the incompetence of one socialist administration. It was 'a crisis of the spirit of the nation' which lay behind the economic crisis (II, pp. 305–6). Invigorated by the highly successful visit she had made to the United States in September – and with her authority reinforced by it – Mrs Thatcher chose as her dominant theme the superiority of the West's free enterprise system over the communist (and socialist) alternative. Contrary to the left's assertions, Britain's problems were a result of a crisis of socialism, not a crisis of capitalism. Moreover, confidence in capitalism was underpinned by confidence in Britain's traditional national character. The passage in which Mrs Thatcher describes her 'total vision of the kind of life we want for our country and our children' (p. 34) is perhaps the best succinct statement of her political beliefs, and one which would be echoed and re-echoed in future years.

The first Conservative Party Conference I ever attended was in 1946 and I came to it as an undergraduate representing Oxford University Conservative Association (I know our Cambridge supporters will not mind). That Conference was held in this very hall and the platform then seemed a long way away and I had no thought of joining the lofty and distinguished people sitting up there, but our Party is the party of equality of opportunity as you can see.

I know you will understand the humility I feel at following in the footsteps of great men like our Leader in that year, Winston Churchill, a man called by destiny to raise the name of Britain to supreme heights in the history of the free world. In the footsteps of Anthony Eden, who set us the goal of a property-owning democracy – a goal we still pursue today; of Harold Macmillan whose leadership brought so many ambitions within the grasp of every citizen; of Alec Douglas-Home whose career of selfless public service earned the affection and admiration of us all; and of Edward Heath who successfully led the Party to victory in 1970 and brilliantly led the nation into Europe in 1973.[1] During my lifetime all the Leaders of the Conservative Party have served as Prime Minister and I hope that the habit will continue. Our Leaders have been different men with different qualities and different styles, but they all had one thing in common: each met the challenge of his time. Now, what is the challenge of our time? I believe there are two: to overcome the country's economic and financial problems, and to regain our confidence in Britain and ourselves.

The economic challenge has been debated at length this week in this hall. Last week it gave rise to the usual scenes of cordial brotherly strife.[2] Day after day the comrades called one another far from comradely names and occasionally, when they remembered, they called us names too. Some of them, for example, suggested that I criticized Britain when I was overseas.[3] They are wrong. It was not Britain I was criticizing, it was socialism, and I will go on criticizing socialism and opposing socialism because it is bad for Britain. Britain and socialism are not the same thing, and as long as I have health and strength they never will be.

Whatever could I say about Britain that is half as damaging as what this Labour Government has done to our country? Let us look at the record. It is the Labour Government that has caused prices to rise at a record rate of 26 per cent a year. They told us the Social Contract[4] would solve everything, but now everyone can see that the so-called 'contract' was a fraud – a fraud for which the people of this country

[1] Winston Churchill was Leader of the Conservative Party 1940–55; Anthony Eden 1955–57; Harold Macmillan 1957–63; Alec Douglas-Home 1963–65; Edward Heath 1965–75.
[2] The Labour Party Conference took place at Blackpool from 29 September to 3 October 1975.
[3] In a speech to the Institute of Socio-Economic Studies in New York in August 1975, Mrs Thatcher had pinpointed current economic problems in Britain, such as inflation, overtaxation, discouragement of enterprise and excessive public spending.
[4] The 'Social Contract' was an informal agreement between the Labour Party and the Trades Union Congress, made in February 1974, whereby the unions promised to refrain from high wage demands in return for social legislation and price controls.

have had to pay a very high price. It is the Labour Government whose past policies are forcing unemployment higher than it need ever have been. Thousands more men and women are losing their jobs every day and there are going to be men and women, many of them youngsters straight out of school, who will be without a job this winter because socialist ministers spent last year attacking us instead of attacking inflation.

It is the Labour Government that brought the level of production below that of the three-day week in 1974.[1] We have really got a three-day week now, only it takes five days to do it. It is the Labour Government that has brought us record peacetime taxation. They have the usual socialist disease: they have run out of other people's money. It is the Labour Government that has pushed public spending to record levels. How have they done it? By borrowing and borrowing. Never in the field of human credit has so much been owed.

Mr President, serious as the economic challenge is, the political and moral challenge is just as grave and perhaps even more so, because economic problems never start with economics. They have much deeper roots in human nature and roots in politics, and they do not finish at economics either. Labour's failure to cope, to look at the nation's problems from the viewpoint of the whole nation and not just one section of it, has led to a loss of confidence, and to a sense of helplessness, and with it goes a feeling that Parliament, which ought to be in charge, is not in charge, and that the actions and decisions are taken elsewhere.

It goes even deeper than that, to the voices that seem anxious not to overcome our economic difficulties, but to exploit them, to destroy the free enterprise society and put a Marxist system in its place. Today those voices form a sizeable chorus in the Parliamentary Labour Party, a chorus which, aided and abetted by the many Constituency Labour Parties, seems to be growing in numbers.

Mind you, anyone who says this openly is promptly accused of seeing reds under the bed, but look who is seeing them now on his own admission. Mr Wilson has at last discovered that his own party is infiltrated by extreme left-wingers, or to use his own words, it is infested with them.[2] When even Mr Wilson gets scared about their success in

---

[1] British industry worked a three-day week from January to March 1974 as a result of the energy crisis caused by a national coal strike.
[2] At the Labour Party Conference on 30 September 1975, Harold Wilson bitterly denounced extremists who were trying to take over constituency organizations.

31

capturing key positions in the Labour Party, should not the rest of us be? Should not the rest of us ask him: 'Where have you been while all this has been going on, and what are you doing about it?' The answer is nothing.

I sometimes think the Labour Party is like a pub where the mild is running out. If someone does not do something soon all that is left will be bitter, and all that is bitter will be Left.

Whenever I visit communist countries their politicians never hesitate to boast about their achievements.[1] They know them all by heart; they reel off the facts and figures, claiming this is the rich harvest of the communist system. Yet they are not as prosperous as we in the West are prosperous, and they are not free as we in the West are free.

Our capitalist system produces a far higher standard of prosperity and happiness because it believes in incentive and opportunity, and because it is founded on human dignity and freedom.

Even the Russians have to go to a capitalist country – America – to buy enough wheat to feed their people – and that after more than fifty years of a state-controlled economy. Yet they boast incessantly; while we, who have so much more to boast about, forever criticize and decry. Is it not time we spoke up for our way of life? After all, no Western nation has to build a wall round itself to keep its people in.

So let us have no truck with those who say the free enterprise system has failed. What we face today is not a crisis of capitalism but of socialism. No country can flourish if its economic and social life is dominated by nationalization and state control.

The cause of our shortcomings does not, therefore, lie in private enterprise. Our problem is not that we have too little socialism. It is that we have too much. If only the Labour Party in this country would act like Social Democrats in West Germany. If only they would stop trying to prove their socialist virility by relentlessly nationalizing one industry after another.

Of course, a halt to further state control will not on its own restore our belief in ourselves, because something else is happening to this country. We are witnessing a deliberate attack on our values, a deliberate attack on those who wish to promote merit and excellence, a deliberate attack on our heritage and our great past, and there are those who gnaw

---

[1] During a visit to Romania in September 1975, Mrs Thatcher heard Nicolae Ceausescu (1918–89), President of Romania 1967–89, relate at length the astonishing (alleged) successes of the Romanian economy.

away at our national self-respect, rewriting British history as centuries of unrelieved gloom, oppression and failure – as days of hopelessness, not days of hope. And others, under the shelter of our education system, are ruthlessly attacking the minds of the young.

Everyone who believes in freedom must be appalled at the tactics employed by the far left in the systematic destruction of the North London Polytechnic[1] – blatant tactics of intimidation designed to undermine the fundamental beliefs and values of every student, tactics pursued by people who are the first to insist on their own civil rights while seeking to deny them to the rest of us.

We must not be bullied or brainwashed out of our beliefs. No wonder so many of our people, some of the best and even the brightest, are depressed and talking of emigrating. Even so, I think they are wrong. They are giving up too soon. Many of the things we hold dear are threatened as never before, but none has yet been lost, so stay here, stay and help us defeat socialism so that the Britain you have known may be the Britain your children will know.

These are the two great challenges of our time – the moral and political challenge and the economic challenge. They have to be faced together and we have to master them both.

What are our chances of success? It depends on what kind of people we are. What kind of people are we? We are the people that in the past made Great Britain the workshop of the world, the people who persuaded others to buy British, not by begging them to do so but because it was best.

We are a people who have received more Nobel Prizes than any other nation except America; and head for head we have done better than America, twice as well in fact.

We are the people who, among other things, invented the computer, the refrigerator, the electric motor, the stethoscope, rayon, steam turbine, stainless steel, the tank, television, penicillin, radar, the jet engine, hovercraft, float glass and carbon fibres, etc. – oh, and the best half of Concorde![2] We export more of what we produce than West Germany, France, Japan or the United States, and well over 90 per cent of these exports come from private enterprise. It is a triumph for the private sector and all who work in it, and let us say so loud and clear.

[1] The North London Polytechnic was subject to repeated disruption between 1971 and 1975 when International Socialists took control of the student union and tried to oust the Director.
[2] The supersonic airliner Concorde was, of course, an Anglo–French joint project.

With achievements like that, who can doubt that Britain can have a great future; and what our friends abroad want to know is whether that future is going to happen.

Well, how can we Conservatives make it happen? Many of the details have already been dealt with in the Conference debates. But policies and programmes should not just be a list of unrelated items. They are part of a total vision of the kind of life we want for our country and our children. Let me give you my vision: a man's right to work as he will, to spend what he earns, to own property, to have the state as servant and not as master – these are the British inheritance. They are the essence of a free country and on that freedom all our other freedoms depend.

But we want a free economy, not only because it guarantees our liberties, but also because it is the best way of creating wealth and prosperity for the whole country, and it is this prosperity alone which can give us the resources for better services for the community, better services for those in need.

By their attack on private enterprise, this Labour Government have made certain that there will be next to nothing available for improvements in our social services over the next few years. We must get private enterprise back on the road to recovery, not merely to give people more of their own money to spend as they choose, but to have more money to help the old and the sick and the handicapped. And the way to recovery is through profits – good profits today leading to high investment, leading to well-paid jobs, leading to a better standard of living tomorrow. No profits means no investment, and that means a dying industry geared to yesterday's world, and that means fewer jobs tomorrow. Other nations have recognized that for years now, and because they have recognized it they are going ahead faster than we are; and the gap between us will continue to increase unless we change our ways, and the trouble here is that for years the Labour Party have made people feel that profits are guilty unless proved innocent.

When I visit factories and companies, I do not find that those who actually work in them are against profits; on the contrary, they want to work for a prosperous concern, a concern with a future – their future. Governments must learn to leave these companies with enough of their own profits to produce the goods and jobs for tomorrow.

If the socialists will not or cannot, there will be no profit-making industry left to support the losses caused by fresh bouts of nationalization. If anyone should murmur that I am preaching *laissez-faire*, let me say I am not arguing and have never argued that all we have to do is to let the economy run by itself. I believe that, just as each of us has an obligation to make the best of his talents, so governments have an obligation to create the framework within which we can do so. Not only individual people but individual firms and particularly small firms. If they concentrated on doing that, they would do a lot better than they are doing now. Some of the small firms will stay small, but others will expand and become the great companies of the future. The Labour Government have pursued a disastrous vendetta against small businesses and the self-employed. We will reverse their damaging policies.

Nowhere is this more important than in agriculture, one of our most successful industries, made up almost entirely of small businesses. We live in a world in which food is no longer cheap or plentiful. Everything we cannot produce here must be imported at a high price.

Yet the Government could not have destroyed the confidence of the industry more effectively if they had tried deliberately to do so with their formula of empty promises and penal taxation. So today what is the picture? Depressed profits, low investment, no incentive, and – over-shadowing everything – Government spending, spending, spending far beyond the taxpayers' means.

To recover, to get from where we are to where we want to be – and I admit we would rather not be here – will take time.

'Economic policy,' wrote Maynard Keynes,[1] 'should not be a matter of tearing up by the roots, but of slowly training a plant to grow in a different direction.'

It will take time to reduce public spending, to rebuild profits and incentives, and to benefit from the investments which must be made. But the sooner that time starts, the better it will be for Britain's unemployed and for Britain as a whole.

One of the reasons why this Labour Government has incurred more unemployment than any Conservative Government since the war is because they have concentrated too much on distributing what we have and too little on seeing that we have more.

We Conservatives hate unemployment. We hate the idea of men and women not being able to use their abilities. We deplore the waste of natural resources and the deep affront to people's dignity from being out of work through no fault of their own. It is ironic that we should

---

[1] John Maynard Keynes (1883–1946), Baron Keynes of Tilton 1942. British economist, author of *The General Theory of Employment, Interest and Money* (1936).

be accused of wanting unemployment to solve our economic problems by the very Government which has produced record post-war unemployment and is expecting more.

The record of Mr Wilson and his colleagues on this is unparalleled in the history of political hypocrisy. We are now seeing the full consequences of nearly twenty months of Labour government. They have done the wrong things at the wrong time in the wrong way, and they have been a disaster for this country.

Now let me turn to something I spoke about in America. Some socialists seem to believe that people should be numbers in a state computer. We believe they should be individuals. We are all unequal. No one, thank heavens, is quite like anyone else, however much the socialists may pretend otherwise. We believe that everyone has the right to be unequal. But to us, every human being is equally important.

Engineers, miners, manual workers, shop assistants, farm-workers, postmen, housewives – these are the essential foundations of our society, and without them there would be no nation. But there are others with special gifts who should also have their chance, because if the adventurers who strike out in new directions in science, technology, medicine, commerce and industry are hobbled, there can be no advance. The spirit of envy can destroy; it can never build. Everyone must be allowed to develop the abilities he knows he has within him – and she knows she has within her – in the way he chooses.

Freedom to choose is something we take for granted, until it is in danger of being taken away. Socialist governments set out perpetually to restrict the area of choice, and Conservative governments to increase it. We believe that you become a responsible citizen by making decisions yourself, not by having them made for you. But they are made for you by Labour all right.

Take education: Our education system used to serve us well. A child from an ordinary family, as I was, could use it as a ladder, as an advancement; but the socialists, better at demolition than reconstruction, are destroying many good grammar schools.[1] Now this is nothing to do with private education. It is opportunity and excellence in our state schools that are being diminished under socialism. Naturally enough, parents do not like this, but in a socialist society parents should be seen and not heard.

[1] The Labour Government aimed to abolish selective grammar schools and establish a fully comprehensive school system.

Another denial of choice is being applied to health. The private sector helps to keep some of our best doctors here, and so available part-time to the National Health Service. It also helps to bring in more money for the general health of the nation; but under Labour, private medicine is being squeezed out, and the result will be to add to the burden of the National Health Service without adding one penny to its income.

Let me make this absolutely clear: when we return to power we shall reverse Mrs Castle's stupid and spiteful attack on hospital pay beds.[1] We Conservatives do not accept that because some people have no choice, no one should have it. Every family should have the right to spend their money, after tax, as they wish, and not as the Government dictates. Let us extend choice, extend the will to choose and the chance to choose.

I want to come now to the argument which Mr Wilson is trying to put across the country: namely, that the Labour Party is the natural party of government because it is the only one that the trade unions will accept. From what I saw on television last week, the Labour Party did not look like a party of government at all, let alone a natural one.

But let us examine the argument, because it is important. If we are to be told that a Conservative Government could not govern because certain extreme leaders would not let it, then general elections are a mockery, we have arrived at the one-party state, and parliamentary democracy in this country will have perished. The democracy for which our fathers fought and died is not to be laid to rest as lightly as that.

When the next Conservative Government comes to power many trade unionists will have put it there. Millions of them vote for us at every election. I want to say this to them and to all of our supporters in industry: go out and join in the work of your unions; go to their meetings and stay to the end, and learn the union rules as well as the far left knows them. Remember that if parliamentary democracy dies, free trade unions die with it.

I come last to what many would put first, the rule of law. The first people to uphold the law should be governments, and it is tragic that the socialist Government, to its lasting shame, should have lost its nerve

---

[1] Barbara Castle (born 1910), Baroness Castle of Blackburn 1990. Labour MP 1945–79; Minister of Transport 1965–68; Employment and Productivity Secretary 1968–70; Social Services Secretary 1974–76; Labour MEP 1979–89. In May 1975 she announced that private pay beds in National Health Service hospitals would be phased out.

and shed its principles over the People's Republic of Clay Cross,[1] and that a group of the Labour Party should have tried to turn the Shrewsbury pickets into martyrs.[2] On both occasions the law was broken and on one violence was done. No decent society can live like that, and no responsible party should condone it. The first duty of government is to uphold the law, and if it tries to bob, weave and duck round that duty when it is inconvenient, the governed will do exactly the same thing and then nothing will be safe – not home, not liberty, not life itself.

There is one part of this country where, tragically, defiance of the law is costing life day after day. In Northern Ireland our troops have the dangerous and thankless task of trying to keep the peace and hold a balance. We are proud of the way they have discharged their duty. This party is pledged to support the unity of the United Kingdom, to preserve that unity and to protect the people, Catholic and Protestant alike. We believe our armed forces must remain until a genuine peace is made. Our thoughts are with them and our pride is with them, too.

Mr President, I have spoken of the challenges which face us here in Britain – the challenge to recover economically and the challenge to recover our belief in ourselves – and I have shown our potential for recovery. I have dealt with some aspects of our strength and approach, and I have tried to tell you something of my personal vision and my belief in the standards on which this nation was greatly built, on which it greatly thrived and from which in recent years it has greatly fallen away. I believe we are coming to yet another turning point in our long history. We can go on as we have been going and continue down, or we can stop and with a decisive act of will say: 'Enough.'

Let all of us here today and others far beyond this hall who believe in our cause make that act of will. Let us proclaim our faith in a new and better future for our Party and our people; let us resolve to heal the wounds of a divided nation, and let that act of healing be the prelude to a lasting victory.

---

[1] In 1973, Labour Councillors at Clay Cross in Derbyshire illegally refused to raise council rents in accordance with the Housing Finance Act 1972 and were consequently surcharged and disqualified from election. The Labour Government passed the Housing Finance (Special Provisions) Act 1975 to relieve them of some of these penalties.
[2] Three men were imprisoned for up to three years in December 1973 for conspiring to intimidate workers at a violent mass picket of a construction site in Shrewsbury during the 1972 builders' strike. Left wingers agitated for their release throughout 1974 and 1975.

6

Speech to Conservatives in Kensington Town Hall, 19 January 1976

The Kensington Town Hall speech in January 1976 marked a return to the Cold War themes of the previous year's Chelsea speech. Nothing had happened to change Mrs Thatcher's gloomy prognosis about the West's prospects if present policies continued. There were as yet no obvious beneficial results from Helsinki. On the contrary, Cuban forces, acting as Soviet surrogates, had overrun Angola. The Soviet Union's military – particularly naval – build-up continued apace. As a result, the tone and message at Kensington were even more urgently challenging, as is shown by the speech's title, 'Britain Awake'. Certainly, one effect of the speech was to wake up the Soviets about the character and approach of Britain's new Leader of the Opposition. It was at this time that the Red Army newspaper Red Star *coined the description of Margaret Thatcher as 'The Iron Lady', from which she never looked back.*

BRITAIN AWAKE

The first duty of any Government is to safeguard its people against external aggression; to guarantee the survival of our way of life. The question we must now ask ourselves is whether the present Government is fulfilling that duty. It is dismantling our defence at a moment when the strategic threat to Britain and her allies from an expansionist power is graver than at any moment since the end of the last war.

Military men are always warning us that the strategic balance is tilting against NATO and the West. The socialists never listen. They do not seem to realize that the submarines and missiles that the Russians are building could be destined to be used against us. Perhaps some people in the Labour Party think we are on the same side as the Russians!

Look at what the Russians are doing. Russia is ruled by a dictatorship

39

of patient, far-sighted men who are rapidly making their country the foremost naval and military power in the world. They are not doing this solely for the sake of self-defence. A huge, largely landlocked country like Russia does not need to build the most powerful navy in the world just to guard its own frontiers.

No. The Russians are bent on world dominance, and they are rapidly acquiring the means to become the most powerful imperial nation the world has seen.

The men in the Soviet Politburo do not have to worry about the ebb and flow of public opinion. They put guns before butter, while we put just about everything before guns. They know that they are a superpower in only one sense – the military sense. They are a failure in human and economic terms.

But let us make no mistake. The Russians calculate that their military strength will more than make up for their economic and social weakness. They are determined to use it in order to get what they want from us.

I warned last year on the eve of the Helsinki Conference that the Soviet Union is spending 20 per cent more each year than the United States on military research and development. Twenty-five per cent more on weapons and equipment. Sixty per cent more on strategic forces. Some military experts believe that Russia has already achieved strategic superiority over America. The balance of conventional forces poses the most immediate dangers for NATO.

I am going to visit our troops in Germany on Thursday. I am going at a moment when the Warsaw Pact forces in Central Europe outnumber NATO's by 150,000 men, nearly ten thousand tanks, and 2,600 aircraft. We cannot afford to let that gap get bigger. Still more serious gaps have opened up elsewhere – especially in the troubled area of southern Europe and the Mediterranean. The rise of Russia as a worldwide naval power threatens our oil rigs and our traditional lifelines, the sea routes.

Over the past ten years, the Russians have quadrupled their forces of nuclear submarines. They are now building one nuclear submarine a month. They are searching for new naval base facilities all over the world, while we are giving up our few remaining bases. They have moved into the Indian Ocean. They pose a rising threat to our northern waters and, farther east, to Japan's vital sea routes. The Soviet navy is not designed for self-defence. We do not have to imagine an all-out nuclear war or even a conventional war in order to see how it could be used for political purposes.

I would be the first to welcome any evidence that the Russians are ready to enter into a genuine détente. But I am afraid that the evidence points the other way. I warned before Helsinki of the dangers of falling for an illusory détente. Some people were sceptical at the time, but we now see that my warning was fully justified. Has deténte induced the Russians to cut back on their defence programme? Has it dissuaded them from brazen intervention in Angola?[1] Has it led to any improvement in the conditions of Soviet citizens, or the subject population of Eastern Europe? We know the answers.

At Helsinki we endorsed the status quo in Eastern Europe. In return we had hoped for the freer movement of people and ideas across the Iron Curtain. So far we have got nothing of substance.

We are devoted, as we always have been, to the maintenance of peace. We will welcome any initiative from the Soviet Union that would contribute to that goal. But we must also heed the warnings of those like Alexander Solzhenitsyn, who remind us that we have been fighting a kind of "Third World War" over the entire period since 1945 – and that we have been steadily losing ground.[2] As we look back over the battles of the past year, over the list of countries that have been lost to freedom or are imperilled by Soviet expansion, can we deny that Solzhenitsyn is right?

We have seen Vietnam and all of Indochina swallowed up by communist aggression. We have seen the communists make an open grab for power in Portugal, our oldest ally – a sign that many of the battles in the Third World War are being fought inside Western countries.

And now the Soviet Union and its satellites are pouring money, arms and front-line troops into Angola in the hope of dragging it into the communist bloc. We must remember that there are no Queensberry rules in the contest that is now going on. And the Russians are playing to win. They have one great advantage over us – the battles are being fought on our territory, not theirs.

Within a week of the Helsinki Conference, Mr Zarodov, a leading Soviet ideologue, was writing in *Pravda* about the need for the Communist

---

[1] When Angola became independent in 1975, civil war continued between rival nationalist armies. The Popular Movement for the Liberation of Angola (MPLA) was armed by the USSR and stiffened by Cuban troops, while South Africa assisted a coalition of the National Front for the Liberation of Angola (FNLA) and the National Movement for the Total Liberation of Angola (UNITA).

[2] In 1975 Solzhenitsyn advanced the controversial thesis: 'The Third World War has already taken place and has ended in defeat' – Yalta 1945 to Helsinki 1975 – through a series of concessions to communism.

Parties of Western Europe to forget about tactical compromises with Social Democrats and take the offensive in order to bring about proletarian revolution. Later Mr Brezhnev made a statement in which he gave this article his personal endorsement. If this is the line that the Soviet leadership adopts at its Party Congress next month, then we must heed their warning. It undoubtedly applies to us too. We in Britain cannot opt out of the world. If we cannot understand why the Russians are rapidly becoming the greatest naval and military power the world has ever seen, if we cannot draw the lesson of what they tried to do in Portugal and are now trying to do in Angola, then we are destined – in their words – to end up on 'the scrap-heap of history'.

We look to our alliance with America and NATO as the prime guarantee of our own security; and, in the world beyond Europe, the United States is still the prime champion of freedom. But we are all aware of how the bitter experience of Vietnam has changed the public mood in America. We are also aware of the domestic circumstances that inhibit action by an American President in an election year.[1] So it is more vital than ever that each and every one of us within NATO should contribute his proper share to the defence of freedom.

Britain, with her worldwide experience of diplomacy and defence, has a special role to play. We in the Conservative Party are determined that Britain should fulfil that role. We are not harking back to some nostalgic illusion about Britain's role in the past. We are saying Britain has a part to play now.

The advance of communist power threatens our whole way of life. It is not irreversible, providing that we take the necessary measures now. But the longer we go on running down our means of survival, the harder it will be to catch up. In other words, the longer Labour remains in government, the more vulnerable this country will be.

What has this Government been doing? Under the last defence review, the Government said it would cut defence spending by £4,700 million over the next nine years. Then they said they would cut a further £110 million. It now seems that we will see further cuts. If there are further cuts, perhaps the Defence Secretary should change his title, for the sake of accuracy, to the Secretary for Disarmament and Insecurity.

We are now spending less per head on defence than any of our major allies. Britain spends only £90 per head on defence. Germany spends

---

[1] In the US presidential election of 2 November 1976, Jimmy Carter (Democrat) defeated Gerald Ford (Republican) by 297 electoral college votes to 241.

£130, not counting its contribution in West Berlin. France spends £115. The United States spends £215. Even neutral Sweden spends £60 more per head than us.

Of course, we are poorer than most of our NATO allies. This is part of the disastrous economic legacy of socialism. But let us be clear about one thing. This is not a moment when anyone with the interests of this country at heart should be talking about cutting our defences. It is a time when we urgently need to strengthen our defences. Of course, this places a burden on us. But it is one that we must be willing to bear if we want our freedom to survive.

Throughout our history, we have carried the torch for freedom. Now, as I travel the world, I find people asking again and again: 'What has happened to Britain?' They want to know why we are hiding our heads in the sand.

Many people may not be aware, even now, of the full extent of the threat. All the same, we expect our Governments to take a more far-sighted view. The Government, to give them their due, spelled out the extent of the peril in their Defence White Paper last year. But, having done so, they drew the absurd conclusion that our defence efforts should be reduced.

The socialists, in fact, seem to regard defence as almost infinitely cuttable. They are much more cautious when it comes to cutting other types of public expenditure. They seem to think that we can afford to go deeper into debt, so that the Government can prop up a loss-making company and waste our money on the profligate extension of nationalization and measures such as the Community Land Act.[1] We can even afford to lend money to the Russians, at a lower rate of interest than we have to pay on our own borrowings.[2] But we cannot afford, in Labour's view, to maintain our defences at the necessary level – not even at a time when, on top of our NATO commitments, we are fighting a major internal war against terrorism in Northern Ireland and need more troops in order to win it.[3]

[1] The Community Land Act 1975 empowered local authorities to acquire land suitable for development and allowed the Department of the Environment to purchase unoccupied office accommodation by compulsion.
[2] In February 1975, Harold Wilson paid an official visit to the USSR and signed an agreement whereby Britain provided credit of £950 million at low rates of interest to finance exports to the USSR.
[3] Over six thousand British troops had been stationed in Northern Ireland since 1969 to prevent sectarian violence and combat terrorism by the IRA and other paramilitary groups.

There are crises farther from home that could affect us deeply. Angola is the most immediate. In Angola, the Soviet-backed guerrilla movement, the MPLA, is making rapid headway in its current offensive, despite the fact that it controls only a third of the population, and is supported by even less. The MPLA is gaining ground because the Soviet Union and its satellites are pouring money, guns and front-line troops into the battle. Six thousand Cuban regular soldiers are still there. But it is obvious that an acceptable solution for Angola is only possible if *all* outside powers withdraw their military support.

You might well ask: why on earth should we think twice about what is happening in a faraway place like Angola?

There are four important reasons. The first is that Angola occupies a vital strategic position. If the pro-Soviet faction wins, one of the immediate consequences will almost certainly be the setting up of Soviet air and naval bases on the South Atlantic. The second reason is that the presence of communist forces in this area will make it much more difficult to settle the Rhodesian problem[1] and achieve an understanding between South Africa and black Africa. The third reason is more far-reaching. If the Russians have their way in Angola, they may well conclude that they can repeat the performance elsewhere. Similarly, uncommitted nations would be left to conclude that NATO is a spent force and that their best policy is to pursue an accommodation with Russia.

Finally, what the Russians are doing in Angola is against détente. They seem to believe that their intervention is consistent with détente. Indeed, *Izvestiya* recently argued that Soviet support for the communist MPLA is 'an investment in détente' – which gives us a good idea of what they really mean by the word. We should make it plain to the Russians that we do not believe that what they are doing in Angola is consistent with détente.

It is usually said that NATO policy ends in North Africa at the Tropic of Cancer. But the situation in Angola brings home the fact that NATO's supply lines need to be protected much further south.

We believe in the Conservative Party that our foreign policy should continue to be based on a close understanding with our traditional ally, America. This is part of our Anglo-Saxon tradition, as well as part of our NATO commitment, and it adds to our contribution to the European Community.

[1] In 1965 the 'Rhodesian Front' Government declared Rhodesia an independent state in defiance of Britain, the colonial power.

Our Anglo-Saxon heritage embraces the countries of the Old Commonwealth that have too often been neglected by politicians in this country, but are always close to the hearts of the British people. We believe that we should build on our traditional bonds with Australia, New Zealand and Canada, as well as on our new ties with Europe.

I am delighted to see that the Australians and the New Zealanders have concluded – as I believe that most people in this country are coming to conclude – that socialism has failed. In their two electoral avalanches at the end of last year,[1] they brought back Governments committed to freedom of choice, Governments that will roll back the frontiers of state intervention in the economy and will restore the incentives for people to work and invest. Our congratulations go to Mr Fraser and Mr Muldoon.[2] I know that we will be able to learn from each other. What has happened in Australasia is part of a wider reawakening to the need to provide a more positive defence of the values and traditions on which Western civilization, and our modern prosperity, have been based.

We stand with that select body of nations that believe in democracy, and social and economic freedom. Part of Britain's world role should be to provide, through its spokesmen, a reasoned and cogent defence of the Western concept of rights and liberties: the kind of defence that America's Ambassador to the UN, Mr Moynihan,[3] has recently provided in his powerfully argued speeches.

But our role reaches beyond this. We have abundant experience and expertise in this country in the art of diplomacy in its broadest sense. It should be used, within Europe, in the efforts to achieve effective foreign policy initiatives. Within the EEC, the interests of individual nations are not identical, and our separate identities must be seen as a strength rather than a weakness.

Any steps towards closer European union must be carefully con-

---

[1] In the New Zealand general election of 29 November 1975, the National Party defeated the Labour Government and won fifty-five of the eighty-seven seats in Parliament. The Liberal–National Country Party coalition won the Australian general election of 13 December 1975 with a 6 per cent swing against Labor.
[2] Malcolm Fraser (born 1930), Australian politician. Leader of the Liberal Party 1975–83; Prime Minister 1975–83. Sir Robert Muldoon (1921–92), New Zealand politician. Leader of the National Party 1974–84; Prime Minister 1975–84.
[3] Professor (Daniel) Patrick Moynihan (born 1927), US diplomat and politician. Ambassador to India 1973–75; Permanent Representative to the UN 1975–76; Democrat Senator 1977–.

sidered. We are committed to direct elections within the Community, but the timing needs to be carefully calculated.[1]

But new problems are looming up.

Among them is the possibility that the communists will come to power through a coalition in Italy.[2] This is a good reason why we should aim for closer links between those political groups in the European Parliament that reject socialism.[3] We have a difficult year ahead in 1976. I hope it will not result in a further decline of Western power and influence of the kind that we saw in 1975, or in further problems in the Middle East.

It is clear that internal violence – and above all political terrorism – will continue to pose a major challenge to all Western societies, and that it may be exploited as an instrument by the communists. We should seek close co-ordination between the police and security services of the Community, and of NATO, in the battle against terrorism. The way that our own police have coped with recent terrorist incidents provides a splendid model for other forces.[4]

The message of the Conservative Party is this. Britain has an important role to play on the world stage. It is based on the remarkable qualities of the British people. Labour has neglected that role.

Our capacity to play a constructive role in world affairs is, of course, related to our economic and military strength.

The excesses of socialism have weakened us on both counts. This puts at risk not just our chance to play a useful role in the councils of the world, but the survival of our way of life.

Caught up in the problems and hardships that socialism has brought to Britain, we are sometimes in danger of failing to see the vast transformations taking place in the world that dwarf our own problems, great though they are. But we have to wake up to those developments, and find the political will to respond to them.

Soviet military power will not disappear just because we refuse to look

---

[1] The first direct elections to the European Parliament were held in June 1979.

[2] After the Italian general election of 20 June 1976, the Christian Democrats did have to rely on communist abstentions in order to remain in office, but there was no coalition.

[3] The European Democratic Union was founded in April 1978 to promote co-operation between Christian Democrats and conservatives from Austria, Denmark, Finland, West Germany, Iceland, Norway, Portugal, Sweden and Britain; but only three of these countries were EEC members at that time.

[4] In December 1975, the police brought a five-day siege of IRA terrorists in Balcombe Street, Marylebone, to a peaceful conclusion, for which they were widely praised.

at it. And we must assume that it is there to be used – as threat or as force – unless we maintain the necessary deterrents.

We are under no illusions about the limits of British influence. We are often told how this country that once ruled a quarter of the world is today just a group of offshore islands. Well, we in the Conservative Party believe that Britain is still great. The decline of Britain's relative power in the world was partly inevitable – with the rise of the nuclear superpowers, with their vast reserves of manpower and economic resources. But it was partly avoidable – the result of our economic decay, resulting from processes that the Labour Government has assisted.

We will reverse those processes when we are returned to government. In the meantime, the Conservative Party has the vital task of shaking the British public out of the effects of a prolonged course of sedation. The sedatives have been applied by people, in and out of government, who have been telling us that there is no external threat to Britain, that all is sweetness and light in Moscow, and that a squadron of fighter-planes or a company of Marine commandos is less important than a new subsidy for a loss-making plant.

The Conservative Party must now sound the warning. There are moments in our history when we have to make a fundamental choice. This is one such moment – a moment when our choice will determine the life or death of our kind of society, and the future of our children. Let us ensure that our children will have cause to rejoice that we did not forsake their freedom.

7

Speech to the Zurich Economic Society, University of Zurich, 14 March 1977

Her lecture to the Zurich Economic Society in March 1977 is the most important economic speech made by Margaret Thatcher during her years in Opposition. The theme was topical and the location appropriate: for the autumn of 1976 had seen the humiliating collapse of the Labour Government's economic policy and the arrival of a team from the International Monetary Fund to work out a stabilization package for Britain's finances. Labour Chancellor Denis Healey's 15 December mini-budget and the IMF 'Letter of Intent' effectively marked the first application of monetarist policies to the British economy.

Remarkably, given the depth of the economic crisis in Britain at the time and the open questioning of whether the reversal of decline was possible, the Zurich speech is full of optimism about the future. It argues that it is not Britain — let alone the capitalist system — which is failing, but rather that failure is the result of too much socialism. And the material benefits of capitalism are shown to flow from the fact that capitalism is itself a morally superior system. Applying language which would become commonplace in ministerial speeches ten years later, Mrs Thatcher even talks of a 'people's capitalism', and concludes that 'we may soon be witnessing the withering away of the class struggle'.

THE NEW RENAISSANCE

You have honoured me by your invitation as a practising politician, not an economist or financier. So I shall not attempt to instruct this highly expert and experienced gathering in economic affairs. Nor would you wish me to come all this way to describe the current situation in Britain, because I could tell you little more than you already know.

What I can offer you of interest is a perspective on the way Britain has developed in the post-war period, and my view of the fundamental change in direction which I believe is about to occur.

Though each country has its own special problems, successes and failures, by and large a similar evolution has taken place; and though I think we in Europe shall sink or swim together, we shall swim only if we will it.

So, though I shall draw my examples from Britain, about which I can speak with more direct knowledge, the trend to which I refer goes well beyond our shores.

Had I spoken to you last year, I should have expressed faith in our nation and civilization, and its capacity for survival. But today, I can offer you much more than faith, I bring you optimism rooted in present-day experience. I have reason to believe that the tide is beginning to turn against collectivism, socialism, statism, dirigism, whatever you call it. And this turn is rooted in a revulsion against the sour fruit of socialist experience. It is becoming increasingly obvious to many people who were intellectual socialists that socialism has failed to fulfil its promises, both in its more extreme forms in the communist world, and in its compromise versions.

The tide flows away from failure. But it will not automatically float us to our desired destination. There have been tides before which were not taken, opportunities which were lost, turning points which came and went. I do not believe that history is writ clear and unchallengeable. History is made by people: its movement depends on small currents as well as great tides, on ideas, perceptions, will and courage, the ability to sense a trend, the will to act on understanding and intuition. It is up to us to give intellectual content and political direction to these new dissatisfactions with socialism in practice, with its material and moral failures; to convert disillusion into understanding.

If we fail, the tide will be lost. But if it is taken, the last quarter of our century can initiate a new renaissance matching anything in our island's long and outstanding history.

I know that many of you in Continental Europe are gloomy about the economic and political condition of the United Kingdom. But I would remind you of the saying: the darkest hour is just before the dawn. I come to you in a mood of optimism, and I base it on two changes which I believe are taking place: a change in ideology, that is to say in people's beliefs and attitudes; and a change in economic circumstances.

For forty years now, the 'progressive' – the up-to-the-moment – thing in Britain has been to believe in the virtues of collectivism. Ever since the 1930s, the intellectual left of British politics has looked through rose-tinted spectacles at the real or imagined successes of planned economies, like those in Eastern Europe. Even Mr Callaghan,[1] for example – not conspicuously a member of the intellectual left – said as recently as 1960:

> I have not the slightest doubt that the economic measures and the socialist measures, which one will find in the countries of Eastern Europe, will become increasingly powerful against the unco-ordinated, planless society in which the West is living at present.

This view has been carrying increasing weight in the Labour Party.

It is true that in what they have said, senior socialist politicians have continued to affirm their faith in the mixed economy. But in the mixed economy, as in a cocktail, it is the mix that counts. In their favoured mix, collectivism has taken an ever larger proportion. The words of these politicians expressed a belief that private enterprise had a major role to play in the economy. But their deeds extended government into almost every part of business life. The 'progressives' had their way.

The nationalized sector of the economy has been extended far beyond the major industries of fuel, transport and steel. In the next few weeks, the aircraft and shipbuilding industries will be nationalized,[2] whilst the Labour Party's programme for the future, published last year, includes plans for taking over banks and insurance companies.[3] Private firms in difficulties have been taken into public ownership. More and more of the taxpayer's money has been pumped into companies that no prudent banker could go on supporting for long, because instead of creating

---

[1] James Callaghan (born 1912), Baron Callaghan of Cardiff 1987. Labour MP 1945–87; Chancellor of the Exchequer 1964–67; Home Secretary 1967–70; Foreign Secretary 1974–76; Leader of the Labour Party 1976–80; Prime Minister 1976–79.
[2] The Aircraft and Shipbuilding Industries Act 1977 created British Aerospace and British Shipbuilders.
[3] On 7 September, the National Executive Committee of the Labour Party published *Banking and Finance*, which advocated the nationalization of the four major clearing banks and seven insurance companies.

wealth they use up wealth created by others.[1] The state sector has come to dominate the mixed economy. Its insatiable demand for finance has inhibited the operation of the market sector. Yet the public sector can only live on private enterprise, on whose surplus it relies. This is where we now stand. But I believe that we have come to the end of the trend.

There is a growing realization in Britain that the 'progressives' were wrong. They are being proved wrong by the failure of the very system they advocated. To finance the extension of socialism on so vast a scale, taxation has risen to penal levels. We have all seen the results – for living standards, for incentive and for enterprise – of the excessive tax burden in Britain.

Yet even these unacceptable levels of taxation have not been enough to finance the public sector. The Government has been borrowing vast sums of money, both within Britain and overseas. But even these borrowings were not enough. The Government turned to printing money in order to finance a public sector deficit that neither taxpayers nor lenders would finance in full. With a huge rise in the money supply, hyper-inflation became a real threat: and that threat does not end with economics. When money can no longer be trusted, it is not only the economic basis for society that is undermined, but its moral basis too. (I shall return to that part of the argument later.)

And when the economic foundations are undermined, those who suffer most are the ordinary working people, the very people in whose name the socialists claim to be acting.

For it is our system, the free enterprise system, which delivers the goods to the great mass of the people. We may have been remiss in not saying this with sufficient vigour in the past; well, I shall not be remiss this evening.

For it is not only in my country that socialism has failed the nation. It is well known that the ultimate aim of every Soviet planner is for his country to equal the levels of production in the USA. It is the West, not the East, which sells off surpluses of grain and other foodstuffs to the planned economies, and also gives them to the countries of the Third World. It is Western technology which the East seeks to acquire. And it is the Western world, those countries with essentially capitalist

---

[1] Since 1974, the Labour Government had nationalized British Leyland and the ship-builders Harland & Wolff, created the British National Oil Corporation, bought 50 per cent of Ferranti Electronics, subsidized Chrysler UK, and set up the National Enterprise Board to facilitate further state intervention.

economies, from which the British Government has recently sought, and received, help for the pound.[1] The socialist countries do not attempt to conceal their admiration for the productive achievements of the free economy. But what they do argue is that the avalanche of goods which the capitalist system produces is available only to the well-to-do.

This is totally false. It misconceives the very essence of capitalist achievement. As Josef Schumpeter[2] put it:

> The capitalist engine is first and last an engine of mass production, which unavoidably means also production for the masses . . . It is the cheap cloth, the cheap fabric, boots, motor cars and so on that are the typical achievements of capitalist production and not as a rule improvements that would mean much to the rich man.

In brief, the material superiority of the free society gives its main benefits to the very people the socialists claim to cherish.

Continuing benefits depend upon innovation. It is innovation which lies at the heart of economic progress, and only the free economy can provide the conditions in which it will flourish.

Alfred Marshall,[3] doyen of nineteenth-century British economists, said the capitalist economy frees constructive genius

> to work its way to the light and to prove its existence by attempting difficult tasks on its own responsibility, and succeeding in them: for those who have done most for the world have seldom been those whom their neighbours would have picked out as likely for the work.

How much more will the remote, central planner fail to pick the winner? This inability to foresee from the centre where the next innovation will come is a key failing of the planned economy. Collectivists may flatter themselves that wise men at the centre – with whom they identify – can make better decisions, and waste fewer resources, than a myriad of individual decision-makers and independent organizations all over the

---

[1] On 3 January 1977, the International Monetary Fund approved standby credits for Britain to the value of £2,300 million.

[2] Josef Schumpeter (1883–1950), Moravian-born US economist and sociologist, whose works include *The Theory of Economic Development* (1911) and *Capitalism, Socialism, and Democracy* (1942).

[3] Alfred Marshall (1842–1924), Professor of Political Economy at Cambridge 1885–1908; author of *Principles of Economics* (1890).

country. Events in Britain have shown that, wise or not, those at the centre lack the knowledge, foresight and imagination required. They are overworked and overwhelmed. They are certainly surprised by events.

I have dwelt so far on the material superiority of the free society. But we must not focus our attention exclusively on the material, because, though important, it is not the main issue. The main issues are moral. In warfare, said Napoleon, the moral to the material is as three to one. You may think that in civil society the ratio is even greater.

The economic success of the Western world is a product of its moral philosophy and practice. The economic results are better because the moral philosophy is superior. It is superior because it starts with the individual, with his uniqueness, his responsibility, and his capacity to choose. Surely this is infinitely preferable to the socialist-statist philosophy which sets up a centralized economic system to which the individual must conform, which subjugates him, directs him and denies him the right to free choice.

Choice is the essence of ethics: if there were no choice, there would be no ethics, no good, no evil; good and evil have meaning only insofar as man is free to choose. In our philosophy the purpose of the life of the individual is not to be the servant of the state and its objectives, but to make the best of his talents and qualities. The sense of being self-reliant, of playing a role within the family, of owning one's own property, of paying one's way, are all part of the spiritual ballast which maintains responsible citizenship, and provides the solid foundation from which people look around to see what more they might do, for others and for themselves. That is what we mean by a moral society; not a society where the state is responsible for everything, and no one is responsible for the state.

I said earlier that the better moral philosophy of the free society underlies its economic performance. In turn, the material success of the free society enables people to show a degree of generosity to the less fortunate unmatched in any other society. It is noteworthy that the Victorian era – the heyday of free enterprise in Britain – was also the era of the rise of selflessness and benefaction.

The second reason why the free society is morally better is because it entails dispersal of power away from the centre to a multitude of smaller groups, and to individuals. On the other hand, the essence of collectivism is the concentration of power in large groups, and in the hands of the state at the centre: as Lord Acton[1] reminded us, absolute power corrupts absolutely.

The left had traditionally argued that the dispersal of power, coupled with the freedom given to the individual, could, and did, lead to the power being unjustly used. But part of the price of freedom is that some will abuse it. And in free societies this problem is dealt with by a strong and impartial legal system, designed to ensure justice between individuals, and to safeguard the weak against the strong. The evolution of such a system was an essential element in the growth of freedom.

It is ironic that many intellectuals espoused the socialist creed because they thought it would prevent the development of harmful monopoly power and that their system would obviate it. They took it for granted that socialism would protect the weak against the strong. They forgot that when the socialists gained power they would become the strong, and would resist any check on their own power.

How shaken and disabused are many of these intellectuals today. And rightly so, for we are now facing the crisis of socialism: economic failure, social and political tensions; a decline in freedom of choice in education, health, economic activity.

Experience has shown that socialism corrodes the moral values which form part of a free society. Traditional values are also threatened by increasing state regulation.

The more the state seeks to impose its authority, the less respect that authority receives. The more living standards are squeezed by taxation, the greater is the temptation to evade that taxation. The more pay and prices are controlled, the more those controls are avoided. In short, where the state is too powerful, efficiency suffers and morality is threatened.

Britain in the last two or three years provides a case study of why collectivism will not work. It shows that the 'progressive' theory was not progressive. On the contrary, it proved retrograde in practice. This is a lesson that democrats all over the world should heed.

Yet I face the future with optimism. Our ills are creating their own antibodies. Just as success generates problems, so failure breeds the will to fight back, and the body politic strives to restore itself.

[1] Sir John Emerich Dalberg-Acton (1834–1902), 1st Baron Acton of Aldenham 1869, British Catholic historian. Liberal MP 1859–66; Professor of Modern History at Cambridge 1895–1902.

The ordinary Briton is neither political philosopher nor economist. He has no clearly articulated theory to tell him why the free society is superior to the collectivist one. But he has felt the shortcomings of collectivism and he senses that something is fundamentally wrong. This explains why many people are giving up their support for socialist ideas and policies.

Nor is the reaction against socialism confined to politics and ideology. It is also practical. Under our very eyes, new forms of free association, free economic activity, great and small, are being born, thanks to the resourcefulness of many men and women.

I am reminded of an observation by Adam Smith,[1] who said:

> The uniform, constant and uninterrupted effort of every man to better his condition, the principle from which public and national, as well as private opulence is originally derived, is frequently powerful enough to maintain the natural progress of things toward improvement, in spite both of the extravagance of government and of the greatest errors of administration. Like the unknown principle of animal life, it frequently restores health and vigour to the constitution, in spite not only of the disease, but of the absurd prescriptions of the doctor.

The great mutual benefit activities, 'the people's capitalism', are burgeoning. Between them, occupational pension funds and life insurance own a good half of all quoted securities on behalf of their members. Thanks to them, and to other charities and non-profit-making activities which hold securities, it is estimated that 85 per cent of the population has an indirect, if not direct, share in British industry. The vast majority of the population is thus participating in capitalism.

The investors and the workers have become the same people. As shareholders and employees, they have an identical interest in industrial and commercial prosperity. We may soon be witnessing the withering away of the class struggle, to adapt a well-known phrase.

Then there are the building societies (which are mutual mortgage banks), which have enabled a good third of the population to buy their

---

[1] Adam Smith (1723–90), Scottish economist. Professor of Moral Philosophy at Glasgow 1752–63; author of *A Theory of Moral Sentiments* (1759) and *The Wealth of Nations* (1776); founder of systematic classical economics.

homes, lending and borrowing without subsidies or assistance, asking only to be allowed to get on with their jobs.

There is the phenomenon that, however many resources are poured into the existing nationalized sector, its employment and share of production tend to fall, while private activities expand, when they have half the chance. The City of London responds to reduced scope for its activities on behalf of British industry (because industry's profits have been eroded) by expanding its services on behalf of the rest of the world. Our manufacturers expand overseas and in Europe, attracting local capital – using the initiative and capacity which, under present circumstances, are only partly used at home. That way they keep their management teams in being for the day when industry will be able to expand in Britain. And were it not for their repatriated earnings, our economic position would be worse.

The great North Sea oil adventure was initiated and financed entirely by free enterprise, without help from Government. The oil companies overcame not only the unprecedented technological problem created by North Sea weather hazards, but also the political hazard posed by hostility to free enterprise and profit. All these developments and potentialities illustrate the inherent vitality of our people. We need have no fear as we engage in the battle of ideas.

We have a ready audience. The younger generation may produce its wild men, but it also produces large numbers of young people for whom the post-war settlement has failed, and who are ready to examine our arguments on their merits. The opportunity is ours if we can grasp it instead of meeting the socialists halfway.

Mr Chairman: When Winston Churchill spoke in this Hall in 1946, he called for an act of faith in recreating the European family.[1] It is an act of faith too which is required today by all of us in restoring the free society.

Not far from Winston Churchill's country home lived one of our best-known national poets, Rudyard Kipling.[2] He and Winston were great friends and mutual admirers. The new renaissance of which I spoke was perhaps best described by Kipling:

[1] In his Zurich speech of 19 September 1946, Churchill appealed for the creation of 'a kind of United States of Europe', based on Franco–German partnership, with the British Commonwealth and the USA as its friends and sponsors.
[2] Rudyard Kipling (1865–1936), English poet and novelist. Lines from 'The Dawn Wind'.

So when the world is asleep, and there seems no hope of waking
Out of some long, bad dream that makes her mutter and moan,
Suddenly, all men arise to the noise of fetters breaking,
And everyone smiles at his neighbour and tells him his soul is his
    own.

8

The Iain Macleod Memorial Lecture, delivered to Greater London Young Conservatives, Caxton Hall, Westminster, 4 July 1977

The Iain Macleod Memorial Lecture of July 1977 can be seen as balancing and complementing the Zurich speech of four months earlier. Zurich had seen a forceful defence of liberty and free enterprise economics. The Macleod Lecture dwells on more orthodox Tory themes – the British nation, the superiority of tradition to ideology, the importance of religion. But perhaps the most original and telling passages are those explaining why self-interest (as Adam Smith – and Mrs Thatcher – understood it) is not to be confused with selfishness (pp. 62–3). An interesting early pointer to the future is provided by the praise for Victorian voluntary effort and the Victorian 'virtues' which lay behind it (p. 66).

DIMENSIONS OF CONSERVATISM

We honour the memory of Iain Macleod[1] by continuing his life's work, the restoration of the Conservative heritage. Some of you here today will remember him; some will have come into politics after he was taken from us. So I shall begin by trying to sum up for you the essence of his contribution to Conservative politics.

He was a great pragmatist in the true meaning of the word: he saw practice as the acid test, and principles as the motivating force. He was the practical man *par excellence* precisely because his every thought and act were so firmly rooted in principle. So when we ask, as all of us do,

---

[1] Iain Macleod (1913–70), Conservative MP 1950–70; Minister of Health 1952–55; Minister of Labour and National Service 1955–59; Colonial Secretary 1959–61; Chairman of the Conservative Party 1961–63; Chancellor of the Exchequer 1970.

what would Iain have done in these circumstances, it is to his underlying principles that we must turn first.

He was a Tory in that he saw himself as part of a continuous and growing Tory tradition going back three whole centuries to the dawn of Parliamentary government in the aftermath of the Civil War, and going forward into a future, presaging changes and challenges of equal magnitude. He was a Christian, for whom Tory politics were a part – a subordinate part – of a great commitment to the Good Life and service of God. He was a national politician, who thought in terms of Britain's needs, ways, and wider contribution to the world, drawing ideas and solutions from the British context, and seeing the statesman's task as finding political solutions for urgent British problems. It is to these dimensions of Conservatism, which he exemplified for us, that I shall devote this talk.

Every generation must restate its values in light of present challenges, but also in light of past experience. There has never been greater need for us Conservatives to do so than there is today. For we have been in danger of allowing our thinking to be dominated by socialism to a point where we even define our own position in terms of how, where and why we differ from socialism and socialists – as though Conservatism was primarily an alternative to socialism. This is a compliment that I for one refuse to pay this recent creed. For we are not just anti-socialists, nor primarily anti-socialists; our opposition to socialism is just one corner of our vision, in which what we are for sets the tone, not what we are against; what we are against stems from what we are for.

The Tory tradition long antedates not only socialism but also what the socialists call capitalism and I prefer to call the free economy. To describe us as the party of free enterprise as opposed to state ownership would be misleading, although we believe in the vital contribution of free enterprise to a free and prosperous Britain, and have good cause to fear the deadening effect of state ownership and control. For to pose our commitment to free enterprise as our main purpose and distinguishing mark would be to describe the whole in terms of one of its many parts.

Free enterprise has a place, an honoured place, in our scheme of things; but as one of many dimensions. For Tories became Tories well before the modern concept of a free market economy meant anything, well before it became a matter of political controversy.

Conservatism will, I believe, continue to be a living, growing creed long after economic controversy gives way to other issues, long after socialism comes to be seen as one of the many blind alleys of history, of interest to the historian alone. The Conservative Party is an integral part of the British tradition, not to be explained in abstract terms, but as part of the living flesh of British life over the generations. So let me begin today, as I learned to do with Iain's help, from a sense of shared history; not just Tory history, but British history.

For we are essentially a British party. We try to the best of our ability to understand Britain's problems and do what is good for Britain, while fulfilling our obligations as members of the world community. We observe what happens elsewhere, and draw lessons from it, but aware that different national traditions, experience and religious values must affect the social, political and economic solutions. We know that there are certain human needs and values, not simply material needs but human rights, dignity, freedom from fear. These should be accorded everywhere. But the further we proceed from these fundamentals to political and economic arrangements, the less competent we feel to do much more than pronounce success or failure.

Our sense of history imparts caution and humility to us. You will have noted how the socialist is happy to lay down the law for all mankind, past, present and future, giving marks, usually bad ones, convinced that he could have done much better. You will have noticed how they claim solidarity with socialist parties and regimes everywhere, in the name of human solidarity, while preaching hatred towards fellow British citizens of differing background or views. You will have noted too how socialists consider themselves qualified to lay down what is good for all countries and societies, for the Chinese and the Chileans, Uruguayans and Paraguayans, South Africans and South Vietnamese, Anguillans and Angolans – and never does a shadow of self-doubt cross their closed little minds.

We beg to differ from them. First, I think it arrogant to claim that our generation is any wiser than previous generations. We are here, they are gone. We can stand on their shoulders, as I hope succeeding generations will be able to stand on ours. But we should not be too hasty in judging them, not simply because we shall be judged in turn, but because to judge requires so much knowledge, such an effort of imagination to put ourselves into their shoes that could well be spent – barring the professional historian – on understanding our own pressing problems. Least of all do we feel qualified to offer advice to more successful nations, on whose bounty this Government's spendthrift measures have made us dependent.

But we are more than just a British party. The Tories began as a Church party, concerned with the Church and state, in that order, before our concern extended to the economy, and many other fields which politics now touches. Religion gives us not only values – a scheme of things in which economic, social, penal policy have their place – but also our historical roots. For through the Old Testament our spiritual roots go back to the early days of civilization and man's search for God. The New Testament takes us on through Greek philosophy, Roman law, the Church Fathers and the great flowering of a specifically Christian civilization in the Middle Ages from which our own characteristic way of life emerged.

Our religion teaches us that every human being is unique and must play his part in working out his own salvation. So whereas socialists begin with society, and how people can be fitted in, we start with man, whose social and economic relationships are just part of his wider existence.

Because we see man as a spiritual being, we utterly reject the Marxist view, which gives pride of place to economics. However much the Marxists and their fellow-travellers, new and old, may try to wriggle and explain away, this was Marx's stated view and a linchpin of his whole system.

The religious tradition values economic activity – how we earn our living, create wealth – but warns against obsession with it, warns against putting it above all else. Money is not an end in itself, but a means to an end.

The letters the Archbishop of Canterbury received in reply to his 'call to the nation' were recently published.[1] One of them was from a country vicar:

'I am concerned,' he wrote, 'that I haven't enough to do my job properly. I am concerned because my parishioners, some of them at least, are not receiving what I ought to be able to provide and be glad to give them, i.e. a visit in emergencies, just because there is no petrol in the tank and no money in the pocket to buy more; or that there is petrol only sufficient to provide transport for my wife to work.'

[1] Donald Coggan (born 1909), Baron Coggan of Canterbury 1980. Archbishop of York 1961–74; Archbishop of Canterbury 1974–80. In his 'call to the nation' of 15 October 1975, he suggested that the British people were drifting on a tide of selfish materialism, advocated a return to basic values, and invited letters about modern problems.

That vicar knew that he needed money, not for itself, but for what he could do with it.

The increased involvement of government with economic life has coincided with a marked worsening of economic performance. It has heightened tensions between different groups of workers, some struggling to keep differentials, others trying to override them; between producers and consumers, landlords and tenants, public services and the public.

To observe these things is not to deny a role to government in economic life; it is not to preach *laissez faire*. That was preached two centuries back when manufacture and commerce were fighting to free themselves from state monopoly and interference which were holding back their development.

There is much that the state should do, and do much better than it is doing. But there are also proper limits which have long since been passed in this country. To understand the reason, and how these limits can be adduced, we must come back to the nature of man. This is a matter where our understanding and our case, based on religion and commonsense, is so much sounder than that of the socialist doctrine. Yet the socialist travesty has succeeded in gaining wide acceptance by default, even among our own people. I refer to the question of self-interest as against the common good. The socialists have been able to persuade themselves and many others that a free economy based on profit embodies and encourages self-interest, which they see as selfish and bad, whereas they claim socialism is based on, and nurtures, altruism and selflessness. This is baseless nonsense in theory and in practice; let me explain why.

Let us start from the idea of self. There is not and cannot possibly be any hard and fast antithesis between self-interest and care for others, for man is a social creature, born into family, clan, community, nation, brought up in mutual dependence. The founders of our religion made this a cornerstone of morality. The admonition 'Love thy neighbour as thyself, and do as you would be done by' expresses this. You will note that it does not denigrate self, or elevate love of others above it. On the contrary, it sees concern for self and responsibility for self as something to be expected, and asks only that this be extended to others. This embodies the great truth that self-regard is the root of regard for one's fellows. The child learns to understand others through its own feelings – at first its immediate family; in course of time the circle grows.

Our fellow-feeling develops from self-regard. Because we want warmth, shelter, food, security, respect and other goods for ourselves, we can understand that others want them too. If we had no desire for these things, would we be likely to understand and further others' desire for them?

You may object that saintly people can well have no personal desires, either material or prestigious; but we do not legislate for saints.

Now, since people in their day-to-day lives are motivated by this complex of attitudes – self-regard and fellow-feeling, group and sectional interests, personal and family responsibility, local patriotism, philanthropy – an economy will be effective only insofar as it can contain and harness all these drives. Perhaps Archbishop Temple[1] had it right when he said: 'The art of Government, in fact, is the art of so ordering life that self interest prompts what justice demands.'

Adam Smith, who came to economics via philosophy (sociology, as we should now call it) and history, described how the interplay between the self-interest of many can further the mutual interest of all. I urge you to read him, both for what he said and for what he did not say, but is often ascribed to him. He did not say that self-interest was good *per se*; he saw it as a major drive which can be a blessing to any society able to harness it and a curse to those who cannot harness it. He showed how the market economy obliges and enables each producer to serve the consumers' interests by serving his own.

People must be free to choose what they consume in goods and services. When they choose through the market, their choice is sovereign. They alone exercise their responsibility as consumers and producers. To the extent that the fruits of their efforts are appropriated by the state, or other coercive bodies, they not only have responsibility taken away from them, but the ability to make their wishes felt. Power accrues more and more to the politician, bureaucrat, state-owned or subsidized providers of goods and services.

Choice in a free society implies responsibility. There is no hard and fast line between economic and other forms of personal responsibility to self, family, firm, community, nation, God. Morality lies in choosing between feasible alternatives. A moral being is one who exercises his own judgement in choice, on matters great and small, bearing in mind their moral dimension, i.e. right and wrong. Insofar as his right and duty to choose is taken away by the state, the party or the union, his moral faculties, i.e. his capacity for choice, atrophy, and he becomes a

---

[1] William Temple (1881–1944), English cleric. Archbishop of York 1929–42; Archbishop of Canterbury 1942–44.

moral cripple, in the same way as we should lose the faculty of walking, reading, seeing, if we were prevented from using them over the years.

In a letter from a person who responded to the Archbishop of Canterbury's 'call to the nation', this point was beautifully put:

> We wish to be self-reliant and do not want to be dependent on the state, nor do we want the state to take so great a proportion of our money in rates and taxes to decide for us what we shall have and not have ... I may be wrong, but I think it weakens character when little by little our freedom of choice is taken from us.

And another person said:

> I am a middle-aged woman, wife of a lower-paid worker. We have struggled through the years to buy our own house, old though it may be. We have asked for nothing. We only had one child, so no child allowance. What we have achieved we did ourselves. When we look round and see all the handouts people are getting from this Welfare State, we sometimes feel so sad that what should be a wonderful thing has really turned out to sap the goodness and initiative from so many of our people.

So let there be no mistake: economic choices have a moral dimension. A man is now enabled to choose between earning his living and depending on the bounty of the state, a choice which comes about because benefits rise and remain tax-free, while earnings rise more slowly if at all, and tax is high at very low income levels.

A man must choose between spending and saving, between housing himself and depending on the state to house him at his fellow-citizens' expense; between paying for his children's education and accepting whatever the state provides; between working for a wage or salary and setting up on his own; between longer hours of work or study and spending more time in leisure with his family; between spending more of his money on himself and more on his family; between joining a union and not joining, even if it means persecution by union and state.

The socialists would take away most or all of these choices. A man would do what he was told by the state and his union, work where work was 'found' for him, at the rate fixed and degree of effort permitted. He would send his children to school where the education authority decided what the children are taught and the way they are taught. Irrespective of his views, he would live in the housing provided, take what he could get, give what he was obliged to give.

This does not produce a classless society; on the contrary it produces the most stratified of all societies, divided into two classes: the powerful and the powerless, the party-bureaucratic élite and the manipulated masses.

And are these rulers better fitted to make choices on our behalf or to dispose of resources? Are they wiser, less selfish, more moral? What reason have we for supposing that they are? As the French economist and critic of socialism, Claude Frédéric Bastiat,[1] asked a century and a half ago, how can the socialists, who have such a low opinion of the people's ability to choose, have such a high regard for their own?

I quote his own words:

> Since the natural inclinations of mankind are so evil that its liberty must be taken away, how is it that the inclinations of the socialists are good? Are not the legislators and their agents part of the human race? Do they believe themselves moulded from another clay than the rest of mankind? They say that society, left to itself, heads inevitably for destruction because its instincts are perverse. They demand the power to stop mankind from sliding down this fatal declivity and to impose a better direction on it. If, then, they have received from Heaven intelligence and virtues that place them beyond and above mankind, let them show their credentials. They want to be shepherds, and they want us to be their sheep.

We know from experience that these self-appointed guardians use their power to perpetuate it. We have seen how the economic considerations, which in a market economy are decisive, are increasingly subordinated in a controlled economy to the party political interests of politicians, to the group interest of state employees, and to workers in some nationalized industries. We pay through the nose in prices and taxes and take what we are given. In that sense, we don't own those industries, they own us.

And have we not seen at home, and particularly abroad, how some socialist politicians soon come to adopt the very 'ruling lifestyles' they rose to power by denouncing?

---

[1] Claude Frédéric Bastiat (1801–50), French economist, social philosopher, and free trade campaigner.

In the market economy, people are free to give of their money and their time for good causes. They exercise their altruism on their own initiative and at their own expense, whether they give directly and personally through institutions, charities, universities, churches or hospitals.

When the state steps in, generosity is increasingly restricted from all sides. From the one side, the idea is propagated that whatever needs doing is best done by the state. Since the state knows best, causes it does not support must be of questionable worth. On the other side, since the state takes more and more of people's earnings, they have less inclination to give what money they still have left for those needs which the Welfare State fails to meet.

When people give directly, personally or through an institution they respect, they feel that the sacrifices they may make in giving, and the effort in earning, are worthwhile. People have always accepted the responsibility to sustain the young and the old, the unfortunate and the needy. But when the money is taken away and spent by Government, the blessing goes out of giving and out of the effort of earning in order to give.

This contrast is borne out by historical experience. The Victorian age, which saw the burgeoning of free enterprise, also saw the greatest expansion of voluntary philanthropic activity of all kinds – the new hospitals, new schools, technical colleges, universities, new foundations for orphans, non-profit-making housing trusts, missionary societies. Dr Barnardo's Homes was founded in 1866. It cares today for 2,251 children in residential accommodation. The Soldiers', Sailors' and Airmen's Families' Association was founded in 1885 and now, with twelve thousand volunteer workers, helps countless families. The National Society for the Prevention of Cruelty to Children, which now handles some eighty thousand cases annually, was founded in 1884. The St John Ambulance Association was founded in 1877 to provide a service still essential to every centre of population. The Church Army, now giving help to 14,800 people, started in 1890. The Royal National Lifeboat Institution was founded in 1824 and now maintains 250 lifeboats at a cost of about £3 million a year, almost entirely from voluntary subscriptions.

The Victorian age has been very badly treated in socialist propaganda. It was an age of constant and constructive endeavour in which the desire to improve the lot of the ordinary person was a powerful factor. We who are largely living off the Victorians' moral and physical capital can hardly afford to denigrate them.

You may remember Lord Acton's aphorism that while only a foolish

Conservative would judge the present by the standards of the past, only a foolish Liberal would judge the past by the standards of the present. There are many foolish Liberals in the socialist camp; we can do without them in ours.

Why then, you may ask, did socialist thought make so much headway? It is not only a fair question but a vitally important one for us. There are many possible answers. But one obvious reason stands out: socialists criticized imperfect human reality in the name of theory. So long as socialism was only a theory, it made criticism of other ways easy for them. They could claim that their way was best. But now we are beyond the days of theory. For decades socialists have extended their power until they control almost half the world's population. How has the thing worked out in practice? Disastrously. Wherever they have imposed their heavy hand, people are worse off and less free.

A leading Labour Party ideologist, Baroness Wootton,[1] recently said proudly that during her lifetime she was glad to see that one-third of the world's population had come to earn its daily bread under socialism. True, she made a brief reference to the fact that they seem to practise tyranny and racism, but very much *en passant*. She neither stopped to ask whether this was not inherent in socialist rule, nor what the quality and quantity of socialism's daily bread was like. Not all Lady Wootton's fellow socialists are as frank as she is in claiming the socialist world as soulmates, and as encouragement for their efforts to clamp down socialism here 'irrevocably and irreversibly', to use one of the present Government's favourite phrases.

True, not all of the Labour Party are happy to accept communist-ruled regimes as fellow socialists. But they are remarkably muted in their opposition to the 'fraternal relations' adopted by a majority of their party and trade union movement. Insofar as some are embarrassed by the behaviour of their fellow socialists in the Soviet Union, Cambodia and East Germany, they have yet failed to produce a coherent explanation of why they believe that a doctrine which has produced such visibly inhuman results in a third of the world or more would lead us to Utopia in Great Britain.

To say that the others are not 'true socialists' – no connection with the firm next door with the same name – gets us no further. Socialism

---

[1] Professor Barbara Wootton (1897–1988), Baroness Wootton of Abinger Common 1958, British social scientist. Her best-known work is *Testament for Social Science* (1950).

is what socialists do, and socialists do more or less the same, as the opportunity permits.

GULAG[1] was the consequence of socialism. It was not the work of one man. It only happened because socialism demoralized the whole nation, replaced the individual conscience with the Party, right and wrong with what was good for the Revolution.

But as I argued earlier, we shall not win simply by showing the dark side of socialism. That is why I began with our vision, and put it in the centre of the stage. I stress: vision, not blueprint; values and principles, not doctrines. We are really in no better position to prophesy than preceding generations were, and they always got it wrong; the more scientific they thought they were, the further they strayed. For the unfolding of human history is richer and more complex than our minds can foresee.

Yet by understanding the present and the past and adducing possibilities and probabilities as best we can, so long as we leave some margin for error, we can influence the shape of things to come. We have learned much from the over-optimism of the immediate post-war era, when we thought Government could do it all. We need healthy scepticism, but not pessimism.

We are not bound to an irrevocable decline. We see nothing as inevitable. Men can still shape history.

Because the post-war Keynesian recipe of endless growth and full employment through high demand levels went sour, this does not mean we turn our backs on the aspirations which underlay the 1944 White Paper on employment policy.[2] Because we see that welfare can be abused, we do not neglect our responsibility to help people back onto their feet and to look after the handicapped.

We know that we must assure a better balance between what people receive and what they can earn, and between the hardship we see and are moved to mitigate through the welfare system and the reaction we create when taxes fall too heavily on the taxpayer.

This is a turning-point in our Party's history, no less than in our nation's, comparable to the situation when Iain Macleod came back into civilian life after the war. He and his generation had been formed under the combined influence of their heavy wartime responsibilities, the high

[1] Russian acronym for Chief Administration of Corrective Labour Camps.
[2] The 1944 White Paper accepted Government responsibility for 'the maintenance of a high and stable level of employment'.

hopes for post-war Britain generated during the war, and the shock of our electoral defeat in 1945.

Iain let none of these put him off balance. He set to work with others of his generation to pick up the pieces, to begin from where they were. He and the 'One Nation' Group[1] set the tone for much of post-war Conservative thought and action. They did not blame their stars, or the voters. They set to work to ask what had gone wrong, and how to put it right.

That was a generation back. We now stand before the new challenges: how to revive the economy, how to enlarge our liberties, how to restore the balance between trade unions and the community, how to further our European partnership while protecting legitimate British interests, how to simplify the welfare maze which often baffles those who most deserve help, how to regain an underlying sense of nationhood and purpose.

Circumstances in the late seventies are different from those of thirty years ago. Once again we have faced electoral defeat, drawn the necessary conclusions and come back with renewed vigour.

Iain Macleod's approach then was, in essence: if it must be done it can be done; if it can be done it must be done. 'We shall prevail,' one of his great speeches ended. We did, and we shall.

[1] The One Nation Group was formed in 1950 by young Conservative MPs who wanted a greater commitment from the Party to social services.

9

Speech at the Church of St Lawrence Jewry, City of London, 30 March 1978

Margaret Thatcher's first speech at the Church of St Lawrence Jewry in the City of London, in March 1978, develops a number of themes which appeared in the Iain Macleod Lecture the previous year, but with a clearer stamp of personal experience and distinctive conviction. Perhaps this is because it is heavily based on the values and beliefs of Mrs Thatcher's upbringing in Grantham (which she describes in Chapter One of Volume II of her memoirs). A politician who is a Christian, she argues, is not compelled by his or her Christianity to adopt a particular set of political beliefs, for 'Christianity offers us no easy solutions to political and economic issues.' But Christians should be wary of the state taking on too many responsibilities, for 'the role of the state in Christian society is to encourage virtue, not usurp it.' Christianity has another – negative – lesson to teach: that man is not perfectable, and that the pursuit of Utopia therefore entails a dangerous illusion. But the theme which is echoed and repeated ever more forcefully in later Thatcher speeches on the relationship between Christianity and politics comes towards the end of this one: 'We are all responsible moral beings with a choice between good and evil.'

I BELIEVE

Need I say that this is not a party political speech? To offer you such a speech would indeed be to abuse your Rector's hospitality. What is more, it would be extremely imprudent, if not quite impossible.

It is a long time since it was said that the Church of England was the Tory Party at prayer.[1] That famous dictum was never wholly true.

---

[1] The origins of this saying have been traced to a speech by Maude Royden (1876–1956), suffragist and preacher, who said in 1917: 'The Church should . . . be no longer satisfied only to represent the Conservative Party at prayer.'

Historically, it would be nearer the mark to say that the Tory Party in its origin was the Church of England in politics, for the old concept of a partnership between Church and state lies very near the heart of traditional Tory thinking, and in that partnership Tories always believed that the Church had primacy because it was concerned with those things which matter fundamentally to the destiny of mankind.

So how does my religion affect my work as a politician? I was brought up, let me remind you, in a religious environment which, by the standards of today, would seem very rigid. We often went to church twice on Sundays, as well as to morning and afternoon Sunday School. We attended a number of church activities during the week. We believed it was wrong to spend very much on personal pleasure. We were taught always to make up our own minds and never to take the easy way of following the crowd.

I suppose what this taught me above everything else was to see the temporal affairs of this world in perspective. What mattered fundamentally was man's relationship to God, and in the last resort this depended on the response of the individual soul to God's grace.

Politics, when I began to think about them, seemed naturally important because they were one of the ways in which individuals could discharge that duty to their neighbours which God has enjoined on mankind. It was also important because, though good institutions and laws cannot make men good, bad ones can encourage them to be a lot worse.

I never thought that Christianity equipped me with a political philosophy; but I thought it did equip me with standards to which political actions must, in the end, be referred. It also taught me that, in the final analysis, politics is about personal relations, about establishing the conditions in which men and women can best use their fleeting lives in this world to prepare themselves for the next. I was also brought up to believe that it was only through whole-hearted devotion to this preparation that true earthly happiness could be achieved. Experience gives me no reason to revise this view.

Now all this may sound rather pious; but in those days religion had not been stripped by certain sophisticated theologians of its supernatural elements. The language in which we express our religious ideas may have changed – that is to say, when we are not too embarrassed to express them at all. But I still believe that the majority of English parents want their children to be brought up in what is essentially the same religious heritage as was handed to me. To most ordinary people, Heaven and Hell, right and wrong, good and bad, matter.

Now if all this is true, it has one very important implication for politics. In the face of all difficulties and temptations we must keep, and not go on diluting, the specifically Christian content of teaching and corporate life in our schools. That was uppermost in my mind when I was at the Department of Education,[1] and will still be there if I am called to another ministerial office.

Today, we live in what the academics call 'a pluralist society'. My Party, like most others, is not only drawn from all Christian denominations and other religions, but also contains some who would hotly deny that religion has anything at all to do with politics or even with morality.

There are, to my mind, some advantages in this variety. I think some of the bitterness of political strife is reduced when we remind ourselves that many of the people who share our deepest convictions about life are on the other side in political controversy.

For the truth of the matter is this: the Bible as well as the tradition of the Church tell us very little directly about political systems or social programmes. The nearest we get is Christ telling his disciples to render unto Caesar that which is Caesar's, and unto God that which is God's. No doubt many political judgements rest on moral assumptions; but many of the issues on which we are passionately divided are disputes about fact and expediency. In politics, as Edmund Burke[2] taught us, there are very few universal and permanent truths.

So when I speak of my political ideals, I am most of the time speaking as the heir to a particular body of beliefs, and I hope insights; I am talking about what seems to me to be right for this country, at this particular time, bearing in mind our past.

I think it is important to avoid confusing moral and political judgements. There is always a temptation, not easily resisted, to identify our opponents with the Devil, to suggest that politics presents us with a series of clear and simple choices between good and evil, and to attribute base motives to all who disagree with us. These are dangerous and evil

---

[1] Margaret Thatcher was Secretary of State for Education and Science 1970-74.
[2] Edmund Burke (1729-97), Irish-born British statesman and author, theorist of conservatism. Whig MP 1765-94; Paymaster-General 1782 and 1783. Works include *Thoughts on the Cause of the Present Discontents* (1770) and *Reflections on the Revolution in France* (1790).

tendencies; they embitter politics, and they trivialize religion and morality.

Certainly Christianity offers us no easy solutions to political and economic issues. It teaches us that there is some evil in everyone and that it cannot be banished by sound policies and institutional reforms; that we cannot eliminate crime simply by making people rich, or achieve a compassionate society simply by passing new laws and appointing more staff to administer them. In politics there are few simplicities and certainties, and loads of dilemmas. Let me give one or two practical examples of what I mean.

Of course, it is true that all men of good will must be concerned with the relief of poverty and suffering; and in most Christian countries this has come to be regarded as one of the primary concerns of politicians. But it is one thing to say that the relief of poverty and suffering is a duty, and quite another to say that this duty can always be most efficiently and humanely performed by the state. Indeed, there are grave moral dangers and serious practical ones in letting people get away with the idea that they can delegate all their responsibilities to public officials and institutions.

We know the immense sacrifices which people will make for the care of their own near and dear – for elderly relatives, disabled children and so on – and the immense part which voluntary effort, even outside the confines of the family, has played in these fields. Once you give people the idea that all this can be done by the state, and that it is somehow second-best or even degrading to leave it to private people (it is sometimes referred to as 'cold charity'), then you will begin to deprive human beings of one of the essential ingredients of humanity – personal moral responsibility. You will in effect dry up in them the milk of human kindness. If you allow people to hand over to the state all their personal responsibility, the time will come – indeed it is close at hand – when what the taxpayer is willing to provide for the good of humanity will be seen to be far less than what the individual used to be willing to give from love of his neighbour.

So do not be tempted to identify virtue with collectivism. I wonder whether the state services would have done as much for the man who fell among thieves as the Good Samaritan did for him?

I am not saying, of course, that the state has no welfare functions. This would be wholly against the tradition of my Party. We have always believed that there must be a level of well-being below which a citizen must not be allowed to fall. Moreover, people cannot realize their

73

potential without educational opportunity. But the role of the state in Christian society is to encourage virtue, not to usurp it.

Let me give a second example. We all feel the need to assist the people of developing countries and recognize that it is our duty to help them. But how much of the Gross Domestic Product can be properly used in this way? Are direct state subsidies to Governments the best way of offering help? Is not a free and open trading system between countries more mutually beneficial than aid handouts by Government? These are questions which honest people can disagree about.

In post-war Britain we have seen a tendency, particularly in some places of learning and even in some churches, to claim or assume a moral superiority for socialist and collectivist ideas. The argument is presented in a compelling way. It is suggested that a system run on a basis of self-interest, profit and competition is somehow immoral and even structurally wrong.

Those who take this view point to some of the bad things in Victorian times, and before that, citing as evidence selected works of contemporary artists and writers. Now no one would deny that in every age and in every society there are features of which we should be ashamed, but can we honestly say that the system built up on private enterprise and freedom of choice has not produced an immense change for the better in the lot of all our people? Would a system dominated by the state have produced the wealth, well-being and freedom that we enjoy today? In this life we shall never achieve the perfect society, in spite of the optimism of much humanist writing; but at least a system based on personal choice allows us to have and pursue ideals and interests.

Today, it seems as if people are made to feel guilty about being well-off. But Christ did not condemn riches as such, only the way in which they were used and those who put their trust in them. It is one of the Church's tasks to guide us about our use of this world's wealth. But it seems strange to me that a man can be appealed to for substantial contributions to many Church and charitable causes, and yet be half-criticized for having the means to give generously.

Let me be quite clear: I am certainly not saying that socialist theory and socialist practice as we know them are contrary to the New Testament. Nor am I saying that you can't be a good and sincere Christian and a dedicated Social Democrat. What we think about the proper organization of society must depend on our own reading of history and on our own view of the circumstances of society today.

Nevertheless, there is one heresy which it seems to me that some political doctrines embrace. It is the belief that man is perfectable. This takes the form of supposing that if we get our social institutions right – if we provide properly for education, health and all other branches of social welfare – we shall have exorcized the Devil. This is bad theology and it also conflicts with our own experience. In my own lifetime, we have expended vast efforts and huge sums of money on policies designed to make people better and happier. Have we really brought about a fundamental improvement in man's moral condition? The Devil is still with us, recording his successes in the crime figures and in all the other maladies of this society, in spite of its relative material comfort.

If I am critical of what I believe to be the fallacies that underlie socialist doctrine, let me add that there are warnings which need to be heeded by those of us who favour a free market economy. As a Christian, I am bound to shun Utopias on this earth and to recognize that there is no change in man's social arrangements which will make him perfectly good and perfectly happy. Therefore I do not claim that the free enterprise system of itself is automatically going to have these effects. I believe that economic freedom is a necessary, but not a sufficient condition of our own national recovery and prosperity.

There is another dimension – a moral one. For a nation to be noted for its industry, honesty and responsibility and justice, its people need a purpose and an ethic. The state cannot provide these – they can only come from the teachings of a faith. And the Church must be the instrument of that work.

Alexis de Tocqueville,[1] writing on democracy in America, pointed out that: 'Religion . . . is more needed in democratic countries than in any others. How is it possible that society should escape destruction,' he asks, 'if the moral tie is not strengthened in proportion as the political tie is relaxed? And what can be done with a people who are their own masters if they are not submissive to the Deity?'

Freedom will destroy itself if it is not exercised within some sort of moral framework, some body of shared beliefs, some spiritual heritage transmitted through the Church, the family and the school. It will also destroy itself if it has no purpose. There is a well-known prayer which refers to God's service as 'perfect freedom'. My wish for the people of this country is that we shall be 'free to serve'.

---

[1] Count Alexis de Tocqueville (1805–59), French historian, civil servant and politician. *Démocratie en Amérique* (1835–9) and *L'Ancien régime et la révolution* (1856) are his principal books.

So we must have freedom and we must have a morality. But even these are not enough: man is inherently sinful and in order to sustain a civilized and harmonious society we need laws backed by effective sanctions.

Looking at this country today, I am bound to say that upholding the law is one area of life where I would wish the state to be stronger than it is. Freedom can only exist on a basis of law to be observed by governors and the governed, and to be rigorously and fairly enforced.

So the state's role in a democracy is first and foremost to uphold the rule of law. But sometimes in history we have been so impressed with this truth that we have forgotten that ultimately true harmony consists in the willing co-operation of free men, and is not served by an over-regulated society. What is more, even when freedom, as it sometimes does, seems to be working against social harmony, we must remember that it has its own intrinsic value, just because men and women were born to be free.

It appears to me that there are two very general and seemingly conflicting ideas about society which come down to us from the New Testament. There is that great Christian doctrine that we are all members one of another, expressed in the concept of the Church on earth as the body of Christ. From this we learn our interdependence and the great truth that we do not achieve happiness or salvation in isolation from each other but as members of society. That is one of the great Christian truths which has influenced our political thinking. But there is also another: that we are all responsible moral beings with a choice between good and evil, beings who are infinitely precious in the eyes of their Creator. You might almost say that the whole of political wisdom consists in getting these two ideas in the right relationship to each other. Of course there are many sincere Christians who will disagree with my practical conclusions. Totalitarian Marxists will disagree with me in principle. They make no bones about rejecting all the assumptions from which I begin. I believe that their philosophy is utterly inconsistent with the Gospel and the teaching of the Church.

What I am working for is a free and responsible society. But freedom is not synonymous with an easy life. Indeed, my own faith in freedom does not rest in the last resort on utilitarian arguments at all. Perhaps it would be possible to achieve some low-grade form of happiness in a thoroughly regimented state; but in such a state men would not be treated as what they are and what Christianity wanted them to be – free and responsible human beings. There are many difficult things about freedom: it does not give you safety; it creates moral dilemmas for you; it requires self-discipline; it imposes great responsibilities. But such is the destiny of man, and in such consists his glory and salvation.

In such too consists our national greatness. As the Book of Proverbs says: 'Righteousness Exalteth a Nation.'

10

Speech to the Conservative Party Conference, Brighton, 13 October 1978

The 1978 Party Conference speech was a difficult one for the Conservative Party and the Leader of the Opposition. The economy was improving. The financial disciplines imposed as a result of the IMF rescue package in 1976 had begun to do their work; inflation and unemployment fell. The Opposition's opinion poll lead fell also and might well have disappeared altogether were it not for the Saatchi & Saatchi 'Labour isn't Working' advertising campaign in the summer of 1978. Tory expectations of an early election had been disappointed. Although Prime Minister James Callaghan's last-minute decision not to call a general election in the autumn of 1978 can now be seen as a fatal error, at the time it disorientated the Conservatives who assembled in Brighton for a Conference that they had expected would never take place.

The Tories also faced splits on policy. The Shadow Cabinet had proved unable to reach a clear decision on its attitude to incomes policy, just at the time when the Labour Government's own incomes policy began to collapse. Ted Heath spoke in favour of Labour's incomes policy at the Conference itself. Somehow, Mrs Thatcher had to persuade her colleagues, political commentators and indeed wage-bargainers to think in entirely different terms. Hence, the most important passages of the speech were addressed directly to trade unionists, arguing that it was in their interests to work with free enterprise – and free collective bargaining – under a Conservative Government.

Political life may be unpredictable. Dull it isn't. Last month the nation was privileged to watch on television the first broadcast ever to present a chronic case of cold feet as a noble act of patriotism. 'Let's see it through together,' said the Prime Minister in his now notorious announcement that there would be no election – 'in the national interest'.[1] Of course, by seeing it through together he meant seeing it through

[1] James Callaghan made a special broadcast on 7 September 1978 to dismiss speculation about an October poll.

with Labour. I am inclined to think that the people of this country will reject that invitation the moment they are given the opportunity. Whenever the moment comes we are ready. As soon as Parliament reassembles we shall do all we can as a responsible Opposition to end the present damaging uncertainty, to defeat the Government and to bring about a general election.

But I must warn you that the dying days of this administration may well see one last wretched round of manipulation and manoeuvre, of private deals or public pacts or cosy little understandings – always, of course, 'in the national interest' – before the Government are finally dragged, kicking and screaming, to the polls. If that should be the case, so be it. I believe that the longer they wait, the harder they will fall. But the harder, too, will be our task of halting and reversing the decline of Britain.

Our Party offers the nation nothing less than national revival, the deeply needed, long awaited and passionately longed-for recovery of our country. That recovery will depend on a decisive rejection of the Labour Party by the people and a renewed acceptance of our basic Conservative belief that the state is the servant not the master of this nation.

But the problems we shall face are daunting. After nearly five years of Labour Government living standards have just got back to where they were when they took office. The Wilson–Callaghan years have left Britain close to the bottom of every international league table in terms of prices, in terms of jobs, and, above all, in terms of what we produce and what we owe to the rest of the world. Where they have left our country in terms of self-reliance and in terms of self-respect, in terms of national security, I hardly have to tell you.

That is the legacy of Labour, and no amount of whistling in the dark by the Prime Minister or the Chancellor can change it. There is only one service they can do the nation now. It is to stand not upon the order of their going, but go.

The damage that they have done to Britain is immeasurable. Our ancestors built a land of pride and hope and confidence in the future, a land whose influence grew out of all proportion to her size, whose Constitution guaranteed a balance between freedom and order which used to be the British hallmark and became a model for the world. That was the heritage they handed down to us.

What would they think of Labour Britain today? A country in which people ask: 'Why work if you can get by without?'; 'Why save if your savings are taxed away, or inflated away, or both?'; 'Why do a good

79

job when you will probably make out just as well if you do a bad one?';
'Why bother to get extra qualifications when differentials and earnings
so often depend on political muscle, not personal merit?'

At home we are a country profoundly ill at ease with ourselves, while
abroad a darkening and dangerous world scene confronts us. This is not
just a Conservative analysis: it is a view shared here and overseas, not
least by those who love this land and wish it well. In their franker
moments even some Labour Ministers subscribe to it.

'Land of hope and glory, mother of the free' sounds as stirring and
moving as ever, but it is less and less like the land we live in today. Why
is that? What has happened to this country of ours that we thought we
knew? It is not just a question of pinning down who is responsible,
important though that is. The first step in clearing your mind about
where to go is to understand how you got where you are.

Does what has happened to Britain over the last four and a half years
imply that we have been governed by remarkably foolish people? No;
though you may be able to think of one or two who would qualify under
that heading.

Is it the result of having been governed by unusually wicked people?
No. There have been enough good intentions to pave the well-worn
path twice over.

The root of the matter is this: we have been ruled by men who live
by illusions: the illusion that you can spend money you haven't earned
without eventually going bankrupt or falling into the hands of your
creditors; the illusion that real jobs can be conjured into existence by
Government decree, like rabbits out of a hat; the illusion that there is
some other way of creating wealth than by hard work and satisfying
your customers; the illusion that you can have freedom and enterprise
without believing in free enterprise; the illusion that you can have an
effective foreign policy without a strong defence force, and a peaceful
and orderly society without absolute respect for the law.

It is these and many other Labour fallacies that have brought Britain
to where we are today. Of course it is true that things have not deterio-
rated quite so quickly since the crisis in 1976. It was then, you will
remember, that Denis Healey was put on probation to the International
Monetary Fund.[1] A strange man, Mr Healey. He seems to think that
being put on probation is some sort of achievement demanding recog-

---

[1] IMF credits were conditional upon the British Government adhering to economic
orthodoxy as pledged in the 'letter of intent' of 15 December 1976.

nition. Someone ought to tell him that you do not give the man who sets fire to your house a medal just because he phones for the Fire Brigade.

Last week at Blackpool[1] he was boasting again about his success. He could see growing confidence throughout the economy. We are poised, he said, for another 'great leap forward'. But, he told the assembled comrades, there were two conditions which Labour had to fulfil to win the election. First, and I quote him again, 'We have got to keep inflation under control.' Agreed. 'And we have got to strengthen, not weaken the authority of Jim Callaghan in this movement and in this country.' Disagreed. 'Those,' said Mr Healey, 'are the things you have got to ponder before you cast your votes.' Well, the brothers pondered and they voted. They voted overwhelmingly to throw overboard the Government's whole economic strategy, and with it, according to the Chancellor, the Prime Minister's authority.[2] The following day Mr Callaghan tried to restore it by speaking of the Government's 'inescapable responsibility' to deal with the present situation. He said nothing about his own inescapable responsibility for bringing that situation about. That is the charge against Mr Callaghan. Ask Sir Harold Wilson and Barbara Castle what they thought of his 'responsibility' nearly ten years ago when he fought tooth and nail against their plan for reforming the trade unions, for making them – yes – more responsible. '*In Place of Strife*' they called it. The unions did not like it. Mr Callaghan saw it straight into the waste-paper basket.[3] The road to Blackpool 1978 was opened in 1969 by Mr Callaghan. He cut the tape; and so long as it suited him he travelled steadily down the road he had himself opened without so much as a backward glance.

In 1974, during the dispute with the miners, how did he define responsibility then? I will tell you how. He went to Wales and said to the miners: 'I am here as Chairman of the British Labour Party because I wanted to come into the mining valleys to place the Labour Party firmly

---

[1] At the Labour Party Conference.

[2] In Blackpool on 2 October 1978, the Labour Party Conference voted by a ratio of two to one to reject the Government's 5 per cent limit on pay increases and 'any wage restraint by whatever method'.

[3] *In Place of Strife* was the title of a White Paper produced by Mrs Castle, Employment and Productivity Secretary, in January 1969. It contained proposals to modernize industrial relations and reduce the number of strikes. James Callaghan led opposition to the policy within the Cabinet, and the Trade Union Reform Bill was abandoned six months later.

behind the miners' claim for a just and honest wage.' What would he say, what would the people of this country say, if the Chairman of our Party had gone down to East London and announced: 'I am here as Chairman of the British Conservative Party because I wanted to come to Dagenham to place the Conservative Party firmly behind the Ford workers' claim for a just and honest wage'?[1]

Well, now that the boot is on the other foot, what will the Conservatives do to him? Let me put his mind at rest. We are not going to follow in his footsteps. We won't accuse him of union-bashing. We won't support a strike in breach of an agreement. We won't act irresponsibly, and he knows it. Nor do we rejoice at his discomfiture, for his problems are the country's problems. But a man who whets the tiger's appetite cannot expect much sympathy when it turns and bites him.

Today the nation has a Prime Minister whose party has disowned his principal policy and destroyed the chief plank in his election strategy. Until last week that strategy was simple. Labour would play its union card, the one called 'special relationship'. The idea was this: a group of union leaders would try to persuade the country that if they were not allowed to call the tune, there would be no music. Mind you, no union leader ever said: 'I shall overturn a Conservative Government.' It was always the union next door that was going to do that. For Labour this device would have had one splendid virtue. It would have made it possible for every Labour candidate to say in effect: 'Suppose Labour has created more unemployment than any Government since 1945; suppose it has produced a stagnant economy; suppose it has doubled prices; suppose it has nothing to offer but more and more nationalization, more and more state control. The fact remains that only it can keep the unions happy, and without this the economy will grind to a halt.'

That, in a nutshell, was to be the Labour case when the election came. But the election did not come. Blackpool came – and with it, the great illumination.

Today, Labour's policies are at a dead end, economically and politically. This is not something to crow about. We do not hope for a country in ruins so that we can take over. We want to be elected so that we can do better, not because we could not possibly do worse.

The country is looking for a sign that we can succeed where socialism

---

[1] Rejecting a pay increase of 5 per cent, Ford workers went on strike from September to November 1978, when they settled for a package of measures equal to nearly 17 per cent in all.

has failed. Labour's dead end has to be our beginning. The idea that only Labour can talk to labour drowned in the sea at Blackpool. Let me now at our Conservative Conference start the Conservative dialogue.

Here are the facts as I see them – and I am talking now straight to the union leaders:

'We Conservatives don't have a blueprint for instant success. There isn't one. But at least we start with this advantage: we know what not to do. That path has been clearly signposted. If a Government takes too much in tax, everyone wants higher wages. If a Government bails out those who bargain irresponsibly, where does the money come from? The pockets of those who bargain responsibly. If a Government tries to level everyone down, with year after year of totally rigid incomes policies, it destroys incentive. If a Government enforces those policies with the underworld sanctions of blackmail and blacklist,[1] it undermines its own authority and Parliament's.

'For years the British disease has been the "us and them" philosophy. Many in industry are still infected with this virus. They still treat the factory not as a workplace but as a battlefield. When that happens the idea of a common interest between employers and employed flies out of the window and so does the truth that if your company prospers, you will too.

'Now, you, the trade union leaders, have great power. You can use it well or you can use it badly. But look at the position of your members today, and compare it with the position of workers in other free countries. Can you really say, can anyone really say, you have used your power well?

'You want higher wages, better pensions, shorter hours, more government spending, more investment, more – more – more – more. But where is the "more" to come from? There is no more. There can be, but there won't be unless we all produce it. You can no more separate pay from output than you can separate two blades of a pair of scissors and still have a sharp cutting edge.

'And here let me say plainly to the trade union leaders: You are often your own worst enemies. Why isn't there more? Because too often restrictive practices rob you of the one thing you have to sell – your productivity. Restrictive practices are encrusted like barnacles on our

---

[1] Employers who agreed to wage rises in excess of 5 per cent risked incurring dividend controls and inclusion on a blacklist of firms to be denied Government contracts and assistance.

industrial life. They've been there for almost a century. They were designed to protect you from being exploited, but they have become the chief obstacle to your prosperity. How can it be otherwise? When two men insist on doing the work of one, there is only half as much for each.

'I understand your fears. You're afraid that producing more goods with fewer people will mean fewer jobs, and those fears are naturally stronger at a time of high unemployment. But you're wrong. The right way to attack unemployment is to produce more goods more cheaply, and then more people can afford to buy them. Japan and Germany, mentioned several times this week – and rightly so – are doing precisely that and have been for years. Both have a large and growing share of our markets. Both are winning your customers and taking your jobs. Of course, we in Britain see the German success and want it here – the same living standards, the same output, the same low rate of inflation. But remember, what they have also had in Germany is strict control of the money supply, no rigid incomes policy, less state control than we have, lower personal tax, and unions which are on the side of the future, not refighting the battles of the past.

'We shall do all that a Government can to rebuild a free and prosperous Britain. We believe in realistic, responsible collective bargaining, free from Government interference. Labour doesn't. We believe in making substantial cuts in the tax on your pay packet. Labour doesn't. We will create conditions in which the value of the money you earn and the money you save can be protected. We will do these things. That I promise you. We'll play our part if you, the trade union leaders, play yours responsibly.

'Responsibility can't be defined by the Government setting a fixed percentage for everyone, because the circumstances are different in every concern in the country, whether nationalized or free. It's up to you, the trade union leaders, to act realistically in the light of all the facts, as the Government must do. If you demand too much, you will bargain your firm into bankruptcy and your members onto the dole. And no one wants that.

'Our approach works in other countries which are doing far better than we are. It worked here during thirteen years of Conservative Government. You did better, Britain did better – infinitely better – than today under Labour.

'Let's make it work again.'

That is our message to the unions.

You can hear the same message in country after country. You can hear distant echoes of it even from Labour Ministers. It would be nice to think that this was due to an irreversible shift in the distribution of common sense. But it's really due to the nearness of an election and a swelling tide of protest from every taxpayer, every home owner, every parent in the land.

I look forward to Labour's continuing conversion to good sense, and, after the election, to their becoming a helpful Opposition in the new House of Commons.

So far I have spoken mainly of the practical and material failure of the last four Labour years and how we shall start to put things right. Let me turn now to something deeply damaging to this country.

Many of us remember the Labour Party as it used to be. In the old days it was at least a party of ideals. You didn't have to agree with Labour to understand its appeal and respect its concern for the underdog. Gradually over the years there has been a change. I have no doubt that those ideals, those principles, are still alive today in the hearts of traditional Labour supporters. But among those who lead the Labour movement something has gone seriously wrong.

Just compare the years of Clement Attlee and Hugh Gaitskell[1] with those of Harold Wilson and James Callaghan. Today, instead of the voice of compassion, the croak of the Quango[2] is heard in the land. There may not be enough jobs for the workers, but there are certainly plenty of jobs for the boys. That is the house that Harold built, to which his successor has not been slow to add a wing or two of his own.

Many in the Labour Party wonder what has happened to it. Socialism has gone sour. Today Labour seems to stand too often for expediency, for greed, for privilege, for policies that set one half of society against the other.

There are many reasons for this. One stems from that least attractive of emotions, envy. This spirit of envy is aimed not only at those privileged

[1] Clement Attlee (1883–1967), 1st Earl Attlee 1955. Labour MP 1922–55; Leader of the Labour Party 1935–55; Lord Privy Seal 1940–42; Deputy Prime Minister 1942–45; Prime Minister 1945–51. Hugh Gaitskell (1906–63), Labour MP 1945–63; Chancellor of the Exchequer 1950–51; Leader of the Labour Party 1955–63.
[2] Acronym for 'quasi-autonomous non-governmental organisation'. A Quango is independent of the Department which created it, save in the appointment of its members, but it is nominally under the control of a Minister, though not fully accountable to Parliament.

by birth and inherited wealth, like Mr Wedgwood Benn.[1] It is also directed against those who have got on by ability and effort.

It is seen in Labour's bias against men and women who seek to better themselves and their families. Ordinary people – small businessmen, the self-employed – are not to be allowed to rise on their own. They must rise collectively or not at all.

Object to merit and distinction and you're setting your face against quality, independence, originality, genius, against all the richness and variety of life. You are pinning down the swift and the sure and the strong, as Gulliver was pinned down by the little people of Lilliput.

A society like that cannot advance. Our civilization has been built by generation after generation of men and women inspired by the will to excel. Without them we should still be living in the Stone Age. Without the strong, who would provide for the weak? When you hold back the successful, you penalize those who need help.

Envy is dangerous, destructive, divisive – and revealing. It exposes the falsity of Labour's great claim that they're the party of care and compassion. It is the worst possible emotion to inspire a political party supposedly dedicated to improving the lot of ordinary working people.

From there it is but a short step to the doctrine of class warfare. The Marxists in the Labour Party preach that this is not only just, but necessary and inevitable. But let me put this thought to you: if it is wrong to preach race hatred – and it is – why is it right to preach class hatred? If it is a crime to incite the public against a man simply because of the colour of his skin – and it is – why is it virtuous to do so just because of his position?

The political organization of hatred is wrong – always and everywhere. Class warfare is immoral, a poisonous relic of the past. Conservatives are as fallible, as human and therefore as given to making mistakes, as the next man. But we don't preach hatred and we are not a party of envy.

Those who claim that we are a class party are standing the truth on its head. So too are those who claim that we are racists. Our determination to deal with the very real and difficult problems of immigration

---

[1] Anthony Wedgwood Benn (born 1925), 2nd Viscount Stansgate 1960 (renounced title 1963). Labour MP 1950–60, 1963–83, 1984–; Minister of Technology 1966–70; Industry Secretary 1974–75; Energy Secretary 1975–79.

control has inspired Labour to a shameful attempt to frighten the coloured population of Britain.[1]

Last month the Liberal Leader added his voice to the chorus.[2] No doubt in an effort to distract attention from his many deep and pressing problems, he too did his best – or worst – to pin the label of 'racism' on the Conservative Party. I realize that a drowning man will clutch at any straw. But let me remind young Mr Steel, millions of Conservatives were among those who spent five years of their lives fighting a war against racialism when he was still in short trousers.

It is true that Conservatives are going to cut the number of new immigrants coming into this country, and cut it substantially, because racial harmony is inseparable from control of the numbers coming in. But let me say a word to those who are permanently and legally settled here, who have made their homes with us. Your responsibilities are the same as those of every other British citizen, and your opportunities ought to be. Compulsory repatriation is not, and never will be, our policy, and anyone who tells you differently is deliberately misrepresenting us for his own ends.

Many other smears and charges will be thrown at us as election day comes nearer. But let us not be too concerned, however large the lie or absurd the charge. They are a sign of our opponents' desperation. For instance, you may have noticed – and so, I suspect, has the public – how often these charges contradict one another. One moment it is said that we have no policy, the next that our policies would bring about every disaster known to man. One moment Shadow Ministers are said to be notorious villains – well, here the 'villains' are. The next minute they are said to be unknown. Unknown? There's a charge from a party with household names like – let me see, now – Stanley Orme, not to mention Albert Booth.[3] But then, no one does, do they? Well, Mr Prime Minister, if there are any unknowns in the Shadow Cabinet, we are

---

[1] In the course of an interview about immigration policy on the ITV programme *World in Action* on 30 January 1978, Mrs Thatcher had said: 'People are really rather afraid that this country might be rather swamped by people with a different culture.' Opposition spokesmen accused her of stirring up racial hatred and contemplating compulsory repatriation.

[2] Sir David Steel (born 1938), Liberal MP 1965–88; Leader of the Liberal Party 1976–88; Liberal Democrat MP 1988–97. He described Margaret Thatcher's remarks on immigration as 'really quite wicked'.

[3] Stanley Orme (born 1923), Labour MP 1964–97; Minister for Social Security 1977–79. Albert Booth (born 1928), Labour MP 1966–83; Employment Secretary 1976–79.

all looking forward to becoming a lot better-known at your earliest convenience.

Until then, national uncertainty continues, and with it the continued weakening of one of our most ancient and deep-rooted traditions – respect for and safety under the law. When a rule of law breaks down, fear takes over. There is no security in the streets, families feel unsafe even in their own homes, children are at risk, criminals prosper, men of violence flourish, the nightmare world of *A Clockwork Orange*[1] becomes a reality.

Here in Britain in the last few years that world has become visibly nearer. We have seen some of the symptoms of the breakdown of the rule of law – the growth in the number of unsolved and unpunished crimes, especially violent crimes; overcrowded courts; an underpaid and undermanned Police Force; judges insulted by a senior Minister of the Crown.[2] Sometimes members of the Labour Party give the impression that as between the law and the law-breakers they are at best neutral.

We Conservatives are not neutral. We believe that to keep society free the law must be upheld. We are 100 per cent behind the police, the courts, the judges, and not least the law-abiding majority of citizens.

To all those engaged in law enforcement we pledge not just our moral but our practical support. As for the law-breakers, whether they are professional criminals carrying firearms or political terrorists, or young thugs attacking the elderly, or those who think they can assault policemen with impunity, we say this: 'You will find in the new Conservative Government a remorseless and implacable opponent.'

The Conservative Party also stands for the defence of our realm. I am often told that there are no votes to be won by talking about defence and foreign policy. Well, I intend to go on talking about them, especially with elections to the European Parliament approaching.[3] And, unlike

---

[1] *A Clockwork Orange* (1962), a novel by Anthony Burgess (1917–1993), depicts young gangsters in a future Britain of violence and desolation. It was filmed by Stanley Kubrick in 1971.

[2] In a speech at Bournemouth on 15 May 1977, Michael Foot – (born 1913), Labour MP 1945–55, 1960–92; Employment Secretary 1974–76; Lord President of the Council and Leader of the House of Commons 1976–79; Deputy Leader of the Labour Party 1976–80; Leader of the Labour Party 1980–83 – said, 'If the freedom of the people of this country – and especially the rights of trade unionists – . . . had been left to the good sense and fair-mindedness of judges, we would have few freedoms in this country at all.'

[3] In direct elections to the European Parliament held in the UK on 7 June 1979, Conservatives won 60 seats, Labour 17, Scottish Nationalists 1, and Ulster Unionists 3.

Labour, we shall work to make a success of our place in the Community, and we shall not need to be prompted to honour our obligations to our NATO allies.

It was nearly three years ago that I warned of the growing danger of Soviet expansion.[1] I was at once attacked by Labour's Defence Secretary[2] and the Soviet leaders – strange company, you might think, for a British Cabinet Minister. What has happened since I made that speech?

The Soviet Union, through its Cuban mercenaries, has completed its Marxist takeover of Angola; Ethiopia has been turned into a communist bastion in the Horn of Africa; there are now perhaps forty thousand Cubans in that continent, a deadly threat to the whole of Southern Africa. And as the Soviet threat becomes stronger, so the Labour Government has made Britain weaker. It has cut our forces time and again. We now have only seventy-four fighter-planes to defend our country. We lost twice as many as that during one week of the Battle of Britain.

I am well aware that modern Phantoms have many times the firepower of the Spitfire or Hurricane, but how does that help if you run out of Phantoms? There is a minimum level below which our defences cannot safely be allowed to fall. They have fallen below that level. And I give you this pledge: to bring them back to that minimum level will be the first charge on our national resources under the Conservative Government. It will not be easy, but there are no short cuts to security. There are only short cuts to defeat.

Conservatives too will see that our armed forces are properly paid. They do an indispensable job abroad and at home, not least in Northern Ireland.

I spent three memorable and moving days in Northern Ireland in June. The constancy and patience of the men and women of the Province who have endured so much pain through ten years of terror is something that I shall never forget. I know that there are those who say: 'Leave them to solve their own problems, and bring our boys back.' To them I must reply: 'If you wash your hands of Northern Ireland, you wash them in blood.' So long as Ulster wishes to belong to the United Kingdom she will do so. That is the policy of the Conservative Party and it will be the policy of the next Conservative Government.

[1] Speech at Kensington Town Hall, 19 January 1976. See pp. 39–47.
[2] Roy Mason (born 1924), Baron Mason of Barnsley 1987. Labour MP 1953–87; President of the Board of Trade 1969–70; Defence Secretary 1974–76; Northern Ireland Secretary 1976–79. He condemned Mrs Thatcher's observations on the USSR in January 1976 as ill-timed and provocative.

The next Conservative Government! I have spoken of what four years of Labour Government have done to Britain, materially and morally, at home and abroad. I hope that after this afternoon it will not be possible for anyone to say again that there is really not much difference between the parties. There is all the difference in the world, and if it is the will of the country, we will show the country – and the world – what that difference is.

May I end on a personal note? Long ago I learned two lessons of political life: to have faith, and to take nothing for granted. When we meet again the election will be over. I would not take the result for granted, but I have faith that our time is coming and I pray that when it comes we use it well, for the task of restoring the unity and good name of our nation is immense.

I look back at the great figures who led our Party in the past, and after more than three years I still feel a little astonished that it has fallen to me to stand in their place. Now, as the test draws near, I ask your help, and not only yours – I ask it of all men and women who look to us today, who share with us our longing for a new beginning.

Of course, we in the Conservative Party want to win, but let us win for the right reason – not power for ourselves, but that this country of ours, which we love so much, will find dignity and greatness and peace again.

Three years ago I said that we must heal the wounds of a divided nation. I say it again today with even greater urgency. There is a cause that brings us all together and binds us all together. We must learn again to be one nation, or one day we shall be no nation. That is our Conservative faith. It is my personal faith and vision. As we move towards government and service, may it be our strength and inspiration. Then not only will victory be ours, but we shall be worthy of it.

II

THE FIRST
PARLIAMENT

(1979–83)

11

Statement on the Doorstep of 10 Downing Street, 4 May 1979

Margaret Thatcher, by her own admission, could be cautious to the point of super-stition. Even when political chickens were long hatched she was reluctant to count them. So there was no serious discussion until the very end of the 1979 election campaign of the first words the incoming Prime Minister, were that to be Mrs Thatcher, should say. But, at her suggestion, Ronnie Millar had been turning the matter over in his mind. In the early hours of Friday 4 May, when sufficient results were through to convince even Mrs Thatcher that victory was hers, Millar read her his suggested passage -- a prayer attributed to St Francis of Assisi. He records the immediate reaction:

> *The lady rarely shows her deep feelings, but this, on a night of high tension and a constant switchback of emotion, proved too much. Her eyes swam. She blew her nose. 'I'll need to learn it,' she said at length.*[1]

She did, and introduced St Francis to the political world on the doorstep of Downing Street.

Her Majesty The Queen has asked me to form a new administration and I have accepted. It is, of course, the greatest honour that can come to any citizen in a democracy. I know full well the responsibilities that await me as I enter the door of No. 10, and I'll strive inceasingly to try to fulfil the trust and confidence that the British people have placed in me and the things in which I believe.

And I would just like to remember some words of St Francis of Assisi which I think are really just particularly apt at the moment:

Where there is discord, may we bring harmony.
Where there is error, may we bring truth.

[1] *A View from the Wings*, p. 266.

Where there is doubt, may be bring faith.
And where there is despair, may we bring hope.

And to all the British people – howsoever they voted – may I say this: now that the election is over, may we get together and strive to serve and strengthen the country of which we're so proud to be a part.

And finally, one last thing: in the words of Airey Neave,[1] whom we had hoped to bring here with us, 'There is now work to be done.'

---

[1] Airey Neave (1916–79), Conservative MP 1953–79; Head of the Leader of the Opposition's Private Office 1975–79; Conservative Spokesman on Northern Ireland 1975–79. He was killed at Westminster on 30 March 1979 by a bomb planted by the Irish National Liberation Army (a breakaway faction of the IRA).

12

Speech to the Conservative Party Conference, Blackpool, 12 October 1979

The new Prime Minister's 1979 Party Conference speech – the first after the election victory – is, at first sight, surprisingly downbeat. Any temptations to triumphalism had been removed by the mounting economic crisis. That this crisis was partly inherited and partly the result of international circumstances did not make the weathering of it any easier. As the speech recalls, the incoming Government had honoured its immediate pledges – cutting income tax (though raising Value Added Tax), paying more to the police and the armed forces, providing for the sale of council houses. But inflation was rising, and public expenditure – particularly public sector pay – was exploding. Above all, there was no sign that the trade unions (whose powers were still unreformed) appreciated the danger of pricing their members out of jobs.

Consequently, much of the speech was a sober lecture in economic realism. Strikes, Mrs Thatcher argued, harmed trade union members and their families as much as anyone else. Nor was their damage to be measured only in terms of inconvenience, but rather of lost profits, investment and jobs. She read out a letter from a small businessman urging the Government to stick to its policy; but the pressures from within the Cabinet, as well as outside, continued to mount.

Mr President, since we last met there have been one or two changes on the political scene. On that occasion, as you so aptly remarked, I spoke to you as Leader of the Opposition. I am very pleased with my promotion to Prime Minister. I much prefer this job to the other.

I am, as you may know, the first research chemist to hold this great position, and I hope that where I have led, others may follow – but not too soon. I mean, there is no rush. In fact, if you are agreeable, I hope to be with you for quite a while.

The job you have given me is at once a supreme honour and the greatest possible challenge. Now, more than ever, my responsibility is not only to the Party but to the nation. I know that you understand that and would not wish it otherwise. But before we turn to the tasks that face our country, perhaps we can allow ourselves, at this great Party gathering, a moment or two to rejoice, to say 'Thank you,' and to remember.

On Thursday 3 May we won a great victory.[1] Yes, it was a victory for realism and responsibility. It was also a victory for conviction and commitment – your conviction and your commitment. And it was a victory for loyalty and dedication – your loyalty, your dedication. Through the long years of Opposition you kept faith; and you will, I know, keep faith through the far longer years of Conservative Government that are to come.

An election victory such as ours is impossible without teamwork. It's invidious to single out this or that person for praise. However, one or two special tributes are due. We owe a tremendous debt to all our agents, who did so magnificently. And I must also thank Lord Thorneycroft.[2] He has been one of the most outstanding Chairmen the Conservative Party has ever had. This year he added another chapter to his memorable record of service to our Party and our country.

Finally, I wish to say a personal thank you to someone who was and is always there to give strength and authority to our cause, not least in time of trouble. No leader of a Party can ever have been given more sound or more loyal advice than I have had from my friend and deputy, Willie Whitelaw.[3] And my husband has been absolutely marvellous, too.

The victory to which all of you in this hall gave so much was five years coming, but when it came it was handsome. We won with the largest swing since the war and the largest majority in votes.

I was particularly pleased by the support we attracted: the largest trade union vote in our history; the young people, so many of whom saw no future under Labour and who turned to us; and all those who

---

[1] General election, 3 May 1979: Conservatives 339, Labour 269, Liberals 11, others 16.

[2] Peter Thorneycroft (1909–94), Baron Thorneycroft of Dunstan 1967. Conservative MP 1938–66; President of the Board of Trade 1951–57; Chancellor of the Exchequer 1957–58; Minister of Aviation 1960–62; Minister of Defence 1962–64; Defence Secretary 1964; Chairman of the Conservative Party 1975–81.

[3] William Whitelaw (born 1918), 1st Viscount Whitelaw of Penrith 1983. Conservative MP 1955–83; Chief Whip 1964–70; Lord President of the Council and Leader of the House of Commons 1970–72; Northern Ireland Secretary 1972–73; Employment Secretary 1973–74; Chairman of the Conservative Party 1974–75; Home Secretary 1979–83; Lord President of the Council and Leader of the House of Lords 1983–88.

have voted Labour before and who, this time, voted Conservative.

Winning an election is a splendid thing, but it is only the prologue to the vital business of governing. The work that the new Conservative Government has begun is the most difficult, the most challenging that has faced any administration since the war.

We have not wasted time. Already we have raised the pay of our police and armed forces, as we promised to do – and they deserved it. We have set in hand the sale of council houses and flats. In June, we introduced our first Budget. We brought down income tax throughout the scale. We took care to protect the pensioners against inflation. Next month's increases will be the largest in cash terms ever paid. And war widows' pensions have been relieved of tax altogether. At last they have received justice.

But all this is only the beginning. For this Government, it is not the first hundred days that count – and they have not been half bad, as you, Mr President, observed. It is the first five years – and the next five after that. We have to think in terms of several Parliaments. We have to move this country in a new direction, to change the way we look at things, to create a wholly new attitude of mind. Can it be done?

Well, the people have taken the first step by electing us: some, like us, with passionate conviction; others, I do not doubt, more in hope than belief, their fingers tightly crossed.

I understand their caution. So much has been promised in the past, so much has come to nothing, no wonder they are sceptical.

And impatient. Already I can hear some of them saying: 'The Conservatives have been in five months. Things do not seem to be that much better. What is happening? Do you think the Conservatives can really do it?'

We say to them this: 'Yes, the Conservatives can do it. And we will do it. But it will take time. Time to tackle problems that have been neglected for years; time to change people's approach to what Governments can do for people, and to what people should do for themselves; time to shake off the self-doubt induced by decades of dependence on the state as master, not as servant. It will take time and it will not be easy.'

The world has never offered us an easy living. There is no reason why it should. We have always had to go out and earn our living – the hard way. In the past we did not hesitate. We had great technical skill, quality, reliability. We built well, sold well. We delivered on time. The world bought British and British was best. Not German. Not Japanese.

97

British. It was more than that. We knew that to keep ahead we had to change. People looked to us as the front-runner for the future.

Our success was not based on Government handouts, on protecting yesterday's jobs and fighting off tomorrow's. It was not based on envy or truculence or on endless battles between management and men, or between worker and fellow worker. We did not become the workshop of the world by being the nation with the most strikes.

I remember the words written on an old trade union banner: 'United to support, not combined to injure.' That is the way we were. Today we still have great firms and industries. Today we still make much of value; but not enough. Industries that were once head and shoulders above their competitors have stumbled and fallen.

It is said that we were exhausted by the war. Those who were utterly defeated can hardly have been less exhausted. Yet they have done infinitely better in peace. It is said that Britain's time is up, that we have had our finest hour and the best we can look forward to is a future fit for Mr Benn to live in. I do not accept those alibis. Of course we face great problems, problems that have fed on each other year after year, becoming harder and harder to solve. We all know them. They go to the root of the hopes and fears of ordinary people – high inflation, high unemployment, high taxation, appalling industrial relations, the lowest productivity in the Western world.

People have been led to believe that they had to choose between a capitalist wealth-creating society on the one hand and a caring and compassionate society on the other. But that is not the choice. The industrial countries that out-produce and out-sell us are precisely those countries with better social services and better pensions than we have. It is because they have strong wealth-creating industries that they have better benefits than we have. Our people seem to have lost belief in the balance between production and welfare. This is the balance that we have got to find. To persuade our people that it is possible, through their own efforts, not only to halt our national decline, but to reverse it. And that requires new thinking, tenacity and a willingness to look at things in a completely different way.

Is the nation ready to face reality? I believe that it is. People are tired of false dawns and facile promises. If this country's story is to change, we the Conservatives must rekindle the spirit which the socialist years have all but exhausted.

Do we have the authority? Last month I was accused of 'waving a phoney mandate'. In a democracy the word 'mandate' does not imply that a voter has read and accepted his party's manifesto from end to end, and so not only knows, but is voting for, everything it contains. It would be absurd if it did. Not everyone who votes for a political party has read everything in its manifesto. Not everyone who votes for a political party has read anything in its manifesto.

But when a voter takes his decision and slips his paper into the ballot box he does know, broadly speaking, what the party of his choice stands for. In these days of mass communication we can hardly help knowing; and those who voted Conservative know the principal policies we stood for, and that in voting for us they were voting for all those policies. That was and is our mandate, and we have every right to carry it out, and we shall.

Let us have a look at four economic issues, because these were central to our Conservative campaign. They are inflation, public spending, income tax and industrial relations. These four are not four separate and distinct issues. You do not take them and discuss them separately on the sort of 'Now I turn to . . .' basis as though they had no relationship to one another. They are closely related. You cannot cut tax unless you curb public spending. Ask the Chancellor. Ask the Chief Secretary. They know. They have the job of doing both. It is your tax which pays for public spending. The Government have no money of their own. There is only taxpayers' money. Of course, if we had the money we could all think of ways in which to spend it. Hospitals which should have been modernized years ago. More help for the elderly, the sick and the disabled. But Government in one form or another already spends nearly half our entire national income. Mr President, if Labour's lavish spending solved all problems we would have no problems left to solve.

So public spending and taxation are linked.

And inflation is a major problem which cannot be cured without curbing public spending. If the Government overspends, and borrows or prints money to meet the deficit, then prices and interest rates will go on rising – there you have inflation – and the poor, and the pensioners, and the young home-buyers will all suffer.

But there are some who think they have a right to contract out of the effects of inflation, if they are organized in a powerful union with enough muscle to impose their will on a suffering public.

What madness it is, that winter after winter we have the great set-piece battles, in which the powerful unions do so much damage to the industries on which their members' living standards depend. The struggles for wage increases disregard output, profit or any other measure of

99

success. They ignore the reality that there is an inescapable link between prosperity and production.

Since 1979 began, scarcely a week has passed without some group calling for higher pay. Listening to the chorus of pay demands you might imagine that a 100 per cent pay rise for everyone in the country would solve all our economic problems. But we all know that the only result would be doubled prices. No one would have more food, more clothing, more anything.

The key to prosperity lies not in higher pay but in higher output. In 1979 you have all heard endless discussions about pay. How often have you heard similar discussions about how to raise output?

The reason why Britain is today the third-poorest nation in the European Community has little to do with pay but it has everything to do with production. We hanker after a West German standard of output. The truth is very simple: West German pay plus British output per man equals inflation. And that is exactly what has been happening.

The unions win pay awards their members have not earned. The company pays out increases it cannot afford. The prices to the customer go up. Government print the money to make it all possible and everyone congratulates them on their success as an honest broker, with or without beer and sandwiches at No. 10.

It has been happening for years. The result has been the most uncompetitive industry, the lowest economic growth rate and the highest rate of inflation in the industrialized world. In the trade unions the lesson is drawn that militancy paid again, that the company did have the money. It did not. The Government just printed their way out of trouble – until next time round.

This Government wants the greatest possible co-operation with both sides and we will go a long way to get it. But we shall not – repeat not – print money to finance excessive pay settlements.

Conquering inflation, controlling public spending and cutting taxes are the first three stages of a long journey, all interrelated. The fourth I mentioned is to make certain limited but essential changes in the law on industrial relations. We have to make these changes because, as we saw last winter, the law is out of keeping with the needs of the time. When the trade union movement began, it set out to secure for its members a fair return for their work from employers. But today the conflict of interest is not so much between unions and employers as between unions and the nation, of which trade unionists and their families form a large part. It is the British people who have to bear the brunt of the suffering which strikes impose on society. We have to bring about a fair and just balance between a man's right to withhold his labour and the determination of a small minority to impose its will upon the great majority.

As a Government, as Jim Prior[1] said yesterday, we cannot and will not coerce people, but we can and we must protect people from being coerced. And so, before the year is out, we shall introduce legislation concerning secret ballots, secondary picketing and the closed shop.[2] The majority of the unions' own rank and file, so many of whom helped to elect this Government, welcomed our proposals. I hope that the union leaders who have said that they will work with the elected Government of the day will accept them too. The days when only employers suffered from the strike are long since past.

Today strikes affect trade union members and their families, just like the rest of us. One union can deprive us all of coal, or food, or transport easily enough. What it cannot do is defend its members against similar action by other unions. If schools and hospital wards are closed, if there is no petrol at the pumps, no raw materials on the factory bench, the trade unions are as powerless as the rest of society, and when the bills come in for the stoppage their members have to pay up too.

Recently there was a strike which prevented telephone bills from being sent out.[3] It is all right now; but wait until they come in. The cost of that strike to the Post Office is £110 million. It will have to be paid for by everyone who uses the telephone. £110 million loss, caused by a strike of only 150 people in a public service. What nonsense it is. The recent two-day-a-week strike by the engineering union lost the industry £2,000 million in sales.[4] We may never make up those sales, and we shall lose some of the jobs which depended on them. And who will send up a cheer? The Germans, the Japanese, the Swiss, the Americans.

---

[1] James Prior (born 1927), Baron Prior of Brampton 1987. Conservative MP 1959–87; Minister of Agriculture 1970–72; Lord President of the Council and Leader of the House of Commons 1972–74; Employment Secretary 1979–81; Northern Ireland Secretary 1981–84.
[2] Secondary picketing means i) picketing by persons who are not party to the dispute, and ii) picketing of premises whose owner is not party to the dispute. A closed shop exists where employers and unions agree to make union membership a condition of employment.
[3] Post Office computer staff went on strike in support of a pay claim in June 1979.
[4] Engineering workers struck from 10 August to 4 October 1979 for higher wages, shorter hours and longer holidays.

Instead of exporting engineering goods we shall have exported engineering jobs. And who will suffer? The members of the trade unions who caused these strikes. I think that the nation recognizes, and has recognized for a long time, that trade union power is out of balance. That is why people are supporting us in legislating for trade union reform.

Let me say a word about these matters. We place special emphasis on the secret ballot. We believe that the great power wielded by unions calls for greater accountability to their members. We are particularly concerned about the working of the closed shop. The closed shop, together with secondary picketing, makes it possible for small groups to close down whole industries with which they have no direct connection.

Cross the picket line to do your job and you risk losing both your union card and your job, as Stan Sorrell said so graphically yesterday. He is a constituent of mine and one of the many union members who supports the Conservative Party so actively.

During the engineers' strike, news reached London of a new resistance movement in East Anglia. Whole factories were actually working, but so afraid were the employees of the consequences that they dared not reveal their identity, or that of the company, to the media. Millions of British workers go in fear of union power. The demand for this Government to make changes is coming from the very people who experience this fear.

It is coming from the trade unionists themselves. They want to escape from the rule of the militants. We heard this in the Conference hall yesterday. They look to us to help them. Today trade unions have more power over working people and their families than any boss has. The irony is that unions can exist only in a free society. Those who seek freedom for their own purposes should not deny that same freedom to others.[1] I have been speaking of the deep and difficult problems of industry – most of it big industry. But the future of this country depends largely on the success of small businesses. I would like to read to you a letter which I have received from a small businessman in the West Midlands. He put it so much better than I could. He wrote:

I thought I would write to you about the profound effect the change of Government has had upon one small businessman. In 1977, at the age of thirty-eight, I was so disillusioned with the socialist regime

[1] The Employment Act 1980 regulated closed shop agreements, ended secondary picketing, and offered to reimburse unions for the cost of secret ballots.

and its policies that I could see no future for the small to medium business and sold my company to a large group and virtually retired. Financially this was a satisfactory state of affairs, but I yearned to get back into what I knew best. When your Government was elected, I hoped there would be a change of emphasis and indeed that is what has happened. The letterhead on which I write to you is of a new company which I have formed recently, and the biggest factor in its creation has been the steps which you have taken to restore incentive to work at all levels of the community. Not only can self-employed proprietors of small businesses keep more of the profits of those businesses but, more important, those good and hard-working employees who are patently worth a high level of wages are also feeling the benefit of more cash in the pocket and it is now worth their while to work that bit harder or longer as the case may be.

He said this:

Please stick to your policy. It is the only way that we shall eventually solve our problems. It may be hard to bear in the short term but I truly believe that the bulk of public opinion is now behind a return to the basic commonsense fact that the country as a whole cannot continue to be paid more and more money for less and less work.

Here we have proof that the policy is working. It is creating more wealth and more jobs. This is exactly the kind of person whom our Government seek to encourage. We rang him up to ask him if we could use the letter because it was so good, and said that we would not dream of embarrassing him by revealing his name or anything like that. 'What?' he said. 'Non-attribution? I want to stand up and be counted.' It is small businessmen like this who, given the chance, will provide more jobs and more wealth, and the only Government from whom they will get the chance is this Conservative Government.

So far I have spoken of matters of absolutely vital concern to us here at home. But we have important responsibilities overseas as well, particularly Rhodesia. In his speech on Wednesday, Peter Carrington[1]

---

[1] Peter Carrington (born 1919), 6th Baron Carrington 1938. Leader of the House of Lords 1963–66; Defence Secretary 1970–74; Energy Secretary 1974; Chairman of the Conservative Party 1972–74; Foreign Secretary 1979–82; Secretary-General NATO 1984–88.

described the progress which has been made in our efforts to bring Rhodesia to independence with the widest possible international recognition. I understand and share your impatience to bring this about. The entire Government and Party care deeply about the future of Rhodesia. There have been too many wasted opportunities.

It is Britain's responsibility and Britain's alone to bring Rhodesia to legal independence. But it is also in Rhodesia's interests that we should bring as many other countries as possible along with us in recognizing an independent Rhodesia. We undertook to give to Rhodesia the kind of independence constitution which we had given to our other former colonies. We have had a great deal of experience of independence constitutions. These constitutions had certain fundamental principles in common. Each also contained provisions to meet the country's own particular circumstances.

Those same things are true of the constitution under which we are ready to give independence to Rhodesia. Bishop Muzorewa[1] has already accepted that constitution. It must be in Rhodesia's interests, and it is an inescapable duty for the British Government, to do everything possible to bring an end to a war which has caused the most cruel suffering.

What is the purpose of continuing this war? It cannot be to bring about majority rule; that has already been accomplished. If it is to win power, then those who wish to do so must be prepared to proceed democratically through the ballot box and not through the bullet.

At Lusaka,[2] the Heads of Government called for free and fair elections, supervised under the British Government's authority. We stand ready to do this. I think that we have some reason to be proud of what has been achieved since Lusaka. I trust that no one will now put that achievement in jeopardy. In view of what has been accomplished on the independence constitution the time for lifting sanctions cannot be far off. There is no longer any vestige of excuse for the conflict in Rhodesia to continue.

Nearer home, in Europe, we are part of a Community of some 250 million people. It is no use joining anything half-heartedly. Five months

[1] Abel Muzorewa (born 1925), Methodist Bishop 1968–; Prime Minister of Zimbabwe/ Rhodesia 1979–. Muzorewa headed a black majority government under an 'internal settlement' constitution, which guerrilla leaders rejected.

[2] The Commonwealth Heads of Government Meeting took place at Lusaka, Zambia, in the first week of August 1979. The Rhodesian Constitutional Conference opened at Lancaster House, London, under the chairmanship of Lord Carrington, on 10 September 1979.

after taking office, we have done much to restore the trust and confidence that the last Conservative Government enjoyed with our partners in Europe, and which the Labour Government did not. We are a committed member of the Community.

But that does not mean that we are content with the way all its policies work. If nothing is done we are faced in 1980 with the appalling prospect of having to pay £1,000 million more to our European partners than we receive from them, even though we have almost the lowest income per head in the Community.

The hard-pressed British taxpayer will not stand for paying still more in order to reduce the tax bills of our wealthier Community partners. At the European Council in Strasbourg in June we persuaded the other Heads of Government to agree to tackle this problem. We shall expect to make very real progress at the next European Council at the end of November.[1] I do not underestimate the problems that face us in the budget, in fisheries, or in reforming the Common Agricultural Policy. But equally we must not underestimate our opportunities as members of the Community. The future of Western Europe is our future too.

What in the end are the objectives of the states which have come to make up the Community? The three most important are international peace and justice, economic prosperity, and freedom under the law.

We in Europe have unrivalled freedom. But we must never take it for granted. The dangers to it are greater now than they have ever been since 1945. The threat of the Soviet Union is ever-present. It is growing continually. Their military spending goes up by 5 per cent a year. A Russian nuclear submarine is launched every six weeks. Every year the Russians turn out over three thousand tanks and 1,500 combat aircraft. Their military research and development is enormous.

The Soviet forces are organized and trained for attack. The Russians do not tell us why they are making this tremendous and costly effort to increase their military power. Heaven knows, they have enough to do on the consumer side. So far the North Atlantic Alliance has preserved our freedom. But in recent years the Soviet Union's growing strength has allowed it to pull ahead of the Alliance in many fields. We and our allies are resolved to make the effort that will restore the balance. We

---

[1] The issue of the British budget contribution dominated the European Councils held in Dublin in November 1979 and Luxembourg in April 1980. Agreement was not reached until 30 May 1980.

must keep up all our defences, whether nuclear or conventional. It is no good having first-class nuclear forces if we can be overwhelmed by an enemy's conventional forces. Deterring aggression cannot be piecemeal. If it is, our effort is wasted.

Recently, we and our allies have all become more and more alarmed at the number of modern Soviet nuclear weapons targeted on Western Europe. At the same time, NATO's own nuclear forces in Europe are out of date. We and our friends in NATO will soon have to decide whether to modernize our nuclear weapons.[1] These will be difficult decisions for some of our allies, and we must expect to see the Soviet Union mount a powerful psychological campaign to prevent the Alliance from redressing the balance. We shall be looking very closely at President Brezhnev's recent speech to see whether it is the opening shot in that campaign or whether it is a genuine attempt to reduce tension in Europe.[2]

Nor will we neglect our conventional forces. Our most precious asset is the men and women who serve in our forces. As you know, Mr President, as our very able Secretary of State for Defence,[3] we faced a grave situation on taking office. Recruitment was poor, and many of our most skilled and experienced servicemen were leaving the forces. We immediately restored the pay of the services to its proper level, and we will keep it there. We have also taken steps to encourage the rebuilding of our Territorial Army and other reserve forces.

After so much neglect it will take time to put right the weaknesses. Nonetheless, we must see that it is done. We owe it to our servicemen and women, who give our country such magnificent service.

Nowhere has that service been more magnificent than in Northern Ireland. More than three hundred of our servicemen have given their lives there, and their bravery is matched by the courage of the Royal Ulster Constabulary and the prison service.

It is hard to speak of Northern Ireland without emotion. One thinks

---

[1] NATO sought a firm decision on new intermediate-range nuclear forces in Europe by the end of 1979. In September, the British Government agreed to the basing of 144 American-owned Cruise missiles in Britain.
[2] In a speech in East Berlin on 6 October 1979, President Brezhnev offered to reduce Soviet intermediate-range nuclear forces if NATO abandoned its plans to deploy comparable missiles in Western Europe.
[3] Francis Pym (born 1922), Baron Pym of Sandy 1987. Conservative MP 1961–87; Chief Whip 1970–73; Northern Ireland Secretary 1973–74; Defence Secretary 1979–81; Leader of the House of Commons 1981–82; Foreign Secretary 1982–83.

of Warrenpoint, of Lord Mountbatten, of Airey Neave.[1] To any who seek to advance their cause by violence, and who claim to be soldiers of an army fighting for freedom, let me say in the words of the Lord Chancellor,[2] 'Such men are not soldiers. They are not an army. They are not fighting for freedom. They are fighting for chaos.'

We who believe in the one true freedom – freedom under the rule of law – far outnumber and outweigh, in the strength of our resolve, those who set out to murder and to maim. No ends could justify such means. The act of murder can have no moral basis whatsoever.

The British Government is doing everything possible to strengthen the security forces in the fight against the men of violence. Our goal is the same peace for which the Pope appealed so movingly during his visit to Ireland.[3] To all the people of the Province of Ulster, I repeat this pledge: we do not forget you, we will not abandon you. We must and we will find a way of restoring to you more control over your own affairs. We must and we will find a way to peace for your deeply troubled part of our United Kingdom.

We come to the closing moments of our victory Conference. It has been a Conference to remember, and it was a victory to remember.

Throughout most of my life, the chief complaint against politicians has been that they shrank from telling the truth, when the truth was in the least unpleasant or controversial; that they were inclined to woo, when it was their duty to warn; and to please, when it was their business to prophesy. Early in my career, I decided that that was one mistake that I would not make. My harshest critics will perhaps agree that I have succeeded in that modest ambition.

For the complaint that they have against me is the opposite one – apparently I am inclined to speak my mind, even occasionally to nag.

Today I have again pointed to the dangers as I see them, and I have

---

[1] Eighteen soldiers and a civilian were killed by an IRA attack at Warrenpoint in Northern Ireland on 27 August 1979. The same day, Earl Mountbatten of Burma (1900–79) and three others were killed by an IRA bomb while boating in County Sligo in the Republic of Ireland. The INLA murdered Airey Neave MP on 30 March 1979.

[2] Quintin Hogg (born 1907), Baron Hailsham of St Marylebone 1970. Conservative MP 1938–50, 1963–70; 2nd Viscount Hailsham 1950 (renounced title in 1963); Minister of Education 1957; Lord President of the Council 1957–59, 1960–64; Chairman of the Conservative Party 1957–59; Lord Privy Seal 1959–60; Leader of the House of Lords 1960–63; Education Secretary 1964; Lord Chancellor 1970–74, 1979–87.

[3] Pope John Paul II made the first Papal visit to Ireland from 29 September to 1 October 1979.

said what I believe the source of those dangers to be. But let us remember that we are a nation, and that a nation is an extended family.

Families go through their hard times; they have to postpone cherished ambitions until they have the means to satisfy them. At times like these, the strength of the family is truly tested. It is then that the temptation is greatest for its members to start blaming one another and dissipating their strength in bitterness and bickering. Let us do all in our power to see one another's point of view and to widen the common ground on which we stand.

As we close our Conference, a caring and united Party, I think for a moment of last week's events in Brighton.[1] I think of those members of the Labour Party and trade unionists who see the movement they serve abandoning the ideals to which they have devoted their lives. They do not yet share our Conservative ideals – at least they think they do not – but they do want free and responsible trade unions to play an honourable part in the life of a free and responsible society. So do we.

I give them my pledge that my colleagues and I will continue to talk to them, to listen to their views, so long as it is understood that national policy is the sole responsibility of Government and Parliament. In return, I would ask every man and woman who is called on in the next few months to take part in disruptive industrial action to consider the consequences for themselves, their children and their fellow countrymen. But our supreme loyalty is to the country and the things for which it stands.

Let us work together in hope and above all in friendship. On behalf of the Government to which you have given the task of leading this country out of the shadows, let me close with these words: You gave us your trust. Be patient. We shall not betray that trust.

[1] At the Labour Party Conference.

13

Speech to the Conservative Party Conference, Brighton, 10 October 1980

Like the previous year's Party Conference speech, that of 1980 was heavily economic – and for good if gloomy reasons. The international economic scene was one of sharply rising inflation, riding on the back of doubled oil prices, and accelerating recession. But the home-grown problems of the British economy were still worse: Britain's inflation, given a sharp if temporary upward jolt by the 1979 Budget's VAT increases, peaked in May 1980 at 22 per cent; and the prospects for growth and jobs looked ever worse. Most alarming was the unplanned growth in public spending.

Some in Government and the Conservative Party had begun to argue that the Government should take advantage of its own failures by claiming credit for the amount of taxpayers' money which was still being pumped into a bloated and voracious public sector. But Mrs Thatcher refused to do this, knowing that it would set the seal on the abandonment of her economic strategy, even in more propitious circumstances.

Saddled with socialism's economic legacy, accorded only limited room to manoeuvre by the recession, but above all weighed down with a Cabinet still dominated by those who regarded the Thatcherite economic analysis as doctrinaire nonsense, there was little as yet which Mrs Thatcher could do to get the strategy back on course. But at least she could defiantly state her intention of pursuing it to what looked to many like an increasingly bitter end. She was, she declared (in a memorable phrase supplied by Ronnie Millar), 'not for turning'.

Mr Chairman, ladies and gentlemen; most of my Cabinet colleagues have started their speeches of reply by paying very well-deserved tribute to their junior ministers. At Number 10 I have no junior ministers. There is just Denis and me, and I could not do without him.

I am, however, very fortunate in having a marvellous deputy who is wonderful in all places at all times in all things – Willie Whitelaw.

At our Party Conference last year I said that the task in which the

Government were engaged – to change the national attitude of mind – was the most challenging to face any British administration since the war. Challenge is exhilarating. This week we Conservatives have been taking stock, discussing the achievements, the setbacks and the work that lies ahead as we enter our second Parliamentary year. As you said, Mr Chairman, our debates have been stimulating and our debates have been constructive. This week has demonstrated that we are a Party united in purpose, strategy and resolve. And we actually like one another.

When I am asked for a detailed forecast of what will happen in the coming months or years I remember Sam Goldwyn's advice: 'Never prophesy, especially about the future.'

Never mind, it is wet outside. I expect that they want to come in.[1] You cannot blame them; it is always better where the Tories are! And you – and perhaps they – will be looking to me this afternoon for an indication of how the Government see the task before us and why we are tackling it the way we are. Before I begin, let me get one thing out of the way.

This week at Brighton we have heard a good deal about last week at Blackpool.[2] I will have a little more to say about that strange assembly later, but for the moment I want to say just this: because of what happened at that Conference, there has been, behind all our deliberations this week, a heightened awareness that now, more than ever, our Conservative Government must succeed. We just must, because now there is even more at stake than some had realized.

There are many things to be done to set this nation on the road to recovery, and I do not mean economic recovery alone, but a new independence of spirit and zest for achievement.

It is sometimes said that because of our past we, as a people, expect too much and set our sights too high. That is not the way I see it. Rather it seems to me that throughout my life in politics our ambitions have steadily shrunk. Our response to disappointment has not been to lengthen our stride but to shorten the distance to be covered. But with confidence in ourselves and in our future what a nation we could be!

In its first seventeen months this Government have laid the foundations for recovery. We have undertaken a heavy load of legislation, a

---

[1] Left-wing groups were staging a noisy 'right to work' demonstration outside the Conference hall.

[2] On 1 October 1980, the Labour Party Conference at Blackpool passed resolutions in favour of unilateral nuclear disarmament and withdrawal from the EEC.

load we do not intend to repeat because we do not share the socialist fantasy that achievement is measured by the number of laws you pass. But there was a formidable barricade of obstacles that we had to sweep aside. For a start, in his first Budget Geoffrey Howe[1] began to restore incentives to stimulate the abilities and inventive genius of our people. Prosperity comes not from grand conferences of economists but by countless acts of personal self-confidence and self-reliance.

Under Geoffrey's stewardship Britain has repaid $3,600 million of international debt, debt which had been run up by our predecessors. And we paid quite a lot of it off before it was due. In the past twelve months Geoffrey has abolished exchange controls over which British Governments have dithered for decades.[2] Our great enterprises are now free to seek opportunities overseas. This will help to secure our living standards long after North Sea oil has run out. This Government thinks about the future. We have made the first crucial changes in trade union law to remove the worst abuses of the closed shop, to restrict picketing to the place of work of the parties in dispute, and to encourage secret ballots.[3] Jim Prior has carried all these measures through with the support of the vast majority of trade union members. Keith Joseph, David Howell, John Nott and Norman Fowler[4] have begun to break down the monopoly powers of nationalization. Thanks to them British Aerospace will soon be open to private investment. The monopoly of the Post Office and British Telecommunications is being diminished. The barriers to private generation of electricity for sale have been lifted. For the first time nationalized industries and public utilities can be investigated by the Monopolies Commission – a long overdue reform.

Free competition in road passenger transport promises travellers a

---

[1] Sir Geoffrey Howe (born 1926), Baron Howe of Aberavon 1992. Conservative MP 1964–66, 1970–92; Minister for Trade 1972–74; Chancellor of the Exchequer 1979–83; Foreign Secretary 1983–89; Deputy Prime Minister and Leader of the House of Commons 1989–90.
[2] Britain abolished exchange controls on 23 October 1979.
[3] The Employment Act 1980.
[4] Sir Keith Joseph (1918–1994), Baron Joseph of Portsoken 1987. Conservative MP 1957–87; Minister of Housing and Local Government 1962–64; Social Services Secretary 1970–74; Industry Secretary 1979–81; Education Secretary 1981–86. Sir David Howell (born 1936), Conservative MP 1966–97; Energy Secretary 1979–81; Transport Secretary 1981–83; Chairman of the Select Committee on Foreign Affairs 1987–97. Sir John Nott (born 1932), Conservative MP 1966–83; Trade Secretary 1979–81; Defence Secretary 1981–83. Sir Norman Fowler (born 1938), Conservative MP 1970–; Transport Secretary 1981; Social Services Secretary 1981–87; Employment Secretary 1987–90; Chairman of the Conservative Party 1992–94.

better deal. Michael Heseltine[1] has given to millions – yes, millions – of council tenants the right to buy their own homes.

It was Anthony Eden who chose for us the goal of 'a property-owning democracy'.[2] But for all the time that I have been in public affairs that has been beyond the reach of so many, who were denied the right to the most basic ownership of all – the homes in which they live.

They wanted to buy. Many could afford to buy. But they happened to live under the jurisdiction of a socialist council, which would not sell and did not believe in the independence that comes with ownership. Now Michael Heseltine has given them the chance to turn a dream into reality. And all this and a lot more in seventeen months.

The left continues to refer with relish to the death of capitalism. Well, if this is the death of capitalism, I must say that it has quite a way to go!

But all this will avail us little unless we achieve our prime economic objective – the defeat of inflation. Inflation destroys nations and societies as surely as invading armies do. Inflation is the parent of unemployment. It is the unseen robber of those who have saved.

No policy which puts at risk the defeat of inflation – however great its short-term attraction – can be right. Our policy for the defeat of inflation is, in fact, traditional. It existed long before Sterling M3[3] embellished the Bank of England Quarterly Bulletin, or 'monetarism' became a convenient term of political invective.

But some people talk as if control of the money supply was a revolutionary policy. Yet it was an essential condition for the recovery of much of Continental Europe.

Those countries knew what was required for economic stability. Previously, they had lived through rampant inflation; they knew that it led to suitcase money, massive unemployment and the breakdown of society itself. They determined never to go that way again.

Today, after many years of monetary self-discipline, they have stable, prosperous economies better able than ours to withstand the buffeting of world recession.

[1] Michael Heseltine (born 1933), Conservative MP 1966–; Environment Secretary 1979–83, 1990–92; Defence Secretary 1983–86; President of the Board of Trade 1992–95; First Secretary of State and Deputy Prime Minister 1995–97.
[2] Anthony Eden (1897–1977), 1st Earl of Avon 1961. Conservative MP 1923–57; Foreign Secretary 1935–38, 1940–45, 1951–55; Dominions Secretary 1939–40; War Secretary 1940; Prime Minister and Leader of the Conservative Party 1955–57. He put forward this idea at the 1946 Party Conference.
[3] A definition of the money supply as cash in circulation plus sterling bank deposits.

So at international conferences to discuss economic affairs many of my fellow Heads of Government find our policies not strange, unusual or revolutionary, but normal, sound and honest. And that is what they are.

Their only question is: 'Has Britain the courage and resolve to sustain the discipline for long enough to break through to success?'

Yes, Mr Chairman, we have, and we shall. This Government are determined to stay with the policy and see it through to its conclusion. That is what marks this administration as one of the truly radical ministries of post-war Britain. Inflation is falling and should continue to fall.

Meanwhile we are not heedless of the hardships and worries that accompany the conquest of inflation.

Foremost among these is unemployment. Today our country has more than two million unemployed.

Now you can try to soften that figure in a dozen ways. You can point out – and it is quite legitimate to do so – that two million today does not mean what it meant in the 1930s; that the percentage of unemployment is much less now than it was then.

You can add that today many more married women go out to work. You can stress that, because of the high birthrate in the early 1960s, there is an unusually large number of school-leavers this year looking for work, and that the same will be true for the next two years.

You can emphasize that about a quarter of a million people find new jobs each month and therefore go off the employment register.

And you can recall that there are nearly twenty-five million people in jobs, compared with only about eighteen million in the 1930s. You can point out that the Labour Party conveniently overlooks the fact that of the two million unemployed for which they blame us, nearly a million and a half were bequeathed by their Government.

But when all that has been said the fact remains that the level of unemployment in our country today is a human tragedy. Let me make it clear beyond doubt: I am profoundly concerned about unemployment. Human dignity and self-respect are undermined when men and women are condemned to idleness. The waste of a country's most precious assets, the talent and energy of its people, makes it the bounden duty of Government to seek a real and lasting cure.

If I could press a button and genuinely solve the unemployment problem, do you think that I would not press that button this instant? Does anyone imagine that there is the smallest political gain in letting this unemployment continue, or that there is some obscure economic religion which demands this unemployment as part of its ritual? This Government are pursuing the only policy which gives any hope of bringing our people back to real and lasting employment. It is no coincidence that those countries, of which I spoke earlier, which have had lower rates of inflation have also had lower levels of unemployment.

I know that there is another real worry affecting many of our people. Although they accept that our policies are right, they feel deeply that the burden of carrying them out is falling much more heavily on the private than on the public sector. They say that the public sector is enjoying advantages but the private sector is taking the knocks, and at the same time maintaining those in the public sector with better pay and pensions than they enjoy.

I must tell you that I share this concern and understand the resentment. That is why I and my colleagues say that to add to public spending takes away the very money and resources that industry needs to stay in business, let alone to expand. Higher public spending, far from curing unemployment, can be the very vehicle that loses jobs and causes bankruptcies in trade and commerce. That is why we warned local authorities that since rates are frequently the biggest tax industry now faces, increases in them can cripple local businesses. Councils must, therefore, learn to cut costs in the same way that companies have to.

That is why I stress that if those who work in public authorities take for themselves large pay increases, they leave less to be spent on equipment and new buildings. That in turn deprives the private sector of the orders it needs, especially some of those industries in the hard-pressed regions. Those in the public sector have a duty to those in the private sector not to take out so much in pay that they cause others unemployment. That is why we point out that every time high wage settlements in nationalized monopolies lead to higher charges for telephones, electricity, coal and water, they can drive companies out of business and cost other people their jobs.

If spending money like water was the answer to our country's problems, we would have no problems now. If ever a nation has spent, spent, spent and spent again, ours has. Today that dream is over. All of that money has got us nowhere, but it still has to come from somewhere. Those who urge us to relax the squeeze, to spend yet more money indiscriminately in the belief that it will help the unemployed and the small businessman, are not being kind or compassionate or caring.

They are not the friends of the unemployed or the small business.

They are asking us to do again the very thing that caused the problems in the first place. We have made this point repeatedly.

I am accused of lecturing or preaching about this. I suppose it is a critic's way of saying, 'Well, we know it is true, but we have to carp at something.' I do not care about that. But I do care about the future of free enterprise, the jobs and exports it provides and the independence it brings to our people.

Independence? Yes, but let us be clear what we mean by that. Independence does not mean contracting out of all relationships with others. A nation can be free, but it will not stay free for long if it has no friends and no alliances. Above all, it will not stay free if it cannot pay its own way in the world. By the same token, an individual needs to be part of a community and to feel that he is part of it. There is more to this than the chance to earn a living for himself and his family, essential though that is.

Of course, our vision and our aims go far beyond the complex arguments of economics, but unless we get the economy right we shall deny our people the opportunity to share that vision and to see beyond the narrow horizons of economic necessity. Without a healthy economy we cannot have a healthy society. Without a healthy society the economy will not stay healthy for long.

But it is not the state that creates a healthy society. When the state grows too powerful, people feel that they count for less and less. The state drains society not only of its wealth but of initiative, of energy, the will to improve and innovate as well as to preserve what is best. Our aim is to let people feel that they count for more and more. If we cannot trust the deepest instincts of our people we should not be in politics at all. Some aspects of our present society really do offend those instincts.

Decent people do want to do a proper job at work, not to be restrained or intimidated from giving value for money. They believe that honesty should be respected, not derided. They see crime and violence as a threat not just to society but to their own orderly way of life. They want to be allowed to bring up their children in these beliefs, without the fear that their efforts will be daily frustrated in the name of progress or free expression.

Indeed, that is what family life is all about.

There is not a generation gap in a happy and united family. People yearn to be able to rely on some generally accepted standards. Without them you have not got a society at all; you have purposeless anarchy. A healthy society is not created by its institutions, either. Great schools and universities do not make a great nation any more than great armies do. Only a great nation can create and involve great institutions – of learning, of healing, of scientific advance. And a great nation is the voluntary creation of its people – a people composed of men and women whose pride in themselves is founded on the knowledge of what they can give to a community of which they in turn can be proud.

If our people feel that they are part of a great nation, and they are prepared to will the means to keep it great, a great nation we shall be, and shall remain. So, what can stop us from achieving this? What then stands in our way? The prospect of another winter of discontent?[1] I suppose it might.

But I prefer to believe that certain lessons have been learned from experience, that we are coming, slowly, painfully, to an autumn of understanding. And I hope that it will be followed by a winter of common sense. If it is not, we shall not be diverted from our course.

To those waiting with bated breath for that favourite media catchphrase, the 'U turn',[2] I have only one thing to say: 'You turn if you want to. The lady's not for turning.' I say that not only to you, but to our friends overseas and also to those who are not our friends.

In foreign affairs we have pursued our national interest robustly while remaining alive to the needs and interests of others. We have acted where our predecessors dithered, and here I pay tribute to Lord Carrington. When I think of our much-travelled Foreign Secretary I am reminded of the advert, you know the one I mean, about 'The peer that reaches those foreign parts that other peers cannot reach.'[3] Long before we came into office, and therefore long before the invasion of Afghanistan,[4] I was pointing to the threat from the East. I was accused of scaremongering. But events have more than justified my words.

Soviet Marxism is ideologically, politically and morally bankrupt. But militarily the Soviet Union is a powerful and growing threat.

Yet it was Mr Kosygin[5] who said: 'No peace-loving country, no person

---

[1] The winter of 1978–79 was so called on account of a surge of especially damaging strikes. Coined by the *Sun* newspaper, the term was derived from the opening words of Shakespeare's *Richard III*: 'Now is the winter of our discontent'.

[2] A U-turn signifies a complete reversal of policy. The term was closely (and understandably) associated with the Heath Government of 1970–74.

[3] The original slogan was an advertisement for a brand of beer.

[4] The USSR invaded Afghanistan on 25 December 1979.

[5] Alexei Kosygin (1904–80), Soviet politician. Chairman of the Council of Ministers 1964–80.

of integrity, should remain indifferent when an aggressor holds human life and world opinion in insolent contempt.' We agree. The British Government are not indifferent to the occupation of Afghanistan. We shall not allow it to be forgotten. Unless and until the Soviet troops are withdrawn, other nations are bound to wonder which of them may be next. Of course there are those who say that by speaking out we are complicating East–West relations, that we are endangering détente. But the real danger would lie in keeping silent. Détente is indivisible and it is a two-way process.

The Soviet Union cannot conduct wars by proxy in South-East Asia and Africa, foment trouble in the Middle East and Caribbean and invade neighbouring countries and still expect to conduct business as usual. Unless détente is pursued by both sides it can be pursued by neither, and it is a delusion to suppose otherwise. That is the message we shall be delivering loud and clear at the meeting of the European Security Conference in Madrid in the weeks immediately ahead.[1] But we shall also be reminding the other parties in Madrid that the Helsinki Accord was supposed to promote the freer movement of people and ideas. The Soviet Government's response so far has been a campaign of repression worse than any since Stalin's day. It had been hoped that Helsinki would open gates across Europe. In fact, the guards today are better armed and the walls are no lower. But behind those walls the human spirit is unvanquished.

The workers of Poland in their millions have signalled their determination to participate in the shaping of their destiny.[2] We salute them.

Marxists claim that the capitalist system is in crisis. But the Polish workers have shown that it is the communist system that is in crisis. The Polish people should be left to work out their own future without external interference.

At every Party Conference, and every November in Parliament, we used to face difficult decisions over Rhodesia and over sanctions. But no longer. Since we last met the success at Lancaster House, and thereafter in Salisbury – a success won in the face of all the odds – has created

---

[1] The European Security Conference met in Madrid in October 1980 to consider progress in East–West relations since the Helsinki Accord of 1975.
[2] The independent trade union movement Solidarity was founded in Gdansk in August 1980, and soon included 75 per cent of the Polish workforce. Its aims included popular consultation over economic policy, the release of political prisoners and a free press.

new respect for Britain.[1] It has given fresh hope to those grappling with the terrible problems of Southern Africa. It has given the Commonwealth new strength and unity. Now it is for the new nation, Zimbabwe, to build her own future with the support of all those who believe that democracy has a place in Africa, and we wish her well.

We showed over Rhodesia that the hallmarks of Tory policy are, as they have always been, realism and resolve. Not for us the disastrous fantasies of unilateral disarmament, of withdrawal from NATO, of abandoning Northern Ireland.

The irresponsibility of the left on defence increases as the dangers which we face loom larger. We for our part, under Francis Pym's brilliant leadership, have chosen a defence policy which potential foes will respect.

We are acquiring, with the co-operation of the United States Government, the Trident missile system.[2] This will ensure the credibility of our strategic deterrent until the end of the century and beyond, and it was very important for the reputation of Britain abroad that we should keep our independent nuclear deterrent as well as for our citizens here.

We have agreed to the stationing of Cruise missiles in this country. The unilateralists object, but the recent willingness of the Soviet Government to open a new round of arms-control negotiations shows the wisdom of our firmness.

We intend to maintain and, where possible, to improve our conventional forces so as to pull our weight in the Alliance. We have no wish to seek a free ride at the expense of our allies. We will play our full part.

In Europe we have shown that it is possible to combine a vigorous defence of our own interests with a deep commitment to the idea and to the ideals of the Community.

The last Government were well aware that Britain's budget contribution was grossly unfair. They failed to do anything about it. We negotiated a satisfactory arrangement which will give us and our partners time to tackle the underlying issues.[3] We have resolved the difficulties

---

[1] The Lancaster House agreement of 21 December 1979 restored British rule in Rhodesia. Following all-party elections and the granting of a new constitution, the colony gained full legal independence as Zimbabwe on 18 April 1980.

[2] The decision to modernize the British nuclear deterrent in the mid-1980s by replacing the Polaris submarine-launched missile system with Trident was announced on 15 July 1980.

[3] On 30 May 1980, EC Foreign Ministers agreed on a rebate to Britain of £710 million and promised a major review of the EC budget.

of New Zealand's lamb trade with the Community in a way which protects the interests of the farmers in New Zealand while giving our own farmers and our own housewives an excellent deal, and Peter Walker[1] deserves to be congratulated on his success. Now he is two-thirds of his way to success in making important progress towards agreement on a common fisheries policy. That is very important to our people. There are many, many people whose livelihoods depend on it.

We face many other problems in the Community, but I am confident that they too will yield to the firm yet fair approach which has already proved so much more effective than the previous Government's five years of procrastination.

With each day it becomes clearer that in the wider world we face darkening horizons, and the war between Iran and Iraq is the latest symptom of a deeper malady.[2] Europe and North America are centres of stability in an increasingly anxious world. The Community and the Alliance are the guarantee to other countries that democracy and freedom of choice are still possible. They stand for order and the rule of law in an age when disorder and lawlessness are ever more widespread.

The British Government intend to stand by both these great institutions, the Community and NATO. We will not betray them.

The restoration of Britain's place in the world and of the West's confidence in its own destiny are two aspects of the same process. No doubt there will be unexpected twists in the road, but with wisdom and resolution we can reach our goal. I believe we will show the wisdom and you may be certain that we will show the resolution.

In his warm-hearted and generous speech, Peter Thorneycroft said that when people are called upon to lead great nations they must look into the hearts and minds of the people whom they seek to govern. I would add that those who seek to govern must in turn be willing to allow their hearts and minds to lie open to the people.

This afternoon I have tried to set before you some of my most deeply held convictions and beliefs. This Party, which I am privileged to serve, and this Government, which I am proud to lead, are engaged in the massive task of restoring confidence and stability to our people.

I have always known that that task was vital. Since last week it has

---

[1] Peter Walker (born 1932), Baron Walker of Worcester 1992. Conservative MP 1961–92; Environment Secretary 1970–72; Trade and Industry Secretary 1972–74; Minister of Agriculture 1979–83; Energy Secretary 1983–87; Welsh Secretary 1987–90.
[2] The Iran–Iraq War broke out on 22 September 1980.

become even more vital than ever. We close our Conference in the aftermath of that sinister Utopia unveiled at Blackpool. Let Labour's Orwellian nightmare of the left be the spur for us to dedicate with a new urgency our every ounce of energy and moral strength to rebuild the fortunes of this free nation.

If we are to fail, that freedom could be imperilled. So let us resist the blandishments of the fainthearts; let us ignore the howls and threats of the extremists; let us stand together and do our duty, and we shall not fail.

14

Speech at the Church of St Lawrence Jewry, City of London, 4 March 1981

The central theme of Mrs Thatcher's second address to an audience in the Church of St Lawrence Jewry is the relationship between individuals and the nation they compose, more specifically 'the spirit of the nation' which they generate and by which they in turn are influenced. It was a bold speech, not just because the left had for so long grown accustomed to claiming the moral high ground for itself, but also because the Government's policies at this time were under sustained attack for being divisive, destructive and callous. In particular, unemployment was rising sharply. The monthly unemployment figures announced on 24 February 1981 recorded a rise of 43,843, to 2,463,294. The total number of unemployed had risen by over 900,000 in a year. Mrs Thatcher insisted on the high value which she placed on work: 'not only a necessity, [but] a duty, and indeed a virtue'.

Thank you, Rector, for inviting me back to your church and giving me the opportunity to share some thoughts on the subject of your Lent Services – 'The Spirit of the Nation'.

Today is Ash Wednesday, the day when traditionally Christians begin a period of thoughtfulness about their relationship with God and how they are trying to serve Him here on earth. It is, therefore, fitting that on this occasion we consider some of the things which have made our nation flourish in the past and some of the challenges we face today.

My theme will be that the virtue of a nation is only as great as the virtue of the individuals who compose it.

Two years ago in this church, I spoke both as a Christian and a politician about how I found my religious convictions affecting the way I approached the responsibility of Government. Since then I have been, as it were, called to higher service! My approach to my present responsibilities remains the same as it was then, and I am indeed thankful that

I was brought up in a Christian family and learned the message of the Christian faith.

This afternoon, I want to consider some of the characteristics of our way of life which have stood our people in such good stead in times past.

John Newton[1] preached a sermon exactly two hundred years ago in a City church only a step away from this one. In the course of it he said: 'Though the occasion will require me to take some notice of our public affairs, I mean not to amuse you with what is usually called a political discourse.'

I too, Rector, will endeavour to keep to this self-denying ordinance.

The concept of the nation is at the heart of Old Testament Judaism, and one which those who wrote the New Testament accepted. But there is an even more fundamental idea which is also common to both – the idea of personal moral responsibility. It is to individuals that the Ten Commandments are addressed. In the statements 'Honour thy father and thy mother,' 'Thou shalt not steal,' 'Thou shalt not bear false witness,' and so on, the 'thou' to whom these resounding imperatives are addressed is you and me.

In the same way, the New Testament is preoccupied with the individual, with his need for forgiveness and for the divine strength which comes to those who sincerely accept it.

Of course, we can deduce from the teachings of the Bible principles of public as well as private morality; but, in the last resort, all these principles refer back to the individual in his relationships to others. We must always beware of supposing that somehow we can get rid of our own guilt by talking about 'national' or 'social' guilt. We are called on to repent our own sins, not each other's sins.

So each person is all-important in the Christian view of life and the universe. But human beings have social needs as well. So it is that, in the course of history, the family, the neighbourhood and the nation come into being. All these communities have certain things in common. However they grew up, they are held together by mutual dependence, by the experience which their members have in common, by common customs and belief.

They all need rules to enable them to live together harmoniously, and the rules must be backed by some kind of authority, however gently

---

[1] John Newton (1725–1807), popular evangelical preacher and hymn-writer, Vicar of St Mary Woolnoth, Lombard Street, 1780–1807.

and subtly exercised. The nation is but an enlarged family. Because of its traditions, and the mutual love and loyalty which bind its members together, it should ideally need little enforcement to maintain its life. But, alas, because of man's imperfection, evil is ever present, and the innocent must be protected from its ravages.

So the first, and in a sense the most important, point I have to make to you is this: we must never think of individual freedom and the social good as being opposed to each other; we must never suppose that where personal liberty is strong, society will be weak and impoverished, or that where the nation is strong the individual will necessarily be in shackles. The wealth of nations, the defence of national freedom, and the well-being of society – all these depend on the faith and exertions of men and women. It is an old and simple truth, but it is sometimes forgotten in political debate.

But what of the common beliefs and habits which hold this British nation of ours together? There was, of course, a time when the Christian religion was the only permitted form of worship in our land. Today we live in what is called a 'plural society', one in which many different traditions of belief exist alongside each other and also alongside other more recent fashions – those of total disbelief or even nihilism. No doubt we have absorbed much from other systems of belief, and contributed much to them. The change, however, has also brought its dilemmas, not least for the legislator.

We now have to concern ourselves not only with how Christians should behave towards each other within the framework of the nation, but with how they should seek to organize the nation's life in a way that is fair and tolerant towards those who do not accept the Christian message. What I am suggesting to you today, however, is that even though there are considerable religious minorities in Britain, most people would accept that we have a national way of life and that it is founded on Biblical principles.

As we emerged from the twilight of medieval times, when for many life was characterized by tyranny, injustice and cruelty, so we became what one historian has described as 'the people of a book, and that book was the Bible'.[1] What he meant, I think, was that this nation adopted – albeit gradually – a system of government and a way of living together which reflected the values implicit in that book. We acknowledged as a

[1] J.R. Green (1837–1883), historian and clergyman, author of the influential and popular *Short History of the English People* (1874).

nation that God was the source of our strength and that the teachings of Christ applied to our national as well as our personal life. There was, however, a considerable gap between the precept and the practice. Even when men had become free to speak for themselves, to invent, to experiment and to lay the foundations of what became known as the Industrial Revolution, considerable blotches remained on the canvas of our national life.

It took the vision and patience of men like Lord Shaftesbury and William Wilberforce[1] to convince Parliament that it was inconsistent for a nation whose life was based on Christ's teachings to countenance slave labour, children and women working in the mines and criminals locked up in degrading conditions. These leaders were motivated first and foremost by their Christian beliefs. It is also significant that most of the great philanthropists who set up schools and hospitals did so because they saw this as part of their Christian service for the people of the nation. Indeed, something of that same vision can be seen today. Wherever there are refugees or suffering or poverty in the world, there you find Christians working to relieve pain, to provide comfort, hope and practical help.

The spirit of our nation also includes some clear convictions about such things as fair play, which we regard as almost a religion in itself, and bullying, which we loathe. Perhaps Kipling put it best in one of his poems called 'Norman and Saxon', set in A.D. 1100:

'My son,' said the Norman Baron, 'I am dying, and you will be heir
To all the broad acres in England that William gave me for my share
When we conquered the Saxon at Hastings, and a nice little handful it is.
But before you go over to rule it I want you to understand this:
The Saxon is not like us Normans. His manners are not so polite.
But he never means anything serious till he talks about justice and right.
When he stands like an ox in the furrow with his sullen set eyes on your own,
And grumbles, 'This isn't fair dealing,' my son, leave the Saxon alone.'

[1] William Wilberforce (1759–1833), philanthropist, pre-eminent British campaigner for the abolition of the slave trade. MP 1780–1825.

This sense of fair play is based on the acceptance by the majority in the nation of some moral absolutes which underpin our social and commercial relationships. In other words, we believe that just as there are physical laws which we break at our peril, so there are moral laws which, if we flout them, will lead to personal and national decline.

If we as a nation had accepted, for instance, that violence, stealing and deception were plausible activities, then our moral fibre would soon have disintegrated.

There is one other characteristic of our nation which is, I think, worth mentioning: we have always had a sense that work is not only a necessity, it is a duty, and indeed a virtue. It is an expression of our dependence on each other. Work is not merely a way of receiving a pay packet but a means whereby everyone in the community benefits and society is enriched. Creating wealth must be seen as a Christian obligation if we are to fulfil our role as stewards of the resources and talents the Creator has provided for us.

These characteristics of our nation – the acknowledgement of the Almighty, a sense of tolerance, an acknowledgement of moral absolutes and a positive view of work – have sustained us in the past. Today they are being challenged. Although we are still able to live on the spiritual capital passed down to us, it is self-deceiving to think we can do so for ever. Each generation must renew its spiritual assets if the integrity of the nation is to survive.

Today, in spite of the work of the Churches, I suspect that only a minority acknowledge the authority of God in their lives. Perhaps that is why we have turned to the state to do so many things which in the past were the prerogative of the family: why crimes of violence are increasing, and a few people are even suggesting that murder can be justified on the grounds that it is political – a view which must be abhorrent to Christians. Furthermore, the respect for private and public property seems to be diminishing, and outside this City we can no longer assume that a man's word is always his bond.[1]

In terms of ethics and national economics, I should like also to refer to what I believe is an evil: namely, sustained inflation. For over thirty years the value of our currency has been eroding. It is an insidious evil because its effects are slow to be seen and relatively painless in the short run. Yet it has a morally debilitating influence on all aspects of our

---

[1] 'My word is my bond' is the motto of the London Stock Exchange.

national life. It reduces the value of savings, it undermines financial agreements, it stimulates hostility between workers and employers over matters of pay, it encourages debt and it diminishes the prospects of jobs. This is why I put its demise at the top of my list of economic priorities. It is, in my view, a moral issue, not just an economic one.

The second and equally great human and economic problem is the level of unemployment, which has been rising for over two decades and is still rising. I cannot conceal that of all difficulties I face, unemployment concerns me most of all. Leaving aside world recession and the details of economic policies necessary to defeat inflation (which would be the subject of a political discourse), what can we as individuals do to help? For none of us can opt out of the community in which we live. Whether we do something or nothing, our actions will affect it.

First, those who are in work fully accept their duty to provide for those who cannot find work.

Second, if we are employers we can try to take on as many young people as possible, to give them experience of the world of work. There are a number of schemes available for this purpose, and I must say that employers are responding splendidly. They too know how depressing it must be for a young person to feel that he is not needed and cannot find a niche for himself.

Third, we could perhaps buy more British-made goods. Not *everything* British-made, because there are jobs in exports, too, and we expect others to buy *our* goods – but we could help our people by buying more 'home-made' products.

Fourth, we can recognize that if at a time when output is not rising we ourselves demand more pay, it can only come from the pockets of others, and it will reduce the amount they can spend on other goods. That kind of pay claim can price your own job out of existence, or cause someone else to lose his job. And that responsibility cannot be shirked – it is a personal responsibility. It is a moral responsibility.

Another factor, which affects us at present, arises in part from the first and second. It is a sense of pessimism brought on because of the frustrations of not seeming to have a national purpose. When this happens to a nation, groups within it tend to work towards their more limited goals, often at the expense of others.

This pessimism is expressed in two ways. There are those who want to destroy our society for their own purposes – the terrorists and other extremists that we all too frequently see in action these days. Then there are those who adopt a philosophy of 'Eat, drink and be merry, for tomorrow we die.' That can result in a grasping of wealth for its own sake and the pursuit of selfish pleasure.

If I am right, we need to establish in the minds of young and old alike a national purpose which has real meaning for them. It must include the defence of the values which we believe to be of vital importance. Unless the spirit of the nation which has hitherto sustained us is renewed, our national way of life will perish. Who is to undertake this task?

Throughout history it has always been the few who took the lead: a few who see visions and dream dreams. There were the prophets in the Old Testament, the Apostles in the New, and the reformers in both Church and state. I well remember hearing a sermon after the Battle of Britain in which this was said about the few pilots to whom so many owed so much. John Stuart Mill once said that 'One person with a belief is a social power equal to ninety-nine who have only interests.' If we as a nation fail to produce such people then I am afraid the spirit of the nation, which has hitherto sustained us, will slowly die.

What then are the institutional means by which these values can be revived – for ideas and sentiments need institutions if they are to survive and be effective. Because we are talking primarily of the values bequeathed to us by a predominantly Christian culture, we must think first of the role of the Church.

The Church, thought of as the bishops, clergy and laity organized for public worship, has clear duties of its own – to preach the gospel of Christ, to celebrate the sacraments and to give comfort and counsel to men and women struggling with the trials and dilemmas of life.

Politicians must respect and accept its authority in these spheres. In our own country the state pays homage to the Church in many ways. The Queen is Supreme Governor of the Church of England and Protector of the Church of Scotland. These arrangements may seem to many to be antiquated, but they express the state's fundamental respect for the Christian religion. I hope we shall never see here what we have seen in other countries – temporal governments trying to usurp the role of spiritual leadership which properly belongs to the Church. That is a recipe for state tyranny as well as the corruption of religion.

The Church, on the other hand, can never resign altogether from what are called temporal matters. It has always rightly claimed to set before us the moral standards by which our public affairs should be conducted.

But I hope you will forgive me, Rector, for stating what I think these days needs to be pointed out – namely the difference between defining standards and descending into the political arena to take sides on those practical issues over which many good and honest Christians sincerely disagree. This, surely, can only weaken the influence and independence of the Church, whose members ideally should help shape the thinking of all political parties. Bernard Shaw,[1] in his Preface to *Androcles and the Lion*, makes the breathtaking statement, 'Christ was a first-class political economist.' But it was Christ himself who said of those who were too preoccupied with material things: 'Seek ye first the Kingdom of God and his righteousness, and all these things shall be added unto you.'

I wonder if some people are not demanding that 'things be added unto them' *before* they seek the Kingdom of God – indeed, regardless of whether they seek it or not.

As for the role of the state (what the Bible calls 'the things that are Caesar's'), I have never concealed my own philosophy. I believe it is a philosophy which rests on Christian assumptions, though I fully recognize that some Christians would have a different view. To me the wisdom of statesmanship consists of: knowing the limits within which government can and ought to act for the good of the individuals who make up society; respecting those limits; ensuring that the laws to which the people are subject shall be just, and consistent with the public conscience; making certain that those laws are firmly and fairly enforced; making the nation strong for the defence of its way of life against potential aggression; and maintaining an honest currency. Only governments can carry out these functions, and in these spheres government must be strong.

But (and here we come to the point from which we started today) every one of these objects depends for its achievement on the faith and the work of individuals. The state cannot create wealth. That depends on the exertions of countless people, motivated not only by the wholesome desire to provide for themselves and their families, but also by a passion for excellence and a genuine spirit of public service.

The state cannot generate compassion; it can and must provide a 'safety net' for those who, through no fault of their own, are unable to cope on their own. There is a need for far more generosity in our national life, but generosity is born in the hearts of men and women; it cannot be manufactured by politicians. And assuredly it will not flourish if politicians foster the illusion that the exercise of compassion can be

---

[1] George Bernard Shaw (1856–1950), Irish dramatist and critic.

left to officials. And so, I repeat, it is on the individual that the health of both Church and state depends.

Perhaps we have lost the idea that is inherent in Christ's parable of the talents. The steward who simply did not use the resources entrusted to him was roundly condemned. The two who used them to produce more wealth were congratulated and given more. To put up with the mediocre, to flinch from the challenge, to mutter 'The Government ought to be doing something about it,' is not the way to rekindle the spirit of the nation.

And so, what should we conclude about the relationship between the individual and the nation? I make no secret of my wish that everyone should be proud of belonging to this country. We have a past which, by any standard, is impressive; much in our present life and culture, too, commands great respect. We have, as a nation, a sense of perspective and a sense of humour; our scholars win international acclaim, our armed forces are renowned for their bravery and restraint, and our industries, in spite of economic recession, continue to do well in the markets of the world.

I want us to be proud of our nation for another reason. In the comity of nations, only a minority have a system of government which can be described as democratic. In these, economic and cultural life flourish because of the freedom their people enjoy. But a democratic system of government cannot be transferred to other nations simply by setting up imitations of our institutions – we have realized this all too clearly in recent times. For democracy to work, it requires what Montesquieu[1] described as a special quality in the people: 'virtue'. And, I would add, understanding. I believe this quality of virtue to be that derived from the Biblical principles on which this nation and the United States among others are founded. I want this nation to continue to be heard in the world and for the leaders of other countries to know that our strength comes from shared convictions as to what is right and wrong, and that we value these convictions enough to defend them.

Let me sum up. I believe the spirit of this nation is a Christian one. The values which sustain our way of life have by no means disappeared, but they are in danger of being undermined. I believe we are able to generate the will and purpose to revive and maintain them.

---

[1] Charles Louis de Secondat (1689–1755), Baron de la Brède et de Montesquieu. French lawyer, historian and philosopher. His principal works are *Considérations sur la grandeur et la décadence des Romains* (1734) and *De l'Esprit des lois* (1748).

John Newton put it elegantly in the sermon to which I earlier referred:

Though the Island of Great Britain exhibits but a small spot upon a map of the globe, it makes a splendid appearance in the history of mankind, and for a long space of time has been signally under the protection of God and a seat of peace, liberty and truth.

I pray we may continue to receive such blessing and retain such qualities.

15

Extracts from a Speech to the Conservative Central Council, Cardiff City Hall, 28 March 1981

Although it was the 1980 Party Conference speech which asserted that 'the lady's not for turning' (see p. 116), 1981 was the year in which that resolution was critically tested. It had begun badly. Public expenditure and public borrowing continued to race ahead of plans. Unemployment went on rising. Above all, in January the Government was forced into an ignominious retreat before a threatened national coal strike. Many, including the leading Cabinet 'wets',[1] assumed that this marked the beginning of a further retreat into reflation. But the Prime Minister, her advisers and a small group of economic Ministers in the Cabinet, including the Chancellor Geoffrey Howe, had other plans.

The Budget on 10 March directly challenged the post-war Keynesian orthodoxy by cutting Government borrowing in a recession, so as to allow interest rates to fall. The decision was roundly condemned by 364 economists in The Times. *More damagingly, it provoked leaked dissent from outraged – because outmanoeuvred – Cabinet Ministers. Margaret Thatcher replied to them with a counter-challenge, contained in these extracts from her speech to the Central Council in Cardiff.*

EXTRACT 1

Ever since the last war, our nation has faced a challenge in some way hardly less testing than the war itself. Then we faced a threat to our free way of life that all could recognize.

Since that great victory, we have faced danger, less tangible but all the more insidious. It is a threat not of invasion from abroad by our country's declared enemies, but of growing internal decline brought on

[1] An expression widely used in Thatcherite circles referring to left-ish Tories.

ourselves by self-deception and self-inflicted wounds. The symptoms of this decline have long been visible, however much we tried to avert our gaze and deceive ourselves that they would pass. From our unchallenged industrial leadership a hundred years ago, the standards of living of our people have fallen further behind those of countries like Germany and Japan, that rose from defeat to overtake us in the markets of the world.

Instead of earning a better living by adapting to changed methods and new opportunities, we stuck to old ways, and struck for more money without more production.

However radical people's words and theories, most are intensely conservative in preferring established working methods and familiar places and modes of life. And it is always tempting to politicians to try and promise an easy option that will avoid disturbing traditional ways.

So we put off adapting our old industries to modern methods, new markets, new competition. In printing, docks, shipbuilding, railways, steel, engineering, unions adhered too long to old practices and managers condoned demarcation. When new machines were installed, managements were forced to agree to overmanning which cancelled out most of the gains from the new equipment.

We politicians made speeches about 'change is our ally',[1] and one even talked about 'the white heat of technological revolution'.[2] But in practice, instead of using subsidies to ease the path of change, they used them to protect old jobs that could not last. The task of pioneering new jobs was put off to another day.

But our competitors did not stand still. In Europe and in the newly industrialized countries – Japan, Korea, Taiwan, Hong Kong, Singapore – new processes, new products and new techniques were developed. And the irony is that many of our workforce, who were resisting change, used their pay to buy the products of our overseas competitors because they recognized value when they saw it.

And so the new jobs were created not here but overseas. The very overmanning, the very refusal to accept new technology that was meant to protect jobs, became the means by which those jobs were destroyed.

It is hardly surprising that in the league tables of real income per head Britain has fallen steadily behind.

[1] *Change is our Ally: A Tory Approach to Industrial Problems* was a book edited by Angus Maude and Enoch Powell and published by the Conservative Political Centre in 1954.
[2] This phrase derives from a passage in Harold Wilson's address to the Labour Party Conference at Scarborough on 1 October 1963.

But if we have lagged in production we have, alas, led the field in inflation. You don't have to be a monetarist to see that to spend more on static output must push prices up.

There are only four ways in which a company can lay its hands on more money to pay higher wages.

First, by increasing efficiency – the way of Germany and Japan, where more pay is earned by more output. Their inflation is much lower than ours. Their unemployment is less than ours.

Second, by taking it out of profits, on money earmarked for investment. And that's what has been happening here for far too long and why investment is too low.

Third, by passing on the cost of increased wages in higher prices. It doesn't require a degree in economics to see that if a company raises its prices above its competitors at home or abroad it is likely to sell less and end up employing fewer people. That has too often been the British way, which helps explain why our unemployment has gone on rising over many years to such appalling levels.

And the fourth is to borrow and borrow and borrow, and finally seek a subsidy to stay afloat.

It isn't difficult to agree that everyone's interest would be best served by ending this painful progression. But until this Government came into power no one had the courage to stick to the remedy for long enough to allow it to work.

We knew that it had been the Government's readiness to print more money that made it possible for inflation to continue.

It once seemed obvious that so long as there were unemployed hands and under-used plants we could put them to work by more or less throwing newly created money in their direction. That was the theory. But in practice, as Governments increasingly discovered, the extra money did less to raise production than to push prices up even higher, and unemployment up even more.

It was this experience which persuaded the Government to give priority to stopping the spiral of ever-higher inflation and unemployment. If we will learn from history or from the example of other countries today, there is only one sure way. It is to set limits to the increase in the supply of money which has always, everywhere, been the fuel that keeps inflation going faster.

Inflation is now declining rapidly – from over 20 per cent last year to around 12 per cent today. That is good news for industry and its customers at home and abroad. It is also good news for the unemployed.

133

If wage and salary negotiations take account of falling inflation, unions and management can price more jobs and goods back into the market.

Inflation can now be seen as a great divider of the nation. So we must find a common cause which will unite all who truly care for the future strength, prosperity and influence of a free Britain.

For a start, we can surely agree that the grievous number of men and women who are out of work are bearing a heavier burden than those with a job and a regular pay packet.

Is it not then a small sacrifice for those in work to settle for pay which, though less than we would like, is as much as can be afforded by private or public employers without bringing still more unemployment?

We have one common cause we can all support. It is to keep inflation moving down as a condition of stopping unemployment moving up, and as a prelude to getting recovery going on a sound and lasting foundation.

EXTRACT 2

We are engaged upon a massive task. It is no less than to rebuild a nation; a nation strong and confident and truly free, whose people live their lives and use their talent unencumbered by the state, but who have both the means and the will to succour those in need.

Our goal is clear, but as we move towards it we are faced with a recession of peculiar ferocity.

Our difficulties are not unique. It is not true that when it rains, it only rains upon the British people. Our friends and competitors abroad are struggling with the same problems as ourselves.

And, in another context, it is not only we, the British, whose future is in the balance. Others look to us for our part in the defence of the free world, menaced as it is almost as gravely as it ever has been in my lifetime.

Others look to us, others believe in us. Can we not believe in ourselves?

We have much on our side. Great material resources, great gifts of heart and mind, and, as I still believe, great courage. If we should fail, what would lie ahead but permanent decline and an eternity of mutual recrimination?

In the past our people have made sacrifices, only to find at the eleventh hour their Government had lost its nerve and the sacrifice had been in vain.

It shall not be in vain this time.

This Conservative Government, not yet two years in office, will hold fast until the future of our country is assured.

I do not greatly care what people say about me; I do greatly care what people think about our country.

Let us, then, keep calm and strong, and let us preserve that mutual friendship in which patriotism consists.

This is the road I am resolved to follow. This is the path I must go. I ask all who have the spirit – the bold, the steadfast and the young in heart – to stand and join with me as we go forward. For there is no other company in which I would travel.

16

Speech to the Conservative Party Conference, Blackpool, 16 October 1981

The challenge to her critics contained in Mrs Thatcher's Central Council speech was taken up. In April and July there were urban riots, which were seized upon as evidence of the divisive and destructive policies she was pig-headedly pursuing. Opposition to the Prime Minister's and Chancellor's economic strategy continued inside the Cabinet: there were bitter disagreements over public expenditure in July.

This opposition also extended beyond financial policy. Mrs Thatcher and her advisers saw the legal restriction of excessive trade union power as an essential counterpart to financial discipline; otherwise, trade union leaders could use that power to ensure that the pressures on the economy to adapt resulted in ever higher unemployment rather than lower wage costs. But the Employment Secretary, James Prior, and others rejected this analysis and opposed further reform. There was further trouble when Francis Pym and Lord Thorneycroft aired doubts in public as to whether the economic recession was ending – though the first (admittedly still faint) signs of recovery appeared in the summer of 1981, to be confirmed by economic statistics in the following quarter.

So, a variety of plans for reflation – that is, increasing government spending and borrowing, so as to increase growth and employment – were offered by Opposition and dissenting Conservative politicians alike. Pressures again began to build on the Prime Minister to change course. As that autumn's Party Conference approached, it was clear that either the Government would need to commit itself fully to the economic strategy – or abandon it. The outcome was the Cabinet reshuffle in September. This fundamentally and – for as long as Margaret Thatcher remained Prime Minister – permanently shifted the balance to the right. Ian Gilmour, Christopher Soames and Mark Carlisle were sacked. Jim Prior moved to Northern Ireland, making way for Norman Tebbit to enact the next step of trade union reform. Nigel Lawson joined the Cabinet as Energy Secretary. Peter Thorneycroft vacated the Party Chairmanship in favour of Cecil Parkinson.

The Prime Minister had asserted her authority within the Government. The question which only the 1981 Party Conference could decide was whether the Government retained the support of the Party. In Blackpool her opponents, including Ted Heath, fought back. But by the end of the week it was clear that they had lost. The Prime Minister's own speech made a significant contribution to that. It took the arguments of the reflationists seriously and showed why both logic and experience disproved them. And if some passages read like a lecture on economics, that is precisely what the occasion – and the audience – required.

Thank you, Mr President, for that wonderful introduction, one so typical of your own generosity and your dedicated service to our cause.[1] I turn now for a moment to another great servant of our Party. Six and a half years ago I asked Peter Thorneycroft to become our Chairman. Of course, I was anxious whether he would agree to take on the very heavy responsibilities that go with the Chairmanship. But my anxiety was misplaced. He, who had already given more than forty years' service to our Party, wanted to do more. We all came to respect his wise judgement, his zeal for our cause, his breadth of vision and his devotion to the enduring honour of our country. It was typical of his magnanimity that he himself suggested that I should appoint a younger Chairman. I know that it is the wish of all of us that we should send to Peter and Carla on the last day of our Conference a message of affection and of gratitude for the unique qualities which he placed unreservedly at the service of the Party in which he believes so deeply.

And to our present Chairman[2] may I say this: I want to let you into a secret. I asked Peter's advice about you. With that characteristic caution and understatement he said, 'I think he'd do it rather well' – and so say all of us.

This week in Blackpool we have had the grand assize of the nation. Once more the Conservative Party has demonstrated that it is the party of all the people. We are not here to manipulate millions of block votes in some travesty of democracy;[3] nor were we drawn here by the tinsel

---

[1] Refers to Sir Edward du Cann (born 1924), Conservative MP 1956–87; Chairman of the Conservative Party 1965–67; Chairman of the 1922 Committee 1972–84.

[2] Cecil Parkinson (born 1931), Baron Parkinson of Carnforth 1992. Conservative MP 1970–92; Chairman of the Conservative Party 1981–83; Chancellor of the Duchy of Lancaster 1982–83; Trade and Industry Secretary 1983; Energy Secretary 1987–89; Transport Secretary 1989–90.

[3] A reference to the trade-union block votes which were decisive at Labour Party conferences.

glamour of a marriage of convenience.[1] We are here as representatives of a myriad of different interests from every constituency in the land. We are here because we share a deep and abiding concern for the future of our country and our Party.

There has been strenuous discussion and dissent – I welcome it. For years as our Conference has assembled I have grown used to the charge that we are bland and anodyne, careful to avoid differences. I do not think that that is a charge that can be levelled at us this year.

We have witnessed here this week a Party conscious of its awesome responsibilities as Government at an immensely difficult time – difficult not only for us but for many other countries in the world as well, for we are not alone in our problems. The diversity of our Party is not a source of weakness; it is a part of our strength, for it is a reflection of the personal commitment that each one of us brings to the task that lies ahead.

Let me say at once that I am glad that Ted Heath[2] addressed our Conference and delighted that he will be helping us in the Croydon by-election.[3] Our country is weathering stormy waters. We may have different ideas on how best to navigate, but we sail the same ocean and in the same ship.

I have listened to much of the debate that has taken place in this hall, and, you know, I seem to have heard a good deal of what has been said to us around and, as you put it, Mr Chairman, in your introduction, even beyond the fringe.[4] This afternoon I want to draw together what seem to me to be the main strands of your wisdom and advice to the Government and to express some of your worries.

First among these is the deep and heartfelt concern for the personal hardship and waste reflected in every factory closure and redundancy. I learned from childhood the dignity which comes from work and, by contrast, the affront to self-esteem which comes from enforced idleness. For us, work was the only way of life we knew, and we were brought up to believe that it was not only a necessity but a virtue.

[1] A reference to the Liberal-SDP 'Alliance'.

[2] Sir Edward Heath (born 1916), Conservative MP 1950–; Chief Whip 1955–59; Minister of Labour 1959–60; Lord Privy Seal 1960–63; Industry Secretary and President of the Board of Trade 1963–64; Leader of the Conservative Party 1965–75; Prime Minister 1970–74.

[3] The Conservatives lost Croydon North-West to the Liberals in the by-election on 22 October 1981, but regained it at the 1983 general election.

[4] 'The Fringe' is the term applied to unofficial meetings on the margins of the Tory Party Conference.

The concern of this Conference is focused on the plight of the unemployed. But we seek not only to display and demonstrate that concern, but to find and pursue those policies which offer the best hope of more lasting jobs in future years.

To do that, we must learn the lessons of the past in order to avoid the mistakes that led to the increase in inflation and unemployment in the first place. Today's unemployment is partly due to the sharp increase in oil prices;[1] it absorbed money that might otherwise have gone to increased investment or to buying the things which British factories produce. But that is not all. Too much of our present unemployment is due to enormous past wage increases unmatched by higher output, to union restrictive practices, to overmanning, to strikes, to indifferent management, and to the mistaken belief that, come what may, the Government would always step in to bail out companies in difficulty. No policy can succeed that shirks those basic issues.

We have to earn our living in a world which can choose between the goods we produce and those of other countries. The irony is that many of our people spend five days of the week making British goods and on Saturday go out and spend their earnings on goods produced abroad, goods made in countries which have embraced more modern technology and where management and workforce understand that they are on the same side.

Oh, yes: unemployment is the most emotional issue in our country, and however much we may explain what has led to it we cannot alter the fact. [Interruption] Yes, in this conference it does matter; it matters enough not only for us to talk about it but to try to do something constructive about it.

However much we may explain what has led to it, we cannot alter the fact that many people who worked loyally and well for firms up and down the country feel bruised and resentful when, after long and devoted service, they suddenly find themselves without a job. I understand this – I would feel the same. But that would make it even more inexcusable if any Minister, let alone the Prime Minister, were to deceive them with false hopes or spurious remedies. We are dealing with one of the most complex and sensitive problems of our time, and neither rhetoric nor compassion is enough, and demonstrating will not help either.

There have been many voices in the past few weeks calling on us to spend our way back towards a higher level of employment, and to cut

[1] Oil prices doubled in 1979–80 under the impact of the Iranian Revolution.

interest rates at the same time. It is a familiar treatment, and it has been tried by many different Governments these past thirty years.

In the early days it worked well enough. In the 1950s a few million pounds of what we learned to call reflation earned a swift reward in jobs and output. But, as time went on, the dose required grew larger and the stimulus achieved grew less. By the 1960s it was needing hundreds of millions of extra spending to lift some hundreds of thousands of our people back into employment. By the 1970s we found that after thousands of extra millions had been spent we still had unemployment at levels which ten or twenty years before would have been unthinkable. The trick had been tried too often. The people, as earners and consumers, had rumbled what the Government was doing to their money. They knew the Government was creating inflation and they took that into account in their wage demands. So all the extra money went into wages and prices and not into more jobs.

So today, if we were to heed the calls to add another thousand million pounds to our plans for spending, we might thereby create an extra fifty thousand jobs in two years' time; and even those would be all too swiftly cancelled out by the loss of other jobs in private industry as the result of what we had done. The fact is that a good chunk of the higher taxes and the higher interest rates needed to find the money for the extra spending would come from the tills of every business in the land.

'Ah,' but we are told, 'don't put up the taxes or the interest rates – put them down instead.' In other words, 'Print the money.' That way, I must tell you, lies a collapse of trust in sterling both at home and abroad, lies the destruction of the savings of every family. It would lead to suitcase money and penury as the sole reward for thrift. That is not what this Government was elected to do.

But these problems are not peculiar to Britain. Governments all over the world are seeking to borrow on a scale hitherto unknown, and that is why interest rates in every major financial centre have been rising steeply. Indeed, if we had been members of the European Monetary System[1] we might very well have found our interest rates going up long before this September.

That is why it is not a question of choosing between the conquest of inflation and the conquest of unemployment. Indeed, as one of our

[1] The European Monetary System was set up by eight EEC member-states in 1978–79 to promote exchange-rate stability and economic convergence.

PARTY CONFERENCE, 16 OCTOBER 1981

speakers reminded us yesterday, we are fighting unemployment by fighting inflation. Of course, there are those who promise success without tears. I wish they were right. Who more than the Prime Minister would benefit from an easy answer to our troubles? But they would not benefit, because there is no easy answer. [Interruption] It makes it much more exciting, doesn't it? As the President said, it is like the Empire Loyalists[1] when we were young and sitting down there.

But if there were a way of beating inflation and unemployment by displeasing no one in the meantime I should take it like a shot. I can tell you unhesitatingly that if I thought Britain could solve her problems more easily, if I found that world conditions opened up a less rugged road, I should not hesitate to take it. There would be no question of sticking doggedly to so-called dogma. I do not want to prove anything, except that Britain can once again succeed and that all of us can share in the fruits of that success.

But, Mr President, I cannot bow to the pressures to take a route which I know will lead us even further from that prospect. That is not obstinacy. It is sheer common sense. The tough measures that this Government have had to introduce are the very minimum needed for us to win through. I will not change just to court popularity. Indeed, if ever a Conservative Government start to do what they know to be wrong because they are afraid to do what they are sure is right, then it is the time for Tories to cry 'Stop.' But you will never need to do that while I am Prime Minister.

Mr President, in the teeth of international competition British business is beginning to win the major orders that for too long went elsewhere. As the Chairman reminded us earlier this week, £1,000 million of British goods are sold abroad every week. In the last month alone, Standard Telephones has won the £170 million contract for a telephone cable right across the Pacific from Australia to Canada – the longest contract that has ever been put out to tender. British Steel has gained contracts worth £70 million in the North Sea and across the world in Hong Kong. The Davy Corporation leads the international consortium to build the £1,250 million steelworks for India. Foster Wheeler has started work on a £140 million petro-chemical plant in Greece. Great international companies like Texas Instruments, Hewlett Packard and Motorola are

---

[1] The League of Empire Loyalists was a pressure group which bitterly criticized the Conservative Government of the late 1950s for granting independence to the colonies, and expressed its opposition by disrupting Tory Conferences.

demonstrating their faith in Britain's future by choosing this country under a Conservative Government as the main location for their expansion.

This is the way to get extra jobs – thousands of extra jobs for Britain. That is the real recovery. And it is happening now. We are winning through.

These are the headline-catching stories; but every bit as important to this Government is the health of the many small and thrusting businesses. We have already taken some sixty measures of direct practical help for small businesses. Indeed, our business start-up scheme is one of the most radical and effective in the Western world. Ten thousand new businesses are starting every month. From them will come so much of the new and lasting employment of the future. I salute their work and their enterprise, and we all wish them well.

But yes, I know. You have said it all week. Private business is still being held to ransom by the giant monopolist nationalized industries. And you are right. They do not price themselves onto the dole queues. They do that to other people. They have captive markets at their beck and call. While free enterprise prices are going up in single figures, prices in the nationalized industries are going up by 20 per cent.

The fact is that only when we introduce the spur of competition in the state-owned industries do they begin to respond to the needs of the customer. That is why, for example, Norman Fowler, when he was at the Ministry of Transport, stripped away the veto powers of British Rail on bus and coach licences. If you can travel now from Manchester to London or from Edinburgh to Bristol by road or rail at fares lower than when we took office, that is thanks to Norman Fowler, just as it is thanks to Freddie Laker that you can cross the Atlantic for so much less than it would have cost you in the early 1970s.[1] Competition works.

You heard Patrick Jenkin[2] speak of companies as different as Cable & Wireless and British Transport Hotels. I never thought that we should be able to make so much progress with denationalization in these first two and a half years. And I can assure you that there will be more of

---

[1] Sir Freddie Laker (born 1922), British businessman. Chairman of Laker Airways 1966–82, 1992–, which introduced cheap 'Skytrain' flights from London to New York in 1977.
[2] Patrick Jenkin (born 1926), Baron Jenkin of Roding 1987. Conservative MP 1964–87; Minister for Energy 1974; Social Services Secretary 1979–81; Industry Secretary 1981–83; Environment Secretary 1983–85.

these measures in the next session of Parliament.[1] Mr President, if this is dogmatism, then it is the dogmatism of Mr Marks and Mr Spencer, and I'll plead guilty to that any day of the week.

But, you know, the thought does sometimes occur to me: if only we had never had all those nice Labour moderates – the sort that now join the SDP[2] – we should never have had these problems in the first place. For it was the Labour moderates who nationalized those industries. They are the guilty men. And they have now shacked up with David Steel[3] – although I do not think that Mr Gladstone would have put it in quite these words. The Liberal Leader seems to have quite a passion for pacts, associations, understandings and alliances – a sort of man for all fusions. But of course there is nothing wrong with pacts, provided they are based on a broad identity of principle. But without any genuine common ground parties that cannot advance on their own two feet tend to be trodden on by their partners'.

The marriage is for one election only. After that either party can call it a day and go its separate way. Well, of course, nothing is for ever. But it is an odd couple that pencils in a date for divorce before they have even sat down to the wedding breakfast. Perhaps the caution is understandable. Little is known about the SDP, except that its four leaders were senior members of Labour Cabinets of the 1960s and 1970s. And if the country is in difficulty today, they played their part in bringing that difficulty about. And they have not repudiated their socialism. Mr Jenkins[4] may remark that, 'Good Lord, he has not used the word "socialism" for years'; but he has not disowned it. Nor have his former Cabinet colleagues, the other leaders of the new party whom the Liberals are being asked to embrace.

At a time of growing danger for all who cherish and believe in freedom, this party of the soft centre is no shield, no refuge and no answer. As

---

[1] Between 1979 and 1983 Amersham International, Associated British Ports, British Aerospace, British Transport Hotels, Britoil, Cable & Wireless, Fairey, Ferranti Electronics and the National Freight Corporation were in whole or in part returned to private ownership.
[2] The Social Democrat Party was formed early in 1981 by the former Labour Ministers Roy Jenkins, David Owen, Shirley Williams and William Rodgers.
[3] On 13 October 1981 the SDP and the Liberal Party announced an electoral pact whereby 'SDP–Liberal Alliance' candidates would contest the next election.
[4] Roy Jenkins (born 1920), Baron Jenkins of Hillhead 1987. Labour MP 1948–76; Home Secretary 1965–67, 1974–76; Chancellor of the Exchequer 1967–70; President of the Commission of the EC 1976–81; Social Democrat MP 1982–87; Leader of the SDP 1982–83; Leader of Social and Liberal Democrat Peers 1988–.

Quintin Hailsham said so vividly a few days ago, 'In a confrontation with the politics of power, the soft centre has always melted away.' And when the soft centre has melted away, we are left with the hard shell of the Labour Party.

And make no mistake, the leadership of the Labour Party wants what it has always wanted – the full-blooded socialism that has been the driving force and purpose of its political life and leadership. Mr Wedgwood Benn says that 'the forces of socialism in Britain cannot be stopped.' They can be and they will be. We shall stop them. We shall stop them democratically – and I use the word in the dictionary sense, not the Bennite sense. What they cannot be is half-stopped, least of all by those who for years helped to nurture and support them.

Some of the most important things in life are beyond economics. Last Sunday I visited the victims of the IRA bomb outrage in Chelsea,[1] the kind of outrage that has occurred time and again in Northern Ireland. After seeing the injured children and young soldiers, the heartbreak of their parents and wives, one began to count one's blessings. For their world has been suddenly and cruelly shattered by the bombers and terrorists who are the enemies of civilized society everywhere.

We are all in it together, because a breakdown of law and order strikes at everyone. No one is exempt when the terrorists and the bully-boys take over. We look to the police and to the courts to protect the freedom of ordinary people, because without order none of us can go about our daily business in safety. Without order, fear becomes master and the strong and the violent become a power in the land.

This was why the first action after the riots in Brixton and Toxteth was to restore order.[2] Nothing, but nothing, could justify the violence that we saw that week.

I listened to every word of the debate on Tuesday. You made your views absolutely plain. Much as we are doing to support the police and uphold the rule of law, you urge us to do even more. I will give you this pledge: above all other things, this Government are determined to maintain order and uphold the Queen's peace.

Order depends upon discipline, overwhelmingly upon self-discipline.

---

[1] The IRA blew up a coach carrying Irish Guardsmen outside Chelsea Barracks in London on 10 October 1981. A civilian was killed and many soldiers and bystanders were injured.
[2] Between 10 and 12 April 1981, the inner London area of Brixton witnessed arson, looting and attacks on the police. Similar disturbances occurred in Toxteth, Liverpool and Moss Side, Manchester, and elsewhere from 4 to 9 July 1981.

It is lamentable that the virtues of self-discipline and self-restraint that mark a mature democracy have lately been so little preached in some homes and schools that they have become so poorly practised in our society.

It is when self-discipline breaks down that society has to impose order. It is in this sense that we Conservatives insist that government must be strong – strong to uphold the rule of law, strong to maintain order, strong to protect freedom. This was the truth which our ancestors knew well, but which some of our generation have managed to unlearn. What is freedom if it does not include freedom from violence and freedom from intimidation?

One of the most revealing things about the rhetoric of the left is the almost total absence of any reference to the family. Yet the family is the basic unit of our society, and it is in the family that the next generation is nurtured. Our concern is to create a property-owning democracy; and it is therefore a very human concern. It is a natural desire of Conservatives that every family should have a stake in society and that the privilege of a family home should not be restricted to the few.

The fact that over 55 per cent own their homes is a tribute to successive Conservative Governments, each one of which has helped to build the property-owning democracy. It is now our turn to take a major step towards extending home ownership to many who, until now, have been deliberately excluded.

Councils, particularly socialist councils, have clung to the role of landlord. They love it, because it gives them so much power. So more than two million families have seen themselves paying rent for ever. Petty rules aid restrictions and bring enforced dependence. These are the marks of this last vestige of feudalism in Britain. It is the arrogance of the socialist creed to insist that they know best. For them, equality of opportunity means their opportunity to make sure that everyone else is equal.

Nowhere is this more true than in education. For every family the chance to give your children a better start than you had is one of the greatest joys. Yet we have been so obsessed with the reorganization of education, and with buildings and equipment, that we have failed to concentrate on the quality and content of what is taught in our schools. This is precisely what is of greatest concern to parents, and that is why this Government have given them so much more say in the way schools are run; so much more choice in which school to pick for their children; so much more responsibility for the next generation.

But the best schools, and the best housing and the best education, will avail us nothing if we lack the means or the resolve to defend the way of life of our people. For abroad, this is a time of danger. We face in the Soviet Union a power whose declared aim is to 'bury' Western civilization.

Experience has taught us that threats such as we now face do not disappear unless they are met calmly, and with ingenuity and strength. We cannot defend ourselves, either in this island or in Europe, without a close, effective and warm-hearted alliance with the United States. Our friendship with America rests not only on the memory of common dangers jointly faced and of common ancestors. It rests on respect for the same rule of law and representative democracy. Our purpose must be not just to confirm but to strengthen a friendship which has twice saved us this century.

Had it not been for the magnanimity of the United States, Europe would not be free today. Nor would the peace have been kept in Europe for what is now thirty-six years. Assuming we hold this peace for eight more years we shall then have enjoyed a longer time free from European war than for two centuries. What a triumph for the Western Alliance!

One thrust of Soviet propaganda is concerned to persuade the world that the West, and the United States in particular, is the armsmonger, not the Soviet Union. Nothing could be further from the truth. But it is not surprising that the Russians have found a ready audience; for none of us has any illusions about the horror of nuclear war, and we all shrink from it. However, that should force us to consider what is the most likely way of securing peace. It is precisely because I believe that the unilateralists make war more likely that I seek another way.

Should we more easily get the Soviet side to the table to negotiate disarmament if we ourselves had already renounced nuclear weapons? Why should they negotiate if we had already laid down our arms? Would they follow our example? There are no unilateralists in the Kremlin. Until we negotiate multilateral disarmament we have no choice but to retain sufficient nuclear weapons to make it clear to any would-be aggressor that the consequences of an attack on us would be disastrous for them.

To those of us who want us to close down the American nuclear bases in this country, let me say this: we in Britain cannot honourably shelter under the American nuclear umbrella and simultaneously say to our American friends: 'You may defend our homes with your home-based

missiles, but you may not base those missiles anywhere near our homes.'
The cost of keeping tyranny at bay is high, but it must be paid; for the
cost of war would be infinitely higher, and we should lose everything
that was worthwhile.

It is in this dangerous world that Britain must live. She cannot escape
it or retreat into an island bunker. Yet that is precisely what the Labour
Party proposes. It has become the 'get out' party – to get out of our
defence obligations, get out of our NATO nuclear commitments, and
get out of the European Community.

It is in European affairs that the contrast with the Conservatives is
particularly marked. When in power, Labour did nothing to improve
the European Community. In two and a half years this Government
have slashed our budget contribution and set the Community on the
road to far-reaching reform. It is vital that we get it right. Forty-three
out of every hundred pounds we earn abroad comes from the Common
Market. Over two million jobs depend on our trade with Europe, two
million jobs which will be put at risk by Britain's withdrawal. And even
if we kept two-thirds of our trade with the Common Market after we
had flounced out – and that is pretty optimistic – there would be a
million more to join the dole queues. That is only the beginning.

American and Japanese firms are coming to this country to build
factories and provide jobs for us, so that they can sell to the whole of
Europe. If we came out, future investors would not come here. They
would go to Germany, France or Greece. Even those who are already
here would not be satisfied with a market of fifty million 'cribb'd, cabin'd
and confined' by import controls, customs duties and tariffs. They would
up sticks and away. They would take their investment, their expansion
and their jobs into the rest of Europe.

For the unspoken assumption behind policies of withdrawal from the
Community and unilateral disarmament is that others will continue to
bear their burdens and pick up ours as well. Others would continue to
accept our products, even though we refused to accept theirs; others
would continue to ensure the defence of Europe and provide a shield
behind which we would shelter.

What a contemptible policy for Britain! Nothing is beyond this nation.
Decline is not inevitable. They say I'm an optimist. Well, in this job you
get called all sorts of things. An optimist is one of the nicer ones, and I
would not deny the label. I remember what our country used to be like,
and I know what we can become again. But first we must rid ourselves
of the idea that the laws of economic gravity can somehow be suspended

in our favour, and that what applies to other nations does not apply to ours.

We must finally come to accept what in some ways we have not accepted since the war – that although then we with superb defiance helped the free world to survive, the world has not since then and on that account owed us a living.

We in the Conservative Party know that you cannot get anything for nothing. We held to the firm foundation of principle, grounded in commonsense, common belief and the common purpose of the British people – the commonsense of a people who know that it takes effort to achieve success, the common belief in personal responsibility and the values of a free society, the common purpose that is determined to win through the difficult days to the victory that comes with unity.

This Government, this Government of principle, are seeking the common consent of the people of Britain to work together for the prosperity that has eluded us for so long. There are those who say our nation no longer has the stomach for the fight. I think I know our people; and I know they do.

17

Speech in a Debate on the Falkland Islands in the House of Commons, 3 April 1982

Argentina invaded the Falkland Islands on Friday 2 April. From the previous Wednesday evening it had been clear to the Prime Minister from reports received via the Ministry of Defence that such an invasion would take place; and on that same Wednesday evening Mrs Thatcher had authorized the assembly of a task force to retake the islands. But before any military engagement was imminent, a storm of public criticism had to be faced. Not surprisingly, in her memoirs Lady Thatcher describes that first Falklands debate in the House of Commons on Saturday 3 April as 'the most difficult I ever had to face'. (I, p. 183)

The almost universal Commons support for the sending of the task force concealed different opinions as to its use, as the future would reveal. Thus the most significant passage of the speech is that in which the Prime Minister set out her and the Government's objectives: the end of Argentinian occupation of the islands and their return to British administration at the earliest possible moment.

The Prime Minister: The House meets this Saturday to respond to a situation of great gravity. We are here because, for the first time for many years, British sovereign territory has been invaded by a foreign power. After several days of rising tension in our relations with Argentina, that country's armed forces attacked the Falkland Islands yesterday and established military control of the islands.

Yesterday was a day of rumour and counter-rumour. Throughout the day we had no communication from the Government of the Falklands. Indeed, the last message that we received was at 21.55 hours on Thursday night, 1 April. Yesterday morning at 8.33 a.m. we sent a telegram which was acknowledged. At 8.45 a.m. all communications ceased. I shall refer to that again in a moment. By late afternoon yesterday it became clear that an Argentine invasion had taken place and that the lawful British Government of the islands had been usurped.

I am sure that the whole House will join me in condemning totally this unprovoked aggression by the Government of Argentina against British territory. [Honourable Members: 'Hear, Hear.'] It has not a shred of justification and not a scrap of legality.

It was not until 8.30 this morning, our time, when I was able to speak to the Governor,[1] who had arrived in Uruguay, that I learned precisely what had happened. He told me that the Argentines had landed at approximately 6 a.m. Falklands time, 10 a.m. our time. One party attacked the capital from the landward side and another from the seaward side. The Governor then sent a signal to us which we did not receive.

Communications had ceased at 8.45 our time. It is common for atmospheric conditions to make communications with Port Stanley difficult. Indeed, we had been out of contact for a period the previous night.

The Governor reported that the Marines, in the defence of Government House, were superb. He said that they acted in the best traditions of the Royal Marines. They inflicted casualties, but those defending Government House suffered none. He had kept the local people informed of what was happening through a small local transmitter which he had in Government House. He is relieved that the islanders heeded his advice to stay indoors. Fortunately, as far as he is aware, there were no civilian casualties. When he left the Falklands, he said that the people were in tears. They do not want to be Argentine. He said that the islanders are still tremendously loyal. I must say that I have every confidence in the Governor and the action that he took.

I must tell the House that the Falkland Islands and their dependencies remain British territory. No aggression and no invasion can alter that simple fact. It is the Government's objective to see that the islands are freed from occupation and are returned to British administration at the earliest possible moment.

Argentina has, of course, long disputed British sovereignty over the islands. We have absolutely no doubt about our sovereignty, which has been continuous since 1833. Nor have we any doubt about the unequivocal wishes of the Falkland Islanders, who are British in stock and tradition, and they wish to remain British in allegiance. We cannot allow

[1] Sir Rex Hunt (born 1926), Governor of the Falkland Islands 1980–82, 1985; Civil Commissioner of the Falkland Islands 1982–85.

the democratic rights of the islanders to be denied by the territorial ambitions of Argentina.

Over the past fifteen years, successive British Governments have held a series of meetings with the Argentine Government to discuss the dispute. In many of these meetings elected representatives of the islanders have taken part. We have always made it clear that their wishes were paramount and that there would be no change in sovereignty without their consent and without the approval of the House.

The most recent meeting took place this year in New York at the end of February between my honourable friend the Member for Shoreham [Mr Luce[1]], accompanied by two members of the islands council, and the Deputy Foreign Secretary of Argentina. The atmosphere at the meeting was cordial and positive, and a communiqué was issued about future negotiating procedures. Unfortunately, the joint communiqué which had been agreed was not published in Buenos Aires.

There was a good deal of bellicose comment in the Argentine press in late February and early March, about which my honourable friend the Minister of State for Foreign and Commonwealth Affairs[2] expressed his concern in the House on 3 March following the Anglo–Argentine talks in New York. However, this has not been an uncommon situation in Argentina over the years. It would have been absurd to dispatch the fleet every time there was bellicose talk in Buenos Aires. There was no good reason on 3 March to think that an invasion was being planned, especially against the background of the constructive talks on which my honourable friend had just been engaged. The joint communiqué on behalf of the Argentine Deputy Minister of Foreign Affairs and my honourable friend read:

The meeting took place in a cordial and positive spirit. The two sides reaffirmed their resolve to find a solution to the sovereignty dispute and considered in detail an Argentine proposal for procedures to make better progress in this sense.

There had, of course, been previous incidents affecting sovereignty before the one in South Georgia, to which I shall refer in a moment. In December 1976 the Argentines illegally set up a scientific station on

---

[1] Sir Richard Luce (born 1936), Conservative MP 1971–92; Parliamentary Under-Secretary for Foreign Affairs 1979–81; Minister of State for Foreign Affairs 1981–82, 1983–85; Minister for the Arts 1985–90.
[2] i.e. Richard Luce.

one of the dependencies within the Falklands group – Southern Thule. The Labour Government attempted to solve the matter through diplomatic exchanges, but without success. The Argentines remained there and are still there.

Two weeks ago – on 19 March – the latest in this series of incidents affecting sovereignty occurred; and the deterioration in relations between the British and Argentine Governments, which culminated in yesterday's Argentine invasion, began. The incident appeared at the start to be relatively minor. But we now know it was the beginning of much more.

The commander of the British Antarctic Survey based at Grytviken on South Georgia – a dependency of the Falkland Islands over which the United Kingdom has exercised sovereignty since 1775 when the island was discovered by Captain Cook – reported to us that an Argentine navy cargo ship had landed about sixty Argentines at nearby Leith harbour. They had set up camp and hoisted the Argentine flag. They were there to carry out a valid commercial contract to remove scrap metal from a former whaling station.

The leader of the commercial expedition, Davidoff, had told our Embassy in Buenos Aires that he would be going to South Georgia in March. He was reminded of the need to obtain permission from the immigration authorities on the island. He did not do so. The base commander told the Argentines that they had no right to land on South Georgia without the permission of the British authorities. They should go either to Grytviken to get the necessary clearances, or leave. The ship and some fifty of them left on 22 March. Although about ten Argentines remained behind, this appeared to reduce the tension.

In the meantime, we had been in touch with the Argentine Government about the incident. They claimed to have had no prior knowledge of the landing, and assured us that there were no Argentine military personnel in the party. For our part we made it clear that, while we had no wish to interfere in the operation of a normal commercial contract, we could not accept the illegal presence of these people on British territory.

We asked the Argentine Government either to arrange for the departure of the remaining men or to ensure that they obtained the necessary permission to be there. Because we recognized the potentially serious nature of the situation, HMS *Endurance* was ordered to the area. We told the Argentine Government that, if they failed to regularize the position of the party on South Georgia or to arrange for their departure, HMS *Endurance* would take them off, without using force, and return them to Argentina.

This was, however, to be a last resort. We were determined that this apparently minor problem of ten people on South Georgia in pursuit of a commercial contract should not be allowed to escalate, and we made it plain to the Argentine Government that we wanted to achieve a peaceful resolution of the problem by diplomatic means. To help in this, HMS *Endurance* was ordered not to approach the Argentine party at Leith but to go to Grytviken.

But it soon became clear that the Argentine Government had little interest in trying to solve the problem. On 25 March another Argentine navy ship arrived at Leith to deliver supplies to the ten men ashore. Our Ambassador in Buenos Aires sought an early response from the Argentine Government to our previous requests that they should arrange for the men's departure. This request was refused. Last Sunday, on Sunday 28 March, the Argentine Foreign Minister[1] sent a message to my right honourable and noble friend the Foreign Secretary[2] refusing outright to regularize the men's position. Instead it restated Argentina's claim to sovereignty over the Falkland Islands and their dependencies.

My right honourable and noble friend the Foreign and Commonwealth Secretary then sent a message to the United States Secretary of State[3] asking him to intervene and to urge restraint.

By the beginning of this week it was clear that our efforts to solve the South Georgia dispute through the usual diplomatic channels were getting nowhere. Therefore, on Wednesday 31 March my right honourable and noble friend the Foreign Secretary proposed to the Argentine Foreign Minister that we should dispatch a special emissary to Buenos Aires.

Later that day we received information which led us to believe that a large number of Argentine ships, including an aircraft carrier, destroyers, landing craft, troop carriers and submarines, were heading for Port Stanley.[4] I contacted President Reagan[5] that evening and asked him to intervene with the Argentine President[6] directly. We promised, in the

[1] Dr Nicanor Costa Mendez (born 1922), Argentinian lawyer and diplomat. Minister of Foreign Affairs 1966–70, 1982.
[2] Lord Carrington.
[3] Alexander Haig (born 1924), US soldier and politician. Supreme Allied Commander, Europe, 1974–79; Secretary of State 1981–82.
[4] The capital of the Falkland Islands.
[5] Ronald Reagan (born 1911), US actor and politician. Governor of California 1967–74; 40th President of the United States 1981–89 (Republican).
[6] Leopold Galtieri (born 1926), Argentinian soldier and politician. Commander-in-Chief of the Army 1979–82; member of the ruling military junta 1979–82; President of Argentina 1981–82.

meantime, to take no action to escalate the dispute for fear of precipitating – [Interruption] – the very event that our efforts were directed to avoid. May I remind Opposition Members – [Interruption] – what happened when, during the lifetime of their Government –

Mr J.W. Rooker[1] (Birmingham, Perry Barr): We did not lose the Falklands.

The Prime Minister. – Southern Thule was occupied. It was occupied in 1976. The House was not even informed by the then Government until 1978, when, in response to questioning by my honourable friend the Member for Shoreham [Mr Luce], now Minister of State, Foreign and Commonwealth Office, the honourable Member for Merthyr Tydfil [Mr Rowlands[2]] said: 'We have sought to resolve the issue through diplomatic exchanges between the two Governments. That is infinitely preferable to public denunciations and public statements when we are trying to achieve a practical result to the problem that has arisen.' [Official Report, 24 May 1978, Vol.950, c.1550–1]

Mr Edward Rowlands (Merthyr Tydfil): The right honourable lady is talking about a piece of rock in the most southerly part of the dependencies, which is completely uninhabited and which smells of large accumulations of penguin and other droppings. There is a vast difference – a whole world of difference – between the 1,800 people now imprisoned by Argentine invaders and that argument. The right honourable lady should have the grace to accept that.

The Prime Minister. We are talking about the sovereignty of British territory – [Interruption] – which was infringed in 1976. The House was not even informed of it until 1978. We are talking about a further incident in South Georgia which – as I have indicated – seemed to be a minor incident at the time. There is only a British Antarctic Scientific Survey there, and there was a commercial contract to remove a whaling station. I suggest to the honourable gentleman that had I come to the House at that time and said that we had a problem on South Georgia with ten people who had landed with a contract to remove a whaling station, and had I gone on to say that we should send HMS *Invincible*, I should have been accused of warmongering and sabre-rattling.

Information about the Argentine fleet did not arrive until Wednesday. Argentina is, of course, very close to the Falklands – a point that the

---

[1] Jeffrey Rooker (born 1941), Labour MP 1974–.
[2] Edward Rowlands (born 1940), Labour MP 1966–70, 1972–; Parliamentary Under-Secretary for Foreign Affairs 1975–76; Minister of State for Foreign Affairs 1976–79.

honourable Member for Merthyr Tydfil cannot and must not ignore – and its navy can sail there very quickly. On Thursday, the Argentine Foreign Minister rejected the idea of an emissary and told our Ambassador that the diplomatic channel, as a means of solving this dispute, was closed. President Reagan had a very long telephone conversation, of some fifty minutes, with the Argentine President, but his strong representations fell on deaf ears. I am grateful to him and to Secretary Haig for their strenuous and persistent efforts on our behalf.

On Thursday, the United Nations Secretary-General, Mr Pérez de Cuéllar,[1] summoned both British and Argentine Permanent Representatives to urge both countries to refrain from the use or threat of force in the South Atlantic. Later that evening we sought an emergency meeting of the Security Council. We accepted the appeal of its President for restraint. The Argentines said nothing. On Friday, as the House knows, the Argentines invaded the Falklands, and I have given a precise account of everything we knew, or did not know, about that situation.

There were also reports that yesterday the Argentines also attacked South Georgia, where HMS *Endurance* had left a detachment of twenty-two Royal Marines. Our information is that on 2 April an Argentine naval transport vessel informed the base commander at Grytviken that an important message would be passed to him after 11 o'clock today our time. It is assumed that this message will ask the base commander to surrender.

Before indicating some of the measures that the Government have taken in response to the Argentine invasion, I should like to make three points. First, even if ships had been instructed to sail the day that the Argentines landed on South Georgia to clear the whaling station, the ships could not possibly have got to Port Stanley before the invasion. [Interruption] Opposition Members may not like it, but that is a fact.

Secondly, there have been several occasions in the past when an invasion has been threatened. The only way of being certain to prevent an invasion would have been to keep a very large fleet close to the Falklands, when we are some eight thousand miles away from base. No Government have ever been able to do that, and the cost would be enormous.

---

[1] Javier Pérez de Cuéllar (born 1920), Peruvian diplomat and international official. Secretary-General of the United Nations 1982–91.

Mr Eric Ogden[1] (Liverpool, West Derby): Will the right honourable lady say what has happened to HMS *Endurance?*

The Prime Minister: HMS *Endurance* is in the area. It is not for me to say precisely where, and the honourable gentleman would not wish me to do so.

Thirdly, aircraft, unable to land on the Falklands because of the frequently changing weather, would have had little fuel left and, ironically, their only hope of landing safely would have been to divert to Argentina. Indeed, all of the air and most sea supplies for the Falklands come from Argentina, which is but four hundred miles away compared with our eight thousand miles.

That is the background against which we have to make decisions and to consider what action we can best take. I cannot tell the House precisely what dispositions have been made – some ships are already at sea, others were put on immediate alert on Thursday evening.

The Government have now decided that a large task force will sail as soon as all preparations are complete. HMS *Invincible* will be in the lead and will leave port on Monday.

I stress that I cannot foretell what orders the task force will receive as it proceeds. That will depend on the situation at the time. Meanwhile, we hope that our continuing diplomatic efforts, helped by our many friends, will meet with success.

The Foreign Ministers of the European Community member-states yesterday condemned the intervention and urged withdrawal. The NATO Council called on both sides to refrain from force and continue diplomacy.

The United Nations Security Council met again yesterday and will continue its discussions today. [Laughter] Opposition Members laugh. They would have been the first to urge a meeting of the Security Council if we had not called one. They would have been the first to urge restraint and to urge a solution to the problem by diplomatic means. They would have been the first to accuse us of sabre-rattling and warmongering.

Mr Tam Dalyell[2] (West Lothian): The right honourable lady referred to our many friends. Have we any friends in South America on this issue?

The Prime Minister: Doubtless our friends in South America will make

---

[1] Eric Ogden (1923–97), Labour MP 1964–81; Social Democrat MP 1981–83; Chairman of the Falkland Islands Association 1983–87.
[2] Tam Dalyell (born 1932), Labour MP 1962–.

their views known during any proceedings at the Security Council. I believe that many countries in South America will be prepared to condemn the invasion of the Falkland Islands by force.

We are now reviewing all aspects of the relationship between Argentina and the United Kingdom. The Argentine chargé d'affaires and his staff were yesterday instructed to leave within four days.

As an appropriate precautionary and, I hope, temporary measure, the Government have taken action to freeze Argentine financial assets held in this country. An order will be laid before Parliament today under the Emergency Laws (Re-enactments and Repeals) Act 1964 blocking the movement of gold, securities or funds held in the United Kingdom by the Argentine Government or Argentine residents.

As a further precautionary measure, the ECGD[1] has suspended new export credit cover for the Argentine. It is the Government's earnest wish that a return to good sense and the normal rules of international behaviour on the part of the Argentine Government will obviate the need for action across the full range of economic relations.

We shall be reviewing the situation and be ready to take further steps that we deem appropriate and we shall, of course, report to the House.

The people of the Falkland Islands, like the people of the United Kingdom, are an island race. Their way of life is British; their allegiance is to the Crown. They are few in number, but they have the right to live in peace, to choose their own way of life and to determine their own allegiance. It is the wish of the British people and the duty of Her Majesty's Government to do everything that we can to uphold that right. That will be our hope and our endeavour and, I believe, the resolve of every Member of the House.

[1] The Export Credits Guarantee Department, a central Government trade body.

18

Speech in a Debate on the Falkland Islands in the House of Commons, 14 April 1982

By the time of the next major Commons debate on the Falklands crisis, Britain was enmeshed in complex and frustrating diplomatic negotiations, as the task force continued to head towards the South Atlantic. US Secretary of State Alexander Haig was conducting what was (in effect if not in name) a mediation between the two sides. British policy at this time was mainly directed towards bringing the Americans to state publicly what they conceded privately, namely that Argentina was in the wrong and should withdraw. This General Haig was extremely reluctant to do, in spite of heavy pressure from the Prime Minister when they met in Downing Street. Haig returned to Washington from where, in the course of the debate in the House of Commons on 14 April, he telephoned to say that the Argentinians were complaining that the United States was not being even-handed and was supplying military assistance to the British. In answer to this charge, Haig wished to issue a statement:

> *Since the outset of the crisis the United States has not acceded to requests that would go beyond the scope of customary patterns of co-operation. That will continue to be its stand while peace efforts are under way. Britain's use of US facilities on Ascension Island have been restricted accordingly.*

The Prime Minister had to break away from the debate in order to protest about the mention of Ascension Island – which was of course British. Her protest succeeded.

Mrs Thatcher's speech set out the Government's objectives and justified them. Britain would continue to insist on Argentine withdrawal from the Falklands and South Georgia. The basis of military action would be the right of self-defence. In any diplomatic solution the wishes of the islanders must remain paramount.

The Prime Minister. It is right, at this time of grave concern over the Falkland Islands and their people, that Parliament should be recalled so that the Government may report and the House may discuss the latest developments.

Our objective, endorsed by all sides of the House in recent debates, is that the people of the Falkland Islands shall be free to determine their own way of life and their own future. The wishes of the islanders must be paramount. But they cannot be freely expressed, let alone implemented, while the present illegal Argentine occupation continues.

That is why our immediate goal in recent days has been to secure the withdrawal of all Argentine forces in accordance with Resolution 502 of the United Nations Security Council,[1] and to secure the restoration of British administration. Our strategy has been based on a combination of diplomatic, military and economic pressures, and I should like to deal with each of these in turn.

First of all, we seek a peaceful solution by diplomatic effort. This, too, is in accordance with the Security Council Resolution. In this approach we have been helped by the widespread disapproval of the use of force which the Argentine aggression has aroused across the world, and also by the tireless efforts of Secretary of State Haig, who has now paid two visits to this country and one to Buenos Aires.

On his first visit last Thursday we impressed upon him the great depth of feeling on this issue, not only of Parliament but of the British people as a whole. We may not express our views in the same way as the masses gathered in Buenos Aires, but we feel them every bit as strongly – indeed, even more profoundly, because Britons are involved. We made clear to Mr Haig that withdrawal of the invaders' troops must come first; that the sovereignty of the islands is not affected by the act of invasion; and that when it comes to future negotiations what matters most is what the Falkland Islanders themselves wish.

On his second visit on Easter Monday and yesterday, Mr Haig put forward certain ideas as a basis for discussion – ideas concerning the withdrawal of troops and its supervision, and an interim period during which negotiations on the future of the islands would be conducted. Our talks were long and detailed, as the House would expect. Some things

---

[1] Adopted on 3 April 1982, UN Resolution 502 called for i) the immediate cessation of hostilities; ii) the immediate withdrawal of Argentine forces from the islands; and iii) a diplomatic solution in accordance with the principles of the UN Charter.

we could not consider because they flouted our basic principles. Others we had to examine carefully and suggest alternatives. The talks were constructive and some progress was made. At the end of Monday, Mr Haig was prepared to return to Buenos Aires in pursuit of a peaceful solution.

Late that night, however, Argentina put forward to him other proposals which we could not possibly have accepted; but yesterday the position appeared to have eased. Further ideas are now being considered and Secretary Haig has returned to Washington before proceeding, he hopes shortly, to Buenos Aires. That meeting, in our view, will be crucial.

These discussions are complex, changing and difficult, the more so because they are taking place between a military junta and a democratic government of a free people – one which is not prepared to compromise that democracy and that liberty, which the British Falkland Islanders regard as their birthright.

We seek, and shall continue to seek, a diplomatic solution, and the House will realize that it would jeopardize that aim were I to give further details at this stage. Indeed, Secretary Haig has been scrupulous in his adherence to confidentiality in pursuit of the larger objective. We shall continue genuinely to negotiate through the good offices of Mr Haig, to whose skill and perseverance I pay warm tribute.

Diplomatic efforts are more likely to succeed if they are backed by military strength. At 5 a.m. London time on Monday 12 April, the maritime exclusion zone of two hundred miles around the Falkland Islands came into effect. From that time any Argentine warships and Argentine naval auxiliaries found within this zone are treated as hostile and are liable to be attacked by British forces.

We see this measure as the first step towards achieving the withdrawal of Argentine forces. It appears to have exerted influence on Argentina, whose navy has been concentrated outside the zone. If the zone is challenged, we shall take that as the clearest evidence that the search for a peaceful solution has been abandoned. We shall then take the necessary action. Let no one doubt that.

The naval task force is proceeding with all speed towards the South Atlantic. It is a formidable force, comprising two aircraft carriers, five guided missile destroyers, seven frigates, an assault ship with five landing ships, together with supporting vessels. The composition of the force and the speed with which it was assembled and put to sea clearly demonstrate our determination.

Morale on board the ships in the task force is very high. The ships and aircraft are carrying out exercises on passage, and by the time the force arrives off the Falklands it will be in a very high state of fighting efficiency.

Mr Tam Dalyell (West Lothian): Am I right in thinking that if the task force arrives off the Falklands there will be sufficient air cover against a land-based air force from the Argentine?

The Prime Minister: I shall have something to say about air cover in a moment. I have every confidence in all aspects of this task force.

A number of civilian ships have now been chartered or requisitioned. These include the *Canberra*, for use as a troop ship, and the *Uganda*, which will be available as a hospital ship. Recourse to the merchant marine is traditional in time of naval emergency and its response has been wholehearted on this occasion as in the past.

Men and equipment continue to be flown out to Ascension Island[1] to meet up with the task force. These additional elements will enhance the fighting capability of the force and the range of operations which can be undertaken. Nimrod maritime patrol aircraft are now patrolling the South Atlantic in support of our fleet.

Sustaining a substantial force eight thousand miles from the United Kingdom is a considerable undertaking. As the Ministry of Defence announced this morning, additional measures are now in hand to provide extra capability for the force over an extended period. In particular, the second assault ship, HMS *Intrepid*, is being recommissioned for operational service. She will significantly add to the amphibious capability of the task force now entering the South Atlantic, which already contains her sister ship HMS *Fearless*.

Arrangements are in hand to adapt a large cargo ship for the sea-lift of additional Harriers. This will nearly double the size of the Harrier force in the South Atlantic. All these aircraft have a formidable air-combat and ground-attack capability.

Our diplomacy is backed by strength, and we have the resolve to use that strength if necessary.

The third aspect of our pressure against Argentina has been economic. We have been urging our friends and allies to take action parallel to our own, and we have achieved a heartening degree of success. The most significant measure has been the decision of our nine partners in

---

[1] A small British dependency in the mid-Atlantic, four thousand miles north-east of the Falkland Islands.

the European Community to join us not just in an arms embargo but also in stopping all imports from Argentina.

This is a very important step, unprecedented in its scope and the rapidity of the decision. Last year about a quarter of all Argentina's exports went to the European Community. The effect on Argentina's economy of this measure will therefore be considerable, and cannot be without influence on her leaders in the present crisis. I should like warmly to thank our European partners for rallying to our support. It was an effective demonstration of Community solidarity. The decision cannot have been easy for our partners, given the commercial interests at stake, but they were the first to realize that if aggression were allowed to succeed in the Falkland Islands, it would be encouraged the world over.

Other friends too have been quick to help, and I should like to thank Australia, New Zealand and Canada for their sturdy and swift action. They have decided to ban imports from Argentina, to stop export credits and to halt all sales of military equipment. New Zealand has also banned exports to Argentina. We are grateful also to many other countries in the Commonwealth which have supported us by condemning the Argentine invasion.

What have the Argentines been able to produce to balance this solidarity in support of our cause? Some Latin American countries have, of course, repeated their support for the Argentine claim to sovereignty. We always knew they would. But only one of them has supported the Argentine invasion, and nearly all have made clear their distaste and disapproval that Argentina should have resorted to aggression.

Almost the only country whose position has been shifting towards Argentina is the Soviet Union. We can only guess at the cynical calculations which lie behind this move. But Soviet support for Argentina is hardly likely to shake the world's confidence in the justice of our cause, and it will not alter our determination to achieve our objectives.

One of our first concerns has been and remains the safety of the British subjects who have been caught up in the consequences of the crisis. They include, apart from the Falkland Islanders themselves, the Marines and the British Antarctic Survey scientists on South Georgia and the British community in Argentina. In spite of all our efforts, we have not been able to secure reliable information about the twenty-two Marines who were on South Georgia and the thirteen British Antarctic Survey personnel who are believed to have been evacuated from Grytviken at the same time.

According to Argentine reports, these people are on a ship heading for the mainland. There are also reports that the six Marines and the one member of the crew of *Endurance* who were captured on the Falkland Islands are now in Argentina.

Finally, there are thirteen members of the British Antarctic Survey team and two other British subjects who remain on South Georgia. The survey team's most recent contacts on 12 April with their headquarters in this country indicate that they are safe and well.

On 5 April, we asked the Swiss Government, as the protecting power, to pursue all these cases urgently with the Argentine Government. We trust that their efforts will soon produce the information which we and their families so anxiously seek. On the same day we also sought the assistance of the International Red Cross with regard to the position of the population in the Falkland Islands. So far the Argentine Government have not responded to its request to visit the islands. Last night, a party of thirty-five people from the islands, including the Chief Secretary, arrived in Montevideo, and a report from the Chief Secretary on conditions in the islands is expected at any moment.

Recently, the Government received a message from the British Community Council in Argentina urging a peaceful solution to the present conflict and asking that due consideration be given to the strong British presence in Argentina and the size of the British community there. We have replied, recognizing the contribution which the British community has made to the development of Argentina, but making it plain that we have a duty to respond to the unprovoked aggression against the Falkland Islands and insisting that Argentina should comply with the Mandatory Resolution of the Security Council calling upon it to withdraw its troops.

Mr Dalyell (West Lothian): Before the right honourable lady comes to the end of her speech, I wish to repeat my question about air power. Does the right honourable lady not remember what happened to *Prince of Wales* and *Repulse*?[1] Does she not know that there are at least sixty-eight Skyhawks as well as the Mirages and R5-30s in the Argentine air force? That is a formidable force if the task force is to go near the Falkland Islands. Will the right honourable lady answer my question?

The Prime Minister. I have indicated to the honourable Member for

[1] HMS *Prince of Wales* and HMS *Repulse* were sunk off Malaya by Japanese air attacks on 10 December 1941, with the loss of 840 lives.

West Lothian and to the House that we have taken steps to double the provision of the Harriers. We believe that that will provide the air cover that the honourable gentleman and the House seek. I trust that he and the House will express confidence in our naval, marine and air forces. That is what they are at least entitled to have from the House.

We are also being urged in some quarters to avoid armed confrontation at all costs and to seek conciliation. Of course, we too want a peaceful solution; but it was not Britain that broke the peace. If the argument of no force at any price were to be adopted at this stage it would serve only to perpetuate the occupation of those very territories which have themselves been seized by force.

In any negotiations over the coming days we shall be guided by the following principles. We shall continue to insist on Argentine withdrawal from the Falkland Islands and dependencies. We shall remain ready to exercise our right to resort to force in self-defence under Article 51 of the United Nations Charter until the occupying forces leave the islands. Our naval task force sails on towards its destination. We remain fully confident of its ability to take whatever measures may be necessary. Meanwhile, its very existence and its progress towards the Falkland Islands reinforce the efforts we are making for a diplomatic solution.

That solution must safeguard the principle that the wishes of the islanders shall remain paramount. There is no reason to believe that they would prefer any alternative to the resumption of the administration which they enjoyed before Argentina committed aggression. It may be that their recent experiences will have caused their views on the future to change. But until they have had the chance freely to express their views, the British Government will not assume that the islanders' wishes are different from what they were before.

We have a long and proud history of recognizing the right of others to determine their own destiny. Indeed, in that respect we have an experience unrivalled by any other nation in the world. But that right must be upheld universally, and not least where it is challenged by those who are hardly conspicuous for their own devotion to democracy and liberty.

The eyes of the world are now focused on the Falkland Islands. Others are watching anxiously to see whether brute force or the rule of law will triumph. Wherever naked aggression occurs it must be overcome. The cost now, however high, must be set against the cost we would one day have to pay if this principle went by default. That is why, through diplomatic, economic and, if necessary, through military means, we shall persevere until freedom and democracy are restored to the people of the Falkland Islands.

19

Statement on the Falkland Islands to the House of Commons, 26 April 1982

The recapture by British forces of South Georgia ought to have provided an important boost to morale. But it was overshadowed by media misinterpretation of Mrs Thatcher's irritated remarks at a press conference with John Nott outside No. 10, when she told the press, probing for more interesting stories, that they should 'Rejoice'. As she notes in her memoirs, she 'meant that they should rejoice in the bloodless recapture of South Georgia, not in the war itself' (I, p. 209). A further – and potentially more serious – problem was that the ease with which South Georgia was recaptured suggested to those unfamiliar with the real difficulties facing the task force that the Falkland Islands themselves could be retaken without great risk.

The Prime Minister: With permission, Mr Speaker, I should like to make a statement about recent developments in relation to the Falkland Islands and South Georgia.

In our continuing pursuit of a negotiated settlement, my right honourable friend the Foreign and Commonwealth Secretary[1] visited Washington on 22 and 23 April. He had many hours of intensive discussions with Mr Haig. Their talks proved constructive and helpful, but there are still considerable difficulties. Mr Haig now intends to pursue his efforts further with the Argentine Government.

However, the Argentine Foreign Minister is reported to be unwilling to continue negotiations at present. I hope that he will reconsider this. As the British task force approaches closer to the Falklands, the urgent need is to speed up the negotiations, not to slow them down. We remain in close touch with Mr Haig.

I now turn to events on South Georgia yesterday. The first phase of the

[1] Francis Pym was appointed Foreign Secretary following the resignation of Lord Carrington on 5 April 1982.

operation to repossess the island began at first light when the Argentine submarine *Sante Fe* was detected close to British warships that were preparing to land forces on South Georgia.

The United Kingdom had already made it clear to Argentina that any approach on the part of Argentine warships, including submarines, or military aircraft, which could amount to a threat to interfere with the mission of British forces, would encounter the appropriate response. The *Santa Fe* posed a significant threat to the successful completion of the operation and to British warships and forces launching the landing. Helicopters therefore engaged and disabled the Argentine submarine.

Just after 4 p.m. London time yesterday, British troops landed on South Georgia and advanced towards Grytviken. At about 6 p.m. the commander of the Argentine forces in Grytviken surrendered, having offered only limited resistance.

British forces continued to advance during the night and are now in control of Leith, the other main settlement on South Georgia. At 10 o'clock this morning the officer commanding the Argentine forces on South Georgia formally surrendered.

British forces throughout the operation used the minimum force necessary to achieve a successful outcome. No British casualties have been notified and it is reported that only one Argentine sustained serious injuries. About 180 prisoners were taken, including up to fifty military reinforcements who had been on the Argentine submarine. The prisoners will be returned to Argentina.

British Antarctic Survey personnel on the island were reported to be safe when we last heard from them early yesterday afternoon. Our forces are making contact with them and arrangements are in hand to evacuate them, if they so wish.

I am sure that the House will join me in congratulating our forces on carrying out this operation successfully, and recapturing the island. The action that we have taken is fully in accord with our inherent right of self-defence under Article 51 of the United Nations Charter.

My right honourable friends and I will continue to keep the House fully informed on the situation as it develops.

I should like to emphasize that the repossession of South Georgia, including the attack on the Argentine submarine, in no way alters the Government's determination to do everything possible to achieve a negotiated solution to the present crisis. We seek the implementation of the Security Council Resolution, and we seek it by peaceful means if possible.

20

Speech in a Debate on the Falkland Islands in the House of Commons, 29 April 1982

By the end of April the first phase of the Falklands crisis, in which diplomacy predominated, was about to yield to the second, in which military action was the decisive factor. The Prime Minister had successfully resisted the Haig/Pym proposals which the British Foreign Secretary had brought back from Washington on Saturday 24 April and which, as she points out in her memoirs, would have constituted 'conditional surrender' (I, p. 205). A total exclusion zone of a two-hundred-nautical-mile radius had been declared around the Falklands; it was the War Cabinet's practice not to announce such measures unless and until they could be enforced. Consequently, it was increasingly clear to all that serious and risk-filled military action would soon take place.

It was the Leader of the Opposition, Michael Foot, who asked for a Commons debate. He and others were beginning to waver when confronted by the prospect of outright hostilities. In her speech, the Prime Minister had to reassure the House that diplomacy was being conducted seriously and vigorously. But she also had to prepare public opinion for the use of force.

The Prime Minister: From the onset of the Falklands crisis, my right honourable friends and I have undertaken to keep the House as closely informed as possible about the situation. Although my last report to honourable Members was only two days ago, such is the seriousness of this matter that my right honourable friends and I were glad to agree to the suggestion of the right honourable gentleman the Leader of the Opposition[1] that time should be found for a debate today – the fourth since the Argentine invasion of the Falkland Islands four weeks ago tomorrow.

During that period, the Government have taken every possible step that had a reasonable prospect of helping us to achieve our objectives

---

[1] Michael Foot.

– the withdrawal of the Argentine forces and the end of their illegal occupation of the islands, the restoration of British administration, and a long-term solution which is acceptable not only to the House but to the inhabitants of the Falkland Islands.

It is the Government's most earnest hope that we can achieve those objectives by a negotiated settlement. We have done everything that we can to encourage Mr Haig's attempts to find a solution by diplomatic means. I shall have something more to say about that in a moment.

As the House knows, the Government have also taken military measures to strengthen our diplomatic efforts. Mr Haig's initiative would never have got under way if the British Government had not sent the naval task force to the South Atlantic within four days of Argentina's aggression against the Falkland Islands. What incentive would there have been for the Argentine junta to give Mr Haig's ideas more than the most cursory glance if Britain had not underpinned its search for a diplomatic settlement with the dispatch of the task force? Gentle persuasion will not make the Argentine Government give up what they have seized by force.

Our military response to the situation has been measured and controlled. On 12 April we declared a maritime exclusion zone. It has been enforced against Argentine warships and naval auxiliaries. It has been completely successful, and the Argentine forces on the Falkland Islands have been isolated by sea. Eleven days later we warned the Argentine authorities that any approach by their warships or military aircraft which could amount to a threat to interfere with the mission of the British forces in the South Atlantic would encounter the appropriate response.

On 25 April, as I reported to the House on Monday, British forces recaptured South Georgia. The operation was conducted in exercise of our right of self-defence under Article 51 of the United Nations Charter. The minimum of force was used, consistent with achieving our objective, and no lives – Argentine or British – were lost in the operation, although, as was announced yesterday, we deeply regret that an Argentine prisoner lost his life in an incident on 26 April. That incident is now being urgently investigated by a board of inquiry in accordance with the terms of the relevant Geneva Convention.

The latest of our military measures is the imposition of the total exclusion zone round the Falkland Islands, of which we gave forty-eight hours' notice yesterday. The new zone has the same geographical boundaries as the maritime exclusion zone which took effect on 12 April. It will apply from noon London time tomorrow to all ships and aircraft, whether military or civil, operating in support of the illegal occupation of the Falkland Islands. A complete blockade will be placed on all traffic supporting the occupation forces of Argentina. Maritime and aviation authorities have been informed of the imposition of the zone, in accordance with our international obligations. We shall enforce the total exclusion zone as completely as we have done the maritime exclusion zone. The Argentine occupying forces will then be totally isolated – cut off by sea and air.

I turn now to the point that the right honourable Member for Roxburgh, Selkirk and Peebles [Mr Steel] raised during Question Time. I am grateful to him for leaving me to deal with the matter in my speech. On the diplomatic side, Mr Haig has put formal American proposals to the Argentine Government and requested an early response. I stress the status of those proposals. They are official American proposals. Mr Haig judged it right to ask Argentina to give its decision first, as the country to which Security Council resolution 502 is principally addressed. He saw Mr Costa Mendez last night, but no conclusion was reached. Mr Haig has also communicated to us the text of his proposals. It is difficult both for the House and for the Government that we are not able to say more about them publicly, especially as in our democratic system we need the interplay of opinions and ideas. But they are Mr Haig's proposals, and we understand from him that it is his present intention to publish them in full. But he of course must judge the appropriate time.

The proposals are complex and difficult and inevitably bear all the hallmarks of compromise in both their substance and language. But they must be measured against the principles and objectives expressed so strongly in our debates in the House. My right honourable friend the Secretary of State for Foreign and Commonwealth Affairs remains in close touch with Mr Haig. I very much regret that I am not in a position to say more today, but I stress that they are Mr Haig's proposals and he has put them first to the Argentine Government. It was the Argentine invasion which started this crisis, and it is Argentine withdrawal that must put an end to it.

The world community will not condone Argentina's invasion. To do so would be to encourage further aggression. As the Commonwealth Secretary-General[1] said on 27 April – a point that was alluded to during Question Time today – 'In making a firm and unambiguous response

---

[1] Sir Sonny Ramphal (born 1928), Guyanese politician and international official; Secretary-General of the Commonwealth 1975–90.

to Argentine aggression, Britain is rendering a service to the international community as a whole.'

As the situation has developed, and as the British Government have made every effort to find a solution, the House has broadly supported both the Government's objectives and their actions. But in the past few days it has been argued in some parts of the House, first, that we should not have resorted to the use of force, and secondly, that we should seek greater involvement by the United Nations.

With regard to the first argument, when the House debated the Falkland Islands on 14 April the Leader of the Opposition supported the dispatch of the task force. He said: 'I support the dispatch of the task force. I support it because I believe that it can have strong diplomatic results.' [Official Report, 14 April 1982; Vol.21, c.1152]

We agreed on that.

But it would be totally inconsistent to support the dispatch of the task force and yet to be opposed to its use. What is more, it would be highly dangerous to bluff in that way. British servicemen and ships would be exposed to hostile action. Argentina would doubt our determination and sense of purpose. The diplomatic pressure would be undermined. Is it really suggested that to use our task force in self-defence for the recapture of British territory is not a proper use of force?

As long as the Argentines refuse to comply with the Security Council Resolution, we must continue to intensify the pressure on them. And we must not abandon our efforts to re-establish our authority over our own territory and to free our own people from the invader.

Let me turn now to the question of greater United Nations involvement. All our action has been based on a Resolution of the United Nations. The Argentine invasion was carried out in defiance of an appeal issued by the President of the Security Council at our urgent request on 1 April. That solemn appeal was endorsed by the whole of the Security Council, but it was ignored. Immediately after the invasion we asked for another meeting of the Security Council. That meeting passed Resolution 502. Since then our efforts and those of Mr Haig and a large part of the international community have been directed to implementing that Mandatory Resolution.

That Resolution calls for Argentine withdrawal and a negotiated solution to the dispute. Without Argentine withdrawal, we have no choice but to exercise our unquestionable right to self-defence under Article 51 of the Charter. Of course, if Argentina withdrew we should immediately cease hostilities and be ready to hold negotiations with a view to solving the underlying dispute. After all, we were negotiating only a few weeks before the invasion.

It is quite wrong to suggest that, because the invader is not prepared to implement the Resolution the principles of the United Nations require, we, the aggrieved party, should forfeit the right of self-defence. Such an argument has no validity in international law. It would be to condone and encourage aggression and to abandon our people.

The question that we must answer is, what could further recourse to the United Nations achieve at the present stage? We certainly need mediation, but we already have the most powerful and the most suitable mediator available, Mr Haig, backed by all the authority and all the influence of the United States, working to implement a Mandatory Resolution of the Security Council. If anyone can succeed in mediation, it is Mr Haig.

Of course, we support the United Nations, and we believe that respect for the United Nations should form the basis of international conduct. But, alas, the United Nations does not have the power to endorse compliance with its Resolutions, as a number of aggressors well know.

Those simple facts are perfectly well understood in the international community. Let me quote the Swedish Foreign Minister,[1] because Sweden is a country second to none in its opposition to the use of force and its respect for the United Nations. The Swedish Foreign Minister said of the South Georgia operation: 'We have no objection to Britain retaking British territory. Time and again one is forced to observe that the United Nations is weak and lacks the authority required to mediate.'

That may not be desirable, but it is a fact of life, and we must make our dispositions and judgements accordingly.

The recapture of South Georgia has not diminished international support. No country that was previously with us has turned against us. On Tuesday, my right honourable friend was able to satisfy himself that the support of the European Community remained robust. The world has shown no inclination to condemn Britain's exercise of the right to self-defence.

In the Organization of American States itself, Argentina was criticized for her use of force. Despite the claims of traditional Latin American solidarity, the only Resolution passed clearly referred to Security Council Resolution 502, and called on Argentina not to exacerbate the situation.

---

[1] Ola Ullsten (born 1931), Swedish politician and diplomat. Prime Minister 1978–79; Minister for Foreign Affairs 1979–82.

The truth is that we have been involved in constant activity at the United Nations. Our representative in New York[1] has been in daily touch with the Secretary-General since the crisis began. He has discussed with him repeatedly and at length all possible ways in which the United Nations could play a constructive role in assisting Mr Haig's mission and, if Mr Haig fails, in securing implementation of Resolution 502. Sir Anthony Parsons has also discussed with Mr Pérez de Cuéllar contingency planning about the part that the United Nations might be able to play in the longer term in negotiating and implementing a diplomatic settlement.

In the light of those discussions, our representative has advised us that, first, the Secretary-General is very conscious of the complexity of the problem and of the need for careful preparation of any initiative that he might take.

Secondly, as the Security Council is already seized of the problem, it would be inappropriate for the Secretary-General to act under Article 99 of the Charter.[2]

Thirdly, the Secretary-General would not wish to take any initiative which he had not established in advance would be acceptable to both the parties.

Fourthly, the Secretary-General would also require a clear mandate from the Security Council before taking any action. Our representative has also reported that the Secretary-General has several times stated in public that he was not prepared to take action while Mr Haig's mission was continuing.

On Tuesday, the Leader of the Opposition suggested that my right honourable friend the Foreign Secretary should go to New York to discuss the crisis with the Secretary-General of the United Nations. I have explained to the House already that our own permanent representative has been in communication daily with Mr Pérez de Cuéllar. But if, at any time, either the Secretary-General or my right honourable friend thought that a meeting between the two of them would be likely to assist in achieving an acceptable solution, then I say to the House that my right honourable friend would of course go to New York straight away.

---

[1] Sir Anthony Parsons (1922–96), HM Ambassador to Iran 1974–79; UK Permanent Representative to the United Nations 1979–82; Special Adviser to the Prime Minister on Foreign Affairs 1982–83.
[2] UN Charter, Article 99: 'The Secretary-General may bring to the attention of the Security Council any matter which in his opinion may threaten the maintenance of international peace and security.'

Although we have no doubt about our sovereignty over the Falkland Islands, South Georgia, South Sandwich or British Antarctic Territory, some of my right honourable and honourable friends have suggested that we refer the matter to the International Court of Justice. Since Argentina does not accept the compulsory jurisdiction of the Court, the issue cannot be referred for a binding decision without her agreement.

We have never sought a ruling on the Falkland Islands themselves from that Court; but we have raised the question of the dependencies on three separate occasions – in 1947, 1949 and 1951. Each time Argentina refused to go to the Court. In 1955, the British Government applied unilaterally to the International Court of Justice against encroachments on British sovereignty in the dependencies by Argentina. Again, the Court advised that it could not pursue the matter, since it could act only if there was agreement between the parties recognizing the Court's jurisdiction.

In 1977, Argentina, having accepted the jurisdiction of an international court of arbitration on the Beagle Channel dispute with Chile, then refused to accept its results. It is difficult to believe in Argentina's good faith with that very recent example in mind.

There is no reason, given the history of this question, for Britain, which has sovereignty and is claiming nothing more, to make the first move. It is Argentina that is making a claim. If Argentina wanted to refer it to the International Court, we would consider the possibility very seriously. But in the light of past events it would be hard to have confidence that Argentina would respect a judgement that it did not like.

May I briefly recall the events that immediately preceded the Argentine invasion of the Falkland Islands.

Sir Derek Walker-Smith[1] (Hertfordshire East): My right honourable friend has observed that going to the International Court could be done only with the consent of the Argentine. Has she taken into account the provisions of Article 53 of the statute of the Court, and Article 96[2] with regard to the Security Council asking for an advisory opinion?

The Prime Minister. Yes, Mr Speaker; but my right honourable and learned friend has just made the point – that is only an advisory opinion. Hitherto, Argentina has not even respected the judgement of a court

[1] Sir Derek Walker-Smith (1910–92), Baron Broxbourne 1983. Conservative MP 1945–83; Chairman of the 1922 Committee 1951–55; Minister of Health 1957–60.
[2] UN Charter, Article 96: 'The General Assembly or the Security Council may request the International Court of Justice to give an advisory opinion on any legal question.'

whose jurisdiction it accepted. We do not doubt our own sovereignty. There seems to be little point, therefore, in our taking the question to court.

Mr Michael English[1] (Nottingham West): I am sure that the right honourable lady agrees that an arbitration is not quite the same thing as a decision of the International Court of Justice. In this case, an advisory opinion has a rather technical meaning. It has been requested in times past by the organs of the League of Nations and the United Nations in matters of great seriousness, and has never been refused by the International Court or the former Permanent Court of International Justice. The problem that we all face is why Britain is so reluctant to ask the Security Council to ask for such an opinion.

The Prime Minister: I have indicated that with regard to the dependencies – not the Falkland Islands themselves – we have on four occasions tried to go to the Court. On each occasion we have been flouted because the Argentine withheld its consent. If we were to ask through the Security Council, the matter would have go to through either the General Assembly or the Security Council and they would have to agree to it. In the end, the opinion would be only advisory. That is in accordance with Article 96, which I have before me at the moment. The decision is only advisory. I took the precaution of being reasonably well prepared.

I shall return to the events that immediately preceded the Argentine invasion of the Falkland Islands. Until the end of February, we were conducting negotiations with the Argentine Government. Our delegation was accompanied by representatives from the islands' councils. The negotiations took place in a constructive atmosphere, and produced an agreed communiqué, though the Argentine Government chose not to publish it.

On 20 March, the South Georgia incident began with the illegal landing of Argentine civilians. We sought to solve that problem by diplomatic means, and proposed that an emissary should travel to Buenos Aires to pursue negotiations over the problem as a matter of urgency. It was Costa Mendez himself who on 1 April told us that the diplomatic channel was now closed. That same day, President Reagan's appeal was rebuffed by the President of Argentina. On Friday 2 April the Argentines invaded and the Falklands were occupied.

The following day the Security Council called for Argentine withdrawal. Since that mandatory instruction, the Government of Argentina

---

[1] Michael English (born 1930), Labour MP 1964–83.

have made no move to comply. On the contrary, they have poured in additional troops and equipment. There can be no doubt where the intransigence lies in this matter.

The key to peace is in the hands of the Argentine Government. The responsibility is theirs.

21

Speech in a Debate on the Falkland Islands in the House of Commons, 20 May 1982

Between the beginning of May and mid-June 1982 the Falklands War was fought in earnest. The Argentinian cruiser General Belgrano *was sunk on 2 May. Two days later the British destroyer HMS* Sheffield *was hit by an Argentine Exocet missile and also sank. The casualties prompted increased pressure for a 'diplomatic solution', not least from the Americans. But on 18 May the War Cabinet, conscious of the risks involved – but conscious also of the unacceptable dangers of keeping British troops on board vulnerable ships longer than was necessary – authorized the landing on the Falklands. From now on the crucial decisions were in the hands of the military.*

The politicians concentrated on establishing the most favourable diplomatic background. Mrs Thatcher had spent much of the previous Sunday at Chequers, the Prime Minister's country residence, with officials drafting Britain's final proposals, which were to be put to the Argentinians by the UN Secretary-General. Unless accepted as a whole and within a prescribed time, they would be withdrawn. Effectively, it was an ultimatum. As expected, the Argentinians rejected the offer, which itself had contained more concessions than Mrs Thatcher would have liked. The proposals were published and were explained in detail by the Prime Minister to the Commons – and thus to the world – in the course of the debate on 20 May. The interruptions during the speech testify both to the heavy pressures still being applied to call off immediate military action and to the political consequences if the attempt to retake the Falklands by force had failed.

The Prime Minister: Seven weeks ago today the Argentine Foreign Minister summoned the British Ambassador in Buenos Aires and informed him that the diplomatic channel was now closed. Later on that same day President Reagan appealed to President Galtieri not to invade the Falkland Islands. That appeal was rejected.

Ever since 2 April Argentina has continued to defy the Mandatory Resolution of the Security Council. During the past twenty-four hours the crisis over the Falkland Islands has moved into a new and even more serious phase.

On Monday of this week our Ambassador to the United Nations handed to the Secretary-General our proposals for a peaceful settlement of the dispute. These proposals represented the limit to which the Government believe it was right to go. We made it clear to Senor Pérez de Cuéllar that we expected the Argentine Government to give us a very rapid response to them.

By yesterday morning we had had a first indication of the Argentine reaction. It was not encouraging. By the evening we received their full response in writing. It was in effect a total rejection of the British proposals. Indeed, in many respects the Argentine reply went back to their position when they rejected Mr Haig's second set of proposals on 29 April. It retracted virtually all the movement that their representative had shown during the Secretary-General's efforts to find a negotiated settlement. I shall have some more to say about his efforts later.

The implications of the Argentine response are of the utmost gravity. This is why the Government decided to publish immediately the proposals that we had put to the Secretary-General and to give the House the earliest opportunity to consider them. These proposals were placed in the Vote Office[1] earlier today. The Government believe that they represented a truly responsible effort to find a peaceful solution which both preserved the fundamental principles of our position and offered the opportunity to stop further loss of life in the South Atlantic.

We have reached this very serious situation because the Argentines clearly decided at the outset of the negotiations that they would cling to the spoils of invasion and occupation by thwarting at every turn all the attempts that have been made to solve the conflict by peaceful means. Ever since 2 April they have responded to the efforts to find a negotiated solution with obduracy and delay, deception and bad faith.

We have now been negotiating for six weeks. The House will recall the strenuous efforts made over an extended period by Secretary of State Haig. During that period my Ministerial colleagues and I considered no fewer than four sets of proposals. Although these presented substantial

---

[1] The Vote Office is the room in the Palace of Westminster where documents are made available to MPs.

difficulties, we did our best to help Mr Haig continue his mission, until Argentine rejection of his latest proposals left him no alternative but to abandon his efforts.

The next stage of negotiations was based on proposals originally advanced by President Belaunde[1] of Peru and modified in consultations between him and Mr Haig. As my right honourable friend the Secretary of State for Foreign and Commonwealth Affairs informed the House on 7 May, Britain was willing to accept these, the fifth set of proposals, for an interim settlement. They could have led to an almost immediate ceasefire. But again it was Argentina that rejected them.

I shall not take up the time of the House with a detailed description of those earlier proposals, partly because they belong to those who devised them, but, more importantly, because they are no longer on the negotiating table. Britain is not now committed to them.

Since 6 May, when it became clear that the United States–Peruvian proposals were not acceptable to Argentina, the United Nations Secretary-General, Senor Pérez de Cuéllar, has been conducting negotiations with Britain and Argentina.

Following several rounds of discussions, the United Kingdom representative at the United Nations was summoned to London for consultation last Sunday. On Monday Sir Anthony Parsons returned to New York and presented to the Secretary-General a draft interim agreement between Britain and Argentina which set out the British position in full. He made it clear that the text represented the furthest that Britain and Argentina would go in the negotiations. He requested that the draft should be transmitted to the Argentine representative and that he should be asked to convey his Government's response within two days.

Yesterday we received the Argentine Government's reply. It amounted to a rejection of our own proposals, and we have so informed the Secretary-General. This morning we have received proposals from the Secretary-General himself.

It will help the House to understand the present position if I now describe briefly these three sets of proposals.

I deal first with our own proposals. These preserve the fundamental principles which are the basis of the Government's position. Aggression

---

[1] Fernando Belaunde Terry (born 1913), Peruvian architect and politician. President of Peru 1963–68, 1980–85. His proposals of 2 May 1982 envisaged withdrawal of military forces by Argentina and Britain and administration of the Falkland Islands by an impartial representative pending a definitive negotiated settlement.

must not be allowed to succeed. International law must be upheld. Sovereignty cannot be changed by invasion. The liberty of the Falkland Islanders must be restored. For years they have been free to express their own wishes about how they want to be governed. They have had institutions of their own choosing. They have enjoyed self-determination. Why should they lose that freedom and exchange it for dictatorship?

Our proposals are contained in two documents. First, and mainly, there is a draft interim agreement between ourselves and Argentina. Secondly, there is a letter to the Secretary-General which makes it clear that the British Government do not regard the draft interim agreement as covering the dependencies of South Georgia and the South Sandwich Islands.

I deal with the dependencies first. South Georgia and the South Sandwich Islands are geographically distant from the Falkland Islands themselves. They have no settled population. British title to them does not derive from the Falkland Islands but is separate. These territories have been treated as dependencies of the Falkland Islands only for reasons of administrative convenience. That is why they are outside the draft agreement.

The House has before it the draft agreement, and I turn now to its main features. Article 2 provides for the cessation of hostilities and the withdrawal of Argentine and British forces from the islands and their surrounding waters within fourteen days. At the end of the withdrawal British ships would be at least 150 nautical miles from the islands. Withdrawal much beyond this would not have been reasonable, because the proximity of the Argentine mainland would have given their forces undue advantage.

Withdrawal of the Argentine forces would be the most immediate and explicit sign that their Government's aggression had failed and that they were being made to give up what they had gained by force. It is the essential beginning of a peaceful settlement and the imperative of Resolution 502.

Article 6 sets out the interim arrangements under which the islands would be administered in the period between the cessation of hostilities and the conclusion of negotiations on the long-term future of the islands.

In this interim period there would be a United Nations administrator, appointed by the Secretary-General and acceptable to Britain and the Argentine. He would be the officer administering the Government. Under Clause 3 of this article he would exercise his powers in conformity with the laws and the practices traditionally obtaining in the islands. He would consult the islands' representative institutions – that is the Legislative and Executive Councils through which the islanders were governed until 2 April. There would be an addition to each of the two Councils of one representative of the twenty or thirty Argentines normally resident in the islands. Their representatives would be nominated by the administrator. The clause has been carefully drawn so that the interim administration cannot make changes in the law and customs of the islands that would prejudge the outcome of the negotiations on a long-term settlement.

The provision would not only go a long way to giving back the Falklanders the way of life that they have always enjoyed, but would prevent an influx of Argentine settlers in the interim period whose residence would change the nature of society there and radically affect the future of the islands. That would not have been a true interim administration. It would have been an instrument of change.

Clause 3 of this article thus fully safeguards the future of the islands. Nothing in this interim administration would compromise the eventual status of the Falklands or the freedom which they have enjoyed for so long.

Clause 4 would require the administrator to verify the withdrawal of all forces from the islands and to prevent their reintroduction.

Mr Jack Ashley[1] (Stoke-on-Trent South): I am grateful to the Prime Minister for giving way. Could she help the House by clarifying one point? She said on the Jimmy Young radio programme the other day that she did not like the word 'veto' as it was applied to the Falkland Islands. Is the Government's position that the Falkland Islanders will be consulted and that their views are still paramount? Can the right honourable lady help the House on that point?

The Prime Minister: I am dealing with the arrangements for the interim between the cessation of hostilities and the negotiations. The right honourable gentleman will notice that we have imported into this agreement Article 73 of the United Nations Charter, which refers to the paramountcy of the interests of the islanders. During the long-term negotiations we shall closely consult the islanders on their wishes, and of course we believe in self-determination. That relates to the long-term negotiations. These articles deal with the interim administration, and I have been trying to make it clear that the interim administration must

---

[1] Jack Ashley (born 1922), Baron Ashley of Stoke 1992. Labour MP 1966–92.

not have provisions within it which, in effect, pre-empt the outcome of the long-term negotiations.

I return to Clause 4 of Article 6. We think it likely that the administrator will need to call upon the help of three or four countries other than ourselves and the Argentine to provide him with the necessary equipment and a small but effective force. The purpose of that is that if our troops leave the islands we must have some way of guarding against another Argentine invasion. The safest way under these arrangements would be for the United Nations administrator to have a small United Nations force at his disposal, of the type I have described.

Articles 8 and 9 are also very important. They deal with negotiations between Britain and Argentina on the long-term future of the islands.

The key sentence is the one which reads: 'These negotiations shall be initiated without prejudice to the rights, claims and positions of the parties and without prejudgement of the outcome.'

We would thus be free to take fully into account the wishes of the islanders themselves. And Argentina would not be able to claim that the negotiations had to end with a conclusion that suited her.

Mr Alexander W Lyon[1] (York): Surely it was implicit in those words that if the rights and claims of the Argentines are being considered, the outcome of the negotiations may be that we shall cede sovereignty to Argentina?

The Prime Minister: I have said that we do not prejudge the outcome. If the islanders wished to go to Argentina, I believe that this country would uphold the wishes of the islanders. After their experience I doubt very much whether that would be the wish of the islanders. Indeed, I believe that they would recoil from it.

I return to Article 9. We have to recognize that the negotiations might be lengthy. That is why Article 9 provides that until the final agreement has been reached and implemented the interim agreement will remain in force.

Although this interim agreement does not restore things fully to what they were before the Argentine invasion, it is faithful to the fundamental principles that I outlined earlier. Had the Argentines accepted our proposals, we should have achieved the great prize of preventing further loss of life. It was with that in mind that we were prepared to make practical changes that were reasonable. But we were not prepared to compromise on principle.

---

[1] Alexander Lyon (1931–93), Labour MP 1966–83.

I turn now to the Argentine response. This revived once again all the points which had been obstacles in earlier negotiations. The Argentine draft interim agreement applied not only to the Falklands but included South Georgia and the South Sandwich Islands as well. The Argentines demanded that all forces should withdraw, including our forces on South Georgia, and return to their normal bases and areas of operation. This was plainly calculated to put us at an enormous disadvantage.

They required that the interim administration should be the exclusive responsibility of the United Nations, which should take over all executive, legislative, judicial and security functions in the islands. They rejected any role for the islands' democratic institutions.

They envisaged that the interim administration would appoint as advisers equal numbers of British and Argentine residents of the islands, despite their huge disparity.

They required freedom of movement and equality of access with regard to residence, work and property for Argentine nationals on an equal basis with the Falkland Islanders. The Junta's clear aim was to flood the islands with its own nationals during the interim period, and thereby change the nature of Falklands society and so prejudge the future of the islands.

With regard to negotiations for a long-term settlement, while pretending not to prejudice the outcome, the Junta stipulated that the object was to comply not only with the Charter of the United Nations but with various Resolutions of the General Assembly, from some of which the United Kingdom dissented on the grounds that they favoured Argentine sovereignty.

And if the period provided for the completion of the negotiation expired, the Junta demanded that the General Assembly should determine the lines to which final agreement should conform. It was manifestly impossible for Britain to accept such demands. [Honourable Members: 'Hear, hear.']

Argentina began the crisis. Argentina has rejected proposal after proposal. One is bound to ask whether the Junta has ever intended to seek a peaceful settlement or whether it has sought merely to confuse and prolong the negotiations, while remaining in illegal possession of the islands. I believe that if we had a dozen more negotiations the tactics and results would be the same. From the course of these negotiations and Argentina's persistent refusal to accept Resolution 502 we are bound to conclude that its objective is procrastination and continuing occupation, leading eventually to sovereignty.

Sir John Biggs-Davison[1] (Epping Forest): I thank the Prime Minister for giving way and I apologize for interrupting her. Are we to understand that the proposed interim agreement, like some earlier proposals, is no longer on the table, having regard to the fact that the proposed provisions for the withdrawal of British forces and a non-British administration have consequences for British sovereignty and for the principle for which the task force was dispatched?

The Prime Minister: The proposals have been rejected. They are no longer on the table.

As I said earlier, the Secretary-General has this morning put to us and to Argentina an *aide-mémoire* describing those issues where, in his opinion, agreement seems to exist and those on which differences remain. The first group of issues – those where he believes there is a measure of agreement – would require further clarification; for on some points our interpretation would be different. The *aide-mémoire* states, for example, that Argentina would accept long-term negotiations without prejudgement of the outcome. This important phrase was, however, omitted from the Argentine response to our own proposals and is belied by a succession of statements from Buenos Aires.

Those points where, in the Secretary-General's judgement, differences remain include: first, aspects of the interim administration; secondly, the timetable for completion of negotiations and the related duration of the interim administration; thirdly, aspects of the mutual withdrawal of forces; and fourthly, the geographic area to be covered. Senor Pérez de Cuéllar has proposed formulations to cover some of those points.

The Secretary-General, to whose efforts I pay tribute, has a duty to continue to seek agreement. But, as our representative is telling him in New York, his paper differs in certain important respects from our position as presented to him on 17 May and which we then described as the furthest that we could go. Moreover, it differs fundamentally from the present Argentine position as communicated to us yesterday. It is not a draft agreement, but, as the Secretary-General himself puts it, a number of formulations and suggestions. Some of his suggestions are the very ones which have already been rejected by the Argentine response to our own proposals. Even if they were acceptable to both parties as a basis for negotiation, that negotiation would take many days, if not weeks, to reach either success or failure.

We have been through this often before, and each time we have been

---

[1] Sir John Biggs-Davison (1918–88), Conservative MP 1955–88.

met with Argentine obduracy and procrastination. Argentina rejected our proposals. It is inconceivable that it would now genuinely accept those of the Secretary-General's ideas which closely resemble our own.

Mr Guy Barnett[1] (Greenwich): Is the Prime Minister aware that, according to the Quaker mission at the United Nations in New York, certain members of the Security Council have prepared a document which it is thought may be the basis for negotiation between ourselves and the Argentines?

The Prime Minister: No, sir. I think that that is covered by what I have already said. This is the seventh set of proposals that we have considered. We have considered them carefully. Each time we have met with tactics the object of which is procrastination leading to continued occupation of the islands. Because of the record on this matter, we thought it best to put up our own specific draft interim agreement in writing so that our position was clear for the world to see, and so that it was clear that we were not compromising fundamental principles, but that we were prepared to make some reasonable, practical suggestions if we could secure the prize of no further loss of life. Those proposals were rejected. They are no longer on the table.

Mr Geoffrey Robinson[2] (Coventry North-West): Will the Prime Minister give way?

The Prime Minister: No, not at the moment. The honourable gentleman is interrupting the flow of what I am saying. What is being considered is what is called an *aide-mémoire*, which is not a draft agreement, but a number of formulations and suggestions. The essence of those formulations and suggestions, where they are clear, is that they are those that have already been rejected by the Argentine response to our proposals.

Mr Robinson: I am grateful to the Prime Minister for giving way. Why have we withdrawn those proposals, even though they have been rejected by Argentina? Why cannot they stay on the table for acceptance by Argentina right up to the last minute?

The Prime Minister: Because they have been rejected and it is the seventh lot of proposals with which we have been involved. This cannot go on and on. Someone has to make a decision and an assessment of the objectives of the Argentine Junta.

Mr Leo Abse[3] (Pontypool): Since, at the end of the day, every rational

[1] Guy Barnett (1928–86), Labour MP 1962–64, 1971–86.
[2] Geoffrey Robinson (born 1938), Labour MP 1976–.
[3] Leo Abse (born 1917), Labour MP 1958–87.

man and woman knows that we cannot sustain indefinitely the sovereignty of those rocks eight thousand miles away, why is the Prime Minister showing such extraordinary impatience? [Interruption] Why will she not continue to seek to negotiate when the alternative is carnage and bloodshed, which will have no good effect at all?

The Prime Minister. Because the Argentines do not want a negotiated settlement. They want sovereignty of the islands and they are using protracted negotiations to procure that objective. I do not believe that they are genuine in their negotiations.

Dr David Owen[1] (Plymouth Devonport): Does the Prime Minister accept that many people believe that the proposals by the British Government are fair? Many people now recognize that the British Government may feel it necessary to take further military measures; but they cannot necessarily understand why the Prime Minister believes it necessary to withdraw the proposals, or why the proposals cannot be held on the table in the hope that the Argentine Government will eventually come to their senses.

The Prime Minister. It seems perfectly clear to me that if the proposals have been rejected it is reasonable to withdraw them. They have been rejected. They are no longer on the table. What we are now considering is an *aide-mémoire* put up by the Secretary-General. It seems right that if one makes an offer and it is rejected, that is the end of the matter – particularly bearing in mind that we are discussing the seventh set of proposals in which I have been involved.

Even if we were prepared to negotiate on the basis of the *aide-mémoire*, we should first wish to see substantive Argentine comments on it, going beyond mere acceptance of it as a basis for negotiation. These are the points that we are making in our reply to the Secretary-General. At the same time, we are reminding him – as my right honourable friends and I have repeatedly said to the House – that negotiations do not close any military options.

The gravity of the situation will be apparent to the House and the nation. Difficult days lie ahead; but Britain will face them in the conviction that our cause is just and in the knowledge that we have been doing everything reasonable to secure a negotiated settlement.

[1] David Owen (born 1938), Baron Owen of Plymouth 1992. Labour MP 1966–81; Foreign Secretary 1977–79; Social Democrat MP 1981–92; Leader of the SDP 1983–87, 1988–92; European Union Co-Chairman of the Conference on Former Yugoslavia 1992–95.

The principles that we are defending are fundamental to everything that this Parliament and this country stand for. They are the principles of democracy and the rule of law. Argentina invaded the Falkland Islands in violation of the rights of peoples to determine by whom and in what way they are governed. Its aggression was committed against a people who are used to enjoying full human rights and freedom. It was executed by a Government with a notorious record in suspending and violating those same rights.

Britain has a responsibility towards the islanders to restore their democratic way of life. She has a duty to the whole world to show that aggression will not succeed, and to uphold the cause of freedom.

22

Statement on the Falkland Islands in the House of Commons, 14 June 1982

The landing by British forces at San Carlos was successful. But there now ensued a series of terrible losses as a result of Argentinian air attacks: HMS Ardent, HMS Coventry, the container ship The Atlantic Conveyor and the landing ship Sir Galahad with the Welsh Guards on board. Finally, on 12 June when the Prime Minister hoped that the worst was over, HMS Glamorgan was hit. But on land British forces were rapidly and overwhelmingly successful. After a hard-fought battle at Mount Tumbledown, they reached the outskirts of Port Stanley and the demoralized Argentinian forces threw down their arms and retreated.

In her memoirs, Lady Thatcher describes how she prepared to tell this news to the House of Commons.

'That evening [Monday 14 June], having learnt the news, I went to the House of Commons to announce the victory. I could not get into my own room; it was locked and the Chief Whip's assistant had to search for the key. I then wrote out on a scrap of paper which I found somewhere on my desk the short statement which, there being no other procedural means, I would have to make on a Point of Order to the House.' (I, p. 235)

The Prime Minister: On a point of order, Mr Speaker. May I give the House the latest information about the battle of the Falklands?

After successful attacks last night, General Moore[1] decided to press forward. The Argentines retreated. Our forces reached the outskirts of Port Stanley. Large numbers of Argentine soldiers threw down their

---

[1] Major-General Sir Jeremy Moore (born 1928), Major-General of Commando Forces, Royal Marines 1979–82; Commander of Land Forces, Falkland Islands, May–July 1982.

weapons. They are reported to be flying white flags over Port Stanley. Our troops have been ordered not to fire except in self-defence. Talks are now in progress between General Menéndez and our Deputy Commander, Brigadier Waters,[1] about the surrender of the Argentine forces on East and West Falkland.

I shall report further to the House tomorrow.

[1] Brigadier-General Mario Benjamín Menéndez, Argentinian soldier; Military Governor of the Falkland Islands during occupation April–June 1982. General Sir John Waters (born 1935), Deputy Commander of Land Forces, Falkland Islands, May–July 1982; Deputy Supreme Allied Commander of Europe, 1993–94.

23

Speech to the United Nations General Assembly, Wednesday 23 June 1982

Victory in the Falklands War ensured for Mrs Thatcher a unique authority when she spoke at the UN General Assembly's Special Session on Disarmament on 23 June 1982. She used this to place her stamp on the whole disarmament debate. Principles relating to the conduct of international affairs, which she had first absorbed in her wartime childhood and then had to apply in the course of the Falklands War, were now brought to bear on the Cold War. Eschewing the usual platitudes, Mrs Thatcher bluntly told the General Assembly that 'the fundamental risk to peace is not the existence of weapons of particular types. It is the disposition on the part of some states to impose change on others by resorting to force.'

This, of course, challenged the prevailing idea that weapons in the hands of the peacefully-intentioned, freedom-loving West could be equated with those in the hands of a Soviet Union and Warsaw Pact which had continued to practise aggression, subversion and destabilization. In taking this line, Mrs Thatcher strongly supported the approach of President Reagan's administration. Such support was timely, for the Americans and the Soviets were locked in a fierce propaganda war on disarmament.

The West Europeans had already gone ahead with plans to deploy Cruise and Pershing II missiles in response to the Soviets' deployment of SS20 missiles. The United States and NATO had also proposed a 'zero option', by which NATO would abandon its deployment plans if the Soviet Union dismantled its equivalent missiles. A similar approach, involving sharp reductions in ballistic missile warheads, had also been put forward by the Americans at the Strategic Arms Reduction Talks (START).

This is the first time I have spoken in the General Assembly. It is an honour to be here and to speak under your Presidency, Mr Kittani, and in your presence Mr Secretary-General.

PEACE - THE PURPOSE OF DISARMAMENT

The stated purpose of this Special Session is disarmament. The underlying and more important purpose is peace: not peace at any price. But peace with freedom and justice.

As President Roosevelt commented during the last war: 'We, born to freedom and believing in freedom, would rather die on our feet than live on our knees.'

Leaders of countries from every part of the globe come to this Session in search of surer ways of preserving that peace. Ways that enable the peoples of each sovereign state to lead their lives as they choose within established borders.

If arms control helps us to achieve those central aims more surely and at less cost, we must pursue it vigorously. But if it is carried out in a way which damages peace, we must resist it, recalling that there have been occasions when the known or perceived military weakness of an opponent has been at least as potent a cause of war as military strength. The true definition of disarmament should be 'the balanced and verifiable reduction of armaments in a manner which enhances peace and security.'

Weapons of War

Discussion on disarmament inevitably turns to the weapons of war. Our generation faces a special responsibility, because the march of modern technology has made ever more deadly the weapons of war. We are most keenly aware of that in the case of nuclear weapons because of their terrifying destructive power, which my generation has witnessed and which none of us will ever forget. However alarmed we are by those weapons, we cannot disinvent them. The world cannot cancel the knowledge of how to make them. It is an irreversible fact.

Mr President, nuclear weapons must be seen as deterrents. They contribute to what Winston Churchill called 'a balance of terror'. There would be no victor in a nuclear exchange. Indeed, to start a war among nuclear powers is not a rational option. These weapons succeed insofar as they prevent war. And for thirty-seven years nuclear weapons *have* kept the peace between East and West. That is a priceless achievement. Provided there is the will and good sense, deterrence can be maintained at substantially reduced levels of nuclear weapons.

Of course, we must look for a better system of preventing war than nuclear deterrence. But to suggest that between East and West there is such a system within reach at the present time would be a perilous pretence.

For us, the task is to harness the existence of nuclear weapons to the service of peace, as we have done for half a lifetime. In that task the duty of the nuclear powers is to show restraint and responsibility. The distinctive role of the non-nuclear countries, I suggest, is to recognize that proliferation of nuclear weapons cannot be the way to a safer world.

Nuclear weapons were a major concern of the 1978 Special Session; and they must remain so for us. But they may mask the facts about what we sometimes call, too comfortably, conventional weapons and conventional war. Since Nagasaki, there have been no conflicts in which nuclear weapons have been used. But there have been something like 140 conflicts fought with conventional weapons, in which up to ten million people have died.

Nuclear war is indeed a terrible threat; but conventional war is a terrible reality. If we deplore the amount of military spending in a world where so many go hungry and so much else needs to be done, our criticism and our action should turn above all to conventional forces, which absorb up to 90 per cent of military spending worldwide.

We are all involved – we all have conventional forces. I am convinced that we need a deeper and wider effort throughout the non-nuclear field, to see what we can do together to lighten the risks, the burdens and the fears.

Causes of War

But in a crucial sense, Mr President, we have not reached the root of the matter. For the fundamental risk to peace is not the existence of weapons of particular types. It is the disposition on the part of some states to impose change on others by resorting to force. This is where we require action and protection. And our key need is not for promises against first use of this or that kind of military weapon[1] – such promises can never be dependable amid the stresses of war. We need a credible assurance, if such can ever be obtained, against starting military action at all. The leaders of the North Atlantic Alliance have just given a solemn collective undertaking to precisely that effect. They said: 'None of our weapons will ever be used except in response to attack.'

Let us face the reality. The springs of war lie in the readiness to resort to force against other nations, and not in 'arms races', whether real or imaginary. Aggressors do not start wars because an adversary has built up his own strength. They start wars because they believe they can gain more by going to war than by remaining at peace. Few, if any, of the 140 conflicts since 1945 can be traced to an arms race. Nor was the world war of 1939–1945 caused by any kind of arms race. On the contrary, it sprang from the belief of a tyrant that his neighbours lacked the means or the will to resist him effectively. Let us remember what Bismarck[2] said some seventy years earlier: 'Do I want war? Of course not – I want victory.'

Hitler believed he could have victory without war, or with not very much or very difficult war. The cost to humanity of disproving that belief was immense; the cost of preventing him from forming it in the first place would have been infinitely less.

The causes which have produced war in the past have not disappeared today, as we know to our cost. The lesson is that disarmament and good intentions on their own do not ensure peace.

Disarmament – In Context

Mr President, there is a natural revulsion in democratic societies against war, and we would much prefer to see arms build-ups prevented, by good sense or persuasion or agreement. But if that does not work, then the owners of these vast armouries must not be allowed to imagine that they could use them with impunity.

But mere words, speeches and resolutions will not prevent them. The security of our country and its friends can be ensured only by deterrence

[1] Soviet spokesmen repeatedly promised that the USSR would not use nuclear weapons in a war unless NATO did so first – a pledge which should be seen in the light of Soviet numerical superiority in conventional forces.
[2] Prince Otto von Bismarck (1815–98), German statesman. Prime Minister of Prussia 1862–90; Chancellor of Germany 1871–90.

and by adequate strength – adequate when compared with that of a potential aggressor.

Mr President, I have explained why in general I do not believe that armaments cause wars and why action on them alone will not prevent wars. It is not merely a mistaken analysis but an evasion of responsibility to suppose that we can prevent the horrors of war by focusing on its instruments. These are more often symptoms than causes. But I have made these points not in any way to decry disarmament and arms control – I believe in them both – but to make quite clear what they can and cannot achieve.

Excessive claims and demands have too often been not an aid to practical measures, but a substitute for them. Arms control alone cannot remove the possibility of war. Nevertheless, the limitation and reduction of armaments can still do a great deal. They can reduce the economic burden of military preparation for legitimate self-defence. They can diminish the inhumanity of conflict. They can restrict the military use of advancing science and technology. They can ease tension between states and lessen the fears of people everywhere. To do these things, and to do them in a way that is balanced, verifiable and dependable, is worth sustained and persistent endeavour.

Disarmament – In the Past

Critics too often play down what has already been done through arms control agreements, whether formal or informal: such agreements as those on outer space, the sea bed, Antarctica, the Partial Test Ban Treaty, the Non-Proliferation Treaty, and the various Geneva Accords over the years. My country was among the architects of some of these successes. Although a comprehensive Test Ban Treaty has not been signed and the recent review of the Non-Proliferation Treaty was unproductive, there has been no additional nuclear weapon state since 1964. We also contributed substantially to the banning of biological and toxin weapons in 1972.

We all wish that the achievements had been greater. But to suggest that what has been done so far is insignificant is both inaccurate and unhelpful to further progress. We have a useful foundation upon which to build. Now we must go a stage further.

Measures for the Future

In the nuclear field, the hopes of the world lie in direct talks between the United States and the Soviet Union, the countries which have by far the largest arsenals. These could be greatly reduced in a way which would not endanger security. Decisive action is needed, not just declarations or freezes. I welcome the radical proposals made by the United States for substantially cutting strategic weapons, and for eliminating a whole class of intermediate-range systems (the 'zero option').[1] The negotiations deserve the wholehearted support of us all.

We are also deeply concerned about the dangers of chemical warfare. When the world community decided in 1972 to ban the possession of biological and toxin weapons, we all looked forward to corresponding action next on chemical weapons. It has not happened. Moreover, there is reason to doubt whether every country which signed the 1972 Treaty is observing it. There have been disquieting and well-documented reports, which urgently need investigation, that chemical weapons and toxins have been used in some countries in Asia. The Committee on Disarmament needs to give renewed and determined impetus to a properly verifiable convention banning development and possession of such weapons.

I spoke earlier about the huge weight of conventional forces. The biggest concentration and confrontation of such forces anywhere in the world lies in Europe. But it is heavily weighted on the side of the Warsaw Pact. This situation is in itself a cause for concern.

But there is the more fundamental question whether the Warsaw Pact can or wishes to sustain a stable relationship with the rest of the world. Do not the events in Poland and Afghanistan call this into question?[2] The one by revealing deep disillusion within the Soviet Empire, the second by demonstrating the Soviet propensity to extend its frontiers?

[1] On 18 November 1981, President Reagan offered to cancel the deployment of Cruise and Pershing missiles in Europe if the USSR dismantled its medium-range missiles targeted on Western Europe. Since such a deal would have resulted in the total absence of intermediate-range nuclear forces from Europe, it became known as the 'zero option'.

[2] The Polish opposition movement Solidarity won mass support in 1980–81, but was forcibly suppressed after the imposition of martial law on 12 December 1981. The USSR invaded Afghanistan in 1979 and fought a ten-year war there.

Both are evidence of an underlying instability – thus the need to secure a better balance in conventional arms becomes even more imperative.

For nine years we have pursued patiently talks in Vienna on mutual and balanced force reductions. Our diplomats involved in those talks must be the most patient of all, but they know that their work is of vital importance for peace. Fresh proposals are being made and we hope that this time we shall see some progress.

Britain would also like to see a special effort made to agree on new mandatory confidence and security-building measures in Europe. These would be a valuable complement to action in Vienna on force levels.

Through all these many negotiations there runs a critical factor – verification. How can we be sure that what it is said will be done will be done? Where national security is at stake we cannot take agreements on trust, especially when some states are so secretive and such closed societies. Agreements which cannot be verified can be worse than useless – they can be a new source of danger, fear and mistrust. Verification is not an optional extra in disarmament and arms control. It is the heart of the matter.

Differences over verification have often proved a stumbling block in arms control negotiations. But we note that the Soviet Union is now prepared to open part of its civil nuclear installations to inspection by the International Atomic Energy Agency – a step that the United Kingdom took years ago. I note also that the Soviet Union now seems ready to accept the need for systematic on-site inspection in respect of a chemical weapons treaty. We need to redouble our efforts to bridge the gaps that still remain.

Britain's record over the years in work on disarmament and arms control stands up to any comparison. We wish to do more – not by rhetoric, still less by propaganda postures, but by steady, relevant work going step by step through these difficult and complex matters. This is a long, patient and unspectacular business. There is no short cut if we are to retain security and peace. These are the considerations which I suggest the Special Session needs to have in mind in discussing a comprehensive programme of disarmament and in its review of progress since the first Special Session.

Mr President, the message I bring is practical and realistic. It is the message of a country determined to preserve and spread the values by which we live. It contains nought of comfort to those who seek only a quiet life for themselves at the expense of the freedom of others. Nor to those who wish to impose their will by force. Peace and security require unbroken effort.

We believe that the human values of civilization must be defended.

We believe that international law and the United Nations Charter must be upheld.

We believe that wars are caused not by armaments but by the ambitions of aggressors, and that what tempts them is the prospect of easy advantage and quick victory.

We believe that the best safeguard of peace lies not only in a just cause but in secure defence.

We believe in balanced and verifiable disarmament, where it can be the servant of peace and freedom.

We believe that the purpose of nuclear weapons should be to prevent war, and that it can be achieved by smaller armouries.

We believe that a balanced reduction in conventional weapons could create greater stability.

We believe we have a right and a duty to defend our own people, whenever and wherever their liberty is challenged.

Mr President, my country seeks the path of peace with freedom and justice.

As Abraham Lincoln[1] put it in his second Inaugural Address: 'With malice towards none, with charity for all, with firmness in the right . . . let us strive on to finish the work we are in.'

---

[1] Abraham Lincoln (1809–65), 16th President of the United States, 1861–65 (Republican).

24

Speech to the Conservative Party Conference, Brighton, 8 October 1982

The Conservative Party gathered in Brighton for the October 1982 Party Conference in better spirits than for some years. The triumph of the Falklands War had changed the political outlook – though this was something which the Prime Minister refused to exploit publicly, as is shown by the limited attention it is given in her Conference speech. The 'Falklands factor' assisted in discrediting the Labour Party, led by Michael Foot – a committed proponent of unilateral nuclear disarmament. It also reinforced the public perception that the Government's resolve in pursuing a painful but necessary economic strategy was now leading to a resumption of soundly-based prosperity. The economy was growing again; inflation was coming down fast; and even though unemployment remained high, the Prime Minister's old argument that it was satisfied customers, not interventionist Governments, which delivered new jobs was now widely accepted. Although Mrs Thatcher had never been tempted to call an early 'khaki election' – and although her instincts, even the following year when others urged an early poll, were to play the political game long – the 1982 Conference speech set many of the themes for the next general election campaign.

This is not going to be a speech about the Falklands campaign, though I would be proud to make one. But I want to say just this, because it is true for all our people: the spirit of the South Atlantic was the spirit of Britain at her best.

It has been said that we surprised the world, that British patriotism was rediscovered in those spring days. It was never really lost. But it would be no bad thing if the feeling that swept the country then were to continue to inspire us. For if there was any doubt about the determination of the British people, it was removed by the men and women who, a few months ago, brought a renewed sense of pride and self-respect to our country.

They were for the most part young. Let all of us here, and in the wider audience outside, pause and reflect on what we who stayed at home owe to those who sailed and fought, and lived and died and won. If this is tomorrow's generation, Britain has little to fear in the years to come. In what by any standards was a remarkable chapter in our island history, it is they who this year wrote its brightest page.

In remembering their heroism, let us not forget the courage shown by those same armed forces nearer home. We see them and the other forces of law and order display these qualities day after day in Northern Ireland. Yes, and even closer at hand. I have seen no more moving sight in the last year than the Blues and Royals bearing their tattered standard proudly past the spot in Hyde Park where their comrades had been murdered in a cruel and cowardly bomb attack only two days before.[1] Terrorism is a deadly threat to our way of life, and we will not be cowed by it. We will continue to resist it with all our power and to uphold the principles of democratic government.

I cannot remember a better Conference. Our debates have been lively, good-humoured – indeed, at one moment I was very proud to think that I had served in John Nott's Cabinet, and I am relieved to know that the Secretary of State for Employment will in future have confidence in the Treasury forecasts about the cost of living. He should. He actually compiles the index.

The debates, as I say, have been lively, good-humoured and humming with ideas, and they have tackled the real issues of the day.

There have been two other Party Conferences before this, and perhaps I will have a word to say about them later.

First, I want to come to something that dwarfs party politics – indeed, to an issue that dwarfs every other issue of our time. We have invented weapons powerful enough to destroy the whole world. Others have created political systems evil enough to seek to enslave the whole world. Every free nation must face that threat. Every free nation must strain both to defend its freedom and to ensure the peace of the world. The first duty of a British Government is the defence of the realm, and we shall discharge that duty.

Ever since the war, the principal threat to our country's safety has come from the Soviet bloc. Twenty-six years ago the Russians marched into Hungary. Twenty-one years ago they built the Berlin Wall. Fourteen

---

[1] On 20 July 1982, the IRA staged a bomb attack on the Household Cavalry in Hyde Park, London, killing four and injuring over twenty.

years go they reconquered Czechoslovakia. Three years ago they entered Afghanistan. Two years ago they began to suppress the first stirrings of freedom in Poland.

They knew the strength of the human spirit. They knew that if freedom were allowed to take root in Poland it would spread across Eastern Europe and perhaps to the Soviet Union itself. They knew that the beginning of freedom spelt the beginning of the end for communism.

Yet, despite these regular reminders of the ruthless actions of the Kremlin, there are still those who seem to believe that disarmament by ourselves alone would so impress the Russians that they would obligingly follow suit. But peace, freedom and justice are only to be found where people are prepared to defend them. This Government will give the highest priority to our national defence, both conventional and nuclear.

I want to see nuclear disarmament. I want to see conventional disarmament as well. I remember the atomic bombs that devastated Hiroshima and Nagasaki. I remember, too, the bombs that devastated Coventry and Dresden. The horrors of war are indivisible. We all want peace, but not peace at any price. Peace with justice and freedom.

We seek agreement with the Soviet Union on arms control. We want to reduce the levels of both conventional and nuclear forces. But those reductions must be mutual, they must be balanced and they must be verifiable.

I understand the feelings of the unilateralists. I understand the anxieties of parents with children growing up in the nuclear age. But the fundamental question for all of us is whether unilateral nuclear disarmament would make a war less likely.

I have to tell you that it would not. It would make war more likely. Aggressors attack because they think they are going to win, and they are more likely to attack the weak than they are to attack the strong.

The springs of war lie not in arms races, real or imaginary, but in readiness to use force or threaten force against other nations. Remember what Bismarck said: 'Do I want war? Of course not – I want victory.' The causes of wars in the past have not changed, as we know to our cost. But because Russia and the West know that there can be no victory in nuclear war, for thirty-seven years we have kept the peace in Europe, and that is no mean achievement. That is why we need nuclear weapons, because having them makes peace more secure.

Yet at Blackpool last week, the Labour Party, by a huge majority, adopted a new official defence policy. It went like this: Polaris to be scrapped; Trident to be cancelled; Cruise missiles in service to be removed.

It is now clear beyond doubt that, given the change the Labour Party wants, they would dismantle Britain's defences wholesale.

Yet do you remember how Aneurin Bevan[1] pleaded with an earlier Labour Party Conference not to send a Labour Foreign Secretary 'naked into the conference chamber'? Well, it is a good thing that there isn't going to be a Labour Foreign Secretary.

Yet the Labour Party wants to keep Britain in NATO, continuing to shelter behind American nuclear weapons – so long as they are not on our soil. What utter hypocrisy. To expect an insurance policy but refuse to pay the premium.

There must be millions of Labour supporters who are thoroughly disheartened by what they saw at Blackpool last week. I say to them: 'Forget about the Militant Tendency[2] – come over and join the Tory Tendency.'

A strong and united Western Alliance is a guarantee of our peace and security. It is also a beacon of hope to the oppressed people of the Soviet bloc. Britain is a reliable ally, and with a Conservative Government will always remain so – reliable in NATO, reliable beyond NATO – an ally and a friend to be trusted. And trusted not least by our partners in the European Community.

Of course, ancient nations do not always find it easy to live together. Yet our commitment to the Common Market is clear. We are all democratic countries, where freedom and the rule of law are basic to our institutions.

At present, as you know, Britain pays quite large sums to Community partners often richer than we ourselves. That is fundamentally unjust. It is also shortsighted. As you know, we have just come to the end of our first three-year arrangement. We shall really have to fight – courteously, of course – to make sure that we have a fair deal for the future. But those who would pull us out of Europe must come to terms with the damage that that would do to our people. Even the threat of withdrawal destroys jobs. Firms that invest in the Common Market often decide to come to Britain. Labour's threat to withdraw makes companies hesitate and look elsewhere. That Labour threat is losing us jobs now.

[1] Aneurin Bevan (1897–1960), Labour MP 1929–60; Minister of Health 1945–51; Minister of Labour 1951; Deputy Leader of the Labour Party 1959–60. He made this plea on 3 October 1957.
[2] Militant Tendency, founded in 1955 and known internally as the Revolutionary Socialist League, was a Trotskyite organization which infiltrated the Labour Party.

The great economies of Germany and France, once the engine of growth of the European Community, are struggling with declining output and a growing army of unemployed. Across the Atlantic, the United States, Canada and the countries of Latin America have been faced with the most prolonged slump for fifty years. Even the miracle economies of the Pacific Basin – Japan, Korea, Taiwan, Hong Kong and Singapore – are now being hit.

But the economies of the Eastern bloc are in a far worse state than the West. Poland and Romania are hard-pressed to pay their debts, and the Soviet bloc countries generally are riven with shortages of everything, from seed corn to sewing thread.

None of us foresaw a world recession of such gravity. Last week in Blackpool, the Opposition suggested that I, singlehanded, had brought it about. What powers they attribute to me! If I had that sort of power I would banish recession for ever. We have no time for dreams and delusions. The main culprit – and there are others – is the greatest sustained inflation in modern times. Almost every developed country has suffered from it.

For more than a decade, economic growth has been thwarted. For more than a decade, savers in America and Europe have been systematically robbed by the steady erosion of their savings; and for more than a decade, the ranks of the unemployed have swollen in the wake of inflation. In 1979 many of us in Europe began the long, hard job of wringing inflation out of the system. But governments had promised to do this over and over again. When the going got tough they resorted to the printing press. No wonder people became cynical.

Journalists, many but not all of them on the left, were almost daily predicting U-turns.[1] Some, indeed, confidently went around the bend. Now most commentators, with attitudes varying from awe to rage, recognize that we are sticking to our policy. Oh yes, we have been to the IMF. But unlike the last Government, we went not as a nation seeking help but as a country giving help to others – a much more fitting role for Britain. From socialist supplicant to Conservative contributor.

With inflation falling, interest rates coming down, and honest finance, confidence is returning. In spite of hostilities in the South Atlantic, the exchange rate held steady. What a tribute to the determined and unruffled Chancellorship of Geoffrey Howe! No longer will the saver find his money devalued. No longer shall we have two nations – those

---

[1] In this instance a change from deflationary monetary policies to reflationary ones.

who profit from inflation and those who lose by it. No longer will paper booms explode in confetti money.

There is no road to inflation-free prosperity, except through our own efforts. Two hundred years ago, Edmund Burke blamed the French revolutionaries for trying everywhere to 'evade and slip aside from difficulty'. He said they had a 'fondness for trickery and short-cuts'.

There are just as many evaders and short-cutters around today, in the Labour Party, the SDP and among the Liberals, taken jointly or severally, according to taste. Inflate a little here, expand a little there; it's all so easy. In real life such short cuts often turn out to be dead ends.

In the fifties and sixties the fashion was to say that the long term does not matter very much because, as Maynard Keynes put it: 'In the long run we are all dead.' Anyone who thought like that would never plant a tree.

We are in the business of planting trees, for our children and grand-children, or we have no business to be in politics at all. We are not a one-generation Party. We do not intend to let Britain become a one-generation society. Let us not forget the lesson of history. The long-term always starts today.

Falling inflation on its own will not ensure growth and jobs. We need other things, too. Whether we like it or not, things are changing. They are changing in technology, as we have seen at this conference, with this lectern, that comes up.[1] We keep abreast of the times. They are changing on the map. Faraway countries scarcely heard of ten years ago now overtake us in our traditional industries. Suddenly we are faced with the need to do everything at once – to wake up, catch up and then overtake, even though the future is as hard to predict as ever.

So we have to look as far into that future as we can, make sure that all the best talents are free to work at full stretch to help to lead this country into that future. Socialists believe that the state can do this better than individuals. Nothing could be more misguided. They are wrong. We cannot opt out of the technology race and try to stand comfortably aside. If we were to do so, we should lose not just particular products but whole industries. We dare not leave our neighbours to inherit the world of the microchip. As one production engineer put it: 'The real threat in new technology is the threat of your worst enemies using it.'

Inflation has not been beaten, even when prices stop rising. It is beaten

---

[1] The speech was given at a lectern of adjustable height which rose and fell when the speaker stood up and sat down.

only when costs stop rising. That makes wage costs vital. Pay must relate to output, as every self-employed person will tell you. In the last five years of the 1970s the amount we in Britain paid ourselves for what we produced went up by nearly 100 per cent. In Germany their increase was only 15 per cent. In Japan it was nought per cent. Of course Japanese workers got more pay, but only from more output.

So they got the orders and we lost the jobs. The CBI[1] put it starkly: 'Because we have lost over 10 per cent of the home market to imports, and 2.5 per cent of world export markets to our competitors in the last twelve years, we have lost 1.5 million jobs.' One and a half million jobs, through losing a fair chunk of our home market to importers and a fair chunk of our export market to our competitors. There is a challenge to management and unions. Get those markets back and we shall get our jobs back.

In the public sector, as you know, the Chancellor of the Exchequer has just announced 3.5 per cent more available for next year's public pay bill. Before you say that that is not much, just remember, for the German civil service it is not going to be 3.5 per cent, but 2 per cent. In Japan, the Japanese civil servants are getting no rise at all. Maybe that will put the 3.5 per cent in perspective.

It is important to keep wage costs down, to accept new technology. But if it is important to do all that, good management and good industrial relations are vital to our future. We heard a lot at Blackpool about how Labour would work with the unions. Of course, they don't really mean that. What they mean is cosy get-togethers at No. 10. That is the old pals' act. It has nothing to do with life on the shop floor; and that is where the real problems are sorted out.

When I travel overseas, time and again they say to me: 'Strikes. You have so many strikes. If it were not for that, we would give you more contracts. We would invest more in Britain.' In vain do I say that private industry has very few strikes. The fact is that the much-publicized disruptions in the public sector do Britain down every time.[2] I only wish that some of those trade union members on strike in the public sector would realize how many jobs their actions lost – not necessarily their own jobs, but the jobs of people in manufacturing industry, whose taxes pay their wages. We cannot say it too often: 'Strikes lose jobs.'

[1] The Confederation of British Industry, the main employers' organization in Britain.
[2] The major strikes of 1980–82 were nearly all in the public sector: steel 1980, civil service 1981, health and railways 1982.

It will take a long time to get employment up sufficiently, to get unemployment down as far as we all want. The task is even harder because we are going through a phase in Britain when the number of people of working age is rising. There are many more young people leaving school and wanting jobs than there are older people reaching retirement. Over a period of eight years there will be one and a quarter million extra people of working age. Even without the recession, we should have needed a lot more new jobs just to stop the number of unemployed rising. That shows the magnitude of the task. Today's unemployed are the victims of yesterday's mistakes.

Government destroyed jobs by fuelling inflation; trade unions destroyed jobs by restrictive practices; militants destroyed jobs by driving customers away. But that is the past and, whatever the problems, we have got to tackle them, not with words, not with rhetoric, but with action. Rhetoric is easy, but it does not produce jobs. Indeed, if rhetoric could cure unemployment we would have jobs galore by this time.

For the future, Norman Tebbit[1] has told you that every sixteen-year-old who leaves school next year will either have a job or a year of full-time training. Unemployment will not then be an option, and that is right. But a Government cannot do everything.

If we are to beat unemployment – and we must – we have to do it together. The Government are getting inflation down, interest rates down, reforming trade union law, cutting regulations and removing restrictions. The rest is up to industry, the workforce and management in partnership. In the end, it is private employers who will produce the great majority of jobs.

Time and again, history beats out the same message: competition is better for the consumer than state control. We are acting on that conviction. Three and a half years ago, defenders of the status quo tried to brand denationalization as irrelevant. Now the critics are finding it harder to ignore the evidence of their own eyes. They cannot help seeing the new long-distance coaches speeding down the motorways, at very much lower fares. They cannot miss the success of Cable & Wireless or British Aerospace. Britoil will be the next to be denationalized and British Telecommunications after that. How absurd it will seem in a few

---

[1] Norman Tebbit (born 1931), Baron Tebbit of Chingford 1992. Conservative MP 1970–92; Employment Secretary 1981–83; Trade and Industry Secretary 1983–85; Chancellor of the Duchy of Lancaster 1985–87; Chairman of the Conservative Party 1985–87.

years' time that the state ran Pickfords removals and Gleneagles Hotel!

We are only in our first term. But already we have done more to roll back the frontiers of socialism than any previous Conservative Government.

In the next Parliament we intend to do a lot more. We are seeing increasing evidence of the savings that can be made. Local authority after local authority has found that even the prospect of contracting out their refuse collection produces amazing economies from their staff. As Dr Johnson[1] nearly said: 'When you know you are going to be privatized in a fortnight, it concentrates the mind wonderfully.'

I hope that every Conservative Councillor in the land will act on what Councillor Chope of Wandsworth told us. Wandsworth has gone out to private contractors and down have come the rates.[2] And don't we all want that? Where Wandsworth has led, let other Conservative councils follow.

I should like to say a word about the Health Service, because value for money is just as important in the Health Service. Our opponents' picture of us as a party that doesn't care about the Health Service is utterly untrue, and is particularly ridiculous from the Labour Party. When they were in office they had nearly two thousand fewer hospital doctors and forty thousand fewer nurses than we have, and every one of them was then much worse-paid than today. But that same Labour Party now supports those who are disrupting the National Health Service and lengthening the very waiting lists that we have brought down. What sort of twisted compassion is that?

'I believe that we should condemn industrial action with its damage to the Health Service, whether it comes from doctors, nurses or anyone else who works in the service.' Those aren't my words; those were the Labour Minister of Health's, David Ennals,[3] when he was in charge. We supported him because it was true then, and it is true now.

We have a magnificent record in the Health Service. We heard that splendid speech from Norman Fowler in one of the best debates in this Conference. This year we are spending 5 per cent more in real terms

---

[1] Samuel Johnson (1709–84), English man of letters. The original quotation reads, 'When a man knows he is to be hanged in a fortnight, it concentrates his mind wonderfully.'

[2] Wandsworth is a Conservative-controlled borough in inner London. The rates were a local government tax levied on residential and commercial property.

[3] David Ennals (1922–95), Baron Ennals of Norwich 1983. Labour MP 1964–83; Minister of State for Foreign Affairs 1974–76; Social Services Secretary 1976–79.

on the Health Service than Labour, so under Conservatives we have more doctors, more nurses, more money. Hardly the behaviour of a Government bent on destroying the Health Service.

Naturally we have a duty to make sure that every penny is properly spent; and that is why we are setting up a team to examine the use of manpower in the National Health Service. Naturally, we have a duty to do that. It is part of our duty towards the taxpayer. Of course, we welcome the growth of private health insurance. It brings in more money; it helps to reduce the waiting lists; and it stimulates new treatments and techniques.

But let me make one thing absolutely clear. The National Health Service is safe with us. As I said in the House of Commons on 1 December last: 'The principle that adequate health care should be provided for all, regardless of ability to pay, must be the foundation of any arrangements for financing the Health Service.' We stand by that.

It is not only in the National Health Service that our record has been very good. Next month, the old-age pension will go up by 11 per cent, and that despite the worst recession since the 1930s. That is some achievement too. Whatever our difficulties, nine million pensioners have been fully protected from inflation. We gave our promise and we kept it.

We do not measure our success merely by how much money the Government spends. The well-being of our people is about far more than the Welfare State. It is about self-reliance – family help, voluntary help – as well as state provision. In a society which is truly healthy, responsibility is shared and help is mutual.

Wherever we can, we shall extend the opportunity for personal ownership and the self-respect that goes with it. 370,000 families have now bought their own homes from councils, new towns and housing associations. That is the result of this Government's housing policy, carried through in the teeth of opposition from the Labour Party. We have fought them all the way and we won. Half a million more people will now live and grow up as freeholders with a real stake in the country and with something to pass on to their children. There is no prouder word in our history than 'freeholder'.

That is the largest transfer of assets from the state to the family in British history, and it was done by a Conservative Government. And this really will be an irreversible shift of power to the people. The Labour Party may huff and puff about putting a stop to the sale of council houses. They may go on making life unpleasant for those who try to take advantage of their legal rights – and what a wicked thing it is to do that. But they do not dare pledge themselves to take those houses back, because they know we are right, because they know it is what the people want. And besides, they would be making too many of their own Councillors homeless – not to mention one or two of their MPs.

We want to bring more choice to parents, too. We as parents have the prime responsibility to set the standards and to instil the values by which our children are brought up. None of us has the right to blame the teachers for failing to make up for our shortcomings. But we have every right to be involved in what goes on in our children's schools. As parents we want to be sure not just about the teaching of the 'three Rs', but about the discipline and about the values by which our children are taught to live. We have given parents more say in the choice of schools. We have put parents on governing bodies.[1] For the first time in modern Britain, a Government is really paying attention not just to school organization, but to the curriculum; not just to the buildings, but to what is taught inside them.

And we are not afraid to talk about discipline and moral values. To us 'law and order' is not an election slogan. It is the foundation of the British tradition. I believe that, looking back on this first Parliament of ours, it will be said that we have done more to support the police than any British Government since the war. There are more of them, we pay them better, we train them better and we equip them better; and for that, you know whom we have to thank. I am eternally grateful for the good sense, good humour and loyalty of Willie Whitelaw. Perhaps only I know how staunch he was throughout the whole of the Falklands campaign, and the difficult decisions we had to take. Thank you very much.

It cannot be the police alone who are on duty. As parents, as teachers, as politicians and as citizens, what we say and do, whether in the home, the classroom or the House of Commons, is bound to leave its mark on the next generation. The television producer who glamorizes violence may find his viewing figures ultimately reflected in the crime statistics. And a public figure who comments to the camera on issues of the day should be especially careful of what he says.

The other day, the last Labour Prime Minister – and I do mean 'the last Labour Prime Minister' – spoke of what he called 'a contingent right' in certain circumstances to break the law.[2] None of us has a right,

---

[1] The Education Act 1980 gave parents the right to elect parent-governors.
[2] On 6 September, James Callaghan, referring to unlawful secondary action organized by the TUC in support of National Health Service workers, said, 'If the law is a bad law, there is always a contingent right to take action that you would otherwise not take.'

contingent or otherwise, to uphold the law that suits us and to break the one that does not. That way lies anarchy.

There are many people in Britain who share the hopes and the ideals of the Conservative Party. They share our great purpose to restore to this country its influence and self-respect. But they are anxious about the future and uncertain about the changes that we have had to make. They have not recognized how far the debating ground of British politics has moved to the left over the last thirty years. Where the left stood yesterday the centre stands today. Yet the British people have not moved with it. Instinctively they know that we have to pull this country back to the real centre again. But the anxious say to us: 'You cannot do everything at once. The recession and the international economic situation make things particularly difficult. Why not adapt your approach a little, give in for the time being until things are getting better, and then you can start again after the next election, when you have longer time to do it?'

To do that would be a betrayal. People in Britain have grown to understand that this Government will make no false promises, and nor will it fail in its resolve. How can the Government urge the people to save and to build for tomorrow, if the people know that that same Government is willing to bend and trim for the sake of votes today? That is not trusting the people; and it is not the way to be trusted by them. Nothing could be more damaging to our prospects as a nation than for this Government to throw away the reputation it has earned for constancy and resolve. It would throw away three years of hard-won achievement.

On what moral basis would we be entitled to ask for the nation's support next time? The only way we can achieve great things for Britain is by asking great things of Britain. We will not disguise our purpose, nor betray our principles. We will do what must be done. We will tell the people the truth, and the people will be our judge.

III

THE SECOND
PARLIAMENT

(1983–87)

25

Speech to the Conservative Party Conference, Brighton, 12 October 1984

More important than the content of the Prime Minister's 1984 Conference speech is the fact that it was delivered at all. For at 2.54 a.m. on the day of the speech a bomb planted by the IRA in Brighton's Grand Hotel narrowly failed to kill Mrs Thatcher and the Cabinet. She spent the rest of the night at the nearby Lewes Police College, having refused to return to Downing Street. After breakfast, the Prime Minister was driven back into Brighton to the Conference Centre, where she and her advisers adapted the speech text to the sombre circumstances in which it was now to be delivered.

As a result, the 1984 Conference speech reads very differently from the others. Jokes and polemic are largely absent. The text has some evident rough edges. And, unusually in a Thatcher Conference speech, there was a certain amount of ad-libbing. Much of the speech dealt with the national miners' strike in which the country was currently plunged: and, of course, the theme of resistance to violence by terrorists (or mass pickets) underlay the whole speech. But it was the first paragraph – powerful, moving and defiant – which drew national and international attention.

The bomb attack on the Grand Hotel early this morning was first and foremost an inhuman, undiscriminating attempt to massacre innocent, unsuspecting men and women staying in Brighton for our Conservative Conference. Our first thoughts must at once be for those who died and for those who are now in hospital recovering from their injuries. But the bomb attack clearly signified more than this. It was an attempt not only to disrupt and terminate our Conference; it was an attempt to cripple Her Majesty's democratically elected Government. That is the scale of the outrage in which we have all shared; and the fact that we are gathered here now – shocked, but composed and determined – is a sign not only that this attack has failed, but that all attempts to destroy democracy by terrorism will fail.

I should like to express our deep gratitude to the police, firemen, ambulancemen, nurses and doctors, to all the emergency services, and to the staff of the hotel; to our ministerial staff and the Conservative Party staff who stood with us and shared the danger.

As Prime Minister and as Leader of the Party, I thank them all and send our heartfelt sympathy to all those who have suffered.

And now it must be business as usual. We must go on to discuss the things we have talked about during this Conference; one or two matters of foreign affairs; and after that, two subjects I have selected for special consideration – unemployment and the miners' strike.

This Conservative Conference – superbly chaired, and of course our Chairman came on this morning with very little sleep and carried on marvellously – and with excellent contributions from our members, has been an outstanding example of orderly assembly and free speech. We have debated the great national and international issues, as well as those which affect the daily lives of our people. We have seen at the rostrum miner and pensioner, nurse and manager, clergyman and student. In government, we have been fulfilling the promises contained in our election manifesto, which was put to the people in a national ballot.[1] This Government, Mr President, is reasserting Parliament's ultimate responsibility for controlling the total burden of taxation on our citizens, whether levied by central or local government, and in the coming session of Parliament we shall introduce legislation which will abolish the GLC and the Metropolitan County Councils.[2]

In the quest for sound local government, we rely on the help of Conservative Councillors. Their task should never be underestimated and their virtues should not go unsung. They work hard and conscientiously in the true spirit of Conservative councils up and down the country in getting better value for money through greater efficiency and putting out work to competitive tender. This is privatization at the local level, and we need more of it.

At national level, since the general election just over a year ago, the Government has denationalized five major enterprises,[3] making a total of thirteen since 1979. Yesterday, you gave Norman Tebbit a standing

[1] General election, 9 June 1983: Conservatives 397, Labour 209, Liberal–SDP Alliance 23, others 21.
[2] By the Local Government Act 1985, the Greater London Council and the six Metropolitan County Councils ceased to exist on 31 March 1986. Their functions devolved onto their component boroughs and some joint authorities.
[3] Associated British Ports, Sealink, Scott Lithgow shipyard, Enterprise Oil and Jaguar.

ovation; today, our thoughts are with him and his family.[1] Again and again, denationalization has brought greater motivation to managers and workforce, higher profits and rising investment; and, what is more, many in industry now have a share in the firm for which they work. We Conservatives want every owner to be an earner, and every earner to be an owner.

Soon, we shall have the biggest ever act of denationalization with British Telecom, and British Airways will follow; and we have not finished yet. There will be more to come in this Parliament.

And just as we have stood by our pledge on denationalization, it is our pride that despite the recession, we have kept faith with nine million pensioners, and moreover, by keeping inflation down, we have protected the value of their savings. As Norman Fowler told the Conference on Wednesday, this Government has not only put more into pensions, but has increased resources for the National Health Service. Our record for last year, to be published shortly, will show that the Health Service today is providing more care, more services and more help for the patient than at any stage in its history. That is Conservative care in practice. And I think it is further proof of the statement I made in Brighton in this very hall two years ago – perhaps some of you remember it – that the National Health Service is safe with us.

Now, Mr President and friends, this performance in the social services could never have been achieved without an efficient and competitive industry to create the wealth we need. Efficiency is not the enemy, but the ally, of compassion.

In our discussions here, we have spoken of the need for enterprise, profits and the wider distribution of property among all the people. In the Conservative Party we have no truck with outmoded Marxist doctrine about class warfare. For us, it is not who you are, who your family is or where you come from that matters. It is what you are and what you can do for our country that counts. That is our vision. It is a vision worth defending and we shall defend it. Indeed, this Government will never put the defence of our country at risk.

No one in their senses wants nuclear weapons for their own sake, but equally, no responsible Prime Minister could take the colossal gamble of giving up our nuclear defences while our greatest potential enemy kept theirs.

---

[1] Norman Tebbit, Trade and Industry Secretary, was seriously injured by the Brighton bomb, and his wife Margaret was paralysed.

Policies which would throw out all American nuclear bases – bases which, mind you, have been here since the time of Mr Attlee, Mr Truman[1] and Winston Churchill – would wreck NATO and leave us totally isolated from our friends in the United States; and friends they are. No nation in history has ever shouldered a greater burden nor shouldered it more willingly nor more generously than the United States. This Party is pro-American.

And we must constantly remind people what the defence policy of the Opposition party would mean. Their idea that by giving up our nuclear deterrent we could somehow escape the result of a nuclear war elsewhere is nonsense, and it is a delusion to assume that conventional weapons are sufficient defence against nuclear attack.

And do not let anyone slip into the habit of thinking that conventional war in Europe is some kind of comfortable option. With a huge array of modern weapons held by the Soviet Union, including chemical weapons in large quantities, it would be a cruel and terrible conflict. The truth is that possession of the nuclear deterrent has prevented not only nuclear war, but also conventional war; and to us, peace is precious beyond price. We are the true peace party. And the nuclear deterrent has not only kept the peace, but it will continue to preserve our independence. Winston Churchill's warning is just as true now as when he made it many many years ago. He said this: 'Once you take the position of not being able in any circumstances to defend your rights against aggression, there is no end to the demands that will be made nor to the humiliations that must be accepted.' He knew, and we must heed his warning.

And yet, Labour's defence policy remains 'no Polaris', 'no Cruise missiles in Britain', 'no United States nuclear bases in Britain', 'no Trident', 'no independent nuclear deterrent'.

There is, I think, just one answer the nation will give: 'No defence – no Labour Government.'

Mr President, in foreign affairs this year has seen two major diplomatic successes. We have reached a detailed and binding agreement with China on the future of Hong Kong.[2] It is an agreement designed to

---

[1] Harry S. Truman (1884–1972), 33rd President of the USA 1945–53 (Democrat).
[2] The ninety-nine-year lease by which Britain held 90 per cent of the colony of Hong Kong was due to expire in 1997, and China did not recognize British rights over the remaining 10 per cent. In September 1984 it was agreed that sovereignty over the whole of Hong Kong would revert to China in 1997, with special arrangements to guarantee stability and prosperity for fifty years thereafter. Mrs Thatcher signed the Joint Agreement on Hong Kong in Peking on 19 December 1984.

preserve Hong Kong's flourishing economy and unique way of life; and we believe that it meets the needs and wishes of the people of Hong Kong themselves.

A few weeks ago, the unofficial members of the Executive Council of Hong Kong came to see me. We kept in touch with them the whole time and they frequently made journeys to No. 10 Downing Street as the negotiations with China proceeded. We were just about to initial the agreement and we consulted them, of course, about its content. Their spokesman said this: he said that while the agreement did not contain everything he would have liked, he and his colleagues could nevertheless recommend it to the people of Hong Kong in good conscience – in good conscience. That means a lot to us. If that is what the leaders of Hong Kong's own community believe, then we have truly fulfilled the heavy responsibility we feel for their long-term future.

That agreement required imagination, skill, hard work and perseverance. In other words, it required Geoffrey Howe.[1] And in Europe too, through firmness and determination, we have achieved a long-term settlement of Britain's budget contributions, a fair deal for Britain and for Europe too. And if we had listened to the advice of other party leaders, Britain would not have done half as well. But patient diplomacy – and occasionally, I confess, a little impatient diplomacy – that did the trick.[2] Also, we have at last begun to curb surplus food production in the Community.[3] Now, we know that for some farmers this has meant a painful adjustment, and we are very much aware of their difficulties. Their work and their success are a great strength to our country. Michael Jopling[4] and his colleagues will continue to fight to achieve a fair deal for them.

We have also won agreement on the need to keep the Community's spending under proper control. The Community can now enter on a new chapter and use its energies and influence to play a greater part in world affairs, as an example of what democracies can accomplish, as a very powerful trading group and as a strong force for freedom.

[1] Geoffrey Howe, as Foreign Secretary, patiently negotiated the contentious details of the Hong Kong Agreement.
[2] At the European Council at Fontainebleau on 26 June 1984 it was agreed that Britain would henceforth receive a 66 per cent rebate on its net contribution to the EC budget.
[3] At Fontainebleau it was also agreed that agricultural spending under the Common Agriculture Policy should rise at a rate lower than the growth in the EEC's income.
[4] Michael Jopling (born 1930), Conservative MP 1964–97; Chief Whip 1979–83; Minister for Agriculture 1983–87.

Now, Mr President, we had one of the most interesting debates of this Conference on unemployment, which we all agree is the scourge of our times. To have over three million people unemployed in this country is bad enough, even though we share this tragic problem with other nations; but to suggest, as some of our opponents have, that we do not care about it is as deeply wounding as it is utterly false. Do they really think that we do not understand how hopeless the world must seem to a young person who has not yet succeeded in getting his first job? Of course we know; of course we see; and of course we care. How could they say that we welcome unemployment as a political weapon? What better news could there be for any Government than the news that unemployment is falling? And the day cannot come too soon for me.

Others, while not questioning our sincerity, argue that our policies will not achieve our objectives. They look back forty years to the post-war period, when we were paused to launch a Brave New World; a time when we all thought that having won the war, we knew how to win the peace. Keynes had provided the diagnosis.[1] It was all set out in the 1944 White Paper on Employment.

I bought it then; I have it still. My name is on the top of it: Margaret H. Roberts. One of my staff took one look at it and said: 'Good Heavens! I did not know it was as old as that!'

Now, we all read that White Paper very carefully; but the truth was that politicians took some parts of the formula in it and conveniently ignored the rest. I reread it frequently. Those politicians overlooked the warning in that Paper that Government action must not weaken personal enterprise or exonerate the citizen from the duty of fending for himself. They disregarded the advice that wages must be related to productivity. And, above all, they neglected the warning that without a rising standard of industrial efficiency you cannot achieve a high level of employment combined with a rising standard of living.

And having ignored so much of that, and having ignored other parts of the formula for so much of the time, the result was that we ended up with high inflation and high unemployment.

This Government is heeding the warnings. It has acted on the basic truths that were set out all those years ago in that famous White Paper. If I had come out with all this today, some people would call it

---

[1] The economic theories of Maynard Keynes suggested that the Government could manage aggregate demand by means of fiscal and monetary policy in order to maintain full employment.

'Thatcherite', but in fact it was vintage Maynard Keynes. He had a horror of inflation. A fear of too much state control, and a belief in the market.

We are heeding those warnings. We are taking the policy as a whole and not only in selected parts. We have already brought inflation down below 5 per cent. Output has been rising steadily since 1981 and investment is up substantially. But if things are improving, why – you will ask – does unemployment not fall?

And that was the question one could feel throughout that debate, even though people know there is always a time lag between getting the other things right and having a fall in unemployment. Why does unemployment not fall?

May I try to answer that question?

Well, first, more jobs *are* being created. As Tom King[1] pointed out, over the last year more than a quarter of a million extra jobs have been created; but the population of working age is also rising very fast, as the baby boom of the 1960s becomes the school-leavers of the 1980s. So, although the number of jobs are rising, the population of working age is also rising. And among the population of working age a larger proportion of married women are seeking work. And so you will see why we need more jobs just to stop unemployment rising – and even more jobs to get it falling.

Now, on top of that, new technology has caused redundancy in many factories; though it has also created whole new industries providing products and jobs that only a few years ago were undreamed of. So it has two effects: the first one redundancies, the second and slightly later, new jobs as new products become possible.

This has happened in history before. A few days ago I visited York, where I saw the first railway engine, Stephenson's *Rocket*.[2] I thought of the jobs, the prospects and the hope that the new steam engines and the railways then brought to many people. Communities queued up to be on a railway line, to have their own station. Those communities welcomed change and it brought them more jobs.

I confess I am very glad we have got the railways. But if we were trying to build those same railways today, I wonder if we would ever

[1] Tom King (born 1933), Conservative MP 1970–; Environment Secretary 1983; Transport Secretary 1983; Employment Secretary 1983–85; Northern Ireland Secretary 1985–89; Defence Secretary 1989–92.
[2] George Stephenson (1781–1848), British engineer. His locomotive, *Rocket*, won the Liverpool & Manchester Railway competition in 1829.

get planning permission – it sometimes takes so long. And that is one thing that can sometimes delay the coming into existence of jobs.

That was one example from history; but let us go through during my lifetime, as we have this same phenomenon: redundancies from new technology, more jobs from new technology. In the 1940s, when I took a science degree, the new emerging industries were plastics, manmade fibres and television. Later it will be satellites, computers and telecommunications; and now it is biotechnology and information technology; and today our universities and science parks are identifying the needs of tomorrow. So there are new industries and new jobs in the pipeline.

I remember an industrialist telling me, when I first went into business – and I have always remembered it – 'Our job is to discover what the customer will buy and to produce it.' And in Wrexham the other day, at a Youth Training Centre, I was delighted to see a poster saying: 'It is the customer that makes paydays possible.' So those young people are not only learning new technology; they are learning the facts of business life and how we create new jobs. Because it is the spirit of enterprise that provides jobs; it is being prepared to venture and build a business.

And the role of Government in helping them to do that? It is in cutting taxes; it is in cutting inflation; it is in keeping costs down; it is in cutting through regulations and removing obstacles to the growth of small businesses. For that is where many of the new jobs will come from – small businesses.

And it is providing better education and training. The Youth Training Scheme, now in its second year, was set up to give young people the necessary skills for the new technologies and the necessary approach to industry.[1] A majority of the first year's graduates are getting jobs. A much bigger proportion of those leaving the Youth Training Scheme are getting jobs than of those who left the Youth Opportunities Scheme; and so they should, because it is a much better training scheme and it will improve again this year.

I was very interested in it. David Young[2] started it and I offered to take a trainee for our office at No. 10 Downing Street. We would love

[1] The Youth Training Scheme was set up in September 1983 to offer suitable training places to unemployed sixteen- and seventeen-year-olds. It replaced all previous youth schemes supported by the Manpower Services Commission, including the Youth Opportunities Programme.

[2] David Young (born 1932), Baron Young of Graffham 1984. Minister without Portfolio 1984–85; Employment Secretary 1985–87; Trade and Industry Secretary 1987–89.

to have one. Now, he or she might not have made it to be Prime Minister in one year. But the work at No. 10, because we have a staff, obviously, to run the office, of about a hundred, is varied and interesting, and we really wanted to take on a trainee, and we also said we would take some trainees into the other parts of the civil service. So we were not unwilling; we were really welcoming this person or people, and looking forward to it. At first, the union said 'yes,' then they said 'no,' and the result is that young people have been denied training places.

The same problem arose at Jaguar. First the union said 'yes,' then they said 'no.' So 130 unemployed teenagers have been denied training, and that means young people were denied jobs.

Mr President, we cannot create jobs without the willing co-operation not only of employers, but of trade unions and all of the workforce who work in industry and commerce as well.

Yesterday, in the debate, we were urged to spend more money on capital investment. It looks a very attractive idea; but to spend more in one area means spending less in another, or it means putting up taxes. Now, in government, we are constantly faced with these difficult choices. If we want more for investment, I have to ask my colleagues in Cabinet: 'What are you going to give up? Or you? Or you? Or you? Or you?' Or should I perhaps ask them: 'Whose pay claim are you going to cut – the doctors', the police, the nurses'?' I do not find many takers; because we have honoured the reviews of pay for doctors, nurses and the police and others in full. And you would not have cheered me if we had not done so; and quite right too. But I am bringing this to you because, although people can say the way to solve unemployment is to give a higher capital allocation, I have to say, 'What are we going to give up?' Or I have to turn to Nigel Lawson[1] and ask him which taxes would he put up. Income tax? The personal income tax is already too high. Value Added Tax? Well, I should get a pretty frosty reception from Nigel and I should get a pretty frosty reception from you. But I would be loath to ask him anyway.

But, you see, Governments have to make these difficult choices; because as you know, whether in your own households or whether in your own businesses, there is a certain amount of income, and you are soon in trouble if you do not live within it.

But what I want to say to you is that we *do* consider these difficult

---

[1] Nigel Lawson (born 1932), Baron Lawson of Blaby 1992. Conservative MP 1974–92; Energy Secretary 1981–83; Chancellor of the Exchequer 1983–89.

choices in the public expenditure annual round. We are just coming up to it; and we have managed to allocate a very considerable sum to capital investment. Indeed, we have found the money for the best investment projects on offer. And, believe you me, it has been because of very good management in each and every Department. It has meant cutting out waste, so we could make room for these things and be certain that we could say to you that we were getting value for money.

Let me just give you a few examples of some of the investment projects for which we have found money by careful budgeting.

There is the M254x road, for example. It is being completed. British Railways have been given the green light to go ahead with electrification, if they can make it pay. We have started or built forty-nine new hospitals since 1979. Capital investment in the nationalized industries as a whole is going up. Of course, we look at those things like new power stations, and in a year after drought we look at things like more investment in the water-supply industry. So we are going ahead with major capital investment.

So what is the conclusion that we are coming to? It is the spirit of enterprise that creates new jobs, and it is Government's task to create the right framework – the right financial framework – in which that can flourish, and to cut the obstacles which sometimes handicap the birth of enterprise; and also to manage our own resources carefully as well.

That is more or less what that Employment Policy White Paper in 1944 said; so let me just return to it. Page 1. (It is getting a bit old.)

Employment cannot be created by Act of Parliament or by Government action alone. The success of the policy outlined in this Paper will ultimately depend on the understanding and support of the community as a whole, and especially on the efforts of employers and workers in industry.

It was true then; it is true now; and those are the policies that we are following and shall continue to follow, because those are the policies that we believe will ultimately create the genuine jobs for the future. In the meantime, it is our job to try to mitigate the painful effects of change; and that we do, as you know, by generous redundancy payments, and also by a Community Enterprise Scheme, which not only finds jobs for the long-term unemployed, but finds them in a way which brings great benefits to the communities. And then, of course, where there are redundancy schemes in steel and now in coal, the industries themselves set up enterprise agencies both to give help to those who are made redundant and to provide new training. All of this is a highly constructive policy both for the creation of jobs and a policy to cushion the effects of change.

May I turn now to the coal industry?

For a little over seven months we have been living through an agonizing strike. Let me make it absolutely clear: the miners' strike was not of this Government's seeking, nor of its making.

We have heard in debates at this Conference some of the aspects that have made this dispute so repugnant to so many people. We were reminded by a colliery manager that the NUM always used to accept that a pit should close when the losses were too great to keep it open, and that the miners set great store by investment in new pits and new seams. And under this Government that new investment is happening in abundance. You can almost repeat the figures with me. £2 million in capital investment in the mines for every day this Government has been in power; so no shortage of capital investment.

We heard moving accounts from two working miners about just what they have to face as they try to make their way to work. The sheer bravery of those men and thousands like them who kept the mining industry alive is beyond praise. 'Scabs', their former workmates call them. Scabs? They are lions! What a tragedy it is when striking miners attack their workmates. Not only are they members of the same union, but the working miner is saving both their futures, because it is the working miners – whether in Nottinghamshire, Derbyshire, Lancashire, Leicestershire, Staffordshire, Warwickshire, North Wales or Scotland – who have kept faith with those who buy our coal. And without that custom thousands of jobs in the mining industry would be already lost.

And then we heard – unforgettably – from the incomparable Mrs Irene McGibbon, who told us what it is like to be the wife of a working miner during this strike. She told us of the threats and intimidation suffered by herself and her family and even her eleven-year-old son; but what she endured only stiffened her resolve. To face the picket line day after day must take a very special kind of courage. But it takes as much – perhaps even more – for the housewife who has to stay at home alone. Men and women like that are what we are proud to call 'the best of British'; and our police who upheld the law with an independence and a restraint perhaps only to be found in this country are the admiration of the world.

To be sure, the miners had a good deal. And to try to prevent a strike the National Coal Board gave to the miners the best ever pay offer, the highest ever investment and (for the first time) the promise that no miner would lose his job against his will. We did this despite the fact that the bill for losses in the coal industry last year was bigger than the annual bill for all the doctors and dentists in all the National Health Service hospitals in the United Kingdom.

Let me repeat it: the losses – the annual losses – in the coal industry are enormous. £1.3 billion last year. You have to find that money as taxpayers.

Mr President, this is a dispute about the right to go to work of those who have been denied the right to go to vote.[1] And we must never forget that the overwhelming majority of trade unionists, including many striking miners, deeply regret what has been done in the name of trade unionism. When this strike is over – and one day it will be over – we must do everything we can to encourage moderate and responsible trade unionism, so that it can once again take its respected and valuable place in our industrial life.

Meanwhile, we are faced with the present Executive of the National Union of Mineworkers. They know that what they are demanding has never been granted either to miners or to workers in any other industry. Why then demand it? Why ask for what they know cannot be conceded?[2] There can only be one explanation: they did not want a settlement; they wanted a strike. Otherwise, they would have balloted on the Coal Board's offer. Indeed, one-third of the miners did have a ballot, and voted overwhelmingly to accept the offer.

Mr President, what we have seen in this country is the emergence of an organized revolutionary minority who are prepared to exploit industrial disputes, but whose real aim is the breakdown of law and order and the destruction of democratic Parliamentary government. We have seen the same sort of thugs and bullies at Grunwick,[3] more recently against Eddie

---

[1] Under the constitution of the National Union of Mineworkers, a national strike required the support of at least 55 per cent in a national ballot. The NUM Executive refused to hold a national ballot, but tried to secure the effect of a national strike by holding area ballots and sending pickets from striking areas to prevent work in nonstriking areas.

[2] The NUM demanded that every pit remain open, regardless of financial loss, until physically exhausted.

[3] Grunwick, a photographic business in north-west London, was subject to prolonged and violent mass picketing in 1977 after the APEX trade union signed up dismissed workers, claimed 'recognition', and demanded their reinstatement.

Shah in Stockport,[1] and now organized into flying squads around the country. If their tactics were to be allowed to succeed, if they are not brought under the control of the law, we shall see them again at every industrial dispute organized by militant union leaders anywhere in the country.

One of the speakers earlier in this Conference realized this fact, realized that what they are saying is: 'Give us what we want, or we are prepared to go on with violence.' And he referred to Danegeld.[2] May I add to what that speaker said?

> We never pay anyone Danegeld,
> No matter how trifling the cost,
> For the end of that game is oppression and shame
> And the nation that plays it is lost!

Yes, Rudyard Kipling. Who could put it better?

Democratic change there has always been in this, the home of democracy. But the sanction for change is the ballot box. It seems that there are some who are out to destroy any properly elected Government. They are out to bring down the framework of law. That is what we have seen in this strike.

And what is the law they seek to defy? It is the common law, created by fearless judges and passed down across the centuries. It is legislation scrutinized and enacted by the Parliament of a free people. It is legislation passed through a House of Commons, a Commons elected once every five years by secret ballot by one citizen, one vote. This is the way our law was fashioned, and that is why British justice is renowned across the world.

'No government owns the law. It is the law of the land, the heritage of the people. No man is above the law and no man is below it. Nor do we ask any man's permission when we require him to obey it. Obedience to the law is demanded as a right, not asked as a favour.' So said Theodore Roosevelt.[3] Mr President, the battle to uphold the rule of law

---

[1] When press proprietor Eddie Shah launched the Messenger group of free newspapers with non-union labour in 1983, the National Graphical Association organized mass picketing of his premises.

[2] Danegeld was a tax imposed in England from A.D. 991 to pay the Vikings to desist from further raids, i.e. a kind of blackmail money. The lines are from Kipling's poem 'Dane-geld'.

[3] Theodore Roosevelt (1858–1919), US statesman. Governor of New York 1898–1900; 26th President of the United States 1901–9 (Republican).

calls for the resolve and commitment of the British people. Our institutions of justice, the courts and the police require the unswerving support of every law-abiding citizen; and I believe they will receive it.

The nation faces what is probably the most testing crisis of our time: the battle between the extremists and the rest. We are fighting, as we have always fought, for the weak as well as for the strong. We are fighting for great and good causes. We are fighting to defend them against the power and might of those who rise up to challenge them. This Government will not weaken. This nation will meet that challenge. Democracy will prevail.

26

The Second Carlton Lecture, Delivered at the Carlton Club, London, 26 November 1984

Not surprisingly, a month after the Brighton bomb and with the miners' strike at its height, it was the theme of the challenge to democracy that dominated Mrs Thatcher's Carlton Lecture, delivered on 26 November 1984. In spite of the optimistic title, it is the vulnerability of democracy that clearly preoccupies the speaker. And it is not the violent opposition to democratic institutions, but rather the opposition of unrepresentative minorities which manipulate their way to power over their fellow citizens that is singled out for the sharpest criticism. This theme also reflects current political conditions: having lost the 1983 general election, fought on the most left-wing platform ever put forward by the Labour Party, the hard left were now using all possible extra-Parliamentary means to achieve their ends – through trade unions, local government and special-interest groups.

WHY DEMOCRACY WILL LAST

Just over two years ago, Mr Harold Macmillan[1] delivered the First Carlton Lecture. All of us who were present to hear it or who have since read it hoped that this would be the first of a distinguished series. You do me a great honour in inviting me to deliver the second.

When he was Prime Minister, Mr Macmillan gave me my first

[1] Harold Macmillan (1894–1986), 1st Earl of Stockton 1984. Conservative MP 1924–29, 1931–64; Air Secretary 1945; Minister of Housing and Local Government 1951–54; Minister of Defence 1954–55; Foreign Secretary 1955; Chancellor of the Exchequer 1955–57; Prime Minister and Leader of the Conservative Party 1957–63.

ministerial job in 1961.[1] Some twenty years later, as Prime Minister myself, it gave me the greatest pleasure to recommend Mr Macmillan for his highly deserved and widely acclaimed earldom on the occasion of his ninetieth birthday.

Today, the Earl of Stockton may have a distinguished title; he may sit in a different Chamber; but he speaks with the brilliance, wit and understanding with which he has always spoken. His lecture was entitled 'Civilization under Threat' because he thought – and I quote his own words – something 'vague and meaningless and a little pompous would be about right'. Needless to say, the lecture was everything but that.

The title I first toyed with for my lecture was 'Democracy under Threat' – because there are, as we know, enemies of democracy both within and without. But that would have been too pessimistic a title, because the defenders of democracy are far the more numerous. The overwhelming majority of the British people are democrats. Britain's democratic institutions are resilient. And the heart of our country is strong.

I have confidence and faith in our people; and have therefore called my lecture: 'Why Democracy will last'.

Democracy

We meet here as practitioners in the craft of democracy. Indeed, this great club is a workshop of that craft.[2] The families of some of those in this room have been practising this skill for several generations. Others have become master-craftsmen in one generation. Still more are serving their apprenticeships for the future.

Democracy has always been, and remains, one of the rarer forms of government. The United Nations now numbers 159 countries, but no more than about sixty could be described as democracies.

So steady and inevitable was our own progress towards democracy – so familiar are the landmarks of Magna Carta in 1215, Simon de Montfort's Parliament in 1265, Habeas Corpus in 1679, the Glorious Revolution of

---

[1] Margaret Thatcher was Joint Parliamentary Secretary to the Ministry of Pensions and National Insurance 1961–64.
[2] The Carlton Club was founded in 1832 specifically as a Conservative political-cum-social club. It was the effective headquarters of the Party until 1870, and its membership has always included leading Conservative politicians.

1688, the Reform Bills from 1832 leading to universal suffrage – that it is easy to forget how unusual is our history.

If we look wider, in the past or the present, we see not only how rare but how vulnerable democracy is: the brief flowering of Athens in the ancient world; the instant destruction of the fledgling Russian democracy in 1917 by Lenin's *coup d'état*; and the infancy of most real democracies outside Europe now.

And even if we look at the kind of representative democracy which we practise in Britain today, we realize how long has been the road from Runnymede.[1]

> At Runnymede, at Runnymede!
> Your rights were won at Runnymede!
> No freeman shall be fined or bound,
> Or dispossessed of freehold ground,
> Except by lawful judgement found
> And passed upon him by his peers.
> Forget not, after all these years,
> The Charter signed at Runnymede.
>
> And still when Mob or Monarch lays
> Too rude a hand on English ways,
> The whisper wakes, the shudder plays
> Across the reeds at Runnymede.
> And Thames, that knows the moods of kings,
> And crowds and priests and suchlike things,
> Rolls deep and dreadful as he brings
> Their warning down from Runnymede!

The first of the great Parliamentary Reform Bills actually occurred in the lifetime of the father of one member of our present House of Lords, Lady Elliot of Harwood.[2] Her father, Sir Charles Tennant,[3] was born in 1823.

---

[1] It was at Runnymede, on the banks of the River Thames in Surrey, that King John put his seal to the Magna Carta on 15 June 1215. The poem, 'The Reeds of Runnymede', is by Rudyard Kipling.

[2] Katharine Elliot (1903–94), Baroness Elliot of Harwood 1958. Conservative Party activist; Roxburghshire County Councillor 1946–75; Delegate to UN General Assembly 1954, 1956, 1957.

[3] Sir Charles Tennant (1823–1906), Scottish businessman and art patron. Liberal MP 1879–86.

Votes for women, albeit for those aged thirty or over, were one of the few beneficial consequences of the First World War. That was the only time when the age of thirty, in the life of women, has been of statutory significance. Votes for women under thirty, on the same terms as men, came during my own lifetime. It was as late as 1950 – by which time the university seats had been abolished – that the first general election was held, based on the principle of 'one person, one vote'.

But freedom depends on more than just a voting system. Long before democracy was valued, long before we had this form of representative government, long before universal suffrage, we prided ourselves on being a free people. We'd freed ourselves from fear of foreign domination. We'd freed ourselves from absolute monarchy. Above all, we'd developed the common law which established protection for the common man against the over-mighty and powerful. The debt we owe to the judges over many centuries has been incalculable.

There is no more eloquent statement of eighteenth-century England's reverence for freedom than that attributed to the Chief Justice, Lord Mansfield,[1] in the case of James Somersett, the slave:

> The air of England has long been too pure for a slave, and every man is free who breathes it. Every man who comes into England is entitled to the protection of English law, whatever oppression he may heretofore have suffered, and whatever may be the colour of his skin.

By the nineteenth century, Tennyson[2] – the great poet of my native Lincolnshire – was able to call this nation 'a land of settled government, a land of just renown'.

But if we are to preserve and indeed strengthen democracy, we must encourage those forces which sustain it, which are friendly to it, and identify and isolate those elements which subvert it, which are its enemies. And the democracy of which we speak is not the counterfeit model of communism, but genuine democracy.

Economists and politicians have not always been the friends of freedom. Indeed, one of them would have led us into serfdom from the middle-class comfort of a house in Highgate and from the publicly

[1] William Murray (1705–93), 1st Earl of Mansfield 1756. MP 1742–56; Solicitor-General 1742–54; Attorney-General 1754–56; Lord Chief Justice 1756–88. His ruling in Somersett's case effectively abolished slavery in England in 1772.
[2] Alfred Tennyson (1809–92), 1st Baron Tennyson 1884. Poet Laureate 1850–92.

provided reading rooms of the British Museum.[1] But others knew more of human nature and had more respect for the importance of the individual.

Democracy and Economic Life

Great political economists, the greatest of them Adam Smith, have shown how a market economy, by devolving the power of consumer choice to customers, runs with the grain of democracy, which disperses the power of political choice to voters. The economic enemies of democracy are those who would impose on people systems of production and distribution based on compulsion, not on people's choice. Many live under systems whose rulers know only too well the connection between economic and political freedom, for they suppress economic freedoms precisely to prevent that political freedom which would ultimately follow. But are there not closer to home some trends and fashions of thought which contain, in more respectable guise, the seed of the same danger?

If some powerful group of producers says to us: 'You've got to buy our product, whether or not you want it. We'll force you to do so by the use of monopoly power or political muscle,' then those producers are taking away from their fellow citizens an economic freedom – and that is true, even if we were feeble enough to vote to allow it because we thought 'Anything for a quiet life.' And if they are prepared to rob us of our economic freedoms, what is to stop them taking away other freedoms as well?

Let us never forget: democracies can, and in the past have, voted for measures which lead to their own destruction. The job of democratic leaders is to warn that measures which may seem easy or even popular, which may end some immediate conflict, must be resisted if in the end they risk destroying democracy itself.

Doubtless consensus politicians mocked Demosthenes when he warned that the blandishments of King Philip of Macedon had only one object – the extinction of freedom in the Greek cities.[2] But he was right. They certainly mocked Churchill in a comparable case. And he was right too.

---

[1] Karl Marx (1818–83), German philosopher and economist, lived in London from 1849 and worked regularly in the British Museum library.
[2] Demosthenes, the great Athenian orator, warned in his 'Philippics' in the fourth century B.C. against the threat to Greek freedom posed by the Macedonian King.

Doubtless we could settle back into allowing industries, which we know should modernize, to levy on us all the compulsory costs of their own inefficiency, of their own protection. But that way lies, in the end, the erosion of the economic freedoms on which democracy rests; just as surely as Greek weakness in the face of the Macedonian King led to the extinction of political freedoms.

Democracy and Technology

Technology too has profound implications for political life.

Huge concentrations of people in great buildings simply repeating mechanical routines will be a thing of the past – and thank goodness for that. We can look forward to more and varied work being dispersed amongst smaller groups; less mass organization of people for mechanical purposes; more dispersal of economic power. All these bode well for a diverse and democratic society.

Other technical developments are more sombre. In the last century the Swiss Cantons, secure in their mountains; Britain, secure behind her navy; the New England cities, far from European dynastic wars; all could live in confident independence because, with reasonable vigilance, there was not much danger of destruction from outside. Powerful modern weapons and nuclear technology will never again allow us to live in so secure a world. Even if every nuclear weapon were destroyed, the knowledge of how to make them cannot be disinvented. Now only a ceaseless vigilance can keep us safe.

Democracy and Morality

Having said all of this, let us never forget that the case for democracy rests ultimately on morality. Somebody once said that when politicians start to talk about morality, you had better count the spoons. But there is no way round the word if we are to discuss what is the greatest internal threat to democracy.

In the old days, political leaders used to argue about something called 'the protection of minorities'. How could minority groups in a democracy be protected against the majority? Surely the 51 per cent might claim legitimacy for persecution of the 49 per cent?

But democracy is about more than majorities. It is about the right of every individual to freedom and justice: a right founded upon the Old and New Testatments, which remind us of the dignity of each individual, his right to choose and his duty to serve. These rights are God-given, not state-given. They are rights which have been evolved and upheld across the centuries by our rule of law: a rule of law which safeguards individuals and minorities; a rule of law which is the cement of a free society.

But what I think we are now seeing is the reverse problem, and we haven't properly faced up to it yet – the problem of the protection of the majority. There has come into existence a fashionable view, convenient to many special-interest groups, that there is no need to accept the verdict of the majority; that the minority should be quite free to bully, even coerce, to get the verdict reversed. Marxists, of course, always had an excuse when they were outvoted: their opponents must have 'false consciousness' – their views didn't count. But the Marxists, as usual, only provide a bogus intellectual top-dressing for groups who seek only their own self-interest.

Plenty of groups operate more simply. They don't care whether they have persuaded their fellow citizens or not, or whether constitutionally elected governments undertake properly approved policies. These minorities will coerce the system to meet their own objectives, if we let them get away with it.

Many of the new 'campaigning' pressure groups, run by professionals who move from campaign to campaign – some in the trade unions; some even in parts of the system of government itself – have seen how our democracy has evolved rules to temper the power of the majority and provide safeguards and rights for the minority. They have spotted that, if minorities bend the rules or simply ignore them, they may succeed in manipulating the whole process. The minority, indeed, may in the end effectively coerce the majority. You may recall that Burke had a phrase for it, as always: 'All that is needed for evil to triumph is for good men to do nothing.'

Now, I hope I won't be thought too provocative if I complain again about the sloppy use of the word 'consensus' in such cases. If there is a national debate and a constitutional vote about some matter, and if a recalcitrant minority says, 'The vote be damned; we are going to do our level best to stop the majority having its way,' then it's no good saying 'We must seek consensus, we must negotiate.' Such a group will never consent, whatever the majority thinks, until it gets what it wants. That is when we have to stand up and be counted; that is when we have to do what we believe to be right. We must never give in to the oldest and least democratic trick of all – the coercion of the many by the ruthless manipulating few. As soon as we surrender the basic rule which says we must persuade our fellow citizens, not coerce them, then we have joined the ranks of the enemies of democracy. Now that democracy has been won, it is not heroic to flout the law of the land, as if we still struggled in a quagmire where civilization had yet to be built. The concept of fair play – a British way of saying 'respect for the rules' – must not be used to allow the minority to overbear the tolerant majority.

Yet these are the very dangers which we face in Britain today. At one end of the spectrum are the terrorist gangs within our borders, and the terrorist states which finance and arm them. At the other are the hard left operating inside our system, conspiring to use union power and the apparatus of local government to break, defy and subvert the laws.

Their course of action is characterized by a calculated hostility towards our courts of justice. Our courts have long been distinguished for their impartiality. Our judges are famous for their fair-mindedness, their objectivity and their learning. But it is precisely because the courts uphold the principles of reasoned justice and equality before the law that the fascist left is contemptuous of them.

Who is there to speak for the majority? The Labour Party cannot. It is itself the victim of a takeover of the passive majority by a ruthless minority. We see moderate Labour politicians having to eat their words and take their leave.

And the Alliance?[1] It is a house divided: divided on principle, divided on policy, divided not once but many times over.

The Role of the Conservative Party Today

A unique responsibility is therefore placed on today's Conservative Party. And speaking to you in this building, it is right that I should dwell for a moment on the role of our Party.

There are in the free world a number of powerful and distinguished parties in the Conservative tradition. But I think it is fair to say that none can rival our own Conservative Party for the length of its service to the nation, the durability of its philosophy, its tenacity of tradition, combined with its willingness to embrace and refine necessary change

[1] The SDP–Liberal Alliance.

and, above all, for the sheer centrality of its role in the political life of our society. It can reasonably claim to be the leading democratic party in the world.

In our long history, the Conservative Party – as our name implies – has sought, successfully, to conserve many things: the Established Church, the Monarchy, the House of Lords, the constitutional integrity of the United Kingdom. But now the mantle has fallen on us to conserve the very principle of Parliamentary democracy and the rule of law itself – to conserve them for all people, of all parties and of none.

Each generation has to stand up for democracy. It can't take anything for granted and may have to fight fundamental battles anew.

My predecessor, in the First Carlton Lecture, dealt eloquently with the whole of civilization: the culture of the cities of Guatemala, the Oxford of 1914, Bretton Woods,[1] even the cumbersome diplodocus roaming in the valley of the Thames who didn't get as far as Oxford – a vast array of lost worlds surveyed with inimitable style.

I have concentrated on one strand of his argument – the uniqueness and vulnerability of our freedoms and our democracy – because I am still in the business of building defences for those freedoms and standing up for that democracy and justice in the immediate hurly-burly of political life. That is why I have pointed both to the dangers and to the opportunities.

If we don't guard against the dangers and rise to the opportunities, Lord Stockton's heirs may, in some distant lecture, add us to his lost worlds.

But I am confident. Britons will never lack brave hearts nor sound laws to defend their freedoms. When injustice threatens, we can mobilize the common sense and common law of Britain; and look to our Parliamentary democracy to signal dangers and shape the laws.

This year, as before in our history, we have seen men and women with stout hearts defying violence, scorning intimidation, defending their rights to uphold our laws. We have seen a new birth of leadership.

Individuals do count. Truth will prevail. Democracy does work and will endure. And we will defend it with our political lives. Let that be the message of this, the Second Carlton Lecture.

---

[1] An International Monetary Conference was held at Bretton Woods, New Hampshire, USA, in July 1944 to plan the post-war exchange system and establish the International Monetary Fund.

27

Address to a Joint Meeting of the American Congress, 20 February 1985

It was a mark of the friendship between the American President and the British Prime Minister, as well as of the respect in which Mrs Thatcher was now generally held in the United States, that she was invited in February 1985 to follow in the footsteps of Winston Churchill by addressing a Joint Meeting of Congress. The speech expresses Mrs Thatcher's high view of America's international vocation, rejects the fashionable notion that the United States and the Soviet Union are 'superpowers . . . of equal worth and equal significance', and restates the importance of strong Western defence. Less obviously, Mrs Thatcher spared President Reagan any blushes about the size of the US budget deficit – which her ministerial colleagues and European Governments were blaming for most of the world's economic ills. She also strongly defended President Reagan's Strategic Defence Initiative (SDI), of which the British Foreign Office and Ministry of Defence were at the time alternately critical or contemptuous.

Mr Speaker, Mr President, Distinguished Members of Congress:

On this, one of the most moving occasions of my life, my first words must be to say thank you for granting me this rare privilege of addressing a Joint Meeting of the United States Congress.

My thoughts turn to three earlier occasions when a British Prime Minister, Winston Churchill, has been honoured by a call to address both Houses.[1] Among his many remarkable gifts, Winston held a special advantage here. Through his American mother, he had ties of blood with you. Alas for me, these are not matters we can readily arrange for ourselves!

Those three occasions deserve to be recalled, because they serve as

[1] Winston Churchill addressed Congress in December 1941, May 1943 and January 1952.

lamps along a dark road which our people trod together; and they remind us what an extraordinary period of history the world has passed through between that time and ours; and they tell us what later generations in both our countries sometimes find hard to grasp – why past associations bind us so closely.

Winston Churchill's vision of a union of mind and purpose between the English-speaking peoples was to form the mainspring of the West. No one of my generation can forget that America has been the principal architect of a peace in Europe which has lasted forty years. Given the shield of the United States, we have been granted the opportunities to build a concept of Europe beyond the dreams of our fathers; a Europe which seemed unattainable amid the mud and slaughter of the First World War and the suffering and sacrifice of the Second.

When, in the spring of 1945, the guns fell silent, General Eisenhower[1] called our soldiers to a Service of Thanksgiving. In the order of service was a famous prayer of Sir Francis Drake:[2]

Oh Lord God, when Thou givest to Thy Servants to endeavour any great matter, grant us to know that it is not the beginning but the continuing of the same until it be thoroughly finished, which yieldeth the true glory!

On this day, close to the fortieth anniversary of that service and of peace in Europe – one of the longest periods without war in all our history – I should like to recall those words and acknowledge how faithfully America has fulfilled them. For our deliverance from what might have befallen us, I would not have us leave our gratitude to the tributes of history. The debt the free peoples of Europe owe to this nation, generous with its bounty, willing to share its strength, seeking to protect the weak, is incalculable. We thank and salute you!

Of course, in the years which separate us from the time when Winston Churchill last spoke to Congress, there have been disappointments as well as hopes fulfilled: the continued troubles in the Middle East; the brutal occupation of Afghanistan; the undiminished agony of tortured Poland; and above all, the continued and continuing division of the European continent.

[1] Dwight D. Eisenhower (1890–1969), US soldier and statesman. Supreme Allied Commander in the West 1944–45; 34th President of the United States 1953–61 (Republican).
[2] Sir Francis Drake (c.1545–96), English buccaneer and explorer.

From these shores, it may seem to some of you that by comparison with the risk and sacrifice which America has borne through four decades, and the courage with which you have shouldered unwanted burdens, Europe has not fully matched your expectations. Bear with me if I dwell for a moment on the Europe to which we now belong.

It is not the Europe of ancient Rome, of Charlemagne, of Bismarck. We who are alive today have passed through perhaps the greatest transformation of human affairs on the continent of Europe since the fall of Rome. In but a short chapter of its long history – and it is your history as much as ours – Europe lost the position which it had occupied for two thousand years.

For five centuries, that small continent had extended its authority over islands and continents the world over. For the first forty years of this century, there were seven great powers: the United States, Great Britain, Germany, France, Russia, Japan, Italy. Of those seven, two now tower over the rest – the United States and the Soviet Union.

To that swift and historic change, Europe – a Europe of many different histories and many different nations – has had to find a response. It has not been an easy passage to blend this conflux of nationalism, patriotism, sovereignty, into a European Community. Yet I think that our children and grandchildren may see this period – these birth-pangs of a new Europe – more clearly than we do now. They will see it as a visionary chapter in the creation of a Europe able to share the load alongside you. Do not doubt the firmness of our resolve in this march towards this goal. But do not underestimate what we already do.

Today, out of the forces of the Alliance in Europe, 95 per cent of the divisions, 85 per cent of the tanks, 80 per cent of the combat aircraft and 70 per cent of the fighting ships are provided, manned and paid for by the European Allies. And Europe has more than three million men under arms, and more still in reserve. We have to. We are right in the front line. The frontier of freedom cuts across our continent.

Members of Congress, the defence of that frontier is as vital to you as it is to us. It is fashionable for some commentators to speak of the two superpowers – the United States and the Soviet Union – as though they were somehow of equal worth and equal significance. Mr Speaker, that is a travesty of the truth! The Soviet Union has never concealed its real aim. In the words of Mr Brezhnev, 'The total triumph of socialism all over the world is inevitable – for this triumph we shall struggle with no lack of effort.' Indeed, there has been no lack of effort!

Contrast this with the record of the West. We do not aim at domination, at hegemony, in any part of the world. Even against those who oppose and who would destroy our ideas, we plot no aggression. Of course, we are ready to fight the battle of ideas with all the vigour at our command; but we do not try to impose our system on others. We do not believe that force should be the final arbiter in human affairs. We threaten no one. Indeed, the Alliance has given a solemn assurance to the world: none of our weapons will be used except in response to attack.

In talking to the Soviet Union, we find great difficulty in getting this message across. They judge us by their ambitions. They cannot conceive of a powerful nation not using its power for expansion or subversion. And yet they should remember that when, after the last war, the United States had a monopoly of nuclear weapons, she never once exploited her superiority. No country ever used such great power more responsibly or with such restraint. I wonder what would have befallen us in Western Europe and Great Britain if that monopoly had been in Soviet hands.

Mr Speaker, wars are not caused by the build-up of weapons. They are caused when an aggressor believes he can achieve his objectives at an acceptable price. The war of 1939 was not caused by an arms race. It sprang from a tyrant's belief that other countries lacked the means and the will to resist him. Remember Bismarck's phrase: 'Do I want war? Of course not – I want victory.'

Our task is to see that potential aggressors, from whatever quarter, understand plainly that the capacity and the resolve of the West would deny them victory in war, and that the price they would pay would be intolerable. That is the basis of deterrence. And it is the same whatever the nature of the weapons. For let us never forget the horrors of conventional war and the hideous sacrifice of those who have suffered in them. Our task is not only to prevent nuclear war, but to prevent conventional war as well.

No one understood the importance of deterrence more clearly than Winston Churchill, when in his last speech to you he said: 'Be careful above all things not to let go of the atomic weapon until you are sure and more than sure that other means of preserving peace are in your hands!'

Thirty-three years on, those weapons are still keeping the peace. But since then technology has moved on; and if we are to maintain deterrence – as we must – it is essential that our research and capacity do not fall behind the work being done by the Soviet Union.

That is why I firmly support President Reagan's decision to pursue research into defence against ballistic nuclear missiles – the Strategic Defence Initiative.[1] Indeed, I hope that our own scientists will share in this research.

The United States and the Soviet Union are both signatories to the 1972 Anti-Ballistic Missile Treaty,[2] a treaty without any terminal date. Nothing in that treaty precludes research, but should that research – on either side – lead to the possible deployment of new defence systems, that would be a matter for negotiation under the treaty.

Mr Speaker, despite our differences with the Soviet Union, we have to talk with them, for we have one overriding interest in common – that never again should there be a conflict between our peoples. We hope too that we can achieve security with far fewer weapons than we have today and at lower cost. And, thanks to the skilful diplomacy of Secretary Shultz,[3] negotiations on arms control open in Geneva on 12 March. They will be of immense importance to millions. They will be intricate, complex and demanding, and we should not expect too much too soon.

We must recognize that we have faced a Soviet political offensive designed to sow differences among us; calculated to create infirmity of purpose, to impair resolve, and even to arouse fear in the hearts of our people. Hope is such a precious commodity in the world today, but some are tempted to buy it at too high a price. We shall have to resist the muddled arguments of those who have been induced to believe that Russia's intentions are benign and that ours are suspect, or who would have us simply give up our defences in the hope that where we led, others would follow. As we learned cruelly in the 1930s, from good intentions can come tragic results. Let us be under no illusions. It is our strength and not their goodwill that has brought the Soviet Union to the negotiating table in Geneva.[4]

Mr Speaker, we know that our Alliance – if it holds firm – cannot be defeated; but it could be outflanked. It is among the unfree and the

[1] The Strategic Defence Initiative, 1983–93, popularly known as 'Star Wars', was a US Government research project to develop a defence system using satellites to detect and destroy enemy missiles.
[2] The Anti-Ballistic Missile Treaty restricted the deployment of anti-ballistic missile defences, but its precise implications for SDI were disputed.
[3] George Shultz (born 1920), US economist and politician. Secretary of the Treasury 1972–74; Secretary of State 1982–89.
[4] The USSR had walked out of arms control talks relating to intermediate nuclear forces in November 1983, in response to the stationing of US Cruise and Pershing missiles in Western Europe. Its agreement to resume negotiations was announced in January 1985.

underfed that subversion takes root. As Ethiopia demonstrated, those people get precious little help from the Soviet Union and its allies.[1] The weapons which they pour in bring neither help nor hope to the hungry. It is the West which heard their cries; it is the West which responded massively to the heart-rending starvation in Africa; it is the West which has made a unique contribution to the uplifting of hundreds of millions of people from poverty, illiteracy and disease.

But the problems of the Third World are not only those of famine. They face also a mounting burden of debt, falling prices for primary products, protectionism by the industrialized countries. Some of the remedies are in the hands of the developing countries themselves. They can open their markets to productive investment; they can pursue responsible policies of economic adjustment. We should respect the courage and resolve with which so many of them have tackled their special problems, but we also have a duty to help.

How can we help? First and most important, by keeping our markets open to them. Protectionism is a danger to all our trading partnerships, and for many countries trade is even more important than aid. And so we in Britain support President Reagan's call for a new GATT round.[2] The current strength of the dollar, which is causing so much difficulty for some of your industries, creates obvious pressures for special cases, for new trade barriers to a free market. I am certain that your Administration is right to resist such pressures. To give in to them would betray the millions in the developing world, to say nothing of the strains on your other trading partners. The developing countries need our markets as we need theirs, and we cannot preach economic adjustment to them and refuse to practise it at home.

And second, we must remember that the way in which we in the developed countries manage our economies determines whether the world's financial framework is stable; it determines the level of interest rates; it determines the amount of capital available for sound investment the world over; and it determines whether or not the poor countries can service their past loans, let alone compete for new ones. And those are

---

[1] By early 1985, over 300,000 people had died in Ethiopia as a result of famine caused by drought. The Ethiopian Government was a client of the USSR, but food relief came chiefly from the West.
[2] President Reagan called, on 7 February 1985, for a new round of the General Agreement on Tariffs and Trade to begin early the following year. The 'Uruguay Round' duly began in 1986, and final agreement on further trade liberalization was reached in 1993.

the reasons why we support so strongly your efforts to reduce the budget deficit. No other country in the world can be immune from its effects – such is the influence of the American economy on us all.

We in Europe have watched with admiration the burgeoning of this mighty American economy. There is a new mood in the United States. A visitor feels it at once. The resurgence of your self-confidence and your national pride is almost tangible. Now the sun is rising in the West.

For many years, our vitality in Britain was blunted by excessive reliance on the state. Our industries were nationalized, controlled and subsidized in a way that yours never were. We are having to recover the spirit of enterprise which you never lost. Many of the policies you are following are the policies we are following. You have brought inflation down. So have we. You have declared war on regulations and controls. So have we. Our civil service is now smaller than at any time since the war. And controls on pay, prices, dividends, foreign exchange – all are gone. You have encouraged small business – so often the source of tomorrow's jobs. So have we.

But above all, we are carrying out the largest programme of denationalization in our history. Just a few years ago in Britain, privatization was thought to be a pipe-dream. Now it is a reality – and a popular one. Our latest success was the sale of British Telecommunications. It was the largest share issue ever to be brought to the market on either side of the Atlantic – some two million people bought shares. Members of Congress, that is what capitalism is: a system which brings wealth to the many and not just to the few.

The United Kingdom economy is in its fourth year of recovery. Slower than yours, but positive recovery. We have not yet shared your success in bringing down unemployment, although we are creating many new jobs. But output, investment and standards of living are all at record levels, and profits are well up. And the pound? It is too low! For whatever the proper international level of sterling, it is a marvellous time for Americans not only to visit Britain but to invest with her – and many are. America is by far the largest direct investor in Britain. And I am delighted to say that Britain is the largest direct investor in the United States. The British economy has an underlying strength; and like you, we use our strength and resolve to carry out our duties to our allies and to the wider world.

We were the first country to station Cruise missiles on our territory. Britain led the rest. In proportion to our population, we station the same number of troops as you in Germany. In Central America, we keep troops stationed in Belize at that Government's request. That is our contribution to sustaining democracy in a part of the world so vital to the United States. We have troops in Cyprus and in the South Atlantic and, at your request, a small force in Sinai. And British servicemen are now on loan to some thirty foreign countries. We are alongside you in Beirut; we work with you in the Atlantic and in the Indian Ocean; our navy is on duty across the world. Mr Speaker, Britain meets her responsibilities in the defence of freedom throughout the world, and she will go on doing so.

Members of Congress: closer to home there is a threat to freedom, both savage and insidious. Both our countries have suffered at the hands of terrorists. We have both lost some of our best young lives; and I have lost some close and dear friends. Free, strong, democratic societies will not be driven by gunmen to abandon freedom or democracy. The problems of the Middle East will not be solved by the cold-blooded murder of American servicemen in Lebanon, nor by the murder of American civilians on a hijacked aircraft.[1] Nor will the problems of Northern Ireland be solved by the assassin's gun or bomb.

Garret Fitzgerald[2] and I – and our respective Governments – are united in condemning terrorism. We recognize the differing traditions and identities of the two parts of the community of Northern Ireland – the Nationalist and the Unionist. We seek a political way forward acceptable to them both, which respects them both. So long as the majority of people of Northern Ireland wish to remain part of the United Kingdom, their wishes will be respected. If ever there were to be a majority in favour of change, then I believe that our Parliament would respond accordingly; for that is the principle of consent enshrined in your Constitution and an essential part of ours.

There is no disagreement on this principle between the United Kingdom Government and the Government of the Republic of Ireland. Indeed, the four constitutional Nationalist parties of Ireland, North and South, who came together to issue the New Ireland Forum Report,[3]

---

[1] On 23 October 1983 a suicide-bomber drove a lorry laden with explosives into the US Marine compound in Beirut, killing 242 American troops on a peacekeeping mission. On 3 December 1984 a Kuwaiti airliner bound for Karachi was hijacked by Shi'ite terrorists, who shot dead two officials of the American Agency for Development.
[2] Dr Garret Fitzgerald (born 1926), Irish politician. Minister for Foreign Affairs 1973– 77; Leader of the Fine Gael Party 1977–87; Prime Minister 1981–82, 1982–87.
[3] The New Ireland Forum Report, published on 2 May 1984, advocated the unification of Ireland by federation or by joint Anglo–Irish authority over Northern Ireland.

made clear that any new arrangements could only come about by consent. And I welcome too their outright condemnation and total rejection of terrorism and all its works.

Be under no illusions about the Provisional IRA. They terrorize their own communities. They are the enemies of democracy, and of freedom too. Don't just take my word for it. Ask the Government of the Irish Republic, where it is an offence even to belong to that organization – as indeed it also is in Northern Ireland.

I recognize and appreciate the efforts which have been made by the administration and Congress alike to bring home this message to American citizens who may be misled into making contributions to seemingly innocuous groups. The fact is that money is used to buy the deaths of Irishmen north and south of the border – and 70 per cent of those killed by the IRA are Irishmen. And that money buys the killing and wounding even of American citizens visiting our country.[1] Garret Fitzgerald – and I salute him for the very brave thing he did yesterday in passing a special law to see that money did not get to the IRA – Garret Fitzgerald and I will continue to consult together in the quest for stability and peace in Northern Ireland. And we hope we will have your continued support for our joint efforts to find a way forward.

Distinguished Members of Congress: our two countries have a common heritage as well as a common language. It is no mere figure of speech to say that many of your most enduring traditions – representative government, Habeas Corpus, trial by jury, a system of constitutional checks and balances – stem from our own small islands. But they are as much your lawful inheritance as ours. You did not borrow these traditions: you took them with you, because they were already your own.

Human progress is not automatic. Civilization has its ebbs and flows. But if we look at the history of the last five hundred years – whether in the field of art, science, technology, religious tolerance or in the practice of politics – the conscious inspiration of it all has been the belief and practice of freedom under law; freedom disciplined by morality, under the law perceived to be just.

I cannot conclude this address without recalling words made immortal by your great President Abraham Lincoln in his Second Inaugural

[1] The IRA exploded a bomb outside Harrods department store in Knightsbridge, London, on 17 December 1983. Six people died, one of them an American, and ninety were injured.

Address, when he looked beyond an age when men fought and strove towards a more peaceful future:

> With malice toward none; with charity for all; with firmness in the right, as God gives us to see the right. Let us strive on to finish the work we are in, to do all which may achieve and cherish a just and lasting peace among ourselves and with all nations!

Members of Congress, may our two kindred nations go forward together sharing Lincoln's vision, firm of purpose, strong in faith, warm of heart, as we approach the third millennium of the Christian era.

Mr Speaker, thank you!

28

Statement on Libya to the House of Commons, 15 April 1986

Just before 11 p.m. on Tuesday 8 April the Prime Minister received a message from President Reagan requesting British support for the use of the American F1-11 aircraft based in Britain for strikes against Libya. Three days earlier a bomb in West Berlin had killed two people (one a US soldier) and injured more than two hundred (sixty of them Americans). The United States was convinced that this and other acts of terrorism could be traced back to Colonel Gaddafi, the Libyan dictator. After much heart-searching and discussion, and after further communication with the American President, Mrs Thatcher promised the Americans her support. This was probably the single biggest favour done by a post-war British Prime Minister to an American Administration, and was immediately recognized as such by the Americans.

It also entailed a high degree of political risk for the Prime Minister, who had recently withstood the crisis precipitated by Michael Heseltine over the future of the Westland helicopter company, and had been heavily criticized over the proposed sale of British Leyland (See I, pp. 423–41). As a result, anti-Americanism was already rife on both sides of the House of Commons at this time. And the bitterly critical reception given to British compliance with the American raids turned out to be all that Mrs Thatcher might have feared.

The Prime Minister: With permission, Mr Speaker, I shall make a statement about Libya. Before I do so, may I first say that my right honourable friend the Leader of the House[1] will shortly be making a business statement indicating that there will be a full day's debate on this matter tomorrow.

The House is aware that last night United States forces made attacks

---

[1] John Biffen (born 1930), Conservative MP 1961–97; Chief Secretary to the Treasury 1979–81; Trade Secretary 1981–82; Leader of the House of Commons 1982–87.

on specific targets in Libya. The Government have evidence showing beyond dispute that the Libyan Government have been and are directly involved in promoting terrorist attacks against the United States and other Western countries, and that they had made plans for a wide range of further terrorist attacks. The United Kingdom has itself suffered from Libyan terrorism. The House will recall the murder of WPC Fletcher in St James's Square.[1] There is no doubt, moreover, of the Libyan Government's direct and continuing support for the Provisional IRA, in the form of money and weapons.

Two years ago, we took certain measures against Libya, including the closure of the Libyan People's Bureau in London, restrictions on the entry of Libyans into the United Kingdom, and a ban on new contracts for the export to Libya of defence equipment. Yesterday the Foreign Ministers of the European Community reaffirmed their grave concern at Libyan-inspired terrorism and agreed on new restrictions against Libya. Since we broke off diplomatic relations with Libya, we have had no choice but consistently to advise British nationals living and working there that they do so on their own responsibility. Our interests there have been looked after by the Italian Government. Our representative in the British Interests Section of the Italian Embassy will continue to advise the British community as best he can.

The United States has tried by peaceful means to deter Colonel Gaddafi[2] and his régime from their promotion of terrorism, but to no effect. President Reagan informed me last week that the United States intended to take military action to deter further Libyan terrorism. He sought British support for his action. He also sought agreement, in accordance with our long-standing arrangements, to the use in the operation of some United States aircraft based in this country. This approach led to a series of exchanges, including a visit by Ambassador Walters[3] on Saturday 12 April.

Article 51 of the UN Charter specifically recognizes the right to self-defence. In view of Libya's promotion of terrorism, the failure of peaceful means to deter it, and the evidence that further attacks were threatened,

---

[1] Policewoman Yvonne Fletcher was killed and eleven others injured on 17 April 1984 when gunmen inside the Libyan People's Bureau in London fired on demonstrators outside.
[2] Colonel Mu'ammar Muhammad al-Gaddafi (born 1942), ruler of Libya 1969–.
[3] Lieutenant-General Vernon Walters (born 1917), US soldier and diplomat. Ambassador for Special Missions 1981–85; US Permanent Representative to the United Nations 1985–88; Ambassador to the Federal Republic of Germany 1988–91.

I replied to the President that we would support action directed against specific Libyan targets demonstrably involved in the conduct and support of terrorist activities; and, further, that if the President concluded that it was necessary, we would agree to the deployment of United States aircraft from bases in the United Kingdom for that purpose. I reserved the position of the United Kingdom on any question of further action which might be more general or less clearly directed against terrorism.

The President assured me that the operation would be limited to clearly-defined targets related to terrorism, and that the risk of collateral damage would be minimized. He made it clear that use of F1-11 aircraft from bases in the United Kingdom was essential, because by virtue of their special characteristics they would provide the safest means of achieving particular objectives with the lowest possible risk both of civilian casualties in Libya and of casualties among United States service personnel.

Terrorism is a scourge of the modern age. Libya has been behind much of it and was planning more. The United Kingdom itself has suffered from Libya's actions. So have many of our friends, including several in the Arab world.

The United States, after trying other means, has now sought by limited military action to induce the Libyan régime to desist from terrorism. That is in the British interest. It is why the Government support the United States action.

29

Speech to the House of Commons During the Debate on Libya, 16 April 1986

The Prime Minister spoke in the emergency debate on Libya, justifying not just British but American policy decisions. She had received the personal thanks of the American President; but in the House that afternoon there was little sympathy for American action. The speech, however, was full of difficulty for another reason. This was that it was necessary to reveal sufficient evidence of Libyan terrorism gathered by British and American intelligence in order to justify the action being taken – but without jeopardizing the sources.

The Prime Minister: My statement yesterday explained the Government's decision to support the United States's military action, taken in self-defence, against terrorist targets in Libya.

Of course, when we took our decision we were aware of the wider issues and of people's fears. Terrorism attacks free societies and plays on those fears. If those tactics succeed, terrorism saps the will of free peoples to resist.

We have heard some of those arguments in this country: 'Don't associate ourselves with the United States,' some say; 'Don't support them in fighting back: we may expose ourselves to more attacks,' say others.

Terrorism has to be defeated; it cannot be tolerated or sidestepped. When other ways and other methods have failed – I am the first to wish that they had succeeded – it is right that the terrorist should know that firm steps will be taken to deter him from attacking either other peoples or his own people who have taken refuge in countries that are free.

Before dealing with that central issue, and the evidence that we have of Libyan involvement, I wish to report to the House on the present position, as far as we know it. There have been reports of gunfire in Tripoli this lunchtime, but we have no further firm information. The

United States action was conducted against five specific targets directly connected with terrorism. It will, of course, be for the United States Government to publish their assessment of the results. However, we now know that there were a number of civilian casualties, some of them children. It is reported that they included members of Colonel Gaddafi's own family. The casualties are, of course, a matter of great sorrow. We also remember with sadness all those men, women and children who have lost their lives as a result of terrorist acts over the years – so many of them performed at the Libyan Government's behest.

We have no reports of British casualties as a result of the American action, or of any subsequent incidents involving British citizens in Libya. I understand that telephone lines to Libya are open and that people in the United Kingdom have been able to contact their relatives there.

As I told the House yesterday, since May 1984 we have had to advise British citizens choosing to live and work in Libya that they do so on their own responsibility and at their own risk. Our consul in the British Interests Section of the Italian Embassy has been and will remain in close touch with representatives of the British community to advise them of the best course of action.

Mr Eric Heffer[1] (Liverpool Walton): The right honourable lady referred to the killing of innocent children and then to terrorist attacks on innocent people in various parts of the world. I think that she and I may have been brought up in the same Christian tradition. Does she remember that two wrongs do not make a right?

The Prime Minister: Had the honourable gentleman been listening, he would have realized that I was trying to tackle that argument in part when I said that terrorism thrives on a free society. The terrorist uses the feelings in a free society to sap the will of civilization to resist. If the terrorist succeeds, he has won and the whole of free society has lost.

We are most grateful for the work of the Italian authorities, as our protecting power, on behalf of the British community in Libya.

In this country, we have to be alert to the possibility of further terrorist attacks – so too do our British communities abroad. Our security precautions have been heightened; but it is, of course, the technique of the terrorist not just to choose obvious targets. Members of the public should therefore be ready to report to the police anything suspicious that attracts their attention. We have also taken steps to defend our interests overseas,

---

[1] Eric Heffer (1922–91), Labour MP 1964–91.

seeking from foreign governments enhanced protection for British Embassies and communities.

The United Nations Security Council met twice yesterday and resumes today. With some significant exceptions, first international reactions have been critical, even to this carefully limited use of force in self-defence; but I believe that we can be pretty certain that some of the routine denunciations conceal a rather different view in reality.

Concern has been expressed about the effects of this event on relations between East and West. The United States informed the Soviet Union that it had conclusive evidence of Libyan involvement in terrorist activities, including the Berlin bomb,[1] that limited military action was being taken, and that it was in no way directed against the Soviet Union. We now hear that Mr Shevardnadze[2] has postponed his meeting with Mr Shultz planned for next month. I must say that that looks to me rather like a ritual gesture. If the Soviet Union is really interested in arms control it will resume senior ministerial contacts before long.

Right honourable and honourable Members have asked me about the evidence that the Libyan Government are involved in terrorist attacks against the United States and other Western countries. Much of this derives, of course, from secret intelligence. As I explained to the House yesterday, it is necessary to be extremely careful about publishing detailed material of this kind. To do so can jeopardize sources on which we continue to rely for timely and vital information. I can, however, assure the House that the Government are satisfied from the evidence that Libya bears a wide and heavy responsibility for acts of terrorism. For example, there is evidence showing that on 25 March, a week before the recent Berlin bombing, instructions were sent from Tripoli to the Libyan People's Bureau in East Berlin to conduct a terrorist attack against the Americans. On 4 April the Libyan People's Bureau alerted Tripoli that the attack would be carried out the following morning. On 5 April the Bureau reported to Tripoli that the operation had been carried out successfully. As the House will recall, the bomb which killed two people and injured 230 had exploded in the early hours of that same morning.

This country too is among the many that have suffered from Libyan terrorism. We shall not forget the tragic murder of WPC Fletcher by

---

[1] For the Berlin bomb, see p. 246.
[2] Eduard Shevardnadze (born 1928), Soviet politician. Minister for Foreign Affairs 1985–90, 1991; President of Georgia 1992–.

shots fired from the Libyan People's Bureau in London just two years ago tomorrow. It is also beyond doubt that Libya provides the Provisional IRA with money and weapons. The major find of arms in Sligo and Roscommon in the Irish Republic on 26 January, the largest ever on the island, included rifles and ammunition from Libya.

There is recent evidence of Libyan support for terrorism in a number of other countries. For instance, only three weeks ago intelligence uncovered a plot to attack with a bomb civilians queuing for visas at the American embassy in Paris. It was foiled and many lives must have been saved. France subsequently expelled two members of the Libyan People's Bureau in Paris for their involvement.

Sir John Biggs-Davison (Epping Forest): My right honourable friend mentioned the considerable arms find by the Garda in County Sligo. Does she recall that they also unearthed a very large supply of small-arms ammunition in boxes with Libyan army markings?

The Prime Minister: I am grateful to my honourable friend. I do recall that piece of evidence.

On 6 April an attempt to attack the United States Embassy in Beirut, which we know to have been undertaken on Libyan Government instructions, failed when the rocket exploded on launch.

It is equally clear that Libya was planning yet more attacks. The Americans have evidence that United States citizens are being followed and American Embassies watched by Libyan intelligence agents in a number of countries across the world. In Africa alone, there is intelligence of Libyan preparations for attacks on American facilities in no fewer than ten countries.

There is other specific evidence of Libyan involvement in past acts of terrorism, and in plans for future acts of terrorism. But I cannot give details because that would endanger lives and make it more difficult to apprehend the terrorists. We also have evidence that the Libyans sometimes chose to operate by using other Middle East terrorist groups.

But we need not rely on intelligence alone, because Colonel Gaddafi openly speaks of his objectives. I shall give just one instance. In a speech at the Wheelus base in Libya in June 1984, he said: 'We are capable of exporting terrorism to the heart of America. We are also capable of physical liquidation and destruction and arson inside America.'

There are many other examples.

Mr Tony Banks[1] (Newham North-West): I am grateful to the Prime Minis-

---

[1] Tony Banks (born 1943), Labour MP 1983–.

ter for giving way. Why is she prepared to support United States aggression against Libya but is not prepared to support United States economic sanctions against Libya?

The Prime Minister: If the honourable gentleman will contain himself in patience, I shall come to that.

Yesterday, many honourable Members referred to the need to give priority to measures other than military, but the sad fact is that neither international condemnation nor peaceful pressure over the years has deterred Libya from promoting and carrying out acts of terrorism.

Mr Robert N Wareing[1] (Liverpool West Derby): (Rose)

The Prime Minister: No, I must carry on at the moment. I am on a new point about non-military measures about which I have been asked, and I must proceed through this evidence carefully.

In 1981 the United States closed the Libyan People's Bureau in Washington and took measures to limit trade with Libya. Later, in January this year, the United States Government announced a series of economic measures against Libya. They sought the support of other Western countries. We took the view, together with our European partners, that economic sanctions work only if every country applies them. Alas, that was not going to happen with Libya.

In April 1984 we took our own measures. We closed the Libyan People's Bureau in London and broke diplomatic relations with Libya. We imposed a strict visa régime on Libyans coming to this country and we banned new contracts for the supply of defence equipment, and we severely limited Export Credits Guarantee Department credit for other trade.

Over the years, there have been many international declarations against terrorism – for example, by the economic summit under British chairmanship in London in June 1984; by the European Council in Dublin in December 1984; and finally by the United Nations General Assembly in December 1985. All those meetings adopted resolutions condemning terrorism and calling for greater international co-operation against it.

Indeed, the Resolution of the United Nations General Assembly unequivocally condemns as criminal all acts, methods and practices of terrorism. It calls upon all states, in accordance with international law, to refrain from organizing, instigating, assisting or participating in terrorist

[1] Robert Wareing (born 1930), Labour MP 1983–.

253

acts in other states. After the *Achille Lauro* incident,[1] the Security Council issued a statement condemning terrorism in all its forms everywhere. But while resolutions and condemnations issued from those cities, in others more terrible events – bombings, hijackings and kidnappings – were happening or were being planned. They are still being planned. It was against that remorseless background of terrorist atrocities, and against the background of the restrained peaceful response, that the case for military action under the inherent right of self-defence to deter planned Libyan terrorist attacks against American targets was raised.

President Reagan informed me last week that the United States intended to take such action. He sought our support. Under the consultation arrangements which have continued under successive Governments for over thirty years, he also sought our agreement to the use of United States aircraft based in this country. Honourable Members will know that our agreement was necessary.

In the exchanges which followed, I raised a number of questions and concerns. I concentrated on the principle of self-defence, recognized in Article 51 of the United Nations Charter, and the consequent need to limit the action and to relate the selection of targets clearly to terrorism.

There were, of course, risks in what was proposed. Many of them have been raised in the House and elsewhere since the action took place. I pondered them deeply with the Ministers most closely concerned, for decisions like this are never easy. We also considered the wider implications, including our relations with other countries; and we had to weigh the importance for this country's security of our alliance with the United States and the American role in the defence of Europe.

As I told the House yesterday, I replied to the President that we would support action directed against specific Libyan targets demonstrably involved in the conduct and support of terrorist activities; further, that if the President concluded that it was necessary, we would agree to the deployment of United States aircraft from bases in the United Kingdom for that specific purpose.

Mr Andrew Faulds[2] (Warley East): Will the right honourable lady give way?

The Prime Minister. No, sir.

---

[1] Four Palestinian terrorists hijacked the Italian cruise liner *Achille Lauro* in the Mediterranean on 7 October 1985 and murdered an American passenger before surrendering to the Egyptian authorities two days later.
[2] Andrew Faulds (born 1923), Labour MP 1966–97.

The President responded that the operation would be limited to clearly defined targets related to terrorism, and that every effort would be made to minimize collateral damage. He made it clear that, for the reasons I indicated yesterday, he regarded the use of F1-11 aircraft from bases in the United Kingdom as essential. There are, I understand, no other F1-11s stationed in Europe. Had we refused permission for the use of those aircraft, the United States operation would still have taken place; but more lives would probably have been lost, both on the ground and in the air.

It has been suggested that, as a result of further Libyan terrorism, the United States might feel constrained to act again. I earnestly hope that such a contingency will not arise. But in my exchanges with the President I reserved the position of the United Kingdom on any question of further action which might be more general or less clearly directed against terrorism.

Mr Faulds: Will the right honourable lady give way?

The Prime Minister: No. This point is particularly important.

Moreover, it is clearly understood between President Reagan and myself that, if there were any questions of using United States aircraft based in this country in a further action, that would be the subject of a new approach to the United Kingdom under the joint-consultation arrangements. Many honourable Members have questioned whether the United States action will be effective in stopping terrorism –

Mr Faulds: Will the right honourable lady give way on that point?

The Prime Minister: Many honourable Members –

Mr Faulds: (Rose)

Mr Speaker: Order. The honourable gentleman knows that he must resume his seat if the Prime Minister does not give way.

The Prime Minister: Many honourable Members have questioned whether the United States action will be effective in stopping terrorism or will instead have the effect of quickening the cycle of violence in the Middle East. Let us remember that the violence began long ago. It has already taken a great many lives. It has not been so much a cycle of violence as a one-sided campaign of killing and maiming by ruthless terrorists, many with close connections with Libya. The response of the countries whose citizens have been attacked has not so far stopped that campaign.

Mr Wareing: Will the Prime Minister give way on that point?

The Prime Minister: I will give way to the honourable gentleman later. Please may I continue with this point?

Mr Faulds: Why not give way to me?

The Prime Minister: Indeed, one has to ask whether it has not been the failure to act in self-defence that has encouraged state-sponsored terrorism. Firm and decisive action may make those who continue to practise terrorism as a policy think again. I give way to the honourable Member for Liverpool West Derby [Mr Wareing].

Mr Wareing: Would the Prime Minister agree that if her argument is correct we should all be feeling very much safer? Can she therefore explain why, for the first time since the early days of my election to the House, I was asked this morning – as all honourable Members have been asked – for my pass, and my car was searched in order to ensure our safety? Am I to feel safe now as a result of this attack?

The Prime Minister: I would have hoped that the honourable gentleman would see the wisdom of taking heightened precautions. It would have been folly not to do so.

It has also been suggested that the United States action will only build up Colonel Gaddafi's prestige and support in the Arab world. In the very short term, one must expect statements of support for Libya from other Arab countries – although one is entitled to ask how profound or durable that support will be. But moderate Arab Governments, indeed moderate Governments everywhere, have nothing to gain from seeing Colonel Gaddafi build up power and influence by persisting in policies of violence and terror. Their interest, like ours, lies in seeing the problems of the Middle East solved by peaceful negotiation, a negotiation whose chances of success will be much enhanced if terrorism can be defeated.

Mr Alan Beith[1] (Berwick-upon-Tweed): (Rose)

The Prime Minister: I shall not give way now.

Let me emphasize one very important point. A peaceful settlement of the Arab–Israel question remains our policy, and we shall continue to seek ways forward with moderate Arab Governments. Indeed, I shall be seeing King Hussein[2] later this week to discuss this very matter.

Mr Beith: To what extent does the Prime Minister think that Colonel Gaddafi's capacity to mount attacks of terrorism has been reduced by the measures taken by the United States?

The Prime Minister: I believe that his capacity and the will of the people to do so have been impaired by the actions that have been taken.

The United States is our greatest ally. It is the foundation of the Alliance which has preserved our security and peace for more than a

---

[1] Alan Beith (born 1943), Liberal MP 1973–88; Liberal Democrat MP 1988–.

[2] Hussein ibn Talal (born 1935), King of Jordan 1952–.

generation. In defence of liberty, our liberty as well as its own, the United States maintains in Western Europe 330,000 servicemen. That is more than the whole of Britain's regular forces. The United States gave us unstinting help when we needed it in the South Atlantic four years ago.

The growing threat of international terrorism is not directed solely at the United States. We in the United Kingdom have also long been in the front line. To overcome the threat is in the vital interests of all countries founded upon freedom and the rule of law. Terrorism exploits the natural reluctance of a free society to defend itself, in the last resort, with arms. Terrorism thrives on appeasement. Of course, we shall continue to make every effort to defeat it by political means. But in this case that was not enough. The time had come for action. The United States took it. Its decision was justified, and, as friends and allies, we support it.

30

Speech to the Conservative Party Conference, Bournemouth, 10 October 1986

The 1986 Conservative Party Conference at Bournemouth was one of the few such events which, by common consent, made a real political difference. Carefully prepared under Party Chairman Norman Tebbit's direction in order to emphasize the Government's achievements and sense of direction, the Conference helped give the Conservative Party momentum for the following year's general election victory. Indeed, so many new announcements had been made in the course of the Conference week that there seemed a danger that the Prime Minister's own speech might be overshadowed.

But from the moment when Mrs Thatcher appeared on the platform, wearing what she called 'the rose of England', in contrast to the Labour Party's rose of socialism which had tactfully replaced the Red Flag as its symbol, the speech was one of her triumphs. Although this was a time of rising prosperity, she chose to emphasize the moral not just the material arguments for Conservative policies. Much of the speech is also a withering attack on Neil Kinnock's defence policies, on which Labour would prove highly vulnerable at the forthcoming election.

Mr President, this week at Bournemouth, we've had a most responsible Conference: the Conference of a Party which was the last Government, is the present Government, and will be the next Government. We have heard from Ministers a series of forward-looking policies which are shaping the future of our country. And not only from Ministers, but from the body of the hall has come speech after speech of advice, encouragement and commitment.

We are a Party which knows what it stands for and what it seeks to achieve. We are a Party which honours the past that we may build for the future.

Last week, at Blackpool, the Labour Party made the bogus claim that it was 'putting people first'.[1] 'Putting *people* first'? Last week Labour voted for the state to renationalize British Telecom and British Gas, regardless of the millions of people who have been able to own shares for the first time in their lives.

'Putting *people* first'? They voted to stop the existing right to buy council houses, a policy which would kill the hopes and dreams of so many families.

Labour may say they put people first; but their Conference voted to put government first, and that means putting people last.

What the Labour Party of today wants is: housing – municipalized; industry – nationalized; the police service – politicized; the judiciary – radicalized; union membership – tyrannized; and above all – and most serious of all – our defences neutralized.

Never! Not in Britain.

We have two other Oppositions who have recently held their conferences, the Liberals and the SDP. Where they're not divided they're vague, and where they're not vague they're divided. At the moment they appear to be engaged in a confused squabble about whether or not Polaris should be abandoned, or replaced, or renewed, or re-examined. And if so, when; and how; and possibly why.[2] If they can't agree on the defence of our country, they can't agree on anything. Where Labour has its Militant Tendency, they have their muddled tendency. I'll have rather more to say about defence later.

Conservative Morality

But just now I want to speak about Conservative policies, policies which spring from deeply held beliefs. The charge is sometimes made that our policies are only concerned with money and efficiency. I am the first to acknowledge that morality is not and never has been the monopoly of any one party. Nor do we claim that it is. But we do claim that it is the foundation of our policies.

Why are we Conservatives so opposed to inflation? Only because it puts up prices? No; because it destroys the value of people's savings.

[1] 'Putting People First' was the slogan of the Labour Party Conference held at Blackpool from 28 September to 3 October 1986.
[2] Alliance defence policy was thrown into disarray on 24 September 1986 when the Liberal Party Conference at Eastbourne passed a resolution in favour of non-nuclear defence, while the SDP explicitly rejected unilateral disarmament.

Because it destroys jobs, and with it people's hopes. That's what the fight against inflation is all about.

Why have we limited the power of trade unions? Only to improve productivity? No; because trade union members want to be protected from intimidation and to go about their daily lives in peace – like everyone else in the land.

Why have we allowed people to buy shares in nationalized industries? Only to improve efficiency? No; to spread the nation's wealth among as many people as possible.

Why are we setting up new kinds of schools in our towns and cities? To create privilege? No; to give families in some of our inner cities greater choice in the education of their children.[1] A choice denied them by their Labour councils.

Enlarging choice is rooted in our Conservative tradition. Without choice, talk of morality is an idle and an empty thing.

Britain's Industrial Future

Mr President, the theme of our Conference this week is 'The Next Move Forward'. We have achieved a lot in seven short years. But there is still a great deal to be done for our country.

The whole industrial world, not just Britain, is seeing change at a speed that our forebears never contemplated, much of it due to new technology. Old industries are declining. New ones are taking their place. Traditional jobs are being taken over by computers. People are choosing to spend their money in new ways: leisure, pleasure, sport and travel. All these are big business today. It would be foolish to pretend that this transition can be accomplished without problems. But it would be equally foolish to pretend that a country like Britain, which is so heavily dependent on trade with others, can somehow ignore what is happening in the rest of the world; can behave as if these great events have nothing to do with us; can resist change.

Yet that is exactly what Labour proposes to do: they want to put back the clock and set back the country. Back to state direction and control. Back to the old levels of overmanning. Back to the old inefficiency. Back to making life difficult for the very people on whom the future of Britain

---

[1] In 1986 the Department of Education announced a new type of secondary school, the City Technology College, to be financed jointly by industry and the state.

depends – the wealth creators, the scientists, the engineers, the designers, the managers, the inventors – all those on whom we rely to create the industries and jobs of the future.

What supreme folly. It defies all common sense.

Jobs

As do those Labour policies which, far from putting people first, would put them out of jobs. The prospects of young people would be blighted by Labour's minimum wage policy, because people could not then afford to employ them and give them a start in life. A quarter of a million jobs could be at risk. Many thousands of jobs would go from closing down American nuclear bases. Labour want sanctions against South Africa. Tens of thousands of people could lose their jobs in Britain – quite apart from the devastating consequences for black South Africans. Out would go jobs at existing nuclear power stations. Whatever happened to Harold Wilson's 'white heat of technological revolution'? On top of all this, jobs would also suffer as would-be investors in Britain took one look at Labour and decided to set up elsewhere. Labour say they would create jobs. But those policies would destroy jobs.

This Government has created the climate that's produced a million extra jobs over the past three years. Here in Britain, it is encouraging that more of the population are in work than in Italy, or France, or Germany. Nevertheless, as you heard yesterday, more has to be done, and is being done. Meanwhile, no other country in Europe can rival our present range of help for people to train, retrain and find jobs. And I would like just to say, Mr President: training is not a palliative for unemployment. Training will play an ever larger part in our whole industrial life. For only modern, efficient industry and commerce will produce the jobs our people need.

Popular Capitalism

Our opponents would have us believe that all problems can be solved by state intervention. But Governments should not run business. Indeed, the weakness of the case for state ownership has become all too apparent. For state planners do not have to suffer the consequences of their mistakes. It's the taxpayers who have to pick up the bill.

This Government has rolled back the frontiers of the state, and will roll them back still further. So popular is our policy that it's being taken up all over the world. From France to the Philippines, from Jamaica to Japan, from Malaysia to Mexico, from Sri Lanka to Singapore, privatization is on the move: there's even a special Oriental version in China. The policies we have pioneered are catching on in country after country. We Conservatives believe in popular capitalism, believe in a property-owning democracy. And it works!

Power to the People

In Scotland recently, I was present at the sale of the millionth council house: to a lovely family with two children, who can at last call their home their own. Now let's go for the second million! And what's more, millions have already become shareholders. And soon there will be opportunities for millions more, in British Gas, British Airways, British Airports and Rolls-Royce.[1] Who says we've run out of steam? We're in our prime!

The great political reform of the last century was to enable more and more people to have a vote. Now the great Tory reform of this century is to enable more and more people to own property. Popular capitalism is nothing less than a crusade to enfranchise the many in the economic life of the nation. We Conservatives are returning power to the people. That is the way to one nation, one people.

Return of National Pride

Mr President, you may have noticed there are many people who just can't bear good news. It's a sort of infection of the spirit, and there's a lot of it about. In the eyes of these hand-wringing merchants of gloom and despondency, everything that Britain does is wrong. Any setback, however small, any little difficulty, however local, is seen as incontrovertible proof that the situation is hopeless.

Their favourite word is 'crisis'. It's a crisis when the price of oil goes up, and a crisis when the price of oil comes down. It's a crisis if you

---

[1] British Gas and the British Airports Authority were privatized in 1986, British Airways and Rolls-Royce in 1987.

don't build new roads, it's a crisis when you do. It's a crisis if Nissan does not come here, and it's a crisis when it does.[1] 'It's being so cheerful as keeps 'em going.'[2] What a rotten time these people must have, running round running everything down.

Especially when there's so much to be proud of. Inflation at its lowest level for twenty years. The basic rate of tax at its lowest level for forty years.[3] The number of strikes at its lowest level for fifty years. The great advances in science and industry. The achievement of millions of our people in creating new enterprises and new jobs. The outstanding performance of the arts and music and entertainment worlds. And the triumphs of our sportsmen and women. They all do Britain proud. And we are mighty proud of them.

Conservatives Care

Our opponents, having lost the political argument, try another tack. They try to convey the impression that we don't care.

So let's take a close look at those who make this charge. They're the ones who supported and maintained Mr Scargill's[4] coal strike for a whole year, hoping to deprive industry, homes and pensioners of power, heat and light. They're the ones who supported the strike in the Health Service which lengthened the waiting time for operations, just when we were getting it down.[5] They're the ones who supported the teachers' dispute which disrupted our children's education.[6] They are those Labour Councillors who constantly accuse the police of provocation when they deal with violent crime and drugs in the worst areas of our inner cities.

---

[1] The Japanese car manufacturer Nissan announced plans to build an assembly plant in Britain on 1 February 1984. The factory opened in Sunderland in 1986.
[2] 'It's being so cheerful as keeps me going' was the catchphrase of the lugubrious comedy character 'Mona Lott' in the BBC radio programme *ITMA* (1939–49).
[3] The 1986 Budget reduced the basic rate of income tax to 29 per cent.
[4] Arthur Scargill (born 1938), President of the National Union of Mineworkers 1981–.
[5] National Health Service workers belonging to the Confederation of Health Service Employees and the National Union of Public Employees took industrial action from May to December 1982 in support of a 12 per cent pay claim. 130,000 operations had to be cancelled.
[6] Two teaching unions, the NUT and NAS/UWT, took selective industrial action from 26 February 1985 in a dispute over pay and conditions which was to last over two years.

Mr President, we're not going to take any lessons in caring from people with that sort of record.

We care profoundly about the right of people to be protected against crime, hooliganism and the evil of drugs. The mugger, the rapist, the drug trafficker, the terrorist – all must suffer the full rigour of the law. And that's why this Party and this Government consistently back the police and the courts of law, in Britain and Northern Ireland. For without the rule of law, there can be no liberty.

It's because we care deeply about the Health Service that we've launched the biggest hospital building programme in this country's history.

Statistics tell only part of the story. But this Government is devoting more resources of all kinds to the Health Service than any previous Government. Over the past year or so, I've visited five hospitals. In the north-west – at Barrow in Furness – I visited the first new hospital in that district since the creation of the Health Service forty years ago. In the north-east, another splendid new hospital, at North Tyneside, with the most wonderful maternity unit and children's wards. Just north of London I went round St Albans' Hospital where new wards have been opened and new buildings are under way. I visited the famous Elizabeth Garrett Anderson Hospital for Women, which this Government saved. The service it provides is very special and greatly appreciated. And then last week I went back to the Royal Sussex County Hospital in Brighton, to open the new renal unit. Many of us have cause to be very thankful for that Brighton Hospital. Everywhere patients were loud in their praise of the treatment they received from doctors and nurses whose devotion and skill we all admire.

This Government's record on the Health Service is a fine one. We're proud of it, and we must see to it that people know how much we've done.

Of course, there are problems still to be solved. The fact that there's no waiting list in one area does not help you if you have to wait for an operation in your area. It doesn't help if there's a new hospital going up somewhere else, but not where you'd really like it. We are tackling these problems. And we shall go on doing so, because our commitment to the National Health Service is second to none. We've made great progress already. The debate we had on Wednesday, with its telling contributions from nurses and doctors in the Health Service, was enormously helpful to us. It's our purpose to work together and to continue steadily to improve the services that are provided in hospital and community alike. This is Conservatives putting care into action.

And we care deeply that retired people should never again see their hard-earned savings decimated by runaway inflation. For example, take the pensioner who retired in 1963 with £1,000 of savings. Twenty years later, in 1983, it was only worth £160. That is why we will never relent in the battle against inflation. It has to be fought and won every year.

We care passionately about the education of our children. Time and again we hear three basic messages: bring back the three Rs into our schools; bring back relevance into the curriculum; and bring back discipline into our classrooms.

The fact is that education at all levels – teachers, training colleges, administrators – has been infiltrated by a permissive philosophy of self-expression. And we are now reaping the consequences which, for some children, have been disastrous.

Money by itself will not solve this problem. Money will not raise standards. But, by giving parents greater freedom to choose, by allowing head teachers greater control in their school, by laying down national standards of syllabus and attainment, I am confident that we can really improve the quality of education. Improve it not just in the twenty new schools but in every school in the land. And we'll back every teacher, head teacher and administrator who shares these ideals.

Defence

Mr President, we care most of all about our country's security. The defence of the realm transcends all other issues. It is the foremost responsibility of any Government and any Prime Minister.

For forty years, every Government of this country, of every political persuasion, has understood the need for strong defences: by maintaining and modernizing Britain's independent nuclear deterrent; by membership of the NATO Alliance, an alliance based on nuclear deterrence; and by accepting, and bearing in full, the obligations which membership brings. All this was common ground.

Last week, Mr President, the Labour Party abandoned that ground. In a decision of the utmost gravity, Labour voted to give up Britain's independent nuclear deterrent unilaterally. Labour would also require the United States to remove its nuclear weapons from our soil and to close down its nuclear bases: weapons and bases which are vital, not only for Britain's defence, but for the defence of the entire Atlantic Alliance. Furthermore, Labour would remove Britain altogether from the protection of America's nuclear umbrella, leaving us totally unable to deter a nuclear attack. For you cannot deter, with conventional weapons, an enemy which has, and could threaten to use, nuclear weapons. Exposed to the threat of nuclear blackmail, there would be no option but surrender. Labour's defence policy – though 'defence' is scarcely the word – is an absolute break with the defence policy of every British Government since the Second World War.

Let there be no doubt about the gravity of that decision. You cannot be a loyal member of NATO while disavowing its fundamental strategy. A Labour Britain would be a neutralist Britain. It would be the greatest gain for the Soviet Union in forty years. And they would have got it without firing a shot.

I believe this total reversal of Labour's policy for the defence of our country will have come as a shock to many of Labour's traditional supporters. It was Labour's Nye Bevan who warned his party against 'going naked into the conference chamber'. It was Labour's Hugh Gaitskell who promised the country to 'fight, fight and fight again' against the unilateral disarmers in his own party. That fight was continued by his successors.

Today the fight is over. The present leadership are the unilateral disarmers. The Labour Party of Attlee, of Gaitskell, of Wilson is dead. And no one has more surely killed it than the present leader of the Labour Party.[1] There are some policies which can be reversed. But weapon development and production takes years and years. Moreover, by repudiating NATO's nuclear strategy Labour would fatally weaken the Atlantic Alliance and the United States's commitment to Europe's defence. The damage caused by Labour's policies would be irrevocable. Not only present but future generations would be at risk.

Of course, there are fears about the terrible destructive power of nuclear weapons. But it is the balance of nuclear forces which has preserved the peace for forty years in a Europe which twice in the previous thirty years tore itself to pieces. Preserved peace not only from nuclear war, but from conventional war in Europe as well. And it has saved the young people of two generations from being called up to fight as their parents and grandparents were. As Prime Minister, I could not remove that protection from the lives of present and future generations.

Let every nation know that Conservative Governments, now and in

---

[1] Neil Kinnock (born 1942), Labour MP 1970–95; Leader of the Labour Party 1983–92; Member of the European Commission 1995–.

the future, will keep Britain's obligations to its allies. The freedom of all its citizens and the good name of our country depend upon it.

This weekend, President Reagan and Mr Gorbachev are meeting in Reykjavik.[1] Does anyone imagine that Mr Gorbachev would be prepared to talk at all if the West had already disarmed? It is the strength and unity of the West which has brought the Russians to the negotiating table.

The policy of Her Majesty's Opposition is a policy that would help our enemies and harm our friends. It totally misjudges the character of the British people.

After the Liberal Party Conference, after the SDP Conference, after the Labour Party Conference, there is now only one party in this country with an effective policy for the defence of the realm. That party is the Conservative Party.

Our Vision

Mr President, throughout this Conference we have heard of the great achievements of the last seven years. Their very success now makes possible the Next Moves Forward, which have been set out this week. And we shall complete the manifesto for the next election – within the next eighteen months. That manifesto will be a programme for further bold and radical steps in keeping with our most deeply held beliefs. We do our best for our country when we are true to our convictions.

As we look forward to the next century, we have a vision of the society we wish to see, the vision we all serve.

We want to see a Britain where there is an ever-widening spread of ownership, with the independence and dignity it brings. A Britain which takes care of the weak in their time of need.

We want to see a Britain where the spirit of enterprise is strong enough to conquer unemployment north and south. A Britain in which the attitude of 'them and us' has disappeared from our lives.

We want to see a Britain whose schools are a source of pride and

---

[1] Mikhail Gorbachev (born 1931), Soviet leader. General Secretary of the Communist Party 1985–91; President of the Presidium of the Supreme Soviet 1988–90; Executive President 1990–91. At the Reykjavik Summit of 11–12 October 1986, Gorbachev offered to eliminate strategic nuclear weapons within ten years if the USA effectively abandoned the Strategic Defence Initiative. This President Reagan refused to do.

where education brings out the best in every child. A Britain where excellence and effort are valued and honoured.

We want to see a Britain where our streets are free from fear, day and night.

And above all, we want to see a Britain which is respected and trusted in the world – which values the great benefits of living in a free society, and is determined to defend them.

Mr President, our duty is to safeguard our country's interests, and to be reliable friends and allies. The failure of the other parties to measure up to what is needed places an awesome responsibility upon us. I believe that we have an historic duty to discharge that responsibility and to carry into the future all that is best and unique in Britain. I believe that our Party is uniquely equipped to do it. I believe the interests of Britain can now only be served by a third Conservative victory.

31

Speech to the Conservative Central Council, Torquay, 21 March 1987

When Mrs Thatcher addressed the Central Council in Torquay on Saturday 21 March 1987, the political world was already in a frenzy of election fever. Within the Conservative Party work had been under way since the previous year on election planning. The writing of the manifesto – on this occasion being prepared under Mrs Thatcher's direct supervision – had begun. Although no decision had been made for a summer election, circumstances looked increasingly favourable for one. The main risk to Conservative re-election appeared to be the defection of 'soft' Tory support to the Liberal–SDP Alliance: hence the pointed criticism of the latter in Mrs Thatcher's speech. More seriously, the speech looks forward to the Prime Minister's imminent visit to Moscow. The attacks on communism and the doubts voiced in the speech about Soviet intentions were such that President Gorbachev would tell her later that on reading them he had wondered whether to withdraw the invitation.

Socialism has Failed

Madam Chairman, may I begin with a public service announcement? I don't know the date of the next election, and neither does anyone else.

What I do know is that whenever that election is declared, this Government and this Party will enter the lists with a greater record of achievement and success than any Government for many a long year. And that record of success is all the more impressive when set against the miserable inheritance that the last Labour Government bequeathed to us: an economy bedevilled by inflation which decimated people's savings; a society dictated to, and dominated by, a handful of trade union leaders; defence forces starved of resources and equipment; living standards further and further behind our European competitors; and, pervading all, a sense of hopelessness and national decline.

Socialism has failed the British people. But in its long years of power, the socialist dogma – of dependence on the state, of a comfortable subservience to the bureaucrat in town hall and Whitehall – had bitten deep into the national spirit. And no wonder. If you were a trade unionist, you were subject to the rule of militants by an undemocratic rulebook. If you were building up a business, or saving for the future, you were hit by red tape and high taxes. And if, like so many of our people, you lived in a council house, you had no right to buy your own home – and many Labour local authorities made jolly sure you didn't.

Socialists, in effect, offered the British people a deal. If you were content not to strive, not to seek a better chance for your children, not to provide for your own future, not to question the *diktat* of your trade union boss, you were patted on the head. But if you struggled, against all the odds, to improve your own and your family's prospects, you were burdened with taxes, pettifogging regulations, and egalitarian envy.

Is it altogether surprising that, in the last years of the seventies, Britain sank into a slough of despond and dependency? This Britain which, only forty years before, had rescued Europe from tyranny.

Fresh Start

Well, eight years ago we made a fresh start. Today, eight years later, Britain is back in the first division. In economic growth and productivity, we are top of the league of major European countries. We have created the wealth to bring about a big improvement in our social services. And our people enjoy the highest standard of living in our history. What's more, this country is listened to abroad with a new respect.

The opposition parties – and not a few pundits – predicted that, after winning through to success, we would throw it all away and try to buy votes with an irresponsible Budget. Well, not for the first time, they were wrong. We don't buy votes – we earn them. We've earned them this week by sticking to the policies of honest money and personal incentives we've pursued from the beginning. This has made it possible in one and the same financial year to increase spending by £4¾ billion on education, health and other public services; to cut borrowing by £3 billion; and to reduce income tax by £2½ billion.

Madam Chairman, that's a hat-trick.

Electioneering? No! Listen to the newspapers. The *Daily Telegraph*: a 'cautious Budget'. The *Independent*: the 'Budget goes for caution'. The *Financial Times*: 'Lawson opts for prudence'. And the *Sun*, with glorious abandon: 'What a lot you got.'

In politics, a budget that is both responsible and popular is something of a curiosity. It was possible only because, slowly but surely, Britain has built its strongest economy for a generation. Don't imagine that this was achieved easily. And don't get the idea that we received much help from opposition parties. Quite the reverse. While this Government was steadily reducing inflation by restoring sound finance, Labour, Liberals and the Social Democrats carped and criticized all the way. In 1981 they had a supporting chorus of 364 economists.[1] This week, it's down to a quintet. And they weren't exactly in tune with the times.

Lib–Lab–SDP

Labour's opposition is predictable enough. It has declined from a great party to a band of zealots which is instinctively hostile to the hopes and dreams of ordinary people. If you want to own your council house, or buy shares in British Telecom or British Gas or British Airways, or oppose the closed shop, Labour is against you. More and more people are waking up to Labour's new extremism.

And what of the Labour Party in exile? By which, of course, I mean the Liberals and the SDP. In the last year or so, in the House of Commons, they have voted eight times more often with Labour than with us. Not much doubt where *their* sympathies lie. Mind you, they haven't changed. Ten years ago, at the peak of trade union power, the Liberals formed the Lib–Lab pact to keep Labour in power.[2] And when this was going on, where were the founders of the SDP? Sitting round Labour's Cabinet table: Mrs Shirley Williams[3] beside Mr Michael Foot,

---

[1] On 30 March 1981, 364 academic economists published a letter in *The Times* calling on the Government to reject monetarism and stop deflating demand.

[2] On 23 March 1977, Liberal MPs agreed to help the Labour Government avoid defeat in Parliament in return for consultation about policy. The pact lasted until the end of the 1978 session.

[3] Shirley Williams (born 1930), Baroness Williams of Crosby 1993. Labour MP 1964–79; Prices and Consumer Protection Secretary 1974–76; Education Secretary 1976–79; Social Democrat MP 1981–83; President of the SDP 1982–87.

Mr William Rodgers[1] next to Mr Denis Healey, and Dr David Owen? – alongside Mr Tony Benn. For the British people that was the Winter of Discontent. For David Steel, David Owen, Shirley Williams, Bill Rodgers, not to mention Roy Jenkins in Brussels, it was the good old days.

I gather at the next election, they are hoping to be asked to give us an encore – the two Davids[2] in that ever-popular musical delight: 'Don't tell my mother I'm half of a horse in a panto'. I'm told Mr Steel has been rehearsing for it this very week.

The Liberals have always put Labour in. They did it in 1924, in 1929, in 1974 and in 1977. And given half a chance they'd do it again. This week, once again, they united against income tax cuts for people like factory workers, teachers, policemen and nurses; and don't forget, many, many pensioners pay income tax too.

The message of all this is clear. There are three types of socialism on offer: the full-blooded Labour variety; the half-hearted Social Democrat variety; and the half-baked Liberal variety.

The Morality of Tax Cuts

We've heard other siren voices in recent weeks. 'Prime Minister,' they sing, 'whatever you do, don't cut taxes, because most people don't need a boost to their standard of living: increase public spending instead, because that creates jobs.'

Madam Chairman, I'm sure you've identified the two fallacies in that argument. First, we've already increased public spending this year – by £4¾ billion. We announced it last autumn. Now the opposition parties want to spend that same money a second, and maybe a third time.

The second mistake is to ignore the fact that cutting taxes itself creates jobs. The truth is that, unlike increased public spending, income tax cuts reward hard work; they develop enterprise; and they stimulate wealth creation. That is why taxes are being cut around the world – especially in Europe and the United States.

It is with these policies, Madam Chairman, that a million new jobs

---

[1] William Rodgers (born 1928), Baron Rodgers of Quarry Bank 1992. Labour MP 1962–81; Transport Secretary 1976–79; Social Democrat MP 1981–83; Vice-President of the SDP 1982–87.
[2] The dual leadership of the SDP–Liberal Alliance, David Owen and David Steel.

have been created here in Britain since 1983. And this week, the nation's confidence has been boosted by the news that unemployment has been falling steadily for the past seven months. This month, we saw the biggest seasonally adjusted fall on record – a fall in unemployment in every region of the country. And prospects for the coming months are good.

But we haven't forgotten those still without a job. Since 1979, this Government has spent £10,000 million on employment and training measures. The fact is, we have done more than any other country in Europe. And David Young has a succession of visitors asking how we do it.

Inner Cities

Despite our economic success, there are still problems to be solved. Look for instance at the inner cities. We have been asked to have 'Faith in our Cities'.[1] We do have faith in our cities. But not always in some of the people who run them: those who talk more about social engineering than about tackling the problems; those who care more about sexual propaganda than helping children read and write; those who seem more concerned with fighting the police than with fighting crime.

How can such people claim to build prosperous cities? When they need more jobs, but drive out small businesses. When they fail to collect rents, but leave houses in disrepair. When they send rates soaring, but spend vast sums on ridiculous projects.

No wonder Robert Kilroy-Silk,[2] who was Labour MP for Knowsley, Liverpool until last year, has said: 'The militants and their ilk in Liverpool are the biggest deterrents to job creation on Merseyside that there have ever been. Dozens of times in the last few years I have tried fruitlessly to persuade companies that I knew were looking for sites for new plants, to locate on Merseyside and in Knowsley, but each time the decision went against us, because of their perception of our militancy.'

Of course, money is needed to solve some of the inner city problems. If, in 1979, we'd said we were going to provide an extra £1 billion for inner cities, people would have thought it would go a long way to solving the problem. In fact, we've provided not £1 billion but over £2 billion. But the problems are still there.

[1] This is an oblique reference to *Faith in the City*, a controversial Church of England report on inner city deprivation published in December 1985.
[2] Robert Kilroy-Silk (born 1942), Labour MP 1974–86.

More public money is powerless in the face of destructive local authorities. If inner cities are once again to be centres of commerce and enterprise, rivalling the vitality of our great cities of the last century, they need more than public spending. They need local leadership committed to enterprise. They need lower rates. They need quicker disposal of surplus land. They need schools of excellence and opportunity open to people of all backgrounds. But without local leadership dedicated to enterprise and renewal, money can do little.

Education

The same is true of education. Ideally, education should give us both the vision of a better life, and the workaday skills to attain it. This Government has a fine record in providing the resources to achieve this goal. More money is being spent per pupil than ever before. More money is being spent on teachers, who are better qualified than ever before. There are more teachers in proportion to pupils than ever before. And more young people are entering higher education than ever before. And in many schools, children are receiving an excellent education. But elsewhere, despite all the extra resources, some pupils still leave school unable to read or write properly or do simple mathematics.

Our task is to ensure that every child is taught certain basic subjects, and is tested on them so that we not only know what pupils should learn, but whether they're learning it.[1] Of course, this still leaves ample room for the more creative side of teaching. But how can a child really profit from that unless he has mastered the basic skills?

Madam Chairman, no one has a greater incentive than parents to see that the school is meeting the needs of their child. That's why our recent legislation involves parents more and more in the life and running of schools. Parents don't want their children banned from taking part in competitive games. Parents don't want what is called 'positive images for gays' being forced on innocent children. Parents don't want their children indoctrinated by Labour's so-called 'peace studies'.

They send them to school for what school is all about – a good education. We must revive that commitment in all state schools – excellence, not just for the few, but for all.

[1] On 24 July 1987 Education Secretary Kenneth Baker announced plans to test schoolchildren at the ages of seven, eleven and fourteen. The first compulsory National Curriculum tests (for seven-year-olds) were held in 1991.

As regards the teachers' dispute, let me say just this: the Government's pay offer to teachers – a 25 per cent increase over eighteen months – is more than generous.[1] We hope that, in response, the teachers will adhere to high standards of professionalism. Above all, it is the children who should and must come first.

Law and Order

Madam Chairman, people have long regarded Conservatives as the Party of law and order. They are right. This Government has increased the forces of law and order; increased police manpower by 16,300 since 1979; increased maximum sentences to life imprisonment for crimes like attempted rape and drug trafficking; encouraged crime prevention; helped set up more than eighteen thousand Neighbourhood Watch schemes[2] – upholding the law cannot be left just to the police and courts.

Thank goodness we have a Conservative Government to give support to the police and the courts. Take a look at a whole batch of Labour authorities which have gone out of their way to undermine the police. In some of these areas, Labour councils are engaged not in crime prevention, but in police prevention.

Labour's leadership does little to restrain these hard-left councils. And indeed, the Labour Party at Westminster is hardly an example. In one day last month, Labour voted against the Prevention of Terrorism Act,[3] an Act designed to help the police catch terrorists; voted against our proposal to refer lenient sentences to the Court of Appeal; voted against life imprisonment for possession of a firearm with intent to commit a crime. Scarcely the way to win the war against crime and terrorism.

Madam Chairman, this Government has shown its determination to defeat the criminal. A great deal has been done. But, as the crime figures reminded us, the battle is far from won – and who can forget the horrific

[1] In March 1987, the Teachers' Pay and Conditions Act 1987 empowered the Education Secretary to impose a pay settlement, though sporadic strikes continued till the summer.
[2] In a Neighbourhood Watch scheme, groups of residents (under the supervision of the police) agree to increase watchfulness in order to prevent crimes in their local area. The first such scheme in Britain started in Cheshire in 1982.
[3] The Prevention of Terrorism (Temporary Provisions) Act, passed in November 1974 and renewed annually, proscribes terrorist organizations, allows terrorist suspects to be held for five days without charge, and gives power to exclude certain persons from mainland Britain.

murder case before the courts this week?[1] The Government has already planned for further increases in police manpower for this coming year. We shall fight on relentlessly until safety is restored to our streets and security to our homes and families.

Defence and Moscow Visit

Madam Chairman, a week today I leave on my visit to the Soviet Union, the first official visit by a British Prime Minister for twelve years. It takes place at an interesting time. We have seen in Mr Gorbachev's speeches a clear admission that the communist system is not working. Far from enabling the Soviet Union to catch up with the West, it is falling further behind. We hear new language being used by their leaders. Words which we recognize like 'openness' and 'democratization'. But do they have the same meaning for them as they do for us?

Some of those who have been imprisoned for their political and religious beliefs have been released. We welcome that. But many more remain in prison or are refused permission to emigrate. We want to see them free, or reunited with their families abroad, if that is what they choose. We shall welcome any movement towards a more humane society in the Soviet Union; towards a society which respects basic human rights.

With the signs that the Soviet Union is at last prepared to negotiate seriously on the reduction of nuclear weapons, we see the strength and resolve of the West beginning to reap its reward. It was the deployment of Cruise and Pershing missiles which brought the Russians back to the negotiating table. The lesson is clear: firmness pays; strength is the surest foundation on which to work for peace.

The people who have not learned that lesson are the Labour Party. They – and the Liberals *and* the SDP – voted in the House of Commons against the deployment of Cruise. The Leader of the Opposition went trotting off to Moscow to lay our independent nuclear deterrent like a bone at Mr Gorbachev's feet.[2] And what did his Party do to

---

[1] At the Old Bailey on 19 March 1987, three men were convicted of the murder of PC Keith Blakelock during the Tottenham riots in 1985.

[2] Neil Kinnock visited the USSR from 21 to 27 November 1984. He was told – in fact by the then Soviet leader, Konstantin Chernenko, not Gorbachev – that if a future Labour Government adopted non-nuclear defence the USSR would dismantle some missiles and aim others away from Britain.

Mr Callaghan, when he dared to disagree?[1] One of his closest former colleagues dismissed him as 'old'. Nothing could show more clearly that to be acceptable in today's Labour Party, you have to be wholeheartedly committed to the CND[2] approach of one-sided disarmament.

The Conservative Party is not prepared to take risks with Britain's security. Nuclear weapons are vital to our defence. Conventional weapons have not succeeded in deterring war. Nuclear weapons have prevented not only nuclear war, but conventional war as well. They have kept the peace in Europe for over forty years.

Peace with freedom and justice is our dearest wish – peace which provides security for both East and West; which will ensure that the younger generation are not called up to fight as their parents and grandparents were. When I go to Moscow to meet Mr Gorbachev next week, my goal will be a peace based *not* on illusion or surrender, but on realism and strength.

But you can't have peace by a declaration of intent. Peace needs confidence and trust between countries and peoples. Peace means an end to the killing in Cambodia, an end to the slaughter in Afghanistan. It means honouring the obligations which the Soviet Union freely accepted in the Helsinki Final Act in 1975 to allow free movement of people and ideas and other basic human rights. If we could have that, it would be the best news the world has known for a long time. So, Madam Chairman, we shall reach our judgements not on words, not on intentions, not on promises; but on actions and on results.

That is the only sure way. And I would not expect Mr Gorbachev to take any different attitude in dealing with us.

The Conservative Vision

Of course, when I go to Moscow, I shall be representing a very different kind of country from that of Mr Gorbachev – and indeed, Britain is now a very different country from that represented by Harold Wilson in 1975. Not so long ago, millions of families thought that they would

---

[1] In a speech in Cardiff on 25 May 1983, James Callaghan rejected the whole idea of unilateral nuclear disarmament. 'Before negotiations begin and unless we reach a satisfactory agreement,' he said, 'Britain and the West should not give up these weapons for nothing in return.'

[2] The Campaign for Nuclear Disarmament was founded in 1955 to mobilize opposition to Britain's independent nuclear deterrent and atomic weapons in general.

never be able to own their own home. Not so long ago, most people thought that they would never have the chance to own shares. What seemed impossible then is happening now. Today more families have a personal stake in the property of Britain than ever before in our history.

We believe that, given opportunity, offered the chance, the human spirit will find a better path than the state could ever devise. You cannot build a successful country without believing that the majority of people will use their talents wisely. One of the gulfs between the socialists and ourselves is this essential faith in the individual.

Conservatives are not in the business of government to forge a standardized society. In states where that is the aim, political liberty is lost. The task of government is to provide a framework within which everyone is free to pursue a better life.

Labour points down one road. We follow another – the creation of wealth, the spread of ownership, the freeing of the human spirit.

That is the vision which we Conservatives have long held. It is a vision which has served Britain well. It is a vision which, when the time comes, we shall once again offer confidently to the British people.

IV

THE THIRD
PARLIAMENT

(1987–90)

32

Speech to the Conservative Party Conference,
Blackpool, 9 October 1987

Emerging from the 1987 general election with an overall majority of 102, Mrs Thatcher entered her third and final term with a set of radical and ambitious proposals for reform in housing, local government finance and education. These had a special bearing on the inner cities, often dogged by dependency, poor schools and badly maintained council estates. Improving life in these areas was a major preoccupation for Mrs Thatcher at this time, as witnessed by her remarks at Conservative Central Office on the night of the election victory and by the contents of this, her first post-election Party Conference speech.

Mr President, a lot has happened since we last met.

There was, for instance, our election victory in June.[1] They tell me that makes it three wins in a row. Just like Lord Liverpool.[2] And he was Prime Minister for fifteen years. It's rather encouraging.

It was an historic victory. And I want to thank all those who did so much. Above all, our Chairman, Norman Tebbit. Norman and Margaret hold, and will always hold, a unique place in our esteem and affection. Thank you, too, Margaret.

And on 11 June we even won some nine seats we failed to gain in 1983. And we won back three we lost at by-elections. To the victors we say – congratulations. To our former colleagues who lost – come back soon. We miss you.

Just why did we win? I think it is because we knew what we stood

[1] General election, 11 June 1987: Conservatives 376, Labour 229, SDP–Liberal Alliance 22, others 23.

[2] Robert Banks Jenkinson (1770–1828), 1st Baron Hawkesbury 1803, 2nd Earl of Liverpool 1808. Tory MP 1790–1803; Foreign Secretary 1801–04; Home Secretary 1804–06, 1807–09; Secretary for War and the Colonies 1809–12; Prime Minister 1812–27.

for, we said what we stood for, and we stuck by what we stood for. And since the election, it sometimes seems we are the only party that does.

From Impossibility to Victory

Mr President, twelve years ago, I first stood on this platform as Leader of the Conservative Party. Now, one or two things have changed since 1975. In that year we were still groaning under Labour's so-called 'Social Contract'. People said we should never be able to govern again.

Remember how we had all been lectured about political impossibility? You couldn't be a Conservative, and sound like a Conservative, and win an election – they said. And you certainly couldn't win an election and then act like a Conservative and win another election. And – this was absolutely beyond dispute – you couldn't win two elections and go on behaving like a Conservative, and yet win a third election. Don't you harbour just the faintest suspicion that somewhere along the line something went wrong with that theory?

Right up to 11 June, the Labour Party, the Liberals and the SDP were busy saying that Conservatism doesn't work. Oddly enough, since 12 June, they've been saying that it does. And so our political opponents are now feverishly packaging their policies to look like ours. And it's interesting that no party now dares to say openly that it will take away from the people what we have given back to the people.

Mr President, Labour's language may alter; their presentation may be slicker; but underneath, it's still the same old socialism. Far be it for me to deride the sinner that repenteth. The trouble with Labour is they want the benefit of repentance without renouncing the original sin. No way!

And the so-called 'Alliance'?

During the election campaign I used to wonder what the Alliance leaders meant by consensus politics. I have a feeling that, if Dr Owen didn't know it before, he knows now: six inches of fraternal steel beneath the shoulderblades.[1] Mr President, we are a successful Party leading a successful nation. And I'm often asked, what's the secret? It's really quite simple. What we have done is to re-establish at the heart of British politics a handful of simple truths.

[1] On 14 June 1987, David Steel proposed that the Liberal Party and the SDP merge to form a single party. David Owen opposed this. The SDP membership voted in favour of a merger on 6 August, and Dr Owen resigned the leadership.

First, no economy can thrive if government debases the coinage. No society can be fair or stable when inflation eats up savings and devalues the pound in everyone's pocket. Inflation threatens democracy itself. We've always put its defeat at the top of our agenda. For it's a battle which never ends. It means keeping your budget on a sound financial footing. Not just one year, but every year – and that's why we need Nigel Lawson.

The second, men and women need the incentive that comes from keeping more of what they earn. No one can say that people aren't interested in their take-home pay. If that were true, a lot of trade union leaders would be out of a job. So as economic growth has taken off, we've cut income tax. And as soon as we prudently can, we'll do it again.[1] And third, as people earn more, they want to own more. They value the security which comes from ownership – whether of shares or homes. Soon there will be more shareholders than trade unionists in this country. Of course, not all trade unionists are shareholders – yet. But I hope that before long they will be.

Home ownership too has soared. And to extend the right to council tenants, we had to fight the battle, as you know, the battle in Parliament, every inch of the way. Against Labour opposition. And against Liberal opposition.

Does the Labour Leader now applaud what has happened? Does the Liberal Leader welcome it? Surely, now that it's proved so popular, it must be the sort of liberating measure of which even he would approve?

For years, we Conservatives had talked about wanting to create a property-owning democracy. Looking back, I wonder whether we did as much as we should have done to achieve that goal. But I don't believe that anyone will be able, in the years ahead, to make a similar charge against this Government; indeed, extending ownership has been one of the achievements of which I am most proud.

And fourth, it is our passionate belief that free enterprise and competition are the engines of prosperity and the guardians of liberty. These ideas have shaped free political institutions and brought unimagined wealth to countries and continents.

Just look at what we have achieved: low inflation; tax cuts, wider ownership, a revival of enterprise and, over the last year, unemployment

[1] The 1988 Budget reduced the basic rate of income tax to 25 per cent and replaced all higher tax bands with a single upper rate of 40 per cent.

has fallen at record speed by 400,000. And we want it to fall further. And with continued economic growth, it should.

And our economic success has enabled Britain to play a more prominent role in the world at large. We are now the second biggest investor in the world, and the very model of a stable economy. And that's why Nigel Lawson has been able to play a leading role in helping to tackle the world debt crisis. International bankers, the Finance Ministers of other nations – they all listen to you a lot harder when they owe you money rather than the other way round.

The old Britain of the 1970s, with its strikes, poor productivity, low investment, winters of discontent, above all its gloom, its pessimism, its sheer defeatism – that Britain is gone. And we now have a new Britain, confident, optimistic, sure of its economic strength – a Britain to which foreigners come to admire, to invest; yes, and to imitate.

I have reminded you where the great political adventure began and where it has led. But is this where we pitch our tents? Is this where we dig in? Absolutely not. Our third election victory was only a staging post on a much longer journey. And I know with every fibre of my being that it would be fatal for us just to stand where we are now. What would be our slogan for the 1990s if we did that?

Would 'consolidate' be the word that we stitch on our banners? Whose blood would run faster at the prospect of five years of consolidation?

Of course, we secure what we've achieved. But we move on – applying our principles and beliefs to even more challenging ground. For our purpose as Conservatives is to extend opportunity – and choice – to those who have so far been denied them.

Education

And Mr President, our most important task in this Parliament is to raise the quality of education. You heard what Kenneth Baker[1] had to say about it in that most interesting, stimulating debate we had the other day. It's in the national interest. And it's in the individual interest of every parent, and above all, of every child. We want education to be part of the answer to Britain's problems, not part of the cause.

[1] Kenneth Baker (born 1934), Conservative MP 1968–97; Environment Secretary 1985–86; Education Secretary 1986–89; Chancellor of the Duchy of Lancaster and Chairman of the Conservative Party 1989–90; Home Secretary 1990–92.

To compete successfully in tomorrow's world – against Japan, Germany and the United States – we need well-educated, well-trained, creative young people. Because if education is backward today, national performance will be backward tomorrow.

But it's the right of individual boys and girls which worries me most. Too often, our children don't get the education they need, the education they deserve. And in the inner cities – where youngsters must have a decent education if they are to have a better future – that opportunity is all too often snatched from them by hard-left education authorities and extremist teachers.

And children who need to be able to count and multiply are learning anti-racist mathematics – whatever that may be. Children who need to be able to express themselves in clear English are being taught political slogans. Children who need to be taught to respect traditional moral values are being taught that they have an inalienable right to be gay. And children who need encouragement – and children do so much need encouragement – so many children – they are being taught that our society offers them no future. All of those children are being cheated of a sound start in life – yes, cheated.

Of course, in the country as a whole there are plenty of excellent teachers and successful schools. And in every good school, and every good teacher, is a reminder of what too many young people are denied.

I believe that government must take the primary responsibility for setting standards for the education of our children. And that's why we are establishing a National Curriculum for basic subjects.[1] It is vital that children master essential skills: reading, writing, spelling, grammar, arithmetic; and that they understand basic science and technology. And for good teachers this will provide a foundation on which they can build with their own creative skill and professionalism.

But the key to raising standards is to enlist the support of parents. The Labour left – hard, soft and in-between – they hate the idea that people should be able to choose. In particular, they hate the idea that parents should be able to choose their children's education.

The Conservative Party believes in parental choice. And we are now about to take two dramatic steps forward in extending choice in education.

---

[1] The Education Reform Act 1988 established the National Curriculum as a single course of study in three core subjects (English, maths, and science) and seven foundation subjects to be followed by all pupils between the ages of five and sixteen.

First, we will allow popular schools to take in as many children as space will permit. And this will stop local authorities from putting artificially low limits on entry to good schools.

And second, we will give parents and governors the right to take their children's school out of the hands of the local authority and into the hands of their own governing body. This will create a new kind of school funded by the state, alongside the present state schools and the independent private schools. These new schools will be independent state schools.[1] They will bring a better education to many children because the school will be in the hands of those who care most for it and for its future.

Mr President, there's no reason at all why local authorities should have a monopoly of free education. What principle suggests that this is right? What recent experience or practice suggests it is even sensible?

In these ways, we are furthering our Conservative tradition of extending opportunity more widely.

This policy will be of the greatest advantage not to those schools where the parents are already satisfied with their children's education, but to those schools where the parents are dissatisfied and believe that their children could do a lot better. Nowhere is this policy more needed than in what have come to be known as 'inner cities'. It will profit those people most.

Inner Cities

Now, Mr President, the phrase 'inner cities' is a kind of convenient shorthand for a host of problems. Cities have risen and declined throughout history. Risen by responding to the opportunities, the markets, the technologies their day have offered. And declined when they clung to old, outdated ways and new markets passed them by. That is what's happened to many of our great cities.

And their decline was sometimes aggravated by the worst form of post-war town planning – a sort of social vandalism, carried out with the best of intentions but the worst of results. All too often, the planners

---

[1] The Education Reform Act 1988 gave secondary schools and larger primary schools the right to 'opt out' of local education authority control and apply for grant maintained status, subject to a ballot of parents. Grant maintained schools are funded directly by the Department of Education and have greater opportunity to manage their own budgets.

cut the heart out of our cities. They swept aside the familiar city centres that had grown up over the centuries. They replaced them with a wedge of tower blocks and linking expressways, interspersed with token patches of grass and a few windswept piazzas, where pedestrians fear to tread.

The planners didn't think: 'Are we breaking the pattern of people's lives? Are we cutting them off from their friends, their neighbours?' They didn't wonder: 'Are we uprooting whole communities?' They didn't ask: 'Can children still play safely in the street?'

They didn't consider any of these things. Nor did they consult the police about how to design an estate in which people could walk safe from muggers and vandals. They simply set the municipal bulldozer to work. What folly, what incredible folly!

And the people who didn't fit into this urban utopia? They dispatched them to outlying estates, without a pub or corner shop or anywhere to go.

Oh, the schemes won a number of architectural awards. But they were a nightmare for the people. They snuffed out any spark of local enterprise. And they made people entirely dependent on the local authorities and the services they chose to provide.

And as if that were not enough, some of our cities have also been dominated by Labour councils implacably hostile to enterprise. So when industries left, they piled higher rates on those that remained. When old markets vanished, they sought not new markets but new subsidies. And they capitalized not on their strengths, but on their weaknesses. And in fact they accelerated decline.

So, dying industries, soulless planning, municipal socialism – these deprived the people of the most precious things in life: hope, confidence and belief in themselves. And that sapping of the spirit is at the very heart of urban decay.

Mr President, to give back heart to our cities we must give back hope to the people. And it's beginning to happen.

Because today Britain has a strong and growing economy. Oh yes, recovery has come faster in some parts of the country than others. But now it is taking root in our most depressed urban landscapes. We all applaud the organization 'Business in the Community' – it is over three hundred major firms that have come together to assist in reviving the urban communities from which so many of them sprang.

So many of the amenities of our towns and cities – the parks and public gardens, the libraries and art galleries, the churches and schools – had their origin in the philanthropy of men who made good themselves;

and they wanted to do good for others. That impulse – that sense of obligation to the wider community – it is that we must enlist today.

I've seen the start of recovery for myself: on Teesside, in Gateshead, in Wolverhampton and in the West Midlands. And in Glasgow, which is undergoing a remarkable revival, thanks largely to the work of George Younger and Malcolm Rifkind.[1] I shall never forget one Glaswegian I met on my visit there. 'How do you do?' I said. 'My name's Margaret Thatcher.' 'Mine's Winston Churchill,' he replied. And astonishingly enough, it was. And he produced a document to prove it. Winston Harry Churchill. Absolutely splendid person.

Mr President, to speed up the process of recovery in these and other places, we have a whole battery of special measures and programmes – you heard about them from Kenneth Clarke:[2] special measures and programmes to clear derelict land, to renovate run-down council estates, to regenerate city centres, and to turn dereliction into development.

But by themselves these measures are not enough. We must also give people in the inner cities the opportunities to improve their own lives and the belief that they can do it.

The major reforms in our programme are of course designed for the whole country. But they will be of particular benefit to inner cities.

We will free tenants from their dependence on council landlords. We will free parents to choose the schools they want for their children. We will free businesses in the urban development areas from irksome planning restrictions and controls. And with our rate reform legislation, socialist councils will no longer be able to drive out small businesses and destroy employment by imposing sky-high rates. And above all, the Community Charge will make local councils far more accountable to all their voters.[3] With all these things taken together, these measures will

---

[1] George Younger (born 1931), Baron Younger of Prestwick 1992. Conservative MP 1964–92; Scottish Secretary 1979–86; Defence Secretary 1986–89. Malcolm Rifkind (born 1946), Conservative MP 1974–97; Scottish Secretary 1986–90; Transport Secretary 1990–92; Defence Secretary 1992–95; Foreign Secretary 1995–97.

[2] Kenneth Clarke (born 1940), Conservative MP 1970–; Paymaster General and Minister for Employment 1985–87; Chancellor of the Duchy of Lancaster and Minister for Trade and Industry (with additional responsibility to co-ordinate policy on inner cities) 1987–88; Health Secretary 1988–90; Education Secretary 1990–92; Home Secretary 1992–93; Chancellor of the Exchequer 1993–97.

[3] The Local Government Finance Act 1988 replaced domestic rates with the Community Charge (often called the Poll Tax). Introduced in Scotland in 1989 and in England and Wales in 1990, the Community Charge was levied at a flat rate on all resident adults (with rebates for those on low incomes). The Local Government Act 1992 replaced the Community Charge with a property-based Council Tax from 1993.

greatly reduce the power of the local council over tenants, parents, pupils and businesses; and greatly increase the opportunities open to those very people. To coin a phrase, it is an 'irreversible shift of power in favour of working people and their families'.[1]

Mr President, the social problems of some inner cities are deep-seated. Quick and easy solutions are not possible. But the philosophy of enterprise and opportunity, which has put the spark back into our national economy, that is the way – and the only way – to rejuvenate our cities and restore their confidence and pride.

The Fight Against Crime

But our greatest concern, in inner cities and elsewhere, is to reverse the tide of crime, for it disfigures all our lives.

On Wednesday, we debated crime with a depth of concern that reflects the feelings of every decent person in the country. Crime invades homes; it breaks hearts; it drags down neighbourhoods; and it spreads fear. The Government is playing its full part in the fight against crime. We have strengthened the police. We have introduced tougher sentences. Violent crime concerns us, above all. It's not just that violent crime is worse than other crime. It's much worse. And that's why we are now taking still tougher action against knives and against guns.

Even so the feeling persists that some of the sentences passed by the courts have not measured up to the enormity of crime. And so, as Douglas Hurd[2] announced this week, we shall be introducing legislation to provide for an appeal against sentences which are too lenient.[3] And may I point out it will be the second time this Government has brought a measure of this kind before Parliament. And I hope that this time it will receive a speedy passage on to the statute book.

But we shall make little progress in the drive against crime if we expect the police and the courts to take on the whole burden. When we are sick, we turn to the doctor; yet we accept responsibility for taking

[1] The Labour Party had concluded its election manifesto of February 1974 with a declaration of intent to 'bring about a fundamental and irreversible shift in the balance of power and wealth in favour of working people and their families'.
[2] Douglas Hurd (born 1930), Conservative MP 1974–97; Northern Ireland Secretary 1984–85; Home Secretary 1985–89; Foreign Secretary 1989–95.
[3] The Criminal Justice Act 1988 empowered the Attorney-General to refer unduly light sentences to the Court of Appeal.

care of our health. When fire breaks out, we call in the fire brigade; yet we know it is up to us to take sensible precautions against fire. So it is with crime.

There is enormous scope for the public to help the police in what, after all, is a common duty: in Neighbourhood Watch; in Business Watch; in crime prevention; in prompt reporting of crime seen or suspected; and in readiness to give evidence.

But even that is not enough. Civilized society doesn't just happen. It has to be sustained by standards widely accepted and unpaid. And we must draw on the moral energy of society. And we must draw on the values of family life.

For the family is the first place where we learn those habits of mutual love, tolerance and service on which every healthy nation depends for its survival. It was Sir William Haley,[1] the great editor of *The Times*, who, twenty years ago, said this: 'There are things which are bad and false and ugly and no amount of argument or specious casuistry will make them good or true or beautiful. It is time that these things were said.' And he said them.

But if we are to succeed today, all those in authority must recover that confidence and speak with a strong, emphatic and single voice. Because too often they speak in different and conflicting voices.

The great majority of crimes are committed by young people, in their teens and early twenties. It is on such impressionable young people that anti-police propaganda and the glamorization of crime can have the most deadly effect.

When left-wing councils and left-wing teachers criticize the police, they give moral sanction to the criminally inclined. When the broadcasters flout their own standards on violent television programmes, they risk a brutalizing effect on the morally unstable. When the Labour Party refuses to support the Prevention of Terrorism Act – an Act that saves lives – they weaken society, they weaken society's resistance to the modern scourge of terrorism. Local councils, teachers, broadcasters, politicians; all of us have a responsibility to uphold the civilized values which underpin the law. We owe it to society, of which we are a part. And we owe it especially to future generations, who will inherit the society that we create.

[1] Sir William Haley (1901–87). Director-General of the BBC 1944–52; editor of *The Times* 1952–66.

Defence

Mr President, our Conference takes place at a time which could prove to be a historic turning-point in world affairs. And we can say – with some pride – that Britain has played a major part in creating the opportunities which now open up before us.

It is, of course, a time of tension and even of danger in the Persian Gulf. But there, too, Britain is giving a strong lead.[1] And I do indeed pay tribute to both Geoffrey Howe and you, Mr President,[2] for the lead which you have given.

May I join you, Mr President, in speaking for this whole Conference – and indeed for the people of this country – when I express our thanks and appreciation to the Merchant officers and seamen who sail that vital waterway; and to the Royal Navy's Armilla Patrol and its minesweepers which protect them? We honour their dedication and their courage.

But today is also a time of hope. Indeed, there is no mistaking the bracing air of change in the Soviet Union. In my many hours of talking with Mr Gorbachev in Moscow earlier this year, his determination to bring about far-reaching reform was plain.[3] The difficulties and obstacles confronting him are massive. But we must recognize that anything which increases human liberty, which extends the boundaries of discussion and which increases initiative and enterprise in the Soviet Union, is of fundamental importance in terms of human rights. And that's why we support it.

That is why we have publicly welcomed and encouraged those aspects of Mr Gorbachev's reforms which do just this. They are genuinely courageous – not least in their admission that, after seventy years, the socialist system has failed to produce the standard of life the Russian people want.

But Mr President, we have yet to see that change carried through into the Soviet Union's policies towards the outside world. The traditional instruments of Soviet power – military strength, subversion, propaganda

[1] Britain deployed the Armilla Patrol of three warships in the Persian Gulf from 1980 to protect neutral shipping during the Iran–Iraq War.
[2] George Younger, Defence Secretary.
[3] Margaret Thatcher was in the USSR from 28 March to 2 April 1987, visiting Moscow and Tbilisi.

– are all being exercised as vigorously as ever. Afghanistan is still occupied. The Berlin Wall still stands, and Soviet weapons are still pouring into Third World countries which need food but not arms. They get the food from the free world and arms from the Soviet Union.

There is however hope in the agreement which now seems certain to be signed later this autumn, by the United States and the Soviet Union, to eliminate medium and shorter-range nuclear missiles.[1] We welcome that agreement. Indeed Britain has contributed in a major way to its achievement. It's a success for the West – especially for the United States and President Reagan.

But let us remember one thing. If we had listened to the Labour Party and to CND – insofar as you can distinguish between the two – that agreement would never have been achieved. The Russians would have kept their thirteen hundred nuclear warheads, while the West would have given away its three hundred, for nothing in return. That lesson must never be forgotten. Reductions in nuclear weapons come about not from weakness, but from strength.

Our Policies

Our policies – Conservative policies – are bearing fruit and we have every reason to be pleased. But we must not let satisfaction turn to euphoria.

We are ready for improved relations with the Soviet Union. But we can't afford to take anything on trust.

Nor should we be deceived by changes in style rather than substance. We shall continue to judge the Soviet Union not by what they say, but by what they do.

We believe that the strategic nuclear weapons of the United States and the Soviet Union could be reduced by 50 per cent without endangering Western security. But, so long as the Soviet Union continues to enjoy massive superiority in chemical and conventional forces, we say that reductions in nuclear weapons in Europe have gone far enough. As the

[1] President Reagan and Mr Gorbachev signed the Intermediate-Range Nuclear Forces Treaty on 8 December 1987. It provided for the elimination over three years of all land-based medium-range and shorter-range nuclear weapons held by the USA and the USSR.

Supreme Allied Commander in Europe[1] reminded us recently: it is not a nuclear-free Europe we want, it is a war-free Europe.

Nuclear weapons will continue to play a vital role in preventing war in Europe – as they have done for forty years. And that is why we will press ahead with Trident and the modernization of our independent deterrent, vital to our security.

Mr President, the British people want peace. But it must be peace with freedom and justice. And that peace is only maintained by keeping our defences strong, by resisting violence and intimidation at home, and by standing up to tyrants and terrorists abroad. That is the true spirit of the British people. That is the spirit which sustained us through two world wars. And it guides us still.

Conclusion

Mr President, you may perhaps have heard that I'm a faithful student of Rudyard Kipling. Occasionally, I've even been known to quote him.

So it won't come as a complete surprise if I refer to his poem 'Recessional', in which he warned us to beware of boasting and to keep 'a humble and a contrite heart'. That's sound advice to any Government.

But may I say today we have both a right and a duty to remind the whole free world that, once more, Britain is confident, strong, trusted. Confident, because attitudes have changed. 'Can't be done' has given way to 'What's to stop us?' Strong, because our economy is enterprising, competitive and expanding. And trusted, because we are known to be a powerful ally and a faithful friend.

All this has been made possible by the national revival which we have carried through. And everyone in this hall, and millions outside it, can claim a share in that revival.

Now, once again, it has fallen to the Conservatives to lead the nation into the 1990s. Let us face that future with quiet confidence born of what we have accomplished in the last eight years.

Britain's institutions are shaped by the character of her people. It's all that is gifted, just and fair in that character which reassures our

[1] General Bernard Rogers (born 1921), US soldier. Chief of Staff, US Army, 1976–79; Supreme Allied Commander, Europe, 1979–87.

friends and allies, and brings hope to those who have yet to know the liberty we take for granted.

Mr President, it is a great trust which has been placed in our care. May we never fail that trust.

33

Speech to the Scottish Conservative Party Conference, Perth, 13 May 1988

Mrs Thatcher could always rely upon a particularly enthusiastic welcome from Scottish Conservatives on her visits north of the border. But it was a source of frustration that the Scots in general, however much they might appreciate particular Conservative policies, could not be wooed away from their traditional collectivist politics. All the more frustrating, because so many of the past thinkers and practical men whom Mrs Thatcher admired were Scottish. Of the many speeches she made in Scotland urging a recognition of and return to rugged Scottish individualism and entrepreneurship, the Perth speech of May 1988 is the most powerful.

Mr President, ladies and gentlemen, I am proud and delighted to speak once again from the platform at Perth. It was here that I made my first speech as Prime Minister. From here I launched the last two successful election campaigns. Today, I launch a third campaign: a campaign to strengthen the Union by winning back Scotland for the Conservative and Unionist cause.

The Conservative Party is the oldest political party in Scotland. We have had our share of triumphs. We have been through challenging times – but we have never ceased to serve the interests of Scotland, indeed of the whole United Kingdom.

Today, we have hard work ahead of us – to turn the electoral map of Scotland blue once more. But your lively and candid Conference these last three days has confirmed that it is we in the Conservative Party who are doing the new thinking for the new Scotland. It is Malcolm Rifkind and his team at the Scottish Office who are setting the policy agenda with style and conviction. As it is Jim Goold, John Mackay[1] and their colleagues at Central Office who are rebuilding the organization that will win our future victories.

The Economy

Mr President, I'm sometimes told that the Scots don't like Thatcherism. Well, I find that hard to believe – because the Scots *invented* Thatcherism, long before I was thought of.

It is more than two hundred years since Adam Smith, David Hume, Adam Ferguson[2] and others first set out their ideas of a world in which wealth would be generated and spread ever more widely. They saw that it is not government which creates wealth – it's people. That people do best when they pursue their own vision. And that a wise Government will harness the efforts of individuals to improve the well-being of the whole community. So they proposed to restrain government and to liberate men and women.

Mr President, those are the ideas I hold most dear. And they had their origins in the Scottish Enlightenment.

Those ideas changed the world. The Industrial Revolution, the expansion of British trade, the development of new nations, the spread of new goods, new technologies, new ideas over the globe, benefiting millions of people who had never heard of Adam Smith, or David Hume, or indeed of Scotland – that's the history of Scottish ideas in action.

It is also the history of Scottish enterprise. Enterprise of every kind. Scottish explorers, Scottish scientists, Scottish missionaries, Scottish businessmen, Scottish doctors, Scottish inventors – men like John Napier, James Watt, Andrew Carnegie, David Livingstone, John McAdam,

---

[1] James Goold (born 1934), Baron Goold of Waterfoot 1987, Chairman of the Scottish Conservative Party 1987–90. John Mackay (born 1938), Lord Mackay of Ardbrecknish, Conservative MP 1979–87; Chief Executive of the Scottish Conservative Party 1987–90, Minister of State for Social Security 1994–97.
[2] David Hume (1711–76), Scottish philosopher, economist and historian. His works include *A Treatise of Human Nature* (1739–40) and *An Enquiry Concerning Human Understanding* (1748). Adam Ferguson (1723–1816), Scottish philosopher and historian. Professor of Moral Philosophy at Edinburgh 1764–85; author of *An Essay on the History of Civil Society* (1767).

Alexander Graham Bell, Alexander Fleming.[1] The British Empire could never have flourished as it did if the Scots had not been there to build the roads, cure the sick, establish industries, promote trading links, and to map out the unknown territories.

Scotland herself flourished in the days when Glasgow was the second city of Empire, and a quarter of the world's ships were launched into the Clyde. But an economy in the forefront of the first Industrial Revolution was bound to face major problems in adapting to the second.

When that challenge came, Governments failed Scotland. They failed Scotland not by doing too little, but by promising too much. Successive Governments promised to insulate Scotland from the reality of industrial change. They told you: 'You don't need to worry. We'll protect you.' But they couldn't – and they didn't.

Shipyards closed. Factories closed. Men lost their jobs. Whole areas turned to wasteland. And the money that might have been invested in new industries, new opportunities, went instead in trying to keep yesterday's jobs alive.

The result was that the economy fell faster, apathy and despair spread wider. And disillusion with government grew deeper. It was as if the Scots concluded: 'If government can't save us, what on earth can we do?'

What had happened to the enterprise of Carnegie, of Weir, of Dunlop, of the Crawfords?[2] Where was the energy which had founded great Scottish companies along the banks of the Clyde? And the canniness which had made Edinburgh one of the first centres of international finance?

Today the Scots have answered those questions by their actions. Those qualities were always there – but they were buried by over-government.

---

[1] John Napier (1550–1617), Scottish mathematician, inventor of logarithms. James Watt (1736–1819), Scottish engineer, who built the first efficient and reliable steam engines. Andrew Carnegie (1835–1919), Scottish-born US industrialist and philanthropist. David Livingstone (1813–73), Scottish missionary and explorer of Africa. John McAdam (1756–1836), Scottish civil engineer, who developed new methods of road construction. Alexander Graham Bell (1847–1922), Scottish-born US inventor of the telephone. Sir Alexander Fleming (1881–1955), Scottish bacteriologist, discoverer of penicillin.
[2] Andrew Weir (1865–1955), 1st Baron Inverforth 1919. Shipping magnate; Minister of Munitions and Supply 1919–21. John Dunlop (1840–1921) developed the pneumatic tyre and founded the Dunlop Rubber Company. The 25th, 26th and 27th Earls of Crawford controlled the Wigan Coal & Iron Company from 1870 to 1940, building it up into a nationwide concern.

This Government has liberated the energies of the Scottish people.

And Scotland is on the march again. New companies are burgeoning, feeding on the benefits of lower company taxes, growing market opportunities, and rising standards of living. In 1987 alone, nearly six thousand new companies were registered in Scotland. Scotland is a world leader in the industries of tomorrow – in electronics, in computer sciences, in financial services. Over £100,000 million of funds is managed and controlled within one square mile of the centre of Edinburgh. And as a result, the 'situations vacant' columns of Scottish newspapers are bursting at the seams – offering real jobs founded on real needs.

The Scottish economy today is one of the fastest-growing economies in the world. Its rise in manufacturing productivity outshines not just the rest of Britain, but also the USA, Japan, Germany, France, Italy and Canada.

Who has benefited most from this great burst of progress? The people of Scotland. Judged by the cold statistics, the Scottish people enjoy greater prosperity than anywhere in the United Kingdom outside the crowded, high-priced south-east. And no statistics can capture the benefits of living in a civilized city within five minutes of some of the finest scenery and fishing in the world – not to mention a handy golf course and a distillery or two. I am told they sometimes go together.

This Scottish miracle didn't happen by accident. Indeed, it could never have happened at all if the Government had been in the hands of the negative, bitter, class-ridden and backward-looking Labour Party that Malcolm Rifkind and I face daily in the House of Commons.

It happened because the Tory Government set the Scottish people free. Free from Labour's controls on their wages. Free from Labour's suffocating restrictions on enterprise. Free from Labour's destructive penalties on investment. Free from Labour's punitive taxes on risk-taking. Free from all the shackles that socialism had imposed on the work and imagination of the people.

Mr President, as someone once said, the people had nothing to lose but their chains. They had a world to win. And they are winning it.

The number of companies coming to Scotland has surged – but first we had to abolish exchange controls. Financial services have mushroomed in Edinburgh and Glasgow – but first we had to deregulate the industry. The unions are now back in the hands of the moderate majority – but first we had to change the law to control the militants. Above all, the

SCOTTISH PARTY CONFERENCE, 13 MAY 1988

Scottish economy is now infused with the spirit of enterprise – but first we had to get taxes down. If Labour's 1979 income tax rates were still in force, a Scotsman on average earnings would be paying almost £15 a week more to the man in Whitehall than he is paying today.

Mr President, this is the great divide in politics. We believe in incentives to create wealth; the Labour Party believes in taxes to redistribute it.

But Labour policy doesn't redistribute income. It redistributes taxpayers – from high-tax countries to low-tax countries. It redistributes work – from honest employment to the black economy. It redistributes accountants – from improving efficiency to avoiding taxes. And under every Labour Government since the war, it has redistributed economic success from this country to West Germany, to Japan and the United States.

What we have done is to reverse that process. We have given everyone more reason to work, to save and to invest. We have encouraged unskilled workers to try for a job and train in new techniques, rather than be demoralized on the dole. We have persuaded the wealth-creators – the scientists, the businessmen, the entertainers – to stay in this country and pay their taxes here, not to our competitors abroad.

We have generated prosperity and, with prosperity, more jobs.

In those difficult days of the early eighties, I used to be asked: 'Where will the new jobs come from?' I had to tell people: 'Governments don't know what the jobs of tomorrow will be. And when they try to guess, they get it wrong.'

Today I can reply: 'Look around you at the new factories, the new industries, the new signs of commerce and prosperity. The jobs of tomorrow are here.'

A month ago, I visited IBM's plant in Greenock. In 1951 it employed ten people. On what? Assembling typewriters. Today, in 1988, it employs 2,500 people and supports four thousand more. The day I was there, it produced its two millionth personal computer. The same day I opened a brand new five-crown hotel in Dundee, built at a cost of £5 million and employing a staff of 130. And for good measure, I was able to announce up to another three hundred new jobs at a new medical science centre at the nearby technology park. Mr President, Scotland is changing before our eyes.

This Government has worked hard for that kind of prosperity. Scotland has worked hard for it too. And that is why I get pretty upset when it's thrown away. Scotland won Ford for Dundee. Labour lost it.[1] But let that be a reminder – a reminder that Scotland's soundly-based, dynamic economic revival could never have happened under a Labour Government. Even out of power, the ghost of Labour stalks the industrial landscape, frightening away foreign investment and chilling the prospects of growth.

As a great Glasgow journalist, Colm Brogan,[2] once remarked: 'Wherever a Labour Government attempts to improve human wealth and happiness, grass never grows again.'

And when Labour is presented with the evidence of Scotland's success in tomorrow's world, they shut their eyes to it. They don't want to know. And sometimes, Mr President, the media shut *their* eyes as well. So perhaps I should take the opportunity to reassure them that news of Scotland's success is not covered by Section Two of the Official Secrets Act.[3]

Agriculture

Mr President, no Tory ever forgets the vital importance of farming to a prosperous economy and a healthy society. Today, Scottish farmers have to compete in a world where trading conditions are tough and surpluses abound. Within the European Community, we have had to put a limit on the budget in order to control surpluses and bring supply more in line with demand. Without such reform, the CAP would, quite simply, have run out of money. And the victims would have been farmers and farm workers alike.[4] So Britain brought our European partners to

[1] The Amalgamated Engineering Union negotiated a single-union deal with the Ford Motor Company to set up a new plant at Dundee with the creation of a thousand jobs. The Transport and General Workers' Union, recognized at other Ford plants, fiercely objected to its exclusion. The inter-union dispute escalated until Ford announced on 25 March 1988 that the project could not go ahead when British unions were unable to guarantee conditions required for competitiveness.

[2] Colm Brogan (1902–77), Scottish journalist, author of anti-socialist polemics. In *Our New Masters* (1947), he wrote, 'Wherever Sir Stafford Cripps has tried to increase wealth and happiness, grass never grows again.'

[3] Section Two of the Official Secrets Act 1911 was a catch-all clause which banned publication of facts concerning the operation of government. It was repealed in 1989.

[4] The European Council held in Brussels from 11 to 12 February 1988 agreed to impose binding limits on spending under the Common Agricultural Policy and to reduce food surpluses by introducing 'stabilizers' (automatic price cuts once a certain level of output is exceeded) and 'set aside' (payment to farmers to leave land uncultivated).

face reality. They haven't always liked that. But Scottish farmers have never been afraid to face reality, never been unwilling to adapt to change. All they ask is that the competition be on equal terms. That's why this Government has repeatedly fought in Brussels for a fair deal for our farmers – in lamb, beef, cereals and much else. That's why we've reformed the tax laws so that the family farm can be passed on to the next generation free of tax – one of the fairest and best tax deals for farmers obtainable in the Community. That's why we have cut the rate of tax sharply on small farmers. As a result, Scottish agriculture is strong and confident enough to establish major export markets.

And while I'm on exports, I must congratulate the Scotch whisky industry, whose exports exceeded £1 billion in value in 1986. I'm told its Scotland's largest export. But, as I told Mr Takeshita[1] this week, it could do still better if foreign countries did not protect their pale imitations behind devices like tax discrimination, which leave a very nasty taste in the mouth.

The Community Charge

Mr President, nobody can tell the Scots that revaluation was fair. It wasn't. That's why the Scots wanted a better system – and that's why we are replacing the old, outdated, arbitrary and unfair system of local rates with the Community Charge.[2] It is absurd that out of almost four million local electors in Scotland, only one million pay full rates, and two million pay no rates at all. Yet all four million use local services and benefit from the rates paid by their neighbours. Where is the fairness in that?

It is equally absurd that the same rate is levied on similar properties, however many people are living in them. Yet local services are used by people, not by houses. Why should a retired widow living alone in the family home pay the same rates as four working adults next door? Where is the fairness in that?

---

[1] Noboru Takeshita (born 1924), Japanese politician. Minister of Finance 1982–86; Prime Minister and Leader of the Liberal Democratic Party 1987–89.
[2] Local government domestic rates were levied on the basis of the rental value of property. In Scotland, the law required this value to be reassessed every five years. The revaluation of 1985 shifted the tax burden from commercial to domestic ratepayers and proved extremely unpopular. Hence the Community Charge was introduced in Scotland in 1989 – a year earlier than elsewhere.

The answer is, Mr President, that there is no fairness in rates. A system of finance which totally separates voting power from financial responsibility is wrong at the root.

If we are to have responsible and accountable local government, a clear link between the services provided and the charge levied is essential. That is the principle behind the Community Charge.

It is designed to ensure that the same level of services delivered with the same degree of efficiency will result in the same community charge for every person in Scotland. And it will be the same system throughout England too.

The charge does not cover the whole of local spending. In Scotland, it will account for only one-seventh of the total. The remaining six-sevenths will continue to be paid out of central government and the Unified Business Rate.

So why do we read so much about gainers and losers? The reason is clear. The Community Charge is not set by the Government. It is set by local councils. And an extravagant and inefficient council will have to charge more, and a prudent and responsible council will be able to charge less.

The councils themselves will create the gainers and losers. The gainers will be those who are fortunate enough to live with careful Tory local government; the losers those who live under free-spending Labour councils.

But there's the rub, Mr President. When every local resident pays a community charge, the councils will have to justify their expenditure to the voters. Voters in Labour Edinburgh will want to know why their community charge is £334 a year, when in Tory Eastwood it is £70 less. Hard-left councils will no longer be able to hide the cost of their political fads and anti-nuclear fancies by passing them on to business and the rate-paying minority. They will have to send the bill to every elector – and face the consequences at the next election.

Education

Mr President, bills are now going through Parliament which will radically change education. They will provide for parents to play a principal role in the education of their children.

In Scotland there is a tradition of excellence in education which our opponents constantly threaten. Some of you may have heard of Paisley

Grammar![1] That school and others like it were under threat from Labour, because their values and traditions were resented. They were popular with parents. They had high academic standards. They enforced high standards of discipline. We saved them. Labour hated it. The parents loved it. Let Labour be in no doubt about the message: we will always defend the parents that they seek to attack.

Social Security

Mr President, for day after day, week after week, in the House of Commons and elsewhere, we have been treated to the sound of sanctimonious Opposition politicians congratulating themselves on their superior compassion – with particular reference to the health and welfare services.

Well, here are the facts. We are not spending less on these services, but more. A lot more. On both of them. On the NHS nearly £2,000 million more this year. On social security another £2,000 million this year.

Labour can't bear the fact that we have increased spending on the social services and the NHS and cut taxes at the same time. They increased taxes and cut nurses' pay and the hospital programme. With this Conservative Government, as you know, the nurses and doctors have had the largest increase ever – a move that has been greatly welcomed.

But in social security it wasn't only a question of spending more: a number of problems had grown up over the years and they simply had to be dealt with. For example, some young people were choosing to leave school and be idle on supplementary benefit. That was wrong – so we stopped it. We offered training instead for those who couldn't get a job – and paid a training grant. That way they are occupied and learn a skill for the future. That was right, and most parents and sensible people agreed.

And then, some families on low wages who had young children found they could do better by going on unemployment benefit. That too was

---

[1] Paisley Grammar School was threatened with closure under local education authority plans announced in September 1987, but the Government ruled that well-attended schools could not be closed without the approval of the Secretary of State, and Paisley was reprieved in June 1988.

wrong – so now we top up their earnings with 'family credit', a new benefit. That has helped 400,000 people to keep the dignity and respect of working to provide for their own families. Another good and necessary reform.

Then we found the cost of housing benefit was rising dramatically, from £1½ billion in 1979 to over £5 billion this year, and that even in times of much greater prosperity it was going to an increasing number of households. In fact, every two households now have to keep not only themselves but contribute to a third. That is still so – even after the reforms which we have just brought in. And even after the extra we have just allocated to housing benefit. But it will not rise so much in future. And this year expenditure will be £5.3 billion. But we had to take the steps we did to contain its growth in future years.

And then we have tried to give special help to the long-term sick and disabled.

But, with something like twenty possible extra allowances, it's hardly surprising that some people didn't know where they were. Or what they could claim. So we have rolled them all into one which covers almost all disabled people. May I say to them: 'It costs more, and it's taking time to sort out, but you'll find it will be much simpler and fairer.' All told, and in real terms, we spend 80 per cent more on this group than when we came to power. That's been a good reform too. An essential reform. A real Tory reform.

And to people who are retired, let me say this: 'It's not only a question of providing more for each pensioner, but providing for more pensioners too: something like a million more, since we took office.' And while the number of pensioners will continue to increase over the next decade, the population of working age will decline. And on top of that, the promises that had been made for the second pension – SERPS[1] – were too great for future generations to be asked to bear.

So we have now safeguarded pensions by putting them on a sound financial basis – one that is fair all round. At the same time, we have honoured our pledge to protect the basic pension against rising prices. Moreover, we have slashed inflation, so your savings are safer with a Conservative Government. We have abolished the investment incomes

---

[1] The State Earnings-Related Pension Scheme came into operation in 1978 under the Social Security Pensions Act 1975, which aimed to provide every employed person with an earnings-related old-age pension in addition to the basic fixed-rate pension. The cost of SERPS spiralled, and the Social Security Act 1986 offered contributors incentives to contract out and join a personal or occupational pension scheme instead.

surcharge. And we have introduced an extra tax allowance for the over eighties.

Those who are now retiring can do so secure in the knowledge that they can look forward to a far better future than was ever possible a few years ago.

That is the measure of our reforms you have heard so much about. They strike a balance between those genuinely in need and those who provide for them. Yes, they have cost more and they will go on costing more; but, like our financial position as a whole, they are sound. So let our noisy critics remember that this Party does not represent only one section or one part of the nation – our purpose is to ensure that the recovery now taking place will benefit all the people.

Devolution

Mr President, since the Act of Union,[1] Scotland has had a proud history as a distinctive nation within the United Kingdom. We in this Party believe in a Scotland that continues to play a full part in the Kingdom, and on equal terms. Now that every other party in Scotland is challenging that role,[2] it is vital that we defend it.

People say that we're not a Scottish party – and they are right. We're not. But neither are we an English party or a Welsh party or an Irish party. We are a party of the whole United Kingdom. We are the Conservative and Unionist Party. And we will always be a Unionist party.

I am delighted that at this Conference you resoundingly rejected the prospect of a second-class Scotland, cut off from the rest of the United Kingdom by tax barriers that would destroy her economy. For just stop to think for one moment how utterly inadequate and superficial the proposals for devolution from the opposition parties really are.

At least the Nationalists have the honesty to say that they want to break up the United Kingdom. Labour say they don't, but their policies say that they would. They want to establish a Scottish Assembly – another layer of government – with the power to raise taxes. Yet they

[1] The Act of Union 1707 combined the English and Scottish Parliaments and created the United Kingdom of Great Britain.
[2] The arguments for and against administrative and legislative devolution to Scotland (and to a lesser degree Wales) long divided both the Conservative and Labour Parties. On becoming Tory leader, Mrs Thatcher shifted her party's policy towards vigorous defence of the Union of the United Kingdom.

leave unanswered questions which are of fundamental importance for Scotland's future.

Why should companies want to invest in an area with higher taxes than the rest of the country? How could Scottish MPs continue to vote on English matters at Westminster if English MPs were excluded from consideration of Scottish issues? Who would foot the bill for the additional bureaucracy? How could Scotland possibly benefit from *losing* influence and representation in Whitehall and Westminster?

More bureaucracy. More taxation. Less representation and less influence for Scotland within the United Kingdom. And for what purpose, Mr President? To undermine the unity of the United Kingdom. It is hardly an attractive political prospectus.

As long as I am Leader of this Party, we shall defend the Union clearly by rejecting legislative devolution unequivocally.

For in debate after debate we have endorsed a very different policy – a policy far bolder and more imaginative than that of our opponents. Not devolution to politicians and bureaucrats – but devolution to the Scottish people themselves. Devolution of housing, devolution of education, devolution of share ownership and devolution of state-run industries to individuals.

It was a *Unionist* Government which gave council tenants in Scotland the right to buy their own homes. And over 113,000 Scots have done so. It was a *Unionist* Government which gave people the opportunity to choose to which school they send their children. And over a hundred thousand Scots have done so. And it was a *Unionist* Government which gave people the opportunity to buy shares in British industry. And today twice as many Scots own shares than was the case in 1979.

This policy of devolution to the people continues with our policy of Scottish privatization. Nationalization took companies out of Scottish hands and into Whitehall; privatization will hand them back to Scotland. It will create major new Scottish companies with vast assets, thousands of employees and a powerful presence in the Scottish economy – and give the Scottish public a new opportunity to acquire a major stake in the ownership of Scottish industry.

These are policies which give real power back to the people. Policies which the people support. The challenge for us all now is to turn support for our policies into support for our Party.

Conclusion

Mr President, I have come here to encourage you to assert our Party's place in the centre of Scotland's national life.

I won't be discouraged by temporary setbacks. I didn't come into politics to take short-cuts, or court easy popularity. My principles are not at the mercy of the opinion polls – neither, I am sure, are yours.

Only the practical application of Tory principles has made the recovery of the Scottish economy possible. As Scotland regains its self-confidence, as more Scots realize that they have every right to be proud of Scotland's economic recovery, so our fortunes will revive. Tory values are in tune with everything that is finest in the Scottish character and with the proudest moments in Scottish history. The values of hard work, self-reliance, thrift, enterprise – the relishing of challenges, the seizing of opportunities. That's what the Tory Party stands for – that's what Scotland stands for.

Speech to the General Assembly of the Church of Scotland, Edinburgh, 21 May 1988

Of the addresses given by Mrs Thatcher on the relationship between Christianity and politics, that to the General Assembly of the Church of Scotland in May 1988 was the most controversial. The clergy generally received it with public disapproval, tempered by some private support. But the contents were hardly different from other, earlier variations on the same theme. Oddly enough, it was the quotation from St Paul's Letter to the Thessalonians (p. 310), rather than any original thoughts from the Prime Minister, that seems to have most irritated her critics.

Moderator and Members of the Assembly: I am greatly honoured to have been invited to attend the opening of this 1988 General Assembly of the Church of Scotland; and I am deeply grateful that you have now asked me to address you.

I am very much aware of the historical continuity, extending over four centuries, during which the position of the Church of Scotland has been recognized in constitutional law and confirmed by successive Sovereigns. It sprang from the independence of mind and rigour of thought that have always been such powerful characteristics of the Scottish people. It has remained close to its roots and has inspired a commitment to service from *all* people.

I am, therefore, very sensible of the important influence which the Church of Scotland exercises in the life of the whole nation, both at the spiritual level and through the extensive caring services which are provided by your Church's department of social responsibility. But I am conscious also of continuous links the Church of Scotland maintains with other Churches.

Christianity – Spiritual and Social

Perhaps it would be best if I began by speaking personally as a Christian, as well as a politician, about the way I see things. Reading recently I came across the starkly simple phrase: 'Christianity is about spiritual redemption, not social reform.'

Sometimes the debate on these matters has become too polarized, and given the impression that the two are quite separate. Most Christians would regard it as their personal Christian duty to help their fellow men and women. They would regard the lives of children as a precious trust. These duties come not from any secular legislation passed by Parliament, but from being a Christian.

But there are a number of people who are not Christians, who would also accept those responsibilities. What then are the distinctive marks of Christianity?

They stem not from the social but from the spiritual side of our lives. Personally, I would identify three beliefs in particular.

First, that from the beginning man has been endowed by God with the fundamental right to choose between good and evil. Second, that we were made in God's own image and, therefore, we are expected to use all our *own* power of thought and judgement in exercising that choice; and further, if we open our hearts to God, He has promised to work within us. And third, that Our Lord Jesus Christ, the Son of God, when faced with His terrible choice and lonely vigil, *chose* to lay down His life that our sins may be forgiven. I remember very well a sermon on an Armistice Sunday, when our preacher said: 'No one took away the life of Jesus. He chose to lay it down.'

I think back to many discussions in my early life when we all agreed that if you try to take the fruits of Christianity without its roots, the fruits will wither. And they will not come again unless you nurture the roots.

But we must not profess the Christian faith and go to church simply because we want social reforms and benefits or a better standard of behaviour; but because we accept the sanctity of life, the responsibility that comes with freedom and the supreme sacrifice of Christ expressed so well in the hymn:

When I survey the wondrous Cross
On which the Prince of Glory died,
My richest gain I count but loss,
And pour contempt on all my pride.

Bible Principles – Relevance to Political Life

May I also say a few words about my personal belief in the relevance
of Christianity to public policy – to the things that are Caesar's?

The Old Testament lays down in Exodus the Ten Commandments
as given to Moses, the injunction in Leviticus to love our neighbour as
ourselves, and generally the importance of observing a strict code of
law. The New Testament is a record of the Incarnation, the teachings
of Christ and the establishment of the Kingdom of God. Again, we have
the emphasis on loving our neighbour as ourselves and to 'Do-as-you-
would-be-done-by.'

I believe that by taking together these key elements from the Old and
New Testaments, we gain: a view of the universe, a proper attitude to
work, and principles to shape economic and social life.

We are told we must work and use our talents to create wealth. 'If a
man will not work he shall not eat,' wrote St Paul to the Thessalonians.
Indeed, abundance rather than poverty has a legitimacy which derives
from the very nature of Creation.

Nevertheless, the Tenth Commandment – Thou shalt not covet –
recognizes that making money and owning things could become selfish
activities. But it is not the creation of wealth that is wrong, but love of
money for its own sake. The spiritual dimension comes in deciding what
one does with the wealth. How could we respond to the many calls for
help, or invest for the future, or support the wonderful artists and crafts-
men whose work also glorifies God, unless we had first worked hard
and used our talents to create the necessary wealth? And remember the
woman with the alabaster jar of ointment.

I confess that I always had difficulty with interpreting the Biblical
precept to love our neighbours 'as ourselves' until I read some of the
words of C.S. Lewis.[1] He pointed out that we don't exactly love *ourselves*
when we fall below the standards and beliefs we have accepted. Indeed
we might even *hate* ourselves for some unworthy deed.

[1] Clive Staples Lewis (1898–1963), English novelist and popular theologian.

Political Action and Personal Responsibilities

None of this, of course, tells us exactly what kind of political and social institutions we should have. On this point, Christians will very often genuinely disagree; though it is a mark of Christian manners that they will do so with courtesy and mutual respect. What is certain, however, is that any set of social and economic arrangements which is not founded on the acceptance of individual responsibility will do nothing but harm.

We are all responsible for our own actions. We cannot blame society if we disobey the law. We simply cannot delegate the exercise of mercy and generosity to others. The politicians and other secular powers should strive by their measures to bring out the good in people and to fight down the bad; but they can't create the one or abolish the other. They can only see that the laws encourage the *best* instincts and convictions of the people, instincts and convictions which I am convinced are far more deeply rooted than is often supposed.

Nowhere is this more evident than the basic ties of the family, which are at the heart of our society and are the very nursery of civic virtue. It is on the family that we in government build our own policies for welfare, education and care.

You recall that Timothy was warned by St Paul that anyone who neglects to provide for his own house (meaning his own family) has disowned the faith and is 'worse than an infidel'.

We must recognize that modern society is infinitely more complex than that of Biblical time, and of course new occasions teach new duties. In our generation, the only way we can ensure that no one is left without sustenance, help or opportunity is to have laws to provide for health and education, pensions for the elderly, succour for the sick and disabled.

But intervention by the state must never become so great that it effectively removes personal responsibility. The same applies to taxation; for while you and I would work extremely hard whatever the circumstances, there are undoubtedly some who would not unless the incentive was there. And we need *their* efforts too.

Religious Education

Moderator, recently there have been great debates about religious education. I believe strongly that politicians must see that religious education has a proper place in the school curriculum.

In Scotland, as in England, there is an historic connection expressed in our laws between Church and state. The two connections are of a somewhat different kind, but the arrangements in both countries are designed to give symbolic expression to the same crucial truth: that the Christian religion – which, of course, embodies many of the great spiritual and moral truths of Judaism – is a fundamental part of our national heritage. I believe it is the wish of the overwhelming majority of people that this heritage should be preserved and fostered. For centuries it has been our very life-blood. Indeed, we are a nation whose ideals are founded on the Bible.

Also, it is quite impossible to understand our history or literature without grasping this fact. *That* is the strong practical case for ensuring that children at school are given adequate instruction in the part which the Judaic–Christian tradition has played in moulding our laws, manners and institutions. How can you make sense of Shakespeare and Sir Walter Scott, or of the constitutional conflicts of the seventeenth century in both Scotland and England, without some such fundamental knowledge?

But I go further than this. The truths of the Judaic–Christian tradition are infinitely precious – not only, as I believe, because they are true, but also because they provide the moral impulse which alone can lead to that peace, in the true meaning of the word, for which we all long.

Tolerance

To assert absolute moral values is not to claim perfection for ourselves. No true Christian could do that. What is more, one of the great principles of our Judaic–Christian inheritance is tolerance. People with other faiths and cultures have always been welcomed in our land, assured of equality under the law, of proper respect and of open friendship. There is absolutely nothing incompatible between this and our desire to maintain the essence of our own identity. There is no place for racial or religious intolerance in our creed.

Christians and Democracy

When Abraham Lincoln spoke in his famous Gettysburg speech of 1863 of 'government of the people, by the people, and for the people', he gave the world a neat definition of democracy which has since been widely and enthusiastically adopted. But what he enunciated as a form of government was not in itself especially Christian, for nowhere in the Bible is the word 'democracy' mentioned. Ideally, when Christians meet, as Christians, to take counsel together their purpose is not (or should not be) to ascertain what is the mind of the majority, but what is the mind of the Holy Spirit – something which may be quite different.

Nevertheless, I am an enthusiast for democracy. And I take that position not because I believe majority opinion is inevitably right or true – indeed no majority can take away God-given human rights – but because I believe it most effectively safeguards the value of the individual, and, more than any other system, restrains the abuse of power by the few. And that *is* a Christian concept.

But there is little hope for democracy if the hearts of men and women in democratic societies cannot be touched by a call to something greater than themselves. Political structures, state institutions, collective ideals are not enough.

We Parliamentarians can legislate for the rule of *law*. *You*, the Church, can teach the life of faith.

Conclusion

For, when all is said and done, a politician's role is a humble one. I always think that the whole debate about the Church and the state has never yielded anything comparable in insight to that beautiful hymn 'I Vow to Thee my Country'. It begins with a triumphant assertion of what might be described as secular patriotism, a noble thing indeed in a country like ours: 'I vow to thee my country all earthly things above; entire, whole and perfect the service of my love.'

It goes on to speak of 'another country I heard of long ago', whose King cannot be seen and whose armies cannot be counted, but 'soul by soul and silently her shining bounds increase'. Not group by group, or party by party, or even Church by Church – but soul by soul – and each one counts.

That, members of the Assembly, is the country which you chiefly serve. You fight your cause under the banner of an historic Church. Your success matters greatly – as much to the temporal, as to the spiritual welfare of the nation.

35

Speech at the College of Europe, Bruges, 20 September 1988

Measured by almost every criterion, the Bruges speech of September 1988 was the most important Mrs Thatcher delivered during her time as Prime Minister. It was a direct response to the increasing interventionism and incipient federalism of the European Commission and its President, Jacques Delors. The pressure for European Economic and Monetary Union (EMU) was increasing. M. Delors had predicted that within ten years the Community would be the source of '80 per cent of our economic legislation, and perhaps even our fiscal and social legislation as well'. In September he had addressed the British Trades Union Congress, advocating measures on collective bargaining to be taken at a European level.

But the Bruges speech was not limited to a rejection of this agenda. It also set out a new, alternative model for Europe – one of voluntary co-operation between independent nation states, free markets and open trade. Within the Conservative'Party it exposed a gap, which in truth already existed, between a minority who were eager to see the merger of Britain with a new European superstate, and the majority who regarded such a prospect as unthinkable. In doing so, the Bruges speech can be said to have contributed towards the overthrow of Mrs Thatcher as Prime Minister in 1990. But it also fundamentally reshaped political patterns and shifted public opinion on Europe, with consequences which, at the time of writing, are still unclear.

First, may I thank you for giving me the opportunity to return to Bruges – and in very different circumstances from my last visit shortly after the Zeebrugge ferry disaster,[1] when Belgian courage and the devotion of your doctors and nurses saved so many British lives. Second, may I

---

[1] The Townsend Thoresen ferry *Herald of Free Enterprise* sank off the Belgian port of Zeebrugge on 6 March 1987, with the loss of 187 lives.

say what a pleasure it is to speak at the College of Europe[1] under the distinguished leadership of its Rector, Professor Lukaszewski. The College plays a vital and increasingly important part in the life of the European Community. Third, may I also thank you for inviting me to deliver my address in this magnificent hall. What better place to speak of Europe's future than in a building which so gloriously recalls the greatness that Europe had already achieved over six hundred years ago?

Your city of Bruges has many other historical associations for us in Britain. Geoffrey Chaucer[2] was a frequent visitor here. And the first book to be printed in the English language was produced here in Bruges by William Caxton.[3]

Britain and Europe

Mr Chairman, you have invited me to speak on the subject of Britain and Europe. Perhaps I should congratulate you on your courage. If you believe some of the things said and written about my views on Europe, it must seem rather like inviting Genghis Khan to speak on the virtues of peaceful co-existence!

I want to start by disposing of some myths about my country, Britain, and its relationship with Europe. And to do that I must say something about the identity of Europe itself.

Europe is not the creation of the Treaty of Rome.[4] Nor is the European idea the property of any group or institution.

We British are as much heirs to the legacy of European culture as any other nation. Our links to the rest of Europe, the Continent of Europe, have been the *dominant* factor in our history. For three hundred years we were part of the Roman Empire, and our maps still trace the straight lines of the roads the Romans built. Our ancestors – Celts,

---

[1] The College of Europe was founded by the European Movement in 1949, with the aim of developing the 'European mind' among international officials and civil servants.

[2] Geoffrey Chaucer (c. 1342–1400), poet and civil servant, travelled in Flanders on diplomatic missions in the 1370s.

[3] William Caxton (c. 1422–91), the first English printer, published *The Recuyell of the Historyes of Troye* at Bruges in 1475.

[4] The Treaty of Rome, dating from 17 April 1957, is the basic text governing the establishment, structure, powers and development of the European Community.

Saxons and Danes – came from the Continent. Our nation was – in that favourite Community word – 'restructured' under Norman and Angevin rule in the eleventh and twelfth centuries.

This year we celebrate the three hundredth anniversary of the Glorious Revolution, in which the British Crown passed to Prince William of Orange and Queen Mary.

Visit the great churches and cathedrals of Britain, read our literature and listen to our language: all bear witness to the cultural riches which we have drawn from Europe – and other Europeans from us.

We in Britain are rightly proud of the way in which, since Magna Carta in 1215, we have pioneered and developed representative institutions to stand as bastions of freedom. And proud too of the way in which for centuries Britain was a home for people from the rest of Europe who sought sanctuary from tyranny.

But we know that without the European legacy of political ideas we could not have achieved as much as we did. From classical and medieval thought we have borrowed that concept of the rule of law which marks out a civilized society from barbarism. And on that idea of Christendom – for long synonymous with Europe – with its recognition of the unique and spiritual nature of the individual, we still base our belief in personal liberty and other human rights.

Too often the history of Europe is described as a series of interminable wars and quarrels. Yet from our perspective today surely what strikes us most is our common experience. For instance, the story of how Europeans explored and colonized and – yes, without apology – civilized much of the world is an extraordinary tale of talent, skill and courage.

We British have in a special way contributed to Europe. Over the centuries we have fought to prevent Europe from falling under the dominance of a single power. We have fought and we have died for her freedom. Only miles from here in Belgium lie the bodies of 120,000 British soldiers who died in the First World War. Had it not been for that willingness to fight and to die, Europe would have been united long before now – but not in liberty, not in justice.

It was British support to resistance movements throughout the last war that helped to keep alive the flame of liberty in so many countries until the day of liberation.

Tomorrow, King Baudouin[1] will attend a service in Brussels to commemorate the many brave Belgians who gave their lives in service with

---

[1] Baudouin I (1930–93), King of the Belgians 1951–93.

the Royal Air Force – a sacrifice which we shall never forget. It was from our island fortress that the liberation of Europe itself was mounted.

And still today we stand together. Nearly seventy thousand British servicemen are stationed on the mainland of Europe. All these things alone are proof of our commitment to Europe's future.

The European Community is *one* manifestation of that European identity. But it is not the only one. We must never forget that east of the Iron Curtain peoples who once enjoyed a full share of European culture, freedom and identity have been cut off from their roots. We shall always look on Warsaw, Prague and Budapest as great European cities. Nor should we forget that European values have helped to make the United States of America into the valiant defender of freedom which she has become.

Europe's Future

This is no arid chronicle of obscure facts from the dust-filled libraries of history. It is the record of nearly two thousand years of British involvement in Europe, co-operation with Europe and contribution to Europe, a contribution which today is as valid and as strong as ever.

Yes, we have looked also to wider horizons – as have others – and thank goodness for that, because Europe never would have prospered, and never will prosper, as a narrow-minded, inward-looking club.

The European Community belongs to *all* its members. It must reflect the traditions and aspirations of *all* its members.

And let me be quite clear: Britain does not dream of some cosy, isolated existence on the fringes of the European Community. Our destiny is in Europe, as part of the Community.

That is not to say that our future lies only in Europe. But nor does that of France or Spain or indeed any other member.

The Community is not an end in itself. Nor is it an institutional device to be constantly modified according to the dictates of some abstract intellectual concept. Nor must it be ossified by endless regulation. The European Community is the practical means by which Europe can ensure the future prosperity and security of its people in a world in which there are many other powerful nations and groups of nations.

We Europeans cannot afford to waste our energies on internal disputes or arcane institutional debates. They are no substitute for effective action. Europe has to be ready both to contribute in full measure to its own security and to compete commercially and industrially in a world in which success goes to the countries which encourage individual initiative and enterprise, rather than to those which attempt to diminish them. This evening I want to set out some guiding principles for the future, which I believe will ensure that Europe does succeed, not just in economic and defence terms but also in the quality of life and the influence of its peoples.

Willing Co-Operation Between Sovereign States

My first guiding principle is this: willing and active co-operation between independent sovereign states is the best way to build a successful European Community. To try to suppress nationhood and concentrate power at the centre of a European conglomerate would be highly damaging and would jeopardize the objectives we seek to achieve. Europe will be stronger precisely because it has France as France, Spain as Spain, Britain as Britain, each with its own customs, traditions and identity. It would be folly to try to fit them into some sort of identikit European personality.

Some of the founding fathers of the Community thought that the United States of America might be its model. But the whole history of America is quite different from Europe. People went there to get away from the intolerance and constraints of life in Europe. They sought liberty and opportunity; and their strong sense of purpose has, over two centuries, helped create a new unity and pride in being American – just as our pride lies in being British, or Belgian, or Dutch, or German.

I am the first to say that on many great issues the countries of Europe should try to speak with a single voice. I want to see us work more closely on the things we can do better together than alone. Europe is stronger when we do so – whether it be in trade, in defence, or in our relations with the rest of the world.

But working more closely together does *not* require power to be centralized in Brussels or decisions to be taken by an appointed bureaucracy. Indeed, it is ironic that just when those countries such as the Soviet Union, which have tried to run everything from the centre, are learning that success depends on dispersing power and decisions away from the centre, some in the Community seem to want to move in the opposite direction. We have not successfully rolled back the frontiers of the state in Britain only to see them re-imposed at a European level, with a

European super-state exercising a new dominance from Brussels.

Certainly we want to see Europe more united and with a greater sense of common purpose. But it must be in a way which preserves the different traditions, Parliamentary powers and sense of national pride in one's own country; for these have been the source of Europe's vitality through the centuries.

Encouraging Change

My second guiding principle is this: Community policies must tackle present problems in a *practical* way, however difficult that may be. If we cannot reform those Community policies which are patently wrong or ineffective and which are rightly causing public disquiet, then we shall not get the public's support for the Community's future development.

That is why the achievements of the European Council in Brussels last February are so important. It wasn't right that half the total Community budget was being spent on storing and disposing of surplus food. Now those stocks are being sharply reduced. It was absolutely right to decide that agriculture's share of the budget should be cut in order to free resources for other policies, such as helping the less well-off regions and training for jobs. It was right too to introduce tighter budgetary discipline to enforce these decisions and to bring total EC spending under better control.

Those who complained that the Community was spending so much time on financial detail missed the point. You cannot build on unsound foundations, financial or otherwise; and it was the fundamental reforms agreed last winter which paved the way for the remarkable progress which we have since made on the Single Market.[1] But we cannot rest on what we have achieved to date. For example, the task of reforming the Common Agricultural Policy is far from complete. Certainly, Europe needs a stable and efficient farming industry. But the CAP has become unwieldy, inefficient and grossly expensive. Production of unwanted surpluses safeguards neither the income nor the future of farmers themselves. We must *continue* to pursue policies which relate supply more

---

[1] The Single Market is 'an area without internal frontiers in which the free movement of goods, persons, and capital is ensured.' By the Single European Act 1987, EC member-states undertook to abolish remaining trade barriers and create a Single Market by 1992.

closely to market requirements, and which will reduce overproduction and limit costs. Of course, we must protect the villages and rural areas which are such an important part of our national life – but not by the instrument of agricultural prices.

Tackling these problems requires political courage. The Community will only damage itself in the eyes of its own people and the outside world if that courage is lacking.

Europe Open to Enterprise

My third guiding principle is the need for Community policies which encourage enterprise. If Europe is to flourish and create the jobs of the future, enterprise is the key. The basic framework is there: the Treaty of Rome itself was intended as a charter for economic liberty. But that is not how it has always been read, still less applied.

The lesson of the economic history of Europe in the seventies and eighties is that central planning and detailed control *don't* work, and that personal endeavour and initiative *do*; that a state-controlled economy is a recipe for low growth, and that free enterprise within a framework of law brings better results.

The aim of a Europe open to enterprise is the moving force behind the creation of the Single European Market by 1992. By getting rid of barriers, by making it possible for companies to operate on a Europe-wide scale, we can best compete with the United States, Japan and the other new economic powers emerging in Asia and elsewhere.

And that means action to *free* markets, action to *widen* choice, action to *reduce* government intervention. Our aim should *not* be more and more detailed regulation from the centre: it should be to deregulate and to remove the constraints on trade.

Britain has been in the lead in opening its markets to others. The City of London has long welcomed financial institutions from all over the world, which is why it is the biggest and most successful financial centre in Europe. We have opened our market for telecommunications equipment, introduced competition into the market for services and even into the network itself – steps which others in Europe are only now beginning to face. In air transport, we have taken the lead in liberalization and seen the benefits in cheaper fares and wider choice. Our coastal shipping trade is open to the merchant navies of Europe. I wish I could say the same of many other Community members.

Regarding *monetary matters*, let me say this: the key issue is *not* whether there should be a European Central Bank. The immediate and practical requirements are: to implement the Community's commitment to free movement of capital – in Britain we have it; and to the abolition throughout the Community of the exchange controls – in Britain we abolished them in 1979; to establish a genuinely free market in financial services, in banking, insurance, investment; to make greater use of the ecu.[1] Britain is this autumn issuing ecu-denominated Treasury bills, and hopes to see other Community Governments increasingly do the same. These are the *real* requirements because they are what Community business and industry need, if they are to compete effectively in the wider world. And they are what the European consumer wants, for they will widen his choice and lower his costs.

It is to such basic practical steps that the Community's attention should be devoted. When those have been achieved, and sustained over a period of time, we shall be in a better position to judge the next moves.

It is the same with the *frontiers* between our countries. Of course we must make it easier for goods to pass through frontiers. Of course we must make it easier for our people to travel throughout the Community. But it is a matter of plain commonsense that we cannot totally abolish frontier controls if we are also to protect our citizens from crime and stop the movement of drugs, of terrorists, and of illegal immigrants. That was underlined graphically only three weeks ago, when one brave German customs officer, doing his duty on the frontier between Holland and Germany, struck a major blow against the terrorists of the IRA.[2]

And before I leave the subject of the Single Market, may I say that we certainly do not need new regulations which raise the cost of employment and make Europe's labour market less flexible and less competitive with overseas suppliers. If we are to have a European Company Statute, it should contain the minimum regulations. And certainly we in Britain would fight attempts to introduce collectivism and corporatism at the European level – although what people wish to do in their own countries is a matter for them.

---

[1] The ecu – or European currency unit – is a notional currency based on the 'basket' of currencies in the European Monetary System.

[2] Two IRA terrorists were arrested on the Dutch–German border on 31 August 1988. During the preceding four months, the IRA had killed three RAF servicemen in Holland and exploded bombs at two British Army bases in West Germany.

Europe Open to the World

My fourth guiding principle is that Europe should not be protectionist. The expansion of the world economy requires us to continue the process of removing barriers to trade, and to do so in the multilateral negotiations in the GATT. It would be a betrayal if, while breaking down constraints on trade within Europe, the Community were to erect greater external protection. We must ensure that our approach to world trade is consistent with the liberalization we preach at home. We have a responsibility to give a lead on this, a responsibility which is particularly directed towards the less developed countries. They need not only aid; more than anything they need improved trading opportunities, if they are to gain the dignity of growing economic strength and independence.

Europe and Defence

My last guiding principle concerns the most fundamental issue: the European countries' role in defence. Europe must continue to maintain a sure defence through NATO. There can be no question of relaxing our efforts, even though it means taking difficult decisions and meeting heavy costs.

It is to NATO that we owe the peace that has been maintained over forty years. The fact is, things *are* going our way: the democratic model of a free enterprise society *has* proved itself superior; freedom *is* on the offensive, a peaceful offensive, the world over for the first time in my lifetime.

We must strive to maintain the United States's commitment to Europe's defence. That means recognizing the burden on their resources of the world role they undertake, and their point that their allies should play a full part in the defence of freedom, particularly as Europe grows wealthier. Increasingly they will look to Europe to play a part in out-of-area defence, as we have recently done in the Gulf. NATO and the WEU[1] have long recognized where the problems with Europe's defences

[1] The Western European Union (WEU) is an organization for collective self-defence based on the Treaty of Brussels, a fifty-year alliance signed by Britain, France, Belgium, Luxembourg and the Netherlands on 17 March 1948. The subsequent adhesion of Italy and West Germany led to the formal inauguration of the WEU on 6 May 1955.

lie, and have pointed out the solutions. The time has come when we must give substance to our declarations about a strong defence effort with better value for money.

It's not an institutional problem. It's not a problem of drafting. It's something at once simpler and more profound: it is a question of political will and political courage, of convincing people in all our countries that we cannot rely for ever on others for our defence, but that each member of the Alliance must shoulder a fair share of the burden.

We must keep up public support for nuclear deterrence, remembering that obsolete weapons do not deter, hence the need for modernization. We must meet the requirements for effective conventional defence in Europe against Soviet forces, which are constantly being modernized. We should develop the WEU, not as an alternative to NATO, but as a means of strengthening Europe's contribution to the common defence of the West. Above all, at a time of change and uncertainty in the Soviet Union and Eastern Europe, we must preserve Europe's unity and resolve, so that whatever may happen our defence is sure.

At the same time, we must negotiate on arms control and keep the door wide open to co-operation on all the other issues covered by the Helsinki Accords.

But let us never forget that our way of life, our vision, and all that we hope to achieve is secured not by the rightness of our cause but by the strength of our defence. On this we must never falter, never fail.

The British Approach

I believe it is not enough just to talk in general terms about a European vision or ideal. If we believe in it, we must chart the way ahead and identify the next steps. That's what I have tried to do this evening.

This approach does not require new documents. They are all there: the North Atlantic Treaty, the revised Brussels Treaty, and the Treaty of Rome, texts written by far-sighted men, a remarkable Belgian – Paul Henri Spaak[1] – among them. However far we may want to go, the truth is that we can only get there one step at a time. What we need now is to take decisions on the next steps forward rather than let ourselves be

---

[1] Paul-Henri Spaak (1899–1972), Belgian statesman. Minister for Foreign Affairs 1936–38, 1939–45, 1945–47, 1954–57, 1961–66; Prime Minister 1938–39, 1947–49; Secretary-General of NATO 1957–61.

distracted by Utopian goals. Utopia never comes, because we know we should not like it if it did.

Let Europe be a family of nations, understanding each other better, appreciating each other more, doing more together but relishing our national identity no less than our common European endeavour. Let us have a Europe which plays its full part in the wider world, which looks outward not inward, and which preserves that Atlantic Community – that Europe on both sides of the Atlantic – which is our noblest inheritance and our greatest strength.

May I thank you for the privilege of delivering this lecture in this great hall to this great College.

36

Speech to the Royal Society, 27 September 1988

It was as a scientist, as much as a politician, that Mrs Thatcher delivered her speech to the Royal Society on 27 September 1988. During the previous year, the Prime Minister had reformed the Government's approach to the funding of scientific research in order to shift the emphasis onto pure science and away from activities which could be better left to the private sector. At about the same time she had become convinced by the scientific arguments suggesting that the global environment was seriously threatened as a result of the depletion of the ozone layer (which protects life from ultra-violet radiation) and the build-up of 'greenhouse gases' (which might lead to climatic change). Inevitably, the Royal Society speech raised more questions than it answered, because (in Mrs Thatcher's view) any 'answers' had both to be based on sound science and be compatible with the economic prosperity that alone could provide the resources to deal with pollution and other environmental dangers.

But media reaction to the speech confirmed its political significance. The Times *commented:*

The Prime Minister, who until now has been widely regarded as a sceptic on the issue, said that protecting the balance of nature was 'one of the great challenges' of the rest of the century.

Her scenario, putting global pollution high on the political agenda, will delight environmentalists and the growing number of Tory backbenchers who want the Government to give a greenish tinge to its free enterprise policies. Her remarks also indicate that Mrs Thatcher recognizes that the electorate is becoming increasingly concerned about the threat to the planet's eco-system and is determined that she will not be outflanked by her political opponents.

Mr President, Your Excellencies, Fellows of the Royal Society, Ladies and Gentlemen: It was at your annual dinner of 1972 that I had the privilege of speaking to *your* Society in my capacity as Secretary of State for Education and Science. This is my first opportunity as *Prime Minister* to address *our* Society, of which I am so proud to be a Fellow.

I confess that I am quite pleased that I didn't continue my work on glyceride monolayers in the early 1950s, or I might never had got here at all! But I am reminded of a reviewer of Solly Zuckerman's[1] recent autobiography, who said that as a rule scientists rarely make successful politicians. From *my* experience let me say this: in today's world it is very good for politicians to have had the benefit of a scientific background.

And not only politicians. Those who work in industry, in commerce, in investment. Indeed, so important has it become that I believe we are right to make science a compulsory subject for all schoolchildren.

Over its 343-year history, the Royal Society has become the leading British academy of science, with over a thousand Fellows and, in keeping with your international tradition and standing, nearly a hundred foreign members.

As you know Mr President, we have tried in No. 10 Downing Street to recognize the enormous contributions that scientists have made and are making to our prosperity and intellectual reputation as a people, by showing prominently portraits of eminent scientists among our pictures of those who have done so much for our country. And so we have Michael Faraday in the hall. We have Isaac Newton in the dining room, and paintings of Robert Boyle, Humphry Davy, Edmund Halley and Dorothy Hodgkin in our other rooms.[2] Indeed, we have just redecorated No. 10, and have changed some of the other pictures, so there are several spaces vacant. I should like to fill them during my years of office with more of today's scientists. Alas, we have found that many distinguished scientists do not devote time to being painted by distinguished artists on canvases of the right size. I should be grateful if you could rectify this state of affairs.

---

[1] Solly Zuckerman (1904–93), Baron Zuckerman of Burnham Thorpe 1981, South African-born zoologist. Professor of Anatomy at Birmingham 1946–68; Chief Scientific Adviser to HM Government 1964–71.

[2] Michael Faraday (1791–1867), British chemist and physicist, pioneer of electricity. Sir Isaac Newton (1642–1727), English physicist and mathematician, founder of modern physics. Robert Boyle (1627–91), Anglo-Irish physicist and chemist, who formulated Boyle's Law on the compressibility of gases. Sir Humphry Davy (1778–1829), British chemist, who discovered the elements sodium, potassium, calcium, boron, magnesium, strontium and barium. Edmund Halley (1656–1742), English geophysicist, meteorologist and astronomer, who identified in 1705 the comet later named after him. Dorothy Hodgkin (1910–94), British biochemist, who analysed the structure of penicillin, insulin, and vitamin B12.

Everyone here, and no one more than myself, will support Whitehead's[1] statement that a nation which does not value trained intelligence is doomed. Science and the pursuit of knowledge are given high priority by successful countries, not because they are a luxury which the prosperous can afford, but because experience has taught us that knowledge and its effective use are vital to national prosperity and international standing.

But we need to guard against two dangerous fallacies: first that research should be driven wholly by utilitarian considerations; and second, the opposite, that excellence in science cannot be attained if work is undertaken for economic or other useful purposes.

We should not forget that *industry* has had its share of Nobel Prizes. AT&T for the transistor; IBM for warm superconductors. EMI for X-ray tomography. It is time we won some more.

In a January White Paper, and on various occasions since, this Government has made it clear that the *commercial* development of scientific principles should mainly be the task of industry. It is in industry's own interest to pursue the research needed for its own business, collaborating with partners as necessary. Industry could also help our academics to spot commercial applications when they arise unexpectedly during the course of more basic work. There are too many stories of British discoveries being published without patent protection, only to make money for foreign lands. Industry is becoming more scientific-minded, scientists more industry-minded. Both have a responsibility to recognize the practical value of the ideas which are being developed.

Basic Science

In your Dimbleby Lecture on knowledge and its power, Mr President,[2] you stressed the importance of basic science in a challenging way. You will know, from our joint attendance at the new Advisory Council on Science and Technology (ACOST),[3] that this is a view which I share. It is mainly by unlocking nature's most basic secrets, whether it be about

[1] A.N. Whitehead (1861–1947), British philosopher and mathematician.
[2] Sir George Porter (born 1920), Baron Porter of Luddenham 1990. President of the Royal Society 1985–90, Professor of Photomolecular Sciences at Imperial College, London 1987–.
[3] The Advisory Council on Science and Technology was created in August 1987 to identify sectors for state-funded research and development.

the structure of matter and the fundamental forces or about the nature of life itself, that we have been able to build the modern world. This is a world which is able to sustain far more people with a decent standard of life than Malthus[1] and even thinkers of a few decades ago would have believed possible.

It is not only material welfare. It is about access to the arts, no longer the preserve of the very few, which the gramophone, radio, colour photography, satellites and television have already brought, and which holography will transform further.

Of course, the nation as a whole *must* support the discovery of basic scientific knowledge through Government finance. But there are difficult choices, and I should like to make just three points.

First, although basic science can have colossal economic rewards, they are totally unpredictable. And therefore the rewards cannot be judged by immediate results. Nevertheless, the value of Faraday's work today must be higher than the capitalization of all the shares on the Stock Exchange! Indeed it is astonishing how quickly the benefits of curiosity-driven research sometimes appear. During the Great War, our then President, J.J. Thomson,[2] cited the use of X-rays in locating and assessing the damage of bullet wounds. The value of the saving of life and limb was beyond calculation, yet X-rays had only been accidentally discovered in 1895.

Second, no nation has unlimited funds, and it will have even less if it wastes them. A commitment to basic science cannot mean a blank cheque for everyone with – if I may put it colloquially – a bee in his bonnet. That would spread the honey too thinly.

So, what projects to support? Politicians can't decide. And, Heaven knows, it is difficult enough for our own Advisory Body of Scientists to say yea or nay to the many applications. I have always had a great deal of sympathy for Max Perutz's[3] view that we should be ready to support those teams, however small, which can demonstrate the intellectual flair and leadership which is driven by intense curiosity and dedication.

A good researcher is keenly competitive and wants to be first. The final stage of the race for the DNA structure was as exciting as any

[1] Thomas Malthus (1766–1834), British economist. His *Essay on the Principle of Population* (1798) argued that population tended to increase at a much faster rate than food supplies.
[2] J.J. Thomson (1856–1940), British physicist who discovered the electron.
[3] Max Perutz (born 1914), Austrian-born British biochemist, best known for work on the structure of the haemoglobin molecule.

Olympic marathon. The natural desire of gifted people to excel and gain the credit for their work must be harnessed. It is a great source of intellectual energy.

We accept that we cannot measure the value of the work by economic output, but this is no argument for lack of careful management in the way specific projects are conducted. The money is not for top-heavy administration, but for research. If only we could cut some £20 million from *very* large-scale projects – where the non-scientists sometimes outnumber the scientists – *that* money could provide support for hundreds of young researchers, whose requirements are measured in thousands of pounds.

My third point is that, despite an increase in the basic science budget of 15 per cent in real terms since 1979, the United Kingdom is only able to carry out a small proportion of the world's fundamental research, and that of course is true of most countries. It is, therefore, very important to encourage our own people to be aware of the work that is going on overseas and to come back here with their broadened outlook and new knowledge. It is also healthy to have overseas people working here.

We already do much to encourage international travel and teamwork. The Royal Society has forty-four exchange agreements with learned societies overseas, leading to a thousand exchanges a year. Through the SERC (the Science and Engineering Research Council), the Government funds some 1,230 post-doctoral fellowships, half of which are tenable overseas for one year, and often more. The recent visits of the Presidents of the Soviet and Chinese Academies and the increased exchanges to which they will lead are most welcome. The Society's work in promoting internationalism has my strongest support.

Mr President, this country will be judged by its contribution to knowledge and its capacity to turn that knowledge to advantage. It is only when industry and academia recognize and mobilize each other's strengths that the full intellectual energy of Britain will be released. In this respect we greatly appreciate your work and that of Sir Francis Tombs,[1] Chairman of ACOST.

---

[1] Sir Francis Tombs (born 1924), Baron Tombs of Brailes 1990. Chairman of the Electricity Council 1977–80; Chairman of Rolls-Royce 1985–92; Chairman of ACOST 1987–90.

The Environment

Mr President, the Royal Society's Fellows and other scientists, through hypothesis, experiment and deduction have solved many of the world's problems. Research on medicine has saved millions and millions of lives, as you have tackled diseases such as malaria, smallpox, tuberculosis and others. Consequently the world's population, which was one billion in 1800, two billion in 1927, is now five billion souls and rising. Research on agriculture has developed seeds and fertilizers sufficient to sustain that rising population, contrary to the gloomy prophecies of two or three decades ago. But we are left with pollution from nitrates and an enormous increase in methane which is causing problems. Engineering and scientific advance have given us transport by land and air, the capacity and need to exploit fossil fuels which had lain unused for millions of years. One result is a vast increase in carbon dioxide. And this has happened just when great tracts of forests which help to absorb it have been cut down.

For generations, we have assumed that the efforts of mankind would leave the fundamental equilibrium of the world's systems and atmosphere stable. But it is possible that with all these enormous changes (population, agricultural, use of fossil fuels) concentrated into such a short period of time, we have unwittingly begun a massive experiment with the system of this planet itself.

Recently three changes in atmospheric chemistry have become familiar subjects of concern. The first is the increase in the greenhouse gases – carbon dioxide, methane and chlorofluorocarbons – which has led some to fear that we are creating a global heat-trap, which could lead to climatic instability. We are told that a warming effect of one degree Centigrade per decade would greatly exceed the capacity of our natural habitat to cope. Such warming could cause accelerated melting of glacial ice and a consequent increase in the sea level of several feet over the next century. This was brought home to me at the Commonwealth Conference in Vancouver last year when the President of the Maldive Islands reminded us that the highest part of the Maldives is only six feet above sea level. The population is 177,000. It is noteworthy that the five warmest years in a century of records have all been in the 1980s – though we may not have seen much evidence in Britain!

The second matter under discussion is the discovery by the British Antarctic Survey of a large hole in the ozone layer which protects life from ultra-violet radiation. We don't know the full implications of the ozone hole, nor how it may interact with the greenhouse effect. Nevertheless, it was common sense to support a worldwide agreement in Montreal last year to halve the world consumption of chlorofluorocarbons by the end of the century. As the sole measure to limit ozone depletion this may be insufficient, but it is a start in reducing the pace of change while we continue the detailed study of the problem on which our (British) Stratospheric Ozone Review Group is about to report.

The third matter is acid deposition, which has affected soils, lakes and trees downwind from industrial centres. Extensive action is being taken to cut down emission of sulphur and nitrogen oxides from power stations, at great but necessary expense.

In studying the system of the earth and its atmosphere we have no laboratory in which to carry out controlled experiments. We have to rely on observations of natural systems. We need to identify particular areas of research which will help to establish cause and effect. We need to consider in more detail the likely effects of change within precise timescales. And to consider the wider implications for policy – for energy production, for fuel efficiency, for reforestation.

This is no small task, for the annual increase in atmospheric carbon dioxide alone is of the order of three billion tonnes. And half the carbon emitted since the Industrial Revolution remains in the atmosphere. We have an extensive research programme at our meteorological office, and we provide one of the world's four centres for the study of climatic change. We must ensure that what we do is founded on good science to establish cause and effect.

In the past, when we have identified forms of pollution we have shown our capacity to act effectively. The great London smogs are now only a nightmare of the past. We have cut airborne lead by 50 per cent. We are spending £4 billion on cleansing the Mersey Basin alone; and the Thames now has the cleanest metropolitan estuary in the world. Even though this kind of action may cost a lot, I believe it to be money well and necessarily spent, because the health of the economy and the health of our environment are totally dependent upon each other.

The Government espouses the concept of sustainable economic development. Stable prosperity can be achieved throughout the world provided the environment is nurtured and safeguarded. Protecting this balance of nature is therefore one of the great challenges of the late twentieth century, and one in which I am sure your advice will be repeatedly sought.

Conclusion

I have spoken about my own commitment to science and to the environment. And I have given you some idea of what Government is doing. I hope that the Royal Society will generate increased popular interest in science by explaining the importance and excitement of your work.

When Arthur Eddington[1] presented his results to this Society in 1919, showing the bending of starlight, it made headlines. It is reported that many people could not get into the meeting, so anxious were the crowds to find out whether the intellectual paradox of curved space had really been demonstrated. Should *we* be doing more to explain why we are looking for the Higgs Boson at CERN and trying to decode the human genome?[2]

This is a Golden Age of discovery and new thought. The natural world is full of fascination, providing the doors of understanding are opened. I applaud our Royal Society for its manifold achievements, and congratulate you Mr President on your splendid leadership.

I ask you to drink a toast to the Royal Society.

---

[1] Arthur Eddington (1882–1944), British astrophysicist, author of *The Expanding Universe* (1933).

[2] The Higgs Bosons are a new class of elementary particles whose existence was first predicted by Edinburgh physicist Peter Higgs on the basis of the Weinberg-Salam theory of interaction. The production of Higgs Bosons by the next generation of particle accelerators would confirm 'gauge' theories of fundamental forces. CERN (the Conseil Européen pour la Recherche Nucléaire) is a nuclear research organization founded in 1954 and based at Meyrin, near Geneva. The genome is the full complement of genes carried by a single set of chromosomes. The human genome project aims to locate and analyze every gene in the human body. The knowledge obtained will be of great value to medical science.

37

Speech to the Conservative Party Conference, Brighton, 14 October 1988

In retrospect, the 1988 Party Conference can be seen to mark a turning point in the Thatcher Government's fortunes. From now on political problems began to mount. The effects of the loose financial policies that would bring first inflation and then recession were already starting to become apparent. From the summer of 1988 interest rates rose steadily, though the sense of economic well-being lasted into the following year. The economic passages of Mrs Thatcher's Conference speech bear witness both to current prosperity and to concern about the future. The speech also covers ground on which Mrs Thatcher had entered earlier in the year, rehearsing the themes of the changes to the global environment and the need to resist European federalism. But perhaps the most enduringly significant passages are those in which she justifies Conservative policies against the (recurring) charges of materialism and selfishness.

Four years have passed since we last came to Brighton for our Conference. We all have memories of that week: memories sad and memories brave. But the human spirit is indomitable. And today we take inspiration from those of our friends, many of them here in this hall, friends who survived to rededicate themselves to the cause of freedom.

Madam President, all elections matter. But some matter more than others. Some elections are not just part of history. They make history. Such was our Conservative victory in 1979. After a series of socialist Governments that said: 'We can't,' Britain wanted a Government that said: 'We can.' It got one.

Nearly ten years in government – how much energy and commitment we have all put into the battle. And no one more so than the great friend and colleague we are delighted to have with us today: Willie Whitelaw. Nearly ten years in government – and a resurgence of freedom and prosperity without parallel. Nearly ten years – yet it's still we

Conservatives who set the pace, generate the ideas, and have the vision. Alone among the political parties, we hold fast to our convictions.

But next year's tenth anniversary is no time to rest on our laurels. It marks the start of our next ten. We are all too young to put our feet up. And I hope you'll excuse me if I include myself.

I'm not so sure though about our political opponents. They don't seem to have had too good a summer. After the two platoons of the old Alliance went their separate ways, up they popped last month at Torquay and Blackpool respectively. The second called the first one names, but seemed to have some difficulty knowing what name to call themselves.[1] All those initials are so confusing, aren't they? I suggest 'SOS' – but clearly things have gone too far for that. In the end, I think that they decided to be one thing in the country and whatever they felt like in the House of Commons. Or was it the other way round?

As for Labour's goings-on at Blackpool, for half an hour or so it seemed that their Leader had seen the light and would shortly be calling his memoirs 'I Did it Her Way'. Whatever happened to socialism?[2] I began to compose a gracious little tribute to get the new session off to a bright start.

Alas for high hopes. Was Labour about to shake off its union shackles and go it alone? Not on your Todd[3] – and that, Madam President, is positively the last Ron Todd joke at this Conference.

So it's back to square one for the socialists. The Labour leopard can't change its spots – even if it sometimes thinks wistfully of a blue rinse.

[1] On 3 March 1988, the Liberal Party and the SDP merged to form the Social and Liberal Democratic Party (SLDP). Three of the five Social Democrat MPs opposed the merger and relaunched 'the continuing SDP' on 8 March. The SLDP later renamed itself the Social and Liberal Democrats (SLD), but the working title of 'the Democrats', adopted by the 1988 Party Conference, never caught on.
[2] In his speech to the Labour Party Conference at Blackpool on 4 October 1988, Neil Kinnock talked about competitiveness and individualism and urged Labour to pay heed to wealth creation.
[3] Ron Todd (born 1927), General Secretary of the Transport and General Workers' Union 1985–92; Chairman of the TUC International Committee 1985–92. At the 1988 Labour Party Conference, he denounced 'sharp-suited cordless-telephone social- ism' and cast the 1.25 million votes of the TGWU in favour of a motion reaffirming unilateral nuclear disarmament, which was consequently passed on 6 October against the wishes of the Party Leader.

Materialism – The Community

Madam President, nearly ten years into this Conservative Government, and everybody knows that our policies work, and Labour's don't; that our policies have produced a standard of living undreamed of by our parents, and the highest standard of social services this country has ever known. The Japanese call it Britain's economic miracle – and who are we to argue? I'm proud that with a Conservative Government people are better off than they've ever been before.

But an odd thing has happened recently. Because we strive to increase the prosperity of the nation and its citizens, we are accused of materialism.

It's a curious charge. For years, one of the main arguments in British politics was how to secure economic growth. Now we've done that, now that we've halted and reversed the years of decline over which Labour presided, we are told that all we care about is 'Loadsamoney'.[1] Because we give people the chance to better themselves, they accuse us of encouraging selfishness and greed. What nonsense.

Does someone's natural desire to do well for himself, to build a better life for his family and provide opportunities for his children, does all this make him a materialist? Of course it doesn't. It makes him a decent human being, committed to his family and his community, and prepared to take responsibility on his own shoulders.

The truth is that what we are actually encouraging is the best in human nature. The prosperity brought about by our policies offers a wider choice to more people than ever before.

Yes, our children can travel to see the treasures and wonders of the world. Yes, older people can enjoy greater comfort and pursue their own interests. Yes, culture and the arts are thriving. Yes, people can expect to enjoy these things. And if that is the charge, I plead guilty.

And there's another reply to Labour's charge of materialism: our approach has meant more to spend on the social services. More on the Health Service. More on the disabled. Indeed, if you measure community concern by community spending – as Labour does – we win hands down every time.

---

[1] 'Loadsamoney' (i.e. loads of money) was the name given by British comedian Harry Enfield to a greedy, materialistic character in his television show 1987–88. Neil Kinnock accused the Government of 'Loadsamoney economics'.

Of course, we don't expect the Labour Party to have anything good to say about us. After all, they have hardly anything good to say about each other.

But it's time we took credit for some of the things we have achieved. For example: the eight million patients treated in hospitals each year; the 80 per cent increase in spending on benefits for the disabled; and an increase in real terms of 45 per cent in nurses' pay.

It's not for Labour, who cut nurses' pay, and cut hospital building, to lecture Conservatives on care and compassion.

Our Government has made enormous increases in the amount spent on social welfare to help the less fortunate – and so have individuals. As prosperity has increased, so the fundamental generosity of our people has prompted far more personal giving. Of course, there will always be a minority whose sole concern is themselves. But those who care – and they are the great majority of us – now have the means to give.

And they are giving in full measure: over £1,500 million a year to boost charities, rebuild churches, help medical research and feed the hungry. And it doesn't stop at individuals. Many businesses are now giving a percentage of their profits to help the community in which they are situated.

Is this materialism? Is this the selfish society? Are these the hallmarks of greed? The fact is that prosperity has created not the selfish society but the generous society. Madam President, Labour's charge is absurd.

Individuals in the Community

So our critics come up with a new charge. They say the individual gains his success only at the expense of the community.

That's wrong, too. Personal effort does not undermine the community; it enhances the community. When individual talents are held back, the community is held back too. Encourage the individual and the community benefits. A parent's success is shared by his family, a pupil's by his school, a soldier's by his regiment. A man may climb Everest for himself, but at the summit he plants his country's flag.

We can only build a responsible, independent community with responsible, independent people. That's why Conservative policies have given more and more of them the chance to buy their own homes, to build up capital, to acquire shares in their companies.

337

But there are some people – such as those living on housing estates controlled by hard-left councils, or parents with children going to inadequate schools – who, by the time of the last election, had not benefited from our policies as much as we'd like. Our last manifesto had those people especially in mind.

That's why we're giving council tenants new rights in housing. We believe that where families have a bigger say in their own home, the whole street looks up. In some areas, it's already happening.

And we're giving parents more say in their children's education. We believe that if parents help run schools, we'll get the best schools not just for their children, but for all children.

But it's not enough to pass new laws at Westminster. We have to see that the benefits reach the people for whom they were intended. And Madam President, we have to do that. We have to help those families. Otherwise they will be browbeaten by socialist Councillors and bombarded by socialist propaganda, calculated to deny them the opportunities we have provided. Greater responsibility gives more dignity to the individual and more strength to the community. That belief is at the heart of Conservatism. We must make it live.

The Economy

Madam President, when we were returned at that historic election in 1979 we were faced with the overriding threat of inflation. It was inflation that had redistributed wealth from the thrifty to the fly-by-night. It was inflation that had undermined confidence first in the currency, then in savings, then in investment, and finally in the country's future. To salvage our economy, we had first to defeat inflation, and only then could the great revival of the British economy begin.

Today we are in our eighth year of growth. Our unemployment figures are below the Community average. We have created more jobs than they have. Other countries come to our shores to see what we do and go home to copy.

Since we took office, we have handed eighteen state enterprises back to the British people – so far. We have encouraged ownership at home and ownership at work. We have turned small business from an endangered species to a vital and rapidly growing part of our economy. The habits of hard work, enterprise and inventiveness that made us great are with us again.

But however firmly rooted our new-found strength, you can't steer an economy on automatic pilot. Success doesn't look after itself. You have to work at it. In economics, there are no final victories.

At home, the fast pace of economic growth has put more money into people's pockets and more money into industry's profits. Some has been invested, but with rapid growth in consumption, imports have grown faster than exports, leaving us with a substantial trade deficit. And too much buying has been paid for by too much borrowing.

To encourage people to spend less and save more, the Chancellor has to raise interest rates. It's never popular to push them up – except perhaps with savers – but, popular or not, the Chancellor has done the right thing. And the right thing is to make sure that we continue to grow steadily, if less fast than in recent months.

Too much borrowing has also meant that inflation today is too high. Make no mistake: we intend to bring inflation down again. That's not an expression of hope. It's a statement of intent. I think the country knows us well enough by now to recognize that we say what we mean and mean what we say.

There are always pressures on Government to spend more than the country can afford. We're not going down that road. Not this year. Not next year. Not any year. We will continue to keep a firm grip on public spending. And I look forward to those who so roundly condemn extravagance with private money giving their wholehearted support to our prudence in handling the public's money.

Protecting our World

Madam President, there is nothing new or unusual about the Tory commitment to protect the environment. The last thing we want is to leave environmental debts for our children to clear up – slag, grime, acid rain and pollution.

For much of human history, man assumed that whatever he did, he could take his natural world for granted. Today we know that simply isn't true. In the last century or so, we have seen an unprecedented increase in the pace of change: the growth in population, the spread of industry, the dramatically increased use of oil, gas and coal, the cutting down of forests.

And these have created new and daunting problems: acid rain, and the greenhouse effect – a kind of global heat-trap and its consequences

339

for the world's climate. In the past, science has solved many problems which at the time seemed insuperable. It can do so again.

We are far too sensible to think that in 1988 we can turn the clock back to a pre-industrial world where Adam delved and Eve span. The Garden of Eden had a population of two. Our world has a population of five billion going on six. It has more than doubled in my own lifetime. Those people need to cook meals, heat homes, clothe themselves, find work. They need factories, roads, power stations. All these things are part of our lives today and the ambition of the Third World tomorrow.

So the choice facing us is not industrial development or a clean environment. To survive we need both. Industry is part of our habitat; economic growth is one of the systems that sustain human life today.

Madam President, pride in these islands – our countryside, our seas and rivers – runs like a thread through our history and literature. Sometimes, it seems a perverse pride. 'Fog, fog everywhere' begins one of Dickens's greatest novels.[1] That was still true in London when I first went to work there. But the Clean Air Act of 1956 – passed by a Conservative Government – banished smog from the air we breathe.

The Thames is now the cleanest metropolitan estuary in the world, and £4 billion is now being spent on the Mersey. I want to see the industrial rivers of the North and Midlands – and of Europe – as clean as the Thames. We have led Europe in banning the dumping of harmful industrial waste in the North Sea.

Given our record, we are well placed to take the lead with other Governments in practical efforts to protect the wider world. We will work with them to end the destruction of the world's forests. We shall direct more of our overseas aid to help poor countries to protect their trees and plant new ones. We will join with others to seek further protection of the ozone layer – that global skin which protects life itself from ultra-violet radiation. We will work to cut down the use of fossil fuels, a cause of both acid rain and the greenhouse effect. And, Madam President, that means a policy for safe, sensible and balanced use of nuclear power.

It's we Conservatives who are not merely friends of the earth[2] – we are its guardians and trustees for generations to come. The core of Tory philosophy and of the case for protecting the environment are the same.

[1] *Bleak House* (1853).
[2] A play on the name of the environmentalist group Friends of the Earth.

No generation has a freehold on this earth. All we have is a life tenancy – with a full repairing lease. This Government intends to meet the terms of that lease in full.

Law and Order

Year in, year out, this Conservative Government has taken action against crime: action on police numbers, on police powers, on firearms, on fraud, on prison building, on compensation for victims, on stiffer penalties.

And action against football hooligans and those who carry knives and firearms. And there is more to come. Witness, for example, the new Criminal Justice Act.[1] I hope that the courts will continue to take account of the strong public support for tough penalties against violent criminals. I am sure they will pay the most careful attention to the longer sentences that are now available to them.

Anyone who mugs an old lady leaving the post office with her pension; anyone who rapes a teenager walking home from an evening with friends; anyone who commits violence against a child, should have no shred of doubt about the severity of the sentence for that sort of brutality. Violent crime is a blight on too many lives. Its reduction has a claim not only on the political energy of the Government, but on the moral energy of the people.

We are not spectators in the battle between the police and criminals. We are all involved. To witness a crime and say nothing about it hinders the police and helps the criminal. To protect our own home from burglary hinders the criminal and helps the police.

There's a breed of left-wing politicians who excuse violence on the grounds that it's not the criminal who is guilty, but the rest of us. That's a specious argument left over from the sixties. In effect it excuses, indeed even encourages, crime by absolving the criminal of guilt in advance. Weasel words can never justify the actions of the robber, the thug or the hooligan.

Conservatives need no sermons from socialists on the role of law. We proposed tougher sentences for criminals who carry guns; they opposed them. We proposed that over-lenient sentences should be referred to

---

[1] The Criminal Justice Act 1988 introduced many technical reforms in respect of the rights of defendants, the admissibility of evidence, the powers of the Court of Appeal, etc.

the appeal court; Labour voted against. We condemned violence on the picket line; they equivocated.

And, year after year, they will not support the Prevention of Terrorism Act – an act which is vital to the defeat of the IRA and which has saved so many lives. I find that very hard to forgive.

Northern Ireland

In this country and in other democracies, the enemies of civilization and freedom have turned to the gun and the bomb to destroy those they can't persuade. The terrorist threat to freedom is worldwide. It can never be met by appeasement. Give in to the terrorist and you breed more terrorism.

At home and abroad our message is the same: we will not bargain, nor compromise, nor bend the knee to terrorists.

In our United Kingdom, the main terrorist threat has come from the IRA. Their minds twisted by hatred and fanaticism, they have tried to bomb and murder their way to their objective of tearing more than a million citizens out of the United Kingdom. The truth is that the whole IRA campaign is based on crushing democracy and smashing anyone who doesn't agree with them.

To all those who have suffered so much at their hands – to the Northern Ireland policemen and prison officers and their families, to the soldiers, the judges, the civil servants and their families – we offer our deepest admiration and thanks for defending democracy and for facing danger while keeping within the rule of law – unlike the terrorist who skulks in the shadows and shoots to kill. We thank too the security forces who had the guts to go to Gibraltar to give evidence to the inquest, demonstrating conclusively that they acted at all times within the law and to save lives.[1] The lives of countless people who would have been killed had the IRA fulfilled their murderous purpose.

What a pity it is that there are still some in this country not prepared to accept the verdict of the jury, so great is their prejudice against the security forces. What comfort that must be to the terrorists.

We will work to increase co-operation in security between the sovereign Governments in London and Dublin. We will work to involve both

---

[1] On 6 March 1988, three IRA terrorists were shot dead in Gibraltar by British security forces. An inquest jury returned a verdict of lawful killing on 30 September.

Protestants and Catholics fully and fairly in the economic and political life of Northern Ireland. But we will never give up the search for more effective ways of defeating the IRA. If the IRA think they can weary us or frighten us, they have made a terrible miscalculation.

People sometimes say that it is wrong to use the word 'never' in politics. I disagree. Some things are of such fundamental importance that no other word is appropriate. So I say once again today that this Government will never surrender to the IRA. Never.

East/West and Defence

Madam President, great changes are taking place in world affairs – no less momentous, no less decisive for our future than those which followed the Second World War.

But there is a crucial difference. This time liberty is gaining ground the world over. Communism is in retreat, democracy and free enterprise are showing that only they can meet the real needs of people.

Britain's resurgence and our close relationship with the United States under President Reagan's strong leadership have put us right at the forefront of these great events. Once again we are playing the part which history and our instincts demand. President Reagan has rebuilt the strength and confidence of the West – not without a little help – and inspired the democracies to go out and win the battle of ideas. It is vital that Britain and America should always stand together. So the next President of the United States too will have the United Kingdom as a staunch ally. The need for strong leadership in America and in Britain will be no less in the period ahead.

Perhaps one day the exciting developments taking place in the Soviet Union will lead to a freer society and less expansionist aims. Let us hope so. But hope is no basis for a defence policy. For all the bold reforms, the Soviet Union remains a one-party state, in which the Communist Party is supreme, and Soviet forces remain far in excess of what they need for defence alone. So we have to keep our sense of perspective, and our defences in good repair.

The old dangers persist, and we have also to be alert to new dangers. Even as relations with the Soviet Union become more hopeful, some other countries have already acquired chemical weapons and missiles. What's more, some seek nuclear weapons.

Madam President, it is in the nature of democracies to relax at the first sign of hope. This we must not do. For great change is also a time of great uncertainty, especially in the countries of Eastern Europe. Now more than ever the West must be united and prepared.

NATO's purpose is to prevent not only nuclear war but all war. Its strategy recognizes that conventional weapons alone cannot provide an effective deterrent against either a nuclear threat or the massive conventional and chemical weapons of the Warsaw Pact.

Yet last week in Blackpool, Labour reduced the defence of the realm to a farce. Their new secret weapon for Britain's defence was revealed. It was a form of words. Labour's leadership proposed a composite resolution embracing unilateral disarmament, bilateral disarmament and multilateral disarmament, all at the same time. Not to defend Britain against her enemies, but to defend the Labour Leader against his enemies.

And, like all forms of appeasement, it failed. The Labour Conference passed a resolution reaffirming Labour's commitment to one-sided disarmament.

But the only resolution that matters is the unswerving resolution of this Conservative Government. The British people know that it is our strength which keeps us safe.

Europe

I spoke recently in Bruges about Britain's views on Europe. It caused a bit of a stir. Indeed, from some of the reactions you would have thought I had reopened the Hundred Years War. And from the avalanche of support, you'd have thought I'd won it single-handed.

And why all the fuss? Because I reminded people that Europe was not created by the Treaty of Rome? Because I said that willing and active co-operation between independent sovereign states is the best way to build a successful European Community? Because I said that to try to suppress nationhood and concentrate power at the centre of a European conglomerate would be highly damaging and would jeopardize the objectives we seek to achieve?

Of course, that wasn't at all convenient for those who want to bring about a federal Europe by stealth. They don't like having these points aired publicly. That was evident from their confusion. First they argued that national identity is not threatened by Brussels. Then they said that the whole idea of nationhood is old-fashioned and out of date anyway. Well, they can't have it both ways!

But I welcome the debate, because it has brought into the open an equally fundamental question – the choice between two kinds of Europe: a Europe based on the widest possible freedom for enterprise; or a Europe governed by socialist methods of centralized control and regulation. There is no doubt what the Community's founders intended. The Treaty of Rome is a charter for economic liberty, which they knew was the essential condition for personal and political liberty. Today that founding concept is under attack from those who see European unity as a vehicle for spreading socialism. We haven't worked all these years to free Britain from the paralysis of socialism only to see it creep in through the back door of central control and bureaucracy from Brussels. That wasn't what we joined the European Community for. Ours is the true European ideal. It is that ideal which will fire our campaign in the European elections. That is why we must win every possible seat in the European Parliament for the Conservative cause.[1] We shall point out that Britain has taken the lead in tackling practical issues in Europe which are of real benefit to people – reform of the Common Agricultural Policy, completion of the Single Market, the fight against terrorism and drugs; that Britain continues to make the second-largest financial contribution to Europe; that Britain stations more forces beyond its borders – nearly seventy thousand of them – than any other European country in defence of freedom. With those sort of credentials no one should doubt Britain's wholehearted commitment to Europe.

Conclusion

Madam President, every year the press tells us in advance that Conservative Conferences are dull affairs in which everyone agrees with everyone else. And every year we have a debate on law and order.

Still, the press is right in one respect. Everyone can see, through all the cut and thrust of debate, that this Party is united on the great fundamentals of politics. The same truths. That individuals have a right to liberty that no state can take away. That Government is the servant of the people, not its master. That the role of Government is to strengthen

[1] European Parliament election, 15 June 1989: Labour 45, Conservatives 32, others 4.

our freedom, not deny it. That the economic role of Government is to establish a climate in which enterprise can flourish, not to elbow enterprise out of the way. That a wise Government will spread opportunities, but that individuals must seize them. That citizens who are protected by the law have a duty to assist in maintaining the law. That freedom entails responsibilities, first to the family, then to neighbours, then to the nation – and beyond. That a strong Britain is the surest guarantor of peace.

As well as these grand themes, we have always believed in what is small and precious, in the value of what is local and familiar, in the patchwork of voluntary groups and associations, each with its own purpose, but all pursuing the common purpose of making the country a better and more civilized place.

These are the beliefs which sustain us. Other parties may discard their principles along with their names, or seek to conceal their beliefs in order to win power. We hold by the principles we know to be right.

Right. Not right because they serve our interests. Not even right just because they work. But right because they express all that is best in human nature.

Nothing less would have sustained us through the difficult early days of this Government. Nothing less would have ensured the loyalty of our supporters and the trust of the British people when the going wasn't so good.

But we had – and have – the great assurance. Our beliefs are not lofty abstractions confined to philosophy lectures. They are the commonsense of the British people. They are what ordinary men and women agree on instinctively.

The Conservative Party occupies the common ground of British politics. Indeed, we staked out that ground. And it is where the great mass of the British people have pitched their tents. And so it has fallen to us to lead Britain into the 1990s. And, who knows, beyond.

There will be new challenges, new problems, new tests. For there are no final victories in politics either. But, Madam President, we will meet them strengthened by our belief in this country. In the talents and wisdom of its people. In their tolerance and fairness. In their decency and kindness. And in their confidence and in their courage.

38

Speech to the Conservative Party Conference, Blackpool, 13 October 1989

By the time the Conservative Party gathered in Blackpool in October 1989, it was clear both to observers and to the Prime Minister and her colleagues that the Government was facing major problems. These were predominantly economic; but they were also personal. Relations between Mrs Thatcher and Chancellor of the Exchequer Nigel Lawson were tense and mistrustful – she blaming him for the policy of shadowing the Deutschmark which had brought a return of inflation, he increasingly sensitive about his reputation. During the Party Conference, tricky negotiations had to take place between the two, even about the wording of references in their speeches to the exchange rate.

There were other problems too. As the Prime Minister had foreseen, the anniversary of her ten years in power prompted critical surveys. The elections for the European Assembly in June had gone badly, which served as an occasion for critics of the Bruges speech to voice their dissent.

But the longer-term significance of the Prime Minister's 1989 Conference speech lies in the way in which it addressed the crumbling of communism that was now taking place. East German refugees had been flooding out through Hungary to the West. The demolition of the Berlin Wall would shortly begin. It was not just the left, however, who would have to come to terms with the end of the Cold War; so would Conservatives, not least those like Mrs Thatcher who were regarded as the archetypal Cold Warriors. In her speech, the Prime Minister repeatedly links the failure of socialism behind the Iron Curtain with its inevitable failure in Western countries, while mocking the Labour Party's conversion of convenience to apparently non-socialist policies.

I can think of no more fitting Chairman for this final session of our Conference than you Mr President,[1] the greatest team player in British

[1] Lord Whitelaw.

politics, a straight bat at the wicket, steady on the green, mighty in the scrum. Your role in Government was invaluable: always wise, often witty, and just occasionally . . . wily. I know that I speak for everyone when I say that this Conference extends to you and Celia the warmest possible thank-you: it's marvellous to see you both here. And may I say thank you to our Party Chairman, Kenneth Baker, for getting our Conference off to a flying start with such a terrific speech.

Mr President, this Conference, as distinct from last week's little exercise in shadow-boxing in Brighton,[1] has addressed, head-on, the real issues of the day. Which is what you would expect from a Party and a Government of real beliefs. Not for us, disposable ideals. Not for us, throwaway conviction. Not for us, rent-a-principle. We Conservatives know what we believe, say what we believe, and stand by what we believe.

The Triumph of Freedom

Mr President, what a fantastic year this has been for freedom. 1989 will be remembered for decades to come as the year when the people of half our continent began to throw off their chains.

The messages on our banners in 1979 – freedom, opportunity, family, enterprise, ownership – are now inscribed on the banners in Leipzig, Warsaw, Budapest and even Moscow. For decades, East Germans had risked their lives to claw their way through the barbed wire to freedom. Now they come not by the brave handful, but by the cheerful thousand. Hungary, turning day by day more confidently towards freedom and dignity, dismantles communism and opens her borders to the West.[2] In Poland, the freely elected representatives of a courageous people move resolutely into the seats of government. Let us never forget Poland's contribution to our own Finest Hour.[3] Mr President, what happened in

[1] The Labour Party Conference was held at Brighton from 1 to 6 October 1989.
[2] Hungary started to dismantle its border fences in May 1989. On 10 September it suspended an agreement with the GDR to send back East Germans without travel documents. Twenty-four thousand East Germans thereupon entered Austria via Hungary. East Germany announced the opening of its border with West Germany on 9 November 1989, and demolition of the Berlin Wall started the next day.
[3] A Solidarity-dominated Government took office in Poland on 12 September 1989 – the first Government in Eastern Europe not to be under communist control since 1948. In 1940, the Polish Air Force fought alongside the RAF in the Battle of Britain.

Russia in 1917 wasn't a revolution. It was a *coup d'état*. The true revolution is what is happening in Russia and Eastern Europe today.

In 1979 we knew that we were starting a British revolution; in fact, we were the pioneers of a world revolution. So it's ironic that as enterprise and liberty rise from the dead ashes of state control, the Labour Party here is still trying to blow life into those old embers.

Imagine a Labour canvasser talking on the doorstep to those East German families when they settle in, on freedom's side of the Wall. 'You want to keep more of the money you earn? I'm afraid that's very selfish. We shall want to tax that away. You want to own shares in your firm? We can't have that. The state has to own your firm. You want to choose where to send your children to school? That's very divisive. You'll send your child where we tell you.'

The trouble with Labour is that they're just not at home with freedom. Socialists don't like ordinary people choosing, for they might not choose socialism. That's why Labour wants the state to take more and more of the decisions.

'But that's all changed,' we're told. If you believe the reports, Brighton last week was the scene of an unprecedented mass conversion. Nothing like it since the Chinese General who baptized his entire army with a hosepipe.

Isn't it amazing? The Party which fought to stop council tenants having the right to buy their homes now tells us it is the Party of home ownership. The Party which called for one-sided nuclear disarmament now stands for strong defence. The Party which took us to the IMF, like some Third World country, now primly poses as a model of financial rectitude. And it's all happened, as dear old Tommy Cooper used to say, 'Just like that.'[1] Would you believe it? Well, no; actually I wouldn't.

You see, one can't help wondering: if it's that easy for the Labour Leader to give up the principles in which he does believe, won't it be even easier for him to give up the principles in which he does not believe?

The truth is: nothing has really changed. Labour just wants power at any price, and they'll say anything to get it. Labour's real prescription for Britain is the disease half the world is struggling to cure.

And as for the leaders of the former Alliance Parties, I will say no

---

[1] Tommy Cooper (1922–84), Welsh comedian and magician. 'Just like that!' was his catch-phrase.

more than this: they have never learned what every woman knows – you can't make a soufflé rise twice.

The Heart of the Matter

Mr President, it is no accident that socialism has failed. Nor that the democracies and free enterprise economies of the West have prospered. These results are the inevitable consequences of two quite different approaches.

It's not a question of a little less planning here or a little less regulation there, or a fraction more private capital in this sector or a touch more competition in that. Socialism is not just about economics. Its central dogma is to make the state the ultimate authority for the whole of life. It's based on coercion. It denies the dignity of people. It is a secular creed which has utterly failed.

The ruins that remain of socialism in Europe today are physical shortages, a corrupt bureaucracy, growing unrest, and the urgent cry of those refugees: 'We want to get out.'

Our creed never set out to dominate the whole of life. At the heart of our belief is the principle of freedom, under a rule of law. Freedom that gives a man room to breathe, to take responsibility, to make his own decisions and to chart his own course. Remove man's freedom and you dwarf the individual, you devalue his conscience and you demoralize him. That is the heart of the matter.

Some talk as if we should be ashamed of harnessing men's talents to the common good. They paint wealth as selfishness, a better standard of living as greed. But only by creating wealth can you relieve poverty. It's what you do with your wealth that counts.

In these ten Conservative years, voluntary giving has doubled. Individuals and companies contribute unprecedented sums to rejuvenate the inner cities and support great charitable causes. Others give their time and their effort.

Of course, there are people who are selfish. There are people who are downright evil. Human wickedness is always with us – but you'll find it's not in this Party that crime and hooliganism are excused. For the most part, freedom enables and moves men and women to be warm-hearted and generous. For every Pharisee our system produces, you will find at least three good Samaritans.

Economy

Ten years ago, we set out together on a great venture. To provide a new lexicon for prosperity. To replace 'It can't be done,' with 'I'll have a go.' And we succeeded.

Yes, there are still serious problems to tackle – and I'll come to them in a moment. But let us set them against the massive achievements of our period in office. Industry: modernized at a pace unrivalled in the post-war years. Productivity in manufacturing: gains far exceeding those in Europe and North America. Profits: the best for twenty years, leading to investment at record levels. Jobs: more people in work in Britain than ever before. Living standards: higher than we have ever known. Reducing the national debt, not piling it up for our children to repay. Privatization: five industries that together were losing over £2 million a week in the public sector, now making profits of over £100 million a week in the private sector.

That is the measure of our achievements.

But if you really want to see how the economy is doing, look at the newspapers. No, I didn't say read them. Just count the ones that didn't exist before 1979 – and weigh the ones that did.

And if you're still not satisfied, talk to the Americans and Japanese. They are investing more in Britain than in any other European country. Moreover, for the first time in years there are as many British as there are German companies in the top hundred in Europe. Further, of these, six of the seven top earners are British or part-British.

And, with all these achievements under our belt, who presumes to advise us on inflation? Labour – who hold the record for the highest inflation for fifty years: 27 per cent.

Mr President, all inflation is painful. So is reducing it. But in 1982 we got it down to 5 per cent, and by 1986 to 3 per cent. Today, inflation is 7.6 per cent. For a Conservative Government that's far too high. We must get it down again. And we will.

But I know what a worry inflation is, especially for pensioners. We have always promised that whatever the rise in inflation, the retirement pension will be fully protected against it. This month's figure for inflation, which came out this morning, is the one used for the pension increase next April. That means that the single pension next April will go up by £3.30 and the married pension by £5.30. This Government keeps its promises.

I also know what a worry high interest rates are for families with mortgages and for those involved in farming and small businesses. But when the choice is between high rates now or persistent higher inflation later, with all the damage that would do, the choice is clear.

Inflation will come down through the use of high interest rates, as it has in the past. And so it must, for the rest of the world isn't standing still. America, Japan, West Germany – they're all investing, modernizing, cutting costs. To stay competitive, we must do the same.

As Nigel Lawson made clear yesterday, industry must not expect to find refuge in a perpetually depreciating currency. Only by steadily improving efficiency will we win and keep our share of the world's markets.

Britain's economy is strong. When inflation is beaten – and it will be – Britain will be stronger still.

Conservatism and Choice

Mr President, we Conservatives have extended ownership of homes, shares and pensions to more people than ever before. We've created that democracy of ownership upon which political democracy depends. We've laid the economic foundations of a decent and prosperous future.

None of this would have been possible without the two finest Chancellors of the Exchequer since the war – Geoffrey Howe and Nigel Lawson.[1] Their achievements have enabled us to provide more resources where they were needed – for schools, for hospitals, for pensioners and disabled people.

But money can't achieve everything. We have to make sure that public services meet the needs of the public, and not just the convenience of those who work in them. It would be wholly wrong if people could only exercise choice in the private sector, and were given no choice in the public sector – if they had simply to take it or leave it. If patients had no choice where they were to be treated, they'd be left on long waiting lists. If parents couldn't choose their children's school, they'd have to go where the local authority sent them. If tenants had no say in the way their estates were run, they'd be under the thumb of their council landlords. What could be more democratic than to give people a direct say in these things?

[1] Nigel Lawson would resign as Chancellor of the Exchequer on 26 October 1989.

What could be more arrogant than to deny it to them? That's why choice matters so much; choice for the less well-off as much as for the comfortably off.

Health

Mr President, in every year since I became Prime Minister more money has been spent on the Health Service; in every year more doctors and nurses have been recruited; and in every year more patients have been treated. These are the actions of a Government determined to make the Health Service one of the best in the world. The advances in the last ten years have – by any standards – been remarkable.

At the same time people rightly worry about waiting lists for operations and also about the time that outpatients have to wait before being seen. The time taken to treat patients can be weeks in one area and years in another.

There are some who say that the only way to improve the NHS further is to give more money. So we have. Two billion pounds more this year than last.

But the truth is that money on its own is not the answer. That's why we are looking at other ways of improving the service to the patient. We want those hospitals and doctors who carry the heaviest burden of work to be rewarded for it. We want people to be able to choose where they can get the best and quickest hospital care. In view of some of the false impressions that have been created, let me emphasize one simple point.

The National Health Service will not be privatized. The National Health Service was never going to be privatized. No matter what the emergency, accident or disease, no matter how long or complicated the treatment, the Health Service is there, the Health Service will always be there, to provide the finest care. There to heal, there to cure and there to tend the needs of the patient.

Education

Mr President, we all want our children to have more opportunity than we had ourselves. We know their individual strengths and capacities. We wish everyone to be able to explore the limits of their own abilities and to find their place in the world. And we fervently believe that parents are the best people to judge what is right for their children.

Socialists, however, are obsessed with equal outcomes at the expense of equal opportunities. Time and again, we erected ladders for children to climb; time and again, the socialist politicians climbed them, and having done so, they tried to kick them away. They did it with grammar schools. They did it with direct grant schools. They want to do it with assisted places[1] and grant maintained schools.

Mr President, they haven't changed. Let me tell you what I found when I opened a new school in Nottingham a fortnight ago. It was a City Technology College. The local Labour-controlled council had told an eleven-year-old girl that she would be thrown out of the council's music school if she attended the CTC where she's been accepted. To deprive an eleven-year-old of her music classes because she goes to a school that the council doesn't control – there's socialist compassion for you.

In the teeth of fierce Labour opposition, we have enlarged the choice of schools for parents and children and brought in major education reforms. We've brought in a National Curriculum of ten subjects which all children have a right and need to know, with mathematics, English and science at their core.

Who now argues that we were wrong? They know that we were right – right to insist on higher standards in the classroom; right to establish a curriculum which gives children the skills for work and the knowledge for a full life; right to pass on the best of our heritage and scholarship to the next generation; right to establish wider opportunities throughout the entire education system.

Passports to Opportunity

But there are still too many ways in which opportunity *after* school can be blocked. For instance, there are prejudices about the age at which people can begin a new career.

Well, I started being Prime Minister at the age of fifty-three. I'd never been Prime Minister before. But I adapted to the work. I did my best. And my employers have twice asked me to stay on.

---

[1] The Education 1980 introduced the Assisted Places Scheme to provide financial support for some pupils in independent education.

Then again, some people find a lot of jobs blocked to them because they don't have the right qualifications. I went to Oxford University, but I've never let it hold me back.[1]

Let there be no mistake: skills, degrees, diplomas, qualifications – these are necessary in the modern industrial world. But opportunity mustn't be cut short at eighteen. We must make sure it lasts a lifetime. We have already set up the first training scheme that's open to all young people – and a new adult training scheme for the long-term unemployed. Incidentally, it's the best of its kind in Europe.

But we also need to remove those obstacles and disincentives which Government itself has erected.

That's why I'm proud that this month we abolished the earnings rule for pensioners.[2] Income tax and National Insurance can also be an obstacle to those starting work – especially the low-paid. So, again, I'm proud that this Government has cut income tax at all levels. This very month we have cut the National Insurance contributions by up to £3 a week. And thanks to the Chancellor, from next April married women will be taxed separately, giving them complete privacy in their tax affairs. And then, Mr President, in 1992 the professions will have the freedom to move throughout Europe. That will open up a much wider vista for all young people.

These and other changes are passports – passports that will enable their holders to overcome a false start in early life, passports with no expiry date, passports to the Conservative world of opportunity.

Environment

Mr President, when I spoke to the Royal Society about the environment over a year ago, I spoke about the global threat of climate change. I set out the magnitude of the challenge we face.

Until recently, we have always thought that whatever progress humanity makes, our planet would stay much the same. That may no longer be true. The way we generate energy; the way we use land; the way industry uses natural resources and disposes of waste; the way our

---

[1] Amid much controversy, Oxford University dons had in 1985 voted against a proposal to bestow an honorary doctorate on the Prime Minister.
[2] The 'earnings rule' refers to the system whereby pensioners earning more than a certain sum had their pensions reduced accordingly.

populations multiply – those things, taken together, are new in the experience of the earth. They threaten to change the atmosphere above us and the sea around us. That is the scale of the global challenge. We have to work to solve these problems on a sound scientific basis so that our remedies will be effective.

It is no good proposing that we go back to some simple village life and halve our population by some means which have not been revealed, as if that would solve all our problems. Indeed, some of the Third World's primitive farming methods created the deserts and denuded the forests. And some of Eastern Europe's crude technologies polluted the skies and poisoned the rivers. It's prosperity which creates the technology that can keep the earth healthy.

We are called Conservatives with good reason. We believe in conserving what is best – the values of our way of life, the beauties of our country.

The countryside has shaped our character as a nation. We have a special responsibility not to let the towns sprawl into it. We will keep the Green Belt[1] green. And to make Britain cleaner, we shall bring in a new Environment Bill to give us much tougher controls on pollution, litter and waste.

Next month, I shall be going to the United Nations to set out our view on how the world should tackle climate change. We have proposed a global convention – a sort of good-conduct guide on the environment for all the world's nations on problems like the greenhouse effect. Britain has taken the lead internationally and we shall continue to do so.

This is not only a question of acting responsibly. There is something deeper in us, an innate sense of belonging, of sharing life in a world that we have not fully understood. As Voyager 2, on its remarkable twelve-year flight, raced through the solar system to Neptune and beyond, we were awestruck by the pictures it sent back of arid, lifeless planets and moons. They were a solemn reminder that our planet has the unique privilege of life.

How much more that makes us aware of our duty to safeguard our world. The more we master our environment, the more we must learn to serve it.

---

[1] The 'Green Belt' is land excluded from development.

Change and Uncertainty

Mr President, there are always new dangers to be faced, new battles to be fought. We are at war against drugs: against those who produce drugs, against those who peddle drugs, against those who launder the profits of the drug trade. Drugs stunt young lives, break up families, injure babies before they are even born.

There are those in Britain who say we should legalize certain drugs. As though burglary could be defeated by legalizing theft. How typical of the muddled thinking of the so-called progressives. In fact, such action would expose many more of our young people to the danger of drugs.

We must continue to protect them with the full force of the law. The police and customs officers deserve our thanks for all they do.

We also face the continuing battle against the terrorists and those who take hostages. We think of Terry Waite, Brian Keenan, John McCarthy[1] – and of their families and friends who endure so much. Any Government which has influence over those who hold hostages should be ready as a matter of course to use that influence to bring about their release. A country cannot support terrorism and still expect to be treated as a member of the international community. To take hostages is to exclude yourself from the civilized world.

In Germany in the last few weeks we have seen the IRA gun down a young army wife sitting alone in her car.[2] And in Britain, we have seen them bomb the young musicians in the Royal Marines Band.[3] Some can't wait to put the blame on security arrangements, as though they were somehow responsible for these appalling crimes. Let us pin the responsibility where it belongs: on the common murderers of the IRA. We thank our servicemen and women and the police for their courage and their dedication.

[1] Brian Keenan, a British-Irish teacher, and John McCarthy, a British journalist, were kidnapped in Beirut by the terrorist group Islamic Jihad on 11 and 17 April 1986 respectively. Terry Waite, the special envoy of the Archbishop of Canterbury, was kidnapped on 20 January 1987 while attempting to negotiate the release of Western hostages in Lebanon. Islamic Jihad released Keenan on 24 August 1990, McCarthy on 8 August 1991 and Waite on 18 November 1991.
[2] Heidi Hazell, the wife of a British soldier, was shot dead by the IRA at Unna Messen in West Germany on 8 September 1989.
[3] Ten bandsmen were killed when the IRA bombed the Royal Marines School of Music at Deal in Kent on 22 September 1989.

Defence

Mr President, in today's rapidly changing world you never know where conflict may arise. In the last ten years we have seen the Soviet invasion of Afghanistan, the Iran–Iraq War, Vietnam's occupation of Cambodia, attacks on shipping in the Gulf, one crisis after another in Lebanon and the Middle East. And, for us, the battle for the freedom of the Falklands. Times of great change are also times of uncertainty and even danger. The lesson is that you must always keep your defences strong, so that you are prepared for any situation.

Some among us remember all too well what happened in the 1920s and 1930s, when we allowed our hopes for a peaceful world to outrun our judgements on the need for defence. The world paid a terrible price. We know now that it's strong defence which protects peace, weakness which brings war. So we have kept our defences strong and we have kept the peace in Europe.

Yes, we are ready to negotiate to reduce the levels of weapons on both sides. But only so long as it can be done without jeopardizing our security. President Gorbachev understands that principle very well. From our very first meeting he has always told me that he would never do anything to put the Soviet Union's security in danger – and he knows that I would never endanger our security.

Yet that's just what Labour would do. Endanger our security. Last week the Labour Party voted overwhelmingly to cut Britain's defence budget by a quarter – almost equivalent to the entire Royal Navy. Of course, Labour says that they would keep our nuclear deterrent. But what for?

Not to defend or deter, certainly not. Only to negotiate it away as quickly as possible in return for a small cut in the Soviet Union's vast nuclear arsenal. We would give up all our nuclear weapons, while the Soviet Union would keep most of theirs. What a bargain!

Labour's supposed conversion to multilateralism is no more than a confidence trick to try to make Labour electable. It's still unilateral disarmament – unilateral disarmament by agreement with the Soviet Union. That isn't a defence policy to see Britain through the 1990s; it's a form of words to see Labour through the next election.

How does one explain the Labour Leader's contortions? Is he being false to his convictions? Or true to his character?

358

Mr President, politicians come in many colours, but if you aspire to lead this nation: 'This above all – to thine own self be true.'[1] You don't reach Downing Street by pretending you've travelled the road to Damascus, when you haven't even left home. It will be our job to expose Labour's defence policy and make sure no one is taken in.

It is Government's responsibility to safeguard our defence. Today, as for the past ten years, only a Conservative Government can be trusted to do that.

Conclusion

Mr President, I spoke to you first as Leader of our Party here in Blackpool, on this platform, at our Party Conference in 1975. I remember it so well. It was not the height of our political fortunes. Nor the height of Britain's.

Freedom was in retreat. The countries of Eastern Europe seemed crushed for ever under the communist heel. But I said then that we were coming up to a turning-point in our history.

Few believed it – but that turning-point came in 1979. For we Conservatives were the pathfinders. We did not know it at the time, but the torch we lit in Britain, which transformed our country – the torch cf freedom that is now the symbol of our Party – became a beacon that has shed its light across the Iron Curtain into the East.

Today that beacon shines more strongly than at any time this century. You can see it reflected in the faces of the young people from the communist countries who have reached the West. Like most young people the world over, they are resolved to make their own way, to achieve success by their own efforts, to live the life they choose as part of a free world they have never known. They are retelling the story of our history.

We cannot know the direction in which free nations in the future will progress. But this we do know – and dare not forget: only those whose commitment to free enterprise and opportunity is a matter of conviction, not convenience, have the necessary strength to sustain them. Only those who have shown the resolve to defend the freedom of the West can be

---

[1] *Hamlet*, I, iii, continuing: 'And it must follow, as the night the day, Thou canst not then be false to any man.'

trusted to safeguard it in the challenging, turbulent and unpredictable times that lie ahead.

Mr President, the decade and the century which open up before us must see the last triumph of liberty, our common cause. The world needs Britain – and Britain needs us – to make that happen.

39

Speech on the Global Environment to the United Nations General Assembly, New York, 8 November 1989

Mrs Thatcher's speech in November 1989 to the UN General Assembly on 'The Global Environment' built on the reputation she had already acquired as an authority on these issues. Although it is population expansion and its effects that she singles out as the main source of environmental problems, and although the threats of global warming and ozone depletion are discussed, the speech also insists – with renewed emphasis – that 'as well as the science, we need to get the economics right'. Economic growth is vigorously defended against the socialist environmentalists, who regarded it as the root of what was wrong, rather than the means to put it right.

Mr President, it gives me great pleasure to return to the podium of this Assembly. When I last spoke here four years ago, on the fortieth anniversary of the United Nations, the message that I and others like me gave was one of encouragement to the organization to play the great role allotted to it. Of all the challenges faced by the world community in those four years, one has grown clearer than any other in both urgency and importance – I refer to the threat to our global environment. I shall take the opportunity of addressing the General Assembly to speak on that subject alone.

During his historic voyage through the South Seas on the *Beagle*, Charles Darwin[1] landed one November morning in 1835 on the shore of Western Tahiti. After breakfast he climbed a nearby hill to find a vantage point to survey the surrounding Pacific. The sight seemed to him like 'a framed engraving', with blue sky, blue lagoon, and white

---

[1] Charles Darwin (1809–82), British biologist, author of *On the Origin of Species* (1859) and *The Descent of Man* (1871).

breakers crashing against the encircling coral reef. As he looked out from that hillside, he began to form his theory of the evolution of coral; 154 years after Darwin's visit to Tahiti we have added little to what he discovered then.

What if Charles Darwin had been able not just to climb a foothill, but to soar through the heavens in one of the orbiting Space Shuttles? What would he have learned as he surveyed our planet from that altitude? From a moon's eye view of that strange and beautiful anomaly in our solar system that is the earth?

Of course, we have learned much detail about our environment as we have looked back at it from space, but nothing has made a more profound impact on us than these two facts. First, as the British scientist Fred Hoyle[1] wrote long before space travel was a reality, 'Once a photograph of the earth, taken from the outside is available . . . a new idea as powerful as any other in history will be let loose.' That powerful idea is the recognition of our shared inheritance on this planet. We know more clearly than ever before that we carry common burdens, face common problems, and must respond with common action.

Second, as we travel through space, as we pass one dead planet after another, we look back on our earth, a speck of life in an infinite void. It is life itself, incomparably precious, that distinguishes us from the other planets. It is life itself – human life, the innumerable species of our planet – that we wantonly destroy. It is life itself that we must battle to preserve.

For over forty years, that has been the main task of this United Nations. To bring peace where there was war. Comfort where there was misery. Life where there was death.

The struggle has not always been successful. There have been years of failure. But recent events have brought the promise of a new dawn, of new hope. Relations between the Western nations and the Soviet Union and her allies, long frozen in suspicion and hostility, have begun to thaw.

In Europe this year, freedom has been on the march. In Southern Africa – Namibia and Angola[2] – the United Nations has succeeded in holding out better prospects for an end to war and for the beginning of prosperity. And in South-East Asia, too, we can dare to hope for the

---

[1] Professor Sir Fred Hoyle (born 1915), British astronomer and science-fiction novelist.
[2] In Namibia, elections were held from 7 to 11 November 1989, which led to independence on 21 February 1990. In Angola, the MPLA and UNITA signed a declaration on 23 June 1989 intended to end the civil war.

restoration of peace after decades of fighting.[1] While the conventional, political dangers – the threat of global annihilation, the fact of regional war – appear to be receding, we have all recently become aware of another insidious danger. It is as menacing in its way as those more accustomed perils with which international diplomacy has concerned itself for centuries. It is the prospect of irretrievable damage to the atmosphere, to the oceans, to earth itself.

Of course, major changes in the earth's climate and the environment have taken place in earlier centuries when the world's population was a fraction of its present size. The causes are to be found in nature itself – changes in the earth's orbit; changes in the amount of radiation given off by the sun; the consequential effects of the plankton in the ocean; volcanic processes. All these we can observe and some we may be able to predict. But we do not have the power to prevent or control them.

What *we* are now doing to the world, by degrading the land surfaces, by polluting the waters and by adding greenhouse gases to the air at an unprecedented rate – all this is new in the experience of the earth. It is mankind and his activities which are changing the environment of our planet in damaging and dangerous ways.

We can find examples in the past. Indeed we may well conclude that it was the silting up of the River Euphrates which drove man out of the Garden of Eden. We also have the example of the tragedy of Easter Island, where people arrived by boat to find a primeval forest. In time the population increased to over nine thousand, and the demand placed upon the environment resulted in its eventual destruction as people cut down the trees. This in turn led to warfare over the scarce remaining resources, and the population crashed to a few hundred people without even enough wood to make boats to escape.

The difference now is in the scale of the damage we are doing. We are seeing a vast increase in the amount of carbon dioxide reaching the atmosphere. The annual increase is three billion tonnes – and half the carbon emitted since the Industrial Revolution still remains in the atmosphere. At the same time as this is happening, we are seeing the destruction on a vast scale of tropical forests which are uniquely able to remove carbon dioxide from the air. Every year an area of forest equal to the surface of the United Kingdom is destroyed. At present rates of

[1] Although an international conference on Cambodia failed to reach agreement in August 1989, Vietnam withdrew its last remaining troops from the country in September.

clearance we shall, by the year 2000, have removed 65 per cent of forests in the humid tropical zones. The consequences of this become clearer when one remembers that tropical forests fix more than ten times as much carbon as do forests in the temperate zones.

We now know, too, that great damage is being done to the ozone layer by the production of halons and chlorofluorocarbons. But at least we have recognized that reducing and eventually stopping the emission of CFCs is one positive thing we can do about the menacing accumulation of greenhouse gases. It is of course true that none of us would be here but for the greenhouse effect. It gives us the moist atmosphere which sustains life on earth. We need the greenhouse effect – but only in the right proportions.

More than anything, our environment is threatened by the sheer numbers of people and the plants and animals which go with them. When I was born the world's population was some two billion. My grandson will grow up in a world of more than six billion.

Put in its bluntest form, the main threat to our environment is more and more people, and their activities: the land they cultivate ever more intensively; the forests they cut down and burn; the mountainsides they lay bare; the fossil fuels they burn; the rivers and seas they pollute. The result is that change in future is likely to be more fundamental and more widespread than anything we have known hitherto.

Change to the sea around us, change to the atmosphere above, leading in turn to change in the world's climate, which could alter the way we live in the most fundamental way of all. That prospect is a new factor in human affairs. It is comparable in its implications to the discovery of how to split the atom. Indeed, its results could be even more far-reaching.

The Latest Scientific Evidence

We are constantly learning more about these changes affecting our environment, and scientists from the Polar Institute in Cambridge and the British Antarctic Survey have been at the leading edge of research in both the Arctic and the Antarctic, warning us of the greater dangers that lie ahead.

Let me quote from a letter I received only two weeks ago, from a British scientist on board a ship in the Antarctic Ocean:

In the polar regions today, we are seeing what may be early signs of man-induced climatic change. Data coming in from Halley Bay and from instruments aboard the ship on which I am sailing show that we are entering a spring ozone depletion which is as deep as, if not deeper than, the depletion in the worst year to date. It completely reverses the recovery observed in 1988. The lowest recording aboard this ship is only 150 Dobson units for ozone total content during September, compared with three hundred for the same season in a normal year.

That's a very severe depletion.

He also reports on a significant thinning of the sea ice. He writes that, in the Antarctic, 'our data confirm that the first-year ice, which forms the bulk of sea ice cover, is remarkably thin and so is probably unable to sustain significant atmospheric warming without melting. Sea ice,' he continues, 'separates the ocean from the atmosphere over an area of more than thirty million square kilometres. It reflects most of the solar radiation falling on it, helping to cool the earth's surface. If this area were reduced, the warming of earth would be accelerated due to the extra absorption of radiation by the ocean.

'The lesson of these polar processes,' he goes on, 'is that an environmental or climatic change produced by man may take on a self-sustaining or "runaway" quality . . . and may be irreversible.'

These are sobering indications of what may happen, and they led my correspondent to put forward the interesting idea of a world polar watch, amongst other initiatives which will observe the world's climate system and allow us to understand how it works.

We also have new scientific evidence from an entirely different area, the tropical forests. Through their capacity to evaporate vast volumes of water vapour, and of gases and particles which assist the formation of clouds, the forests serve to keep their regions cool and moist by weaving a sunshade of white reflecting clouds and by bringing the rain that sustains them. A recent study by our meteorological office on the Amazon rainforest shows that large-scale deforestation may reduce rainfall and thus affect the climate directly. Past experience shows us that without trees there is no rain, and without rain there are no trees.

The Scope for International Action

Mr President, the evidence is there. The damage is being done. What do we, the international community, do about it?

In some areas, the action required is primarily for individual nations or groups of them to take. I am thinking of action to deal with pollution of rivers – and many of us now see the fish back in rivers from which they had disappeared. I am thinking of action to improve agricultural methods – good husbandry which ploughs back nourishment into the soil, rather than the cut-and-burn which has damaged and degraded so much land in some parts of the world. I am thinking of the use of nuclear power which – despite the attitude of so-called 'Greens' – is the most environmentally safe form of energy.

But the problem of global climate change is one that affects us all, and action will only be effective if it is taken at the international level. It is no good squabbling over who is responsible or who should pay. Whole areas of our planet could be subject to drought and starvation if the pattern of rains and monsoons were to change as a result of the destruction of forests and the accumulation of greenhouse gases.

We have to look forward, not backward. We shall only succeed in dealing with the problems through a vast international co-operative effort. Before we act, we need the best possible scientific assessment; otherwise we risk making matters worse. We must use science to cast a light ahead, so that we can move step by step in the right direction.

The United Kingdom has taken on the task of co-ordinating such an assessment within the inter-governmental panel on climate change, an assessment which will be available to everyone by the time of the Second World Climate Conference next year. But that will take us only so far. The report will not be able to tell us where the hurricanes will strike, who will be flooded, or how often and how severe the droughts will be. Yet we will need to know these things if we are to adapt to future climate change.

That means we must expand our capacity to model and predict climate change. We can test our skills and methods by seeing whether they would have successfully predicted past climate change for which historical records exist.

Britain has some of the leading experts in this field, and I am pleased to be able to tell you that the United Kingdom will be establishing a new centre for the prediction of climate change, which will lead the effort to improve our prophetic capacity. It will also provide the advanced computing facilities scientists need. And it will be open to experts from all over the world, and especially from the developing countries, who can come to the United Kingdom and contribute to this vital work.

But as well as the science, we need to get the economics right. That means, first, we must have continued economic growth in order to generate the wealth required to pay for the protection of the environment. But it must be growth which does not plunder the planet today and leave our children to deal with the consequences tomorrow. Second, we must resist the simplistic tendency to blame modern multi-national industry for the damage which is being done to the environment. Far from being the villains, it is on them that we rely to do the research and find the solutions. It is industry which will develop safe alternative chemicals for refrigerators and air-conditioning. It is industry which will devise bio-degradable plastics. It is industry which will find the means to treat pollutants and make nuclear waste safe – and many companies already have massive research programmes.

The multinationals *have* to take the long view. There will be no profit or satisfaction for anyone if pollution continues to destroy our planet. As people's consciousness of environmental needs rises, they are turning increasingly to ozone-friendly and other environmentally safe products. The market itself acts as a corrective: the new products sell, and those which caused environmental damage are disappearing from the shelves. And by making these new products and methods widely available, industry will make it possible for developing countries to avoid many of the mistakes which we older industrialized countries have made.

We should always remember that free markets are a means to an end. They would defeat their object if by their output they did more damage to the quality of life through pollution than the well-being they achieve by the production of goods and services.

On the basis of sound science and sound economics, we need to build a strong framework for international action. It is not new institutions that we need. Rather we need to strengthen and improve those which already exist: in particular the World Meteorological Organization and the United Nations Environment Programme. The United Kingdom has recently more than doubled its contribution to UNEP. We urge others, who have not done so and who can afford it, to do the same. The central organs of the United Nations, like this General Assembly, must also be seized of a problem which reaches into virtually all aspects of their work, and will do so still more in the future.

The most pressing task which faces us at the international level is to negotiate a framework convention on climate change – a sort of good-conduct guide for all nations. Fortunately, we have a model in the action already taken to protect the ozone layer. The Vienna Convention in 1985 and the Montreal Protocol in 1987 established landmarks in international law.[1] They aimed to prevent rather than just cure a global environmental problem.

I believe we should aim to have a convention on global climate change ready by the time the World Conference on Environment and Development meets in 1992. That will be among the most important conferences the United Nations has ever held. I hope that we shall all accept a responsibility to meet this timetable.

The 1992 Conference is indeed already being discussed among many countries in many places. I draw particular attention to the very valuable discussion which members of the Commonwealth had under the Prime Minister of Malaysia's Chairmanship at our recent Commonwealth Heads of Government Meeting in Kuala Lumpur.

But a framework is not enough. It will need to be filled out with specific undertakings – or protocols, in diplomatic language – on the different aspects of climate change. These protocols must be binding, and there must be effective régimes to supervise and monitor their application. Otherwise, those nations which accept and abide by environmental arguments, thus adding to their industrial costs, will lose out competitively to those who do not.

The negotiation of some of those protocols will undoubtedly be difficult. And no issue will be more contentious than the need to control emissions of carbon dioxide, the major contributor – apart from water vapour – to the greenhouse effect. We can't just do nothing; but the measures we take must be based on sound scientific analysis of the effect of the different gases and the ways in which these can be reduced. In the past, there has been a tendency to solve one problem at the expense of making others worse. The United Kingdom, therefore, proposes that we prolong the role of the inter-governmental panel on climate change

---

[1] The Vienna Convention 1985 obliged twenty states to take measures to protect human health and the environment from the adverse affects of modification of the ozone layer, and to pool relevant research. The Montreal Protocol 1987 provided for the halving of global production of chlorofluorocarbon gases by the year 2000.

after it submits its report next year, so that it can provide an authoritative scientific basis for the negotiation of this and other protocols.

We can then agree targets to reduce the greenhouse gases, and how much individual countries should contribute to their achievement. We think it important this should be done in a way which enables all our economies to continue to grow and develop.

The challenge for our negotiators on matters like this is as great as for any disarmament treaty. The inter-governmental panel's work must remain on target, and we must not allow ourselves to be diverted into fruitless and divisive arguments. Time is too short for that.

Before leaving the area where international action is needed, I would make a plea for a further global convention, one to conserve the infinite variety of species – of plant and animal life – which inhabit our planet. The tropical forests contain a half of the species in the world, so their disappearance is doubly damaging. It is astonishing but true that our civilization, whose imagination has reached the boundaries of the universe, does not know, to within a factor of ten, how many species the earth supports. What we do know is that we are losing them at a reckless rate – between three and fifty each day, on some estimates – species which could perhaps be helping us to advance the frontiers of medical science. We should act together to conserve this precious heritage.

Britain's Contribution

Every nation will need to make its own contribution to the world effort. I want to tell you how Britain intends to contribute, either by improving our own national performance in protecting the environment, or through the help which we give to others.

First, we shall be introducing over the coming months a comprehensive system of pollution control to deal with all kinds of industrial pollution, whether to air, water or land. We are encouraging British industry to develop new technologies to clean up the environment and minimize the amount of waste it produces – and we aim to recycle 50 per cent of our household waste by the end of the century.

Secondly, we will be drawing up over the coming year our own environmental agenda for the decade ahead. This will cover energy, transport, agriculture, industry – everything which affects the environment. With regard to energy, we already have a £2 billion programme of improvements to reduce acid rain emissions from our power stations.

We shall be looking more closely at the role of non-fossil fuel sources, including nuclear, and our latest legislation requires companies which supply electricity positively to promote energy efficiency. On transport, we shall look for ways to strengthen controls over vehicle emissions and to develop the lean-burn engine, which offers a far better long-term solution than the three-way catalyst in terms of CO^2 and the greenhouse effect.[1] We have already reduced the tax on lead-free petrol to encourage its use. This is an example of using market-based incentives to promote good environmental practice. We shall see whether there are other areas where this same principle can be applied.

With regard to agriculture, we recognize that farmers not only produce food – which they do with great efficiency – they need to conserve the beauty of the priceless heritage of our countryside. We are therefore encouraging them to reduce the intensity of their methods and to conserve wildlife habitats. We are planting new woods and forests – indeed there has been a 50 per cent increase in tree planting in Britain in the last ten years. We also aim to reduce chemical inputs to the soil, and are bringing forward measures to deal with the complex problems of nitrates in water.

Third, we are increasing our investment in research into global environmental problems. I have already mentioned the climate change centre that we are establishing. In addition, we are supporting our own scientists', and in particular the British Antarctic Survey's, crucial contribution to the world ocean circulation experiment, as well as the voyages of our aptly-named research ship, the *Charles Darwin*. We have also provided more money for the climate and environment satellite monitoring programmes of the European Space Agency.

Fourth, we help poorer countries cope with their environmental problems through our aid programme. We shall give special help to manage and preserve the tropical forests. We are already assisting twenty countries, and have recently signed agreements with India and Brazil. As a new pledge, I can announce today that we aim to commit a further £100 million bilaterally to tropical forestry activities over the next three years, mostly within the framework of the Tropical Forestry Action Plan.

---

[1] The lean-burn engine is an internal combustion engine (usually with additional valves) designed to burn more efficiently, thus reducing fuel consumption and modifying exhaust emissions. The three-way catalyst reduces toxic emissions by converting oxides of nitrogen back into nitrogen.

Conclusion

Mr President, the environmental challenge which confronts the whole world demands an equivalent response from the whole world. Every country will be affected. No one can opt out. We should work through this great organization and its agencies to secure worldwide agreements on ways to cope with the effects of climate change, the thinning of the ozone layer, and the loss of precious species. We need a realistic programme of action and an equally realistic timetable. Each country has to contribute, and those countries which are industrialized must contribute more to help those which are not. The work ahead will be long and exacting. We should embark on it hopeful of success, not fearful of failure.

I began with Charles Darwin and his work on the theory of evolution and the origin of the species. Darwin's voyages were among the high points of scientific discovery. They were undertaken at a time when men and women felt with growing confidence that we could not only understand the natural world, but master it too.

Today, we have learned rather more humility and respect for the balance of nature. But another of the beliefs of Darwin's era should help to see us through – the belief in reason and the scientific method. Reason is humanity's special gift. It allows us to understand the structure of the nucleus. It enables us to explore the heavens. It helps us to conquer disease. Now we must use our reason to find a way in which we can live with nature, not dominate nature.

At the end of a book which has helped many young people to shape their own sense of stewardship for our planet, its American author quotes one of our greatest English poems, Milton's[1] *Paradise Lost*. When Adam in that poem asks about the movements of the heavens, Raphael refuses to answer.

'Let it speak,' he says,

> 'the maker's high magnificence, who built
> So spacious, and his line stretched out so far,
> That man may know he dwells not in his own;
> An edifice too large for him to fill,

---

[1] John Milton (1608–74), English poet.

Lodged in a small partition, and the rest
Ordained for uses to his Lord best known.'

We need our reason to teach us today that we are not, that we must not try to be, the lords of all we survey. We are not the lords, we are the Lord's creatures, the trustees of this planet, charged today with preserving life itself – preserving life with all its mystery and all its wonder.

40

Speech to the Conservative Central Council, Cheltenham, 31 March 1990

By the time of the March 1990 Central Council it was clear that the Prime Minister would have to fight for her political life. Nigel Lawson's resignation the previous October, though it had shaken the Government, had at least cleared the way for a new Chancellor – John Major – to apply the necessary remedy of high interest rates to bring down inflation. But high mortgage rates were deeply unpopular. Even more so was the Community Charge (the replacement for the rates). More precisely, it was the levels of the Charge, rather than the system, which were causing outrage among hitherto steadfast Conservative supporters – though most media attention focused on the left-wing rioters who, even as Mrs Thatcher was addressing the Central Council in Cheltenham, were storming their way up Whitehall. The Prime Minister had hoped to be able to announce at Central Council rigorous new measures to curb Community Charge bills; but partly as a result of Ministerial obstruction, partly simply because of the technical difficulties, this did not prove possible.

Madam Chairman, it's a very great pleasure to be in Cheltenham once again. To avoid any possible misunderstanding, and at the risk of disappointing a few gallant colonels, let me make one thing absolutely clear: I haven't come to Cheltenham to retire.

This Central Council has assumed a great importance in the life of our Party. And the lively debate you had on the Community Charge showed the Tory Party at its best. It dealt with the anxieties which many people have, and which I shall be addressing in a moment. But your debates have also shown that our Party is optimistic about the future and loyal to the vision which unites us.

That vision is the same which we proclaimed when you, Sir David,[1]

---

[1] Sir David Davenport-Handley (born 1919), Chairman of the National Union of Conservative and Unionist Associations 1979–80; President of the National Union of Conservative and Unionist Associations 1990–91.

chaired our Party Conference of 1979 after that first triumphant general election victory. Those qualities are the ones which you, Willie Whitelaw, our outgoing President, have represented throughout your whole political life. As Deputy Leader of our Party, your warm friendship, wise counsel and coolness under fire are an example to us all.

Community Charge

Madam Chairman, many of the bills for the Community Charge which people are now receiving are far too high. I share the outrage they feel.

But let's be clear: it's not the way the money is raised, it's the amount of money that local government is spending that's the real problem. No scheme, however ingenious, could pay for high spending with low charges.

There is no ideal tax which will pay for local spending without raising some objections. But the greatest objections of all were reserved for the rating system. The public protests lasted not months but decades. It was grossly unfair that of the thirty-seven million people who had a vote for local councils, only seventeen million paid rates. Unfair to the elderly couple in one house who paid the same as four or five adults in good jobs next door. Unfair to the widow who had to leave her family home because of the burden of rates.

That was why all of us fought the last election on a pledge to abolish the rates. The Community Charge means that all adults pay something towards the cost of local services. But those on low incomes or social security benefit get substantial rebates – all paid for by the taxpayer. Indeed, general taxation and business together pay the lion's share of what local councils spend. The Community Charge meets only £30 out of every £100.

In spite of that, many of the actual bills are a scandal. Too many councils, most of them Labour, have piled on the spending, and all of the extra has gone onto Community Charge.

It costs £96 more for the privilege of living in Labour Warrington than in neighbouring Tory Trafford; £108 more in Labour Liverpool than in next-door Tory Wirral; and an appalling £339 more in Labour Camden than in adjoining Tory Westminster.

Many residents of Camden would be astonished to learn they live in an area that's more expensive than Belgrave Square!

We thought that even Labour would have some consideration for local citizens. But not a bit of it. All those speeches about compassion! – Forget them. Labour was cynically using ordinary families as political cannon-fodder, hoping people would blame the Government for the high charges Labour imposed. The Labour Association of London Authorities recommended Labour councils to consider setting 'the highest [charge] you can get away with'. Mark those words: 'the highest *you can get away with*'. Well, don't let them get away with it!

We have put in place some additional help already. For example, transitional relief, when the change from rates to Community Charge is just too big for people to bear. That will help seven and a half million people. And people in areas who have had to contribute to the safety net this year will be relieved of the burden next year.[1] And in this year's Budget, John Major[2] took the welcome step of doubling the capital limits, so that prudent savers would no longer be disqualified from help. But there is more to do.

First, where council budgets are excessive, the Environment Secretary has power to cap the Community Charge to bring it down. He will soon be announcing which councils will be charge capped this year. But his powers are limited.

Second, the Standard Charge, which applies where people live in one house but maintain a second. Some enjoy a country cottage or a holiday home. But others have no choice. They may have had to go to look after a sick relative, or moved house to another job and can't sell their old one, or can't sell a house which has been left to them, or have to live in one home as a condition of their job and have bought another for their retirement.

In some of these cases Government has forbidden any charge for a certain length of time. In others it has given local authorities discretion to charge up to two Community Charges in respect of the house which is not the main home. Some councils are exercising this discretion sympathetically, in favour of the citizen. Others are not, and people are

---

[1] The replacement of rates by the Community Charge shifted the local tax burden between individuals and between areas. To ease the impact of this, the Government 1) provided 'transitional relief' to assist those former ratepayers who would have to pay more under the Community Charge, and 2) devised a self-financing 'safety net' whereby areas which gained from the change would initially subsidize areas which lost from it.

[2] John Major (born 1943), Conservative MP 1979–; Chief Secretary to the Treasury 1987–89; Foreign Secretary 1989; Chancellor of the Exchequer 1989–90; Prime Minister 1990–97.

unexpectedly faced with large bills. If this goes on, we shall have to limit the councils' discretion in time for next year.

Third, some councils are complaining about their Standard Spending Assessments. Chris Patten[1] has agreed to look at any fresh evidence you care to place before him about those assessments. I am sure you will take advantage of this offer in good time for next year's grant settlement.

But the real problem is very high spending, and that an increased grant from the taxpayer is not passed on in a lower Community Charge but is used for still higher expenditure.

Madam Chairman, Conservative councils cost you less. Labour costs you more. So the real answer is to get rid of Labour councils. Many of you will have a chance to do just that in a few weeks' time. But everyone has the right to look to Government and Parliament to protect them as Community Charge-payers from overpowering taxation. They will not look in vain.

Roof Tax

And what is Labour's alternative? A Roof Tax. That is, a tax on the capital value of your house whether or not you own it. And who would gain from that? Certainly not the council tenant who had no stake in the increased value of his home, yet saw his Roof Tax going through the roof. Certainly not those who needed an extension or made any improvements to their home, which increased in value. The council would soon be there, estimating how much more you'd have to pay, questioning whether your improvements were socially useful. It would bring a whole new meaning to the phrase 'Neighbourhood Watch'. You and your neighbours would be the ones being watched.

Madam Chairman, however deeply we feel, political disagreement is no excuse for breaking the law. Yet thirty Labour Members of Parliament are supporting those who refuse to pay the Community Charge. In recent weeks, Marxist agitators and militants have organized mob violence.[2] Policemen have been punched, councillors assaulted and shopkeepers

---

[1] Chris Patten (born 1944), Conservative MP 1979–92; Environment Secretary 1989–90; Chancellor of the Duchy of Lancaster and Chairman of the Conservative Party 1990–92; Governor of Hong Kong 1992–97.
[2] On the day this speech was delivered, 31 March 1990, a mass demonstration against the Community Charge in Trafalgar Square, London, ended in large-scale violence and looting. The police made over 340 arrests.

have seen their shops looted. When hard-left campaigns of law-breaking are organized by Labour Party members, and publicly defended by Labour MPs, no weasel words from the Leader of the Opposition can alter the plain fact that they are inescapably Labour's responsibility.

Economy

Madam Chairman, you may just possibly have noticed that I seem lately to have been subjected to a certain amount of criticism.

Not, by the way, for the first time. Nor, I dare say, for the last. You might say, Madam Chairman, that being criticized is one of the perks of being Prime Minister. It comes along with the job, which may be one reason why the job is never advertised.

In fact, I have often wondered what such an advertisement would say. Perhaps something like:

Senior position in Government involving long hours, short holidays and tall orders. Expertise required in the whole range of Government policy and especially in carrying cans. Tied cottage. Makes job ideal for someone used to living above the shop. Experience in this line of work preferred but impossible. Current status: 650 applicants *and no vacancy*.

Let me say this to you and to the country: hard choices are never popular at the time you make them, just as soft options are never popular six months later. The war against inflation is an example of what I mean. It has to be fought year in, year out. Today, inflation is too high. And mortgage rates and the high Community Charges of Labour councils will for a time take it a little higher.

The unavoidable price of beating inflation is a temporary period of high interest rates to slow down spending, cut borrowing and increase saving. Alas, that price falls heavily on those who have sacrificed so much to buy their own homes and who now see their mortgage payments rising further than they had ever imagined.

No one in the Conservative Party takes that lightly. No one in this Government takes it lightly. We know that in homes all over the country people are having to cut down on other things in order to meet their monthly payments.

The hard truth is that we faced a choice between a short-term rise in interest rates and a long-term rise in inflation. And that really is no choice at all. Labour tell you, Madam Chairman, that all our problems could be solved by putting up spending, running up the nation's over-draft, slashing interest rates and controlling credit by some means as yet unspecified.

If ever that happened, money would pour out of this country so fast, Labour wouldn't be worried about controlling credit – credit would be controlling them. The confidence of the world's markets can be kept only by sound financial policies.

The Budget

And who better to retain that confidence than John Major? His savers' Budget, Madam Chairman, was the right Budget for 1990.[1] And the more the people save, the less the Government needs to tax. Only by encouraging high levels of saving can we sustain the high level of invest-ment needed for growth without inflation.

But savings are good not only for the economy. The habit of thrift provides the security for a comfortable retirement and an inheritance for children and grandchildren.

Here there is a great divide of principle between us and Labour: socialists borrow and pass on debts; Conservatives save and pass on assets. For years, it was not possible for people to build up capital out of earnings. Now they can. And millions more are doing so, under our Government.

Last week's Budget marked a milestone for women. The earnings and savings of a married woman will no longer be treated as though they were her husband's. Tax penalties on marriage will disappear and millions of women will be better of. I'm proud to be a member of a Government which has brought in this overdue measure of justice for women.

Madam Chairman, the British economy is strong. Of course, to hear the left-wing talk, you wouldn't think that British industry has never invested so heavily; that British companies have never exported so much; British businesses have never multiplied so fast; and that there have never been so many jobs in Britain. All of those things are signs of a strong economy.

---

[1] The Budget of 20 March 1990 introduced 'tax exempt special savings accounts' (TESSAs) and made certain means-tested social security benefits available to pensioners with a level of savings higher than hitherto.

Socialism at Home and Abroad

Madam Chairman, in the next election there will be over three million first-time voters too young to remember what socialism was like. I would be hard put to describe to someone whose entire adult experience is of Tory freedom and prosperity that grey world of strikes and union control. Inflation at 27 per cent, punitive levels of income tax, and then that gravediggers' strike which finally dug Labour's grave – it all sounds as remote as ration books and petrol coupons.

But I don't have to explain it to them. They can see socialism for themselves in the Eastern European countries which are now struggling to free themselves from its depressing legacy: the shortages and shabbiness of everyday goods, the tyranny of petty bureaucrats, and the survivor's maxim, 'If you see a queue, join it.'

To young people, I say: 'When you visit Eastern Europe, learn from them about the socialist past that didn't work, and tell them about the Conservative future that will. And then come home and tell your friends of the excitement of people who are tasting freedom for the first time.'

It's no surprise to us when conservative parties win elections in Hungary and East Germany.[1] The people of those countries have learned not to take freedom for granted. And under the sheep's clothing of social democracy they recognize the wolf's face of socialism.

Madam Chairman, I don't think Labour's intervention in the Hungarian elections has altogether received the attention it deserves. Labour decided to back the Hungarian Social Democrats and Mr Hattersley,[2] doubtless fortified by the goulash at the Gay Hussar,[3] went out to Budapest to throw his full weight behind them. With devastating effect.

Alerted by Mr Hattersley's presence to the fact that the Social Democrats had something to do with socialism, the electorate gave them 3½ per cent of the votes. They didn't even qualify for a seat in the parliament.

We must hope, Madam Chairman, that the Deputy Leader of the

---

[1] The Alliance for Germany, formed by Christian Democrats, gained 48 per cent of the vote in the East German elections on 18 March 1990. The centre-right Hungarian Democratic Forum and the liberal Alliance of Free Democrats emerged as the largest parties in the first round of the Hungarian elections on 25 March.

[2] Roy Hattersley (born 1932), Labour MP 1964–97; Prices and Consumer Protection Secretary 1976–79; Deputy Leader of the Labour Party 1983–92.

[3] The Gay Hussar is a well-known Hungarian restaurant in London.

Labour Party doesn't rest on these laurels. Let him campaign in every constituency in the country and alert the British voters also to the fact that the Labour Party has something to do with socialism.

For the problem Conservatives face is that the lure of socialism today is strongest in countries which haven't recently experienced it. People who have never lost their freedom don't always realize how precious it is. We must do everything we can to remind them.

Youth and Opportunity

But we must do more than that. We must make sure that wider opportunities are available to all our young people. Each of them endowed with unique talents and abilities. Each with his own dreams and ambitions. Education opens new doors to a fuller life. And each generation must open those doors to give the next a better start.

Madam Chairman, no one gave his children a better start in life than my father gave me – because he took the view that what was good enough for him wasn't good enough for me. And he encouraged me to keep on learning.

For opportunity must not stop short at the age of sixteen. Yet too often it does. We are seeing to it that children leave school with the right basic education. That's what the National Curriculum is all about. But for some children it's hard to find the right opening or get the right advice. Many feel they want to leave school and train – though they don't quite know what to train for.

We want to help them. We're getting industry interested in young people during their school life. We're also creating new Training and Enterprise Councils under business leadership.[1] They know the jobs of the future.

But our approach isn't limited to providing young people with training and a job. It is to motivate, enthuse and involve each of them by offering a real choice. So we intend to offer sixteen- and seventeen-year-olds a credit worth at least £1,000 – an experiment to start with – to enable them to train with a local company of their choice.

The skills they'll get won't be those of a narrow, time-serving appren-

[1] Training and Enterprise Councils (TECs), consisting of groups of local employers, were set up from 1988 as a key part of the decentralization of state-funded training programmes.

ticeship: these can trap people in a dying trade. They must be skills which can be adapted to new techniques and new industries as they arise, skills to which young people can add as they go through life.

Madam Chairman, for many young people this will offer a chance they never had before. They need the training – and we need them.

Labour

I don't think I need say much about Labour's policies. They're mostly under wraps – understandably – but one or two slipped out of the bag.

For example, shareholders in privatized companies could kiss goodbye to their dividends. Labour's credit controls could stop you buying a bigger home as your family grew. And Labour want an extra tax on your savings.

With policies like these, Madam Chairman, small wonder that the Labour Leader tries to drown them in verbiage. What did Shakespeare say? 'He draweth out the thread of his verbosity finer than the staple of his argument.'

And that came from *Love's* Labour's *Lost*.

Madam Chairman, socialism simply does not work. Its adherents have fellow-travelled the world to find just *one* successful variety. And come away empty-handed.

In the 1930s it was off to Moscow, where Stalin had attained the Promised Land. But the Promised Land turned out to be the Gulag. In the 1960s it was Cuba's turn. 'At last,' they cried, 'a happy revolution.' Then Fidel Castro[1] spoke for seven hours. And finally Nicaragua. The results of the election were confidently awaited. A Sandinista victory was assured – after all, half Hampstead was on their side. What could go wrong? Everything, it seems. The Order of Lenin was replaced by the order of the boot. And now there's a woman in charge.[2] Madam Chairman, there is nothing like a dame.

---

[1] Fidel Castro Ruz (born 1927); Cuban politician. Prime Minister 1959–76; First Secretary of the Communist Party 1965–; President of Cuba 1976–.
[2] In the Nicaraguan general election of 25 February 1990, the National Opposition Union, led by Violeta Barrios de Chamorro, defeated the Sandinista National Liberation Front which had taken power in 1979.

Environment

We Conservatives are not only friends of the earth, we are its trustees. But concern for the environment is not, and never has been, a first priority for socialist governments. As we peel back the moral squalor of the socialist régimes in Eastern Europe, we discover the natural and physical squalor underneath. They exploited nature every bit as ruthlessly as they exploited the people. In their departure, they have left her choking amidst effluent, acid rain and industrial waste.

Marxist governments sacrificed every other value to industrial production. But they weren't very good at it. So they created both poverty and pollution, muck without brass – the Yorkshireman's nightmare.

Let me give you one particularly horrific example, drawn entirely from Soviet sources. The Aral Sea shrank by half in the last thirty years. On the mudflats left by the retreating waters, millions of tons of salt, chemicals and fertilizer waste were spread by the winds to people and crops hundreds of miles away. On one coast, a majority of children have serious illnesses; most men called up by conscription are rejected as unfit; more than half the population suffer from hepatitis, typhoid or throat cancer; and infant mortality has reached one in ten in the first year.

Capitalism is not the enemy of the environment, but its friend and guardian. As more people own property, so more people have an incentive to protect it from pollution. This we have learned from experience, and no more so than in the last ten years in Britain. So much of the wealth created by a flourishing economy has been ploughed back directly into measures to protect and enhance our environment.

In the last five years, we have cut the level of lead in our air by half. In last week's Budget, John Major widened the differential in the price of petrol still further. And from October this year, all new cars will have to be able to run on unleaded fuel.

This is not the record of a Government with no time for the environment. We stand for clean streets, clear seas, fresh air, green acres. These are the values of a Government green in policy but not in judgement.

The Victory of Freedom

Madam Chairman, it is a privilege to be alive at a time when freedom is advancing, and tyranny retreating, throughout the world.

And who would have guessed that our actions here would have helped bring about such vast historical changes? For these events would never have happened if the West had succumbed to the sleeping-sickness of socialism.

Nor would the Soviet grip have been released if the anti-nuclear appeasement advocated by Labour had won the day. It was the unwitting ally of communism's Old Guard.

It was not the spiritual attractions of freedom which converted communist rulers to reform and democracy. It was sheer necessity — the blunt, hard fact that they could not compete with free capitalist countries on their own chosen ground of material prosperity and social advance.

What is liberating those under communism, Madam Chairman, is the spectre of capitalist competition.

Our struggle is their struggle; our success is their inspiration; their victory our vindication. Let us not falter at the very moment when the walls of their prison are collapsing.

Let me tell you how I see the way ahead for Britain. I see a Britain of enterprise: a Britain in which new industries, small businesses, the self-employed and the latest technologies flourish; in which British goods beat the competition in markets throughout the world; in which companies support the local community, give to local charities, foster local arts and improve the local environment; and in which industry combines with science to overcome disease, poverty and disaster.

I see a Britain of choice and responsibility: a Britain in which schools, run by teachers and parents, not bureaucrats, achieve new standards of excellence; in which self-governing hospitals compete to provide patients with a higher quality of care; in which tenants run their own estates or choose between a range of landlords.

I see a Britain of wider ownership: a Britain in which not two in three, but four in five families own their own homes; in which more state industries are transferred to profit and success in the private sector; in which more employees have a stake in their companies — and in other people's companies; in which each generation can save out of its income the capital to give the next generation a better start; in which ownership is not a privilege, but a matter of course.

And I see a Europe of free nations. A Europe united in its belief in democracy, in the power of free enterprise and in the diversity of its national cultures. A Europe where national frontiers are respected by all European countries; where free trade extends from the Atlantic to the Soviet border; where countries freely co-operate to advance the prosperity of their peoples; where an open, single market broadens our children's horizons and widens their opportunities.

Just eighteen months ago in Bruges, when I recalled that the European Community was not synonymous with Europe and that Warsaw, Prague and Budapest were European cities, it may have seemed to some a fanciful excursion into history. Yet today, their countries have rejoined European democracy.

So I see also a wider world of freedom – a family of independent nations in close alliance with the United States, standing together in defence of liberty and democracy and raising anew the torch of Western civilization. Flourishing enterprise. Choice and responsibility. A democracy of ownership. Freedom with security. These are the goals we set for Britain in the years and in the century which lie ahead.

Conclusion

And that's why, Madam Chairman, our struggle with the Labour Party has never been a matter just of economics. It concerns the way of life we believe is right for Britain, now and in the future. It concerns the values by which we live.

Socialism is a creed of the state. It regards ordinary human beings as the raw material for its schemes of social change. But we put our faith in people – in the millions of people who spend what they earn – not what other people earn. Who make sacrifices for their young family or their elderly parents. Who help their neighbours and take care of their neighbourhoods. The sort of people I grew up with. These are the people whom I became Leader of this Party to defend. The people who gave us their trust.

To them I say: of course I understand your worries. They are part of the fabric of my life too, and I share the aspirations which you hold.

You don't expect the moon. But you do want the opportunity to succeed for yourselves and for your children. A decently paid job to go to. A home which you can call your own, improve and furnish and take pride in. Savings you can invest for a rainy day. A modest stake in the business for which you work. Schools which will give your children a chance to get on in life. A Health Service to fall back on when you or your family are sick. A neighbourhood free of litter, vandalism and fear.

These are the things I want too. And they are the things for which this Party stands.

Being loyal to our Conservative vision has never been more vital. Around us, the values for which we in this Party stand are becoming established as the ethos of the new decade. And, for all its raucous protest and its arrogant, assumed self-confidence, socialism in Britain quakes before a future which it sought to kill at birth and whose triumph it still dreads.

Our economy is strong. Our defences are sure. Our policies are right. Let the storm clouds swirl. Before us, a shining future is within our reach. Let us have the spirit – and yes, the sheer guts – to press on and grasp it.

I have the stomach for that fight. So do you. And so, I believe, does Britain.

41

Speech to the North Atlantic Council, Turnberry, 7 June 1990

The collapse of Soviet control in Eastern Europe and the diminution of the Soviet military threat required a fundamental reassessment of NATO strategy and weaponry. But Mrs Thatcher's approach was more cautious than that favoured by President Bush; indeed, not just over NATO, but also in their attitudes to German reunification and to the European Community more generally, a gap had opened up between the two leaders, which would not be closed until the Gulf crisis later that summer. It now fell to the North Atlantic Council – that is, essentially NATO Foreign Ministers – to reach conclusions about the reshaping of NATO which would later be discussed at the full NATO Summit that the Americans were urging. In her speech at Turnberry, Mrs Thatcher argued for the development of NATO's role as a wider transatlantic forum – a view that was shared by American Secretary of State James Baker – and for an extension of NATO's 'out of area' role. The latter passage, with its warnings about potential dangers in the Gulf, came to have a prophetic ring.

First, may I welcome you very warmly to the United Kingdom. We are delighted to be hosting this important occasion;[1] and we look forward to seeing many of you again at the NATO Summit in London next month.[2] You may think it slightly strange that we chose Turnberry, which is geographically on the outer fringes of NATO, to hold a meeting to discuss issues which are central to NATO's future.

So let me tell you a little of the local history to show that, far from

---

[1] The North Atlantic Council is the governing body of NATO, composed of representatives of the sixteen member countries. Its Ministerial Meetings, held twice yearly, are attended by Foreign Ministers. Margaret Thatcher addressed the opening session at Turnberry, Scotland, as Prime Minister of the host country.

[2] The NATO Summit held in London on 5 and 6 July 1990 formalized the end of the Cold War and made a start on redefining the military strategy and political goals of the alliance.

being some remote and windswept shore, Turnberry has played its part in defence and in the affairs of Europe over many centuries – with a few lessons for NATO even today.

Turnberry Castle, whose ruins you will see nearby, was home in the thirteenth century to the Earls of Carrick. It was from here that one of them left for the Crusade in 1268 under the banner of King Louis IX of France, only to die in the Holy Land two years later – an early and not entirely successful example of Franco–British defence co-operation. His widow subsequently married a member of the Bruce family, and their son was Robert the Bruce, King of Scotland. He inflicted a certain amount of damage on the English at the Battle of Bannockburn in the year 1314.

For the English, it was an early example that forward defence does not work unless backed up by an adequate deterrent, kept up to date as necessary. I would also point out that the victorious Scots forces were armed with pikes, while the defeated English horsemen had lances: perhaps there is a moral there too![1] Subsequently Scotland and England came together by the Act of Union – that was in the days before you needed a two-plus-four group to deal with the external consequences.[2] And since then Britain has led the way in having the sort of multi-national forces which are only just now coming into vogue in NATO.

So you see, Mr Secretary-General, we may be on the fringes geographically; but the tradition of strong defence and involvement in Europe really does go back a long way in this part of the world.

NATO's Success

Mr Secretary-General, this meeting takes place shortly after President Gorbachev's visits to Canada and to the United States for the very successful summit with President Bush.[3] President Mitterrand[4] visited

[1] An allusion to LANCE, the NATO ground-launched short-range nuclear missile. Mrs Thatcher wanted to see an upgraded follow-on to LANCE (FOTL) developed by the USA and deployed in the mid-1990s, but the Germans were reluctant to modernize NATO short-range nuclear forces, and cancelled FOTL in 1990.
[2] The 'two-plus-four' group (East and West Germany plus Britain, France, the USA and the USSR) met from May 1990 to deal with the security implications of German reunification. Its work came to a close with the signing in Moscow on 12 September 1990 of the Treaty on the Final Settlement on Germany.
[3] George Bush (born 1924), US politician. Vice-President of the United States 1981–89; 41st President of the United States 1989–93 (Republican).
[4] François Mitterrand (1916–96), French politician. First Secretary of the Socialist Party 1971–81; President of the Fifth Republic 1981–95.

the Soviet Union just before that. And I am on my way there now.[1] Such an intense series of high-level meetings between Western and Soviet leaders would have seemed quite remarkable only a couple of years ago. Today it does not seem unusual; a measure of how far we have come in a short time – and of how much we have to thank NATO for.

I think the simplest explanation for NATO was given by one of its great architects, President Harry Truman. 'We hoped that it would prevent World War III,' he said. And it has.

But it has done more than that. NATO has surely been the most successful alliance in history. It has deterred war, without ever having to fight a war. It halted the spread of communism. It has demonstrated unprecedented unity and resolve among its members, reaching a high point in the decision to deploy Cruise and Pershing 2 in 1979, despite Soviet intimidation. It kept the hope of freedom alive in the hearts of millions beyond the Iron Curtain. And it finally convinced the Soviet leaders that the Cold War, which they had instigated, had done far more damage to their own country and cause – economically, politically and morally – than ever it did to the democratic nations.

All this required something in addition to weapons and an alliance: we had to keep our faith, our resolve and our nerve. We did.

As a result, we are probably more secure now than we have ever been. NATO has been the foundation for everything else we enjoy: our freedom, our rule of law, our prosperity.

In this centenary year of President Eisenhower's birth, we pay special tribute to the staunchness and generosity of the United States and Canada in stationing their forces in Europe through all these years. We in Europe have been fortunate to have such allies.

New Challenges

But success creates new problems. For much the greater part of NATO's existence, our task has been to defend our way of life against an aggressive enemy with an expansionist ideology. The issues were stark. We knew where we stood and what we stood for.

Now the landscape with which we became so familiar as we looked eastward is changing radically. Communism has crumbled. It has lost

---

[1] Margaret Thatcher flew to Moscow on the evening of 7 June 1990 for a three-day official visit which included trips to Ukraine and Armenia.

all credibility, even among nominal believers. The countries of Eastern Europe are reaching out to the West. We no longer think of them as potential enemies or as part of a wider threat to our way of life. They are friends in need of help, wanting to return to their rightful place in Europe. Soviet forces are withdrawing from almost all of Eastern Europe.

Politically NATO no longer has a clear front line. Militarily, the Defence Planning Committee concluded in its recent communiqué: 'The implementation of a CFE Treaty[1] will virtually eliminate the possibility of a surprise attack on NATO.' Not an attack, but a surprise attack. In short, things look very different even from a year ago.

This does not diminish the need for NATO. Confronted with the sort of turbulence and uncertainty about the future which we see in the Soviet Union and parts of Eastern Europe, it would be folly to believe disarmament could never again become rearmament, that ploughshares could not be refashioned into swords or worse. The Soviet Union still has a formidable military capability, and will continue to do so for the foreseeable future. And there could be new threats to our security originating from outside Europe altogether.

We must keep our capacity effectively to deter and to defend ourselves. You don't cancel your home insurance policy just because there have been fewer burglaries in your street in the last twelve months. To anyone who asks: 'Has NATO a future?', we reply with a resounding 'Yes.'

But that does not rule out changes to face a new situation – indeed it strengthens the case for them. The eclipse of other defence organizations like SEATO and CENTO illustrates what can happen if an alliance fails to move with the times once it has fulfilled its immediate purpose.[2] The task of your meeting and the NATO Summit which we shall hold in London next month is to strike the right balance between preserving the essentials of NATO as it is now, and adapting it to new circumstances.

We need to consider how to extend NATO's role from preventing war to building peace; to identify the threats we shall face in future and

---

[1] The Treaty on Conventional Armed Forces in Europe (CFE), signed in Paris on 19 September 1990, restricted NATO and the Warsaw Pact to equal numbers of tanks, artillery-pieces, armoured combat vehicles, combat aircraft and attack helicopters between the Atlantic Ocean and the Ural Mountains. In accepting parity, the Warsaw Pact undertook to reduce its total arsenal by as much as 40 per cent.

[2] The South-East Asia Treaty Organization (SEATO) was an alliance between Australia, Britain, France, New Zealand, Pakistan, the Philippines, Thailand and the USA which existed from 1954 to 1977. The Central Treaty Organization (CENTO), an alliance created in 1959, formally lapsed in 1979 when the withdrawal of Iran, Pakistan and Turkey left Britain the only member.

the forces and strategies we need to meet them; and to look at how NATO will fit with the many other organizations which will be managing Europe's future. If we succeed, we ensure that NATO remains as relevant, indeed as pivotal, in the next phase as in the past.

NATO's Enduring Principles

Some absolutely fundamental elements of NATO we must take with us into the future.

First, we must maintain secure defence. Past history, in particular our experience with the League of Nations,[1] has shown that political commitments and undertakings alone cannot provide security. Our predecessors in 1919 were idealists, but they led us into dreamland. At this new turning-point in Europe's history, even fuller of promise than 1919 and 1945, we must not make the same mistake. Sufficient forces and weapons keep us secure, not fine words.

Second, we should continue to provide for our defence and our security collectively. Stability in Europe depends on the Western countries standing together. Were we to let NATO's integrated structure fall apart because the military threat is no longer perceived as so acute, we should take a big step backwards towards the bad old days of European power politics, pursued ultimately by force.

A very important part of this will be to ensure that a united Germany is a full member of NATO and its integrated military structure. The people of both parts of Germany want that. NATO's members want that. And most of the countries of Eastern and Central Europe want that.

There will need to be transitional arrangements for Soviet forces in the former GDR,[2] together with other safeguards to meet Soviet concerns, and we shall have to work at those. But once we have all accepted the right of the German people to determine their future and unite, we cannot dictate their associations or alliances. Indeed the Helsinki Agreements specifically reaffirm the right of countries to choose whether or not to belong to an alliance.

[1] The League of Nations, the predecessor of today's United Nations, was instituted in the aftermath of the First World War. It has become almost synonymous with impractical internationalism largely as a result of its members' feeble response to aggression in the 1930s.
[2] The German Democratic Republic, i.e. East Germany.

Third, we must preserve the United States's presence in Europe – in both conventional forces and nuclear weapons. President Bush's strong commitment to America's continuing role is very welcome indeed. The presence of US forces in Europe is essential to balance Soviet strength, even after recent changes.

But more than that, the Atlantic community, the drawing together of the United States and Europe, is the very heart of NATO. If the price of reconstructing Europe were to be the disintegration of that Atlantic community, I should fear for the future.

Fourth, our defence will continue to require nuclear weapons in Europe. Without adequate nuclear weapons, kept up to date and based forward in Europe, our defence would be very much less secure. The lesson of the last forty years is that nuclear deterrence in Europe works. It remains the best guarantee of our defence and security, and that applies particularly for those who would be in the front line of any new conventional war.

We should keep the numbers of nuclear weapons and the types of delivery systems which we need under review. President Bush's decision to terminate work on the successor to LANCE and on modernization of nuclear artillery showed that we are ready to take account of changed circumstances. We can also start to think about our objectives in negotiations to reduce short-range, ground-launched nuclear missiles.

But we must retain sufficient nuclear weapons, and the means of delivering them, to meet our long-term security needs. Our job, as Ministers responsible for our countries' defence and security, is to take the long view. That is what our predecessors in the 1940s and 1950s did; and as a result we have enjoyed peace.

New Directions

Those principles – secure collective defence, the transatlantic connection and credible deterrence – should be strongly reaffirmed by the Summit. They represent the enduring pillars of NATO – as important for the future as they were in the past.

But there are other areas where we can and should adapt NATO to the new situation it faces. And it is to these I now turn. First, we should be ready to update NATO's military strategy to deal with the new situation created by Soviet troop withdrawals and the prospect of a CFE Agreement.

There are many questions to be answered. Does forward defence in the Central Region still make sense in these circumstances? Or should we think more in terms of defence in depth and greater reliance on mobility, flexibility and reserves? Such a change would have implications for the size of the forces which a country like Britain stations forward in Europe.

Second, ought NATO to give more thought to possible threats to our security from other directions? There is no guarantee that threats to our security will stop at some imaginary line across the mid-Atlantic.

It is not long since some of us had to go to the Arabian Gulf to keep oil supplies flowing. We shall become very heavily dependent on Middle Eastern oil once again in the next century. With the spread of sophisticated weapons and military technology to areas like the Middle East, potential threats to NATO territory may originate more from outside Europe. Against that background, it would be only prudent for NATO countries to retain a capacity to carry out multiple roles, with more flexible and versatile forces.

The arguments for rationalizing military production, with a greater role for competition, will become more compelling. We should examine the feasibility of making NATO forces more multi-national. As we reduce our forces, NATO must remain at the forefront of new military technology. I believe that President Reagan's Strategic Defence Initiative and his determination to keep it going had an important part in bringing about the change of approach in Moscow some years ago.

All these matters need to be considered, and they amount to a very full agenda. But while NATO's primary role will remain defence, we should also be thinking about how to give the Alliance a more effective political role, because that too can contribute to our security.

There are two aspects to this. First, we should make NATO the main forum for transatlantic dialogue. I remember many years ago President Kennedy proposed a declaration of interdependence of the two sides of the Atlantic.[1] I would hope we could revive that spirit.

We owe a very great debt to the United States for the enormous contribution which they make to preserving peace not only in Europe and the Atlantic, but in the Pacific and indeed right round the globe.

---

[1] John Fitzgerald Kennedy (1917–63), US politician. 35th President of the United States 1961–63 (Democrat). He proposed a declaration of transatlantic interdependence in a speech at Philadelphia on 4 July 1962.

We should do everything we can, individually and collectively, to support and underpin them.

As part of that, we should give greater weight to political consultation on wider world problems within NATO, as the forum which brings together the United States, Canada and Europe. Indeed, I would like to see us build up the transatlantic relationship in other areas such as trade and finance as well – as we are doing between the European Community and the United States – so that the network of common interests linking the two sides of the Atlantic is strengthened as we go into a new millennium.

The world is changing faster than our ways of thinking. We need to be more imaginative and to work on a bigger canvas.

More emphasis on NATO's political role and activities such as arms control and verification should also make it easier for the Soviet Union to come to terms with NATO's continued existence and German membership of it, while at the same time helping us to maintain public understanding and support for NATO in our own countries.

Second, we need to help the Eastern European countries feel more secure.

By keeping NATO intact, we risk making them feel excluded at the very time that we want to draw them back into the main stream of Europe. Yet NATO cannot itself offer them security guarantees, nor is it realistic to think of extending NATO's membership at present.

What we can do is to build up the CSCE[1] as the body within which political and security issues affecting Europe as a whole can be discussed.

President Mitterrand has spoken of a confederation of European states. I have myself called for a great alliance for democracy, which would one day extend from the Atlantic to the Urals and beyond. I think we are all after the same objective: an area of political stability and economic progress, in which democracy and market economies are firmly rooted.

That is the best guarantee of the sovereign independence of the Eastern European countries. The CSCE can never be a substitute for the defence guarantee that NATO provides. But it can provide a framework of growing trust and confidence which will make both East and West feel more secure.

---

[1] The Conference on Security and Co-Operation in Europe, which first met at Helsinki in 1975, embraced all the states of Europe (except Albania) plus the United States and Canada. In 1995 it was renamed the Organization for Security and Co-Operation in Europe (OSCE).

In this way, Europe's future would be determined by three principal institutions: the European Community with a network of association agreements with Eastern Europe, as the engine of Europe's economic development and prosperity; NATO, as the guarantee of our security and the focus of transatlantic partnership; and the CSCE, as the wider forum bringing in also the Soviet Union and Eastern Europe for discussion of East/West issues.

That would be a sturdy construction to ensure continuing peace and stability.

Conclusion

Mr Secretary-General, I am leaving from this meeting to travel to Moscow to meet President Gorbachev. The message I shall take is that NATO flourishes and will continue to do so, not as an alliance against anyone – NATO has never attacked anyone and will not in future – but as an alliance for freedom, justice and democracy, values which are now ever more widely accepted across Europe. I hope your endeavours here and those of our Summit in July will enable us to preserve the best from NATO's successful past, while ensuring that our alliance is just as strong and influential in the new world of the future.

42

The Pankhurst Lecture, Delivered to the 300 Group, London, 18 July 1990

Issues of social policy – the tax treatment of families, social security dependency, divorce, illegitimacy – became increasingly politically important at the end of the Thatcher Government. Within the Conservative Party, there was some tension between the feminist and family lobbies – those who believed a woman's role lay in challenging men in politics, business and the professions, and those who believed her place was in the home. As someone who had combined a professional career with bringing up a family, Mrs Thatcher found it easy to understand the competing demands on time and resources which this combination entailed. But her view was, as she put it, that 'while the home must always be the centre of one's life, it should not be the boundary of one's ambitions' (II, p. 81). The Pankhurst Lecture accordingly combines a defence of the right of mothers to go out to work, strictures against single parenthood and the announcement of the setting up of a new Child Support Agency to ensure that absent parents paid proper maintenance for their children.

This is the first time that I have had the privilege to address the 300 Group,[1] though I have attended a number of the group's events over the years, and I am honoured to be asked to deliver the 300 Group address at this, the Pankhurst Lunch.

You have a specific goal, which I applaud and support. I, too, wish to see more women in Parliament and in public life as a whole. Not because I think women should be granted special favours. I haven't received special favours in politics at Westminster or outside it. And I very much doubt if you have either. Rather, I want to see more women in public life because this country will be better served if it draws fully on the rich talents of women as much as men.

---

[1] The 300 Group was founded in 1980 to campaign for equal representation of women in Parliament – three hundred women MPs being the target.

Women have had to fight over many years to gain the opportunities we now have. Among the standard-bearers of this crusade were many of those whose names are recalled here today: Nancy Astor, the first woman Member of Parliament; Margaret Bondfield, the first woman Cabinet Minister; Amy Johnson, the first woman aviator; and Elizabeth Garrett Anderson, who became the first woman qualified doctor in Britain.[1]

Mrs Pankhurst

But no one could surpass the achievement of Emmeline Pankhurst.[2] Mrs Pankhurst was a fighter. Not everyone, even now, would approve of every tactic she used. But it's sometimes forgotten that it was the example given by Mrs Pankhurst and her colleagues in wartime, as much as their militancy in peacetime, which brought, first grudging respect, and then enthusiastic support for her cause. The reward of that sacrifice was the enfranchisement in 1918 of women over thirty; and in the same year it became possible for women to enter Parliament. The gratitude of the nation brought justice for women.

The Influence of Women

Not, of course, that women before this time lacked influence. Certainly the idea of a woman as a frail, sheltered junior partner in the business of life is alien to the Judaeo-Christian tradition.

Chapter 31 of the Book of Proverbs talks about the qualities of a capable woman, whose 'worth is far beyond rubies'. And what does she do? In addition to getting on with her work at home and making every effort to give the best to her husband and children, we also read: 'She seeks wool and flax, and works with willing hands . . . She rises while it is yet night (Well, I can certainly testify to that!) and provides food for

---

[1] Nancy Astor (1879–1964), Viscountess Astor. Conservative MP 1919–45. Margaret Bondfield (1873–1953), Labour MP 1923–24, 1929–31; Minister of Labour 1929–31. Amy Johnson (1903–41), British aviator, who made a solo flight from England to Australia in 1930. Elizabeth Garrett Anderson (1836–1917), first woman member of the British Medical Association.
[2] Emmeline Pankhurst (1858–1928), suffragette, founder of the Women's Social and Political Union 1903. Conservative Prospective Parliamentary Candidate 1926–28.

her household (Some things never change!). She considers a field and buys it; with the fruit of her hands she plants a vineyard . . . She perceives that her merchandise is profitable . . . She makes linen garments and sells them . . . She opens her mouth with wisdom, and the teaching of kindness is on her tongue. She looks well to the ways of her household, and she does not eat the bread of idleness.'

Well, there's nothing new about women working!

This thoroughly admirable lady, who is at the same time a good wife, a good mother, a practical provider for her own, generous to others and a very good businesswoman, balanced her responsibilities rather well. And, essentially, it is the balancing of responsibilities which I want to deal with today.

Women in Public Life

Since the days of Mrs Pankhurst, the economic, social and political condition of women in Britain has been transformed.

In 1918 there were seventeen women Parliamentary candidates. Only one came to Parliament. At the 1987 general election there were 325 women candidates. Forty-one were elected.

Not enough, I agree. We need more – lots more. Every one of us will be delighted when there are so many that our presence there is no longer a matter of comment. In this Government there are four women Ministers of State and two Junior Ministers – oh, and one Prime Minister . . . not a bad record, if you consider we have only seventeen women Conservative Members of Parliament, and that five of these are Ministers in the Commons. The two others are Ministers in the Lords. And earlier in the lifetime of this Government, Baroness Young[1] was the first woman to lead the House of Lords, and of course she was in the Cabinet.

I was delighted that four out of the eight new peers whom I recommended in the last Working Peers List were women, distinguished in their own right. This was the first time that half the list were women.

Just as important, though, is the advance of women outside Parliament in public life. In the professions, in management, in self-employment, and generally. Two out of five jobs are now done by women.

[1] Janet Young (born 1926), Baroness Young of Farnworth 1971. Chancellor of the Duchy of Lancaster 1981–82; Lord Privy Seal 1982–83; Leader of the House of Lords 1981–83; Minister of State at the Foreign Office 1983–87.

We have come a long way since the days when Marie Curie[1] was forced to publish her early research under her husband's name. Or from the days when Lady Ada Lovelace[2] – a gifted mathematician but condemned to obscurity – was providing the basis of the first computer programmes.

We are also trying to ensure that girls and young women are educated and trained for jobs which would in the past have been the preserve of men. Around half the students in medicine and dentistry are now women, and the latest figures for the legal and accountancy professions show a similar picture. Alas, in engineering we still lag far behind, in spite of the fact that it is over seventy years ago that Dame Caroline Haslett[3] founded the Women's Engineering Society and set such a marvellous example herself.

This is doubly ironic, because science and technology have done so much for women throughout this century. The spirit of enterprise has translated advances into equipment which has removed most of the drudgery from household chores, leaving so much more time both for the family and for work outside the home. And technological progress and push-button equipment has opened up for women jobs once physically impossible for them to do.

But legislation has been necessary too, both to stamp out discrimination and to tackle other problems. One of the most important tax reforms of this Government has been the introduction of independent taxation for married couples – giving them two separate personal allowances as well as a married couples' allowance. This means that up to £7,700 of the family income is now tax-free.

Three million married women will pay less as a result of these changes, three-quarters with incomes less than £5,000 per year. These reforms have promoted women's independence and protected their privacy.

---

[1] Marie Sklodowska Curie (1867–1934), Polish/French physicist and chemist, who investigated radioactivity.
[2] Ada Byron (1815–52), Countess of Lovelace. British mathematician who assisted computer pioneer Charles Babbage.
[3] Dame Caroline Haslett (1895–1957), British electrical engineer. A founding member of the Women's Engineering Society 1919; Founder-Director of the Electrical Association for Women 1924–56.

Where we are Now

So there is much to applaud. The horizons of women have widened immeasurably. And women's way of life has changed accordingly.

Far more women now go out to work. Some married women are working because they prefer a career to having children. Others want to combine a career with having a family. Others yet again are working, at least part-time, to bring in extra money for the family. And of course many of us want not only to spend time bringing up our family, but also to be able to use our talents and abilities elsewhere, feeling that otherwise they would be wasted and we should lose the satisfaction, stimulation and independence that such work brings.

But let me say this: it is wrong to describe the choice as between working and not working. Anybody who has tried to bring up children knows that there is no more demanding – or fulfilling – work. And if we who work outside the home do not make enough time to be with our children, we should regret it for ever.

There can be no single solution that applies to everyone: family and economic circumstances are so different, and so are temperaments and aptitudes. It's not for the state or anyone else to dictate whether and how much women should work. It is a decision for the husband and wife to take together. Otherwise there will be friction; and nothing could be worse for the family.

Sometimes I am asked how I managed to combine a successful career with a family, and I can only draw on my own experience. I've always found that to get the most out of life you have to work really hard. And the more effort you put in, the more satisfaction you get out.

But you have to think ahead: you have to organize your life and your family's life with great care. You have to make swift decisions – and the right ones – often at the start of the day, or quite late at night. And you have to see they are put into effect with the minimum of fuss. Yet, no matter how hard you work or how capable you are, you can't do it all yourself. You have to seek reliable help – a relative, or what my mother would have called 'a treasure'. Someone who brought not only her work but her affections to the family. And, as at other times, the existence of the wider family is so very important – the grandparents, the uncles and aunts and the friends who help us to cope; although of course today grandparents are often working themselves![1]

It is also clearly in the interests of business to give women the chance to combine bringing up a family and having a job. Major companies such as Esso, BP, ICI, IBM, the leading banks, and the Government as an employer are setting an example, providing flexible conditions, career breaks for children, good-quality nursery facilities, working from home and part-time working. These are all things that help women go back to work. And I would like to see many more employers follow their lead.

Families under Pressure

And there is a less happy aspect of the background against which women today must balance their responsibilities. Sadly, no fewer than one in five children will experience a parental divorce before they are sixteen. And one in four children are born to unmarried parents. Last year nearly 800,000 lone-parent families were receiving income support. And these families are often concentrated in areas where children can hardly know what an ordinary married family life is like. In the United Kingdom we have one of the highest proportions of lone-parent families of all the European Community countries.

No matter how sympathetic we are to the difficult circumstances which lie behind these figures, they should cause us the greatest unease. Unease because of the interests of the children – and unease because of the effects on the life of our country as a whole.

Of course, there's never been a golden age of universal marital bliss. But the worry is that what was once the exception may now become the rule.

And it is, of course, the children who suffer most. I remember the late Mia Kellmer Pringle[2] stressing again and again that children must be brought up in a stable, loving environment in which parents offer time, affection and guidance. The children need security. These things are most likely where the parents are married – and stay married. Because there is always home to go to.

In some cases that ideal is just not attainable, and in others – where

[1] Mrs Thatcher had become a grandmother in February 1989.
[2] Mia Kellmer Pringle (1920–83), Austrian-born psychologist. Director of the National Children's Bureau 1963–81; author of *The Needs of Children* (1974).

for example there is violence – it is undoubtedly better where the parents are separated. We must be supportive of lone parents left to bring up children on their own.

Just recently I met Mrs Margaret Harrison, who runs Homestart, an organization with some six thousand voluntary workers who are themselves parents.[1] They visit families in their homes, giving other parents – especially single parents – friendship and support in the practical things involved in running a home and bringing up their children. It's not officious; it's not intrusive; it's not patronizing. Homestart volunteers put the people they help on an equal footing right from the start by indicating that perhaps they too in time could use their experience to help others – those who have been helped help too. Homestart seeks to break the cycle of deprivation, by helping today's children grow up in happiness and security to become tomorrow's parents.

Maintenance

Government too must be concerned to see parents accept responsibility for their children. For even though marriages may break down, parenthood is for life. Legislation cannot make irresponsible parents responsible. But it can and must ensure that absent parents pay maintenance for their children. It is not fair for them to expect other families to foot their bills too.

At present, only one in three children entitled to receive maintenance actually benefit from regular payments; and three-quarters of lone parents have to rely on social security. Earlier this year I announced that we were looking at ways to stop absent parents just walking away from their duty to maintain their children. We have been examining the policy and practices of other countries, and we have decided that we must have a simpler system of maintenance available to all. The present one is too inconsistent, too slow and too complicated.

In future, we will set up a new Child Support Agency[2] which will have access to the information necessary to trace absent parents and make them accept their financial obligation. We will move to assessing maintenance through a standard administrative formula which will take

---

[1] Keith Joseph, an enthusiast for Homestart's work, introduced Mrs Harrison and her organization to the Prime Minister.
[2] The Child Support Agency was set up under the 1990 Social Security Act.

account of the parents' ability to pay, of the cost of bringing up a child – *and* the right of that child to share in their parents' rising living standards. Complicated cases may still have to be referred to the courts, but the existence of such a formula will help in these cases too.

These proposals will help lone parents, who are often overwhelmed by the sheer scale of the task of making absent parents face up to their responsibilities. The whole process will be easier, more consistent and fairer. The morale and confidence of the mother will then be restored. Then she will be able to better use and develop her own abilities for the benefit of her children and herself. She can then break out of the cycle of loneliness. We will publish the full details of these proposals in a White Paper this autumn.

Conclusion

Today I have covered a wide range of issues. And I have tried to put them in the context of balancing responsibilities.

What Mrs Pankhurst would have made of questions like this it isn't easy to know. And certainly, I don't claim to. But I am interested to note that her daughter, Christabel,[1] wrote of her mother that she was 'no revolutionary in her views on marriage'.

The great and valuable revolution which has taken place since Mrs Pankhurst's victory over the forces of prejudice and reaction, which has allowed us to be here today, will go on. The vistas of opportunity for women will continue to widen – and widen further as we enter the EC Single Market and women add languages to our enormous range of attributes.

There is an enormous reserve of wisdom and ability on which to draw. Let's have three hundred women Members of Parliament to do just that!

---

[1] Christabel Pankhurst (1880–1958), suffragette and religious propagandist.

43

Speech to the Aspen Institute, Aspen, Colorado,
5 August 1990

In her August 1990 Aspen speech, the Prime Minister set out for the first time her detailed thoughts about the shape of the post-Cold War world – what was now being called the New World Order. At the time, it was the crisis caused by Saddam Hussein's invasion of Kuwait which was the main focus at Aspen. By common consent, Mrs Thatcher's presence by the side of President Bush had the effect of stiffening the West's response. But it is the passages in which the Prime Minister defined democracy in universally applicable terms and then proposed the means to apply it that constitute the core of the speech and give it enduring importance. The call to ensure that the West – and Europe in particular – should open its markets and provide generous assistance for the reforming Soviet Union and the East European countries emerging from communism would be repeated by Mrs Thatcher with ever greater insistence in the years after she left office.

SHAPING A NEW GLOBAL COMMUNITY

First, thank you, Henry,[1] for your very kind words and for the honour of being invited to address this fortieth-anniversary Conference. It must be rare for an American President and a British Prime Minister to address the same Conference of a private institute. It is a great tribute to the Aspen Institute's[2] prestige and, of course, has absolutely nothing

[1] Henry Catto (born 1930), US politician and diplomat. Assistant Secretary of Defense 1981–83; Ambassador to Britain 1989–91; Director of the US Information Agency 1991–93.
[2] The Aspen Institute, founded in 1949, organizes conferences and seminars which bring together business, educational, cultural and political leaders to discuss contemporary problems.

403

whatsoever to do with the climate and the beauty of Aspen at this time of year – they are purely coincidental. We are extremely fortunate to have Henry Catto as Ambassador to Britain and he and Jessica do an outstanding job.

Of course, diplomacy has changed a bit since the first American Ambassador came to London just over two hundred years ago. I am told that a memorandum survives from President Jefferson[1] to his Secretary of State. The President wrote: 'We have not heard anything from our Ambassador to France for three years. If we do not hear from him this year – let us write him a letter.'

I am sure American Ambassadors are much more communicative these days.

Mr Chairman, it is a great honour to receive the Aspen Institute's Statesman Award, and I am most grateful to Mr Phelan[2] for what he said about me in presenting it. The only two previous recipients have been men of the highest distinction, both associated with different aspects of Europe: Jean Monnet[3] with the founding of the European Community; and Willy Brandt[4] with Germany's reconciliation with its eastern neighbours, which reached its fulfilment with Chancellor Helmut Kohl's[5] recent visit to the Soviet Union. As a European, and a passionate admirer of all that the nations of Europe have given to the world – in art, in literature, in political ideas – it is a privilege to be in such company.

Britain's destiny lies in Europe as a full member of the Community. We shall not be standing on the sidelines or, as you would say, watching from the bleachers. On the contrary, we shall bring to it our own distinctive point of view – practical and down to earth. We fight hard for what we believe in, namely: a Europe based on willing co-operation

---

[1] Thomas Jefferson (1743–1826), US statesman. Secretary of State 1789–93; Vice-President of the United States 1797–1801; 3rd President of the United States 1801–9 (Democrat-Republican).

[2] John Phelan, Jr (born 1931), US financier. President of the New York Stock Exchange 1980–84.

[3] Jean Monnet (1888–1979), French economist and civil servant. Deputy Secretary-General of the League of Nations 1919–23; President of the European Coal and Steel Community 1952–55; Chairman of the Action Committee for the United States of Europe 1956–75.

[4] Willy Brandt (1913–92), German politician. Mayor of West Berlin 1957–66; Foreign Minister 1966–69; Chancellor of the Federal Republic 1969–74.

[5] Helmut Kohl (born 1930), German politician. Minister-President of the Rhineland Palatinate 1969–76; Chancellor of the Federal Republic 1982–.

between independent sovereign states; a Europe which is an expression of economic freedom, without which political freedom could not long endure; a Europe which rejects central control and its associated bureaucracy; a Europe which does not resort to protectionism, but remains open to the outside world; and – of supreme importance for Britain – a Europe which always seeks the closest possible partnership with the United States.

Mr Chairman, you have chosen for this Conference the theme 'Shaping a New Global Community'. That theme reflects the boldness, energy and vision of this remarkable country which has led the free world for over four decades. The willingness to think ahead on a world scale, when many countries are self-absorbed, preoccupied, even obsessed with their regional problems, is very refreshing and very necessary.

The President gave you his vision of the way ahead in a marvellous speech on Thursday.[1] Anyone who had doubts – and I certainly had none – about America's willingness to continue to give leadership to the world will realize how wrong they were. I am an undiluted admirer of American values and the American dream, and I believe they will continue to inspire not just the people of the United States but millions upon millions across the face of the globe.

Your theme is also very timely, because it has been given to us, in the last decade of this century, to fashion a new global community. For today we are coming to realize that an epoch in history is over, an epoch which began in 1946 when an American President and a former British Prime Minister shared a platform here in the United States at Fulton, Missouri. They saw with foreboding what Winston Churchill famously called an Iron Curtain coming down across Europe. And they forged the great Western Alliance which bound us together through a common sense of danger to the lives of free peoples.

For more than forty years that Iron Curtain remained in place. Few of us expected to see it lifted in our lifetime. Yet with great suddenness the impossible happened. Communism is broken, utterly broken. And Soviet citizens are talking democracy. The Mayors of Moscow and Leningrad discuss Milton Friedman[2] – I have heard them. And anyone who talks to Mr Gorbachev and other Soviet leaders recognizes a complete change in the nature of their aspirations.

---

[1] President Bush opened the Aspen Institute Conference on 2 August 1990.
[2] Milton Friedman (born 1912), US economist. Professor of Economics at Chicago 1948–82; foremost exponent of monetarism.

We do not see this new Soviet Union as an enemy, but as a country groping its way towards freedom. We no longer have to view the world through a prism of East–West relations. The Cold War is over.

As the Iron Curtain goes up, a new drama unfolds before us, and one in which we are both the authors and the players. Our freedom of action is enlarged and our horizons broaden. The unity and strength which we in the West have found from joining together in defence can now be turned to serve more positive and ambitious purposes.

The first and most exalted of these is to create a world in which true democracy and the rule of law are extended far and wide.

In its heyday, communism believed that it would inevitably dominate the world, subsuming all national feeling and everything which gives life its infinite variety, replacing it with what was alleged to be a scientific system of conformity and uniformity. The very inhumanity and arrogance of the proposition makes one wonder how anyone could ever have believed in it, for communism is so plainly contrary to the human spirit.

Not that there is anything inevitable about the spread of democracy. If anything, the difficulties of sustaining it are greatly underestimated. The heady sense of freedom which comes from throwing off totalitarian rule is short-lived. Building a true democracy is a lengthy and painstaking task.

It is easy enough to transfer the institutions of democracy from one country to another, as Britain did to much of Africa in the 1960s. But it soon becomes apparent that is no guarantee that democracy, as we know it, will be practised. The one-party state in which there is no possibility of choosing an alternative Government is hardly what we mean by democracy.

Mr Chairman, what are the fundamental tenets of true democracy? For me they are these:

First, a sense of personal responsibility. People need to realize that they are not just pawns on a chessboard, to be moved around at the whim of politicians. They can influence their destiny by their own efforts.

And second, democracy means limitation of the powers of government and giving people the greatest possible freedom. In the end, the strength of a society depends not on the big battalions but on the foot-soldiers, on the willingness of ordinary men and women who do not seek fame or glory or high office, to play an active part in their community, not as conscripts but as volunteers.

And third, democracy and freedom are about more than the ballot and universal suffrage. At the beginning of this tumultuous century, Britain rightly believed herself a free country. Yet we went into the First World War with only a 30 per cent franchise. A strong rule of law is the essential underpinning of democracy. The steady growth of the common law over centuries, the process by which statute law is passed by an elected Parliament or Congress, the independence of the judiciary – these are as much the pillars of democracy as its Parliamentary institutions.

And the fourth essential, Mr Chairman, is an economy based on market principles and a right to private property. Wealth is not created by regulation and instruction, but by ordinary enterprising people. It is hard for those who have only experienced life in totalitarian societies to think in these terms, because it is outside anything they have ever known. That is why one sometimes wonders whether some of the countries trying to introduce economic reform have yet understood what a market economy is really about.

So the challenge of spreading democracy and the rule of law is an awesome one. But we must not be pessimistic. One can point to countries – for example, Spain, Portugal, Chile, Nicaragua – where the transition from authoritarian rule to democracy has succeeded. And to those who suggest that some countries are perhaps too large for democracy, there is the remarkable example of India with its seven hundred million people, where democracy is well established.

Mr Chairman, it will take the united efforts of the West to shape a new global community based on democracy, the rule of law and market principles. And we need a plan of campaign; and I suggest that these should be its main elements:

At the East–West Summit of thirty-five nations to be held in the autumn I propose that we should agree on a European Magna Carta to entrench for every European citizen, including those of the Soviet Union, the basic rights which we in the West take for granted. We must enshrine certain freedoms for every individual: freedom of speech, of worship, of access to the law, and of the marketplace.[1] Freedom to participate in genuinely democratic elections, to own property, to maintain nationhood; and, last, freedom from fear of an over-mighty state.

Next we must bring the new democracies of Eastern Europe into closer association with the institutions of Western Europe. And I propose

---

[1] These ideas were the basis of the ten principles set out in Section One of the *Charter of Paris for a New Europe*, signed by CSCE participants on 21 November 1990.

that the Community should declare unequivocally that it is ready to accept all the countries of Eastern Europe as members if they want to join, provided that democracy has taken root and that their economies are capable of sustaining membership. We cannot say in one breath that they are part of Europe, and in the next our European Community club is so exclusive that we will not admit them.

Of course, it will be some time before they are ready for membership, so we are offering them intermediate steps such as Association Agreements. But the option of eventual membership should be clearly, openly and generously on the table. The European Community has reconciled antagonisms within Western Europe; it should now help to overcome divisions between East and West in Europe.

This does not mean that the further development of the existing Community has to be put on ice. Far from it. The completion of the Single Market by 1992 will be an enormous change, one of the biggest since the Community began in 1957. It should herald a fair and open Europe, and one which will be immensely attractive to the newly free peoples of Eastern Europe. And the same is true of closer co-operation in foreign policy.

But if, instead, we set off down the path of giving more and more powers to highly centralized institutions, which are not democratically accountable, then we should be making it harder for the Eastern Europeans to join. They have not thrown off central command and control in their own countries only to find them reincarnated in the European Community. With their new freedom, their feelings of patriotism and national identity flooding out again, their newly restored Parliaments are full of vitality. We must find a structure for the Community which accommodates their diversity and preserves their traditions, their institutions and their nationhood. And we need to do this without introducing the concept of first- and second-class membership of the Community, which would be divisive and defeat much of the purpose of bringing their countries into Europe.

Mr Chairman, all the messages we are getting indicate that the Soviet Union and Eastern Europe desperately want to have the policies of economic freedom, but they just do not know how to acquire them. Many of us are providing practical assistance through 'Know-How Funds'[1] and

---

[1] The British Know-How Fund was developed from June 1989 to assist the transition to a market economy in Eastern Europe by providing training and advice on management, banking, accountancy, commercial law, etc. It is administered by the Foreign Office and paid for by the Overseas Development Agency.

joint ventures. But such is the scale of the problem that we shall need to devise new and more imaginative ways to help. For example, we might identify a whole sector of the Soviet economy such as transport and distribution or food processing or oil exploration or the banking system, and offer to help run it on market principles to demonstrate what can be achieved.

After all, the Soviet Union has natural wealth in abundance. It is not resources it lacks, but the ability to turn them to advantage. One day the Soviet Union will be a highly prosperous country – and so will China – and it is not too soon to be thinking how to bring them into the world economy.

But the most difficult step is for Governments which have been accustomed to running a regimented economy to think in a different way. If we can begin to associate them with the international institutions which have done so much to help ensure our own prosperity, in particular the GATT and the IMF, that could make it easier for them. We might also bring the Soviet Union gradually into closer association with the Economic Summit. Britain will be hosting next year's Economic Summit in London, and if my colleagues agree, I would not be averse to taking a first step along that road on that occasion.[1]

So there are three points in our plan of campaign: a European Magna Carta; closer association of East and West in Europe; and eventually bringing the Soviet Union into the Economic Summit and the Western economy.

But there is a further crucial point. None of this could be contemplated unless we in the West had been resolute to maintain a secure defence. The fact that our peoples were willing to bear the burdens, sustain the expense and brave the dangers of defence for over forty years is a proof of how much they value liberty and justice.

We failed to do this after the First World War. Instead, armies were disbanded, weapons were laid aside, and American forces went home. The result was once again world war – war in Europe and war in the Pacific – and a whole generation paid a terrible price.

After the Second World War we were wiser. We threatened no one, but we kept up our defences. We halted the great expansion of communism. Today, nations and peoples are free who would otherwise be in

---

[1] The G7 Economic Summit was held in London from 15 to 17 July 1991. President Gorbachev joined Western leaders on the final day.

bondage, were it not for our perseverance and, above all, that of the United States.

But now, in the moment of success, it is wise to be cautious. History has seen too many false springs. The Soviet Union, as the President said, remains a formidable military power. Even the Russian Republic – on its own – would be the largest country in the world, stretching from the Baltic to the Pacific across eleven time zones. Moreover, with the spread of bailistic missiles and chemical weapons, it is all too likely that we shall face ugly situations in other parts of the world, as we are seeing now.

We shall continue to need NATO. And that means we shall continue to need American forces in Europe – in your own interests as well as in ours. Do you remember some of the lines from T.S. Eliot's[1] 'Chorus on the Rock'? He said this:

It is hard for those who live near a police station to believe in the triumph of violence.
Do you think that the faith has conquered the world and that lions no longer need keepers?
Do you need to be told that whatever has been, can still be?

What a pity more poets were not also politicians. That is marvellous language, and its meaning so wonderfully clear.

Mr Chairman, as we look to the future, there are other issues which call for a much higher level of international co-operation, more intensive than anything we have achieved so far: the spread of drugs, terrorism and intimidation, a decaying environment. No country is immune from them.

Our ability to come together to stop or limit damage to the world's environment will be the greatest test of how far we can act as a world community. Science is still feeling its way, and some uncertainties remain. But we know that very high population growth is putting an enormous pressure on the earth's resources. Primitive methods of agriculture are extending deserts and destroying tropical forests, and as they disappear, nature's capacity to correct its own imbalance is seriously affected.

We know, too, that our industries and way of life have done severe damage to the ozone layer. And we know that within the lifetime of our

---

[1] Thomas Stearns Eliot (1888–1965), American-born British poet, playwright and critic.

grandchildren the surface temperature of the earth will be higher than at any time for 150,000 years; the rate of change of temperature will be higher than in the last ten thousand years; and the sea level will rise six times faster than has been seen in the last century.

Mr Chairman, the costs of doing nothing, of a policy of wait and see, would be much higher than those of taking preventive action now to stop the damage getting worse. And the damage will be counted not only in dollars, but in human misery as well. Spending on the environment is like spending on defence – if you do not do it in time, it may be too late.

Most of us have been brought up to give praise and thanks for the miracles of creation. But we cannot give thanks with our words if our deeds undermine the beauty of the world to which we are born.

The same lessons apply to the evil of drugs. We must warn all, by all means: we must use every means to warn young people of the blandishments which will be used to entice them into drug addiction. We must ram home that to succumb would utterly ruin their lives and devastate their families. The contemptible and callous men who prey upon the young for their own material gain must be hunted ruthlessly until they are brought to justice.

This problem is not limited to a handful of countries. There are now forty million addicts worldwide and the number continues to rise. We have to grapple with every aspect of the problem: cutting the demand, the production, the money-laundering and the international networks.

Hard as we have tried, we are still far from success. And there is only one way to attack the problem, wherever it occurs, and that is by bringing together all the resources and knowledge of every country to slay this dragon.

That goes for terrorism and intimidation too. The terrorists fight with the weapons of war. We respond with the rule of law. The dice are loaded against the law-abiding and the innocent. Terrorism will only be beaten when all civilized Governments resolve that they will never harbour or give safe haven to terrorists. Anything less than a proven total dedication to hunting down the terrorists within should make those countries the outcasts of the world.

Let it be plain – we shall never surrender to terrorism.

Mr Chairman, intensified economic international co-operation is needed just as much on more familiar problems. A world which formed itself into inward-looking blocs of nations would be taking a sad step backwards.

Yet I see a real danger of that: a European bloc based on the European Community's proposed economic and monetary union; a Western-hemisphere bloc based on a United States–Canada–Latin American free trade area; and then a Pacific bloc with Japan and some of the East and South-East Asia countries. Such an arrangement would encourage protectionism and stifle trade at the very time we need to be driving forward to a positive outcome for the Uruguay Round of world trade negotiations. That means we shall all need to make concessions, particularly on agriculture, where we are all far from perfect. To slide back into protectionism would be damaging for every one of us, and none more than the developing countries who, as well as aid, need trade.

Of course they need help, particularly the poorest, and they all seek investment. But there is going to be unprecedented demand for the world's savings over the next decade.

When you look at the problems of developing countries, you frequently find it is the politics which have led the economics astray. These problems do not always stem from lack of resources or natural wealth or some other similar handicap. Quite often they are the result of bad government, corruption, and the breakdown of law and order, or cynical promises which could never be kept. And that is not a view which I have invented; in case you thought it sounded like me, it comes from an excellent report by the World Bank. The problems will not be solved by abstractions such as a new international economic order, nor by the verbose vocabulary of the North/South dialogue.

The developing countries need sustained help. But they also need democracy, good government, and sensible economic policies which attract foreign investment. That investment will go to the countries which offer the best prospect of stability, which welcome enterprise, and give a fair rate of return, with the right to repatriate a reasonable proportion of the profits. Investment will not come into a country unless it can also get out.

All these problems underline the need for an effective global institution where we can agree on certain basic standards, resolve disputes and keep the peace. We thought we had created that at San Francisco in 1946 when we founded the United Nations. Sadly, it has not quite worked out that way.

Iraq's invasion of Kuwait[1] defies every possible principle for which the United Nations stands. If we let it succeed, no small country can

---

[1] Iraq invaded Kuwait on 2 August 1990.

ever feel safe again. The law of the jungle would take over from the rule of law.

The United Nations must assert its authority and apply a total economic embargo unless Iraq withdraws without delay. The United States and Europe both support this. But to be fully effective it will need the collective support of all the United Nations' members. They must stand up and be counted, because a vital principle is at stake: an aggressor must never be allowed to get his way.

As East/West confrontation diminishes, as problems which have long dominated the United Nations' agenda, such as apartheid in South Africa, are being resolved, we have an opportunity to rediscover the determination that attended the founding of the United Nations. And the best time is now, with our present very able and widely respected Secretary-General.[1] It was never realistic to think of the United Nations as a world government. But we can make it a place where truth is told and objective standards prevail. The five Permanent Members of the Security Council have acquired authority in recent times by working together. Not enough, but a basis on which to build.

Some would say all this is a triumph of hope over experience. But let us not be hypnotized by the past, otherwise we shall always shrug our shoulders and walk away. Shakespeare reminded us:

> Our doubts are traitors
> And make us lose the good we oft might win,
> By fearing to attempt.[2]

Mr Chairman, may I thank you most warmly for giving me this occasion to explain how I believe we can shape the future, as we move into the third millennium. If we are to do better than our best, Europe and the United States must continue to make common cause, attracting others as we go, but remaining faithful to the principles which have brought us so far.

Winston Churchill expressed so well the positive approach we shall need. In his description of the Journey of Life he said this:

Let us be contented with what has happened to us and thankful for all we have been spared.

[1] Javier Pérez de Cuéllar.
[2] *Measure for Measure*, I, iv.

413

Let us treasure our joys but not bewail our sorrows.
The glory of light cannot exist without its shadows.
Life is a whole, and good and ill must be accepted together.[1]

We must work together for more joy and less sorrow, to ensure more light and less shadow. If we achieve that, we shall have done well. I wish you well in all your endeavours.

[1] Winston Churchill, *Thoughts and Adventures.*

44

Speech to the House of Commons During the Debate on the Gulf Crisis, 6 September 1990

The weeks which followed Iraq's invasion of Kuwait on Thursday 2 August were full of diplomatic and, increasingly, military activity. Mrs Thatcher was in regular contact with President Bush as the latter sought to assemble a coalition of powers to force Saddam Hussein to withdraw. On Thursday 6 September the House of Commons was recalled to debate the crisis.

Naturally, the Prime Minister began by giving a full account of what was known of the situation and of the measures, including the UN Security Council Resolutions, which had been taken to exert pressure on Iraq. But the second half of the speech – and the string of hostile Labour interventions it provoked – show Mrs Thatcher preparing the ground for the military action which she had always believed would prove necessary. The experience of the Falklands War made her extremely reluctant to return to the United Nations for authorization of the use of force when Article 51 of the UN Charter (that is, the right of self-defence) sufficed. This was to be a source of disagreement not just with Opposition MPs but also with Secretary Baker and the Americans.

The Prime Minister. May I first express our deep sorrow at the loss of a greatly loved colleague, Ian Gow,[1] and our sympathy to his family; and also express our sadness at the loss of the two other honourable Members to whom Mr Speaker referred, Mr Adams and Mr Wall,[2] who were taken from us so suddenly, and extend our sympathy to their families, too.

---

[1] Ian Gow (1937–90), Conservative MP 1974–90; Parliamentary Private Secretary to the Prime Minister 1979–83. He was killed by an IRA car-bomb in Hankham, East Sussex, on 30 July 1990.
[2] Allender Steele Adams (1946–90), Labour MP 1979–90. Patrick Wall (1933–90), Labour MP 1987–90.

The Government have asked for Parliament to be recalled to discuss the grave developments in the Gulf over the last few weeks.

In the early hours of 2 August, Iraq invaded and occupied Kuwait, a peaceful, independent country and a member of the United Nations since 1963. It was a flagrant and blatant case of aggression.

The United Nations Security Council responded promptly, demanding first Iraq's immediate and unconditional withdrawal, and subsequently restoration of the legitimate Government of Kuwait. When after a few days Iraq had failed to respond, the Security Council imposed comprehensive sanctions and later authorized the use of force to implement them.

Meanwhile, in response to requests from King Fahd of Saudi Arabia[1] and other Gulf rulers, the United States, closely followed by Britain, immediately deployed ground, air and naval forces to deter further aggression by Saddam Hussein,[2] and in support of the Security Council's decisions. More than twenty other countries, including several Arab nations, have now sent or committed themselves to sending forces.

British and other foreign citizens in Iraq and Kuwait have been caught up in the crisis, and are being used by Iraq as hostages in a way which has caused revulsion throughout the world. Embassies in Kuwait have been forcibly prevented from carrying out their duty of looking after their citizens.

The Government have responded to this extremely serious situation vigorously and in close co-operation with our allies and friends. Our resolute response has received wide support in this country and elsewhere and the gratitude and appreciation of many Arab Governments.

Honourable Members naturally wished to debate these matters at a convenient moment, and I welcome the opportunity to give the House a fuller account of events and of the Government's actions. Both my right honourable friends the Secretaries of State for Foreign and Commonwealth Affairs and Defence[3] have just returned from visiting the area and are in a position to give first-hand reports to the House.

I shall first say a word about the origins of the present crisis. In July, Iraq and Kuwait became involved in a dispute over oil pricing and

---

[1] Fahd ibn Abdul Aziz (born 1923), King of Saudi Arabia 1982–; Prime Minister 1982–.
[2] Saddam Hussein (born 1937), President of Iraq 1979–.
[3] Douglas Hurd and Tom King.

production levels, and over Iraqi debts to Kuwait. Iraq's principal demand was that Kuwait and the United Arab Emirates should cut oil production in order to maintain prices. Iraq also demanded it should not have to repay the loans of many billions of dollars received from Kuwait during the Iran–Iraq War. As the dispute developed, Iraq deployed substantial numbers of troops to positions near the border of Kuwait.

Active diplomatic efforts, notably by President Mubarak of Egypt,[1] were made to defuse the situation. As a result, Iraq and Kuwait agreed to bilateral talks in Jeddah on 1 August, with the prospect of a further round of discussions in Baghdad. The Iraqi Government gave explicit and categorical assurances to the Governments of Egypt and Saudi Arabia that they had no intention of invading Kuwait.

Saddam Hussein introduced into this dispute the further question of Iraqi territorial claims on Kuwait. These claims are without legal foundation. The Al-Sabah family has ruled Kuwait since the eighteenth century, long before Iraq itself was created in the break-up of the Ottoman Empire following the First World War.

Kuwait's borders with the newly created Iraq were drawn in 1923. They were accepted by Iraq when it became an independent state in 1932. None the less, Iraq resuscitated its territorial claim against Kuwait in 1961, when British protection of Kuwait came to an end. British forces were despatched at the request of the ruler to protect Kuwait's independence and sovereignty. They were subsequently replaced by an Arab League force. The existing border was then finally reaffirmed between Iraq and Kuwait in 1963.

That is the history. To return to recent events. Despite having assured other Arab Governments and leaders that he had no aggressive intent, Saddam Hussein ordered Iraqi forces to invade Kuwait in the early hours of 2 August. They did so under the pretext of responding to a request for assistance from a non-existent revolutionary government which they alleged had overthrown the Government of Kuwait.

Saddam Hussein then established a puppet régime consisting of Iraqi officers. That so-called Government have now disappeared without trace, and Saddam Hussein claims to have annexed Kuwait, which he now describes as a province of Iraq. History has many examples of perfidy and deceit. This ranks high among them and shows that nothing

---

[1] Lieutenant-General Hosni Mubarak (born 1928), Egyptian air force officer and politician. Commander-in-Chief 1972–75; Vice-President 1975–81; President 1981–.

Saddam Hussein says can be trusted. Moreover, it is an outrageous breach of international law.

Iraq's actions raise very important issues of principle as well as of law. There can be no conceivable justification for one country to march in and seize another, simply because it covets its neighbour's wealth and resources. If Iraq's aggression were allowed to succeed, no small state could ever feel safe again. At the very time when at last we can see the prospect of a world governed by the rule of law, a world in which the United Nations and the Security Council can play the role envisaged for them when they were founded, Iraq's actions go back to the law of the jungle.

The issue is one of importance to the whole world. It affects world security, world oil supplies and world economic stability. It affects the confidence of all small states, not only those in the Middle East. We have bitter memories of the consequences of failing to challenge annexation of small states in the 1930s. We have learned the lesson that the time to stop the aggressor is at once. The international response has been swift and resolute, and for that we owe much to the United States and to the co-operation of the Soviet Union.

On 2 August, the very day of the invasion, the Security Council adopted Resolution 660, condemning the invasion and calling for Iraq's immediate and unconditional withdrawal.

On 4 August, the European Community and its member states took measures to protect Kuwaiti assets, to freeze Iraqi assets, to embargo oil and to stop arms sales to Iraq. It also agreed to work for comprehensive economic sanctions in the Security Council.

Two days later, as Iraq had failed to comply with the original Resolution 660, the Security Council adopted a further Resolution – 661 – which demanded the restoration of the legitimate Government of Kuwait and imposed comprehensive mandatory sanctions on Iraq under Chapter VII.[1] A committee of the Security Council was also set up to monitor and report on the implementation of sanctions.

Subsequently, the Security Council has adopted three further Resolutions. They declare Iraq's annexation of Kuwait null and void; condemn Iraq's actions against foreign nationals in Kuwait and Iraq, and demand

---

[1] Chapter VII of the UN Charter outlines 'Action with Respect to Threats to the Peace, Breaches of the Peace, and Acts of Aggression', and states that the Security Council may call upon UN members to interrupt economic relations and communications (Article 41).

that they be allowed to leave; and Resolution 665 calls upon United Nations member states to take necessary measures against shipping to ensure the strict implementation of sanctions. As was pointed out at the time, that includes the use of minimum force.

Not a single country voted against any of those Resolutions, although the Yemen and Cuba abstained on some of them.

Let me stress: our objectives are those set out in those Resolutions – unconditional Iraqi withdrawal from Kuwait and restoration of the legitimate Kuwaiti Government. The preferred method is comprehensive economic sanctions, collectively and effectively implemented.

Iraq is vulnerable to sanctions. Its economy is based almost totally on the export of a single commodity, oil, through a limited number of identifiable outlets. That is why the action of Turkey and Saudi Arabia in preventing the export of Iraqi oil through the pipelines was of such critical importance. Other outlets are being effectively blockaded, and the embargo on the sale of oil from Iraq and Kuwait is so far working well.

Iraq is also heavily dependent on imports of food and other commodities; and it has limited currency reserves following the war with Iran. That is why it was so important to freeze Kuwaiti accounts and assets abroad on the very first day, and so prevent Iraq from exploiting them. Rigorous implementation of sanctions by the whole world is vital to make the policy work.

The leaders of Saudi Arabia, Egypt and Turkey have shown great steadfastness, as have the Gulf Co-operation Council and many members of the Arab League. Saudi Arabia and other members of OPEC[1] have helpfully agreed to increase oil production substantially to compensate for the loss of Iraqi and Kuwaiti oil on the world market.

For a number of countries, backing sanctions will bring serious economic hardship. An international initiative to find financial and other ways to help them is already under way. I saw Secretary Brady[2] yesterday to discuss that, and said that Britain would play its part; and while we must all contribute, it is only fitting that a special effort should be made by those who, for one reason or another, are not contributing to the multi-national force in the Gulf.

I have been dealing with sanctions and their enforcement. The

[1] The Organization of Petroleum-Exporting Countries.
[2] Nicholas Brady (born 1930), US businessman and politician. Secretary of the Treasury 1988–93.

419

question has arisen whether further authority would need to be obtained from the Security Council for military action beyond that required to enforce sanctions. We have acted throughout in accordance with international law, and we shall continue to do so. Resolution 661, which called for comprehensive economic sanctions, expressly affirms the inherent right of individual or collective self-defence, in response to the armed attack by Iraq against Kuwait, in accordance with Article 51 of the United Nations Charter. We hope that economic sanctions will prove to be sufficient. That is why they must be strictly enforced. But we are not precluded by reason of any of the Security Council Resolutions from exercising the inherent right of collective self-defence in accordance with the rules of international law.

Mr Tony Benn (Chesterfield): This is the nub of the whole debate. As I understand it, what the right honourable lady has said is that the United Nations Charter, and the resolutions that have been passed, have already, here and now, given her legal authority, if it comes to it and it is decided, to take military action against Iraq. I take it that, if we vote in the right honourable lady's Lobby tomorrow night, she will claim that to be an endorsement of that view. Is that her view? She knows the real anxiety. People think that America may go to war and Britain, which is quite a minor part of the operation, will be dragged into it before the House resumes.

The Prime Minister. The nub of the debate is to secure the withdrawal of Iraq from Kuwait and the legitimate restoration of the Government of Kuwait. [Interruption.] If the right honourable gentleman will wait a moment, he will hear my view when I have finished this section of my speech.

May I repeat what I have said? We have acted throughout in accordance with international law and we shall continue to do so. I pointed out that Resolution 661, which called for comprehensive economic sanctions, expressly affirms the inherent right of individual or collective self-defence in response to the armed attack by Iraq against Kuwait. [Interruption.] This is from the Resolution, in accordance with Article 51 of the United Nations Charter.

We hope that economic sanctions will prove to be sufficient. That is why they must be strictly enforced. But we are not precluded, by reason of any of the Security Council Resolutions, from exercising the inherent right of collective self-defence in accordance with the rules of international law.

To undertake now to use no military force without the further authority of the Security Council would be to deprive ourselves of a right in international law expressly affirmed by Security Council Resolution 661; it would be to do injustice to the people of Kuwait, who are unable to use effective force themselves; it would be to hand an advantage to Saddam Hussein; and it could put our own forces in greater peril. For these reasons, I am not prepared to limit our legitimate freedom of action.

Mr Tam Dalyell (Linlithgow): If the Prime Minister is so sure about the rightness of her cause, why the reluctance to seek United Nations authority?

The Prime Minister. I have made my position absolutely clear. May I repeat it? To undertake now to use no military force without the further authority of the Security Council would be to deprive ourselves of a right in international law expressly affirmed by Resolution 661; it would be to do injustice to the people of Kuwait, who are unable to use effective force themselves; it would be to hand an advantage to Saddam Hussein; and it could put our own forces in greater peril.

I have full legal authority for everything that I say on these matters, and for those reasons I am not willing to limit our legitimate freedom of action. I have made the position clear, and there is nothing further that I can add. For the reasons that I have given, I am not prepared to limit our legitimate freedom of action. If right honourable or honourable Members think to the contrary, I am sure that they will have time to put their views. My views have been approved by the topmost legal opinions that we can get.

Our first objective has been to make sanctions effective as a means of bringing pressure on Saddam Hussein to withdraw from Kuwait. Our second but no less urgent objective was to deter further Iraqi aggression. Saddam Hussein could have gone on to invade the north-eastern territories of Saudi Arabia and seize its oilfields. Had he succeeded in that, he could have taken the smaller Gulf states too. It is thanks to rapid action by the United States in sending forces to the area, and prompt support by Britain and France, that the aggressor has been halted.

We have worked throughout in the closest possible co-operation with the United States. I have been in frequent contact with President Bush, and my right honourable friends the Secretary of State for Foreign and Commonwealth Affairs and the Secretary of State for Defence have remained in the closest touch with their American colleagues. That pattern has been repeated at every diplomatic and military level. The

President of the United States has given a lead that deserves the widest support; and the commitment of American forces has been on a tremendous scale.

The House will be familiar with Britain's response, which of course is on a much smaller scale – and I will summarize it briefly. We have deployed a squadron of Tornado F3 air defence aircraft, a squadron of Tornado ground attack aircraft, and a squadron of Jaguar aircraft for ground support. They are stationed in Saudi Arabia, Bahrain and Oman. They are backed up by VC10 tanker aircraft and Nimrod maritime patrol aircraft.

One Royal Navy destroyer and two frigates are in the Gulf. A second destroyer is on its way, as are three mine-clearance vessels. There are also a number of support ships in attendance. A limited number of ground forces are deployed to defend airfields and to provide security generally.

That is already a valuable contribution to the defence of Saudi Arabia and the Gulf, but we believe some additional forces will be needed, and their composition is under consideration.

I wish to stress three points about our armed forces. First, they have been deployed in the area at the request of the Governments of Saudi Arabia, Kuwait and other Gulf states – and, in the case of Bahrain, that Government have invoked our treaty of friendship.

Secondly, they arrived quickly – a factor that contributed enormously to their effect, because the greatest need to deter was in the very early days of the crisis. That is a tribute to the efficiency, skill and dedication of our servicemen and servicewomen.

Thirdly, our forces are part of a much wider international effort, including not only United States forces but those of our European allies, of many Arab countries and others, including members of the Commonwealth. It is a truly multi-national force.

The plight of British and other foreign nationals in Iraq and Kuwait has shocked everyone. Every norm of law, of diplomatic convention and of civilized behaviour has been offended by the way in which those citizens have been rounded up, treated as hostages, and used as a human shield.[1] It is strange for someone who claims to be the leader of the

---

[1] There were some four thousand British citizens in Kuwait, and six hundred in Iraq. They were ordered to surrender themselves to the Iraqi authorities on 16 August 1990, and some were moved to potential military targets such as airfields and oil facilities to deter air raids.

Arab world, a latter-day Saladin,[1] to hide behind women and children. Through the United Nations and bilaterally, we have done everything possible to press Iraq to let our people go, just as theirs are free to go from Britain. There has been particularly good co-operation with other European countries on this matter. The International Committee of the Red Cross is seeking but has not yet obtained the right of access to all hostages held in Iraq and Kuwait, which they are entitled to under the Geneva Convention.

The recent release of some women and children is very welcome, and more are expected in the next few days.[2] But they should never have been detained in the first place; and their release does not make the detention of their husbands, fathers and sons any less evil and reprehensible.

Mr Tony Banks (Newham North-West): Has the Prime Minister seen the complaint in a letter to *The Times* today from one of the released hostages, which said that the British presence in Kuwait – the Embassy – was not giving sufficient and proper advice to those people who remained? Secondly, it said that there has been no debriefing of those people who have come back from Kuwait. Will the Prime Minister tell us what action is being taken to debrief those who have fortunately been released? Thirdly, will she tell us why the British Airways flight was allowed to land in Kuwait five hours after the invasion had taken place? Why was it not warned and allowed to be diverted?

The Prime Minister: I shall answer the honourable gentleman's questions in reverse order. The British Airways flight landed, its passengers disembarked, and the crew handed over to a successor crew and went to their hotels. All that took place before the invasion: the invasion was later. I think that there will be a letter setting out the full facts – a legal letter, so I cannot go further into the matter. Some people would most strenuously argue against some of the misinformation which has unfortunately occurred.

Secondly, with hindsight, people expected us to be able to give advice on things that we could not possibly foresee. Our Embassy deserves praise. When it was suggested that our people should go to hotels, volunteers immediately went to those hotels to look after them. We did

[1] Saladin (1137–93), the chivalrous Sultan of Egypt and Syria 1174–93, who led the Muslims against the Crusaders in Palestine.
[2] Saddam Hussein announced on 28 August that foreign women and children would be permitted to leave. Thousands flew out of Baghdad on 1 September, including hundreds brought from Kuwait on coaches organized by British diplomats there.

not know what would occur. There was no one there to meet them, so they returned to their homes. It is suggested that people should have been advised to try to escape. I do not know how the honourable gentleman can think that we could possibly have given such advice. Will he recall that one of our citizens who tried to do that was shot dead?[1] We have not even been able to recover his body.

The third matter that the honourable gentleman raised was debriefing. These people arrived back at 4.45 in the morning, having suffered terrible experiences. I and all my right honourable friends were concerned that somebody from the Department of Social Security should be at the airport to give immediate help if required, also doctors in case medical attention was needed, and that there should be someone there to get accommodation should that be needed. That was at 4.45 a.m. Had we attempted to debrief them then, we should have been extremely culpable. It would have been said that we were hard and unthinking. Many of those people have already reported, voluntarily, every single thing that they knew. Of course, we shall do everything that we can to ensure that we obtain as much information as possible because it may be helpful to others.

The honourable gentleman's criticisms are not well-founded, and I should like to thank our people in Kuwait.

The recent release, as I said, is welcome, but these people should not have been detained. Their release does not make the detention of their husbands, fathers and sons any less evil and reprehensible.

Our Ambassador[2] and his staff in Baghdad are doing their utmost to help and protect our people. In Kuwait, we and nearly thirty other countries have refused to comply with Iraq's utterly illegal attempt to close foreign Embassies.

Although our Embassy is surrounded by armed soldiers, and its water and electricity cut off, our Ambassador and his small staff of volunteers continue to offer what help they can to the beleaguered British community. The House – most of it – will join me in paying tribute to their work, and, even more so, to the courage and fortitude of all the British people in both countries who are living through this terrible time. Our thoughts go also to their families. We are all very grateful to the work

---

[1] Donald Croskery, a British businessman, was shot dead by Iraqi forces on the Kuwaiti–Saudi border on 12 August 1990.
[2] Sir Harold Walker (born 1932), HM Ambassador to Bahrain 1979–81; the United Arab Emirates 1981–86; Ethiopia 1986–90; Iraq 1990–91.

done by the helpline run by my honourable friend the Member for Kingswood [Mr Hayward][1] and others. It is splendid work, and we thank the many who have given their time and effort.

Mr Ronnie Campbell[2] (Blyth Valley): The Prime Minister just mentioned the helpline. We all agree that it has been marvellous and has helped in all our constituencies. Does the Prime Minister agree, however, that the families of the people affected should be able to use 'Freephone', so that obtaining the information that they need does not cause their telephone bills to build up?

The Prime Minister: As well as the helpline – which, I believe, is turning itself into a charity so that we are better able to supply it with money voluntarily – there is a twenty-four-hour emergency unit at the Foreign Office which I believe people can telephone without expense.

The Minister of State, Foreign and Commonwealth Office (Mr William Waldegrave[3]: Not yet.

The Prime Minister: They cannot telephone without expense yet; however, they are telephoning. People are on duty there for twenty-four hours a day, and are receiving many calls. We are doing everything possible in that regard.

Mr Robert Hayward (Kingswood) rose.

The Prime Minister: I shall give way to my honourable friend: I hope that then I can get on with the rest of my speech.

Mr Hayward: May I thank my right honourable friend for her comments about the efforts of the helpline and all its helpers? May I also clarify the position in relation to charitable trusts? We are in the process of forming such a trust, and if we have enough money we shall give assistance to those who face financial difficulties as a result of the actions taken in Iraq and Kuwait.

The Prime Minister: I believe that I am right in saying that the Foreign Office is also giving some money to help the helpline in its very valuable work.

We shall do our utmost to obtain the freedom of the hostages, keeping their plight constantly before the world. We shall not give in to threats and blackmail. We have made it known that we shall hold Saddam

---

[1] Robert Hayward (born 1949), Conservative MP 1983–92.
[2] Ronnie Campbell (born 1943), Labour MP 1987–.
[3] William Waldegrave (born 1946), Conservative MP 1979–97; Minister of State for Foreign Affairs 1988–90; Health Secretary 1990–92; Chancellor of the Duchy of Lancaster 1992–94; Minister of Agriculture 1994–95; Chief Secretary to the Treasury 1995–97.

Hussein and Iraqi officials individually responsible at law under the Geneva Conventions – to which Iraq is a party – for any harm that befalls them.

I believe that the House will agree that we cannot be deflected from the determined course of action on which we have embarked, and which alone will ensure that the aggressor is not allowed to benefit from his crime. Indeed, by taking hostages, and by his treatment of them, Saddam Hussein only increases the world's abhorrence and stiffens its determination not to let aggression succeed.

Our resolve, and that of our partners and allies, to bring about Iraq's withdrawal from Kuwait and the restoration of the legitimate Government is absolute. There can be no compromise solutions which limit or diminish that objective, and attempts to devise them only postpone the moment when Iraq realizes that there is no option but to withdraw.

Mr Dave Nellist[1] (Coventry South-East): Will the Prime Minister give way?

The Prime Minister. I would prefer to go on, because I am now biting into other Members' time.

There are also some wider lessons to be drawn from these events. First, I believe that the whole House will welcome the prompt and effective manner in which the United Nations has responded to this crisis. At last we are seeing the United Nations act with the determination and purpose that its founders envisaged. I cannot remember a time when we had the whole world so strongly together against an action as now.

Secondly, I would make particular mention of the part played by the five Permanent Members of the United Nations Security Council. They have worked together to an unprecedented degree to ensure that United Nations action is effective. I believe that in this we are seeing the first results of post-Cold War diplomacy: confrontation has been replaced by a new atmosphere of co-operation. We would never have succeeded in getting this response three or four years ago. We hope that the forthcoming meeting between President Bush and President Gorbachev will further strengthen this new accord.

Thirdly, some of the countries bordering Iraq are facing severe difficulties from the flood of refugees – Egyptians, Indians, Pakistanis and Bangladeshis, already numbering hundreds of thousands – all fleeing from Saddam Hussein. Those countries, and the refugees themselves,

[1] David Nellist (born 1952), Labour MP 1983–91; Independent Labour MP 1991–92.

need help until their passage home can be arranged. I can announce today an immediate contribution of a further £2 million to the relevant international organizations. That brings our refugee relief from this crisis so far to £5.4 million.

Fourthly, we must not lose sight of other fundamental issues in the region, above all the need for a just solution to the Palestinian problem. Unfortunately, the Palestinians' support for Iraq's action in seizing the territory of another state has grievously damaged their cause,[1] but nevertheless these events must not stop us from trying to find a solution to this long-standing issue. Peace and security will not come to the region until it is solved.

Ms Clare Short[2] (Birmingham Ladywood): Will the Prime Minister give way?

The Prime Minister. I should like to get on and finish my speech now.

Fifthly, we will need to look to the future, the time when Iraq has withdrawn from Kuwait, as it must, and the legitimate Government have been restored. There will then need to be arrangements to ensure Kuwait's security and that of other countries in the region. I believe that this will need to involve the United Nations, and it is not too early to plan for this situation now.

Sixthly, while East–West relations have improved enormously, these events remind us that dangers can arise elsewhere in the world, and we must always have a strong defence and the capability to operate beyond the borders of NATO, for threats to our security can arise there just as much as in Europe.

Seventhly, we must renew our efforts to outlaw not only the use of chemical weapons but their possession, and no effort must be spared to prevent Iraq from obtaining the materials or technology to manufacture nuclear weapons.

Mr Jeremy Corbyn[3] (Islington North): Will the Prime Minister give way?

The Prime Minister. No. I am not far from the end of my speech and I intend to go straight through to the end of it.

The crisis also underlines the importance of continuing international efforts to prevent the spread of ballistic missiles.

[1] Yasser Arafat, Chairman of the Palestinian Liberation Organization, and Saddam Hussein issued a joint statement in Baghdad on 2 August 1990, saying that Palestinians and Iraqis were united in a common struggle against Israeli occupation and American intervention in the Gulf.
[2] Clare Short (born 1946), Labour MP 1983–.
[3] Jeremy Corbyn (born 1949), Labour MP 1983–.

Mr Eric Heffer (Liverpool Walton): Will the right honourable lady give way?

The Prime Minister: I shall give way to the honourable gentleman, very specially.

Mr Heffer: Will the right honourable lady explain why it was that, when the Kurds were gassed and chemical weapons were used against them[1] – I know that this Government made protests – the United States, for example, ensured that that was not discussed in the Security Council at the time, when there should have been a great movement by the entire world against that terrible thing which Saddam Hussein did?

The Prime Minister: There should, and we were one of the countries. Indeed, I think that we were the country that made the most vigorous protests in every forum where we were. That was quite right. I am grateful to the honourable gentleman for bringing out the point that it was we who made the most vigorous protests.

In the coming weeks we must persist in the determination that we have shown hitherto. There will be those who say that the international effort is costing too much and is not worth it. Some people will forget the awfulness of what Saddam Hussein has done. There will be calls for compromise, attempts to fudge the issues and blur the principles, attempts to undermine the virtually unanimous opposition of the world to what Iraq has done. Of course we prefer a peaceful solution, but that must involve Iraq's total and unconditional withdrawal from Kuwait and the restoration of the lawful Government.

Let us not forget that in Saddam Hussein we are dealing with a person who, without warning, has gone into the territory of another state with tanks, guns and aircraft, has fought and taken the state against international law and against the will of its people. A person who will take such action against one state will take it against another if he is not stopped and his invasion reversed.

We are dealing with a person who has rejected the efforts of the Secretary-General of the United Nations to achieve a peaceful solution on the basis of the United Nations' Resolutions.

We are dealing with a person who plunged his country into eight years of war against Iran, costing the lives of countless thousands of Iraq's young men – and many hundreds of thousands more casualties

---

[1] During a large-scale military operation against Kurdish guerrillas in August 1988, the Iraqi air force dropped chemical bombs on Kurdish villages and refugee columns in northern Iraq.

– without achieving anything other than destruction and desolation.

We are dealing with a man who has used chemical weapons even against his own people. Such a man must be stopped; and we shall persevere until he is.

45

Speech to the Conservative Party Conference, Bournemouth, 12 October 1990

Mrs Thatcher's final Party Conference speech as Prime Minister was as clear, authoritative and successful as any. In spite of the Party's poor showing in the opinion polls, high interest rates, still-rising inflation, the running sore of the Community Charge, splits on Europe and speculation about a possible leadership challenge from Michael Heseltine, Mrs Thatcher remained convinced that problems were soluble and the next election winnable.

Policy work for a manifesto had already begun. Some of this thinking about the extension of choice in housing, education and training made its way into the Conference speech. Above all, the defence of British national and Parliamentary sovereignty against Euro-federalist incursions would clearly be a decisive (and undoubtedly popular) cause. Moreover, the build-up for all-out war in the Gulf, in order to force Saddam Hussein to disgorge Kuwait, had both strengthened the Anglo–American relationship and focused public attention on Mrs Thatcher's known strengths of leadership. The reception given to the speech confirmed that the Constituency parties had lost none of their enthusiasm.

I want to begin on a personal note, and I think you will understand why. Since we met last year, I have lost the best of friends, Ian Gow, and we have all lost one of our wisest and bravest colleagues. Before he was murdered by the IRA, Ian taught us how a civilized community should respond to such an outrage. This is what he said:

> The message that should go out from all decent people – and 99 per cent of people in Northern Ireland and 99 per cent of people in Great Britain are decent people – is that we will never, never surrender to people like this.

Let us pledge to Ian's memory that we will never waver from the steadfast courage he showed in defence of our fellow citizens in Ulster, their rights and their liberties. Ian was a brave man. It is brave men and women who will ensure that democracy triumphs over darkness.

Mr President, this year the world seems to have relived the opening sentence of *A Tale of Two Cities*: 'It was the best of times, it was the worst of times.'

The worst of times as a tyrant struck down a small country that stands at the gateway to the Gulf; the best of times as tyranny crumbled and freedom triumphed across the continent of Europe.

The toppling of the Berlin Wall. The overthrow of Ceausescu by the people he had so brutally oppressed.[1] The first free elections in Eastern Europe for a generation. The spread of the ideas of market freedom and independence to the very heart of the Soviet Leviathan.

Who could have foreseen all this? Who will ever forget the testimonies of courage we heard yesterday in this very hall?[2] Our friends from Eastern Europe reminded us that no force of arms, no walls, no barbed wire can for ever suppress the longing of the human heart for liberty and independence. Their courage found allies. Their victory came about because for forty long, cold years the West stood firm against the military threat from the East. Free enterprise overwhelmed socialism.

This Government stood firm against all those voices raised at home in favour of appeasement. We were criticized for intransigence. Tempted repeatedly with soft options. And reviled for standing firm against Soviet military threats.

When will they learn? When will they ever learn?

Now again, in the sands of the Middle East, principle is at stake. Mr President, dictators can be deterred, they can be crushed – they can never be appeased.

These things are not abstractions. What changed the world and what will save the world were principle and resolve. Our principles: freedom, independence, responsibility, choice – these and the democracy built upon them are Britain's special legacy to the world.

[1] President Nicolae Ceausescu of Romania was overthrown and then executed (with his wife Elena) in December 1989.
[2] On 11 October 1990 the Conservative Party Conference was addressed by József Antall (1932–93), Prime Minister of Hungary 1990–93, and by Pastor Paul Negrut from Romania, Dr Sabine Bergmann Pohl from the former East Germany, Dasha Havel from Czechoslovakia, and Professor Andrzej Zacwislak from Poland. They were members of a delegation of sixteen distinguished democrats from Eastern Europe.

Everywhere those who love liberty look to Britain. When they speak of Parliaments they look to Westminster. When they speak of justice they look to our common law. And when they seek to regenerate their economies, they look to the transformation we British have accomplished.

Principles and resolve: they are what changed Britain a decade ago. They are what the Conservative Party brings to Britain. They alone can secure her freedom and prosperity in the years ahead.

Mr President, this has been the Conference of a Party and a Government with a clear message. Kenneth Baker has given us two fizzing speeches. And our Government's plans for the 1990s have been set out by Ministers. We've heard John Major, Peter Lilley and Michael Howard[1] spell out the policies that will maintain Britain's prosperity. We've heard Douglas Hurd and Tom King make clear that Saddam Hussein will be forced to disgorge Kuwait. We've heard Cecil Parkinson outline bold plans for new investment in transport, and from John Gummer[2] our Party's commitment to farming and the countryside. We've heard David Waddington, Ken Clarke, Chris Patten, Tony Newton and John MacGregor[3] describe how their reforms will make Britain a safer, cleaner, healthier, more secure and better-educated country.

Meanwhile, quietly in the background, Norman Lamont,[4] our Chief Secretary to the Treasury, has been making some of the most effective

---

[1] Peter Lilley (born 1943), Conservative MP 1983–; Trade and Industry Secretary 1990–92; Social Security Secretary 1992–97. Michael Howard (born 1941), Conservative MP 1983–; Employment Secretary 1990–92; Environment Secretary 1992–93; Home Secretary 1993–97.

[2] John Selwyn Gummer (born 1939), Conservative MP 1970–74, 1979–; Chairman of the Conservative Party 1983–85; Minister of Agriculture 1989–93; Environment Secretary 1993–97.

[3] David Waddington (born 1929), Baron Waddington of Read 1990. Conservative MP 1968–74, 1979–90; Chief Whip 1987–89; Home Secretary 1989–90; Lord Privy Seal and Leader of the House of Lords 1990–92; Governor of Bermuda 1992–. Tony Newton (born 1937), Conservative MP 1974–97; Chancellor of the Duchy of Lancaster and Minister for Trade and Industry 1988–89; Social Security Secretary 1989–92; Lord President of the Council and Leader of the House of Commons 1992–97. John MacGregor (born 1937), Conservative MP 1974–; Chief Secretary to the Treasury 1985–87; Minister of Agriculture 1987–89; Education Secretary 1989–90; Lord President of the Council and Leader of the House of Commons 1990–92; Transport Secretary 1992–94.

[4] Norman Lamont (born 1942), Conservative MP 1972–97; Chief Secretary to the Treasury 1989–90; Chancellor of the Exchequer 1990–93. In the autumn, it was the job of the Chief Secretary to negotiate with Government Departments on their spending plans for the coming year.

speeches of all. They're quite short speeches. Monosyllables even. Short monosyllables. But they seem to have an effect on his audience quite out of proportion to their length.

What a fabulous team we've got.

We in this Government all realize that if we are to continue generating the wealth to finance better public services tomorrow, we must have sound money and control of public spending today.

As always, some of the best speeches have come from the floor. I was glad to see even more women speakers this year. Some years ago, I heard a speaker here – a young man – deliver the line: 'Women are the backbone of the Conservative Party. They must be brought to the fore.' That showed an uncertain knowledge of anatomy, but a very sound grasp of politics.

Mr President, a decade ago we revived this country by setting out in a new Conservative direction. We didn't seek a more comfortable way of muddling through, some means of making socialism work in a less destructive way. We too had learned what our Polish guest had experienced far more bitterly: that socialism can't be improved, it has to be removed.

So we cut taxes, reduced controls, denationalized state industries, widened share ownership. And we put the union bosses in their rightful place – under the control of their own members.

It wasn't easy. And it was only possible because we had faith in the country's enterprise and talent – and because we had the tenacity to see our policies through – 'The Strength to Succeed'.[1] Remember the strikes that were supposed to bring Britain to a halt. The steel strike ten years ago – backed by Labour. The violent coal strike which lasted a year – backed by Labour. And a host of other strikes – backed by Labour.

We stood firm. And last year in Britain there were fewer strikes than at any time since the war. And there's a record number of people in jobs.

Yesterday's jobs have been replaced by new jobs. Better jobs. Cleaner jobs. In modern industries.

Young people now face a brighter working future. Our scientific research is second to none. Our universities, our polytechnics, our colleges of further education – they're doing a superb job.

Industry now has a new underlying strength. As a recent survey shows, of the fifty most successful European companies, the French have eight,

[1] 'The Strength to Succeed' was the slogan of the Conference.

Germany has two, and twenty-eight are British. It can be and often is better made in Britain.

Mr President, exactly a week ago, John Major dropped one of his quiet surprises on an unsuspecting press. Well, they surprise us sometimes too. He announced that interest rates would be cut by 1 per cent and that Britain would enter the Exchange Rate Mechanism.[1] Of course, we have long been committed to joining the ERM – but only when our own policies of firm financial discipline were seen to be working. The signs are clear that our policies to bring down inflationary pressures are succeeding and that monetary growth is back within its limits. It was this which enabled us to cut interest rates.

Inflation announced this morning is 10.9 per cent. But it will soon begin to decline.

Joining the ERM will reinforce our own financial discipline against it. And it will require industry to remain competitive.

But inflation is still too high. It must and will be beaten.

Mr President, our entry into the ERM has been warmly welcomed by our Community partners. But as John Major made absolutely clear yesterday, this Government has no intention of agreeing to the imposition of a single currency.[2] That would be entering a federal Europe through the back-Delors.[3] Any such proposal involves a loss of sovereignty which Parliament would not accept.

I hope that the Community will agree to John Major's important proposals for a common currency, to be used alongside existing national currencies. Europe works better when we respect one another's different national and Parliamentary traditions.

But meanwhile we must continue the prudent policies of successive Tory Chancellors. They have enabled us, out of the budget surpluses of the last three years, to repay £26,000 million of the national debt –

[1] The Exchange Rate Mechanism (ERM) was set up in 1979 as part of the European Monetary System of the European Community. ERM currencies were fixed against each other within a prescribed band of fluctuation (either +/−2.25 per cent or +/−6 per cent) but float against non-member currencies. Britain entered the ERM on 5 October 1990 – with considerable misgivings on the part of Margaret Thatcher.
[2] Proposals for an EC single currency were set out in the Delors Report on Economic and Monetary Union of 22 April 1989. The European Council held at Strasbourg on 8 and 9 December 1989 decided to call an Inter-Governmental Conference (IGC) on the issue. The IGC on Economic and Monetary Union opened at Rome on 15 December 1990 and concluded at Maastricht on 10 December 1991.
[3] A pun on the name of Jacques Delors (born 1925), French politician. Finance Minister 1981–84; President of the European Commission 1984–94.

that is well over £1,000 pounds for every household in the land.

We have kept control of public finances, but we have also honoured our pledge to protect the value of pensions against inflation. We will continue to do so. It means that next April the single pension will go up by £5.10 a week, and the married pension by £8.15 to £83.25 a week. This Party keeps its promises.

Last week, Mr President, I seemed to hear a strange sound emanating from Blackpool. I thought at first it was seagulls. Then I remembered that Labour was holding its annual Conference there. And I realized it wasn't seagulls, it was chickens – chickens being counted before they were hatched – except for Labour's call to enter the ERM and cut interest rates. A case of counting chickens after they'd flown the coop.

Then, I heard voices getting all worked up about someone they kept calling 'the Prime Minister in Waiting'.[1] It occurs to me, Mr President, that he might have quite a wait. I can see him now, like the people queuing up for the winter sales. All got up with his camp bed, hot thermos, woolly balaclava, CND badge . . . Waiting, waiting, waiting . . .

And then when the doors open, in he rushes – only to find that, as always, there's 'that woman' ahead of him again. I gather there may be an adjective between 'that' and 'woman', only no one will tell me what it is. But I'll tell you this, 'that man' is going to trip over his promises in the rush if he's not careful.

There is his promise, for example, not to cut taxes 'for many years to come'. That's the one Labour promise it's safe to believe. Indeed, the Labour Leader was being unduly modest. He won't cut taxes ever.

Why? Because he's a socialist – and they just don't like the idea. In government they put taxes up, and in opposition they fight our proposals to bring taxes down. And taxes would go up – up and up – if Labour spends as much of your money as they've promised.

But they say, 'We're reformed characters, next time it will be different, we've paid our debt to society.' If that were true, it would be the first debt Labour has ever paid. We Conservatives say that society must be protected from such a persistent offender – and a sentence of eleven years in opposition is nowhere near enough.

Then Labour say they're going to introduce 'freedom and fairness' in trade union law. In other words, freedom to force their members out on strike against their will. Freedom to organize secondary strikes against third-party employers, other workers and the general public.

---

[1] i.e. Neil Kinnock, the Labour leader.

And freedom to give wings to flying pickets to go round the country and bring it to a halt.

Those aren't freedoms. They're powers to hurt others; and there's nothing fair about them.

Labour's third pledge is to replace the Community Charge by the unfairness of rates, with all the additional horrors of a revaluation. What Labour wants is for local authorities to be accountable not to the citizen but to its own left wing. For years, council after council has been hijacked by socialist extremists. The residents wanted litter-free zones, but what they got was nuclear-free zones. The Community Charge is making them more accountable and less electable. No wonder Labour councillors don't want it.

Then there's this plan of Labour's for smaller, more decentralized government – which would contain two brand new ministries, a couple of new departments of state, nine different bodies in each region, a hundred new committees, Heaven knows how many councils and commissions on top, and a great herd of quangos thundering up Whitehall. A mere 2,012 new bureaucratic bodies in all.

It's the oldest law of politics: government tends to expand, and socialist government expands absolutely.

Mr President, that's four impossible pledges so far. And I could go on for hours quoting from Labour's lexicon of logical contradictions. There is its pledge to cut emissions of carbon dioxide – by burning more coal. And its promise to improve educational standards – by phasing out tests.

But the really remarkable thing about Labour is, they want you to swallow that they're now a party of moderation.

Labour's Blackpool Conference was the amateur dramatics of the season, a grand masquerade at which militants and Trots peeped out from behind a painted smile. Glenda[1] had given them a few professional tips. The audience had learned its lines. The rehearsals had gone splendidly. Ron Todd gave a dazzling performance as Mr Moderation.

Alas, on the night, the extras got everything mixed up and voted the wrong way – to emasculate defence, to bump up public spending, to ditch our electoral system, to deselect moderate MPs. The audience applauded like mad. Only Dennis Skinner[2] remained glued to his seat. The theatre of the absurd was clearly not for him.

---

[1] Glenda Jackson (born 1936), British actress and politician. Labour MP 1992–.
[2] Dennis Skinner (born 1932), Labour MP 1970–.

Well, Mr President, they can produce all the assurances in the world. They can say that they never read their own manifestos or understood their own speeches. But there's one thing they can't do. They can't tell the nation why it should trust a Party whose only claim to office is that it has ditched its principles, disguised its policies and denied its past. And when a Party does that, how could anyone trust its promises for the future?

That brings me to the Liberal Party. I gather that during the last few days there have been some ill-natured jokes about their new symbol, a bird of some kind, adopted by the Liberal Democrats at Blackpool. Politics is a serious business, and one should not lower the tone unduly. So I will say only this of the Liberal Democrat symbol and of the party it symbolizes: this is an ex-parrot. It is not merely stunned. It has ceased to be, expired and gone to meet its maker. It is a parrot no more. It has rung down the curtain and joined the choir invisible. This is a late parrot.[1] And now for something completely different . . .

Mr President, most of us remember a time when, although people saved for a rainy day, they couldn't hope to leave what one might call a capital sum to their children. These days, it's different. Many more people have homes and shares and savings to pass on. Indeed, the average real value of what pensioners can leave to their children is almost twice what it was only ten short years ago. So as time goes by, capital passes from one generation of a family to another, bringing a wealth of opportunity and an opportunity for wealth.

Labour's response to people's well-being is to sneer at it as materialism – when they are not denying it as myth. They relish class division. They depend on it. It's the root of all socialism.

We relish opportunity for all – in health, in schools, in housing. So that people get what they want, not what politicians want. The more we foster these things, the more we break down barriers – barriers between workers and bosses, skilled and unskilled, tenants and owners, barriers between private and public. That's the kind of open, classless Britain I want to see. And it's the kind of Opportunity Britain the Conservative Party stands for. A Britain where people begin by improving their own lives and end by helping to improve the lives of others.

---

[1] This passage derives from a comedy sketch in the BBC television series *Monty Python's Flying Circus*, in which a dissatisfied customer strives to convince a pet-shop owner that a recently purchased parrot is dead. Six days later, the Liberal Democrats demonstrated that they were alive by winning the Eastbourne by-election with a swing of 20 per cent from the Conservatives.

Much has been done. But more remains to be done.

So far we've slashed income tax, abolished seven taxes, and given married women their own separate tax allowance. That's good. But not good enough. So as soon as it's safe to do so, we'll cut income tax again.

We've trebled the number of shareholders in Britain and privatized twenty major industries. That's good, but not good enough. We want more shareholders and more workers to own shares. So we'll privatize the major ports; then tackle British Rail – with more to come.

We have enabled three million more people – half of them council tenants – to become new home-owners. Good – but not enough. So we'll introduce a pilot scheme in England to allow New Town[1] tenants to turn their rents into mortgages – as we did with great success in Scotland and Wales. If this scheme succeeds like those, we'll extend it nationwide.

Mr President, children leaving school – and some adults who've missed out – deserve the chance to learn a skill. We need more flexible training. So we've put it into the hands of local businessmen, who know the skills needed for the future. That's good – but not enough. Now we're giving a brand new voucher to trainees in eleven pilot areas so they can use it to get the training they want. If that's a success, we shall make them available nationwide. This training voucher gives real motivation and power to young people. It's the first voucher scheme we've introduced – and I hope it won't be the last.

Mr President, this Government has made education a top priority. By providing the framework for higher standards. By establishing a national curriculum. By spending more on each child than ever before. By the smallest class sizes ever.

But, above all, by freedom, choice and competition.

Some fifty grant maintained schools – that is, the new independent state schools – are the first to relish their freedom from local authority control and the extra resources that freedom brings. That's good, but not good enough. I want to see far more schools becoming independent state schools. As John MacGregor announced on Wednesday, we shall give every primary and secondary school in the country the opportunity to have independent status.

But let us be perfectly clear: Governments can determine the structure of education. They can't determine its soul. It's for parents to use their new power to insist on the best. It's for teachers and heads to provide

---

[1] The New Town Corporations act as public sector landlords in a number of areas.

it. And it's for the examination boards and the Inspectorate to be rigorous in monitoring the results.

Asking too little of our children is not only doing them an injustice, it's jeopardizing our national future. They tell us: 'Spelling doesn't matter.' It does if you're after a job. They say: 'Grammar is old-fashioned.' Not if you want to make sense. They add: 'Doing sums is outdated.' I'm glad nobody told me that when I was negotiating the return of our money from Europe.

And then the education specialists tell us: 'It depends what you mean by standards.' If they don't know that, what are they doing in education?

Let me give them some clues: we are open to new methods of teaching. But not if they mean our children can't read. Yes, we do want more learning for work. But not at the cost of academic achievement for the most gifted children. Of course we want more examination successes. But not a confetti of meaningless qualifications. Employers will soon see through that one. A new battle for Britain is under way in our schools.

Labour's tattered flag is there for all to see. Limp in the stale breeze of sixties ideology. But let's be fair. They've promised us action.

That's what alarms me. Action to close down the newly independent state schools, the grammar schools, the City Technology Colleges. Action to stamp out choice for ordinary people, and to impose state uniformity. Action to rob parents of power and give it to unions and administrators.

Labour is stuck fast in the egalitarian sands from which the rest of the world is escaping. We Conservatives have run up our flag. Choice, high standards, better teachers – a wider horizon for every child from every background. The Labour Leader has chosen education to be his Party's battleground. So be it. We need have no fear of the result.

Mr President, I know the importance this Conference attaches to reducing crime. Crime and violence injure not only the victim, but all of us, by spreading fear and making the streets no-go areas for decent people.

Government has strengthened police numbers, improved police pay and revolutionized police technology. We've provided stiffer sentences for the men of violence. When the courts hand down severe sentences for violent crimes they will receive this Government's unqualified support.

To be soft on crime is to betray the law-abiding citizen. And to make excuses for the criminal is to offer incentives to dishonesty and violence. Crime flourishes in a culture of excuses. We Conservatives know, even if many sociologists don't, that crime is not a sickness to be cured – it's a temptation to be resisted, a threat to be deterred, and an evil to be punished.

Mr President, this year we celebrated the fiftieth anniversary of the Battle of Britain. We remembered 'the few': and as the Hurricanes, the Spitfires and the lone Lancaster flew over London, we looked back to a time when our nation stood alone and showed its true mettle.

That spirit is just as much alive today. The world knows it can count on Britain to be staunch in defence. That's why London was chosen for NATO's summit meeting last July, one of the most important ever held. Now at last we can afford to reduce our forces in Europe. But we mustn't weaken our defence: we adapt it to meet new threats – to prepare for the unexpected.

Danger never sleeps. Governments which assume that there are no clouds on the horizon risk finding themselves at the heart of the storm.

When NATO Foreign Ministers met in Scotland in June, I warned that our dependence on Middle Eastern oil will grow again in the next century, and that we must have the capacity to defend our trade routes. These warnings were more timely than I knew.

In the Gulf today we face an attempt to extinguish liberty and nationhood. Saddam Hussein took Kuwait by war, with no respect for her people, for property or for international law. And every day he remains is a new act of war. This tyrant has taken our people hostage.

Not a day goes by without our thinking of their plight and how we can bring them safely home to their families.

Mr President, Saddam Hussein must withdraw from Kuwait and the legitimate Government must be restored.

As Winston Churchill said in the thirties: 'If you give in to aggression there will be no end to the humiliation you have to suffer.'

In times of great crisis, Britain and the United States stand as always together – and President Bush deserves our admiration and full support for the lead he has given.

Sanctions are being drawn tighter and tighter and we most earnestly hope they will work. If not, the military option is there and the build-up of forces continues. We must be ready for any contingency.

Some people suggest there should be negotiations. But what is there to negotiate about? You don't negotiate with someone who marches into another country, devastates it, killing whoever stands in his way. You get him out, make him pay and see that he is never in a position to do these things again. Saddam Hussein can't do these things without paying compensation. He and those who carry out his orders must be made answerable for their crimes.

Never before have the nations of the world been so united in a single resolve: that aggression shall not pay.

But if this Government had not kept Britain's defences strong, we would not have had the forces and equipment to send to the Gulf: our Tornadoes, Jaguars, frigates, minesweepers, and the Desert Rats. Our servicemen and servicewomen have already demonstrated their superb professionalism.

Yet, even at a time when tyrants like Saddam Hussein are getting closer to having nuclear weapons of their own, Labour would still give up our nuclear deterrent. Mr President, this Government will maintain our nuclear deterrent, guardian of the peace for forty years. We shall keep Britain strong and secure. We will never take risks with our defences.

Mr President, when the call came to send forces to the Gulf it was independent nations – above all the United States and Britain – which took rapid and decisive action. Many other nations followed, especially in the Arab world. Nationhood remains the focus of loyalty and sovereignty in the modern world.

The revolutions of 1989 in Eastern Europe showed how deep that feeling is. As the Eastern Europeans detach themselves from the aberration of communism, they look to their own country and heritage. So, too, do the people of newly united Germany. The speeches on the day of unification echo and re-echo with references to sovereignty and independence.

Europe cannot be built by ignoring or suppressing this sense of nationhood, by trying to turn us into regions rather than nations. The way forward lies in willing co-operation between independent sovereign states.

Nor do we see the Europe of the future as a tight little inward-looking protectionist group which would induce the rest of the world to form itself into similar blocs. We want a Europe which is outward-looking, and open to all the countries of Europe once they are democratic and ready to join.

We do not judge how European you are by how much you want to increase the power of the unelected Commission. Intervention, centralization and lack of accountability may appeal to socialists. They have no place in our Conservative philosophy. We shall resist unnecessary regulation and bureaucracy: but when rules have been agreed, our fellow members of the European Community will find that Britain has the best record for implementing them openly and honestly.

We are careful about money and rightly so. We're the second-biggest net contributor to Europe, paying over £2 billion a year.

But – and it is a crucial but – we shall never accept the approach of those who want to use the European Community as a means of removing our ability to govern ourselves as an independent nation. Our Parliament has endured for seven hundred years and has been a beacon of hope to the peoples of Europe in their darkest days. Our aim is to see Europe become the greatest practical expression of political and economic liberty the world over. We will accept nothing less.

Mr President, this was the year when time ran out on socialism. Marxist socialism is not yet buried, but its epitaph can now be written. It impoverished and murdered nations. It promoted lies and mediocrity. It persecuted faith and talent. It will not be missed.

We have entered an age in which the people increasingly yearn for the path of freedom, free enterprise and self-reliance. Even in the newly liberated East, they are not seeking some third way between free enterprise and socialism: they know, if Labour doesn't, that the third way leads only to the Third World.

Labour's vision has been shattered. Beneath its contrived self-confidence lies a growing certainty that the world and history have passed it by; and that if Britain rejects them yet again, as I believe it will, socialism must return for ever to its proper place – the Reading Room of the British Library where Karl Marx found it. Section: History of Ideas; Subsection: Nineteenth Century; Status: Archaic.

The new world of freedom into which the dazzled socialists have stumbled is not new to us. What to them is uncharted territory is to us familiar and well-loved ground. For Britain has returned to those basic truths and principles which made her great – personal liberty, private property and the rule of law, on which democratic freedoms everywhere are based.

Ours is a creed which travels and endures. Its truths are written in the human heart. It is the faith which once more has given life to Britain and offers hope to the world.

We pledge in this Party to uphold these principles of freedom and to fight for them. We pledge it to our allies overseas. And we pledge it to this country we are proud to serve.

46

Speech to the House of Commons in the Debate on a Motion of No Confidence in Her Majesty's Government, 22 November 1990

Soon after the end of the October 1990 Party Conference the final act of the tragedy began to be played out. Later that month Mrs Thatcher was isolated at the Rome European Council, where the other Heads of Government proved implacably determined to press ahead with plans for political and monetary union. On 1 November Geoffrey Howe resigned from the Cabinet and later proceeded to deliver a venomous personal attack on Mrs Thatcher in his resignation statement. Michael Heseltine, spotting his opportunity, announced that he would contest the Conservative Party Leadership. On Tuesday 20 November Mrs Thatcher, then in Paris for the CSCE Summit, learned that she had narrowly failed to win enough votes to avoid a second ballot. Subsequent discussions with individual Cabinet members revealed to her that she could no longer rely on their support. On Thursday morning (22 November) the Prime Minister told the Cabinet of her decision to resign.

Mrs Thatcher's final speech as Prime Minister to the House of Commons in the 'No Confidence' Debate on 22 November – the same day as the announcement of her resignation – is widely regarded as one of her greatest triumphs. This was largely the result of the delivery rather than the content of the speech. In fact, it is only in the responses to interventions that the written account takes life.

As the Prime Minister spoke, shame, embarrassment and awkwardness on the Government benches were transformed into relieved and enthusiastic applause. The strange, supercharged atmosphere of the occasion made an indelible impression on all who experienced it.

The Prime Minister: It is, of course, the right and duty of Her Majesty's Opposition to challenge the position of the Government of the day. It is also their right to test the confidence of the House in the Government if they think that the circumstances warrant it. I make no complaint about that. But when the windy rhetoric of the right honourable Member for Islwyn [Mr Kinnock] has blown away, what are their real reasons for bringing this motion before the House? There were no alternative policies – just a lot of disjointed, opaque words.

It cannot be a complaint about Britain's standing in the world. That is deservedly high, not least because of our contribution to ending the Cold War and to the spread of democracy through Eastern Europe and the Soviet Union – achievements that were celebrated at the historic meeting in Paris from which I returned yesterday.

It cannot be the nation's finances. We are repaying debts, including the debts run up by the Labour Party.

It cannot be the Government's inability to carry forward their programme for the year ahead, which was announced in the Gracious Speech[1] on 7 November. We carried that debate by a majority of 108.

The Opposition's real reason is the leadership election for the Conservative Party, which is a democratic election according to rules which have been public knowledge for many years – one member, one vote. That is a far cry from the way in which the Labour Party does these things. Two in every five votes for its Leader are cast by the trade union block votes, which have a bigger say than Labour Members in that decision: precious little democracy there.

The real issue to be decided by my right honourable and honourable friends is how best to build on the achievements of the 1980s, how to carry Conservative policies forward through the 1990s, and how to add to three general election victories a fourth, which we shall surely win.

Eleven years ago, we rescued Britain from the parlous state to which socialism had brought it. I remind the House that, under socialism, this country had come to such a pass that one of our most able and distin-

---

[1] The 'Gracious Speech': i.e. the Queen's Speech, written by the Government, announcing proposals for legislation.

guished Ambassadors[1] felt compelled to write in a famous dispatch, a copy of which found its way into the *Economist,* the following words: 'We talk of ourselves without shame as being one of the less prosperous countries of Europe. The prognosis for the foreseeable future,' he said in 1979, was 'discouraging'.

Conservative government has changed all that. Once again, Britain stands tall in the councils of Europe and of the world, and our policies have brought unparalleled prosperity to our citizens at home.

In the past decade, we have given power back to the people on an unprecedented scale. We have given back control to people over their own lives and over their livelihood – over the decisions that matter most to them and their families.

We have done it by curbing the monopoly power of trade unions to control, even to victimize, the individual worker. Labour would return us to conflict, confrontation and government by the consent of the TUC.

We have done it by enabling families to own their homes, not least through the sale of 1.25 million council houses. Labour opposes our new rent-to-mortgages initiative,[2] which will spread the benefits of ownership wider still.

We have done it by giving people choice in public services – which school is right for their children, which training course is best for the school-leaver, which doctor they should choose to look after their health and which hospital they want for their treatment.

Labour is against spreading those freedoms and choice to all our people. It is against us giving power back to the people by privatizing nationalized industries. Eleven million people now own shares, and 7.5 million people have registered an interest in buying electricity shares.[3] Labour wants to renationalize electricity, water and British Telecom. It wants to take power back to the state and back into its own grasp – a fitful and debilitating grasp.

Mr Martin Flannery[4] (Sheffield Hillsborough): The right honourable

---

[1] Sir Nicholas Henderson (born 1919), HM Ambassador to Poland 1969–72; to West Germany 1972–75; to France 1975–79; to the United States 1979–82. His leaked despatch from Paris of 31 March 1979 was reproduced in the *Economist* on 2 June 1979.

[2] The rent-to-mortgages initiative, for which a pilot scheme began in Scotland in March 1990, encouraged public sector tenants to buy their own homes by converting their weekly rent into a mortgage repayment.

[3] Dealing in shares of the twelve privatized regional electricity companies began on 11 December 1990.

[4] Martin Flannery (born 1918), Labour MP 1974–92.

lady says that she has given power back to the people, but more than two million of them are unemployed. Has she given power back to them? Inflation is 10.9 per cent. Is that giving power back to the people, compared with rates throughout the rest of Europe? Is the frittering away of £100 billion worth of North Sea oil, which no other country has had, giving power back to the people? Will she kindly explain that – and how pushing many people into cardboard boxes and taking power away from them is somehow giving power back to them?

The Prime Minister: Two million more jobs since 1979 represent a great deal more opportunity for people.

Yes, 10.9 per cent inflation is much higher than it should be, but it is a lot lower than 26.9 per cent under the last Labour Government.

Yes, we have benefited from North Sea oil. The Government have made great investments abroad that will give this country an income long after North Sea oil has ceased. We have provided colossal investment for future generations. Labour Members ran up debts, which we have repaid. We are providing investment for the future; we do not believe in living at the expense of the future.

Mr Dave Nellist (Coventry South-East): If things are as good as the Prime Minister is outlining, why are her colleagues not happy for her to continue in the job of defending that record?

The Prime Minister: These are the reasons why we shall win a fourth general election. We have been down in the polls before when we have taken difficult decisions. The essence of a good Government is that they are prepared to take difficult decisions to achieve long-term prosperity. That is what we have achieved and why we shall handsomely win the next general election.

I was speaking of the Labour Party wanting to renationalize privatized industry. Four of the industries that we have privatized are in the top ten British businesses, but at the very bottom of the list of one thousand British businesses lie four nationalized industries. Labour's industries consume the wealth that others create and give nothing back.

Because individuals and families have more power and more choice, they have more opportunities to succeed – two million more jobs than in 1979, better rewards for hard work, income tax down from 33p in the pound to 25p in the pound, and no surcharge on savings income. Living standards are up by a third, and 400,000 new businesses have been set up since 1979 – more than seven hundred every week. There is a better future for our children, thanks to our hard work, success and enterprise. Our people are better off than ever before. The average pensioner –

Mr Simon Hughes[1] (Southwark and Bermondsey): Will the right honourable lady give way?

The Prime Minister: If the honourable gentleman will just listen, he might hear something that he did not know.

The average pensioner now has twice as much to hand on to his children as he did eleven years ago. They are thinking about the future. This massive rise in our living standards reflects the extraordinary transformation of the private sector.

Mr Hughes: There is no doubt that the Prime Minister, in many ways, has achieved substantial success. There is one statistic, however, that I understand is not challenged, and that is that, during her eleven years as Prime Minister, the gap between the richest 10 per cent and the poorest 10 per cent in this country has widened substantially.

At the end of her chapter of British politics, how can she say that she can justify the fact that many people in a constituency such as mine are relatively much poorer, much less well housed and much less well provided for than they were in 1979? Surely she accepts that that is not a record that she or any Prime Minister can be proud of.

The Prime Minister: People on all levels of income are better off than they were in 1979. The honourable gentleman is saying that he would rather that the poor were poorer, provided that the rich were less rich. That way one will never create the wealth for better social services, as we have. What a policy. Yes, he would rather have the poor poorer, provided that the rich were less rich. That is the Liberal policy.

Mr Hughes: No.

The Prime Minister: Yes, it came out. The honourable Member did not intend it to, but it did.

The extraordinary transformation of the private sector has created the wealth for better social services and better pensions – it enables pensioners to have twice as much as they did ten years ago to leave to their children.

We are no longer the sick man of Europe – our output and investment grew faster during the 1980s than that of any of our major competitors.

---

[1] Simon Hughes (born 1951), Liberal MP 1983–88; Liberal Democrat MP 1988–.

447

Several Hon. Members rose.

The Prime Minister: If honourable Members would be a little patient, it would allow me to get a little further.

No longer a doubtful prospect, when American and Japanese companies invest in Europe, we are their first choice. Britain no longer has an overmanned, inefficient, backward manufacturing sector, but modern, dynamic industries.

The right honourable gentleman referred to the level of inflation. Yes, in 1987 and 1988 the economy did expand too fast. That is why we had to take the tough, unpopular measures to bring the growth of money supply within target. Inflation has now peaked and will soon be coming down. Inevitably, the economy has slowed, but we firmly expect growth to resume next year. For the fundamentals are right.

Our industry is now enterprising. It has been modernized and restructured. In sector after sector, it is our companies which lead the world – in pharmaceuticals, in telecommunications and in aerospace. Our companies have the freedom and talent to succeed – and the will to compete.

Mr James Sillars[1] (Glasgow Govan): The Prime Minister is aware that I detest every single one of her domestic policies, and I have never hidden the fact. [Interruption.]

Mr Speaker: Order.

Mr Sillars: However, it is always a greater pleasure to tackle a political heavyweight opponent than a lightweight Leader of the Opposition – [Interruption.] – who is afraid to explain why, after a lifetime of campaigning to get rid of nuclear weapons, he is going to plant three Trident missiles in my country.[2]

Can I take the Prime Minister back to the question of the poor getting poorer? Does she not realize – even at this point, five minutes after midnight for her – that, because of the transfer of resources from the poor to the wealthy, the poll tax was unacceptable, and that it was because of the poll tax that she has fallen?

The Prime Minister: I think that the honourable gentleman knows that I have the same contempt for his socialist policies as the people of East Europe, who have experienced them, have for theirs. I think that I must have hit the right nail on the head when I pointed out that the logic of

[1] James Sillars (born 1937), Labour MP 1970–76; Scottish Labour MP 1976–79; Scottish Nationalist MP 1988–92.
[2] The Trident nuclear submarines are, of course, based on the Clyde in Scotland.

those policies is that they would rather the poor were poorer. Once they start to talk about the gap, they would rather that the gap were that − [indicating] − down here, not this − [indicating] − but that [indicating]. So long as the gap is smaller, they would rather have the poor poorer. One does not create wealth and opportunity that way. One does not create a property-owning democracy that way.

Can I now get back to the subject of industry and an industrial policy from which Scotland has benefited so much, and from which it could never have benefited under the Government that the honourable Member for Glasgow Govan [Mr Sillars] used to support, and under the political policy he espouses now?

Yes, our companies have the freedom and talent to succeed, and the will to compete. And compete we must. Our competitors will not be taking a break. There must be no hankering after soft options and no going back to the disastrous economic policies of Labour Governments. No amount of distance lends enchantment to the lean years of Labour, which gave us the lowest growth rate in Europe, the highest strike record and, for the average family, virtually no increase in take-home pay. Labour's policies are a vote of no confidence in the ability of British people to manage their own affairs. We have that confidence. Confidence in freedom and confidence in enterprise. That is what divides Conservatives from socialists.

Our stewardship of the public finances has been better than that of any Government for nearly fifty years. It has enabled us to repay debt and cut taxes. The resulting success of the private sector has generated the wealth and revenues which pay for better social services − to double the amount being spent to help the disabled, to give extra help to war widows, and vastly to increase spending on the National Health Service. More than one million more patients are being treated each year and there are eight thousand more doctors and fifty-three thousand more nurses to treat them.

Mr Jack Ashley (Stoke-on-Trent South) rose.

The Prime Minister. That is the record of eleven and a half years of Conservative government and Conservative principles. All these are grounds for congratulation, not censure, least of all from the Leader of the Opposition, who has no alternative policies.

Mr Ashley rose.

The Prime Minister. I shall give way to the right honourable gentleman, but then I should like to move on to say something about Europe, because what the Leader of the Opposition said about it was, to say the least, opaque.

Mr Ashley: The Prime Minister mentioned disabled people, and as she is always anxious to be honest with the House, would she care to give a wider perspective about what has happened to disabled people under her Government?[1] Would she care to confirm the official figures, which show that in the first ten years of her reign, average male earnings rose by 20 per cent in real terms, whereas benefits for disabled people in that period rose 1 per cent in real terms? How well did disabled people do out of that?

The Prime Minister: The right honourable gentleman is very selective indeed. He knows full well that, in the past eleven years, we have spent twice as much on the disabled, over and above inflation – not twice as much in cash terms, but twice as much in terms of what the benefits will buy – especially in the mobility allowance and the Motability scheme.[2] This has been quite outstanding and has been brought about because, under our policies, we have been able to create the wealth which created the resources to do that, among other things.

During the past eleven years, this Government have had a clear and unwavering vision of the future of Europe and Britain's role in it. It is a vision which stems from our deep-seated attachment to parliamentary democracy and commitment to economic liberty, enterprise, competition and a free market economy. No Government in Europe has fought more resolutely against subsidies, state aids to industry and protectionism, unnecessary regulation and bureaucracy and increasing unaccountable central power at the expense of national Parliaments. No Government has fought more against that in Europe than we have.

We have fought attempts to put new burdens and constraints on industry, such as the Social Charter[3] which would take away jobs, in particular part-time jobs. For us, part of the purpose of the Community is to demolish trade barriers and eliminate unfair subsidies, so that we

---

[1] Jack Ashley, deaf himself, was an active campaigner for the disabled.

[2] The mobility allowance is an annual grant to disabled people who run a vehicle. Motability is a voluntary organization, created in 1978 and supported by the Government, which helps the disabled buy and maintain cars and electric wheelchairs.

[3] The so-called Community Charter of the Fundamental Rights of Workers was first proposed by the EC Commission in May 1989.

can all benefit from the great expansion of trade both within Europe and with the outside world.

The fact is that Britain has done more to shape the Community over the past eleven years than any other member state. Britain is leading the reform of the Common Agricultural Policy, getting surpluses down, putting a ceiling on agricultural spending. We have been the driving force towards the Single Market which, when it is completed, will be the most significant advance in the Community since the Treaty of Rome itself. We have done more than any other Government to resist protectionism, keep Europe's market open to trade with the rest of the world, and make a success of the GATT negotiations.

We have worked for our vision of a Europe which is free and open to the rest of the world, and above all to the countries of Eastern Europe as they emerge from the shadows of socialism. It would not help them if Europe became a tight-knit little club, tied up in regulations and restrictions. They deserve a Europe where there is room for their redis-covered sense of nationhood and a place to decide their own destiny after decades of repression.

With all this, we have never hesitated to stand up for Britain's interests. The people of Britain want a fair deal in Europe, particularly over our budget contribution. We have got back nearly £10 billion which would otherwise have been paid over to the EC under the arrangements negoti-ated by the Labour Party when it was in power.

Indeed, what sort of vision does the Labour Party have? None, accord-ing to the Leader of the Opposition. Labour Members want a Europe of subsidies, a Europe of socialist restrictions, a Europe of protectionism. They want it because that is how they would like to run – or is it ruin? – this country.

Every time that we have stood up and fought for Britain and British interests, Labour Front Bench spokesmen have carped, criticized and moaned. On the central issues of Europe's future, they will not tell us where they stand. Do they want a single currency? The right honourable gentleman does not even know what it means, so how can he know? [Laughter.]

Mr Kinnock: It is a hypothetical question.

The Prime Minister: Absolute nonsense. It is appalling. He says that it is a hypothetical question. It will not be a hypothetical question. Someone must go to Europe and argue knowing what it means.

Are Labour Members prepared to defend the rights of this United Kingdom Parliament? No, for all that the right honourable gentleman said. For them, it is all compromise – 'Sweep it under the carpet,' 'Leave it for another day,' and 'It might sort itself out' – in the hope that the people of Britain will not notice what is happening to them, and how the powers would gradually slip away.

The Government will continue to take a positive and constructive approach to the future of Europe. We welcome economic and monetary co-operation: indeed, no other member state has gone further than Britain in tabling proposals for the next stage, including the hard ecu.[1] But our proposals would work with the market and give people and Governments real choice.

We want the Community to move forward as twelve: and from my talks in Paris with other European leaders over the past few days, I am convinced that that is their aim too. Europe is strongest when it grows through willing co-operation and practical measures, not compulsion or bureaucratic dreams.

Mr Alan Beith (Berwick-upon-Tweed): Will the Prime Minister tell us whether she intends to continue her personal fight against a single currency and an independent central bank when she leaves office?

Mr Dennis Skinner (Bolsover): No. She is going to be the Governor. [Laughter.]

The Prime Minister: What a good idea! I had not thought of that. But if I were, there would be no European central bank accountable to no one, least of all national Parliaments. The point of that kind of Europe with a central bank is no democracy, taking powers away from every single Parliament, and having a single currency, a monetary policy and interest rates which take all political power away from us. As my right honourable friend the Member for Blaby [Mr Lawson] said in his first speech after the proposal for a single currency was made, a single currency is about the politics of Europe, it is about a federal Europe by the back door. So I shall consider the proposal of the honourable Member for Bolsover [Mr Skinner]. Now, where were we? I am enjoying this.

Mr Michael Carttiss[2] (Great Yarmouth): Cancel it. You can wipe the floor with these people.

The Prime Minister: Yes, indeed – I was talking about Europe and the

---

[1] On 20 June 1990, Chancellor of the Exchequer John Major outlined British proposals for a fixed-value ecu to float in the ERM alongside national currencies, which it could conceivably supplant in time.

[2] Michael Carttiss (born 1938), Conservative MP 1983–97.

socialist ideal of Europe. Not for us the corporatism, socialism and central control. We leave those to the Opposition. Ours is a larger vision of a Community whose member states co-operate with one another more and more closely to the benefit of all.

Are we then to be censured for standing up for a free and open Britain in a free and open Europe? No. Our policies are in tune with the deepest instincts of the British people. We shall win the censure motion, so we shall not be censured for what is thoroughly right.

Under our leadership, Britain has been just as influential in shaping the wider Europe and the relations between East and West. Ten years ago, the Eastern part of Europe lay under totalitarian rule, its people knowing neither rights nor liberties. Today, we have a Europe in which democracy, the rule of law and basic human rights are spreading ever more widely; where the threat to our security from the overwhelming conventional forces of the Warsaw Pact has been removed; where the Berlin Wall has been torn down and the Cold War is at an end.

These immense changes did not come about by chance. They have been achieved by strength and resolution in defence, and by a refusal ever to be intimidated. No one in Eastern Europe believes that their countries would be free had it not been for those Western Governments who were prepared to defend liberty, and who kept alive their hope that one day East Europe too would enjoy freedom.

But it was no thanks to the Labour Party, or to the Campaign for Nuclear Disarmament of which the right honourable gentleman is still a member. It is this Government who kept the nuclear weapons which ensured that we could never be blackmailed or threatened. When Brezhnev deployed the SS-20s, Britain deployed the Cruise missiles and was the first to do so. And all these things were done in the teeth of the opposition of the honourable gentlemen opposite – and their ladies.[1] [Laughter.] The SS-20s could never have been negotiated away without the bargaining strength which Cruise and Pershing gave to the West.

Should we be censured for our strength? Or should the Labour Party be censured for its weakness? I have no doubt that the people of Britain will willingly entrust Britain's security in future to a Conservative

---

[1] Glenys Kinnock, wife of the Labour Party Leader, was a strong supporter of unilateral nuclear disarmament.

Government who defend them, rather than to socialists who put expediency before principle.

Sir Eldon Griffiths[1] (Bury St Edmunds): May I offer my right honourable friend one measurement of the immense international respect and affection that she enjoys as a result of her policies of peace through strength? An opinion poll published on the west coast of America last month – [Laughter.]

Mr Speaker. Order. This takes up a great deal of time. The honourable gentleman is seeking to participate in the debate. Will he please ask a question?

Sir Eldon Griffiths: The figures are Gorbachev 74 per cent, Bush 75 per cent and Thatcher 94 per cent.

The Prime Minister. I am sure that they were quite right, too.

I wish to say a word or two about the situation in the Gulf, because it will dominate politics until the matter is resolved. It is principle which is at stake, as well as the rule of international law.

In my discussions with other Heads of Government at the CSCE Summit in Paris, I found a unanimous and impressive determination that Iraq's aggression must not succeed. The Resolutions of the United Nations must be implemented in full. That is the peaceful option, Mr Speaker, and it is there to be taken, if Saddam Hussein so chooses. There was also a widespread recognition among my colleagues in Paris that the time was fast approaching when the world community would have to take more decisive action to uphold international law and compel Saddam Hussein to leave Kuwait.

No one can doubt the dangers which lie ahead. Saddam Hussein has many times shown his contempt for human life, not least for the lives of his own people. He has large armed forces. They are equipped with peculiarly evil weapons, both chemical and biological.

Mr Tam Dalyell (Linlithgow): Will the Prime Minister give way?

The Prime Minister. No, not now.

Twice in my time as Prime Minister we have had to send our forces across the world to defend a small country against ruthless aggression: first to our own people in the Falklands, and now to the borders of Kuwait. To those who have never had to take such decisions, I say that they are taken with a heavy heart and in the knowledge of the manifold dangers, but with tremendous pride in the professionalism and courage of our armed forces.

---

[1] Sir Eldon Griffiths (born 1925), Conservative MP 1964–92.

454

There is something else which one feels. That is a sense of this country's destiny: the centuries of history and experience which ensure that, when principles have to be defended, when good has to be upheld and when evil has to be overcome, Britain will take up arms. It is because we on this side have never flinched from difficult decisions that this House and this country can have confidence in this Government today.

V

AFTER
DOWNING STREET

(1990–96)

47

Speech at a Lunch Sponsored by the Hoover Institution, the *National Review*, the Heritage Foundation and the American Enterprise Institute, Washington DC, 8 March 1991

Mrs Thatcher's first major speech after leaving Downing Street was, significantly, made to four leading American conservative think-tanks. She found the seriousness with which American conservatives regarded high policy refreshing; for their part, they had no doubt about the contribution that Britain under her leadership had made to winning the Cold War. In her speech Mrs Thatcher, while extolling the West's achievements, warned of the dangers of complacency and the need for imaginative measures to help bring the Soviet Union towards democracy and free enterprise. She reminded her audience of the importance of American leadership in what the commentators had begun to call a 'uni-polar' world. She cautioned against learning wrong lessons from the coalition's success in the Gulf War: that victory might have taken place with the authorization of United Nations Security Council Resolutions, but it required nation states to achieve it. True internationalism – the co-operation between sovereign nation states – rather than supra-nationalism, offered the best hope of peace and stability.

We have before us today the opportunities created by two great victories: President Reagan's victory over communism in the Cold War, and President Bush's victory over aggression in the Gulf.

Both those victories were hard-won. They required courage, the vision to see what was possible when others could not, and the persistence to fight through to a full and final conclusion.

Very few leaders possess that combination of qualities. But in the Gulf War, President Bush has shown leadership of the very highest order.

He built a grand coalition of twenty-eight allies; he assembled overwhelming force from around the world; he gave full backing to a brilliant military concept which produced one of the greatest feats of arms with the fewest casualties in history; and he helped lay the foundations of future stability in the region. We can truly say, as Pitt[1] said in 1804:

> Amid the wreck and misery of nations, it is our just exaltation that we have continued superior to all that ambition or that despotism could effect; and our still higher exaltation ought to be that we provide not only for our own safety but hold out a prospect for nations now bending under the iron yoke of tyranny of what the exertions of a free people can effect.

But that victory was not won solely in the last six months. It was the culmination of a decade's achievement:
– The military build-up of the 1980s
– The recovery of America's and the West's self-confidence
– The technological advance that created the Patriot missile and the Apache attack helicopter
– And the revival of our economies that made these miracles possible.
Someone once said that 'The past is another country – they do things differently there.'[2] It is difficult today to conjure up the despairing and defeatist atmosphere of the post-Vietnam seventies. But in those days, the West was on the decline and on the defensive.

Our defences were neglected. The Soviet Union steadily reinforced its military superiority.

Our allies felt abandoned. They felt they could no longer rely on a hedonistic West. We coined the cynical joke: 'Lose a country, gain a restaurant.'

In the battle of ideas, we had all but ceased to aim at furthering freedom and had settled for containing communism.

This political weakness only mirrored deeper weaknesses in our societies. Every such crisis is ultimately a crisis of the spirit.

We knew we had lost time, lost nerve and lost ground.

---

[1] William Pitt the Younger (1759–1806), British statesman. Tory MP 1781–1806; Chancellor of the Exchequer 1782–83; Prime Minister 1783–1801 and 1804–06.
[2] L.P. Hartley (1895–1972), English novelist.

The Eighties: A New Direction

So, as the eighties began, we in the United States and Britain set out in a new direction.

We wrestled with the challenge of reviving our economies.

We rebuilt our shattered defences.

We faced up to the threat of a Soviet empire at the peak of its military might, made still more dangerous by knowledge of its own economic weakness and social fragility.

We made it clear that arms control would proceed on the basis of genuine equality of weaponry between East and West – or not at all. The Soviet Union built up its SS-20s. We deployed Cruise and Pershing missiles. The result – the first ever agreement to reduce nuclear weapons.

When the Soviet Union said that Germany could only be united if it left NATO, President Bush and I stayed firm. The result – a reunified Germany fully within NATO.

At home we liberated enterprise and cut taxes, producing higher living standards, more jobs and the spread of ownership.

Capitalism made our people prosperous at home and enabled us to feed the hungry abroad. Socialism, by contrast, proved the road to poverty and serfdom.

As Eastern Europe emerges from the darkness, the truth is now fully known, and told even by communists:

– Behind statistics boasting of bumper crops, food rotted

– As economic growth rates soared on paper, people queued for hours to buy goods that a Western supermarket couldn't even give away

– As five-year plan followed five-year plan, command economies turned out products that no one wanted to buy and created an environment in which no one wanted to live.

But the world was strangely reluctant to observe these facts.

A World Bank report praised the Romanian economy for achieving high rates of growth from the early fifties on. A perceptive economist whose name is not unknown to you, Alan Walters,[1] calculated backward from the current Romanian living standards to show that if these figures

---

[1] Sir Alan Walters (born 1926), British economist. Professor of Economics at Johns Hopkins University 1976–91; Personal Economic Adviser to the Prime Minister 1981–84, 1989.

had been accurate, the Romanian people would have all been dead in 1950.

Since then, the life has drained out of communism entirely. And with it, the heart went out of socialism.

Make no mistake. These communist régimes were not some unfortunate aberration, some historical deviation from a socialist ideal. They were the ultimate expression, unconstrained by democratic and electoral pressures, of what socialism is all about:

- State ownership at the expense of private property
- Government control at the expense of individual enterprise
- In short, the state was everything and the individual nothing.

I freely acknowledge that socialists and statists often begin by finding injustices and wanting to remove them. But they go on to the notion that only state ownership and state regulation can solve such problems. You can only believe that by ignoring the lessons of history, the lessons of politics and the lessons of economics. After the experience of this century and the testimony of Eastern Europe, intellectual irresponsibility on this scale is also moral irresponsibility.

We knew that communism was spiritually bankrupt, and we said so. We knew that the Stalinist system would always produce misery and tyranny but could never produce prosperity, and we said so.

We knew that 'captive nations' under communism wanted and deserved to be free, and we said so. We even dared use the phrase 'captive nations'.

And the more we told the truth, the more we restored our own people's self-confidence and the hopes of those still living under tyranny.

In the decade of the eighties, Western values were placed in the crucible and they emerged with greater purity and strength. So much of the credit goes to President Reagan. Of him it can be said, as Canning[1] said of Pitt, he was the 'pilot that weathered the storm'.

The world owes him an enormous debt, and it saddens me that there are some who refuse to acknowledge his achievements.

For the whole world has changed:

- The Cold War was won without a shot being fired
- Eastern Europe regained its freedom; its people elected democratic governments and they announced their intention to leave the Warsaw Pact

[1] George Canning (1770–1827), British statesman. Tory MP 1793–1827. Foreign Secretary 1807–09, 1822–27; President of the India Board 1816–21; Prime Minister 1827.

– The Berlin Wall came down, and Germany was reunified within NATO; she and Japan, the vanquished nations in the Second World War, prospered mightily and ironically became the creditors in the new world of peace

– A weakened Soviet Union was compelled by the West's economic and military competition to reform itself; a new, more realistic and clear-sighted leadership came to the top

– *Glasnost* was launched, *perestroika*[1] was started and we saw the beginnings of democratic politics

– As the Soviet Union abandoned its revolutionary role in the world, the United Nations became a more effective forum for active diplomacy

– And the United States once again became the pre-eminent power in the world.

These are great and for the most part beneficial changes. They have been confirmed by the progress of the Gulf War in which America led, and Britain and France have helped militarily, together with many Arab nations; Germany and Japan have contributed financially; the United Nations has given its blessing; and the Soviet Union, while pursuing her own diplomatic course at times, never quite departed from the UN Resolutions she had originally supported.

A new world means new problems and the need for new approaches. How do we deal with the crisis in the Soviet Union? How do we reshape NATO in the post-Cold War world? How do we preserve and strengthen the economic foundations of the Western Alliance? How do we defend Western interests elsewhere and extend stability beyond the West in the aftermath of the Gulf War? In my view, we shall tackle all of these problems more effectively, as we won the Gulf War, by the tested policy of Western unity, based on the firm US leadership of sovereign nations in alliance.

Nationhood / East–West

But not every change in recent months has been for the better.

In the Soviet Union there is accumulating evidence that progress towards reform has been slowed, possibly halted. Dark forces of reaction are on the rise. At such a time, it is vital that all those committed to reform

---

[1] *Glasnost* and *perestroika* (Russian 'openness' and 'restructuring') were the reform slogans of Mikhail Gorbachev from 1985–86 onward.

should not falter. No doubt some reformers never expected reform to extend to multi-party democracy and a free economy. 'But no man can fix the boundaries of the march of a nation.'[1] And divisions among reformers now would only hand victory to the hard-liners, whom I at least refuse to call 'conservatives'. The Soviet people have not gone so far to have the prize of freedom and genuine democracy wrested from their grasp.

But the task of reforming and liberalizing the Soviet Union is a far more difficult one than any of us had supposed a few years ago.

How do you persuade people brainwashed by egalitarian propaganda that inequities are the side-effects of rising prosperity for all? How do you tell them that higher living standards can only be attained at the short-term price of higher unemployment? And how do you do any of this while the demoted bureaucrats, the discredited politicians and all those who flourished under totalitarian mediocrity are out to undermine everything you do?

I am often asked: Can we still do business with Mr Gorbachev?

We should not underestimate the future reforming zeal of a man who allowed Eastern Europe to grasp its freedom; who has begun the withdrawal of Soviet troops; accepted arms reduction for the first time; and cut support for communist insurgencies across the world. We have to go on doing business with him. In the same way, he has to do business with the democratic reformers if he is to succeed.

The pessimists among you will perhaps reply that the Soviet leader embarked on reform so as not to be left behind the military build-up and economic progress of the West in the 1980s. I am the last person – or maybe the second to the last person – to deny that these played a major role in Mr Gorbachev's calculations. We had an economy driven by information technology; he had an economy fuelled by vodka!

And the very realism that prompted these reforms will persuade him to step up liberalization, if he can, when the present slowing of *perestroika* pushes the Soviet economy further into crisis, as it must.

Perhaps it does not really matter whether the optimists or the pessimists are right, because optimism and pessimism dictate the same policy. If Mr Gorbachev remains a reformer at heart, as I believe, he will privately welcome Western pressure for reform and employ it against

---

[1] Quoted from a speech delivered at Cork on 21 January 1885 by Irish politician Charles Stewart Parnell (1846–91), Home Rule MP 1875–91; Leader of the Home Rule Party 1880–91.

the hard-liners. If he himself has succumbed to the hard-liners, as others believe, the West's pressure will push him too in the direction of reform.

So what kind of reform should we be seeking for these people who have rejected a false ideology but have not yet learned the ways of freedom?

It is fashionable in some circles to argue for credits for the Soviet Union. But to give large credits to fill shops will not help to build the necessary structures of liberty: they would be dissipated quickly, leaving an increasing burden of debt.

Any assistance to the Soviet Union must, therefore, be granted only in response to practical economic reforms. Helping the present structures will only keep reform at bay. We must instead encourage the dispersal of power from Moscow to the republics. Five Soviet republics are now negotiating for such a dispersal of power[1] – let us hope those negotiations succeed.

Second, we have to stress to the Soviets just how essential private property is to freedom. History teaches that human rights will not long survive without property rights; nor will prosperity be achieved without them.

Nor is freedom secure without independent courts and a rule of law. Here we have experience and knowledge totally denied to people who have grown up in a totalitarian system. Perhaps we should consider extending the Know-How Funds for the Soviet Union to go towards developing an independent judiciary.

We must also draw the Soviet Union closer to the institutions of the international trading and payments system. Associating the Soviet economy more closely with these will, over time, help to transform that economy internally. Their rules will help promote sound money, competition and genuine trade. No economy will prosper if it is strangled by regulations and bureaucrats.

So, let us say to Mr Gorbachev that he can count on our help when he makes reforms. But the reverse of this is that any evidence of a return to repression must prompt from the West a swift and effective response. The constant raising of human rights cases in the Soviet Union over many years, especially since the Helsinki Accords, did undoubtedly have an effect – we must remember that lesson and act upon it.

In particular, we cannot overlook or condone the disgraceful abuses

---

[1] Lithuania, Latvia, Estonia, Georgia and Armenia were by this time refusing to recognize the constitutional legitimacy of the USSR.

of those rights which we have seen in the Baltic states.[1] These states were seized by the Soviet Union not by law, but by fraud and violence. That seizure has never been regarded as legal by the West. We fully support the right of the Baltic states to determine their own future. We must make it clear to the Soviet Union that it is not a question of whether they will be free – but only of when they will be free. And they will be free.

NATO and Defence

There are signs that the Soviet Union is failing to fulfil either the letter or the spirit of the terms of the treaty for reduction of conventional forces in Europe, signed in Paris.[2] And there are signs of pressure by the Soviet military to reassert its position.

Moreover, the re-emergence of tension and uncertainty on Europe's eastern border ought to remind NATO's Continental European members both that international dangers can rarely be predicted and that sustained commitment is necessary to deal with them.

We must never forget that it is NATO – because it is strong defence – which underpins that peace with freedom and justice that we in the West enjoy and now have the opportunity to extend to others. NATO has been uniquely successful in maintaining liberty. It is not just a military alliance, but an alliance in defence of a way of life. NATO must not be discarded.

It is in the interests of Europe that the United States should continue to play that dominant role in NATO to which we have become accustomed. Indeed, as was demonstrated in the Gulf, for all the assistance that Britain and other powers gave, only one nation has the power to defend freedom and security in the world today. That is and for the foreseeable future will remain the United States.

---

[1] Soviet paratroopers were sent into the Baltic states between 7 and 30 January 1991, ostensibly to enforce conscription. They stormed the television station in Vilnius on 13 January, killing thirteen protestors, and six people died in violent incidents in Riga during the following three days.

[2] In early 1991 the USSR tried to avoid disbanding three motorized divisions by reclassifying them as naval shore-defence units. It was also accused of surreptitiously withdrawing over sixty thousand items of military equipment to the east of the Urals. CFE talks in Vienna were adjourned on 21 February at NATO's request, and agreement on these matters was not reached until June.

The pursuit of a new defence role for the countries of Europe is much discussed. It is certainly true that, within NATO, the European countries should make a greater contribution.

The European countries should also be prepared to take a more active military role in response to events outside NATO's present area. Germany's interpretation of its constitution has so far prevented it making a military contribution. But a full commitment to the defence of international freedom and stability requires risking life as well as treasure.

NATO has been a great success. We should be wary of creating new institutions to replace or complement its unique and indispensable role. Perhaps the most extraordinary suggestion yet to come out of Brussels is that the disunity and half-heartedness of most European nations during the Gulf crisis demonstrate the need for a united European foreign and defence policy.

A new structure, even if it were necessary, can never be a substitute for will. Any arrangements which denied Britain and France sovereign control of their foreign and military commitments, especially determining these vital questions by a majority vote, would almost certainly have excluded Anglo–French forces from the Gulf – or at least long delayed their arrival and limited their number. In those grim early days after Iraq's invasion, America would have been left to stand alone. And it is far from certain that, even after prolonged deliberations, the European Community would have contributed military assistance. The methods of compromise which underpin such decisions would almost certainly have left Europe on the sidelines.

For many years, successive American Governments believed that progress towards a United States of Europe would relieve America of the burden of defending freedom. That hope, alas, turned out to be greatly exaggerated. Moreover, this kind of geopolitical grand strategy should be regarded with the greatest scepticism. If a European superstate were to be forged, it would almost certainly develop interests and attitudes at variance with those of America. We would thereby move from a stable international order with the United States in the lead to a more dangerous world of new competing power blocs. This would be in no one's interest, least of all America's.

So NATO must remain the principal defence organization of the West: instead of seeking to supplant it, we should aim to adapt and extend it to meet the challenges of the post-Cold War world.

Enlarging NATO's Role

Our first step should be to enlarge its political role. This great transatlantic partnership should not confine itself to matters of defence but should extend its discussions into other political and economic areas. This would be of benefit to countries on both sides of the Atlantic.

Second, those Eastern European countries which have left the Warsaw Pact[1] should be given a new, special status in NATO – something short of full membership but well beyond mere observer status. Perhaps France has pointed the way in this respect.[2] Such a new status could be an added source of stability in a traditionally unstable area and reassure these countries in troubled times. Even in periods of warmer relations, you can have a chilly spell.

Third, I believe that NATO's role should be extended to threats which are out-of-area. When I addressed the NATO Council at Turnberry last June, I warned that:

There is no guarantee that threats to our security will stop at some imaginary line . . . With the spread of sophisticated weapons and military technology to areas like the Middle East, potential threats to NATO territory may originate from outside Europe.

Within two months, Saddam Hussein had invaded Kuwait. Fortunately, although there was no co-ordinated NATO response, several NATO nations acted vigorously to ensure that aggression did not pay.

Saddam Hussein has been defeated.

But Iraq is not alone in acquiring the technology and power to turn regional conflict into global crisis. Defense Secretary Richard Cheney[3] has reminded us that:

[1] On 21 January 1991, Czechoslovakia, Hungary and Poland announced their withdrawal from the Warsaw Pact with effect from 1 July 1991, when the organization was in fact wound up.

[2] Since 1966, France has possessed a unique status within NATO as a member whose armed forces are not part of the integrated military command structure.

[3] Richard Cheney (born 1941), US politician. Congressman 1978–89 (Republican); Secretary of Defense 1989–93.

... by the year 2000, more than two dozen developing nations will have ballistic missiles, fifteen of those countries will have scientific skills to make their own, and half of them either have or are near to getting nuclear capability as well. Thirty countries will have chemical weapons and ten will be able to deploy biological weapons.

This means that the NATO countries under America's leadership must be in a position to deter aggression by these countries and, if it occurs, to make a swift and devastating response.

Strong defence will continue to be necessary – and costly. For technology does not stand still. It was the coalition's technological superiority which, with the courage of our fighting men, enabled us to defeat the world's fourth-largest army after just four days' ground war. For myself, I believe we must keep up the rate of technological advance which gave us the Patriot missile and which gave us SDI.

All too often after wars, democracies rush to cut back defence and increase domestic public spending. The end of the Cold War led to a similar reaction. It is time to consider whether the plans to reduce spending on defence should be revised. Resolve is not enough; you must have the military capability too.

Perhaps the single most important point to be made today is that the only real peace dividend is, quite simply, peace. Our generation has enjoyed it because of the investment of billions of dollars and pounds in defence.

So the first way to ensure that freedom prevails is to defend it – principally through NATO.

But no less important is the second means – the maintenance of world prosperity, founded upon an open system of free trade. And if there are risks to our security, the risks today to the open trading system are just as great.

Let us remember that the West's post-war prosperity could never have been achieved without the orderly framework of free trade provided by the GATT. Our response to the stock market crash of 1929 was rising protectionism, which transformed it into a catastrophic economic depression, slashing world trade in manufactured goods by some 40 per cent – and all but undermining the credibility of capitalism itself.

By contrast, our response to the world recession of the early 1980s was to resist protectionist pressures. Free enterprise and open trade duly swept us into years of unparalleled prosperity.

Yet the temptation to erect or retain tariff and other barriers is understandable. Managing trade through a network of bilateral agreements and tariff barriers has superficial political attractions. But in the long term, it would make home industries less efficient; consumers pay more for less choice; and condemn the Third World to lower living standards by denying them markets.

It would serve no purpose for me now to attribute blame for the failure, so far, of the Uruguay Round of the GATT.[1] We might both be embarrassed by the degree of our agreement. Anyway, I have had a thing or two to say about this at European Councils.

But the dangers to free trade are now greater than for forty years. And paradoxically, they have been increased by the end of the Cold War. Solidarity on these matters between the United States and Western Europe in the face of the threat of communism has inevitably waned – and with it the will to compromise in the common economic interest.

Of course, people are impatient after four years of negotiations in the GATT. However, if there is evidence of a real and urgent commitment to reach a settlement and more time is needed, it should be given. Some of the best agreements have been reached after the clock has stopped.

It would be a tragedy if the GATT talks were to fail because the US, the Cairns Group[2] and the European Community could not reach an agreement on cutting farm subsidies. We cannot expect the Third World to agree to what the West wants – protecting intellectual property rights and liberalizing services – when we deprive them of their main export market, agricultural commodities, and hence of the funds to improve and diversity their economies.

The stakes are high. If GATT should fail, we would gradually drift into a world of three powerful, protectionist trade blocs – based on America, Europe and Japan – engaged in mutually destructive trade wars. That would not only threaten world prosperity, but it could also damage the common sympathy vital to defence ties across the Atlantic.

We should be moving in precisely the opposite direction. Europe and North America, staying within GATT rules, should move steadily to cut tariffs and other trade barriers between them. In the short term, special

[1] The Uruguay Round of the General Agreement of Tariffs and Trade was dominated by disputes over agricultural subsidies. The United States proposed to cut internal farm support by 75 per cent and export subsidies by 90 per cent, but the EC refused to cut subsidies by more than 30 per cent.
[2] The Cairns Group was a negotiating bloc in the GATT comprising fourteen agricultural exporting countries, among them Australia, Brazil, Canada, Hungary and Indonesia.

provision would have to be made for the more difficult problems like agriculture; and over the decades, we would create a free trade area in embryo across the Atlantic. It would be the greatest concentration of wealth and skills in history, encompassing 58 per cent of the world's GNP, and it would be a force for free trade rather than a restraint upon it. The very size and prosperity of the group would give it enormous influence in setting liberal rules for open world trade. The inclusion of America would reassure against the fears, whether justified or not, of some European countries about German economic dominance. And, above all, it would provide the economic underpinning for NATO and its out-of-area role. It is a visionary prospect, but we need a distant star to steer by.

The European Community's response to the challenges and opportunities of free trade will be crucial.

Europe is now at the crossroads. Amid the apparently technical arguments on monetary union, institutional change and social dimension, a struggle is under way for Europe's future.

Only recently, perhaps, has America begun to recognize that it too has a stake in the outcome. A democratic Europe of nation-states could be a force for liberty, enterprise and open trade. But, if creating a United States of Europe overrides these goals, the new Europe will be one of subsidy and protection.

The European Community does indeed have a political mission. It is to anchor new and vulnerable democracies more securely to freedom and to the West. This is what happened after the end of authoritarian rule in Spain, Portugal and Greece. So the offer of full Community membership must be open to the countries of Eastern and Central Europe just as soon as democracy and the free market have taken root. In the meantime, we must strengthen links of trade, investment and culture.

The false political mission which some would set for the European Community is to turn it into an inward-looking and protectionist United States of Europe. A Europe in which individual nations, each with its own living democracy, would be subordinated within an artificial federal structure which is inevitably bureaucratic. A Community lacking a common language can have no public opinion to which the bureaucrats are accountable.

Americans and Europeans alike sometimes forget how unique the United States of America is. No other nation has so successfully combined people of different races and nations within a single culture. Both

471

the Founding Fathers of the United States and successive waves of immigrants to your country were determined to create a new identity. Whether in flight from persecution or from poverty, the huddled masses have, with few exceptions, welcomed American values, the American way of life and American opportunities. And America herself has bound them to her with powerful bonds of patriotism and pride.

The European nations are not and can never be like this. They are the product of history, and not of philosophy. You can construct a nation on an idea, but you cannot reconstruct a nation on the basis of one.

You have only to consider the consequences of trying, as did the architects of the French Revolution of 1789, to reconstruct France on the basis of a slogan. Alas, it was not 'liberty, equality and fraternity' which were the result. In exactly the same period as the Americans have lived under one Constitution, our French friends notched up five. A *Punch* cartoon has a nineteenth-century Englishman asking a librarian for a copy of the French Constitution, only to be told: 'I am sorry, sir. We do not stock periodicals.'

It is in this light that we should consider the attempt which is being made to create a European superstate. That aspiration has many origins – some noble, some cynical, some just naive. But, in any case, utopian aspirations never made for a stable polity. Political institutions cannot be imposed if they are to endure. They have to evolve and they have to command the affection, loyalty and respect of populations living under them. The kind of Europe which all of us – on both sides of the Atlantic and, not least, in the countries of Central and Eastern Europe so recently emerged from the thrall of communism – must see is no less visionary and far more practical than the alternative. Our kind of Europe, of sovereign states proud of their national identity, enjoying the prosperity which free enterprise brings, a force for open trade, democracy and liberty, would look outward to the world where freedom must be defended and extended. And when we look westward, we see not threatening rivals but staunch friends with common purposes. That's my vision of a European future.

Middle East / UN

Whether it is in Europe or the wider world, we have to know clearly what we should expect from international institutions. The Gulf War posed a sudden dramatic challenge to the international community.

Indeed, 'The Gulf' was hardly on our agenda until the sudden invasion of Kuwait on 2 August last year. Yet, since then, the Gulf has dominated all else.

The war is now over and we are working to build a secure and lasting peace. It is precisely the right time both to look again at the issues which have so long divided the peoples of the Middle East and to take stock of the future role of the United Nations.

It is not for others to come up with precise formulas for solving the problems of the Middle East. Agreement will only come from painstaking and persistent negotiation between the peoples involved. An international conference could play a part in this – not to arbitrate, but its members could provide advice on the preparation of an agenda, the development of proposals, the framing of security agreements and the course of diplomacy.

I believe that six items, among others, should be on our agenda for peace in the Middle East.

– First, the Gulf must be protected as an international seaway. Our navies will have to stay there, and those from the European countries must take a bigger and more prominent share of the duty.

– Second, military equipment and supplies may need to be pre-positioned in the area, both to deter further aggression and to enable the rapid deployment of Western troops should that deterrent fail.

– Third, arrangements must be made to safeguard the security of Kuwait. For who will be prepared to invest the enormous sums required to rebuild Kuwait, unless security is properly guaranteed? I believe a United Nations force policing a demilitarized zone would be right for this purpose.

– Fourth, there is the question of biological, chemical and nuclear weapons. We must be satisfied by direct observation that Iraq's have been destroyed. We should have sanctions against supplying them with equipment that could be used for that purpose. And Iraq's territory must be open to rigorous inspection to ensure that production has not begun again.

– Fifth, countries which engage in aggressive war cannot expect to be allowed freely and quickly to build up their military strength. We must take steps to ensure that the advanced weapons of war are withheld from Iraq, which has, twice in ten years, invaded the territory of neighbouring Islamic states.

– Finally, there is the Palestinian question, so long encased in suspicion and hostility. It can only be tackled by direct negotiation with the representatives of the Palestinian people. But those leaders who supported Saddam Hussein do not come to seek equity with clean hands. One favourable development is that the Soviet Union is now playing a very different role than in the past. So some of the fears that a Palestinian state – even though part of a confederation with Jordan – would be prey to communist subversion have receded. But we can well understand Israel's concern for secure borders, and indeed the concern of all states in the area for a system of regional security.

The United Nations was tested by the crisis in the Gulf. And it came through with an enhanced reputation. The Permanent Members of the UN Security Council worked together for the first time since 1945 to defeat aggression – and not for one Resolution, but for twelve.

But the UN Resolutions had to be enforced by the actions and commitment of individual countries – both America and her NATO allies, and the other Arab countries of the region which saw their interests threatened by Saddam Hussein's aggression. This combination of international authority by the United Nations and enforcement by the United States and other sovereign countries may well prove to be the best model for future contingencies. A UN armed force, operating under the instructions of a UN committee representing the interests of opposed countries, would be paralyzed and helpless.

The counterpart to increased United Nations authority is for all of its members to take seriously their obligations under the Charter. It is no good individual states condemning abuses of human rights abroad if they do not practise freedom at home.

Freedom and the Future

There can be no better time or place to consider the future of our nations than here – at the heart of the free world. The role of practical statesmen in any age is to create or adapt political structures for prosperity and peace. Today, I have suggested how this may now be done – in NATO, in the GATT, in the Soviet Union, in Europe and in the United Nations.

But true statesmanship in a free country must be measured by more than that. It requires an unswerving commitment to make the sovereignty of justice prevail. It requires an ability to inspire others with the rightness of a cause. It requires strong arms and great hearts.

We look to America for these things. And we do not look in vain.

After victory in the Cold War and in the Gulf, we face a still nobler, still more challenging task – to advance the reign of freedom and free enterprise throughout the world. It is now, more than ever, America's destiny, supported by her faithful friends – and no friends are truer than her friends in Britain – to press ahead with that endeavour.

In the words of Abraham Lincoln: 'Let us strive on to finish the work we are in.'

48

Speech to the Economic Club of New York, 18 June 1991

Mrs Thatcher's June 1991 speech to the Economic Club of New York is essentially a defence of financial orthodoxy – that is, firm control of public expenditure, balanced budgets, low taxes and sound money. It explains how inflation took off in Britain in the late 1980s because, while Nigel Lawson was Chancellor of the Exchequer, policy shifted away from orthodox monetarism to sterling's shadowing of the Deutschmark. But this policy is shown to be the result of a wider international attempt to manage exchange rates. Mrs Thatcher's criticism of this approach was so strong that it was widely taken as an attack on the European Exchange Rate Mechanism (ERM) and so of John Major's Government's policy. The speech is also notable in that it spells out for the first time in some detail Mrs Thatcher's proposal for an 'Atlantic Economic Community' – a free trade area embracing Europe on the one hand and North America on the other. This project has since been taken up (without attribution) by British Government Ministers and others.

It is a great honour to be asked to address this distinguished audience – and a great pleasure also to be back in New York, which never ceases to astonish, delight, intimidate, inspire, elevate, and widen one's horizons. New York remains the economic and financial capital of the world's greatest military power, the world's greatest defender of liberty and, despite your real but short-term difficulties, the world's greatest economic power. So this is the right place to discuss the future direction of economic policy and, following the great victory of Desert Storm,[1] the right place to discuss the economic aspects of President Bush's 'New World Order'.[2]

---

[1] 'Operation Desert Storm' was the code-name of the military offensive to liberate Kuwait which lasted from 16 January to 28 February 1991.

[2] Speaking of the Gulf War in his State of the Union Address on 29 January 1991,

Inflation and the Economy

It is also the right time to do so. For, after a decade of rising prosperity, both our countries are suffering from a recession that has been more prolonged than some expected. I am delighted to hear that some economists are forecasting a speedy recovery – and even some central bankers have been detected smiling in private. But many of the businessmen I meet are more cautious.

Recovery will, of course, come – and with it revived investment and higher living standards. Let us hope it will match the long period of growth of the 1980s. But there is bound to be another recession in the course of time. For the trade cycle is a permanent fact of economic life, which politicians can ameliorate by sensible policies, or aggravate by foolish ones, but which they can't abolish altogether.

It should be the aim of a prudent Government to improve the nation's general economic performance at all stages of the cycle by removing obstacles to enterprise and mobility. In that way, growth will be more sustainable, the inevitable setbacks less painful, and inflation less of a temptation to short-sighted administrations.

What Government should *not* do is attempt to compensate for the trade cycle by fiscal and monetary manipulation. This policy has been likened to 'bringing out sunshades in October', either stimulating the economy when recovery is already under way, or pushing an incipient recession even deeper.

The facts of financial life make this a hopelessly hit-or-miss affair. A central bank inevitably has difficulties in controlling money supply growth, principally in predicting the demand for money. This is extremely difficult to achieve in the very short term. But over a period of six months – and certainly on an annual basis – it is much easier and, indeed, can be done.

So there is a strong case, as Milton Friedman has long argued, for a regular and predictable increase in the money supply calculated on a long-term basis. And there is no case at all for any attempt at 'fine tuning'.

President Bush said: 'What is at stake is more than one small country, it is a big idea – a New World Order, where diverse nations are drawn together in common cause to achieve the universal aspirations of mankind: peace and security, freedom, and the rule of law.'

What, then *is* the proper role of Government in a free enterprise economy?

Government has the fundamental duty to provide a sound financial framework by controlling monetary growth in pursuit of a currency which holds its value. It must control its budget deficit so as not to build up debt for future generations. And it must do so *mainly* by controlling its expenditure.

These are not truths of merely temporary application. They go to the root of Government's fundamental tasks at all times and in all places.

As soon as politicians, economists or bankers devise ways to try to circumvent them – the trouble begins. It is no good departing from financial orthodoxy when political pressures mount. That is precisely the time you must stick to it.

If you tolerate a little inflation, it quickly leads to a lot of inflation. As with any addictive drug, increasing the doses is required to achieve the same results. If you ease up in the battle to curb public spending and allow Government budget deficits to rise, you put an unnecessary interest burden on business borrowers and starve the wealth-creating industries. Or if your response to increased public spending is to put up taxes, you lose out even sooner, as talent departs, investment is postponed and hard work discouraged.

Britain in the 1980s

Britain was a perfect demonstration of that lesson.

For most of the post-war period the British economy had been in relative decline. Some argued that this was inevitable, that it reflected fundamental weaknesses in British society or even the British character. Government intervention was therefore regarded as the answer to these alleged weaknesses.

It only slowly dawned on people that the exact opposite diagnosis was the correct one. Government was doing *too* much, and the wrong things.

It was stoking up the money supply, and therefore inflation, in order to prop up companies that otherwise would have priced themselves out of the market. And when inflation took hold, it then intervened *ad hoc* to fix specific costs and prices and to bail out particular companies.

Whitehall – not the British people – was to blame for the resulting

478

stagflation. We had to reverse all that. We provided a sound financial framework to beat inflation. We cut back Government borrowing. But in the words of my friend and colleague Keith Joseph, contained in a lecture at that time, we realized that 'monetarism is not enough'.[1] So we also set out to create a framework favourable to enterprise.

We cut penal rates of income tax and the tax on companies, and we abolished some taxes altogether. We slashed burdensome regulations to encourage small businesses, the seedcorn of economic growth. We restored the balance in law both between trade unions and employers, and between unions and their members. We embarked on a vigorous programme of privatization – forty-four major businesses so far – spreading ownership of capital and property ever more widely.

These policies were dramatically successful. The performance of the British economy was transformed. And in spite of the difficulties of our present recession, the great gains made in the 1980s are not being lost. Britain now has a soundly based free enterprise economy.

Experience – The Name we Give to our Mistakes.

But how, if we learned those lessons in the 1980s, did we allow the renewed inflation – which prompted this recession – to occur? Why was money supply allowed to grow too rapidly?

Part of the explanation lies in the general response of *all* Western countries to the collapse of the stock market in late 1987.[2] Some people were talking of a Great Depression on the scale of the 1930s. It seemed imperative that all Western countries should respond by making sure that the financial market and the banking system were not short of liquidity. And we did.

But though this may have contributed something to the inflationary pressures we have seen, I do not believe it accounts for them fully. For the real explanation, we must go back to first principles. We must rethink the basis of co-ordination of policies within the G7,[3] and especially the co-ordination of exchange-rate intervention.

---

[1] Sir Keith Joseph's Stockton Lecture 1976 was published under the title 'Monetarism is not Enough'.

[2] In New York on 19 October 1987, the Dow Jones Average fell 508.32 points (23 per cent), precipitating large falls in share values across the world.

[3] The G7 group of seven industrialized countries comprises the USA, Japan, Germany, France, Italy, Britain and Canada. Since 1975, their Heads of Government have met annually to discuss economic and political problems.

With the Louvre and Plaza Agreements[1] in the mid-1980s, we sought to put the objective of greater stability of international exchange rates *above* that of the control of inflation.

In Britain, we compounded this error when in 1987–88 we tried to shadow the Deutschmark. Again, the objective of a stable exchange rate was pursued at the expense of monetary discipline.

These policies led to falls in interest rates to artificial and unsustainable levels, which in turn prompted excessive monetary and credit growth. That produced the inflation with which we are all too familiar, and which is the underlying cause of the present recession.

'Experience,' said Oscar Wilde,[2] 'is the name we give to our mistakes.' And the conclusion to be drawn from our experience in both the 1970s and the 1980s is that Governments should commit themselves to price stability – which can only be achieved by reduced monetary growth – and leave it to companies and individuals in the marketplace to calculate the various other risks in the business of wealth creation.

Targeting exchange rates injects excessive monetary pressure when central bankers 'guesstimate' the wrong rate and, like fine-tuning, can produce wild swings towards inflation or deflation when the rate is either undervalued or overvalued, as East Germany is currently discovering.[3] When that happens, the 'stability' that makes fixed exchange rates superficially attractive to businessmen is either abandoned in dramatic devaluation or maintained at the cost of far more damaging instabilities, like rapid inflation and higher interest rates. In the ERM Britain is fortunate to have a margin of 6 per cent to accommodate variations in the exchange rate.

In general, however, I recall the words of Karl Otto Pöhl,[4] former Governor of the Bundesbank: 'Interest rates should be set according to domestic monetary conditions and the exchange rate should be left to go where

[1] By the Plaza Agreement of 22 September 1985, the Finance Ministers of the United States, Japan, West Germany, France and Britain undertook to co-ordinate intervention in exchange rates to bring down the value of the US dollar. The Louvre Accord of 22 February 1987 was an agreement between the Finance Ministries of the G7 (minus Italy) to act to check the fall of the dollar and bring about a wider stabilization of currencies.
[2] Oscar Wilde (1854–1900), Irish-born poet, dramatist and novelist.
[3] A surge of inflation followed economic and monetary union between East and West Germany on 1 July 1990, when Ostmarks were converted into Deutschmarks at a rate of one-to-one (for personal savings up to four thousand marks).
[4] Karl Otto Pöhl (born 1929), German civil servant and banker. Governor of the Deutsche Bundesbank 1980–91.

it will.' To which I will add: if you fix the exchange rate, then interest rates and domestic monetary conditions go where *they* will. And Finance Ministers are left like innocent bystanders at the scene of an accident.

International Order

Let me now attempt to draw from the economic experience of the past fifteen years four broad lessons. They are:

1. An economy will work best when it is built on a framework of clear and predictable rules on which individuals and companies can depend when making their own plans.

2. Government's primary economic task is to frame and enforce such rules.

3. Within such rules individuals, families, companies, and other social organizations should be free to pursue success at the risk of failure.

4. Although Governments will sometimes break the first three rules, public opinion should as far as possible make them ashamed of doing so and eager to return to observing them.

But do not the same rules – or something very like them – apply also to the 'New World Order' envisaged by President Bush in the aftermath of America's two great victories in the Cold War and the Gulf War?

For make no mistake: America now has a unique, even awesome, responsibility. It alone occupies the position of the three wartime allies in 1944 and 1945 when the blueprints for the great international institutions like the GATT, the IMF, the World Bank and the UN were laid down. It will be an American President and Congress who will have the dominant voice in drawing up any new blueprints.

Some of those institutions are flourishing – notably the UN now that the automatic Soviet veto has been removed. Some, like the International Atomic Energy Agency, will need strengthening to take on a greater role in combating nuclear proliferation to 'rogue' states. And some face the challenges of new organizations – like the GATT facing the erosion of free trade as regional economic blocs attempt to assert their identities.

And what is true for organizations is also true for the rules of world order, laid down in 1945.

One of those rules – that states should not commit unprovoked aggression against other states – has just been triumphantly vindicated by President Bush's successful liberation of Kuwait. So triumphantly, indeed, that it is unlikely to be challenged in any clear-cut way for some considerable time to come.

But should there perhaps be new – and more ambitious – rules in the future? Must we continue to turn a blind eye to utterly appalling violations of human rights provided that they are confined within a country? Even if those violations send thousands of people like the Kurds fleeing into neighbouring states as refugees, destabilizing those neighbours in the process?[1] And if we are to have such wider rules – which would surely be a step towards a more civilized world – who is to enforce them? And under what authority?

Then there is the erosion of existing rules – principally in the field of trade and economics. Can GATT be given a new lease of life? Does it need strengthening? Or the support of new organizations committed firmly to free trade? And if so, what?

And perhaps the biggest question of all: will the American people be prepared to undertake the role of Atlas holding up this new world order? Or, as in the 1920s, will the ingratitude of the rest of the world persuade them to retreat into a hemispheric economic isolationism?

Let me answer that last question at once!

I believe that the American people will be prepared to accept this burden of world leadership and to act as the international community's enforcer of last resort – but only if the United States can rely on the support of its allies, not only in *ad hoc* military coalitions but in a wider alliance encompassing trade and economic relations as well as the occasional rare military action.

I think you know I am not a Marxist! So I do not think that economics determine everything. But I do believe that you cannot have political and diplomatic unity in a West that is bitterly divided over trade and economic relations.

---

[1] In March 1991, when Iraqi Government troops crushed the Kurdish insurgency which had overrun areas of northern Iraq in the aftermath of the Gulf War, hundreds of thousands of Kurds sought refuge in Turkey and Iran. Margaret Thatcher added her voice to calls for action, and in mid-April the United States, Britain and France committed forces to the defence of a 'safe haven' for the Kurds in northern Iraq.

Trade Politics

Let us remember that the world order established in 1945 was sustained on the basis of Western economic co-operation. The West's military alliance and post-war prosperity could never have been achieved without, first, the Marshall Plan,[1] and, later, the growth of trade within the orderly framework of rules provided by the GATT, the IMF and the World Bank.

However, that picture has to be qualified. Since the mid-1970s the volume of trade has continued to grow – but at a slower rate in relation to total world output than before. This is in part because there has been a growth in covert forms of protection.

Our current challenge is to prevent the world slipping back into protection, and instead to give a new momentum to freer trade. How is this to be done?

We must honour the rules of the GATT and, where possible, widen their application. We must ensure that the problems over agriculture, services and intellectual property rights – but above all agriculture – are resolved. And that the Uruguay Round is thereby salvaged. For there is a harsh rule of politics, to which international bodies are not immune. If things are not going forward, then they are going backwards. At present, in trade they are going backwards. Other moves towards free trade – provided these conform to GATT rules – should therefore be encouraged.

I welcome the creation of a US–Canada free trade area and the prospect of its extension to Mexico.[2] These reforms should strengthen the economies of your two neighbours and hold down the cost of living for Americans.

It is vital, however, that these should not be steps towards a world of three protectionist blocs built around the US, the European Community and Japan. There are those in Europe who regard the prospect of two

[1] The Marshall Plan (officially known as the European Recovery Program) provided Western Europe with $13,000 million of US economic aid between 1948 and 1952.
[2] The US–Canada Free Trade Agreement was signed on 2 January 1988 and came into operation on 1 January 1989. The North American Free Trade Agreement (NAFTA), signed by the United States, Canada and Mexico on 17 December 1992, provides for the elimination of all tariffs and other barriers over ten to fifteen years from 1 January 1994.

such blocs, engaging in managed trade with a new European superstate, with apparent equanimity and even enthusiasm. I am not among them.

Nor, I believe, should anyone be who has at heart the interests of America or the West as a whole. For it would undermine the sense of Western solidarity under American leadership, which is the only sure foundation of any new world order built to last.

So these new blocs must be steps not towards protectionism, but towards a world of freer trade.

When the Uruguay Round has been successfully completed therefore – and that will require the full co-operation of the European Community – we must take the next step towards wider economic integration.

We must begin to lay the foundations of an Atlantic Economic Community, embracing Europe (namely the European Economic Community, EFTA[1] and the new democratic states of Eastern Europe) on the one hand, and North America on the other. This proposal has all the merits which are attached to any extension of free trade – greater economic efficiency leading to greater wealth, benefiting all those taking part. But it has two other important advantages as well.

Given the liberal economic tradition of the US, Britain and several European Community countries, and given the fierce commitment to free market economics of the former communist states, such a bloc would be imbued with the philosophy of free trade.

And because it would account for no less than 58 per cent of world GNP, other trading blocs and potential trading blocs would have to follow its lead in such matters. It would give the GATT real clout – halting and reversing the drift towards a world of protectionist blocs.

The second advantage is that, by moving in this direction, it would strengthen the vital ties of defence and culture which link America and Europe, and which the drift to protectionism and trade wars threatens to undermine. It would, in effect, be the economic underpinning of NATO – and make a great deal more sense than the various half-baked schemes for giving a defence identity to the European Community.

This proposal is only the beginning of what would be a very long road. It certainly needs close and detailed study.

We would need to lay out very carefully the steps to merging a European Single Market and a North American Free Trade Area and what mechanisms would be required to settle disputes over obstacles to

---

[1] The European Free Trade Association (EFTA), founded in 1960, consisted in 1991 of Austria, Finland, Iceland, Liechtenstein, Norway, Sweden and Switzerland.

trade. No one with experience of negotiating the Single Market in Europe would pretend that will be easy. We would need also to work out transitional arrangements for some industries, particularly steel, agriculture and some services.

But none of those need be insuperable obstacles. I hope that in the months ahead a group could be formed to look at all these matters with a view to a practical timetable for such a scheme. Because, to repeat the political law I quoted above: if things are not going forward, then they are going backwards. And in matters of free trade they *are* going backwards.

The Future

But I am encouraged, Mr Chairman, by remembering the role that America and Britain played at the end of the Second World War at Bretton Woods in laying earlier foundations for the free world's economy. Our countries were both closely involved in setting up the IMF, the IBRD, the OECD[1] and, of course, the GATT.

Like NATO, these international institutions have stood the tests of time and stress. Like NATO, they have always depended on trust and on common goals. And no matter how many institutions you create – or how elaborate their acronyms – if they do not have such a basis they will not long endure.

One such basis is provided by the special relationship between the United States and Britain. Our shared commitment to free enterprise capitalism, to free trade and to liberal democracy will be tested in many ways in the years ahead.

So let us now resolve that the triumph of these Western values should not be some transient phenomenon. Let us hold fast to the truths by which we set our compass. And let us extend a helping hand to those who follow us on the glorious trail to a freer and more peaceful world.

---

[1] The International Bank for Reconstruction and Development (IBRD), commonly known as the World Bank, began operations in June 1946. The Organization for Economic Co-Operation and Development (OECD) aims to help formulate and co-ordinate the economic and social policies of industrialized nations. It was founded in 1961 to replace the Organization for European Economic Co-Ordination, established in 1948.

49

The First Clare Boothe Luce Lecture,
Washington D.C., 23 September 1991

In the Clare Boothe Luce Lecture, Mrs Thatcher confronts the issue of what should be the conservative programme in the post-Cold War world. Although she touches on domestic policy – in particular the growth of social security dependency – the answer is essentially given in international terms. The three guiding principles of conservatism are shown to be: the pursuit of stability (which, however, is not a justification for trying to preserve ossified, inflexible arrangements); the fulfilment of nationhood (which means respecting, not repressing, nationalist impulses); and the promotion of free trade (which is a force for political, not just economic, harmony).

It's always a pleasure to be in the United States, and it is an additional pleasure to be here tonight to attend the presentation of the Clare Boothe Luce award and to deliver the first annual Clare Boothe Luce lecture.

Clare Boothe Luce[1] was both a remarkable woman and a remarkable diplomat. So it is entirely fitting that an award named after her should have gone tonight to Mrs Kathryn Davis and Ambassador Shelby Cullom Davis[2] – a remarkable woman and a remarkable diplomat. Between them they have a combined record of devotion to public service and philanthropy that is rare even in the United States, but that would astonish those countries where such traditions have withered under the influence of socialism.

Nor has Ambassador Cullom Davis forgotten, as Chairman of the

[1] Clare Boothe Luce (1903–87), US journalist, playwright, politician and diplomat. Congresswoman 1943–47 (Republican); Ambassador to Italy 1953–57.
[2] Kathryn Davis (born 1907), US writer and lecturer on foreign affairs. Shelby Cullom Davis (1909–94), US banker and diplomat; Ambassador to Switzerland 1969–75.

Heritage Foundation's[1] Trustees, that among the legitimate aims of philanthropy is the nourishing of the values of freedom and the free economy that underpin the prosperity of this country and of the West as a whole.

I congratulate them both on deserving their award.

Mr Chairman, it is sometimes asked if women can combine a career with motherhood – and, to be sure, it is not always easy to do so. But Clare Boothe Luce did far more than that: she combined being a wife and mother with the roles of magazine editor, playwright, war correspondent, Congresswoman, presidential advisor, painter, art collector, *raconteur* and scuba diver. Could any *man* have done all that and still had the energy left to be a good father? I must ask Denis.

But if Clare had been simply a very successful woman, excelling in a number of careers, we would not be celebrating her here tonight. She was more than that. And she is remembered with particular admiration because in her political life she fought – fought bravely and fought wittily – on the side of freedom and against the evils of fascism and communism that threatened it. Not everyone in those years – the 1930s and 1940s – did so. But as a friend of Winston Churchill, she supported, endorsed and helped to spread his warnings against the twin totalitarianisms.

The collapse of communism we have just witnessed would never have been possible if people like Clare had not resisted it in the days when it seemed likely to overwhelm Europe. I am delighted to be one of those paying tribute to her tonight.

The End of Communism

We have lived through a decade of momentous events. An iron curtain has *lifted* from the continent of Europe. All the capitals of the ancient states of Central and Eastern Europe – Warsaw, Berlin, Prague, Kiev, Budapest, Bucharest, Sofia, Talinn, Riga, Vilnius, and now Moscow itself – all these famous cities and the populations around them, which lie in what was once the Soviet sphere, now enjoy a high and increasing measure of freedom.

An empire has crashed – but not just an empire of armies, slaves and

[1] The Heritage Foundation, founded in 1973 and based in Washington D.C., is a public policy research institute dedicated to the principles of free enterprise, limited government, individual liberty and strong defence.

tyrants. The empire was also one of ideas and dogmas. And when those failed, an empire of lies and propaganda fell too.

It fell because it was resolutely opposed. Opposed not simply by an alliance of free peoples – though certainly by that – but by the ideas of liberty, free enterprise, private property and democracy.

And it failed for another reason too.

Throughout the long years of that twilight struggle we call the Cold War, we in the West had allies in the enemy camp: the Russian people, the Czech people, the Hungarian people, the Polish people, the people of the Baltic states. They were our allies, the best allies we could have had. All we had to do to ensure their support was to tell the truth, to declare what no one now denies: that the system under which they lived was wicked, brutal and founded on force. And its fall is a Russian, a Polish, a Czech and a Hungarian victory every bit as much as it is an American or a Western victory. For it is the victory of truth over lies.

The power of truth, the power of ideas. Ultimately, they amount to the same thing, because only truthful ideas – ideas that are in tune with the essential dignity of man – can prevail across the years. The ruins of Marxist communism in Eastern Europe and the Soviet Union testify most eloquently to that.

But communism was only the extreme form of the socialist plague. Its failure was only the extreme failure of socialist doctrines throughout the world. And in its downfall it has pulled down the neighbouring houses of socialism too. This has opened up enormous opportunities for the next stage of conservatism in all our countries.

The Rebirth of Conservatism

We conservatives can claim to have foreseen, predicted and explained this collapse almost from the beginning, when socialism was merely an intellectual theory. But the more it was put into practice, the more we could point out its inevitable flaws and inherent unworkability.

In the 1970s, we saw this failure in a system of high taxation and suffocating regulation that discouraged hard work, deterred enterprise and imposed stagflation on our economies.

In the 1980s, we saw this failure in an educational system that couldn't teach all children the essentials of language, maths and civic virtues.

And today, we see this failure in a welfare system that keeps millions of people hooked on dependency.

488

Until the 1980s, we conservatives failed to mount an effective challenge to the socialist policies that led to these disasters. In office, we stood pat, and preserved much of the legacy of the previous socialist Government. In Opposition, we criticized the actions of the left – but failed to offer convincing alternatives.

As a result, politics produced what my friend and mentor Keith Joseph has described as 'the socialist ratchet'. Once a socialist reform had been introduced, it remained; but a law passed by a conservative Government was open to repeal by the next socialist Government. As a result, we moved convulsively but inexorably to the left.

There were three reasons for this.

First, far too many on the right of centre had accepted a socialist way of thinking. Many conservatives felt that there was something better about the collectivist approach. Indeed, there seemed a sort of inevitability about it. The fact that it denies the human spirit and substitutes state judgement for personal responsibility was not considered.

Second, conservative politicians lacked the toughness and resolve to put conservative policies into practice.

Third – and this itself reflected the other two problems I have mentioned – we sometimes did not, when we came into office, have the practical policies worked out to put our principles into effect. It was in order to fill *this* gap that the conservative think tank was born.

As early as the 1960s, scholars had banded together to think long-range thoughts, building the foundations for future policies. In Britain, the independent Institute of Economic Affairs[1] pioneered discussion of such ideas as monetarism, deregulation and the power of private property rights. In this country the American Enterprise Institute and the Hoover Institution[2] laid similar intellectual foundations.

The innovation of the 1970s was the creation of what one might call the activist conservative think tank. These institutions took the long-range ideas of their elder brothers and applied them to practical problems.

In Britain, I was one of the founders, with Keith Joseph, of the Centre for Policy Studies, which was deeply involved in the reshaping

[1] The Institute of Economic Affairs was established in 1955 by Anthony Fisher and Oliver Smedley to promote research into economic and political science.

[2] Founded in 1943, the American Enterprise Institute is a private research group which seeks to preserve and improve free enterprise, limited government and cultural and political values. The Hoover Institution on War, Revolution, and Peace, created in 1919, is dedicated to advanced research in the social sciences and public policy.

of Conservative policy between my election as Party Leader in 1975 and my election as Prime Minister in 1979.

Here in America, Ed Feulner[1] was among those who launched the Heritage Foundation in the same period. I need hardly tell this audience of its achievements. You didn't just advise President Reagan on *what* he should do; you told him *how* he could do it. And as a practising politician I can testify that that is the only advice worth having.

But perhaps I should tell this audience one other thing: however brilliant the ideas of intellectuals, they will get nowhere without politicians of courage who are prepared to fight to implement them. I am afraid I had to make this point rather brutally to a dinner given by a British think tank at which politicians counted for little and it was the ideas and influence of intellectuals that really ruled the world. I was forced to remind them that although the cock may crow, it is the hen that lays the egg.

Mr Chairman, it is not my job to intrude into the domestic politics of the United States, and I do not intend to do so tonight.

My purpose instead is to examine those larger questions of political philosophy and strategy which affect us both – because we share the same values and political culture.

In the 1980s, Ronald Reagan and I found ourselves not only following but pioneering the same great themes in economic, social and foreign affairs. And, with a little help from friends, many of them here tonight, we translated those conservative themes and aspirations into concrete policies.

Our belief in the virtues of hard work and enterprise led us to cut taxes. Our belief in private property led to the sale of state industries and public housing back to the people. Our belief in sound money led to the monetarist policies that attacked inflation. Our belief in individual initiative over bureaucratic control led to the successful deregulation of finance and industry.

And, taken together, all these policies led to a freer society and the greatest period of uninterrupted growth in our history.

---

[1] Edwin Feulner, Jr (born 1941), US research foundation executive. President of the Heritage Foundation 1977–.

Three Items of Unfinished Business

But, as conservatives, we should be the last people to imagine that the world has finally and irreversibly changed. Yes, it is true that the collapse of socialism has settled the argument in favour of free market capitalism. However, this remains a time for vigilance, not just celebration. The very scale of the West's achievements throws up new problems which we conservatives have to face. Here are three of the most pressing.

First, the practical case for democracy and capitalism is proven almost beyond dispute. But what of the moral case?

Let me immediately say that no political or economic system itself makes men good – and democracy is no exception. Some virtues, like tolerance and honesty, are necessary to sustain freedom; and some virtues, like industry, thrift and acceptance of responsibility, are even encouraged by it. But the fundamental moral argument for freedom is not that it moulds people in its own image, but that it allows them to create theirs. And it does this because it alone protects those rights without which none of us enjoys the full dignity of human personality.

Freedom has to be valued for itself – not just for its material benefits. And the life of free men and women has to be a life of self-discipline, self-control and – for family and country – self-sacrifice. There will always be new or retread socialists anxious to persuade our peoples that wealth can be redistributed before it is generated, and that ease can be purchased without effort.

So we conservatives must preach the hard truths – and not just the more comforting half-truths – about the free political and economic system which we value.

The second challenge follows closely on.

The great economic advances which capitalism has made possible have allowed us to provide better welfare for those who cannot cope for themselves. But in doing so it has led indirectly to that very dependency culture which is weakening our countries and demoralizing the poor.

Of course, there will always be a point at which providing welfare benefits significantly diminishes the recipients' desire to regain economic and social independence. That can't be totally avoided. But the scale of the problem in some places today is quite new.

491

When welfare benefits are paid to a considerable proportion of the population; when they are specially directed at reducing the painful consequences of previous irresponsibility; when personal taxation strikes hard at those near the bottom of the income scale; and when, more generally, traditional standards are under attack – in these circumstances the very foundations of our society are put at risk.

If we in the affluent West refuse to face up to these issues, we will weaken our ability not only to defend the values of freedom at home, but the security of freedom throughout the world.

Indeed, the final piece of unfinished business concerns the rest of the world.

In Eastern Europe and in the republics which constitute the old Soviet Union an heroic struggle has begun to create Western-style democracy and free enterprise economies – a struggle as heroic in its way, perhaps, as those more moving and dramatic scenes which precipitated the downfall of communism. The Governments and peoples there need no convincing about *what* they have to do: but they need to be shown *how* to do it. And, yes, I say it to this audience, they have to be *helped* to do it.

We may argue about the precise means and the scale of assistance: but the responsibility to bring freedom and free enterprise fully within the grasp of those who long for it falls on *us* too. We have to help these millions of people to enjoy that life, liberty and the pursuit of happiness which the American Declaration of Independence promises to mankind.

International Affairs: Three Conservative Principles

Mr Chairman, one of Clare Boothe Luce's sharper epigrams was: 'A great man is one sentence.'

Well, I will sum up the achievements of President Reagan in a sentence too: Ronald Reagan won the Cold War without firing a shot. He had a little help – at least that's what he tells me. But that imperishable achievement will be seen by history as belonging primarily to him.

That victory led to the freedom that the Russian and other peoples of the Soviet empire now enjoy. It led to the liberty of the Baltic states, the independence of the nations in Eastern Europe, and to the greater freedom of all the republics in the loose Soviet Confederation that is now being built.[1] But, Mr Chairman, some people have pointed at these developments as harbingers of a dangerous instability in the international system. They therefore seek to prop up existing but unfree federal structures like Yugoslavia today,[2] or, until a few weeks ago, an unreformed USSR.

Let us be very clear about our conservative principles here. I will refer to three: stability, nationhood and free trade.

Stability

Stability is a conservative principle. It makes it possible for people to work, save and invest, because it gives them some reason to believe that their present sacrifices will bear fruit later. It persuades people to take out mortgages, found companies, plant trees, and do all the things that assume that their property will be protected, their lives and persons secure, and their children likely to survive to inherit what they have earned.

But conservatives do not make the opposite error either.

We do not confuse stability with the diplomatic error of propping up whatever unstable status quo happens to be at hand. The conflict in Yugoslavia, the communal conflicts in Armenia and Azerbaijan, the ethnic feuding which pervades the old Soviet empire – these things are the consequences of Marxism and of attempting to crush, ignore and override legitimate national feelings in pursuit of an artificial bureaucratic supra-nationalism with no real roots and precious little freedom. True stability lies in creating looser structures of inter-national co-operation in which legitimate nationalisms can both express themselves and forge links based on common interests.

---

[1] On 19 August 1991, hardline communists led by Vice-President Gennady Yanayev seized power in Moscow. President Gorbachev was reinstated after two days, but the state institutions of the USSR had been fatally compromised in the coup attempt. The majority of the constituent republics declared independence and the Communist Party was suspended. On 21 December 1991, the USSR was replaced by a Confederation of Independent States, grouping eleven of the republics in a loose alliance without central governing bodies.

[2] Croatia and Slovenia declared independence on 26 June 1991, after the Serbian-led Yugoslav Federal Army began to take action against separatists. A ceasefire held in Slovenia from 3 July, but by early September Croatia had lost one-third of its territory. Margaret Thatcher strongly supported the Croats and Slovenes, arguing that Western Governments should recognize their independence and supply them with arms.

Nationhood

In other words, Mr Chairman, the conservative virtue of stability leads directly to accepting the legitimacy of nationalism as a basis for independent statehood. National pride, in combination with liberty and the rule of law, powerfully strengthens democratic government. We conservatives recognize that people will consent to be governed, and accept common sacrifices most readily, when they feel themselves to be part and parcel of one another in a larger community. And that sentiment cannot be created by bureaucratic *fiat*. It is the product of many things – a shared history, dynastic loyalties, the same songs and myths, but above all of a common language and culture.

There is no great mystery as to why this should be so. When people share a common language – words, concepts, ideas, philosophies can be debated among them because they understand them in the same sense. That vital ingredient of democracy – public opinion – can more easily come into being; a public debate on political questions that can then become something real and popular – a sport of taxi-drivers, housewives, businessmen, blue-collar workers and football fans – rather than a thing of élites, special interests and remote bureaucracies.

In these circumstances democracy lives. Societies can then enjoy democratic politics in a real, popular sense – however extensive geographically or however varied ethnically. The United States is itself a glorious example of how a common language, culture and institutions have made one people out of immigrants from every quarter of the globe.

True, the United States is also united by a common philosophy of freedom, elaborated in a great Constitution. But would that common philosophy be enough to unify 280 million Americans if their common language and culture were to be broken down into a patchwork quilt of multi-culturalisms? I doubt it.

So the conservative response to the problem of disintegrating empires, like the Soviet Union and Yugoslavia, is to allow their constituent nations and republics to establish their own democratic, independent identities in an orderly and agreed way if they wish to do so. This also involves their collectively or individually accepting the international responsibilities of their predecessor bodies. In particular, arms agreements must be upheld and debt obligations accepted.

To such an argument, the conventional objection is that this would

result in a multitude of small, economically inefficient mini-states –
unviable because of the legacy of their years as part of a wider command
economy. But such a view merely shows that people have adopted statist
thinking. For with the advent of economic freedom the vast majority of
industrial and commercial decisions never come within the purview of
government at all: they fall to individuals and businesses who establish
their own voluntary relationships.

Free Trade

Indeed, nation-states, large and small, can form a complex economic
network, co-operating in their mutual interests – *provided* that a third
conservative virtue is applied: free trade.

I wish I could say that this was an original insight, Mr Chairman.
But the fact is that such ideas only seem original because they are ideas
that our modern age has forgotten or ignored.

Free trade has both economic and political merits. Economically, it
is the truest form of international co-operation, enabling people in all
five continents to contribute to the manufacture and distribution of goods
as varied as a computer or a matchbox. Politically, it means the size
and extent of government need not be dictated by economic efficiencies
of scale; they can be based instead on what I might call democratic
efficiencies of closeness to the people. With free trade you can have *both*
large-scale economic efficiency *and* small-scale political decentralization.

It is only socialism that requires government to be large, remote and
bureaucratic in order to control people and companies over a wide area.
Free trade forces *governments* to compete – to offer lower tax rates and
lighter régimes of regulation in order to satisfy people and companies.
And because it disciplines governments in this way, Mr Chairman, it is
a bulwark of political freedom as well as of economic liberty.

A Federal Europe?

Stability, democratic nationalism, free trade – where have these conservative principles brought us? What are their implications for the
United States in its relationships with its old NATO allies, and its new
ex-communist friends in Europe?

A strong body of opinion, dominant in Brussels, influential in all

495

European capitals, and with friends in this city, argues that Western interests will best be advanced by the development of a strong federal European superstate that would provide the second pillar of a strong Atlantic alliance. Such a body, in effect a United States of Europe, would, it is argued, be an independent player on the world stage, of course – but also a strong and reliable ally in whatever international struggles follow the Cold War.

Yet would such a supra-nation-state be an ally or a rival? Friendly or hostile? A force for democratic and liberal values or for their opposites? Let us test this hypothetical superstate against the conservative values I outlined earlier.

Nationalism?

Advocates of a federal Europe seek to replace French, British, Italian nationalisms, which are deep-rooted sentiments, with a new European nationalism, which is a bureaucratic fiction. They cannot succeed.

But, like the inventors of Soviet nationalism, they can sow seeds of great bitterness in the process. And the institutions they create, such as a common foreign policy, are likely to amount to very little in themselves, while crippling the actual foreign policies of real nations.

The Gulf War and the Croatian crisis have tested the idea of a common foreign policy to destruction – as the Croatian people know all too well. Let us hope most earnestly that the new ceasefire will hold.[1]

Under cover of previous ceasefires, the attacks have continued against Croatia by the Yugoslav army, consisting of largely communist Serbian forces, whose ambition is to create a Greater Serbia. Some five hundred or more Croatians have been killed, some of them massacred and mutilated – as, for example, old people at Cetkovci.

The matter is now before the Security Council. In the meantime the tanks and guns advance into Croatia, taking more towns and cities, and the cries for help have received no practical response. Hardline communism is not beaten yet.

Democracy?

Whatever the theoretical democratic powers of a European Parliament, it would in reality be an adjunct of a remote bureaucracy. Transferring powers from national Parliaments to Brussels would reduce real democratic accountability. And no amount of increasing the Strasbourg Parliament's powers can supply this so-called 'democratic deficit'. More-

---

[1] The ceasefire in Croatia agreed on 22 September 1991 lasted only nine days. It was one of nine ceasefire agreements in six months.

over, debate conducted in ten languages is not the kind of vibrant debate *we* know.

Free trade?

Once I would have felt compelled to argue at length the case that a federal Europe would be inherently protectionist. Not today. Pasta wars, steel wars, the willingness to sink GATT's Uruguay Round in order to keep the CAP[1] intact, the unwillingness to admit industrial and farm goods from Eastern Europe, the attempt to include cars made in Britain by Japanese firms as part of the Japanese car import quota – all these have convinced fair-minded people that the nearer the EC approaches federalism, the further it departs from free trade – and the more it becomes Fortress Europe.

Stability?

A federal Europe, Mr Chairman, would contribute to *instability*. Let me count the ways. It would construct a rich countries' set of economic and political arrangements that would keep out the poorer East European economies indefinitely, thus prolonging and aggravating the problems of new and fragile democracies. By its own protectionism, it would encourage protectionist trends in Japan and the US, thus nudging world trade in the wrong direction. It would continue to destroy Third World agriculture by subsidizing the exports of food surpluses that its Common Agricultural Policy inevitably generates. And it would be unstable, because in the long term separate national interests and allegiances, becoming stronger and more incompatible the longer they are suppressed, will eventually shatter the supra-national institutions intended to contain them.

So, on every account, the concept of a federal Europe fails. And, as an equal partner of the United States, upholding a new post-communist world order, it is – to borrow Clare Boothe Luce's most famous line – 'Globaloney'.[2]

---

[1] CAP: Common Agricultural Policy.

[2] In the House of Representatives on 9 February 1943, Clare Boothe Luce said that much of what US Vice-President Wallace called 'his global thinking is, no matter how you slice it, still Globaloney'.

An Atlantic Future?

Is there a more practical vision, a more generous vision, a more conservative vision? I believe that there is. It points to what I have called an Atlantic Economic Community, and to what Secretary of State James Baker[1] called a 'Euro-Atlantic Community' in a significant speech that deserves more attention – including more attention from conservatives. That is, a large, free trade area, encompassing the United States, Canada and Mexico, the European Community enlarged by Eastern Europe, and perhaps later by former Soviet republics, and the countries of the European Free Trade Area. And this must not be a fortress against free trade – but rather a way of extending free trade more widely and helping fulfil the objectives of the GATT.

When Secretary Baker talked of a free trade zone stretching 'from Vancouver to Vladivostock' only a few months ago, it seemed desirable but utopian. Following the Russian Revolution, it no longer seems quite so utopian. But let us keep our first speculations more cautious by confining them to a zone encompassing the US, the European Community and Eastern Europe.

It would be, in a sense, an economic equivalent – and economic underpinning – of an enlarged NATO. Because it would account for almost 60 per cent of the world's GNP, it would exercise a profound influence in favour of free trade and free markets in other parts of the world. It would spread prosperity and political stability in the new emerging nations in Eastern Europe and the Soviet Union. It would help to avert the increasing danger of a series of trade wars across the Atlantic which inevitably poison Alliance relations and undermine defence co-operation.

[1] James Baker (born 1930), US politician. White House Chief of Staff 1981–85, 1992–93; Secretary of the Treasury 1985–88; Secretary of State 1989–92. In a speech to the Aspen Institute in Berlin on 18 June 1991, he called for a democratic 'Euro-Atlantic community that extends east from Canada to Vladivostok'.

A Second American Century?

Mr President, Henry Luce[1] called this 'the American century'. But would that it had truly been so. For this has also been the totalitarian century, a century of collectivism, mass murder, wars, tension and fleeing refugees.

Only now do we dare to trust, as this twentieth century is coming to an end, both in years and in philosophy, that the cause of liberty will prevail throughout the world; and that the coming century will be the American century – because people everywhere are turning to what have become American ideas – ideas of liberty, democracy, free markets, free trade and limited government.

Mr Chairman, the world is giving this country a mandate for leadership, a mandate which by your actions you have already shown you are prepared to accept.

---

[1] Henry Luce (1898–1967), US magazine editor and publisher, husband of Clare Boothe Luce.

50

Address to the Senate of the Polish Republic, Warsaw, 3 October 1991

In October 1991 Mrs Thatcher made her first visit to post-communist Poland. The political circumstances were very different from those she had encountered during her visit in 1988. Lech Walesa was no longer under semi-house arrest: he was President of the Republic. A liberal reforming Government had, since the Solidarity victory in 1989, been pressing ahead with 'Thatcherite' economic policies. There was, however, a strong political reaction against the painful changes required by those policies, worsened by disillusionment with capitalism as a result of widespread corruption. Mrs Thatcher's arrival coincided with an election campaign for the lower house of the Polish Parliament.

The speech constitutes a classic explanation to an East European audience of capitalism in general and the conservative message in particular. Adapting themes which are to be found in her 1990 Aspen speech, she emphasizes that democracy requires a particular set of assumptions and institutions – not least broadly-based political parties – in order to function. Similarly, capitalism is not to be confused with a lawless free-for-all in which a predatory class allots all the benefits to itself.

FOR YOUR FREEDOM AND OURS

It is a great honour to have been asked to address the Polish Senate, Poland's first democratically elected Parliamentary body for well over half a century. I know that later this month the lower house will also have its first truly free elections. All this represents a triumph for democracy and for the people of Poland.

The bonds of affection and respect which bind your country and mine have been forged in our common struggle for liberty: liberty in the face of the evil tyranny of Nazism from 1939 to 1945; and liberty during the terrible years which followed, when Poland was in the grip of the no less evil dictatorship of communism.

Historians will long debate the consequences of the Yalta Agreements,[1] but let it be said now: many in Britain, including myself, will never forget the way in which the fate of your country was left in the hands of Stalin and his Polish communist allies.

In a sense, victory in the Second World War – a war which was fought to defend Polish freedom – was only achieved in 1989. No country put more effort into that struggle than yours; none bore heavier sacrifices; none gained less when peace was signed. For all these reasons Poland's fate and Poland's freedom have a unique significance for the history of Europe and the future of democracy.

Poland and Britain have more in common even than our shared experience: we have a shared vocation to liberty. For both of us, the idea we have of our country is inseparable from our mission to defend and extend the reign of freedom. The defiant words emblazoned on the banners of Poland's freedom fighters in the nineteenth century would find an echo in any British heart: 'For Your Freedom, and Ours.'

And let me add that we will never forget the courage and sacrifice of Polish airmen who defended our skies and our liberty in the Battle of Britain in 1940.

You will all have been especially pleased that this year, when communism was uprooted in Russia, has also seen the celebration of the two hundredth anniversary of your famous Constitution of 1791 – the first written constitution in mainland Europe to set out a framework for free government. For the Polish people have known throughout your history that freedom must be indivisible and universal.

Ladies and gentlemen, surely no people – except perhaps for the Jews, Armenians and Kurds – has been so repeatedly subject to attempts by others to destroy it. In 1795 Russia, Prussia and Austria swore to abolish everything which might recall the existence of the Poland they had torn from the map of Europe. In 1939 the Nazis promised that the concept of Poland would be erased from the human mind. In 1945, with torture,

---

[1] At the Yalta Conference of 4–11 February 1945, the USA, the USSR and Britain agreed that 'interim governmental authorities broadly representative of all democratic elements' should be established in liberated countries. To this end, in respect of Poland, they called upon the Polish Government in London to confer with the puppet provisional Government installed by the Red Army, which thus achieved a measure of Western recognition, to the dismay of non-communist Poles.

imprisonment, purges, assassination and deportation the communists tried to extinguish the Poland of your fathers.

Polish patriotism defeated them. Two great Polish patriots – President Walesa and Pope John Paul II[1] – inspired the Polish nation to cast off its chains. And I am struck today, as I was when I came here three years ago, how loyalty to the nation itself is allowing painful changes to be endured in hope of a better future.

The Polish nation knows that, whatever the difficulties which lie ahead, it has come through the valley of the shadow of death – and witnessed dawn.

Making Democracy Work

Since 1989, you have been recreating political freedom. And you will have found that this is almost as heroic a task as winning freedom in the first place.

You can draw confidence from three considerations. First, Poland's passion for liberty has never been and can never be extinguished: and you *must* have a passion for liberty if it is to survive. Second, political and economic freedom correspond to men's natural aspirations: certainly there are institutions to be created and techniques to be learned, but human instincts and interests are on your side. Third, democracy and free enterprise are on the march across the continents: not necessarily irrevocably, and certainly not universally – as the tragedy of Croatia shows[2] – but the tide of ideas is flowing in your direction.

Different countries find different democratic paths and patterns. That is only to be expected. But when they reach their destination with democracy they will: be governed through the consent of the majority – expressed in free elections, which must take place regularly within a specified period; the electorate will be able to choose between different parties which, alone or together, can form a Government; and there will be a just rule of law which applies equally to everybody, guaranteeing their fundamental rights, and enforceable by an impartial and independent judiciary – a rule of law is what makes freedom work.

[1] Lech Walesa (born 1943), Polish politician. Leader of Solidarity 1981–90; President of Poland 1990–95. Karol Wojtyla (born 1920), Archbishop of Krakow 1964–78; Pope John Paul II 1978–.
[2] The autumn of 1991 saw the height of the bloody war waged against Croatia: Vukovar finally fell to the Serbs in November.

These are the political foundations of a free society. As such they are vital. But they are not sufficient to make democracy work *well*.

For democracy also depends heavily on the character and calibre of those who aspire to govern – and on the sense of responsibility of the people.

A democratic electorate will insist on being told the whole truth by politicians about the country's circumstances. It also demands clear principles and policies – not ones geared just to short-term requirements but to the needs of the long-term future. It will respect and be inclined to support those whose character and convictions mark them out as leaders – not just followers of fashion.

I have no intention of interfering in Poland's internal politics, especially at such a time as this. But I will say two things.

First, those who willingly supported socialist policies which shored up tyranny and led to economic collapse are least likely to make freedom work now. Those who fearlessly criticized the old system and have set about building the new are most likely to secure for the Polish people all the benefits it can bring.

Second, I urge you all to recognize the huge advantages which properly established political parties can bring. So often people speak as if political parties were an unwelcome and undignified distraction. They are not. One of my own country's greatest political thinkers, the acknowledged father of conservatism, Edmund Burke, described the purpose of a political party in these words: 'Party is a body of men united for promoting by their joint endeavours the national interest upon some particular principle in which they are all agreed.'

Please note it is the *broad principle* which counts – not the details, about which party members may legitimately differ. I have seen in other European countries what happens when the reformers of the centre-right do not work together. Fragmentation has been a prescription for powerlessness. Liberty requires unity of purpose and unity of action among her friends.

Yet to underpin democracy here in Poland – and indeed in any country – politics is not enough; even law is not enough. You need the security provided by strong defence. You need free enterprise and private property. And you need a moral basis to sustain freedom. Let me now say a word on each of these topics.

Security and Defence

Ladies and gentlemen, your country's history, like mine, has taught us that liberal ideals and democratic institutions have to be defended by force if they are to survive. The tragedies which Poland has suffered have all resulted from the fact that your predatory and aggressive neighbours had military superiority.

So democracy requires its security to be assured by strong defence. And that applies just as much in the new world order as it did in the old.

Freedom would not have been allowed to triumph in the Cold War if the West had permitted the Soviet Union to gain military superiority. It was only when – under American and British leadership – NATO showed that it would not be intimidated, that it could not be beaten militarily, and that it was determined to remain technologically ahead, that the Soviet grand strategy had to change.

This was what first prompted the Soviet Communist Party to choose a different kind of leader in Mr Gorbachev. This was what gave him the advantage over his hard-line opponents. This was what must have convinced enough people even in the Soviet security apparatus earlier this year that the perpetrators of the *coup* had no real alternative way forward.

I know that you in Poland are deeply conscious of the need to assure your security at this time of uncertainty. And for this you and your neighbours look to us in the West, and in particular NATO.

It would be impractical for your countries to join NATO as full members. But I do feel that NATO should offer you some form of participation and assistance within its framework, to the extent that conditions in your countries permit. The more you are seen to be friends and partners of the NATO alliance, the greater your security.[1] I know that there is a long tradition of regional co-operation – going back, I understand, all the way to the time when the sons of your fifteenth-century King Kazimierz[2] were simultaneously on the Polish, Lithuanian

[1] Lady Thatcher now believes that NATO should have welcomed Poland, Hungary, the Czech Republic and Slovakia into full membership, as they requested. See her memoirs (II, pp. 532–3).

[2] King Kazimierz IV Jagiellonczyk (1427–92), Grand Duke of Lithuania 1440–92; King of Poland 1447–92. His eldest son, Wladyslaw, became King of Bohemia in 1471 and King of Hungary in 1490, while his second and third sons, Jan Olbracht and Aleksander, succeeded him in 1492 as King of Poland and Grand Duke of Lithuania respectively.

and Hungarian thrones. Not that I wish to suggest that you repeat this model of regional co-operation today!

But there *is* much that the three leading reforming countries of the area – yourselves, Czechoslovakia and Hungary – can do together. You face common problems with the collapse of your eastern markets, you have common security concerns, and you face common political challenges in terms of your relations with the West. So I think there is ample scope for co-ordinating your reform efforts and working out common positions, and so strengthening your arguments in relation to both your eastern and your western neighbours.

Inevitably, the developing situation in the Soviet Union and the distribution of powers between the centre and republics will have a great influence on your security. We must all know with whom we are dealing; that agreements are being honoured; and that duties are being discharged.

But we should also be clear that the best – indeed the only acceptable – basis for stability is national self-determination, democracy and respect for human rights. So whatever uncertainty there may be at present, the long-term security of Poland will have been enhanced by the fall of Soviet communist domination over your eastern neighbours.

We in the West share Poland's concern about the continued presence of Soviet troops in your country. We understand, of course, the practical problems for the Soviet army of withdrawing their forces from several countries over the same period. But we hope that the negotiations to ensure their removal will soon be successfully completed.[1] Poland is seeking to normalize her relations with the Soviet Union on a new basis. The Soviet Union must fully respect Poland's sovereignty in the Friendship Treaty that is under discussion.[2]

Capitalism and Democracy

The security provided by defence is one necessary condition for democracy: a free enterprise economy is another. To some, this may seem less evident. But it is no coincidence that democracy and capitalism were both on the retreat in the 1970s – nor that now they are both advancing together.

[1] The last remaining Soviet troops left Poland on 17 September 1993.
[2] A Treaty of Friendship and Co-Operation between Poland and the USSR was initialled in Moscow on 10 December 1991.

I know that here in Poland capitalism has been given a bad name because some of those who held influential positions under the old communist system abused them to gain benefits for themselves under the new system. Nor, among the former communist countries, is Poland unique in this.

The capitalism which I support – and which is practised in the West – is not a free-for-all in which the powerful are able to exploit their position at the expense of fairness, decency and the common good. Capitalism can only function when there is a strong and just rule of law to which everyone, including government, is answerable. Corruption is almost entirely absent from public administration in the West; in the rare cases where it occurs it is severely punished. And we set the highest possible standards of impartiality for our courts of justice.

All these things are not qualifications or modifications to capitalism. They are essential to it. Capitalism above all requires confidence in order to operate. And such confidence can only be created by a just rule of law applying to everyone equally – never by the law of the jungle.

So capitalism not only needs a rule of law to underpin it; it shares a common root with democracy.

For capitalism, like democracy, gives real power to the people. In even the most active form of political democracy, individuals are not asked to cast their votes on the performance of politicians more than once or twice a year locally, or after a period of years nationally. Yet in the marketplace, men and women, through the goods they buy, are making economic choices every day.

Free enterprise capitalism is *economic* democracy. It limits the power of government by maximizing the power of the people. Free enterprise capitalism is a necessary – though not a sufficient – condition for *political* democracy itself.

Once you permit personal choice to rule through the market, it will in time extend to the ballot box too. You in Poland know all about this. In retrospect, we can see that it was when the communists were unable to destroy private ownership and enterprise in agriculture that the limits of communism itself were recognized.[1] Not that the end came quickly: nor that it could have come at all without extraordinary courage and sacrifice. But when the communists were forced to accept that collec-

---

[1] Wladyslaw Gomulka announced the end of compulsory collectivization of agriculture when he was restored to the First Secretaryship of the Polish Communist Party in October 1956.

tivism could not feed the people, the system was ultimately doomed.

As you know, by looking at Russia alone, a country is not rich just because of its natural resources. If that were so, Russia would already be the richest country in the world. Countries are prosperous only in so far as the system of government encourages the enterprise of the people. For it is enterprise which creates wealth. Hence the countries with few natural resources – such as Switzerland, Japan, Hong Kong, Taiwan and Singapore – are the most prosperous, because there enterprise is encouraged.

Let me make three practical points here. First, only in so far as factories produce goods that people want to buy will the jobs in them be secure. And only if businesses are encouraged to generate wealth first can there be any question of redistributing it. Second, it is businesses that generate wealth, not Governments; and only when wealth has been created can you begin to consider its redistribution. Thirdly, it follows that Governments should not decide their expenditure before they know what their revenue will be. It is income that determines your expenditure: not your wish to spend.

So the proper tasks of government are: to see that money keeps its value; to privatize state-owned industries, break up monopolies, and replace them with the spur of competition; to provide a framework of law for business, and to protect investors; to set some consumer and safety standards; and, of course, to provide a safety net of social benefits for those genuinely unable to cope for themselves.

Making Capitalism Work

Ladies and gentlemen, you are moving in the right direction – but you have further to go. Your Prime Minister and Finance Minister[1] have charted the course you need to follow – and in which you must persist. Inflation has been coming down. You were one of the first Central European countries to make your currency convertible. By opening your economy to the outside world, your own industries have at last had to compete and produce better-quality goods.

Let me say, however, that in my view Poland and her neighbours

---

[1] Jan Krzysztof Bielecki (born 1951), Polish economist and politician. Prime Minister 1991. Leszek Balcerowicz (born 1947), Polish economist and politician. Finance Minister and Deputy Prime Minister 1989–91.

have so far been selfishly and short-sightedly treated by the European Community.[1] The very products – textiles, steel and farming – which are so crucial to Poland's industrial prospects are those which, for the sake of minor short-term political gain, some Community Governments are determined to exclude. This is not just harmful to Poland: it restricts the choice and puts up the price of goods to consumers within the European Community.

It is not good enough for the Community to hold out the prospect of free trade in ten years' time. I would like to see immediate agreement on opening up Community markets to the widest possible range of Polish products; and I want to see Poland admitted as soon as possible to full membership of the European Community. You have not only much to gain – you have much to contribute: you should be allowed to do so.

Poland's economic difficulties stem, above all, from the legacy of socialism. They are not the result of policies for free enterprise capitalism. Rather, too much still remains of the old system and the attitudes and interests which perpetuated it. You need to make a clean break with the past.

There is a very human and understandable temptation which any country experiences when deliberately setting out in a new direction. Fear of the unknown can lead us: to try to buy time through accepting just a little inflation, just a little larger budget deficit, just a little more taxation; to seek refuge in more state intervention in industry as a means of resisting fundamental changes required by the market; and to regard foreign companies and investment as a threat, rather than as a boost to economic progress and a source of jobs.

But from my own experience in tackling a much lesser legacy of socialism in Britain, I know that the faster, the more radical and the more coherent your programme of economic reform, the sooner it will yield benefits and the greater these will be. Like most medicines, it is unpalatable at first. But you persist until it brings about a cure.

Be as bold in transforming your economy as you have been in fighting communism; and become an example to peoples everywhere who wish to enjoy the fruits of freedom.

---

[1] The EC signed association agreements with Poland, Hungary and Czechoslovakia in Brussels on 16 December 1991, providing for a ten-year transition to mutual free trade, with large EC tariff cuts over the first five years in all sectors except agriculture, steel and textiles.

Moral Foundations of Democracy

The third condition for a successful democracy is, as I have said, a moral order which nourishes and sustains freedom. Here in Poland it is impossible to speak of these things without speaking about the role of the Church in your country's glorious struggle for freedom.

It is no surprise to me that it is a Polish Pope who has now given explicit and powerful recognition, in his encyclical *Centesimus Annus*, to the moral and practical arguments for the free economy.[1] But let me immediately say that no political or economic system itself makes men good – and democracy is no exception. Some virtues, like tolerance and honesty, are necessary to sustain freedom; and some virtues, like industry, thrift, self-reliance and taking responsibility for one's family, are encouraged by it. But the main moral argument for freedom is not that it moulds people in its own image, but that it allows them to create theirs. It protects those rights without which none of us enjoys the full dignity of human personality.

It is not just that capitalism works. It is not just that capitalism is morally right. What we have to recognize and proclaim with the most intense conviction is that capitalism works *because* it is morally right.

Poland's Inner Strength

Ladies and gentlemen, your fight against communism had ultimately to be a spiritual fight. This is because communism – as the most extreme and odious variety of socialism – seeks to deny man's God-given and unequal talents, seeks to pervert the natural aspirations of human nature and seeks to crush the human spirit. Communism is the *ultimate* materialism. And it commits the *ultimate* infraction of the First Commandment – because it demands the worship of the *state*.

From the struggle for national rebirth, Poland has acquired an inner strength which it is now for you to use to create a new and better life.

---

[1] The Papal Encyclical *Centesimus Annus*, issued on 2 May 1991 to mark the hundredth anniversary of the Encyclical *Rerum Novarum*, echoed the earlier document in its advocacy of social justice, but strongly emphasized the importance of the market economy.

The way to freedom is exhilarating – but it can be hard. And only those prepared to live a life of effort can travel far along it.

Some forty years ago, when I fought my first Parliamentary campaign in Britain, I remember being inspired by words attributed to Abraham Lincoln, who knew more about freedom than most of us could forget. I have kept them by me ever since.

The passage runs:

You cannot bring about prosperity by discouraging thrift. You cannot keep out of trouble by spending more than you earn. You cannot further the brotherhood of Man by encouraging class hatred. You cannot help men permanently by doing for them what they could and should do for themselves. You cannot build character and courage by destroying Man's initiative and independence.

Treasure these sentiments. Act upon them. And let Poland's example give faith and hope to those who love liberty in every corner of the world.

51

Speech to the 'Global Panel', The Hague,
15 May 1992

The Hague speech of May 1992 is the offspring and worthy successor of the Bruges speech of September 1988. As with the latter, in The Hague Mrs Thatcher was addressing a wider international audience in the hope of influencing attitudes towards Europe's future destination. Now out of government, she was free to be still more direct in her criticisms of European federalism than at Bruges. Above all, the reunification of Germany, which had thus emerged as the dominant European power, and the planned establishment under the Maastricht Treaty of the framework for a European superstate, made the debate sharper and more urgent. Mrs Thatcher argued that a politically united Europe, far from checking German power, would in practice increase it – thus standing on their head the arguments of the Euro-federalists in general, and the French in particular. She argued instead for a return to a (modified) application of the old principle of the balance of power to restore the political equilibrium.

EUROPE'S POLITICAL ARCHITECTURE

We are fortunate to be meeting in The Hague, a beautiful city kept beautiful by a country which values its architectural heritage. Goethe[1] described architecture as 'frozen music'. And in a city like this it is not hard to imagine the grand symphonic melodies that might be released if we could defrost the Town Hall and the great urban squares.

Architecture tells us a lot about ourselves, about our idea of God, about our relationship with our fellow men, and about our vision of man's destiny.

[1] Johann Wolfgang von Goethe (1749–1832), German poet, dramatist, novelist and scientist.

The great medieval cathedrals gave us an exalted spiritual view of man's place in a universe governed by an all-loving and all-seeing Creator.

The Age of Reason pictured civilized man in a neat, geometrically ordered landscape dotted with neo-classical structures at regular intervals – with no more than one small folly to each estate.

And in our own day, the vision of New European Man walking purposefully towards the Common Agricultural Policy was exquisitely realized in the Berlaymont building in Brussels.[1] What music would Goethe hear if he could look upon the Berlaymont, perhaps while acting as an advisor to the Commissioner responsible for developing a policy for European culture (which has languished so long without one)?

And what a climax of discord and disharmony! For the Berlaymont – its halls lined with cancer-causing asbestos – is to be pulled down.

Look at the architecture of the last fifty years – in particular, at the architecture that went beyond the modern to the futuristic. It was certainly very dramatic, but the one thing it no longer expresses is the future. What it expresses is yesterday's vision of the future – one captured by the poet John Betjeman[2] in 1945:

> I have a vision of the future, chum.
> The workers' flats, in fields of soya beans,
> Tower up like silver pencils, score on score.

But the Berlaymont school of architecture is a convenient symbol for the *political* architecture of the European Community. For it too is infused with the spirit of 'yesterday's future'.

Mr Chairman, the European Community we have today was created in very different circumstances to deal with very different problems. It was built upon very different assumptions about where the world was heading. And it embodied political ideas and economic theories that in the light of recent history we have to question. Today I want to do exactly that. In particular, I shall try to answer three questions.

First, how can we best deal with the imbalance in Europe created by the reunification and revival of Germany?

Second, how can we reform European institutions so that they provide

[1] The Berlaymont, a huge four-winged building on the Schuman roundabout, was the seat of the EC Commission. It was built in 1967 and the architects were L. de Vestal, J. Gilson and A. & J. Polak.
[2] Sir John Betjeman (1906–84), English poet and essayist, Poet Laureate 1972–84.

for the diversity of post-communist Europe and be truly democratic? Third, how can we ensure that the new Europe contributes to – rather than undermines – the world's economic prosperity and political stability?

Our answers to these questions can no longer be bound by the conventional collectivist wisdom of the 1940s and fifties. That is yesterday's future. We must draw on the ideas of liberty, democracy, free markets and nationhood that have swept the world in the last decade.

The Beginning of the Community

It was Winston Churchill who, with characteristic magnanimity, in 1946, with his Zurich speech, argued that Germany should be rehabilitated through what he called 'European union' as 'an association between France and Germany' which would 'assume direction'. This could not be done overnight, and it took American leadership.

In 1947, after travelling through Europe in that terrible winter, when everything froze over, George Marshall,[1] the then Secretary of State, promoted the idea of American help. Marshall Aid was administered by institutions set up *ad hoc* – it had to be, if only because most European states did not have adequate machinery, the Greek delegate being found one day simply making up figures for his country's needs – and I expect there were others besides.

The initial impetus was for European recovery. It owed much to simple American good-heartedness. It owed something to commercial calculation: the prosperity of Europe, in free-trade conditions, would also be the prosperity of America. But the main thing was the threat from Stalin. Eastern Europe had shown how demoralized peoples could not resist cunningly executed communist takeovers, and Marshall Aid was intended to set Western Europe back on its feet. It was a prodigious success.

But we have found, again and again, that institutions devised for one set of problems become obstacles to solving the next set – even that they become problems in their own right. The Common Agricultural Policy is an example. As originally devised, it had a modest aim that was not unreasonable.

---

[1] General George Marshall (1880–1959), US soldier and politician. Chief of Staff, US Army 1939–45; Secretary of State 1947–49; Secretary of Defense 1950–51.

Yet we all know that the CAP is now an expensive headache, and one quite likely to derail the Uruguay Round. Because of agricultural protection we stop food imports from the poorer countries. They themselves are nowadays vehement supporters of market principles: it is from the Cairns Group of developing countries that you hear demands for free trade. Yet in the industrialized part of the world, the taxpayer and the consumer stump up $270 billion in subsidies and higher costs; and the World Bank has calculated that if the tariff and other barriers were cut by half, then the poorer countries would gain at once, in exports, $50 billion. In case you might think that these sentiments are somehow anti-European, I should say that they come from an editorial in the economic section of the *Frankfurter Allgemeine Zeitung* of 4 May.

Here we have a prime example of yesterday's solutions becoming tomorrow's problems. You could extend this through the European institutions as a whole. They were meant to solve post-war problems, and did so in many ways extremely well. Western Europe did unite against the Soviet threat, and, with Anglo–American precepts, became free and very prosperous. That prosperity, denied to the peoples of Eastern Europe and Russia, in the end caused demoralization among their rulers, and revolt from below. We are now in a quite different set of circumstances, with the Cold War over.

Looking at European institutions today, I am reminded of a remark made about political parties in the French Third Republic. Some of them had names which reflected radical republican origins from the 1870s, but years later they had become conservative. These radical names, ran the remark, were like the light reaching earth from stars that were long extinct. Equally, with the end of the Cold War we have to look again at the shape of Europe and its institutions.

The German Question

Mr Chairman, let me turn first to the new situation created by the reunification of Germany. And let me say that if I were a German today, I would be proud – proud, but also worried. I would be proud of the magnificent achievement of rebuilding my country, entrenching democracy and assuming the undoubtedly preponderant position in Europe. But I would also be worried about the European Community and its direction. The German taxpayer pays dearly for his place in Europe.

Britain and Germany have a strong joint interest in ensuring that the other Community countries pay their fair share of the cost – and control the Community's spending more enthusiastically – without leaving us to carry so much of the burden.

Germany is well-equipped to encourage such financial prudence. Indeed, I would trust the Bundesbank more than any other European Central Bank to keep down inflation – because the Germans have none-too-distant memories of the total chaos and political extremism which hyper-inflation brings. The Germans are therefore right to be increasingly worried about the terms they agreed for economic and monetary union. Were I a German, I would prefer the Bundesbank to provide our modern equivalent of the gold standard rather than any committee of European central bankers.

But there is an understandable reluctance on the part of Bonn to defend its views and interests so straightforwardly. For years the Germans have been led to believe by their neighbours that their respectability depends on their subordinating their national interest to the joint decisions of the Community. It is better that that pretence be stopped.

A reunited Germany can't and won't subordinate its national interests in economic or in foreign policy to those of the Community indefinitely. And sometimes Germany will be right when the rest are wrong, as it was over the recognition of Croatia and Slovenia.[1] Indeed, if the Federal Republic had led the way in recognizing these countries earlier, Serbian aggression might have been deterred and much bloodshed prevented. Whether rightly or wrongly exercised, however, Germany's new pre-eminence is a fact. We will all be better off if we recognize that modern democratic Germany has come of age.

Nevertheless, Germany's power is a problem – as much for the Germans as for the rest of Europe. Germany is too large to be just another player in the European game, but not large enough to establish unquestioned supremacy over its neighbours. And the history of Europe since 1870 has largely been concerned with finding the right structure to contain Germany.

It has been Germany's immediate neighbours, the French, who have

---

[1] The EC announced its decision to recognize Croatia and Slovenia as independent states on 15 January 1992, after Germany had done so unilaterally on 23 December 1991.

seen this most clearly. Both Briand in 1929 and Schuman[1] after the Second World War proposed structures of economic union to achieve this. Briand's proposal was made just at the moment when the rise of the Nazis made such a visionary scheme impossible, and it failed. But Schuman's vision of a European Community was realized because of an almost unique constellation of favourable circumstances: the Soviet threat made European co-operation imperative; Germany was itself divided; other Western nations sought German participation in the defence of Western Europe; West Germany needed the respectability that NATO and the Community could give; and American presence in, and leadership of, Europe reduced the fears of Germany's neighbours.

With the collapse of the Soviet Union and reunification of Germany, the entire position has changed. A new Europe of some thirty states has come into being, the problem of German power has again surfaced, and statesmen have been scrambling to produce a solution to it. At first France hoped that the post-war Franco–German partnership, with France as the senior partner, would continue. Chancellor Kohl's separate and successful negotiations with Mr Gorbachev quickly showed this to be an illusion.[2]

The next response of France and other European countries was to seek to tie down the German Gulliver within the joint decision-making of the European Community. Again, however, this quickly proved to be an illusion. Germany's preponderance within the Community is such that no major decision can really be taken against German wishes. In these circumstances, the Community augments German power rather than containing it.

Let me illustrate this point with two examples where I agree with the German position. The first, as I have mentioned, was the German decision to recognize Croatia and Slovenia, which compelled the rest of Europe to follow suit. The second is the refusal of the Bundesbank to pursue imprudent financial policies at the urging of some of the countries

---

[1] Aristide Briand (1862–1932), French politician. Prime Minister 1909–11, 1913, 1915–17, 1921–22, 1925–26, 1929. He proposed the creation of a federal European union in a speech to the League of Nations Assembly in September 1929, and set out his plans in a memorandum of 1 May 1930. Robert Schuman (1886–1963), French politician. Finance Minister 1946; Prime Minister 1947–48; Foreign Minister 1948–52; President of the EEC Assembly 1958–60. The Schuman Plan of 1950 was the genesis of the European Coal and Steel Community.

[2] On 11 February 1990, Chancellor Kohl – without consultation with his allies – went to Moscow and won Soviet agreement that 'the unity of the German nation must be decided by the Germans themselves'.

of the G7. However much I may sympathize with these policies, the blunt fact is that Germany has followed its own interests rather than the advice of its neighbours, who have then been compelled to adjust their own stance.

The Balance of Power

What follows from this is that German power will be best accommodated in a looser Europe in which individual nation-states retain their freedom of action. If Germany or any other power then pursues a policy to which other countries object, it will automatically invite a coalition against itself. And the resulting solution will reflect the relative weight of the adversaries. A common foreign policy, however, is liable to express the interests of the largest single actor. And a serious dispute between EC member states locked into a common foreign policy would precipitate a crisis affecting everything covered by the Community.

The general paradox here is that attempts at co-operation that are too ambitious are likely to create conflict. We will have more harmonious relationships between the states of Europe if they continue to have room to make their own decisions and to follow their own interests – as happened in the Gulf War.

But it would be idle to deny that such a balance of power – for that is what I have been describing – has sometimes broken down and led to war. And Europe on its own, however organized, will still find the question of German power insoluble. Europe has really enjoyed stability only since America became a European power.

The third response, therefore, is to keep an American presence in Europe. American power is so substantial that it dwarfs the power of any other single European country. It reassured the rest of Europe in the face of Soviet power until yesterday; and it provides similar comfort against the rise of Germany today – as the Germans themselves appreciate.

Why aren't we worried about the abuse of American power? It is difficult to be anxious about a power so little inclined to throw its weight around that our principal worry is that American troops will go home.

And there's the rub. There is pressure from isolationist opinion in the USA to withdraw from Europe. It is both provoked and encouraged by similar thinking in the Community which is protectionist in economics and 'little European' in strategy. In trade, in the GATT negotiations, in NATO's restructuring, we need to pursue policies that will persuade America to remain a European power.

Europe Free and Democratic

If America is required to keep Europe secure, what is required to keep Europe free and democratic?

When the founders of the European Community drew up the Treaty of Rome, they incorporated features from two quite different economic traditions. From liberalism they took free trade, free markets and competition. From socialism (in guises as various as social Catholicism and corporatism) they took regulation and intervention. And for thirty years – up to the signing of the Single European Act – these two traditions were in a state of perpetual but unacknowledged tension.

Now – with the Commission exploiting the Single European Act to accumulate powers of greater direction and regulation – Europe is reaching the point at which it must choose between these two approaches. Is it to be a tightly-regulated, centralized bureaucratic federal state, imposing uniform standards throughout the Continent? Or is it to be a loose-knit decentralized free-market Europe of sovereign states, based upon competition between different national systems of tax and regulation within a free trade area?

The federalists at least seem to be clear. The Maastricht Treaty[1] met the Commission's requirement for a 'single institutional framework' for the Community. Yet, before the ink was even dry on the Treaty, it was reported that the President of the European Commission was seeking more money and more powers for the Commission which would become the Executive of the Community – in other words a European Government. There would seem to be no doubt about the direction in which the European federalists are now anxious to proceed – towards a federal Europe.

Nor is there any mystery about the urgency with which they press the federalist cause. Even though they may wish to defer the 'enlargement' of the Community with the accession of Eastern Europe, they realize it is

---

[1] The Treaty on European Union signed at Maastricht on 7 February 1992 created a political union, introduced new areas of EC competence, increased the powers of the European Parliament, set a timetable for economic and monetary union, and provided for closer co-operation in foreign and defence policy outside existing EC machinery.

impossible. A half-Europe imposed by Soviet tyranny was one thing; a half-Europe imposed by Brussels would be a moral catastrophe depriving the Community of its European legitimacy.

The Commission knows it will have to admit many new members in the next few decades. But it hopes to construct a centralized superstate in advance – and irrevocably – so that the new members will have to apply for entry on federalist terms.

And it's just not on.

Imagine a European Community of thirty nations, ranging in their economic productivity from Germany to Ukraine, and in their political stability from Britain to Poland,

– all governed from Brussels;

– all enforcing the same conditions at work;

– all having the same worker rights as the German unions;

– all subject to the same interest rates, monetary, fiscal and economic policies;

– all agreeing on a common foreign and defence policy;

– and all accepting the authority of an Executive and a remote foreign Parliament over '80 per cent of economic and social legislation'.[1] Mr Chairman, such a body is an even more utopian enterprise than the Tower of Babel. For at least the builders of Babel all spoke the same language when they *began*. They were, you might say, *communautaire*.

Mr Chairman, the thinking behind the Commission's proposals is essentially the thinking of 'yesterday's tomorrow'. It was how the best minds of Europe saw the future in the ruins after the Second World War.

But they made a central intellectual mistake. They assumed that the model for future government was that of a centralized bureaucracy that would collect information upwards, make decisions at the top, and then issue orders downwards. And what seemed the wisdom of the ages in 1945 was in fact a primitive fallacy. Hierarchical bureaucracy may be a suitable method of organizing a small business that is exposed to fierce external competition – but it is a recipe for stagnation and inefficiency in almost every other context.

Yet it is precisely this model of remote, centralized, bureaucratic organization that the European Commission and its federalist supporters

---

[1] In a speech to the European Parliament on 6 July 1988, Jacques Delors predicted that within ten years the EC would be the source of '80 per cent of our economic legislation and perhaps even our fiscal and social legislation as well'.

seek to impose on a Community which they acknowledge may soon contain many more countries of widely differing levels of political and economic development, and speaking more than fifteen languages. '*C'est magnifique, mais ce n'est pas la politique.*'

The larger Europe grows, the more diverse must be the forms of co-operation it requires. Instead of a centralized bureaucracy, the model should be a market – not only a market of individuals and companies, but also a market in which the players are Governments.

Thus Governments would compete with each other for foreign investments, top management and high earners through lower taxes and less regulation. Such a market would impose a fiscal discipline on Governments, because they would not want to drive away expertise and business. It would also help to establish which fiscal and regulatory policies produced the best overall economic results. No wonder socialists don't like it.

To make such a market work, of course, national Governments must retain most of their existing powers in social and economic affairs. Since these Governments are closer and accountable to their voters, it is doubly desirable that we should keep power at the national level.

The Role of the Commission

Mr Chairman, in 1996, when the arrangements agreed at Maastricht are due to be reviewed, and probably a good deal earlier, the Community should move in exactly the opposite direction to that proposed by the European federalists.

A Community of sovereign states committed to voluntary co-operation, a lightly regulated free market and international free trade does not need a Commission in its present form. The Government of the Community – to the extent that this term is appropriate – is the Council of Ministers, consisting of representatives of democratically elected national Governments. The work of the Commission should cease to be legislative in any sense. It should be an administrative body, like any professional civil service, and it should not initiate policy, but rather carry it out. In doing this it should be subject to the scrutiny of the European Parliament, acting on the model of Commons Select Committees. In that way, whatever collective policies or regulations are required would emerge from deliberation between democratic Governments, accountable to their national Parliaments, rather than being imposed by a bureaucracy with its own agenda.

Co-Operation in Europe

But need this always be done in the same 'single institutional framework'? New problems arise all the time. Will these always require the same level and type of co-operation in the same institutions? I doubt it. We need a greater flexibility than the structures of the European Community have allowed until very recently.

A single institutional framework of its nature tends to place too much power with the central authorities. It is a good thing that a common foreign policy will continue to be carried on under a separate treaty and will neither be subject to the European Court nor permit the Commission to fire off initiatives at will. If 'Europe' moves into new areas, it must do so under separate treaties which clearly define the powers which have been surrendered.

And why need every new European initiative require the participation of all members of the Community? It will sometimes be the case – especially after enlargement – that only some Community members will want to move forward to another stage of integration.

Here I pay tribute to John Major's achievement in persuading the other eleven Community Heads of Government that they could move ahead to a Social Chapter,[1] but not within the Treaty and without Britain's participation. It sets a vital precedent. For an enlarged Community can only function if we build in flexibility of that kind.

We should aim at a multi-track Europe in which *ad hoc* groups of different states – such as the Schengen Group[2] – forge varying levels of co-operation and integration on a case-by-case basis. Such a structure would lack graph-paper neatness. But it would accommodate the diversity of post-communist Europe.

---

[1] The Social Charter was incorporated in the draft treaty on European Union as the Social Chapter. It was removed from the final text on 11 December 1991 at British insistence and signed by the eleven other member states as a separate Social Protocol.
[2] Originally conceived at Schengen in Luxemburg in 1985 and signed by nine EC countries between 1990 and 1992, the Schengen Agreement provides for the abolition of frontier controls on common borders. It came into force on 26 March 1995 and is currently being observed by six nations.

The European Parliament

Supporters of federalism argue, no doubt sincerely, that we can accommodate this diversity by giving more powers to the European Parliament. But democracy requires more than that.

To have a genuine European democracy you would need a Europe-wide public opinion based on a single language; Europe-wide political parties with a common programme understood similarly in all member states; a Europe-wide political debate in which political and economic concepts and words had the same agreed meaning everywhere.

We would be in the same position as the unwieldy Habsburg Empire's Parliament.

The Habsburg Parliament

That Parliament was a notorious failure. There were dozens of political parties, and nearly a dozen peoples were represented – Germans, Italians, Czechs, Poles and so on. For the Government to get anything through – for instance, in 1889 a modest increase in the number of conscripts – took ages, as all the various interests had to be propitiated. When one or other was not satisfied, its spokesmen resorted to obstruction – lengthy speeches in Russian, banging of desk-lids, throwing of inkwells, and on one occasion the blowing of a cavalry trumpet by the Professor of Jurisprudence at the German University of Prague. Measures could not be passed, and budgets could only be produced by decree. The longest-lasting Prime Minister, Count Taaffe,[1] remarked that his highest ambition in politics was the achievement of supportable dissatisfaction on all sides – not a bad description of what the European Community risks becoming.

And because of the irresponsibility of Parliaments, the Habsburg Monarchy could really only be ruled by bureaucrats. It took twenty-five signatures for a tax payment to be validated; one in four people in employment worked for the state in some form or another, even in 1914; and so many resources went to all of this that not much was left for

[1] Count Eduard von Taaffe (1833–95), Austrian statesman. Prime Minister 1868–70, 1879–93.

defence: even the military bands had to be cut back, 'Radetzky March' and all. Of course it was a tremendous period in cultural terms both in Vienna and in Budapest. We in England have done mightily well by the emigration, often forced, to our shores of so many talented people from Central Europe. But the fact is that they had to leave their native lands because political life became impossible.

This example could be multiplied again and again. Belgium and Holland, which have so much in common, split apart in 1831. Sweden and Norway, which have even more in common, split apart in 1905. It does seem simply to be a straightforward rule in modern times that countries which contain two languages, even if they are very similar, must in the end divide, unless the one language absorbs the other. It would be agreeable to think that we could all go back to the world of the Middle Ages, when the educated classes spoke Latin, and the rulers communicated in grunts. But we cannot. Unless we are dealing with international co-operation and alliances, freely entered into, we create artificial structures which become the problem that they were meant to address. The League of Nations, when the Second World War broke out, resolved to ignore the fact and to discuss, instead, the standardization of level-crossings.

A Federal Europe

Mr Chairman, I am sometimes tempted to think that the new Europe which the Commission and Euro-federalists are creating is equally ill-equipped to satisfy the needs of its members and the wishes of their peoples. It is, indeed, a Europe which combines all the most striking failures of our age.

The day of the artificially constructed megastate has gone. So the Euro-federalists are now desperately scurrying to build one.

The Swedish-style welfare state has failed – even in Sweden. So the Euro-statists press ahead with their Social Chapter.

Large-scale immigration has in France and Germany already encouraged the growth of extremist parties. So the European Commission is pressing us to remove frontier controls.

If the European Community proceeds in the direction which the majority of member-state Governments and the Commission seem to want, they will create a structure which brings insecurity, unemployment, national resentment and ethnic conflict.

Insecurity – because Europe's protectionism will strain and possibly sever that link with the United States on which the security of the Continent ultimately depends.

Unemployment – because the pursuit of policies of regulation will increase costs, and price European workers out of jobs.

National resentment – because a single currency and a single centralized economic policy, which will come with it, will leave the electorate of a country angry and powerless to change its conditions.

Ethnic conflict – because not only will the wealthy European countries be faced with waves of immigration from the south and from the east.

Also, within Europe itself, the effect of a single currency and regulation of wages and social costs will have one of two consequences. Either there will have to be a massive transfer of money from one country to another, which will not in practice be affordable; or there will be massive migration from the less successful to the more successful countries.

Yet if the future we are being offered contains so very many risks and so few real benefits, why, it may be asked, is it proving all but irresistible?

The answer is simple. It is that in almost every European country there has been a refusal to debate the issues which really matter. And little can matter more than whether the ancient, historic nations of Europe are to have their political institutions and their very identities transformed by stealth into something neither wished nor understood by their electorates. Yet so much is it the touchstone of respectability to accept this ever-closer union, now interpreted as a federal destiny, that to question is to invite affected disbelief or even ridicule. This silent understanding – this Euro-snobbism – between politicians, bureaucracies, academics, journalists and businessmen is destructive of honest debate.

So John Major deserves high praise for ensuring at Maastricht that we would not have either a single currency or the absurd provisions of the Social Chapter forced upon us: our industry, workforce, and national prosperity will benefit as a result. Indeed, as long as we in Britain now firmly control our spending and reduce our deficit, we will be poised to surge ahead in Europe. For our taxes are low; our inflation is down; our debt is manageable; our reduced regulations are favourable to business.

We take comfort from the fact that both our Prime Minister and our Foreign Secretary have spoken out sharply against the forces of bureaucracy and federalism.

The Choice

Our choice is clear: either we exercise democratic control of Europe through co-operation between national Governments and Parliaments which have legitimacy, experience and closeness to the people; or we transfer decisions to a remote multi-lingual Parliament, accountable to no real European public opinion and thus increasingly subordinate to a powerful bureaucracy. No amount of misleading language about pooling sovereignty can change that.

Europe and the Wider World

Mr Chairman, in world affairs for most of this century Europe has offered problems, not solutions. The founders of the European Community were consciously trying to change that. Democracy and prosperity in Europe were to be an example to other peoples in other continents. Sometimes this view took an over-ambitious turn, with talk of Europe as a third force brokering between two superpowers of East and West. This approach was always based upon a disastrous illusion – that Western Europe could at some future date dispense with the military defence offered by the United States.

Now that the forces of communism have retreated and the threat which Soviet tanks and missiles levelled at the heart of Europe has gone, there is a risk that the old tendency towards decoupling Europe from the United States may again emerge. This is something against which Europeans themselves must guard – and of which the United States must be aware.

This risk could become reality in several ways.

Trade

First, there is the question of trade. It is a terrible indictment of the complacency which characterizes the modern post-Cold War world that we have allowed the present GATT round to be stalled for so long. Free trade is the greatest force for prosperity and peaceful co-operation.

It does no good to the Western alliance when Europe and the United

States come to regard each other as hostile interests. In practice, whatever the theory may be, economic disputes do sour political relations. Agricultural subsidies and tariffs lie at the heart of the dispute, which will not go away unless we in Europe decide that the Common Agricultural Policy has to be fundamentally changed. That will go far to determine what kind of Europe we are building.

For, as I have said before, I would like to see the European Community – embracing the former communist countries to its east – agree to develop an Atlantic free trade area with the United States. That would be a means of pressing for more open multilateral trade throughout the world. Europe must seek to move the world away from competing regional trade blocs – not promote them. In such a trading arrangement, Britain would have a vital role bridging that Atlantic divide – just as Germany should provide Europe with a bridge to the east and to the countries of the former Soviet Union.

Eastern Europe

Secondly, we must modify and modernize our defence. The dangers on Europe's eastern border have receded. But let us not forget that on the credibility of NATO's military strength all our wider objectives depend – reassurance for the post-communist countries, stability in Europe, transatlantic political co-operation.

Communism may have been vanquished. But all too often the communists themselves have not. The chameleon qualities of the comrades have never been more clearly demonstrated than in their emergence as democratic socialists and varieties of nationalist in the countries of Central and Eastern Europe. From the powerful positions they retain in the bureaucracy, security apparatus and the armed forces, from their places in not-really-privatized enterprises, they are able to obstruct, undermine and plunder.

The systems of proportional representation which so many of these countries have adopted have allowed these tactics to succeed all the more, leading to weak Governments and a bewildering multiplicity of parties. All this risks bringing democracy into discredit. If Eastern European countries which retain *some* links with a pre-communist past, and have *some* sort of middle class on which to draw, falter on the path to reform, how will the leaders of the countries of the former Soviet Union dare to proceed further upon it?

We can help by allowing them free access to our markets. I am delighted that association agreements have been signed between the European Community and several of these countries. I would like speedy action to include the others in similar arrangements. But ten years is too long to wait before the restrictions on trade are removed. And I would like to see these countries offered full membership of the European Community rapidly.

Above all we must offer these countries greater security. Russian troops are still stationed on Polish territory. Moreover, it is understandable that the Central and Eastern European countries are alarmed at what conflict in the old USSR and the old Yugoslavia may portend. Although I recognize that the North Atlantic Co-Operation Council[1] has been formed with a view to this, I still feel that the European ex-communist countries are entitled to that greater degree of reassurance which a separate closer relationship with NATO would bring.

Security

But, Mr Chairman, most of the threats to Europe's and the West's interests no longer come from this continent. I believe – and I have been urging this on NATO members since 1990 – that the Americans and Europeans ought to be able to deploy our forces under NATO outside the area for which the present North Atlantic Treaty allows. It is impossible to know where the danger may next come. But two considerations should make us alive to real risks to our security.

First, the break-up of the Soviet Union has led to large numbers of advanced weapons becoming available to would-be purchasers at knockdown prices: it would be foolish to imagine that these will not, some of them, fall into the worst possible hands.

Second, Europe cannot ignore its dependence for oil on the Middle East. Saddam Hussein is still in power. Fundamentalism is as strong as ever. Old scores are still unsettled. We must beware. And we must widen our ability to defend our interests and be prepared to act when necessary.

---

[1] The North Atlantic Co-Operation Council (NACC) was established in December 1991 as a forum for consultation and co-operation between NATO and the countries of the former Warsaw Pact.

The Community's Wider Role

Finally, the European Community must come to recognize its place in what is called the new world order.

The ending of the Cold War has meant that the international institutions created in the post-war years – the UN, the IMF, the World Bank, the GATT – can work much more effectively. This means that the role for the Community is inevitably circumscribed. Within Europe, a wider role for NATO and the CSCE should also be reflected in more modest ambitions for the Community's diplomacy. In Yugoslavia, the Community has shown itself incapable of dealing effectively with security questions. Outside Europe, GATT, with its mandate to reduce trade barriers, should be the body that establishes the rules of the game in trade. The Community must learn to live within those rules. All in all, the Community must be prepared to fit in with the new internationalism, not supplant it.

Conclusion

Mr Chairman, I end as I began – with architecture. The Hague is a splendid capital, and how much we should admire the Dutch for keeping it together so well, as they have done with so many other of their towns. The Mauritshuis[1] is a testimony to the genius which they showed. It was here, and in Amsterdam, that so much of the modern world was invented in the long Dutch fight for freedom.

Dutch architecture has its own unmistakable elegance and durability – it was copied all around the north European world, from Wick in northern Scotland to Tallinn in Estonia. Some architecture does last. Other architecture does not. Let us make sure that we build a Europe as splendid and lasting as the Mauritshuis, rather than one as shabby and ephemeral as the Berlaymont.

---

[1] The Mauritshuis, which stands beside the Court Lake in The Hague, was built in the seventeenth century for Prince John Maurice of Nassau. The architect was Pieter Post, working from plans by Jacob van Campen. The Mauritshuis now houses the Royal Picture Gallery.

52

Speech in a Debate in the House of Lords on 'The European Community: United Kingdom Presidency', 2 July 1992

Translation to the Upper House involves, for any instinctive House of Commons man (or woman), a difficult culture shock. But Lady Thatcher had little opportunity to adjust to the atmosphere of the House of Lords before she felt compelled to speak in the debate on the United Kingdom Presidency of the European Community to express her criticisms of the Maastricht Treaty. What she and a few others had begun as a lonely, much misunderstood and much criticized stand against her successor's European policy, now already showed signs of broadening into a Europe-wide popular revolt against the federalist project. The Danes had voted 'No' to Maastricht. A French referendum was in prospect. And it still seemed possible that the governing political class might start to listen.

Baroness Thatcher. My Lords, it is a privilege to take my place on these distinguished and tranquil benches after thirty-three testing years before the mast in another place. I thank my noble friend[1] for her kind reference to me, and I greatly thank the noble Lord, Lord Jenkins,[2] for parts of his speech.

Mine is a somewhat delicate position. I calculate that I was responsible as Prime Minister for proposing the elevation to this House of 214 of its present members. That must surely be considerably more than most

---

[1] Lynda Chalker (born 1942), Baroness Chalker of Wallasey 1992. Conservative MP 1974–92; Minister of State at the Foreign Office 1986–97; Minister for Overseas Development 1989–97.
[2] Roy Jenkins, Baron Jenkins of Hillhead.

of my predecessors – and my father did not know Lloyd George![1]

As Prime Minister I made a point of following your Lordships' debates and the reports of your Select Committees, and found them invaluable for the wealth of experience and worldliness which they contained. I must confess that your Lordships' voting record occasionally gave rise to other and more violent emotions, particularly when the votes were on matters of finance. My frustration was too often and unfairly visited on the thankfully broad shoulders of my noble friends Lord Whitelaw and Lord Denham.[2] I am sure that the view from here will look quite different.

I ask for your Lordships' forbearance for speaking so soon after my arrival in your Lordships' House rather than allowing a decent interval to elapse. But Britain's Presidency of the Community comes round only once every six years, and in future it may be longer than that. Notorious as I am for patience and restraint, I can hardly wait that long.

As the noble Lord, Lord Richard,[3] said, I find that the late Lord Stockton managed thirty-three minutes,[4] during which he was not exactly complimentary about the then Government's economic policies or its handling of the miners' strike. Therefore speeches are not always non-controversial. The noble Lord, Lord Wilson, for his part spent twenty minutes trampling politely on the Government's record on training and higher education. I therefore take heart that the non-controversial tradition may sometimes be honoured in the breach. But of course, what is controversial to one may be music to the ears of another. Without differences of view there would be no debate; and if Parliament lost its powers to another body there would be little point in debate.

I notice from the speeches that have already been made that one point has forcibly emerged. Bearing in mind that all three parties are

---

[1] David Lloyd George (1863–1945), 1st Earl of Dwyfor 1945. Liberal MP 1890–1945; President of the Board of Trade 1905–08; Chancellor of the Exchequer 1908–15; Minister for Munitions 1915–16; War Secretary 1916; Prime Minister 1916–22; Leader of the Liberal Party 1926–31. This allusion to the facetious song 'Lloyd George Knew my Father' gains its point from the fact that Lloyd George is notorious for having proposed the creation of an unusually high number of peerages.
[2] Bertram Bowyer (born 1927), 2nd Baron Denham of Weston Underwood 1948. Conservative Chief Whip in the Lords 1978–89.
[3] Ivor Richard (born 1927), Baron Richard of Ammanford 1990. Labour MP 1964–74; UK Permanent Representative to the United Nations 1974–79; Member of the EC Commission 1981–84.
[4] Lady Thatcher here refers to the maiden speeches in the House of Lords of two former Prime Ministers, Harold Macmillan and Harold Wilson.

of the same view about ratifying Maastricht, the electorate has had no way during the general election of expressing its view.[1] It had in fact no choice.

Britain has usually set itself rather modest and limited objectives during its turn at holding the Presidency of the EC. True, our last Presidency launched the Single Market; and in view of some of the comments in regard to the Single European Act which I heard in this House on Tuesday, I shall have something to say in that regard later, and my noble friend has already referred to it. But generally we have concentrated on organizing the Community's business efficiently, and drawing precise conclusions from wordy and chaotic debates.

That was necessary, but it will certainly not be enough this time. Rarely, if ever, has the Community had a greater number of important issues demanding its attention than now. Most of them were mentioned by my noble friend the Minister of State,[2] and I shall not repeat the list which she gave so ably, but start with what is on everyone's lips and the most pressing question – that is to say, what to do about Maastricht after the Danish referendum.[3]

Many people who travel through Europe, as I have done in recent months, are struck by the very sharp change in attitudes towards the European Community brought about by the Maastricht Treaty. Scepticism, justifiable scepticism, is on the increase. People feel that their Governments have gone ahead too fast, so that now the gap between Government and people is too wide. Perhaps that is not surprising when in the modern political world European Ministers spend so much time in each other's company: they get out of touch with the people and too much in touch with themselves.

The particular concerns are different in each country, but the basic misgivings are mostly the same. People feel that too many of the powers and rights, which have been theirs for decades and in some cases for centuries, are being given away to the centre in Brussels. We had echoes of that in the speech of the noble Lord, Lord Jenkins. I find it very difficult to understand that two arguments are being run alongside and

---

[1] General election, 9 April 1992: Conservatives 336, Labour 271, Liberal Democrats 20, others 24.
[2] Lady Chalker.
[3] On 2 June 1992, Danish voters rejected the Maastricht Treaty by 50.7 per cent in a referendum (turnout 82.3 per cent). Following the negotiation of special Danish 'opt-outs', a second referendum on 18 May 1993 approved the Treaty by 56.7 per cent (turnout 86.2 per cent).

they are mutually exclusive. There is far too much centralization going on; far too much bureaucracy going on which we do not like; but nevertheless we are going to ratify the Maastricht Treaty. To me, these things do not add up.

There is also among people a good, healthy understanding that bigger is not always better and that variety is more desirable than conformity. The Danish 'No' to Maastricht is just one sign of those things. A recent opinion poll shows that seven out of ten Germans do not want a single currency, and that seven out of ten do not want either to surrender significant powers in order to have a common foreign policy.

People understand that Maastricht is more, much more, than just a technical adjustment to the Treaty of Rome. The people of Denmark saw that when they received their copies – free copies, I would stress – of the Maastricht text. One figure illustrates better than anything else the scale of the extra intrusion into the authority of national Parliaments and Governments and into people's lives, which Maastricht would bring about.

The Treaty of Rome provides for the Commission to have the sole right of initiative in eleven areas of policy. In Maastricht that reaches twenty, to which one has to add at least five other areas of co-operation where the Commission is fully involved – that is to say, monetary, judicial and immigration matters as well as foreign policy and defence. No wonder people feel that they have a right to be consulted about such a major change in the way in which they are governed, especially in the light of M. Delors' notorious statement to the European Parliament that 80 per cent of the decisions taken on economic and social matters will soon be taken by the European Community rather than by national Governments and Parliaments.

It is being alleged that no less substantial powers were conceded to the Community in the Single European Act. I hope that your Lordships will not accept that assertion, but will look at the debates in another place in 1986 about the Single European Act. I hope that noble Lords will look in particular at the assurances given at the that time by the then Foreign Secretary, now my noble friend Lord Howe, and by my noble friend the Minister of State who opened the debate.[1]

---

[1] There were in fact two debates. Lynda Chalker opened the Debate on the European Community on 5 March 1986 (House of Commons Debates, 6th Series, Vol. 93, col. 335–41). Sir Geoffrey Howe spoke during the Second Reading of the European Communities (Amendment) Bill on 23 April 1986 (House of Commons Debates, 6th Series, Vol. 96, col. 316–26).

Qualified majority voting is of course in the Treaty of Rome itself. My noble friend, the then Foreign Secretary, made clear that in the Single European Act qualified majority replaced unanimity only for the measures which were major components of the construction of the Common Market. He said explicitly that their scope was not indefinite. He pointed out that:

> some subjects were of such importance to the national policies of individual member states that they should remain subject to unanimity voting – namely, tax measures, measures relating to the free movement of individuals and measures affecting the rights and interests of employed persons.

He recognized that there would be some people who would be anxious that, in extending qualified majority voting to promote the achievement of an internal market, we might diminish the essential protection of our national interest. He concluded: 'I would not accept that.'

He gave his reasons for doing so.

The suggestion that there is any comparison between the powers transferred to the Community in the Single European Act and in the Maastricht Treaty is misplaced.

Bearing in mind the burning and urgent problems of the moment, one also has to ask: What is the relevance of the Maastricht Treaty to these? What, for example, does it do for fragile democracy in Eastern and Central Europe? It makes it more difficult for those countries to join. Last week the European Council refused even to open negotiations with the much more advanced EFTA countries. The attitude is that we have to form our own tight little huddle before we can even contemplate admitting others.

What does Maastricht do to help lift Europe out of recession? It shackles and burdens our economies with the extra restrictions and intrusive regulations imposed by the Social Charter. We found out last week that the Commission is still trying to do that despite our having opted out of that chapter of the Maastricht Treaty, thanks to the Prime Minister.[1] Unfortunately, the Commission has not yet had its action challenged in the European Court. The Government have indicated

[1] In Luxemburg on 24 June 1992, EC Social Affairs Ministers accepted in principle a Commission proposal to introduce a maximum working week of forty-eight hours throughout the EC, despite strong British opposition.

that they may do so and I hope that they will. We shall then know where we stand on this matter.

The reason for all this is that Maastricht does not tackle today's problems. There has been a hint of that in the other speeches. The world has changed dramatically in the past two years. The Community must adapt to that or it will lose its purpose and lose support. The result of the Danish referendum is an opportunity to think again, but there is regrettably little sign from last week's European Council that the Community as a whole is ready to do that.

Certainly, it will take more than a self-denying ordinance on the part of the Commission, or a promise to give back some of the powers which it has arrogated. Its record of evading the unanimity provisions of the Single European Act deprives it of the good faith that we should otherwise have accorded it.

I am very glad that the Foreign Secretary has said (my noble friend has repeated it today) that Denmark cannot be coerced and cannot be excluded. If that were to happen the Community would be breaking its own laws, which state with absolute clarity that Maastricht has to be ratified by all twelve member states if it is to come into force. If we allow that to be overridden in Denmark's case, each and every one of us will become vulnerable to being coerced or excluded on some other issue or on some other occasion in the future.

We are an association of free peoples, free to take a democratic vote. Denmark has exercised that freedom. Is it now to be suggested that she did something wrong, or somehow she must change her mind? After all, fortunately our Prime Minister exercised our right to be different and not to be governed by the Social Charter, and not to be governed automatically by a single currency, although we agreed the idea. We have done it. We are perhaps the oldest democracy and the freest. It is not for us to criticize others. If ever it is suggested that the people of any member state cannot say 'No' without an attempt at duress, that is a very serious matter for the Community, and one would need to revise one's views about whether it is a community now of free peoples.

Searching for a definition of subsidiarity[1] is not a satisfactory way

---

[1] Subsidiarity is the principle that decisions should be taken at as low a level as possible. Article 3b of the Maastricht Treaty stated that the EC would act 'only if and insofar as the objectives of the proposed action cannot be sufficiently achieved by the member states'. It is the EC Commission which makes the necessary judgement.

forward either, if only because it is based on the notion that it is the Community which has the power which it then parcels out to the member states. The true situation should be the reverse. It should be the member states which exercise all powers, except those which are specifically and legally granted to the Commission.

My own immediate, albeit limited, suggestion at this stage is that the Government should propose a formal and binding restatement of the Luxemburg Compromise.[1] It is not a lot, but it is a little. Your Lordships will recall that this provides that if any member state considers that its vital national interest is at stake, then no vote will be taken. It can be postponed until agreement is reached between all parties. I believe that that would go some way to restore people's confidence in the Community – and, hard as it will be to get agreement, I hope that the Government will consider it, because technically the Luxemburg Compromise is still there. In practice, there is some doubt as to whether and how effectively it can be used.

I make one further plea before concluding this particular section of my speech: the plea that the Maastricht Treaty be not discussed in terms of personalities – it is too important for that – but in terms of the issues involved. The Government have a most difficult and complex task on their hands with this whole issue during the British Presidency. I am sure that they will acquit themselves with distinction in dealing with it and uphold the freedoms of our respective peoples.

I shall deal with the other issues that will affect our Presidency more briefly. My noble friend has already dealt with enlargement. As urgent for the President as the Maastricht agreement is the issue of enlargement of the Community. And it is depressing that, despite our Government's best efforts in Lisbon, other member states have refused to embark on the necessary formal negotiations.[2] I sometimes wonder whether other Governments fully comprehend the scale and the consequences of the bloodless victory over communism in Eastern Europe and the Soviet Union. In the space of two years, it has become a different world – not

---

[1] The Luxemburg Compromise is the informal arrangement within the EC Council of Ministers whereby a member state can claim the right to veto a decision if its 'very important interests' are at stake. The Compromise, which has no legal status, stems from a statement by France when ending a six-month boycott of the Council in Luxemburg in 1966.

[2] The European Council held at Lisbon on 26 and 27 June 1992 decided to postpone enlargement negotiations until after ratification of the Maastricht Treaty and agreement on the 'Delors II' package to increase EC spending.

the end of history, as some foretold, but the return of history. First Yalta was swept away – and a very good thing too. Now Versailles is following it, which some of us do not find surprising.[1]

The real urgency now is to stretch out a hand to the countries of Eastern and Central Europe. We were not able to free them from communist tyranny. When they escaped, it was by their own efforts. Now we have a pressing moral obligation to sustain democracy and free economies – just as we did in earlier times for Greece and Spain and Portugal – by bringing these East European countries into the Community as soon as possible, even though it would require a very long transition period. This is not just in their interests, but also in ours.

We do not want the Community to be in the position of Dr Johnson. Your Lordships will recall his reply to Lord Chesterfield's[2] congratulations after he had completed his dictionary in the cold and poverty of his garret. He said: 'Is not a patron, my Lord, one who looks with unconcern on a man struggling for life in the water, and when he has reached ground encumbers him with help?'

I recognize that we have association agreements with East European countries, but that is not enough for the assurance that they need. The widening of Europe to include the post-communist countries is, I believe, of much more importance than the early admission of other countries. If the European Community does not respond more rapidly to the needs of Eastern Europe, the problem will still arrive on our doorstep, because many peoples from those countries will join the Community even if their Governments cannot. They will vote with their feet and arrive in even larger numbers. I hope that the Government, undaunted by last week's setback in Lisbon on enlargement, will return to the charge.

There are many other pressing issues for the Presidency, but I shall touch on them only very briefly. On finance, there is still plenty of room under the present own resources ceiling to do the things which are most urgent. We heard at Question Time that all the money is apparently

---

[1] 'Yalta' refers to the 1945 Yalta Conference and is shorthand for the division of Europe into a free West and an unfree communist-controlled East. 'Versailles' refers to the post-First World War Treaty of Versailles in 1919 and is shorthand for the diplomatic 'solutions' then devised to Europe's national problems, leading to the creation of the new states of Czechoslovakia and Yugoslavia.

[2] Philip Stanhope (1694–1773), 4th Earl of Chesterfield 1726. Whig MP 1715–23; HM Ambassador to the Netherlands 1728–32; Lord Lieutenant of Ireland 1745–46; Secretary of State for the Northern Department 1746–48. Johnson made his remarks in a letter of 7 February 1755.

not being well used and could be put to better use. I commend the Government for their robust refusal to contemplate additional funds for the Community. There will no doubt be attempts to reopen the issue of the British rebate. I had some great budget battles in my day. The noble Lord, Lord Jenkins of Hillhead, was there and witnessed some of them, and understood the point that I was trying to make. I always found that the most effective weapon was: 'No' – or sometimes, 'No, no, no.' I am glad that this continues to be the policy, even if it is more sweetly expressed.

Britain, with the Commission, was the main driving force behind the launch of the Single Market, and I pay particular tribute, joining my noble friend, to the work which my noble friend Lord Cockfield[1] did to bring about free trade within Europe – one of the original objectives of the old EEC. I hope that we shall use our Presidency for a final drive towards its completion. This is especially important, as my noble friend says, for our service industries. They are one of our particular strengths, yet their opportunities have been greatly constrained by protectionism in other member states, often masquerading under the false flag of restrictions required for regulatory purposes. The remaining obstacles should be removed quickly, and no new bureaucracies created. Indeed, in a sensible world, we would never have gone ahead with a new treaty at all until the Single Market had been first completed and was in operation.

At long last the Community is realizing that statements, declarations and even sanctions are not a strong enough response to the terrible slaughter in what was part of Yugoslavia[2] – not in some remote country, but little more than a two-hour flight from London, and in the heart of Europe. Some of us have been warning for a time that the use of force might become necessary. I am sure that one of the first actions of our Presidency will be to help organize sustained relief supplies for Sarajevo and for other places where people have been brutally attacked and their cities devastated. If attempts are made to interfere with those supplies, I believe that we should be ready to use the air power available to NATO in the area to deal with them. After all, we gave the Kurds air

---

[1] Francis Cockfield (born 1916), Baron Cockfield of Dover 1978. Trade Secretary 1982–83; Chancellor of the Duchy of Lancaster 1983–84; Vice-President of the EC Commission 1985–88.
[2] War broke out in Bosnia-Herzegovina after its declaration of independence on 3 March 1992.

power, and there is no reason why we should not have given it earlier to some of those people in Yugoslavia.

It is sad that once again the lead had to come from America, in particular from James Baker,[1] rather than from the European Community, although we applaud President Mitterrand for his visit to Sarajevo[2] which raised the morale of those suffering people. The fact is that with a common foreign policy we would be dependent on the lowest common denominator among the Twelve – and we all saw what that meant in the Gulf War. Tyrants are not defeated by the action of the United Nations – it does the Resolutions – not by the action of the Community; tyrants are defeated by the lead of nation states which have sufficient defence to go and to do the necessary task.

I agree with my noble friend about the importance of the GATT negotiations. I recall very well that at the last European Council, which I attended as Prime Minister just over two years ago, despite all my efforts my fellow Heads of Government refused even to discuss the negotiations, even though the deadline for the Uruguay Round was only three months away. It has, in fact, been extended twice, and the matter is still not resolved. In the meantime, we have in fact perhaps lost a very great deal of trade which would have helped us during the recession had we come to agreements earlier.

This debate about the Presidency coincides with one of the great constitutional issues of our time. In such matters your Lordships' advice carries very great weight, and I am sure that we shall come back to the Maastricht Treaty, and I hope that we shall debate its implications in full after the Recess.

It will be obvious to your Lordships by this time that I have never knowingly made an uncontroversial speech in my life. Nevertheless, I hope to be more controversial when we get down to discussing the details. I believe that my right honourable friend the Prime Minister can have a very great influence on the whole future of the Community. I have made my view clear on the Maastricht Treaty. For the reasons that I have indicated, I do not believe that the situation will be resolved during our Presidency. I think that noble Lords know how I would vote.

---

[1] Speaking before the US Senate Foreign Relations Committee on 23 June 1992, Secretary of State James Baker suggested that US forces might be sent to Bosnia to get relief supplies into the besieged city of Sarajevo.
[2] President Mitterrand of France made an unexpected six-hour visit to Sarajevo on 28 June 1992. He met President Izetbegovic of Bosnia and Radovan Karadzic, leader of the Bosnian Serb Democratic Party.

But there are so many other things which are more immediate, and which I am certain that our Prime Minister is the best person to address. I am sure that he will do that with effectiveness and distinction. I wish him well during Britain's Presidency.

53

Speech to the CNN World Economic Development Congress, Washington D.C., 19 September 1992

As the first lines of Lady Thatcher's speech to a CNN Conference in Washington on Saturday 19 September 1992 noted, she could hardly have been speaking on international finance at a more appropriate moment. For the previous Wednesday, after a huge and costly commitment of reserves and after real interest rates reached 8.4 per cent (with 11.4 per cent in prospect), sterling was finally withdrawn from the European Exchange Rate Mechanism. Lady Thatcher's earlier warnings and criticisms were grudgingly but almost universally now accepted as having been correct. By a nice irony, the Chancellor of the Exchequer, Norman Lamont, who was in Washington for the International Monetary Fund Conference, was staying elsewhere in the British Embassy as Lady Thatcher and her advisers worked through the night on her speech.

The CNN speech firmly resisted any temptation to indulge in 'I told you so.' Instead, it sought to draw out of the crisis the important lessons for the future. The general conclusion was that the pursuit of 'stability' through pegged exchange rates had been tested to destruction and must be abandoned. More particularly, there should be no going back into the ERM and no truck with a European single currency. And the whole Maastricht project, with its enormous inherent tensions and rigidities, should be discarded.

May I begin by warmly congratulating whoever decided to schedule an Economic and Financial Conference at the end of this past week. It showed foresight of an almost astrological order – maybe some country should ask him to be its Finance Minister! It also forced us to rewrite our speeches – well, some more than others!

What we have lived through this past week has been a lesson in practical economics. As my favourite poet wrote:

Let us admit it frankly,
As a business people should,
We have had no end of a lesson,
It will do us no end of good.[1]

It has been, in particular, a lesson to Governments. The role of Government in trade and commerce, as in much else, is to create a framework of stability within which enterprise can flourish. But the rigid stability of fixed exchange rates threatened to stifle enterprise and obstruct commerce. It required heavy burdens to be placed on companies, including efficient companies. It made imports artificially cheap and exports artificially expensive. It starved firms of capital. It was bad for business. And it meant that home-owners watched anxiously as the cost of their investment rose inexorably.

Yet the stability which fixed rates offered was a false one. It prevented currencies from adjusting gradually to market realities, and in the end it produced wild swings of instability. There's nothing new about fixed exchange rates collapsing. What might be new is to finally learn the lesson that fixed rates don't – and can't – work in free markets.

So I congratulate John Major and Norman Lamont for taking off this economic straitjacket and letting the pound find a level at which it can be sustained without imposing intolerable burdens and disrupting economic life.

Not all political leaders have shown such realism. In 1931 a Labour Government lost power through trying to stick to an overvalued rate of exchange. When the incoming National Government went off gold and floated the pound, a member of the previous Labour Cabinet said plaintively, 'They never told us we could do that!'

That Minister would have been extremely popular with the European Commission. Just imagine the things they wouldn't have told him he could do!

Once that lesson is learned, however, it cannot be unlearned. If a Government could alter its exchange rate in 1931, it could do so again in 1949, in 1967, in 1971 when Bretton Woods itself foundered, this week, or whenever its currency comes under strong market pressures. No system of fixed rates will ever again have the prestige of the pre-1914 gold standard. Nor will there ever again be a general acceptance by the voters and by politicians of the harsh deflationary medicine that its

[1] Rudyard Kipling, 'The Lesson' (1899–1902).

prestige made possible. We all know – currency markets above all – that Government cannot achieve stability by *fiat* in the face of the speed and volume of capital movements in today's world. We now need to rediscover, or re-invent, a framework of stability that encourages growth, enterprise and trade rather than strangling them.

The Eighties

That framework of stability is especially needed today, because the 1980s unleashed a burst of creative enterprise and capitalist endeavour unequalled in this century.

If I may be permitted a personal note, in the last decade Ronald Reagan and I found ourselves pioneering the same great causes in economic, social and foreign affairs.

We started a revolution almost without realizing it. And our policies led to a freer society, one of the longest periods of economic growth with stable prices, and the victory of freedom over communism.

Our first task was to restore economic vitality. We both had to confront dispirited peoples and stagnant economies, marked by low growth and high inflation.

We set about creating a framework favourable to enterprise. In Britain that meant cutting penal rates of income tax, cutting the tax on companies, and abolishing some taxes altogether.

It meant cutting back trade union privileges that had multiplied strikes and restrictive practices, put up industrial costs and increased unemployment.

As a result, productivity in Britain rose faster than in Japan, and by the mid-eighties our rate of growth outpaced that of our European competitors.

I need hardly remind this audience of the success of Reaganomics in America – or perhaps I *do* need to remind you. For in the United States, a myth of the eighties as a decade of individual greed and national bankruptcy seems to have been widely disseminated and accepted. The actual record – increased economic well-being for all classes at the cost of a manageable increase in national indebtedness – is now regularly dismissed as the 'illusions' of the Reagan years.

We are asked to treat the millions of jobs, houses, cars, consumer goods, new companies, personal computers, VCRs, original technologies, modern industries and greatly increased charitable giving as 'transient phantoms', while regarding an increase in the federal deficit as the only solid economic reality.

Mr Chairman, I am reminded of a remark by George Orwell:[1] 'You have to be an intellectual to believe such nonsense. No ordinary man could be such a fool.'

Our second step was to secure sound money and the reduction of inflation. We had learned at Milton Friedman's knee that inflation is a monetary phenomenon; that it can only be controlled and reduced by a gradual squeezing of the money supply; and that a successful cure for inflation will inevitably be accompanied by a temporary rise in unemployment.

To cut inflation, therefore, required some courage as well as the right principles. But we succeeded. Inflation, in Britain, fell from over 20 per cent to less than 4 per cent by mid-1983. And all this outside the ERM.

Thanks to President Reagan and Paul Volcker[2] there was a similar achievement here.

Indeed, in my last four years of office, we had a budget surplus and were able to reduce debt – thus lightening the burden on our children and grandchildren.

Thirdly, I faced a problem which Ronald Reagan did not. Long years of socialism in Britain had created two complementary phenomena: sluggish, inefficient, subsidized state-owned industries, and a people with little prospect of accumulating capital.

We solved both problems with the same policy. We privatized state industries – steel and airlines, for example, which once absorbed billions in subsidies, began paying taxes rather than swallowing them – and we did so in ways that spread shares as widely as possible among workers and small investors.

Mr Chairman, we created millions of new shareholders, new home-owners, new entrepreneurs. The impact of this was not just economic. It brought about a profound change in the attitudes – social, political, even spiritual – of our people. They became more self-reliant, more responsible, more independent, more forward-looking. They have a stake in the future. And they are more resistant to the tenets of socialism.

That is why our Labour Party, like the socialists of Eastern Europe, are hastily abandoning or at least concealing their socialist principles.

---

[1] George Orwell (Eric Arthur Blair, 1903–50), English novelist and essayist, author of *Animal Farm* (1945) and *1984* (1949).

[2] Paul Volcker, Chairman of the Federal Reserve 1979–87.

543

Socialism has a very limited appeal to a capital-owning democracy. Americans have long known that. But in the 1980s America ceased to be exceptional in its deafness to the siren call of socialism. We are all anti-socialists now – even the Swedes![1]

But not even this audience, Mr Chairman, is likely to appreciate the sheer scale of global privatization. Some $400 billion of major sales have either taken place or are in progress. The total number of employees transferred from the state to the private sector is about equal to the population of a medium-sized European country.

The rate of privatization, moreover, is speeding up. It is now sweeping through Latin America and Central Europe and, at long last, even the former Soviet Union.

Indeed, in Eastern Europe communist elites that treated state property as their own and political power as their birthright were forced to surrender these to the mass of people. In international affairs, the revival of Western economies and the defence build-up launched by President Reagan forced the Soviet Union to abandon its aggressive military posture and to embark on internal reforms.

By the end of the 1980s, the former communist countries had become democracies, but were still struggling to transform themselves into market economies.

Even China is pursuing a vigorous enterprise policy. For practical purposes the world economy is almost entirely capitalist.

But this achievement is marred by serious recession; by the slowness of GATT negotiations on world trade; and by the instability induced by artificial constraints hindering trade and commerce – an instability all too vividly encapsulated in this week's events.

An Unusual Recession

The recession into which we have drifted is, therefore, quite different in origin and nature from those of the seventies and early eighties.

It was not imposed on us by external forces like the two OPEC oil-price shocks of the seventies and early eighties.

It was not a necessary side-effect of long-overdue economic reforms

---

[1] The Social Democratic Party, which governed Sweden almost without interruption from 1932 to 1976 and again from 1982, lost the general election of 15 September 1991. A centre-right coalition took office under Carl Bildt of the Moderate Party.

to restrain inflation and revive enterprise, such as President Reagan and I pushed though a decade ago.

It is not weeding out only inefficient, overmanned and subsidized companies. Our trade union and supply-side reforms had already brought about a fundamental economic restructuring in the mid-eighties. This recession is attacking healthy and profitable companies – generally those of small or medium size. And it is doing so savagely. Personal bankruptcy and company liquidations in Britain are running at levels significantly higher than those of earlier recessions.

For all these reasons, the psychology of this downturn is different.

When I was navigating my way through the 1982 recession, I found people understood that certain fundamental changes were necessary and in fact overdue – that there had to be an economic restructuring, and the transformation of industry to fit it for the information age. People will endure hardships if they understand the reason for them and if they can see that the changes will make life better for the future.

But they find the same hardships intolerable when they have done all the right things – when companies have invested in new technology, when home-owners have taken out mortgages at interest rates which seemed reasonable at the time, when workers on the factory floor have co-operated in better working practices, and when they still find themselves out of work, bankrupt or facing repossession.

And when the recession seems not only inexplicable, but is also prolonged beyond the time they had been led to expect, they tend to lose hope and confidence in the future.

What Went Wrong?

What went wrong? The achievements of the 1980s were based on a marriage of two principles: stability in financial policy, and the encouragement of enterprise. Both were essential.

No one can subsist on a diet of change and competition alone. We would all suffer a nervous breakdown without some stability in our lives. A successful policy of enterprise requires, above all, the financial and monetary stability we enjoyed in the eighties.

That stability disappeared in the late 1980s. The 1987 stock market crash convinced Western Governments that a sharp increase in the money supply was needed to avert a slump of thirties dimensions. But the crash was merely a market correction of overvalued stocks. The money thus fed directly into high inflation.

Meanwhile, in Britain, attempts to shadow the Deutschmark attracted funds into the country and expanded the money supply further.

Inflation duly occurred. Among its effects were rises in asset and property prices, large-scale borrowing on inflated assets, and what the British columnist William Rees-Mogg[1] called 'the financing of nonsense'.

Nonsense cannot be sustained. In due course, Governments had to prick this inflationary bubble with monetary restraints and high interest rates. When they did so, property prices fell, over-indebted businesses went broke, home-owners received larger mortgage bills, and the euphoric expectation that asset values would go on rising for ever evaporated.

Recession followed inflation.

Fixed exchange rates – now embodied in the ERM – were having a damaging secondary effect. They acted as a transfer mechanism transmitting the problems of one country to its partners in the system.

Germany's reunification had been purchased with a vast injection of money into East Germany financed by borrowing. That duly threatened inflation throughout the country. To prevent this, the Bundesbank raised interest rates, and through the perverse alchemy of the ERM, Germany's anti-inflationary pressure was transformed into deflation throughout the rest of Europe.

Nations like Britain have found themselves raising interest rates in a recession – real interest rates in Britain this week rose to over 10 per cent. But, in the end, reality was bound to burst through these barriers – and this week Britain resumed control of its own economic destiny.

In effect, the conservative revolution went wrong by forgetting some of its own principles. By making a well-intentioned attempt (that owed more to Keynes than to either Friedman or Hayek[2] to stimulate demand, conservative Governments blundered into monetary instability. By attempting to rig the markets, they perpetuated their error.

---

[1] William Rees-Mogg (born 1928), Baron Rees-Mogg of Hinton Blewitt 1988. Editor of *The Times* 1967–81; Chairman of the Arts Council 1982–89; Chairman of the Broadcasting Standards Council 1988–93.

[2] Friedrich A. Hayek (1899–1992), Austrian-born British economist and political philosopher. Professor of Economic Science at London 1931–50; Professor of Social and Moral Science at Chicago 1950–62. His works include *The Road to Serfdom* (1944) and *The Constitution of Liberty* (1960).

And the monetary instability they reaped then undermined the successful enterprise on which their other economic and social achievements were based.

A New Beginning

Yet if I may coin a phrase, Mr Chairman, we have nothing to fear but fear itself.[1] What we have seen this week is not the destruction of European unity and international co-operation, but the inevitable collapse of rigid economic structures that could not accommodate change and diversity, did not reflect popular wishes, and inflicted unnecessary recessions. As the rise in the London share market demonstrated, we in Britain have been liberated. We are now free to pursue an economic policy that will reduce interest rates to stimulate recovery as the Fed[2] has done here.

More vital, we in the West as a whole are free to devise looser, more flexible but more durable arrangements for European and international co-operation: flexible exchange rates; free trade under a revived GATT, incorporating all the countries of the Pacific Rim; a Europe of nation-states encompassing the new democracies of Central Europe; a more active assistance to Russia by the IMF and the G7 countries; and continuing US leadership of a NATO prepared to uphold international law in and out of area, and strengthened by moves towards transatlantic free trade. We have it in our power today to establish a framework of stability for the world economy so that world enterprise can flourish.

Freeing Money

May I now deal in more detail with the last few days of turbulence, the effective devaluation of the pound sterling and the future of the EMS exchange rate mechanism?

It was not the collapse of the British Government's policy, but the policy itself, which was the problem. It may be embarrassing to go back on a pledge to defend a particular exchange rate come hell or high water. But if the pledge was misguided in the first place, the act of

[1] A quotation from Franklin D. Roosevelt's Inaugural Address of 4 March 1933.
[2] The Federal Reserve, central bank of the United States.

547

breaking it should provoke a round of applause, not condemnation.

There is no point in the opposition parties in Britain or indeed most of the Government's other critics saying 'I told you so.' Not least because they said nothing of the sort.

Indeed, they constantly urged the Prime Minister and Chancellor to embrace monetary union even more rigidly and with greater doctrinaire commitment to the idea of European integration.

And if this was somehow meant to persuade the French to vote 'Yes' to Maastricht, it was hardly worth it, even on those grounds. If you were a Frenchman voting on your country's future,[1] you would hardly be flattered to know that the Germans thought you were worth precisely a quarter of a per cent off the Lombard rate.[2]

Nor would I myself search for scapegoats – either inside or outside Britain. What we do have to do is to learn the lessons of what has happened. The first and general lesson is that if you try to buck the market, the market will buck you. The state is not there to gamble with the nation's savings. Consequently, intervention in the exchange markets should be embarked upon with the greatest caution and within clearly understood limits.

The second lesson is that the ERM in its present form, and with its present purpose, is a grave obstacle to economic progress. I do not myself believe that sterling should re-enter it, and I have yet to be convinced that other currencies benefit from its combination of rigidity and fragility.

I agreed to sterling entering the ERM because I felt that it, like a gold standard, would give some great credibility to our financial policy. But I was clear that I would have been prepared to alter the parity rather than pour out reserves on the one hand or – if we reached the top of the band – irresponsibly loosen monetary policy on the other. I would not have had sterling enter the narrow band,[3] and I would not have gone any further towards a single currency.

Of course, if you are trying to prove to the world – and perhaps

---

[1] The French referendum on the Maastricht Treaty was to be held the following day.
[2] The Deutsche Bundesbank reduced its Lombard rate (one of the bank's two official interest rates) from 9.75 per cent to 9.5 per cent on 14 September 1992. Given that the depreciation of the pound, lira and peseta was threatening to wreck the ERM and undermine the credibility of the Maastricht timetable for monetary union, there was widespread disappointment at the small size of the cut in German interest rates.
[3] The narrow band of the ERM permitted currency fluctuations of +/− 2.25 per cent. The pound entered the ERM in the broad band of +/− 6 per cent fluctuation.

yourself – that you can move forward from the wide band of the ERM towards the single currency, you are forced to pursue a quite different policy. You have to go on defending the currency whatever happens – or at least until your reserves and other countries' patience runs out. And as we have seen, you fail even at that.

The real question now is whether it is either possible or desirable to get back to that limited degree of exchange rate co-ordination and management in Europe which was the original intention of the ERM. My own view is that it is not.

It might in theory be possible to have an ERM which is regarded as something more like a gold standard than a halfway stage to a single European currency. But I doubt it. Old habits die hard. The federalists will use it to keep pushing towards a single currency. It will tempt politicians and bankers again to treat the exchange rate as a virility symbol. And if a simple standard of value is required, what is wrong with the existing Deutschmark protected by an independent Bundesbank without Euro-interference? That is what the Germans want – and I can well see why.

Since countries differ in their level of economic development and potential, their fiscal policies and their rates of inflation, the most flexible and realistic method of economic adjustment is a system of floating exchange rates. Each country can then order its monetary policy to suit its domestic conditions – and then there is no need for any ministerial shouting across the exchanges.

The fundamentals of economic policy can then become again – as they were through the eighties – a domestic monetary policy with the long-term aim of keeping down inflation; firm control on Government spending and borrowing; and a system of tax and regulation which encourages rather than inhibits business.

Limited government, small government, honest government: these are themes not just for reforming the post-communist states, but for getting our own economies back on track.

Après *Maastricht*

The third lesson concerns the Maastricht Treaty, aimed at creating a 'European Union'. Even before the unnerving events of the last few days, I believe that sentiment in Europe and particularly in Britain was moving against ratification.

It was already difficult for people to harbour affection for Maastricht.

Indeed, the Government itself considered our exemption from EMU and the Social Chapter to be its main negotiating success – and yet urged the French to endorse the Treaty without those same exemptions. People were also indignant that the French were allowed a referendum while we were denied one.

It is high time to make as complete a reversal of policy on Maastricht as has been done on the ERM. And of course the connection is very close, economically and politically.

If the divergence between different European economies is so great that even the ERM cannot contain them, how would those economies react to a single European currency? The answer is that there would be chaos and resentment of the sort which would make the difficulties of recent days pale by comparison.

Huge sums would have to be transferred from richer to poorer countries and regions to allow them to take the strain. Even then unemployment and mass migration across now open frontiers would follow. And a fully-fledged single currency would allow no escape hatch.

The political consequences can already be glimpsed: the growth of extremist parties, battening on fears about mass immigration and unemployment, offering a real – if thoroughly unwelcome – alternative to the Euro-centrist political establishment.

If in addition you were to create a supra-national European federation, and the people could no longer hold their national Parliaments to account, extremism could only grow further.

It is time for the European politicians to sit up and take note. Time to stop their endless rounds of summits – summitry is fast becoming a substitute for decision-making – and observe the reality around them.

There is a growing sense of remoteness, an alienation of people from their institutions of government and their political leaders. There is a fear that the European train will thunder forward, laden with its customary cargo of gravy, towards a destination neither wished for nor understood by electorates. But the train can be stopped.

Tomorrow, the French people will vote on the future of Europe.[1] It is not for me to instruct them on French interest. But I must stress that the referendum is not a vote on whether we should have a European Community – but on what kind of European Community it should be.

Whatever the result, France will continue to build Europe, because

---

[1] The French referendum of 20 September 1992 approved the Maastricht Treaty by 51.04 per cent (turnout 69.7 per cent).

Europe cannot be built without France. But is it to be a *Europe des Bureaux?* Or a *Europe des Patries?* The Europe of Delors? Or the Europe of de Gaulle?[1] If I were a Frenchwoman, I would rally to the General's standard and cry: *'Vive l'Europe Libre!'*

Nationhood and Europe's Future

What kind of Europe should that be? *Any* policy or programme which fails to recognize the power of national loyalties is doomed to ultimate failure.

The larger Europe grows, the more diverse must be the forms of co-operation it requires. We should aim at a multi-track Europe in which groups of different states forge varying levels of co-operation and integration on a case-by-case basis. Such a structure would lack graph-paper neatness. But it would accommodate the variety of post-communist Europe.

Instead of a centralized bureaucracy laying down identical regulations, national Governments should offer different mixes of taxes and regulations, competing with each other for foreign investments, top management and high earners. Such a market would impose a fiscal discipline on Governments because they would not want to drive away expertise and business. It would also help to establish which fiscal and regulatory policies produced the best overall economic results.

And that Europe must not only be diverse internally, it must be outward-looking in trade and foreign policy. It will be no real gain if greater trade within Europe is bought at the cost of less trade between Europe and the rest of the world.

Still more serious, however, are the political risks. And these are barely grasped.

Eastern Approaches

We in Britain wish to enlarge Community membership to include the new East European democracies. That would help to bring greater prosperity and much-needed stability to a region which has twice this

[1] Charles de Gaulle (1890–1970), French soldier and statesman. Leader of the Free French 1940–44; Head of the Provisional Government 1944–46; President of the Fifth Republic 1958–69. De Gaulle strongly opposed the growth of supranationalism in the EEC.

century generated conflicts drawing both our countries into world wars, and which today suffers from both political and economic troubles.

Communism may have been vanquished, but communists themselves have not. From the powerful positions they retain in the bureaucracy, security apparatus and the armed forces, from their places in not-really-privatized enterprises, they are able to obstruct, undermine and plunder.

The systems of proportional representation in these countries have allowed such tactics to succeed, leading to weak Governments and a bewildering multiplicity of parties. All this risks bringing democracy into discredit.

But we can help by allowing them free access to our markets. I would like to welcome President Bush's far-sighted proposal in his Detroit speech to extend free trade to Central Europe.[1] I see it as perhaps the first step towards the goal of transatlantic free trade, to which I shall return. But in any event it is a typically American combination of generosity and far-sighted self-interest.

I am also delighted that association agreements have been signed between the EC and several of these countries. But ten years is too long to wait before restrictions of trade are removed. I would like to see these countries offered full membership of the Community as rapidly as possible.

If the EC does not respond rapidly to the needs of Eastern Europe, the problem will still arrive on our doorstep, because the people of Eastern Europe will join the Community even if their Governments cannot. They will vote with their feet and arrive in vast numbers.

Trading and GATT

Our final challenge is to prevent the world slipping back into protection, and instead to give a new momentum to freer trade.

We must ensure that the Uruguay Round is completed – and soon. But other moves towards free trade should be encouraged.

Free trade is the truest form of international co-operation, daily enabling people in different continents to contribute to the manufacture and distribution of goods as varied as a computer or a matchbox. It

[1] In his speech to the Economic Club of Detroit on 10 September 1992, President Bush set the goal of free trade agreements with Poland, Hungary and Czechoslovakia, as well as with Latin American and Pacific countries.

enables nation-states, large and small, to form a complex economic network, co-operating in their mutual interest, without the need for any centralized bureaucracy to direct the process or level the playing field.

Indeed, in conditions of free trade, the size and extent of government need not be dictated by economies of scale; they can be built instead on democratic efficiencies of closeness to the people. With free trade, you can have both large-scale economic and small-scale political decentralization.

I welcome the creation of a US–Canada free trade area and its extension to Mexico. These reforms should strengthen the economies of your two neighbours and hold down the cost of living for Americans.

It is vital, however, that these should not be steps towards a world of three protectionist blocs built around the US, the European Community and Japan. There are those in Europe who regard the prospect of two such blocs, engaging in managed trade with a new European superstate, with apparent equanimity and even enthusiasm.

I am not among them. Nor, I believe, should anyone who has at heart the interest of America or the West as a whole. For it would undermine the sense of Western solidarity under American leadership which is the only sure foundation of any new world order built to last.

So these new blocs must be steps not towards protectionism, but towards a world of freer trade. When the Uruguay Round has been successfully completed, therefore, we must take the next step towards wider economic integration.

We must begin to lay the foundations of an Atlantic Economic Community, embracing Europe (namely the European Economic Community, EFTA and the new democratic states of Eastern Europe) on the one hand and North America on the other.

This proposal has all the merits which are attached to any extension of free trade – greater economic efficiency, leading to greater wealth, benefiting all those taking part. But it has two other important advantages as well.

Given the liberal economic tradition of the US, Britain and several European Community countries, and given the fierce commitment to free market economics of the former communist states, such a bloc would be imbued with the philosophy of free trade.

And because it would account for no less than 58 per cent of world GNP, other trading blocs and potential trading blocs would have to follow its lead in such matters. It would give the GATT real clout – halting and reversing the drift towards a world of protectionist blocs.

The second advantage is that, by moving in this direction, it would strengthen the vital ties of defence and culture which link America and Europe, and which the drift to protectionism and trade wars threatens to undermine.

It would, in effect, be the economic underpinning of NATO – and make a great deal more sense than the various schemes for giving a defence identity to the European Community.

For, as the Gulf War showed, when the chips are down, American leadership and American military technology are essential to decisive military intervention. A common European defence and foreign policy is both a recipe for paralysis and an excuse for others to avoid action.

Most threats however to both the West's strategic interests and to world order are nowadays likely to occur out of NATO's area. NATO's Constitution needs to be revised to take that into account.

But the American people – and who can blame them? – will not be the policemen of the world alone. This has to be a collective task, with the burdens, both financial and military, fairly shared and agreed in advance.

Conclusion

Mr Chairman, to some people these last few days may have seemed like a nightmare. But that is a wrong perception. The trauma and the turbulence have brought home to Governments the limits of their ability to shape the world on lines of political convenience. That is profoundly healthy.

This was the week when the British and other economies broke free of largely self-imposed constraints. And, as a result, new possibilities have opened up – not just to end our recessions, but for more enduring and productive international co-operation.

The histrionics of this time will soon be forgotten. The benefits will be increasingly appreciated. Dire warnings of what will happen when the economic straitjacket is removed will quickly prove false. The patient may perhaps wave his arms around a bit at first. He may even make a noise. But his odd behaviour reflects the torture of the straitjacket, not an inherent disordered condition. And the long-concealed truth quickly dawns that this patient was perfectly sane all the time.

Mr Chairman, let us never again forget that the market has its own spontaneous order, on which the most effective economic co-operation will always be based. Free trade, flexible exchange rates, domestic policies to encourage enterprise, and sound money – these amount to an open international system of co-operation that can accommodate both the dynamic capitalist economies of the Far East and the new democracies of Eastern Europe struggling towards a market order. And on that foundation let us go forward to overcome the remaining obstacles to our prosperity and progress, bringing a better, stabler, freer future within our grasp.

54

Speech to the Boyden Forum, Frankfurt, 25 November 1992

Lady Thatcher's November 1992 speech to a predominantly business audience in Frankfurt develops many of the themes of the earlier Hague and CNN speeches, and gives these a strongly German focus. The speech argues that Germany would be better off, as would its neighbours, if it reconciled itself to being a rich, powerful, successful but essentially 'normal' European power. So the Germans should keep their own currency, managed by their own central bank, and not abandon the Deutschmark in favour of a single European currency; they should openly pursue their own foreign policy interests, rather than pretend to subordinate them within Europe; in short, they should embrace the liberal politics and economics in which the Frankfurt liberals of the nineteenth century believed.

It is a great privilege to address this distinguished audience. It is you who, within a framework of law favourable to enterprise, create the wealth of nations. That wealth not only enhances material standards of living but raises the quality of life, enriching the arts, music, literature and the environment. Germany has a cardinal place in such matters.

It is fitting that we should be meeting in the historic city of Frankfurt, once the capital of the Holy Roman Empire, and the birthplace of Goethe. It was also the town where, in 1848, Germany saw the contest between the liberal and the authoritarian philosophies that did so much to shape her modern history. It was in St Paul's Church, after the revolutions of that year, that liberals debated Germany's future; alas, their words were stronger than their actions. And as the Irish poet Yeats observed in another connection: 'the centre cannot hold ... the best lack all conviction, while the worst are full of passionate intensity.'[1]

How often history has reflected those words. Incidentally, I am

[1] 'The Second Coming' by William Butler Yeats (1865–1939), Irish poet.

delighted to see Professor Lothar Gall[1] among you tonight: his outstanding biography of Bismarck has been a key document which illuminates that bygone era.

Perhaps I should not have said 'bygone', for the contest between the liberal and the authoritarian views is ever-present. Modern Germany has been a splendid exponent of liberal values. The *Ordoliberalen*, who were responsible for the German recovery, inherited the mantle of that liberal tradition of 1848. Their concept of the state was moral, not mechanical. Freedom was established under the rule of law. Honest money in the form of a hard currency put an end to the nightmares of inflation which Germany had known so well. She became a nation built on sound money and the energy of trade.

In his recent Ludwig Erhard Memorial Lecture on economic and monetary union, Dr Hans Tietmeyer[2] pointed out that in the mid-1950s, 'no other country called so strongly for comprehensive liberalization as did Germany'. He also reminded us that Ludwig Erhard's[3] goal of free trade 'was never restricted to Europe. He always saw matters from a global perspective.' Erhard's vision should be just as applicable to the Europe of the 1990s as it was in the 1950s.

I greatly admire the liberalism that is enshrined in the post-war Constitution. It was this which led Germany to be extremely generous in granting refuge to the victims of the killing-fields in Bosnia.[4] Frau Inge Trautluft, in Zagreb, who has organized much of this, has been one of the saints of our time; and the journalists of the *Frankfurter Allgemeine Zeitung*, in particular, have been brave and outspoken on the side of right. Germany has generously taken on a burden which most other European countries have refused.

But how much better it would have been if the West had not only given humanitarian aid, but had struck at this problem's very root by preventing the terrible atrocities which have occurred. Alas, we tried to act on the basis of consensus and, as so often happens, consensus led to paralysis, when effective leadership was needed.

---

[1] Lothar Gall (born 1936), German historian. Professor of Recent History at Frankfurt 1975–. His *Bismarck: The White Revolutionary* appeared in English translation in 1986.
[2] Hans Tietmeyer (born 1931), German banker and civil servant. President of the Deutsche Bundesbank 1993–.
[3] Ludwig Erhard (1897–1977), German economist and politician. Economics Minister 1949–63; Chancellor of the Federal Republic 1963–66.
[4] Germany accepted some 200,000 Croat and Muslim refugees from the former Yugoslavia in 1992.

The contrast with the Gulf War is all too apparent, for then we had the United States willing to take the lead, and the aggressor was stopped. In the new world order Europe must have the courage to show conviction. As the poet Grillparzer[1] said of the old Habsburg Monarchy:

> This is the curse of our old house,
> half-way means and half-way steps
> warily treading to half-way aims.

Tonight I shall deal first with the economic aspects of the challenge ahead, and then go more deeply into the political problems, in the context of both history and the present. We all understand that this is a time for deep reflection about the future of your country, of mine, and indeed of Europe.

The Monetary Challenge of the Late Twentieth Century

Since the discovery of money in the ancient Near East about 850 B.C., the management of the currency has been one of the most difficult tasks facing mankind. The problems and the debates sometimes appear to be entirely theoretical in character, but they always have important practical consequences. I want to talk today about perhaps the greatest ever challenge in currency management.

For most of recorded history man chose a *commodity* to serve as his money, a precious metal, such as gold. The choice of precious metals has been ridiculed as primitive and superstitious, even – in one of John Maynard Keynes's famous phrases – as 'barbarous'. But the gold standard had one overwhelming virtue which must never be forgotten.

The quantity of gold was limited to the stock of the metal inherited from the past and the small annual increases in that stock due to mining. Apart from the chance discovery of rich new sources, these increases were only a tiny fraction of the existing stock. This was of immense benefit to mankind. When gold was the only kind of money, and when later paper money had to be converted into gold at a fixed rate, the slowness of the increase in the quantity of money prevented inflation. While gold was the basis of nations' currencies, no currency suffered from high and systematic inflation over a prolonged period.

---

[1] Franz Grillparzer (1791–1872), Austrian poet and dramatist.

Britain was the traditional defender of the gold standard, but it abandoned this role in 1931. Nevertheless, gold remained the bedrock of the Bretton Woods system of fixed exchange rates in the 1950s and 1960s, with the American Government pledged to maintain the fixed gold price of $35 an ounce. Since 1971, when President Nixon[1] suspended the dollar's convertibility into gold, no major currency has been pegged to a precious metal. Inflation is no longer checked, as it had been for all those centuries, by keeping the value of a currency stable in terms of gold. We have to find new ways of providing a sound currency which is both stable in value and widely acceptable in payment.

That is the monetary challenge of the late twentieth century. Man has to develop a stable currency based exclusively on paper ·and his intelligence, rather than on a precious metal and his superstitions. Keynes saw this new problem in his short 1923 book, *A Tract on Monetary Reform*. He said: 'And – most important of all – in the modern world of paper currency and bank credit there is no escape from a "managed" currency, whether we wish it or not.'

The Achievement of the Bundesbank: A Role-Model for Other Central Banks

The task of management falls on Governments and central banks, with the relative importance of the Government's and central bank's role varying from country to country. In Germany you have decided that the stability of the currency should be entrusted mainly to an independent central bank, the Bundesbank. In Britain we decided after the Second World War that our central bank, the Bank of England, should have a subordinate position in monetary policy, taking its instructions from the Government of the day. There is an active and lively debate in our country on whether that was a good decision.

Here, may I pay you a tribute? From the twenty years of experience since the Americans broke the link with gold, it is clear that the Bundesbank – more than any other central bank in the world – has understood how a *fiat* currency system can be made to work. You realized early on that the best way to maintain the *value* of money was to keep the *quantity* of money under tight control. You were right to introduce money supply

---

[1] Richard M. Nixon (1913–1994), US politician. Vice-President of the United States 1953–61; 37th President of the United States 1969–74 (Republican).

targets in late 1974, and you have been right to continue to base interest rate decisions primarily on domestic monetary trends since then. The Bundesbank has gone further than any other central bank in meeting the monetary challenge of the last part of the twentieth century.

I should perhaps add that usually it has been free from political interference, and its actions have not been undermined by a lax fiscal policy.

External Versus Domestic Objectives in Monetary Policy

Compared with Germany, you may wonder why Britain has had a poor record of monetary management in the last forty years. There are many possible answers. One is that the German people are frightened of inflation, because they have suffered from two catastrophic hyper-inflations in the twentieth century, and are therefore willing to accept the disciplines of sound monetary control.

But I wonder whether that identifies the root of the explanation for the contrasting inflation performances of our two countries. We British have shown over the last twenty years that we are prepared to undergo severe recessions in order to combat inflation, far more severe recessions than those seen in Germany in the same period. Instead, I think that much of the answer reflects the beliefs of influential economists, both in British universities and Whitehall.

The standard British economist's answer to the inflation problem is to fix the exchange rate and to impose an incomes policy, because – as far as he is concerned – a falling exchange rate and rapid wage increases are responsible for inflation. The standard German economist's answer is to recommend a reduction in monetary growth.

Perhaps I am simplifying. But I think that I am being fair – I have had to listen to far too many economists in the last fifteen years! Fortunately, I had Alan Walters as my advisor, who took the monetary view, as did the famous Liverpool six.[1] But there were 364 economists on the other side!

---

[1] The Liverpool six were members of the Economics Department of Liverpool University, headed by Patrick Minford, who advocated monetarism from the late 1970s.

European Economic and Monetary Union

Britain has not been alone in failing to find an adequate response to the monetary challenge of the late twentieth century. Most European currencies have been devalued against the Deutschmark at some point or other in the last twenty years, and every European country has suffered from a measure of continuous inflation. The question arises: 'Why have the Governments of Europe been so inadequate in their efforts to control inflation?' Is the explanation to be sought in a lack of political will, or in widely shared weaknesses of analysis and interpretation?

Large Countries

It should not be controversial that the only viable approach for a large country, an economic superpower, is for monetary policy to focus on the quantity of money, by a deliberate policy of money supply targets. The United States of America is clearly in this position. The American Federal Reserve cannot sensibly let the dollar's exchange rate against any other country dominate the behaviour of its own interest rates, because the American economy is more than twice the size of the world's second-largest, namely Japan. Similarly, Japan has such a large economy that it must – to a large degree – be autonomous in monetary policy.

Small Countries

At the other extreme are some small countries, where the share of traded goods in economic activity may be remarkably high, and cross-border capital flows can dwarf domestic savings. They have sometimes chosen to fix the value of their currencies to that of a larger country because the level of economic activity depends on that of their larger neighbours.

Medium-Sized Countries

But where does that leave medium-sized countries like Germany, France, Britain and Italy? In particular, what is the appropriate monetary regime for the four significant European nations, which – in a world context – are all only medium-sized countries? There is no obvious criterion for choosing between a domestic focus for monetary policy and an external focus.

In practice, the nations of Europe have met this challenge by associating themselves, to a greater or lesser degree, with the monetary policies of Germany, with the consequences we now know.

At the time Britain joined the ERM in 1990, it was not a rigid system. Recent events since then have confirmed the view that Britain would do best to organize its monetary policies with its own domestic economic situation as its central concern, just as the Bundesbank does.

An even more dangerous response to our monetary problems is to try to overcome the dilemmas created by our medium-sized status by forging a larger monetary area, by concocting an ambitious scheme for European economic and monetary union in which we adopt the same currency. I think that the most generous interpretation of this enterprise is that it is intended to ensure that all European nations play their fair share in international monetary matters.

Specifically, the thinking may be that, when the dollar is weak, the obligation to intervene in its defence should be shared between the central banks of Germany, France, Britain and Italy, and even some of the smaller countries. This was, after all, the original motive for creating the ERM in 1978, when Mr Helmut Schmidt[1] thought that Germany was having to do too much intervention to help the dollar.

One theme in the case for EMU[2] today is undoubtedly that Europe would have a currency which in global importance may match, or even exceed, the dollar. My view is that these technical arguments about desirable patterns of foreign exchange intervention are minor compared with the wider consequences of EMU.

---

[1] Helmut Schmidt (born 1918), German politician. Defence Minister 1969–72; Finance Minister 1972–74; Chancellor of the Federal Republic 1974–82.
[2] Since 1989, Economic and Monetary Union (EMU) has signified the three-stage process leading to a single European currency (as set out in the Maastricht Treaty).

EMU would involve massive upheaval, not just in our monetary affairs but in our economic and political institutions.

As Karl Blessing[1] pointed out as early as 1963, after the first proposal for monetary union:

> The final goal of the Commission is a European Monetary Union ... As a European, I would be ready to approve of European Monetary Union and to accept a centrally directed federal banking system; as a responsible central banking practitioner, and realist, I cannot however avoid pointing out the difficulties which stand in the way. A common currency and a federal central banking system are only feasible if, apart from a common trade policy, there is also a common finance and budget policy, a common economic policy, a common social and wage policy – a common policy all round. In brief, this would only happen if there was a [European] Federal State with a European Parliament with a legislative power in respect of all member countries.

Got it in one!

Europe: Where Next? The Political Choice

This point brings us face to face with the political choices between the two different visions of Europe.

First, a Europe of nation states based upon the idea of co-operation between independent sovereign countries, loosely linked in a free trade area with competition between tax and regulatory systems and their own currency. Second, the federalist vision of Europe, run increasingly from Brussels, united by a common citizenship, harmonized by bureaucratic regulation, equipped with common economic, foreign and defence policies, using a single currency, and acquiring all the flags, anthems and symbols of nationhood.

It was the first vision that inspired the post-war international order and led to the formation of the United Nations, the IMF and the GATT. In such a world, multi-lateral and non-discriminatory, a small nation had nothing to fear because it was small – its independence was unimpaired.

[1] Karl Blessing (1900–71), German banker. President of the Deutsche Bundesbank 1958–69.

This kind of Europe would accommodate the countries of Eastern Europe and give them reasonable stability. It would maintain and not jeopardize our relations with our great friend and defender the United States. But some people object to this vision: they equate nationhood to nationalism, which they argue has been responsible for many of the world's troubles.

But the concept of nationhood is as old as the Bible itself:

'Righteousness createth a nation.' (Proverbs 14)
'Nation shall not lift up sword against nation.' (Isaiah 2)

National pride, in combination with liberty and the rule of law, powerfully strengthen democratic government. The vital ingredient of democracy – public opinion – can then come into being. People will consent to be governed and accept common sacrifices most readily when they feel themselves to be part and parcel of one another, with a shared history, similar institutions and loyalties, above all a common language and culture. This is precisely what has happened with the unification of East with West Germany.

It is true that nations can fall under the sway of a tyrant like Saddam Hussein. But, as we discovered in the Gulf War, it takes nation states to defeat the despot.

We must not confuse the nation state with whatever unstable *status quo* happens to be at hand. There were those who wanted to retain the Soviet Union as a structure, as others wanted to keep Yugoslavia. They were wrong. What we are witnessing is the collapse of communism and artificial states with no real roots and precious little freedom. The fact is, we have now seen the collapse of both the Versailles and the Yalta Treaties. We should by now have learned that national sentiment cannot be created by bureaucratic *fiat*.

The conventional objection to this approach is that it creates a multitude of economically inefficient small states. But free trade under the GATT creates its own economic network, regardless of the size of the nation. Taiwan, a nation of twenty million, is a bigger creditor nation than China – or for that matter the United States. With free trade you can have *both* large-scale economic efficiency *and* small-scale political decentralization. People then enjoy the stability of their own nationhood, the benefits of free trade and local and international co-operation.

It is only socialism that requires government to be large, remote and bureaucratic to contain people and companies over a wide area.

This argument leads me to address the second vision, that of a European Union with rights of citizenship, a single currency, monetary and economic policy, a common defence and foreign policy, and an enlarged bureaucracy.

As I have already pointed out – and events this week have once again demonstrated[1] – fixed exchange rates between countries with vastly different economies just won't work; and the suggestion that they could, especially in today's circumstances, has led to deeper recession than we need have suffered and to turmoil in the markets.

At least under the ERM there is an escape hatch, which would not be the case with a single currency. In my view, the Bundesbank cannot and should not be blamed for carrying out its statutory duty of protecting the value of the Deutschmark. But as the ERM transmits your high interest rates to other countries when their need is for a low interest rate, the answer has to be to realign or to leave the system. And there should be nothing unusual or shameful about that. There is no substitute for each nation taking responsibility for running its own economic and financial and fiscal affairs.

Naturally your own people wish to keep the Deutschmark, and so would I in their position.

During the debate on the matter in the Bundestag, all parties agreed on the necessity of another vote before Germany decides whether or not to join EMU.[2] I think that is sensible and right; but with respect, that's not what the Treaty of Maastricht says. The UK has a protocol to that effect before the third stage of EMU, but Germany did not request one. The UK also has a protocol against the Social Charter.

Why do some people contend that every new European initiative requires the participation of all members of the Community? It will sometimes be the case – especially after enlargement – that only some Community members will want to move forward to another stage of integration. For an enlarged Community can only function if we build in flexibility of that kind.

Within a common market, we should aim at a multi-track Europe in which *ad hoc* groups of different states, such as the Schengen Group already, forge varying levels of co-operation and integration, on a case-

---

[1] Intense speculation forced Spain and Portugal to devalue their currencies within the ERM on 22 November 1992.
[2] On 8 October 1992 the Bundestag approved ratification of the Maastricht Treaty, on condition that it be given the final say over the replacement of the Deutschmark by a single European currency.

by-case basis. We should not try to pour different countries into the same mould. The test should be: will it work? And do the peoples of those countries want it? That way you avoid the strains and fractures that will otherwise occur.

The fact is that the people of many European countries are unhappy about the Maastricht Treaty. Scepticism is on the increase. People feel that their Governments have gone ahead too fast – and they are not sure about the direction, either. The trouble is that European Ministers spend so much time in each other's company, they get out of touch with the people and too much in touch with themselves. People do not want to become citizens of a European superstate. Denmark exercised her freedom to say 'No.' And let no one try to bully her out of it.[1] The veto is at the root of the Rome Treaty. Each nation, large or small, must have equal rights in this respect.

It is argued that the undefinable word 'subsidiarity' will prevent the centre from becoming stronger. On the contrary, that thought is based on the notion that the Community has the power, which it then parcels out to member states. The true situation should be the reverse.

Maastricht is much more than just a technical adjustment to the Treaty of Rome. That provides for the Commission to have sole right of initiative in eleven areas of policy. In Maastricht that reaches twenty, to which have to be added five other areas of co-operation where the Commission is fully involved – monetary, judicial and immigration matters, as well as foreign policy and defence. This alternative model is spawning bureaucracy at the expense of democracy.

Further, most federal states have experienced a steady trend towards centralization, as central Governments have a natural appetite for more expenditure and therefore more taxation. The Commission is already demanding more resources, and yet more again, for 'cohesion'. Germany is the largest contributor, but has enough to cope with at present without being called upon for more. The UK is second-largest. This year £2.6 billion net (DM 6.25 billion) will go to the EC; that exceeds the amount we give to the developing world. And already both we and Germany are having to borrow more than we think wise.

---

[1] But 'bully her' the Europeans did. See footnote 3, p. 531.

Which Europe?

In deciding between the two visions of Europe it is not a question of whether we are 'European' or not, but of what kind of a Europe we wish to build.

We are all bound – and will remain bound – by the Treaty of Rome and by the Single European Act, which does not fully take effect until next year. No member nation can be excluded from these two Acts.

But in considering the future, and especially the Maastricht Treaty, we must learn from past experience and take into account the vastly changed circumstances and the feelings of the people.

Would it not be better to pause and consider the matter afresh? There are so many urgent tasks requiring our immediate attention.

For you, there is still the problem of the full integration of East Germany. You know only too well the strains this has caused. We have all watched with great distress some of the extremist demonstrations in your country. We share your anxieties, and I know that you are profoundly aware of the importance of defending Germany's liberal culture.

But we must look further afield too. In Central Europe, memories of the rule of law, Parliamentary institutions and private property were still just alive in 1989. They have returned now – and with some vigour – in countries such as Poland, Hungary and in the Czech Republic.

But in Russia, where since 1917 communism, the most total tyranny of all, has been enforced, recollection of these traditions was virtually dead. And although the communist system has collapsed, there are still communists around who can frustrate political freedom and the emergence of an enterprise economy.

Yet there is something astonishing about Russia. If her talent and resources were harnessed she would be one of the richest nations in the world. She has the second-largest oil reserves, and is the largest exporter of natural gas – of which you are a big consumer; and there is hardly a raw material, rare or abundantly encountered, that she does not produce.

When, before 1914, the rule of law extended across Tsarist Russia, her economy flourished. In the old days, we maybe accepted the Stalinist lies that old Russia had been backward. Not so. When she had a gold standard in place, with a legal system and a growth of private property, she did astonishingly well. In fact, she had the highest growth rates in the world, and if you go to some of the old cities – Kiev, St Petersburg

– you can still see quite easily that these were European cities of energy and promise. That excellent German historian, Professor Heinz Dietrich Loewe,[1] even tells us that the Russian peasants had more calories in their diet in 1900 than the West German population of 1952!

It was a German Chancellor, Bethmann Hollweg,[2] who said in 1914: 'Russia grows and grows, and weighs upon us like a nightmare.'

In Bethmann Hollweg's time this caused panic in Central Europe, and an alliance against Russia. Now our problem is quite different: it is how to bring Russia back to the concert of European nations that communism forced her to abandon. The task is enormous. Yes, she has gained political liberty thanks to President Gorbachev's reforms and President Yeltsin's[3] courage. But the fruits of economic liberty are far harder to win, and it can only be achieved with international co-operation.

In Germany, at the heart of Europe, you understand this more than others. East Germany, plugged into the whole economic structure of liberty – central bank, single currency, rule of law, private property, available financial resources. Nevertheless she is encountering very real human and practical difficulties in making the transition. But in East Germany, whatever the faults of the one-to-one exchange between your own and the old communist currency, you have not had to face hyperinflation along with everything else. That is the danger in Russia now and in other countries of the former Soviet empire. I feel that we should all be doing far more than we have done to help untangle the financial chaos there.

If Russia does not succeed economically and politically, then future generations may apportion quite a lot of the blame to us. Should we not therefore be more generous in our help? And may I say at once that Germany has set an example. But let them not say we hid our heads in the Maastricht sands, and haggled with the Americans over rapeseed oil, while Russia burned.

---

[1] Heinz Dietrich Loewe (born 1944), German historian. Lecturer in Russian History at Oxford 1990–92; Professor of Eastern European History at Heidelberg 1992–.
[2] Theobald von Bethmann Hollweg (1856–1921), German politician. Imperial Chancellor 1909–17.
[3] Boris Yeltsin (born 1931), Russian politician. Secretary of the Central Committee of the Communist Party 1985–86; First Secretary of the Moscow City Party 1985–87; President of the Russian Federation 1991–.

Conclusion

Ladies and gentlemen, Germany is the greatest economic power in Europe, and will for the foreseeable future remain so. Her post-war success in entrenching democracy and building prosperity is one of the wonders of our age.

I have said that a multi-track Europe, in which Germany finds herself on one track and Britain on another, holds no worries for me – nor should it for you. But, that said, Germany is in a special way the heart of Europe – culturally, geographically, and now, more than ever, economically. It is, therefore, vital to Europe that Germany's approach to Europe's future development is sound – and not just for your people, but for mine.

There is always a danger that countries come to forget the sources of their security and strength. We did so in the 1960s and 1970s in Britain – and then had to retrace once more the path back to liberal economics from which we had strayed. It is vital that you in Germany do not make the same mistake. Complacency, corporatism and consensus – these three perpetual temptations to all successful, civilized countries – are always waiting to do their worst: and they must be resisted.

This is even more important at a time when extremists are challenging our institutions. For there is no more favourable climate for extremism than one in which the respectable established political parties become remote from the worries of ordinary people.

The main threat to Germany's, Britain's and Europe's well-being is a failure to remember the foundations of past success – compounded by a failure to look outwards to the new world emerging beyond our shores and frontiers.

The nineteenth-century liberals who met in Frankfurt were unsuccessful. Until 1945 Germany chose under different regimes to adopt various formulae of cartels, state intervention and protectionism. But since then the principles of the liberal economy and the limited state have brought Germany to a pinnacle of prosperity and influence. Germany sets the tone in Europe, even more than she sets the monetary disciplines. I would like to hear the arguments for free enterprise and open trade put still more vigorously – and then carried through – by Europe's most powerful participant.

I would also like to see Germany and Britain ensure that truly global thinking replaces the narrow Europeanism which plagues the European Community. The Community has to realize that the world is changing fast. Economic power is passing to the Far East: it is crucial that we combine, not to keep their products out, but to bring our ideas in, ensuring that freedom and democracy march side by side with economic liberty and growing wealth. And let us not have any doubt that Russia will remain a great power. It is in our interests, as well as being our moral duty, that she looks to our European countries as a source of help and ideas.

Nor are these matters of global policy to be left to learned professors or smooth-talking diplomats. Global issues are now national issues.

If we lose sight of the arguments for global free trade, excluding the products of the poorer ex-Communist countries, desperate for access to our markets, then those streams of immigrants will, legally or illegally, pour across our borders, fuelling a racist reaction.

If we fail to export democracy along with our goods, then armed dictators may come to power and pose new threats to our security.

If we indulge in the fantastic nonsense of seeking to create a European superstate, competing with the United States, we will have only ourselves to blame if our countries have to raise taxes to pay for stronger armaments necessitated by American withdrawal from the defence of Europe and from the leadership of NATO.

That flame of liberal democracy which flickered in Frankfurt all those years ago has since lit up Germany and the rest of Europe too. Of course, the enemies of freedom remain – Nazis chanting hatred on the streets, crypto-communists slipping quietly back into power. The totalitarian tendency is always with us. But it is only a tendency. The bracing creed of liberty is the more potent. In memory of the Frankfurt liberals – and in memory of all those other Germans who lost their lives in the prison camps and torture chambers devised with equal, devilish ingenuity by left and right – let us resolve to mark the coming millennium with freedom's triumph in every corner of our earth.

55

The Keith Joseph Memorial Lecture, London, 11 January 1996

Widely (and accurately) billed as Lady Thatcher's first major speech on domestic political issues since leaving office, her Keith Joseph Memorial Lecture in January 1996 was also much more than that. It restated the principles which she and Joseph had placed at the centre of Conservatism some twenty years earlier and applied them to contemporary politics. Lady Thatcher argued that the fundamental political issue was still the limitation of the powers and scope of government.

Although it was her criticism of the Conservative Government's management of the public finances since 1990 that received most (and disproportionate) media attention, Lady Thatcher's analysis led her to conclude that the return of a Labour Government must be resisted, as must pressures for greater integration within the European Union. Both of these – the Labour Party because it is interventionist by instinct, the new class of Euro-politicians because they are interventionist by interest – would reverse the economically and morally beneficial trend towards small government. In the Keith Joseph Memorial Lecture Lady Thatcher offered the Conservative Party a principled and positive right-wing platform on which to fight the next general election.

LIBERTY AND LIMITED GOVERNMENT

Keith Joseph

Keith Joseph,[1] in whose honour this lecture is delivered, had the charm of a hundred paradoxes. He was a modest man; but, unlike so many modest men, he had really nothing to be modest about. He was (that

---

[1] Sir Keith – later Lord – Joseph (1918–94); his first Cabinet post was as Housing Minister under Harold Macmillan in 1962; in the Thatcher Cabinet he was Industry Secretary 1979–81 and Education Secretary 1981–86.

overworked, but in this case appropriate word) 'brilliant'; yet he never indulged in intellectual virtuosity. He was brave; yet by nature he was timid. He could seem cerebral and remote; but he had a warm heart and impish humour that made his friendship an inexpressible delight.

Keith was also unusual in that, even when quite old and frail, he seemed somehow to remain young. The secret of this youthful spirit was the opposite to that of Faust. For in Keith's case it was the fruit of innocence. Not the innocence of inexperience, let alone of insensitivity. This was the innocence of the pure of heart – of those who have wrestled with the evils of humanity, while remaining unspotted by the world.

Keith's goodness was shown by the little kindnesses which marked his dealings with both political friends and opponents – he had no enemies. But Keith was more than good; he was also great. And his greatness lay in his integrity.

Integrity is an old-fashioned word. There are even some who will tell you it is an old-fashioned thing. But, for a politician, integrity is everything. It is not just a matter of avoiding bribes and inducements. In our remarkably financially honest British politics, it is not even mainly about that – whatever learned judges may say about the matter.[1] In politics, integrity really lies in the conviction that it's only on the basis of truth that power should be won – or indeed can be worth winning. It lies in an unswerving belief that you have to be *right*.

It was not that Keith wore a hairshirt from preference. He was averse to any kind of suffering, especially other people's – and applying the right remedies to the British disease was bound to require suffering.

But Keith's integrity was absolute. When he became convinced – finally convinced, after the endless discussions which were a mark of his open-minded, open-hearted style – that a proposition was correct, he felt he had to defend it. He had to fight for it. When he faced those raging, spitting Trotskyist crowds at our great liberal centres of learning, I suspect he wondered sometimes whether he would have to die for it.[2] But there he stood. He could do no other.

This lecture is not, however, intended as a eulogy. The purpose of

[1] The oblique reference is to the work of (Appeal Court Judge) Lord Nolan's Committee, appointed to report on standards in public life.

[2] Between 1975 and 1979, Sir Keith Joseph gave 150 speeches at universities and polytechnics to put the moral case for capitalism. He often faced violent hostility, and on six occasions was prevented from speaking at all.

recalling the turbulent times of twenty years ago when Keith Joseph and I reshaped Conservatism – with the help of a handful of others, whose dedication compensated for their fewness – is that the same qualities as Keith's are required in our Party today.

Rethinking Conservative Policy

Keith Joseph's name will always be closely associated with the rethinking of Conservative principles and policies in preparation for the Conservative Government of the 1980s.

You will recall that the Party was out of office – having lost the February 1974 election – when Keith began delivering, in the summer and autumn, a series of speeches analyzing what had gone wrong, and suggesting a change of direction. In June came the Upminster speech.[1] Keith dared to talk about what he called the 'inherent contradictions [of the] . . . mixed economy'. This, in the eyes of the Tory establishment, whose only real criticism of the socialists was that they were mixing the economy in the wrong proportions, was bad enough.

But it was the Preston speech in September – delivered almost on the eve of a second general election – which most horrified Keith's critics. In it, he dared to tell the truth about inflation: and that truth was inevitably damning for the previous Conservative Government, of which he and I had been a part.

Inflation was properly to be ascribed to the excessive growth of the money supply. And since, as Keith devastatingly observed, there was a time lag of as much as a year or two between the monetary cause and the inflationary effect, the high inflation of the summer of 1974 – 17 per cent and rising – was the responsibility of the Conservatives.

Keith also rightly noted that the root of the Conservative Government's failure to control inflation was fear of unemployment. But – as he and I would go on to argue on other occasions – unemployment was not an alternative to inflation, but one result of it. Ever higher doses of inflation were required in order to have even a short-term effect on jobs. And in the longer term inflation undermined confidence, pushed up wage costs, promoted inefficiency and aborted new employment.

For saying such things, Keith was publicly ridiculed and privately

[1] The principal speeches were delivered at Upminster on 22 June, Leith on 8 August, Preston on 5 September, and Edgbaston on 19 October 1974.

vilified. His colleagues accused him of disloyalty, splitting the Party and so on. Those whom Hayek had described as 'the socialists of all parties'[1] united to denounce him. For Keith in their eyes was demonstrating the worst possible political seamanship. He was 'rocking the boat'. But in fact it was Keith's compass that was true – and it was the boat that was already adrift and threatened by total shipwreck.

Most of the economic analysis which Keith Joseph offered has since been accepted. But Keith was not only, or even primarily, interested in economics. It was simply that in the 1970s the economics had gone so devastatingly wrong that this was where any new analysis had to focus. Indeed, that remained true to a large extent in the 1980s. Reversing Britain's economic decline was such a huge and painful undertaking that, at least until the later years, the economy had to come first.

Keith himself, though, was even more interested in social than in economic issues. He had come into politics not from personal ambition but from an idealistic urge to diminish the misery of poverty. But his one foray at this time into rethinking social policy, in the form of the Edgbaston speech, went badly wrong. In fact, though flawed in some respects, the speech, with its emphasis on remoralizing society and on strengthening the family, deserves rereading. It does not, though, reveal much about his essential philosophy, which with Keith – as with most professional politicians – remained below the surface.

The kind of Conservatism which he and I – though coming from very different backgrounds – favoured would be best described as 'liberal', in the old-fashioned sense. And I mean the liberalism of Mr Gladstone,[2] not of the latter-day collectivists. That is to say, we placed far greater confidence in individuals, families, businesses and neighbourhoods than in the state.

But the view which became an orthodoxy in the early part of this century – and a dogma by the middle of it – was that the story of human progress in the modern world was the story of increasing state power. Progressive legislation and political movements were assumed to be the ones which extended the intervention of government.

It was in revolt against this trend and the policies it bred that Hayek

---

[1] F.A. Hayek's *The Road to Serfdom* is dedicated 'To the socialists of all parties'.

[2] William Ewart Gladstone (1809–98), British statesman. Tory MP 1832–45; President of the Board of Trade 1843–45; Colonial Secretary 1846; Peelite MP 1847–59; Liberal MP 1859–95; Chancellor of the Exchequer 1852–55, 1859–66, 1873–74, 1880–82; Prime Minister 1868–74, 1880–85, 1886, 1892–94; Leader of the Liberal Party 1867–75, 1880–94.

wrote *The Road to Serfdom*, which had such a great effect upon me when I first read it – and a greater effect still, when Keith suggested that I go deeper into Hayek's other writings.

Hayek wrote:

How sharp a break – with the whole evolution of Western civilization the modern trend towards socialism means – becomes clear if we consider it not merely against the background of the nineteenth century, but in a longer historical perspective. We are rapidly abandoning not the views merely of Cobden and Bright, of Adam Smith and Hume, or even of Locke[1] and Milton, but one of the salient characteristics of Western civilization as it has grown from the foundations laid by Christianity and the Greeks and Romans. Not merely nineteenth- and eighteenth-century liberalism, but the basic individualism inherited by us from Erasmus and Montaigne, from Cicero and Tacitus, Pericles and Thucydides[2] is progressively relinquished.

So, ladies and gentlemen, against that background, it is not surprising that the left claimed all the arguments of principle, and that all that remained to the right were the arguments of accountancy – essentially, when and how socialism could be afforded. It was this fundamental weakness at the heart of Conservatism which ensured that even Conservative politicians regarded themselves as destined merely to manage a steady shift to some kind of socialist state. This was what – under Keith's tuition – we came to call the 'ratchet effect'.

But all that was not just bad politics. It was false philosophy – and counterfeit history.

Let me remind you why this is so.

---

[1] Richard Cobden (1804–65), Radical MP 1841–57, 1859–65; a leader of the Anti-Corn Law League 1838–46. John Bright (1811–89), Radical MP 1843–89; a leader of the Anti-Corn Law League 1838–46; President of the Board of Trade 1868–70; Chancellor of the Duchy of Lancaster 1873–74, 1880–82. John Locke (1632–1704), English philosopher, whose works include *An Essay Concerning Human Understanding* (1690) and *On Government* (1689).

[2] Desiderius Erasmus (1469–1536), Dutch scholar and humanist; author of *Encomium Moriae* (1509) and *Colloquia* (1519). Michel de Montaigne (1533–92), French essayist. Marcus Tullius Cicero (106–43 BC), Roman statesman, lawyer, scholar and orator. Publius (or Gaius) Cornelius Tacitus (c.55–120), Roman historian. Pericles (c.495–429 B.C.), Athenian general and statesman, who presided over the 'Golden Age' of Athens. Thucydides (c.460–400 B.C.), Athenian historian of the Peloponnesian War.

Creativity is necessarily a quality which pertains to *individuals*. Indeed, perhaps the one immutable law of anthropology is that we are all different. Now, of course, individuals can't fulfil their potential without a society in which to do so.

And to set the record straight – once again – I have never minimized the importance of society, only contested the assumption that society means the state rather than other people.[1] Conservatives do not take an extreme atomistic view of society. We need no lectures now, or at any other time, about the importance of custom, convention, tradition, belief, national institutions or what the ancient Romans would describe as 'piety'. Nor do we dispute that the bonds of society need ultimately to be guaranteed by the state. It is Marxists, not Conservatives, who imagined – or at least pretended to imagine – that the state would wither away.

No. What marks out our Conservative vision is the insight that the state – government – only *underpins* the conditions for a prosperous and fulfilling life. It does not *generate* them. Moreover, the very existence of this state, with its huge capacity for evil, is a potential threat to all the moral, cultural, social and economic benefits of freedom.

States, societies and economies, which allow the distinctive talents of individuals to flourish, themselves also flourish. Those which dwarf, crush, distort, manipulate or ignore them cannot progress.

Those eras in which a high value has been placed on the individual are the ones which have known the greatest advances. By contrast, although the great monolithic states, empires and systems can produce impressive monuments and a high level of cultural sophistication, they are not able to mobilize the initiative of their populations to ensure that each generation can expect a better life than its predecessor.

It is only Western civilization that has discovered the secret of continual progress. This is because only Western civilization has developed a culture in which individuals matter, a society in which private property is secure, and a political system in which a range of competing views and interests is accommodated. The *moral* foundation of this system – which is so spontaneous as hardly to seem a system – is the Judaeo–

---

[1] In an interview published in *Woman's Own* on 31 October 1987, Margaret Thatcher made the much-publicized statement, 'There is no such thing as society.' The critics failed to read the continuation of her remarks: 'There are individual men and women, and there are families. And no Government can do anything except through people, and people must look to themselves first. It's our duty to look after ourselves and then to look after our neighbour.'

Christian outlook. The system's *institutional* foundation is the rule of law. Expressed like this, it all sounds very abstract. But we in Britain are extraordinarily, indeed uniquely, lucky. Because, with us, these things have become second nature and a way of life. Over the centuries, the habits of freedom became ever more established in these islands. They and the institutions which came to embody them – independent courts, the common law, above all Parliament – were in a special sense democratized: that is, they came to be regarded as the birthright not of any class or group, but of the nation as a whole. In a more doctrinal form they have found their way into the Constitution of the United States.

All this meant that when Keith and I were struggling to shift Britain back from the socialist state, we were also acting as conservatives, with a small 'c'. We were seeking to re-establish an understanding of the fundamental truths which had made Western life, British life, and the life of the English-speaking peoples what they were. This was the foundation of our Conservative revolution. It remains the foundation for any successful Conservative programme of government.

And that is the first lesson which needs to be drawn from the rethinking of Conservatism, which Keith inspired and led. The principles which he restated, and which formed the basis of the policies the Conservative Government pursued while I was Prime Minister, are as true and as relevant now as they were two decades ago – or indeed, give or take a little economics, two centuries ago.

The cause of limited government – in which the state is servant not master, custodian not collaborator, umpire not player – is the one beneath whose standard Keith Joseph and I gathered all those years ago. It is time to take it out of mothballs, brush off the odd collectivist cobweb that's hung on to it, and go forth to meet the foe.

The second lesson is that avoiding debate about the large issues of government and politics leads to directionless failure. Being prepared to state uncomfortable truths, as Keith insisted in doing, is the precondition for success. It is extremely doubtful whether the Conservative Party lost support because of Keith's controversial Preston speech in September 1974. But I am quite sure that without it we would never have embraced the approach that yielded, first victory in 1979, and then a remarkable string of achievements in the years which followed. Splits and disagreements over important issues never did a Party so much harm as the absence of honest, principled debate.

There is, however, one apparent lesson that we would be most unwise to draw. That is the suggestion, which one hears from time to time, that the only hope for the Conservative Party is a period in opposition. The situation today in the Party is entirely different from that in 1974, when Keith was making his great speeches. In the present Prime Minister, the Party has a leader who shares the broad analysis that Keith Joseph and I put forward.

It is no secret that between John Major and me there have been differences . . . on occasion. But these have always been differences about how to achieve objectives, rather than what those objectives should be. What is required now is to ensure that those objectives are clearly explained, so that a re-elected Conservative Government can go further towards fulfilling them. The attractions of opposition are greatly exaggerated by those who have not experienced it.

What has Gone Wrong?

But, judging from the opinion polls, opposition is where the electorate is at present inclined to send us. For a variety of reasons, which I shall describe shortly, I believe that this would be ill-judged on their part. The Conservative Party still has much to offer. And from Mr Blair's[1] New – or not so new – Labour Party there is much to fear. But we must not ignore the present discontent.

Some of it is more or less inevitable. A constant struggle is required to ensure that long-serving Governments don't run out of steam. I always regarded it as necessary to combine my role as Prime Minister with that of Chief Stoker so as to keep up the pressure.

It is also true that the political world is more complicated than in the eighties. The sharp divide between the forces of freedom, represented by the Conservative Party and the West on the one hand, and the forces of collectivism, represented by the Labour Party and the Soviet bloc on the other, is a thing of the past. The extent of the success we achieved in the 1980s has, in this sense, caught up with us.

That may be politically inconvenient; but I for one would not change it. During most of my political life, freedom in this country was under a direct challenge from fellow-travelling socialists and an aggressive Soviet Union. These challenges were overcome because the Conservative Party in Britain and other right-of-centre parties elsewhere – under the inter-

---

[1] Tony Blair (born 1953), Labour MP 1983–; Leader of the Labour Party 1994–; Prime Minister 1997–.

national leadership of Ronald Reagan – proved too much for them.

The fashionable expression is that communism and indeed socialism 'imploded'. If that means that their system was always unviable, so be it – though many of the people who now say this scarcely seemed to believe it true before the 'implosion' occurred. But, anyway, let's not forget that the system collapsed because it was squeezed by the pressure that we on the right – I repeat, on the right – of politics applied. And the left should not be allowed to get away with pretending otherwise.

But, of course, in politics there is only gratitude for benefits yet to be received. That is why, however successful they've proved to be, Governments and Parties have to keep on re-applying their enduring principles to new circumstances.

The Conservative Party today has problems not because our analysis has been wrong or our principles faulty. Our difficulties are due to the fact that, in certain limited but important respects, our policies and performance have not lived up to our analysis and principles.

That is why the current idea, put around by some malcontents, that the Conservative Party is in trouble because it has moved to the right, and that this is what needs to be remedied, is baloney – and Denis might be able to suggest a still more telling description. The test is simple. Just ask yourself: is it because the Government has not spent, borrowed and taxed *enough* that people are discontented? Or is it that we have gone *too far* towards increasing government spending, borrowing and taxation? The answer is obvious. We are unpopular, above all, because the middle classes – and all those who aspire to join the middle classes – feel that they no longer have the incentives and opportunities they expect from a Conservative Government.

I am not sure what is meant by those who say that the Party should return to something called '*One Nation* Conservatism'.[1] As far as I can tell by their views on European federalism, such people's creed would be better described as '*No Nation* Conservatism'. And certainly anyone who believes that salvation is to be found further away from the basic Conservative principles which prevailed in the 1980s – small government, a property-owning democracy, tax cuts, deregulation and national sovereignty – is profoundly mistaken.

That mistake in most cases has its origins in the acceptance of the

---

[1] Derived from a passage in Disraeli's novel *Sybil* (1845) about the two nations of the rich and the poor, the label 'One Nation' is nowadays loosely applied to Conservatives who favour a more paternalistic and interventionist approach to economic and social policy.

picture of the 1980s which has been painted by the critics. That decade changed the direction of Britain to such an extent that it is unlikely that even a Labour Government would altogether reverse it – try as they might.

Inflation was brought down, without the use of the prices and incomes controls which the great and the good all agreed were indispensable. Public spending as a share of GDP fell, which allowed tax rates to be cut – and government borrowing was reduced. We repaid debt. 364 economists who claimed that it was madness to think you could get economic growth by cutting government borrowing were proved wrong: I'm told they were never the same again.

Reform of the public finances was matched by reform of the trade unions, deregulation and privatization of industries and a great extension of ownership of houses, shares and savings – quite a lot of 'stakeholding',[1] in fact . . .

The economic growth and the improvement of living standards which resulted from these reforms were so great that for a time materialism, rather than poverty, became the main accusation against us. 'Hunting the yuppie'[2] became the favourite sport of the neo-puritan, liverish left. But, of course, the reality was that the success which free enterprise brought over those years was not just expressed in conspicuous consumption – though what would we give for a few more of those yuppies today! It also allowed a doubling – that's over and above inflation – of voluntary giving to good causes.

Moreover, though we made mistakes of financial management by allowing the economy to overheat and inflation to rise towards the end of that period, the general advance of prosperity was solidly based upon real economic improvements. Above all, there was a rapid and sustained rise in industrial productivity, which has continued. And as a result of the control of public expenditure over those years – particularly the reining back of future commitments on pensions – Britain advances towards the next millennium with a large advantage over our European competitors as regards taxation and costs.

The message from all this is not that everything in the 1980s was perfect, or that everything that has followed it in the 1990s has been

---

[1] In a speech in Singapore on 8 January 1996, Opposition Leader Tony Blair talked about his vision of a 'stakeholding democracy' in which the citizen is regarded as an investor in society. See also below, p. 639.
[2] 'Yuppie' is an informal acronym for a young urban (or 'upwardly mobile') professional; a species of the new rich.

bad. Every Prime Minister has his – and her – regrets. The important message, rather, is that in Britain we have seen from the 1980s what works – just as we saw in the 1970s what did not. And what works here, as elsewhere, is free enterprise and *not* big government.

So it would make no economic sense at all for us to move closer to the policies of our opponents. Rather, the economic challenge is to cut back the burden of state spending, borrowing and taxation still further.

And trying to move towards the centre ground makes no political sense either. As Keith used to remind us, it is not the centre ground but the common ground – the shared instincts and traditions of the British people – on which we should pitch our tents.[1] That ground is solid – whereas the centre ground is as slippery as the spin doctors[2] who have colonized it.

The Labour Party

Ladies and gentlemen, one of Keith Joseph's most admirable characteristics – and one which secured for him respect and affection – was that he never cast doubt on the motives of his opponent. So, following in his footsteps, I am not going to cast doubt on the motives of the Leader of the Opposition.

But what about the Party he leads? The Labour Party itself may have changed many of its policies, but it hasn't changed its spots. You can tell this from the unpleasant noises it makes when anything like profits is mentioned. There is still virtually nothing that Labour spokesmen wouldn't spend more taxpayers' money on, or wish to control more tightly. They have learned to accompany these prescriptions with Conservative-sounding rhetoric, and even some Conservative-sounding policies. But the distinctive mark of every Labour policy, from health to education, from privatized utilities to the labour market, is more government interference.

All sorts of worthy people believe that Mr Blair in office would control

---

[1] Sir Keith Joseph advanced this idea in his speech to the Conservative Party Conference in October 1975, and developed it in his pamphlet 'Stranded on the Middle Ground?', published by the Centre for Policy Studies in 1976.
[2] A 'spin doctor' is a public-relations expert, attached to a political party, whose job is to channel information to the media in a way which puts the most favourable construction on events. This American expression originally related to the spin given to a baseball by a pitcher in order to deceive the batter.

his Party, and not they him. But this would be a large gamble to take.

Moreover, Mr Blair is not only human; he is also (as his record shows) by instinct a man of the left. Confronted with the sort of choices you face in government – decisions which often go unmentioned in the manifestos – it is the Prime Minister's gut instincts which count. The pressures to solve problems and assuage demands by more public spending, intervention and controls can become almost irresistible – even for an instinctive free marketeer. Mr Blair may believe with his head that government spending is not the universal panacea: but what about his heart – and, indeed, his gut?

In any case, government is not about generalities but about specifics. Only if you have the conviction – the Conservative conviction – that it is wrong to spend more taxpayers' money unless the reasons for doing so are overwhelming – and even if *then* you don't sleep easily after doing so – are you likely, as Prime Minister, to face down the pressure.

Suspicions that a Labour Government would in practice become too soft a touch on public spending are compounded by all the misty talk about boosting communities and community values. Now, communities can be sustained in two ways only – either by the state, which is what community politics, community leaders, community health, community housing, community centres and so on ultimately rely on; *or* communities can be based on genuine volunteers, sometimes local businesses, sometimes individuals with a common, freely chosen goal – like those who founded the great voluntary movements of the Victorian era which are still with us.

In some cases, to be sure, the state – often in the form of local government – can play a modestly useful part in 'community projects'. But the risk is that community comes to mean collective; collective comes to mean state; and thus the state expands to replace individual effort with subsidized activism. It is free, enterprising, self-reliant, responsible individuals that Britain needs. It's when we have more of *them*, our communities will take better care of themselves.

But I believe there is a still more important reason why Labour should not be entrusted with government. They may protest that they are no longer socialists: but they have lost none of their zeal for constitutional upheaval. The Labour Party's proposals on devolution threaten chaos, and possibly the dissolution of the Union of the United Kingdom itself. Moreover, by embracing European federalism – through the European Social Chapter and, above all, the European single currency – a Labour

Government could deal a terminal blow to the traditions of British Parliamentary democracy.

Cutting the State Down to Size

Traditionally, the socialists believed that the state must make people equal; though an honest look at the perks and privileges of the communist *nomenklatura*[1] might have set them right about that. The New-look Labour Party now apparently wants the state to make people high-minded and socially aware; though a thought for how difficult the churches find it to change people's behaviour ought to induce some doubts when mere politicians start to preach.

It seems to me that New Labour has a new song – one that was made famous by Dame Vera Lynn:[2]

> Wishing will make it so,
> Just keep on wishing, and cares will go . . .
> And if you wish long enough, wish strong enough,
> You will come to know
> Wishing will make it so.

But it won't – any more than you can make people good by legislation. So the limitation of government is *still* the great issue of British politics – and indeed to a remarkable degree of global politics. The threat to limited government did not end with the collapse of communism and the discrediting of socialism. It remains an issue in Western – particularly European – democracies.

There is a constant tendency, in which pressure groups, vested interests and the media play a part, for government to expand. One of Thatcher's laws – for which I owe something to Lord Acton – is that all government tends to expand, and socialist government expands absolutely. If you start with their view of the state – that it exists to right social wrongs rather than to create a framework for freedom – you can never find the definitive justification for saying 'no'. Above all, you cannot say 'no' to demands for more spending on welfare.

[1] In communist countries, the *nomenklatura* were those people listed by the Party for promotion and privileges.
[2] Dame Vera Lynn (born 1917), British singer, who was especially popular during the Second World War.

That is why in Sweden the share of national income the Government took reached some 70 per cent. It's why it's several points higher in Europe on average than here. The dominant political philosophies of those countries have been Socialist, or Social Democrat or Christian Democrat – all of them views which hold that the state, rather than individuals, is ultimately responsible for what happens in society.

This is in marked contrast to the United States which, even when the Democratic Party is in charge, has never been converted to the idea that government – let alone the Federal Government – has the right to intervene whenever it wants. It is also in marked contrast to those Asia Pacific countries – like Hong Kong, the Little Tigers[1] and, of course, the mighty Japan – where government's share of GDP remains very low.

Spending at just over a third of GDP in the United States, and a quarter or less in the Asia Pacific, has resulted in low taxes and high growth rates. Their example, like that of Britain in the 1980s, shows what works – just as the overspent and over-regulated Scandinavian model shows what does not.

It was with the best intent that post-war Governments spent more on welfare, believing that as the standard of living rose, people would do more to look after themselves. What we had to do, as Keith often said in earlier years, was to break the 'cycle of deprivation'.[2] But the more we spent, the greater the dependency, illegitimacy and crime became. And of course the tax burden rose.

Western countries have now woken up to the problem. But they are still paralyzed by it. Here, though, Peter Lilley has been advancing steadily with social security reform, making important changes to reduce future burdens. Yet, as Peter himself often reminds us, social security still accounts for over 40 per cent of central government spending, and costs every working person £15 every working day.

Certainly, the proposals increasingly favoured by the Labour Party for a much higher compulsory second pension[3] – paid for by much higher compulsory contributions – offer no way out. It is one thing to

---

[1] 'The Little Tigers' is a nickname for the new industrializing economies of East Asia, such as South Korea, Taiwan and Singapore.

[2] Sir Keith Joseph first spoke of the 'cycle of deprivation', in which 'the problems of one generation appear to reproduce themselves in the next', in a speech as Social Services Secretary to the Pre-School Playgroups Association in June 1972.

[3] Frank Field (born 1942), Labour MP 1979–, proposed universal compulsory savings for a second pension in his book *Making Welfare Work*, published in 1995.

encourage people to make provision for themselves, as we do with housing, health and pensions. It is also acceptable in some cases to *ensure* that people make some *minimum* contribution towards benefits, as we do through the National Insurance system. But the Labour Party's plans would involve a large increase in compulsory saving which – as you would expect from them – results in a large decrease in personal liberty.

Alleviating the burden of the social security budget is a thankless but vital task, for which real Tory stamina is required. It will not be done by financial sleight of hand.

But the possibility of a really radical approach to spending, requiring large-scale removal or transferral of government functions, must also remain on the agenda. Last November, a brilliant and provocative Centre for Policy Studies pamphlet by Patrick Minford[1] – 'Public Spending – A Twenty-Year Plan for Reform' – reminded us how far we still might go, and how great the potential gains. The spending cuts he proposes would also lead to dramatic tax cuts – with a big impact on growth.

Whether Professor Minford's proposals are deemed acceptable or not, they are extremely valuable in illustrating the possibilities.

So I welcome the determination of the Chancellor of the Exchequer to bring public spending below 40 per cent of GDP.[2] And I hope that at the next election we will be equipped with plans to bring it down over a period of years by much more.

Limited government doesn't mean weak government, only less government. This is shown by the courageous and far-reaching reforms which Michael Howard has been making in the criminal justice system.[3] The strength of the opposition he faces from the vested interests shows he is right – almost as much as do the encouraging recent crime figures.

[1] Patrick Minford (born 1943), British economist. Professor of Applied Economics at Liverpool 1976–.
[2] In his budget of 28 November 1995, Chancellor of the Exchequer Kenneth Clarke reaffirmed his aim to reduce government spending to under 40 per cent of Gross Domestic Product by 1997–98.
[3] Following the Criminal Justice and Public Order Act 1994, Home Secretary Michael Howard promised new powers to impose longer prison terms in his speech to the Conservative Party Conference on 12 October 1995.

'Our New [European] Masters'

But today the main challenge to limited government comes not from within these shores at all, but rather beyond them – from the European Union. There is, of course, also a challenge to *self*-government – and the two are closely connected.

The activity of the European Court, which can only ultimately be checked by amending the European Communities Act[1] itself, is increasingly undermining our judicial system and the sovereignty of our Parliament. Proposals are being made for common European defence – proposals which Michael Portillo[2] has roundly and rightly attacked. They too are a threat to national independence. But most important, of course, is the proposed single European currency which, as John Redwood[3] has argued, 'would be a major step on the way to a single European nation'.

The Prime Minister will have the support of all of us who wish to see these dangerous and damaging proposals resisted, and the present trends reversed, as he argues Britain's case at the forthcoming Inter-Governmental Council.[4] And we look forward to a successful outcome.

But vital as the issue of *self*-government is, it is *limited* government that concerns me today. For the European Union not only wishes to take away *our* powers; it wishes to increase its *own*. It wants to regulate our industries and labour markets, pontificate over our tastes, in short to determine our lives. The Maastricht Treaty, which established a common European citizenship and greatly expanded the remit of the European Commission, shows the outlines of the bureaucratic superstate which is envisaged. And Maastricht is the beginning, not the end of that process.

Indeed, we are increasingly seeing the emergence of a whole new international political class. Some of them are politicians who have failed

---

[1] The European Communities Act 1972 was the essential legislation for British EEC membership.

[2] Michael Portillo (born 1953), Conservative MP 1984–97; Chief Secretary to the Treasury 1992–94; Employment Secretary 1994–95; Defence Secretary 1995–97.

[3] John Redwood (born 1951), Conservative MP 1987–; Welsh Secretary 1993–95; Party Leadership challenger 1995.

[4] Inter-Governmental Councils are the means by which the European Community seeks to reach agreement on important institutional changes.

in their own countries, and so have tried their luck overseas. Some are officials who understand nothing of our British distinction between the legitimate powers of the elected and those of the unelected.

Almost fifty years ago, the Conservative journalist Colm Brogan wrote an incisive critique of the post-war Labour Government, with its arrogant bossiness and intrusive cackhandedness. He called it *Our New Masters.*[1] The title is equally appropriate to the 'new *European* masters'. And it is no surprise to me – as someone who always recognized the socialist destination of this Euro-federalist dream – that now the Labour Party welcomes it all so warmly. What they can't achieve in an independent, free enterprise Britain, they can hope to secure in a Euro-federalist Britain, whose people's instincts are ignored and whose Parliamentary institutions are overridden.

Self-government, limited government, our laws, our Parliament, our freedom: these things were not easily won. And if we Conservatives explain that they are now in peril, they will not be lightly surrendered.

In 'The Reeds of Runnymede', celebrating the signing of Magna Carta, Rudyard Kipling puts it like this:

> At Runnymede, at Runnymede,
> Oh, hear the reeds at Runnymede: –
> 'You mustn't sell, delay, deny,
> A freeman's right or liberty.
> It wakes the stubborn Englishry,
> We saw 'em roused at Runnymede!'

> ... And still when Mob or Monarch lays
> Too rude a hand on English ways,
> The whisper wakes, the shudder plays
> Across the reeds at Runnymede.
> And Thames, that knows the mood of kings,
> And crowds and priests and suchlike things,
> Rolls deep and dreadful as he brings
> Their warning down from Runnymede!

---

[1] The title of Colm Brogan's 1947 book derived from a remark by Sir Hartley Shaw-cross (born 1902), Baron Shawcross of Friston 1959, Labour MP 1945–58, Attorney-General 1945–51. In a House of Commons debate in 1946, Shawcross declared, 'We are the masters at the moment, and not only at the moment, but for a very long time to come.'

56

The John Findley Green Foundation Lecture, Delivered at Westminster College, Fulton, Missouri, 9 March 1996

Lady Thatcher used the opportunity accorded by an invitation to speak at Fulton, Missouri, fifty years on from Sir Winston Churchill's Fulton 'Iron Curtain' speech, to deliver some sobering warnings about threats to the post-Cold War world and offer some prescriptions to deal with them. Although she welcomed the overall balance of changes created by the West's victory over the old Soviet Union, she drew attention to less welcome effects which the West was still too complacent to face: in particular, the proliferation of nuclear, chemical and biological weapons and of the means to deliver them to their chosen targets, i.e. ballistic missiles, which were increasingly falling into the hands of rogue states. This was, however, she argued, just one aspect – if the one with gravest potential consequences – of a general failure of the institutions of the 'New World Order' to deliver the peace and prosperity expected of them. The specific challenge of proliferation could only be dealt with by the construction by America (with the support of its allies, co-ordinated through NATO) of a global ballistic missile defence system. The general challenge of international disorder required a rebirth of Atlanticism, that is the recreation of a united West under US leadership, with new or revivified institutions to support it.

NEW THREATS FOR OLD

When my distinguished predecessor delivered his Fulton speech, exactly fifty years ago, he journeyed hither by train in the company of the President of the United States. On the way, they played poker to pass the time. And the President won $75 – quite a sum in those non-inflationary times for an unemployed former Prime Minister. But in view of the historic impact of his speech on American opinion and subsequently on US foreign policy, Sir Winston Churchill later recorded that his loss was one of the best investments he had ever made.

I did not travel here by train; nor in the company of the President of the United States; nor did I play poker. I don't have the right kind of face for it. But there is some similarity in the circumstances of fifty years ago and today.

Mr Churchill spoke not long after the Second World War. Towards the end of that great conflict, the wartime allies had forged new international institutions for post-war co-operation. There was in those days great optimism, not least in the United States, about a world without conflict presided over benevolently by bodies like the United Nations, the IMF, the World Bank and the GATT. But the high hopes reposed in them were increasingly disappointed as Stalin lowered the Iron Curtain over Eastern Europe, made no secret of his global ambitions and became antagonist rather than ally. Churchill's speech here was the first serious warning of what was afoot, and it helped to wake up the entire West.

In due course, that speech bore rich fruit in the new institutions forged to strengthen the West against Stalin's assault.

The Marshall Plan laid the foundations for Europe's post-war economic recovery.

The Truman Doctrine made plain that America would resist communist subversion of democracy.[1]

The North Atlantic Treaty Organization mobilized America's allies for mutual defence against the Soviet steamroller.

And the European Coal and Steel Community,[2] devised to help reconcile former European enemies, evolved over time into the European Community.

Stalin had overplayed his hand. By attempting to destroy international co-operation, he succeeded in stimulating it along more realistic lines – and not just through Western 'Cold War' institutions like NATO. As the West recovered and united, growing in prosperity and confidence, so it also breathed new life into some of the first set of post-war institutions like the GATT and the IMF. Without the Russians to obstruct them,

[1] Proposing assistance for Greece and Turkey on 12 March 1947, President Truman said, 'I believe it must be the policy of the United States to support free peoples who are resisting attempted subjugation by armed minorities or by outside pressures.'
[2] The European Coal and Steel Community (ECSC) was established in 1952 by France, Italy, West Germany, Belgium, the Netherlands and Luxemburg.

these bodies helped to usher in what the Marxist historian Eric Hobsbawm[1] has ruefully christened the 'Golden Age of Capitalism'. The standard of living of ordinary people rose to levels that would have astonished our grandparents; there were regional wars, but no direct clash between the superpowers; and the economic, technological and military superiority of the West eventually reached such a peak that the communist system was forced into first reform, then surrender, and finally liquidation.

None of this, however, was pre-ordained. It happened in large part because of what Churchill said here fifty years ago. He spoke at a watershed: one set of international institutions had shown themselves to be wanting; another had yet to be born. And it was his speech, not the 'force' celebrated by Marx, which turned out to be the midwife of history.

Today we are at what could be a similar watershed. The long twilight struggle of the Cold War ended five years ago with complete victory for the West and for the subject peoples of the communist empire – and I very much include the Russian people in that description. It ended amid high hopes of a New World Order. But those hopes have been grievously disappointed. Somalia,[2] Bosnia and the rise of Islamic militancy all point to instability and conflict rather than co-operation and harmony.

The international bodies, in which our hopes were reposed anew after 1989 and 1991, have given us neither prosperity nor security. There is a pervasive anxiety about the drift of events. It remains to be seen whether this generation will respond to these threats with the imagination and courage of Sir Winston, President Truman and the wise men of those years.

The Post-Cold-War World

But, first, how did we get to our present straits?

Like the break-up of all empires, the break-up of the Soviet empire wrought enormous changes way beyond its borders.

Many of these were indisputably for the good:

---

[1] Eric Hobsbawm (born 1917), British historian. Professor of Economic and Social History at London 1970–82.

[2] US and, later, UN forces intervened in Somalia from December 1992 to March 1995 to protect famine relief from the effects of civil war, but they failed to secure peace and stability.

– a more co-operative superpower relationship between the US and Russia;

– the spread of democracy and civil society in Eastern Europe and the Baltics;

– better prospects for resolving regional conflicts like those in South Africa and the Middle East, once Soviet mischief-making had been removed;

– the discrediting of socialist economic planning by the exposure of its disastrous consequences in Russia and Eastern Europe;

– and the removal of Soviet obstruction from the United Nations and its agencies.

These were – and still are – real benefits for which we should be grateful.

But in the euphoria which accompanied the Cold War's end – just as in what Churchill's private secretary called 'the fatal hiatus' of 1944 to 1946 – we failed to notice other, less appealing, consequences of the peace.

Like a giant refrigerator that had finally broken down after years of poor maintenance, the Soviet empire in its collapse released all the ills of ethnic, social and political backwardness which it had frozen in suspended animation for so long:

– suddenly, border disputes between the successor states erupted into small wars in, for instance, Armenia and Georgia;[1]

– within these new countries the ethnic divisions aggravated by Soviet policies of Russification and forced population transfer produced violence, instability and quarrels over citizenship;

– the absence of the legal and customary foundations of a free economy led to a distorted 'robber capitalism', one dominated by the combined forces of the mafia and the old communist *nomenklatura*, with little appeal to ordinary people;

– the moral vacuum created by communism in everyday life was filled for some by a revived Orthodox Church, but for others by the rise in crime, corruption, gambling and drug addiction – all contributing to a spreading ethic of luck, a belief that economic life is a zero-sum game, and an irrational nostalgia for a totalitarian order without totalitarian methods;

---

[1] The conflicts between Armenia and Azerbaijan over Nagorno Karabakh, and between Georgia and the separatist republic of Abkhazia, escalated into wars in 1991 and 1992 respectively. Ceasefires were agreed in 1994, and peace talks and border clashes continue.

– and, in these Hobbesian conditions,[1] primitive political ideologies which have been extinct in Western Europe and America for two generations surfaced and flourished, all peddling fantasies of imperial glory to compensate for domestic squalor.

No one can forecast with confidence where this will lead. I believe that it will take long years of civic experience and patient institution-building for Russia to become a normal society. Neo-communists may well return to power in the immediate future, postponing normality; but whoever wins the forthcoming Russian elections[2] will almost certainly institute a more assertive foreign policy, one less friendly to the US.

New Threats for Old

A revival of Russian power will create new problems – just when the world is struggling to cope with problems which the Soviet collapse has itself created outside the old borders of the USSR.

When Soviet power broke down, so did the control it exercised, however fitfully and irresponsibly, over rogue states like Syria, Iraq and Gadaffi's Libya. They have in effect been released to commit whatever mischief they wish, without bothering to check with their arms supplier and bank manager. Note that Saddam Hussein's invasion of Kuwait took place after the USSR was gravely weakened and had ceased to be Iraq's protector.

The Soviet collapse has also aggravated the single most awesome threat of modern times: the proliferation of weapons of mass destruction. These weapons – and the ability to develop and deliver them – are today acquired by middle-income countries with modest populations such as Iraq, Iran, Libya and Syria – acquired sometimes from other powers like China and North Korea, but most ominously from former Soviet arsenals, or unemployed scientists, or from organized criminal rings, all via a growing international black market.

According to Stephen J. Hadley, formerly President Bush's Assistant Secretary for International Security Policy: 'By the end of the decade, we could see over twenty countries with ballistic missiles, nine with nuclear weapons, ten with biological weapons, and up to thirty with chemical weapons.'

---

[1] In *Leviathan* (1651), English philosopher Thomas Hobbes (1588–1679) described the state of nature as an anarchic struggle of each against all.
[2] Presidential elections were scheduled to be held in Russia on 16 June 1996.

According to other official US sources, all of North-East Asia, South-East Asia, much of the Pacific and most of Russia could soon be threatened by the latest North Korean missiles. Once they are available in the Middle East and North Africa, all the capitals of Europe will be within target range; and on present trends a direct threat to American shores is likely to mature early in the next century.

Add weapons of mass destruction to rogue states, and you have a highly toxic compound. As the CIA has pointed out: 'Of the nations that have or are acquiring weapons of mass destruction, many are led by megalomaniacs and strongmen of proven inhumanity or by weak, unstable or illegitimate Governments.' In some instances, the potential capabilities at the command of these unpredictable figures is either equal to – or even more destructive than – the Soviet threat to the West in the 1960s. It is that serious.

Indeed, it is even more serious than that. We in the West may have to deal with a number of possible adversaries, each with different characteristics. In some cases their mentalities differ from ours even more than did those of our old Cold War enemy. So the potential for misunderstanding is great, and we must therefore be very clear in our own minds about our strategic intentions, and just as clear in signalling these to potential aggressors.

And that is only the gravest threat. There are others.

Within the Islamic world the Soviet collapse undermined the legitimacy of radical secular regimes and gave an impetus to the rise of radical Islam. Radical Islamist movements now constitute a major revolutionary threat not only to the Saddams and Assads[1] but also to conservative Arab regimes, who are allies of the West. Indeed they challenge the very idea of a Western economic presence. Hence the random acts of violence designed to drive American companies and tourists out of the Islamic world.

In short, the world remains a very dangerous place, indeed one menaced by more unstable and complex threats than a decade ago. But because the risk of total nuclear annihilation has been removed, we in the West have lapsed into an alarming complacency about the risks that remain. We have run down our defences and relaxed our guard. And to comfort ourselves that we were doing the right thing, we have increasingly placed our trust in international institutions to safeguard our future.

---

[1] General Hafiz Assad (born 1930), Syrian politician. Secretary of the Ba'ath Party 1970–; President of Syria 1971–; Commander-in-Chief 1973–.

But international bodies have not generally performed well. Indeed, we have learned that they cannot perform well unless we refrain from utopian aims, give them practical tasks, and provide them with the means and backing to carry them out.

Institutional Failure

THE UNITED NATIONS

Perhaps the best example of utopian aims is multilateralism; this is the doctrine that international actions are most justified when they are untainted by the national interests of the countries which are called upon to carry them out. Multilateralism briefly became the doctrine of several Western powers in the early nineties, when the United Nations Security Council was no longer hamstrung by the Soviet veto. It seemed to promise a new age in which the UN would act as world policeman to settle regional conflicts.

Of course, there was always a fair amount of hypocrisy embedded in multilateralist doctrine. The Haiti intervention by US forces acting under a United Nations mandate,[1] for instance, was defended as an exercise in restoring a Haitian democracy that had never existed; but it might be better described, in the language of Clausewitz,[2] as the continuation of American immigration control by other means. But honest multilateralism without the spur of national interest has led to intervention without clear aims.

No one could criticize the humane impulse to step in and relieve the suffering created by the civil war in Somalia. But it soon became clear that the humanitarian effort could not enjoy long-term success without a return to civil order. And no internal force was available to supply this.

Hence, the intervention created a painful choice: either the UN would make Somalia into a colony and spend decades engaged in 'nation-building'; or the UN forces would eventually withdraw and Somalia revert to its prior anarchy. Since America and the UN were unwilling

---

[1] US Marines landed in Haiti on 19 September 1994 to restore President Jean-Bertrand Aristide and quell civil strife.

[2] Karl von Clausewitz (1780–1831), Prussian general and military theorist. In *On War* (1833) he wrote that 'War is . . . a continuation of political relations . . . by other means.'

to govern Somalia for thirty years, it followed that the job of feeding the hungry and helping the sick must be left to civilian aid agencies and private charities.

Conclusion: military intervention without an attainable purpose creates as many problems as it solves.

This was further demonstrated in the former Yugoslavia, where early action to arm the victims of aggression so that they could defend themselves would have been far more effective than the UN's half-hearted, multilateral intervention. A neutral peacekeeping operation, lightly armed, in an area where there was no peace to keep, served mainly to consolidate the gains from aggression. Eventually, the UN peacekeepers became hostages, used by the aggressor to deter more effective action against him.[1] All in all, a sorry episode, ended by the Croatian army, NATO airpower and American diplomacy.[2]

The combined effect of interventions in Bosnia, Somalia and, indeed, Rwanda[3] has been to shake the self-confidence of key Western powers and to tarnish the reputation of the UN. And now a dangerous trend is evident: as the Haiti case shows, the Security Council seems increasingly prepared to widen the legal basis for intervention. We are seeing, in fact, that classically dangerous combination – a growing disproportion between theoretical claims and practical means.

BALLISTIC MISSILE DEFENCE

Compare this hubris with the failure to act effectively against the proliferation of nuclear, chemical and biological weapons, and the means to deliver them. As I have already argued, these are falling into dangerous hands.

Given the intellectual climate in the West today, it is probably unrealistic to expect military intervention to remove the source of the threat, as

---

[1] The Bosnian Serbs detained 377 UN personnel as hostages against NATO air strikes between 26 May and 18 June 1995.
[2] Croatia retook the Krajina region from the Serbs in August 1995. From 30 August to 14 September, NATO subjected the Bosnian Serbs to sustained air attacks in 'Operation Deliberate Force'. A ceasefire took effect on 5 October. Peace talks opened at Dayton, Ohio, on 1 November and ended in agreement on 21 November 1995.
[3] Large-scale ethnic violence erupted in Rwanda in April 1994, leading to the deaths of over 200,000 people and the displacement of some five million. Neither a UN presence nor French intervention from June to September 1994 made much impact on the situation.

for example against North Korea – except perhaps when the offender invites us to do so by invading a small neighbouring country. Even then, as we now know, our success in destroying Saddam's nuclear and chemical weapons capability was limited.

And we cannot be sure that the efforts by inspectors of the International Atomic Energy Authority to prevent Saddam putting civil nuclear power to military uses have been any more successful; indeed, we may reasonably suspect that they have not.

What then can we do? There is no mysterious diplomatic means to disarm a state which is not willing to be disarmed. As Frederick the Great[1] mordantly observed: 'Diplomacy without arms is like music without instruments.' Arms control and non-proliferation measures have a role in restraining rogue states, but only when combined with other measures.

If America and its allies cannot deal with the problem directly by pre-emptive military means, they must at least diminish the incentive for the Saddams, the Gaddafis and others to acquire new weapons in the first place. That means the West must install effective ballistic missile defence which would protect us and our armed forces, reduce or even nullify the rogue state's arsenal, and enable us to retaliate.

So the potential contribution of ballistic missile defence to peace and stability seems to me to be very great.

– First and most obviously, it promises the possibility of protection if deterrence fails; or if there is a limited and unauthorized use of nuclear missiles.

– Second, it would also preserve the capability of the West to project its power overseas.

– Third, it would diminish the dangers of one country overturning the regional balance of power by acquiring these weapons.

– Fourth, it would strengthen our existing deterrent against a hostile nuclear superpower by preserving the West's powers of retaliation.

– And fifth, it would enhance diplomacy's power to restrain proliferation by diminishing the utility of offensive systems.

Acquiring an effective global defence against ballistic missiles is therefore a matter of the greatest importance and urgency. But the risk is that thousands of people may be killed by an attack which forethought and wise preparation might have prevented.

It is, of course, often the case in foreign affairs that statesmen are

[1] Frederick II (1712–86), King of Prussia 1740–86.

dealing with problems for which there is no ready solution. They must manage them as best they can.

THE EUROPEAN UNION AND CENTRAL EUROPE

That might be true of nuclear proliferation, but no such excuses can be made for the European Union's activities at the end of the Cold War. It faced a task so obvious and achievable as to count as an almost explicit duty laid down by history: namely, the speedy incorporation of the new Central European democracies – Poland, Hungary and what was then Czechoslovakia – within the EU's economic and political structures.

Early entry into Europe was the wish of the new democracies; it would help to stabilize them politically and smooth their transition to market economies; and it would ratify the post-Cold War settlement in Europe. Given the stormy past of that region – the inhabitants are said to produce more history than they can consume locally – everyone should have wished to see it settled economically and politically inside a stable European structure.

Why was this not done? Why was every obstacle put in the way of the new market democracies? Why were their exports subject to the kind of absurd quotas that have until now been reserved for Japan? And why is there still no room at the inn?

The answer is that the European Union was too busy contemplating its own navel. Both the Commission and a majority of member Governments were committed to an early 'deepening' of the EU (that is, centralizing more power in the EU's supranational institutions), and they felt that a 'widening' of it (that is, admitting new members) would complicate, obstruct or even prevent this process.

So, while the 'deepening' went ahead, they arranged to keep the Central Europeans out by the diplomat's favourite tactic: negotiations to admit them. In making this decision, the European Union put extravagant and abstract schemes ahead of practical necessities, in the manner of doctrinaire 'projectors' from Jonathan Swift[1] down to the present.

And with the usual disastrous results. The 'visionary' schemes of 'deepening' either have failed or are failing.

The 'fixed' exchange rates of the European Exchange Rate Mechan-

---

[1] Jonathan Swift (1667–1745), Irish satirist, political journalist and churchman, whose works include *A Tale of a Tub* (1704) and *Gulliver's Travels* (1726).

ism have made the yo-yo seem like a symbol of rigidity; they crashed in and out of it in September 1992 and have shown no signs of obeying the diktats of Brussels since then.

The next stage of monetary union agreed at Maastricht – the single currency – is due in 1999, when member states will have to achieve strict budgetary criteria. With three years to go, only Luxemburg fully meets these tests; the attempts by other countries to meet them on time have pushed up unemployment, hiked interest rates, depressed economic activity, and created civil unrest.

And for what? Across the continent businessmen and bankers increasingly question the *economic* need for a single currency at all. It is essentially a political symbol – the currency of a European state and people which don't actually exist, except perhaps in the mind of a Brussels bureaucrat.

Yet these symbols were pursued at a real political cost in Central Europe. The early enthusiasm for the West and Western institutions began to wane. Facing tariff barriers and quotas in Western Europe, the Central Europeans began to erect their own. And those politicians who had bravely pursued tough-minded policies of economic reform, believing that they were following the advice of European leaders, found themselves left in the lurch when the going got rough. Only the Czech Republic under the leadership of Vaclav Klaus[1] has remained on course to a normal society.

In the last few years, the democratic reformers have fallen one by one in the former communist satellites, to be replaced by neo-communist Governments promising the impossible: transition to a market economy without tears. This is a tragedy in itself, and an avoidable one. But with Russia lurching politically into a more authoritarian nationalist course, and the question of Central Europe's membership of NATO still unsettled, it has more than merely economic implications.

NATO

Which brings me to my last example of institutional failure, mercifully a partial one counterbalanced by some successes, namely NATO. NATO is a very fine military instrument; it won the Cold War when it had a clear military doctrine. But an instrument cannot define its own purposes,

---

[1] Vaclav Klaus (born 1941), Czech economist and politician. Finance Minister 1989–92; Prime Minister 1992–.

and since the dissolution of the Warsaw Pact, Western statesmen have found it difficult to give NATO a clear one.

Indeed, they have shilly-shallied on the four major questions facing the Alliance:

– Should Russia be regarded as a potential threat or a partner? (Russia may be about to answer that in a clearer fashion than we would like.)

– Should NATO turn its attention to 'out-of-area', where most of the post-Cold War threats, such as nuclear proliferation, now lie?

– Should NATO admit the new democracies of Central Europe as full members with full responsibilities as quickly as prudently possible?

– Should Europe develop its own 'defence identity' in NATO, even though this is a concept driven entirely by politics and has damaging military implications?

Such questions tend to be decided not in the abstract, not at inter-governmental conferences convened to look into the crystal ball, but on the anvil of necessity in the heat of crisis. And that is exactly what happened in the long-running crisis over Bosnia.

At first, the supporters of a European foreign policy and a European defence identity declared the former Yugoslavia 'Europe's crisis' and asked the US to keep out. The US was glad to do so. But the European Union's farcical involvement only made matters worse and, after a while, was effectively abandoned.

Then the United Nations became involved, and asked NATO to be its military agent in its peacekeeping operations.

Finally, when the UN–NATO personnel were taken hostage, the US intervened, employed NATO airpower with real effect, forced the combatants to the conference table, for better or worse imposed an agreement on them, and now heads a large NATO contingent that is enforcing it.

In the course of stamping its authority on events, the US also stamped its authority on the European members of NATO. And since the logis-tical supply chain goes through Hungary, it drew the Central Europeans into NATO operations in a small way. Whether NATO will apply the logic of this crisis in future strategic planning remains to be seen; but for the armchair theorists of a closed, passive and divided NATO, Bosnia has been no end of a lesson.

These various institutional failures are worrying enough in their own terms and in our own times. If we look ahead still further to the end of the twenty-first century, however, an alarming and unstable future is on the cards.

Consider the number of medium-to-large states in the world that have now embarked on a free market revolution: India, China, Brazil, possibly Russia. Add to these the present economic great powers: the USA and Japan, and, if the federalists get their way, a European superstate with its own independent foreign and defence policy separate from, and perhaps inimical to, the United States. What we see here in 2096 is an unstable world in which there are more than half a dozen 'great powers', all with their own clients, all vulnerable if they stand alone, all capable of increasing their power and influence if they form the right kind of alliance, and all engaged willy-nilly in perpetual diplomatic manoeuvres to ensure that their relative positions improve rather than deteriorate. In other words, 2096 might look like 1914 played on a somewhat larger stage.

That need not come to pass if the Atlantic Alliance remains as it is today: in essence, America as the dominant power surrounded by allies which generally follow its lead. Such are the realities of population, resources, technology and capital that if America remains the dominant partner in a united West, and militarily engaged in Europe, then the West can continue to be the dominant power in the world as a whole.

What is to be Done?

I believe that what is now required is a new and imaginative Atlantic initiative. Its purpose must be to redefine Atlanticism in the light of the challenges I have been describing. There are rare moments when history is open and its course changed by means such as these. We may be at just such a moment now.

REVIVING THE ALLIANCE

First, security. As my discussion of the Bosnian crisis demonstrated, the key lies in two reforms: opening NATO membership to Poland, Hungary and the Czech Republic; and extending NATO's role so that it is able to operate out-of-area.

Both reforms will require a change in NATO's existing procedures. An attack on the territory of one member must, of course, continue to be regarded unambiguously as an attack on that of all; but that principle of universality need not apply to out-of-area activities. Indeed, it needs to be recognized that a wider role for NATO cannot be achieved if every member state has to participate in an out-of-area operation before it can go ahead. What is required are flexible arrangements which, to use a fashionable phrase, permit the creation of 'coalitions of the willing'.

Would NATO expansion mark a new division of Europe and give Russia the right to intervene in states outside the fold? Not in the least. Among other reasons, we could hold out the possibility of admitting those countries which subsequently demonstrate a commitment to democratic values and which have trained military forces up to an acceptable standard. That would be a powerful incentive for such states to pursue the path of democratic reform and defence-preparedness.

NATO also provides the best available mechanism for co-ordinating the contribution of America's allies to a global system of ballistic missile defence: that is, one providing protection against missile attack from whatever source it comes.

If, however, the United States is to build this global ballistic defence system with its allies, it needs the assurance that the Alliance is a permanent one resting on the solid foundations of American leadership. That raises, in my view, very serious doubts about the currently fashionable idea of a separate European 'defence identity' within the Alliance.

Essentially, this is another piece of political symbolism, associated among European federalists with long-term aspirations for a European state with its own foreign and defence policy. It would create the armed forces of a country which does not exist. But, like the single currency, it would have damaging practical consequences in the here and now.

In the first place, it contains the germs of a major future transatlantic rift. And in the second, it has no military rationale or benefits. Indeed, it has potentially severe military drawbacks. Even a French General admitted that during the Gulf War the US forces were 'the eyes and ears' of the French troops. Without America, NATO is a political talking shop, not a military force.

Nor is that likely to be changed in any reasonably foreseeable circumstances. Defence expenditure has been falling sharply in almost all European states in recent years. Even if this process were now halted and reversed, it would take many years before Europe could hope to replace what America presently makes available to the Alliance by way of command and control facilities, airlift capacity, surveillance and sheer firepower. Defence policy cannot be built upon political symbolism and utopian projects of nation-building which ignore or even defy military logic and fiscal prudence.

TRANSATLANTIC FREE TRADE

But even a vigorous and successful NATO would not survive indefinitely in a West divided along the lines of trade and economics. One of the great threats to Atlantic unity in recent years has been the succession of trade wars, ranging from steel to pasta, which have strained relations across the Atlantic. So the second element of a new Atlantic initiative must take the form of a concerted programme to liberalize trade, thereby stimulating growth and creating badly needed new jobs. More specifically, we need to move towards a Transatlantic Free Trade Area, uniting the North American Free Trade Area with a European Union enlarged to incorporate the Central European countries.

I realize that this may not seem the most propitious moment in American politics to advocate a new trade agreement. But the arguments against free trade between advanced industrial countries and poor Third World ones – even if I accepted them, which I do not – certainly do not apply to a Transatlantic Free Trade deal.

Such a trade bloc would unite countries with similar incomes and levels of regulation. It would therefore involve much less disruption and temporary job loss, while still bringing significant gains in efficiency and prosperity. This has been recognized by American labour unions, notably by Mr Lane Kirkland[1] in a series of important speeches. And it would create a trade bloc of unparalleled wealth (and therefore influence) in world trade negotiations.

Of course, economic gains are only half of the argument for a TAFTA. It would also provide a solid economic underpinning to America's continued military commitment to Europe, while strengthening the still-fragile economies and political structures of Central Europe. It would be, in effect, the economic equivalent of NATO and, as such, the second pillar of Atlantic unity under American leadership.

---

[1] Joseph Lane Kirkland (born 1922), US trade unionist. President of the American Federation of Labor/Congress of Industrial Organizations (AFL-CIO) 1979–.

POLITICAL FOUNDATIONS

Yet, let us never forget that there is a third pillar – the political one.

The West is not just some Cold War construct, devoid of significance in today's freer, more fluid world. It rests upon distinctive values and virtues, ideas and ideals, and above all upon a common experience of liberty.

True, the Asia Pacific may be fast becoming the new centre of global economic power. Quite rightly, both the United States and Britain take an ever closer interest in developments there.

But it is the West – above all, perhaps, the English-speaking peoples of the West – that has formed that system of liberal democracy which is politically dominant and which we all know offers the best hope of global peace and prosperity. In order to uphold these things, the Atlantic political relationship must be constantly nurtured and renewed.

So we must breathe new life into the consultative political institutions of the West such as the Atlantic Council and the North Atlantic Assembly.[1] All too often, they lack influence and presence in public debate. Above all, however – loath as I am to suggest another gathering of international leaders – I would propose an annual summit of the Heads of Government of all the North Atlantic countries, under the chairmanship of the President of the United States.

What all this adds up to is *not* another supranational entity. That would be unwieldy and unworkable. It is something more subtle, but I hope more durable: a form of Atlantic partnership which attempts to solve common problems while respecting the sovereignty of the member states. In the course of identifying those problems and co-operating to solve them, Governments would gradually discover that they were shaping an Atlantic public opinion and political consciousness.

---

[1] The Atlantic Council is the British section of the Atlantic Treaty Association, which was founded in 1954 to promote the objectives and ideas of NATO in all its member states. The North Atlantic Assembly was established in 1955 as the Conference of Members of Parliament from the NATO Member Countries to strengthen co-operation and understanding within the alliance and foster a common feeling of Atlantic solidarity. It was renamed in 1966.

Fifty Years on

The reaction, fifty years ago, to that earlier Fulton speech was swift, dramatic and, at first, highly critical. Indeed, to judge from the critics, you would have imagined that it was not Stalin but Churchill who had drawn down the Iron Curtain.

But for all the immediate disharmony, it soon became evident that Fulton had struck a deeper chord. It resulted in a decisive shift in opinion: by May, the opinion polls recorded that 83 per cent of Americans now favoured the idea of a permanent alliance between the United States and Britain, which was subsequently broadened into NATO.

By speaking as and when he did, Churchill guarded against a repetition of the withdrawal of America from Europe which, after 1919, allowed the instability to emerge that plunged the whole world – including America – into a second war.

Like my uniquely distinguished predecessor, I too may be accused of alarmism in pointing to new dangers to which present institutions – and attitudes – are proving unequal. But, also like him, I have every confidence in the resources and the values of the Western civilization we are defending.

In particular, I believe (to use Churchill's words) that: 'If all British moral and material forces and convictions are joined with your own in fraternal association, the highroads of the future will be clear, not only for us but for all, not only for our time, but for a century to come.'

That at least has not changed in fifty years.

57

Speech at a Congress of the New Atlantic Initiative, Prague, 11 May 1996

Two months after her speech in Fulton, Lady Thatcher returned to international themes at a 'Congress' of conservative politicians, economists, journalists and intellectuals assembled in Prague to launch a 'New Atlantic Initiative', designed to strengthen the relationship between America and Europe – including Central Europe. She emphasized starkly the incompatibility between Atlanticism and Europeanism, as the latter was being developed by those resolved on the creation of a European superstate with its own currency, laws, citizenship and armed forces. Such a Europe was destined to become a rival to America, not an ally. And the implications of this in a world where the West faced new and unpredictable security threats, as for instance from the proliferation of ballistic missiles, through the 'mail-order missile business', were grave. Only Atlantic solutions offered hope for tackling common Western problems.

THE COMMON CRISIS: ATLANTIC SOLUTIONS

Prague – The Heart of Europe

I must begin by congratulating most warmly the organizers of this glittering Congress.

It is not, of course, the first European Congress. And in the past, I must admit, such Congresses have achieved mixed results.

The Congress of Vienna in 1815 was called to restore order in Europe after the Napoleonic Wars; it began a series of such gatherings designed to achieve a Concert of Europe. But, as is usually the case in European affairs, the concert was distinctly discordant. The style was too rigid and inflexible. And finally, amid Europe-wide upheaval, Austria's Chancellor

Metternich,[1] who had orchestrated the system, had to flee to England.

The Congress of Berlin in 1878 was called to resolve the Eastern Question, this time with Germany's Chancellor Bismarck holding court as an 'honest broker'. Again, great-power politics was relied upon to manage awkward national aspirations, particularly in the Balkans. But the Eastern Question stayed unresolved, the Balkans became more Balkan, the shaky empires staggered on and, with fateful consequences, Germany emerged as the arbiter in Europe.

Here at our Congress in Prague, however, we have a very different purpose: the defence, entrenchment and extension of our Western inheritance of freedom. And the only concert we shall be hearing from is that performed this evening by the excellent Prague Symphony Orchestra.

The British, indeed, have a special fondness for Czech music: Dvořák and Janácek both spent some time in England.[2] And although the phrase has since been used to rather different effect, it was Janácek who memorably remarked – on a visit to London – that the Czech nation was (I quote) 'the heart of Europe – and Europe needs to be aware of its heart'.[3] Magnificent buildings, superb art galleries, in fact on every side the accumulated evidence of a continuously rich intellectual life – anyone visiting this most beautiful of the cities of Central Europe needs no persuading of the justice of Janácek's observation.

Moreover, here in Prague we are not just surrounded by beauty, but by beauty which was paid for by business success. In the last century, Bohemia was the industrial heartland of the Habsburg Empire. And before the last war Czechoslovakia was one of the world's leading economies, enjoying an income per head equal to that of France. It is in keeping with that tradition of industrial prowess that the Czech Republic today is the outstanding economic success story of Central Europe: where others have flinched under the pressures of free enterprise reform, Vaclav Klaus – my other favourite Prime Minister – has kept going down the right track. And the results are internationally recognized and admired.

Yet, we know also the darker side of Central European history, whose

[1] Prince Klemens von Metternich (1773–1859), Austrian statesman. Foreign Minister 1809–48; State Chancellor 1821–48.
[2] Czech composer Antonin Dvořák (1841–1904) paid nine visits to Britain, and British musical societies commissioned four major works. Czech composer Leoš Janácek (1854–1928) visited London in 1926.
[3] A playful allusion to Prime Minister John Major's controversial speech on 11 March 1991, in which he said that he wanted Britain to be 'at the heart of Europe'.

shadows in successive generations fell over Prague. That too makes our meeting here appropriate. We dare not forget that the freedom of this cultured, enterprising people was snuffed out by each of the two monstrous, totalitarian systems of our century – intimidated, dismembered and absorbed by Nazi Germany; subverted, betrayed and enslaved by communist Russia; and each time with the West standing impotently aside. These are blots on the history of the civilized world. They came about because the West was selfish and unprepared. And they confirm an important truth about international affairs. In the language of Hobbes: 'Covenants without the sword are but words.' No amount of promises by world leaders, no amount of guarantees by international bodies without firepower, mattered when the tanks rolled in. Such experience provides a poignant lesson for today's multilateralists, who retain a naive conviction that international institutions, rather than alliances of powerful nation-states, can be relied upon to preserve the peace.

The Post-Cold War Crisis

The fact that now the Czech and Slovak peoples – and the Hungarians, the Poles and other former captives of the Evil Empire – are free to express their nationhood, rebuild their economies and rejoin the international community as sovereign states is, therefore, a cause not just for rejoicing but for deep reflection.

We should reflect that it was not the United Nations, or the World Bank, let alone the European Community, which overthrew communism. It was a united West, under American leadership, enjoying the support of brave dissident patriots in the lands of the Eastern bloc; together we applied irresistible pressures on the Soviet system. And it was the inherent and cumulative failures of that system that caused it to collapse in the face of our challenge. Had we waited upon international consensus and its diplomatic practitioners to win the Cold War for freedom, we would be waiting still.

But, as so often, with victory also came complacency. And it was not long before signs emerged that all was not well with the so-called New World Order. Even the expression, 'New World Order', with its echoes of utopian euphoria from the League of Nations, should have sounded the alarm.

For the post-Cold War Western leaders had made a fatal confusion between two quite distinct propositions. The first – true – proposition was that international institutions, above all the United Nations, could at last begin to work as originally designed, in a world free from Soviet obstruction and aggression. The second – untrue – proposition was that these institutions could themselves perform all the essential functions required to uphold global peace, prosperity and justice.

There was a counterpart of this post-Cold War confusion in the domestic policies of our own nation-states. Again, the release of tension induced a slackness of political muscle. With the lifting of the forty-year threat to our very existence, the general cry was for Governments to cultivate the arts of peace. The demand was for a peace dividend – and politicians were too timid to explain that the only true peace dividend is simply the dividend of peace itself. Furthermore, the dividend is only yielded if sufficient is first invested in defence. But, in any case, the resulting – often imprudent – reductions in defence spending did not lead to Governments spending less overall: quite the contrary. For the state-welfare complex proved more rapacious than the left's favourite ogre, the defence-industrial complex, ever was. To pay for increased welfare, Governments weakened their own financial disciplines, ran deficits and hiked taxes. And all these actions in turn worsened deep-seated social problems like welfare dependency, family breakdown and juvenile crime.

These tendencies, as the experts have been explaining during this morning's sessions, are so general – and their results so deleterious – that we can without exaggeration talk of a 'common crisis'. But it is not, of course, a crisis of capitalism.

Indeed, outside the hefty, unreadable tomes of the Marxist pseudo-economists, there was no crisis of capitalism, only a crisis of socialism – wherever and whenever it has been applied. Its sour fruits are still with us.

Where socialism has left its deepest impression – in most of the former Soviet Union – we see not Western-style democracy and free economies, but corruption, cartels and gangsterism. There is a pervasive lack of trust and civility, the breakdown of civil society in matters large and small. A dour Russian parable on the history of Soviet communism says it all:

> That's how it is with a man. He makes a bad start in his youth by murdering his parents.
> After that he goes downhill: He takes to robbing people in the streets.

Soon he sinks to telling lies and spreading gossip.
Finally, he loses all shame, descends to the depths of depravity, and
enters a room without knocking at the door first.

That's how it was with communism. It began in terror and mass
murder and it ended in petty corruption, inefficiency, bad service, ill
manners, the loss of every social grace, and a society pervaded by rampant egoism. And the social desert thus created was unpromising ground
for the economic transition to a market economy.

All the more credit then to our hosts here in Prague, and to the
democratic reformers in other Central European countries (like my fellow
patron Leszek Balcerowicz,[1] that they succeeded so well in their market
revolution.

Alas, in some countries we have seen a reversion. There is a progressive
disillusionment among ordinary people with pseudo-capitalism and –
worse – a growing nostalgia for the false security of socialism. Former
communists, sometimes in disguise, are returning to power in ex-
communist countries. In Russia itself, there is the possibility of a Government that combines communist economics with an imperialistic foreign
policy.

Such a reversion is not uncommon. Kipling wrote about this as a sort
of natural law:

As it will be in the future, it was at the birth of Man –
There are only four things certain since Social Progress began:
That the Dog returns to his Vomit and the Sow returns to her
    Mire,
And the burnt Fool's bandaged finger goes wabbling back to the
    Fire . . .
. . . As surely as Water will wet us, as surely as Fire will burn,
The Gods of the Copybook Headings with terror and slaughter
    return![2]

We can and must provide against the dangers – the 'terror and slaughter' – that this reversion threatens. To do so effectively, we must turn
to those Atlantic solutions – which our distinguished panels will be
debating this afternoon.

[1] Leszek Balcerowicz (born 1947), Polish economist and politician. Finance Minister
and Deputy Prime Minister 1989–91.
[2] 'The Gods of the Copybook Headings' (1919).

Security Challenges

Mr Chairman, the world is today a freer, and in many ways better, place than it was when the two superpowers – America supported by her European allies, and the Soviet Union conscripting her European satellites – confronted each other. But the world is also more complex, more volatile and more dangerous. Let me give you three reasons why.

First of all, there was a kind of unholy symmetry in international affairs created by a balance of terror. Deterrence – above all nuclear deterrence – worked as it was designed to do. Neither the West nor the Soviets could afford to let any regional crisis so destabilize the system that either side was pushed to the brink; for beyond that brink lay the abyss of mutual destruction. This does not, of course, mean that the Soviet ideological commitment to global revolution in those years was mere bravado. Had they been able to achieve their goals at a sustainable cost they would undoubtedly have done just that. But, accepting that attrition was the only possible strategy, and regarding their client states as pawns, not players, they kept those client states under firm control. The breakdown of Soviet power, however, brought that discipline to an end: it allowed rogue states, often connected with terrorist movements, to emerge and set their own violent agendas.

Second, with the collapse of the Soviet Union there was also a dispersal of weapons of mass destruction and of the technologies to produce them. This has gone much further than we envisaged; and it now constitutes quite simply the most dangerous threat of our times. Yet there is still a conspiracy of silence among Western Governments and analysts about it. We have, of course, known for some time about the danger of the so-called 'back pack' nuclear weapon. The ability of rogue states to produce chemical and biological weapons, without detection, is a constant worry.

But it is the proliferation of advanced missiles and missile technology that has fundamentally altered the threat over the last few years. The North Koreans have developed (and continue to develop) a range of missiles which are even available for sale in a catalogue to all comers. The mail-order missile business is no fantasy of science fiction: it is a fact.

There are many imponderables in precisely assessing the time-scale of the threat: but they should increase our vigilance. On present trends, it is likely that the United States will be threatened by such missiles early in the next century. And, once they are available in the Middle East and North Africa, all the capitals of Europe will be within target range. We thus face the appalling possibility – for which we are at present unprepared – of an attack on a Western city involving thousands of deaths.

It is not only the terrible consequences of their actual use, but the implications of their threatened use, that should disturb us. For that threat casts doubt on the ability of the West to project its power beyond our shores. The North Korean missiles are, for example, a threat to American defence of its allies in the Pacific. And would we have taken the punitive action we did against Libya in 1986, if Gaddafi had been able to strike with his missiles at the heart of our cities? Gaddafi himself has no doubt of the answer (and I quote him): 'If [the Americans] know that you have a deterrent force capable of hitting the United States, they would not be able to hit you. Consequently, we should build this force so that they and others will no longer think about an attack.'[1]

Of course, the Gaddafis may be wrong. We must maintain all possible diplomatic pressure against proliferation. And we should not forswear the possibility of pre-emptive strikes. But, in face of all this our response must also urgently include ballistic missile defence.

Third, we are seeing today a fundamental shift of economic power – which will certainly have political consequences – away from the West to Asia and the Pacific Rim. Unlike the first two challenges – the emergence of rogue states and the proliferation of weaponry – this should not be regarded in itself as a threat to us. Although Asian countries may initially grow wealthier at the expense of our industries by capturing our markets, they will increasingly themselves offer new markets for our goods. All the classic arguments for free trade and against protection remain valid.

The danger, though, lies in the fact that these Asian countries, which are making such rapid economic advances, generally lack the liberal traditions which we in the West take for granted. America is worthy of its superpower status because it has been not only economically but politically liberal. Therefore the advance of American interests in particular, and the West's in general, have been more or less synonymous with the advance of liberty. By contrast, China's extraordinary economic progress is occurring despite, not because of, its political tradition – which

---

[1] Tripoli television, 19 April 1990.

has always been one of tyranny. China's behaviour towards Taiwan demonstrates that the economic challenge from the Far East could easily become a security challenge too.

So the task we face now is to devise a framework of international co-operation which allows these and future threats to be met successfully. It is one which requires principle and shrewdness, tenacity and flexibility, resolve to apply our strength but prudence in conserving it. Above all, it requires the unity of the West under American leadership.

The West

This, however, is far from universally recognized. Irving Kristol[1] once wrote that: 'No modern nation has ever constructed a foreign policy that was acceptable to its intellectuals.' This was true during the Cold War years. It is true now. And in recent years we have heard repeated suggestions that the West was essentially a Cold War construct, rendered irrelevant by the end of a bi-polar world.

In fact, it was – and is – nothing of the sort. The distinctive features of the Western political, judicial, social and economic system existed before communism and will continue after it. Those features are: the longstanding historic commitment to human rights, the rule of law, representative democracy, limited government, private property and tolerance.

Attempts today to suggest that American civilization is antithetical and antipathetic to European civilization, which itself is portrayed by contrast as some homogeneous whole, are bad history and worse politics. American civilization began its life as a branch of the English oak. It has since had the cultures and traditions of other European countries grafted onto it. It is today the centre of an English-speaking civilization with cultural and ethnic links to every European country. And in our present age, in which communications increasingly obliterate distance, culture is a more important fact of life than geography.

In truth, America is a European power – and must remain one. And even if we could overlook our common history and cultural ties, we dare not ignore the politics of Atlantic co-operation. Any ideology that

---

[1] Irving Kristol is a distinguished American neo-conservative commentator. The quotation is from 'American Intellectuals and Foreign Policy', *Foreign Affairs*, July 1967.

threatens Atlantic unity is one that ultimately imperils our collective security.

Europe – Dreams and Nightmares

And here I must touch on the relationship between the Atlantic countries and the European Union. I realize that there are some amongst us here today – and among supporters of Atlanticism outside this hall – who are strong devotees of European integration.

Now, I take it as a sign of the strength of the Atlantic idea – and as a sign of its broad political appeal – that it has captured the imagination of many people who differ on other political questions.

But imagination must also be complemented by clear thinking.

Of course, some of the lesser dreams which went into Europeanism are by no means ignoble. The dream of peace in Europe by permanent reconciliation of the old enemies, France and Germany. The dream of reuniting a continent divided by the Iron Curtain, so that nations like the Czechs could rejoin the free West. The dream – of a less inspirational kind – of a single European market without barriers to trade.

But the overall European federalist project, which was envisaged by some from the start but which has only in recent years come out into the open, is in truth a nightmare. For the drive towards a European superstate – with its own Government, its own laws, its own currency and its own citizenship – would achieve none of the goals which enthusiasts on either side of the Atlantic claim for it.

Were it to come about, another great power would have been born – equal or nearly equal in economic strength to the United States. Does anyone suppose that such a power would not soon become a rival to America? That it would not gradually discover different interests from those of the United States? That it would not by degrees move towards a different public philosophy – one less liberal, more statist? And that it would not eventually seek to establish its own military forces separate from those of the United States?

If this new Europe were not to follow the path to separate great-power status, it would be the first such power in history to renounce its independent role. It would have pioneered a new course in self-abnegation. It would have chosen moral influence over political power. The history of Europe – bloodstained as well as idealistic – should not encourage us in these fantasies.

Europe separated from the United States would in my view be unequivocally a bad thing – bad for America, bad for Europe, and bad for the world at large.

For America, it would transform an ally into a rival – or, at the very least, permanently threaten to do so.

For the world at large, it would increase instability by dividing the West and so hasten the move to a multi-polar world.

And for Europe itself, it would remove from our continent the one power which has kept the peace for fifty years – and which no European really fears.

How quickly lessons are forgotten and deductions from events distorted! Two world wars have flowed from American disengagement from Europe. By contrast, the Cold War was won because America defended Western Europe's security as its own. So talk by some Continental political leaders of the possibility of war unless Europe moves towards political unity is profoundly misguided – as well as unbelievably insensitive.[1] Only if America, as a global superpower, remains directly engaged in Europe is there a guarantee against any Continental European power asserting dominance.

The shortcomings of a common European foreign and security policy have been shown by Europe's feebleness in the former Yugoslavia. There is no reason to believe that attempts to apply a common European defence policy would be any less risible or chaotic – though they could do untold harm to the Atlantic Alliance.

All this means that our energies must be directed towards strengthening NATO, which is as important in the post-Cold War world as in the circumstances of its creation. NATO's role should be expanded. It must be prepared to go out-of-area, where so many of today's threats lie. It must be prepared to accept the Czech Republic and other Central European countries as full members, giving them much-needed reassurance in a time of growing fear about future instability to the east. NATO can also co-ordinate support for the construction of that system of global ballistic missile defence which is now an imperative requirement. And if, as I hope, there is a renewed enthusiasm for such a system in the United States, Britain and other European countries must make a fair contribution.

---

[1] In a speech at the University of Louvain on 2 February 1996, Chancellor Kohl of Germany said: 'The policy of European integration is in reality a question of war and peace in the twenty-first century.'

Atlanticism

Mr Chairman, economic integration on an Atlantic basis can nurture this vital Atlantic relationship in defence and foreign policy. It will also help to counter some unwelcome trends in European economics. For Europe today is far from being synonymous with free enterprise and open trade: it too often also stands for burdensome controls. In fact, that classic victim of Austro-Hungarian bureaucracy, the Good Soldier Švejk, might have felt gloomily at home in today's highly regulated Europe, where like then (and I quote), 'Every day brought new instructions, directives, questions and orders.'[1]

The most practical way forward, I believe, is to merge the North American Free Trade Area with the European Community, including the countries of Central and perhaps in time Eastern Europe. Of course, in terms of pure economic analysis global free trade is the ideal. But trade cannot be divorced from politics, no matter how hard we try: it is politically realistic as well as economically beneficial to concentrate now on creating a Transatlantic Free Trade Area. Such a bloc would be able to push effectively towards global trade liberalization. It would prevent transatlantic trade wars from jeopardizing wider transatlantic links. It would bring our Atlantic civilization closer together.

Finally, as part of this endeavour we must try to develop a real Atlantic political consciousness and public opinion. Of course, this will take time to emerge. Such transformations come about organically and subtly – or not at all. So, I am not talking here about cultural politics. The stupidities of attempts to remould old national identities into new artificial forms – whether ruthlessly in the Soviet Union, or absurdly in the European Union – should not be repeated. But the Atlantic political consciousness is different – for three reasons.

It reflects the realities of recent history.

It does not seek to eliminate national identity, it respects it.

And it makes excellent strategic and economic sense.

For that we may need new institutions; we may need revived ones; but we certainly need more contact. This will follow our Atlantic Initiative, and it is not the least of its advantages – and pleasures.

---

[1] *The Good Soldier Švejk and his Fortunes in the World War* (1920–23) is a satirical novel by the Czech writer Jaroslav Hašek (1883–1923).

Spring in Prague

Ladies and gentlemen, my first visit to Prague was as Prime Minister six years ago. Memories of communism's inelegant death throes were still fresh and the joy of national liberation still sweet. Vaclav Havel's[1] translation from prison as dissident to Palace as President seemed to symbolize not so much a new era as a new world, in which the meek – and the brave and true – would finally inherit the earth.

We in the West won a great victory in the Cold War. Let us not now forget why we fought. The mission of this Congress is to recapture that sense of purpose and clothe it with practical action. Spring in Prague is the time – and the place – to do so.

---

[1] Vaclav Havel (born 1936), Czech dramatist and politician. President of Czechoslovakia 1989–92; President of the Czech Republic 1993–.

58

Speech to an *International Herald Tribune* Conference, Beijing, China, 14 November 1996

Lady Thatcher has taken a very close interest in developments in Hong Kong and China since leaving office, and has made numerous visits to the Asia-Pacific region. She has also been a strong supporter of Hong Kong Governor Chris Patten's attempts to entrench democracy before the 1997 handover under terms which she herself negotiated as Prime Minister. The speech she delivered in Beijing in November 1996 was prepared with the greatest care and based on her understanding of Chinese objectives and sensibilities. It was at the same time respectful and direct, applauding China's advances under Deng Xiaoping's leadership but criticizing – to the evident irritation of the communist Chinese officials who later responded – the continuing abuses of human rights.

To be the last to speak at a Conference which has heard so many important people – Premiers, Ministers, Central Bankers, Chief Executives of great corporations – talk about issues so crucial to China's future is no mean challenge. What is there left to say? But I am not famous for remaining silent. Nor has the *International Herald Tribune* invited me here to do so.

So I shall give my own perspective on China's future. If now and again I am forthright, it is my style rather than any disrespect for our hosts. I speak as a great admirer of the Chinese people and their achievements.

We are privileged to have at the British Museum in London a superb exhibition – one of the most remarkable most of us have ever seen – of the Mysteries of Ancient China. There could not be a more graphic way to remind us that no other nation in history has ever created such a distinctive and culturally rich society, spread across such an immense area, and over such a length of time. China is the only country in the world whose writings of three thousand years ago are still readable in the language of today. That tells us the enormous strength which modern China draws from the continuity of its culture and tradition. Contrary to accepted wisdom, China's culture has also been remarkably inventive. Many of its discoveries – the technique of casting iron, the rudder for steering ships, the compass, and of course gunpowder – predate Europe's assimilation of those techniques by many centuries.

But brilliant though China's civilization has been, it has also had a darker side, represented by the unshakeable conviction that China is sufficient unto itself and can afford to shut out the world beyond its borders. Only in the lifetime of many of us here has that belief begun to crumble. It was Mr Deng Xiaoping's[1] vision and energy which finally set China on a course of opening up to the outside world, a course now being continued by his successors.

China has paid a price for its centuries of self-imposed exclusion from the great currents of change which have flowed so strongly elsewhere in the world. The Western countries have to take some share of the blame for that, because of the humiliations which they inflicted on China in the last century – and Japan for its savage treatment of China in the first part of the present century.

But there has also been a consistent thread running throughout China's own history of guarding against outside intrusion, whether it be trade or ideas or people. It runs from the burning of books in the Qin Dynasty over two thousand years ago right up to the death of Chairman Mao.[2] Imperial China scorned progress, scorned science and scorned the spirit of enterprise, the very qualities which allowed Western societies to advance so rapidly over the past two hundred years. China lost much as a result.

With the next millennium almost upon us, the years of introspection and self-absorption lie in the past. The future is a place in which markets are worldwide and politics and finance know no frontiers. That new world is propelling China to look outward and become much more closely integrated into the world trading system, into the multilateral financial institutions and into regional defence and security relationships.

The question is: how can this seismic shift in China's historic vocation

---

[1] Deng Xiaoping (1904–97), Chinese communist leader, returned to government in 1977 after years in political disgrace, soon becoming effective ruler of China and introducing economic but only very limited political reforms.

[2] Mao Zedong, the Chinese leader, died on 9 September 1976.

be accomplished in ways which benefit *both* China *and* the rest of us? The world has to make room for China to play a role appropriate to its size, its history and its economic weight, as a major world power with important strategic interests. But what does that require from China? How can we avoid the collisions which have been so much a feature of past encounters between China and the Western world? Those are the questions I shall explore.

A term which we very frequently hear nowadays is globalization. It means in essence that a country's economy is no longer influenced just by national or regional conditions, but that *all* economies – save those like North Korea – are exposed to the same influences and market forces in a worldwide marketplace. That has happened first because of the opening of markets through the GATT negotiations, with the considerable reduction of tariffs and other barriers to trade and investment; and second because of the extraordinary power and speed of modern communications, which link the world's economies instantaneously, in ways which we would never have imagined even a few years ago. The result is that we are all exposed to the same competitive pressures, driving us to produce ever more efficiently.

This process is not merely unstoppable: it is highly desirable, because it provides an unrivalled stimulus to growth and prosperity. It should be doubly welcome to China, with her highly talented people, her inexhaustible reserves of labour and her ambition to raise living standards and catch up with other countries in the region.

The question is not whether China is a beneficiary of globalization: it quite clearly is. The evidence for that lies in the impressive growth rates achieved over the last few years. The question is rather whether China can benefit even more, and my answer to that is, 'Yes, if she pursues the right policies.'

China is at the heart of the fastest-growing area of the world, where success has come from allowing markets to operate freely within the framework of a rule of law. The overseas Chinese diaspora in Hong Kong, in Singapore and elsewhere in the region have shown what can be achieved. Indeed there is no better example than Hong Kong. There the natural entrepreneurship of Chinese people, operating within a framework of the rule of law and high standards of public administration provided by Britain, has created extraordinary wealth and prosperity on barren and unpromising terrain – indeed a higher GNP per capita than Britain itself enjoys.

A great deal has already been done by Mr Deng Xiaoping and his successors to reform and liberalize China's economy, and increase the role of the private sector. Indeed, today China is a very different place than the China I first visited in April 1977, almost twenty years ago. But reform is not a process which can be turned on and off at will. If China is to meet the expectations of her people and to go on attracting the foreign investment which is crucial to its future growth, the lessons are clear:

– the work being done to introduce a system of law which is fair and equal for all, and is applied fairly and equally to all, must be carried forward;

– there must also be a fair and equitable system for upholding contracts and for adjudicating commercial disputes;

– the reforms of China's financial system, and the development of capital markets, need to be taken further. A sound financial system is essential in China to derive full benefit from growing trade and investment;

– the private sector needs to be continuously expanded, and as far as possible the disciplines of private-sector businesses applied to the state-owned enterprises which are the main drag on China's economic advance. Reform of these state enterprises is surely one of the most urgent tasks for China's leaders. We faced a not dissimilar problem with the nationalized industries in Britain in the 1980s, and solved it with the policy of privatization which is now widely copied round the world;

– business must have direct and instant access to the information available through the Internet and other systems. It is absolutely right to prevent misuse of these channels for disseminating pornography and violence. But countries which deny or delay access to information will find they miss opportunities and stunt their growth. Speed of decision is vital in the modern business world;

– international rules on intellectual property must be strictly observed, because that goes to the heart of a country's reputation as a reliable and dependable trade partner with whom other countries want to do business.

In other words, if China is to benefit to the fullest extent from the rising tide of Asia's prosperity, she will need to go further and faster in releasing market forces and creating a dependable framework for business. And by taking those steps China will make its case for early entry into the World Trade Organization irresistible, thus taking the final step towards its full involvement in the world economy – a huge step forward from the situation less than twenty years ago, when Mr

Deng Xiaoping embarked on his bold crusade of opening up China.

That is bound to lead in time to change in the way in which China is governed. It is for the people of China to decide for themselves on their political system, not for any of us to dictate to them. Indeed, it would be counter-productive to attempt to do so.

But as one looks round the Asia-Pacific region, it is striking how economic growth and greater prosperity have consistently brought political change in their wake, with Governments becoming steadily more accountable in fully democratic elections. Indeed it's not just Asia's experience: in Europe, the Industrial Revolution was followed by new constitutions and new legal systems. I do not find that surprising, because as people achieve higher living standards and accumulate more wealth, they want a greater say in running their own lives, they want a rule of law and a system of government which is fair and equitable. China has its own distinctive history of strong and highly centralized government, but I do not believe that in the long term it will be immune from the same processes which have affected its neighbours.

Indeed, much has changed already. If one compares the China of today with the China of twenty years ago, let alone with the Soviet Union of Brezhnev and Andropov,[1] it is plain that there have been many improvements in freedom of speech, of information, of movement, of choice of occupation. Government has loosened its control over the lives of individual citizens. We see elections at village level which are genuinely contested, in a way which we in the Western world recognize, with a choice of candidates and much greater information to enable people to exercise that choice. Perhaps it is only a small step, but it is starting from below at the grassroots rather than being imposed from above.

The same gradual progress is visible with the introduction of a rule of law, which enhances civil, corporate and property rights. That is in good part a response to the spread of the market economy and foreign investment. A market cannot operate properly without a fair, transparent and impartial legal system, nor will foreigners invest. At the same time the criminal law is being revised, and the rights of defendants strengthened. And the number of lawyers is growing rapidly – though I am not certain whether that is an unmixed blessing.

But I do not want to paint an overly rosy picture. There are still

[1] Yuri Vladimirovich Andropov (1918–84), Soviet political leader. Succeeded Leonid Brezhnev as Communist Party General Secretary 1982, became President of the USSR 1983.

aspects of life in China which are deeply worrying to those of us fortunate enough to live in democracies and under a full rule of law. And I have to say the recent harsh sentences imposed on Mr Wei and Mr Wang[1] have caused dismay in the wider world.

But there is some better news. We are seeing the beginnings of a system of elections which will I believe move steadily up the scale from the village to the province, and ultimately to the highest national level. That will not be brought about by outsiders. But by expanding the channels which link China to the outside world – through trade, through investment, through the tens of thousands of Chinese students who now study abroad and through the influence of the overseas Chinese – we indirectly encourage this growing constitutionalism. It is what is commonly known as a policy of engagement, and, at the end of the day, that will be far more effective and more positive than sanctions or other attempts at compulsion.

I am not so rash as to predict a precise time-scale for political change in China. I would only observe that it took countries like South Korea and Taiwan at least twenty years of economic progress from the levels at which China finds itself now before they had more open and democratic political systems. That may seem a long time, but in the scale of China's history, it is the blink of an eye.

The event which will have the most direct and immediate bearing on China's reputation in the world is Hong Kong's return to Chinese sovereignty next year – indeed now only just over six months away.

Hong Kong is a creation of which both China and Britain can be enormously proud: China because the vast majority of Hong Kong's people are of Chinese origin, and Britain because its good stewardship has provided the basis for Hong Kong's success.

Hong Kong has achieved for its people one of the highest standards of living in the world. It ranks as one of the three or four most important and sophisticated financial centres. Its soaring skyline is a testimony to the boldness, energy and appetite for risk of its businessmen. The suspension bridge and new airport are simply the latest in a string of remarkable building projects. The whole story of Hong Kong is yet another example of how so often in history it has been the small countries and city-states – Athens, Venice, Elizabethan England – which have been the most

---

[1] Chinese pro-democracy dissidents persecuted by the Communist authorities. Wei Jingsheng was sentenced to fourteen years' and Wang Dan to eleven years' imprisonment.

lively and adventurous and which have put mankind and posterity most in their debt.

But what makes Hong Kong unique is its spirit: that spark of life which comes from freedom under a rule of law. Extinguish the spark and Hong Kong would rapidly become humdrum, a shell of its former self.

Recognition that Hong Kong is, and for many many years will remain, very different from China lies behind Mr Deng Xiaoping's creative and subtle concept of 'One country, two systems'. I remember him explaining that to me in 1984. He reasoned that Hong Kong's continued success and prosperity are important for China, and could only be achieved by preserving the system which created Hong Kong's success and by allowing Hong Kong's people to run their own affairs in their own way.

That is the only basis on which I agreed – or could have agreed – to sign the Joint Declaration on Hong Kong's future in 1984.[1] And despite the doubts that have sometimes been cast in the intervening twelve years on whether 'One country, two systems' will really preserve Hong Kong's way of life, I still profoundly believe in Mr Deng Xiaoping's commitment and that of his successors to honouring his pledges in China's name.

On my own visits to Hong Kong I find people increasingly confident about 1997. It is clear too that they are proud of being Chinese and of what is being achieved in China.

So I am optimistic about Hong Kong's future, despite the bureaucratic battles which have ebbed and flowed since 1984, despite the hard words exchanged in negotiations, and despite the gloomy predictions that China will seek to interfere in how Hong Kong people run their own affairs. I believe the essentials of what makes Hong Kong unique are still intact and will continue after 1997.

But China will need to show great understanding for Hong Kong's traditions, above all its tradition of free speech. Every signal from Beijing will be scrutinized with great care. Statements which imply that free speech will be qualified after 1997 risk undermining the foundations on which Hong Kong's enterprise society is built. The best possible start for China in 1997 would be to keep the present members of the elected legislature unchanged until the due time of the next elections. But if this is not the case, then I hope that China will take the earliest steps to

[1] The (Sino–British) Joint Declaration of December 1984 provided for the return of Hong Kong to China in 1997, to be governed as a Special Administrative Region according to the conditions contained in the 'Basic Law'.

organize free and fair elections to the new legislative body. As Winston Churchill often quoted: 'Magnanimity in politics is not seldom the truest wisdom.'

Be under no illusion: next year's transition will take place amid unprecedented international interest and unprecedented media attention. The world will be watching for any sign that China is not honouring its obligations. It's not a case of foreign Governments interfering in Hong Kong: it is a simple fact of life in the modern world that events are subject to the most detailed scrutiny by television and a free press.

I hope that China's response to this challenge will be to strain every sinew to ensure that the transition is a success – not only for Hong Kong, but for China itself. A smooth and peaceful transition, in which the transfer of sovereignty has virtually *no* perceptible effect on Hong Kong's everyday life, would earn China untold credit with the rest of the world. 1997 is a year of opportunity for China, and I hope the opportunity will be grasped.

The fact is that the success of the transition is now in China's hands, and in China's hands alone. Britain will do its duty so long as the Union Jack flies over Hong Kong, and interest in what happens will last far beyond that. But the future is China's to determine, in conjunction with the people of Hong Kong.

Because I am confident that China *will* get it right, I intend to be in Hong Kong, among its exceptional and brave-hearted people, to experience next year's events at first hand and to witness the undertakings so solemnly given by China in 1984 being put into practice.

In parallel with the great changes going on within China, we have the immensely difficult but important task of integrating an emerging China into the systems, rules and values of a world which, because of its self-imposed seclusion, it did not have a hand in shaping.

Our starting point should be unequivocal: it is in our Western interest that China should be open, stable and prosperous, and a full partner in the international community. That is the only rational policy for the West to pursue with a country which has the world's largest population, a veto in the United Nations, nuclear weapons and is an enormous market.

The opposite policy – a policy of containing China rather than working with it – would forfeit China's co-operation on a whole range of international issues, including arms control, the environment and UN matters. Containment would be a self-fulfilling prophecy, turning China into an enemy when we want a friend.

China has legitimate strategic interests just as the rest of us do, and is entitled to be treated with respect and consistency, in accordance with its status. In recent years the consistency has too often been lacking, as the United States in particular has given China a bewildering mixture of signals rather than a clear and consistent statement of its intentions.

So our – Western – policy must be to build relations with an evolving China and find ways to manage differences.

But China cannot sit and wait for the world to come to her. The international community is built on a balance of interest and on readiness to accept constraints. The most important of these constraints is that countries accept that in no circumstances should they use or threaten force to extend their power. Problems including those in China's relations with Taiwan must be settled peacefully.

Equally, it is in all our interests to see China play an active part in regional affairs. That is already happening in APEC[1] and in the Asia–Europe Summit. It has been visible too in China's constructive approach to solving Cambodia's problems and the discreet influence which it has exerted on North Korea.

There are important issues in the South China Sea involving both natural resources and sovereignty, where China also has a perfectly legitimate interest in being involved when they are discussed and negotiated. But many other countries have interests as well, both those bordering the South China Sea and trading nations all round the world who have a major interest in seeing the sea-lanes kept open.

Given the scale of her exports, China should also be present in the World Trade Organization once she brings her trading practices fully into line with international standards.

And I hope China will follow its acceptance of the Non-Proliferation Treaty and the Nuclear Test Ban Treaty by also becoming a member of Missile Technology Control Regime, thus joining the international effort to stop the export of weapons of great destructive power to countries which would have no scruples about their use.

The most sensitive area of all is defence and national security. There are no great alliances in the Asia-Pacific to match the role of NATO in Europe. But the American presence in the Pacific is a major contribution to the stability of the area, reassuring countries which might otherwise feel threatened and ensuring that no single power can aspire to dominate militarily.

[1] The Asia-Pacific Economic Co-Operation Organization.

A regular dialogue between China and the United States on strategic issues, as well as regional security and arms control, would be a way of avoiding misunderstandings about each other's intentions and lead on to other confidence-building measures of the type which have proved to be effective in Europe. The most vital task of all is to avoid a gratuitous second Cold War. It will require great efforts both by China and by the West, but the prize for both is too great to let slip.

Thankfully, the days when China and the West snarled at each other in mutual incomprehension and suspicion are behind us. We should no longer dwell on the indignities of the past, but should both look to the opportunities of the future.

And the key to that future?

As Winston Churchill put it: 'Trust the people, the mass of the people in almost any country.'

Trust the people.

59

The Fourth Nicholas Ridley Memorial Lecture, London, 22 November 1996

The Nicholas Ridley Memorial Lecture delivered to a dinner held by the Conservative Way Forward Group was intended as Lady Thatcher's last major speech before the 1997 general election campaign. In spite of the advice she had offered in her earlier Keith Joseph Memorial Lecture to revive Conservative fortunes by pursuing popular, radical right-wing policies, the Government was currently involved in yet another damaging quarrel with its own backbenchers, who demanded a clearer line on the question of a European single currency. This partly overshadowed the Ridley Lecture's prime purpose, which was to set out in the starkest terms why socialism remained a threat. Distinguishing between the old socialism of Marxism in its various guises and the new socialism, which Lady Thatcher describes as 'a system of pervasive state control and influence over people's lives,' she finds the latter occurring in many different manifestations – Tony Blair's ideas of a 'stakeholding economy', the incursions of bureaucracy and corporatism from Europe, the political correctness which plagues America, and the predominance of corrupt socialist governing cliques in most of the ex-communist world. The Keith Joseph and Nicholas Ridley Memorial Lectures between them combine to give a philosophically-based and comprehensive programme for radical Conservatism at the start of the new millennium.

NICHOLAS RIDLEY

If Thomas Carlyle was even partly right in suggesting that history is the biography of great men,[1] anyone studying the history of *our* times should also study the character and career of Nicholas Ridley.

---

[1] Thomas Carlyle (1795–1881), Scottish essayist and historian, wrote 'The history of the world is but the biography of great men' in a lecture entitled 'On Heroes, Hero-Worship, and the Heroic in History' (1841).

Nick defied every stereotype. He was what used to be called 'an original'. His temperament combined in equal measure the opposing elements of the classical and the romantic.

He had a clear, analytical mind, which made him the best technical problem-solver I ever worked with. As he put it after leaving office: 'I was educated as a mathematician and engineer. I see a problem and I want to put it right . . . This perhaps explains why I am not a good politician.'

I wish we had more such 'bad politicians' today!

Free-market economics was always Nick's passion. And he had a longer, better pedigree in that respect than most Thatcherites – or indeed, I may add, than Thatcher herself. His first vote against a Conservative Government baling out nationalized industries was in *1961*. To be so right, so early on, is not to have *seen* the light – it is to have *lit* it.

Yet the other side of Nick's complex personality was his sensitivity. As befits the grandson of Sir Edwin Lutyens,[1] he was a gifted and prolific painter. His cool, atmospheric watercolours conveyed his sense of wonder at the beauties of nature.

This leads to one further revealing fact about Nick's character. He could not, of course, in any terms be considered 'classless'. In fact, like the Labour Leader, he must have had a whole wardrobe of old school ties.[2] But he was also quite convinced that the bourgeois values of enterprise, thrift and effort were what drove our country and society forward, and that government must create the climate for these things to flourish.

And of course there was Nick's integrity. The really honest, honourable man is not always popular. He makes people uneasy because he says what they half-thought – and would rather they hadn't. But whenever you meet such people you come away feeling better for it – and the country feels better too, knowing that it can produce them.

Nick enjoyed high office, but he was usually surprised to be offered it. I think he had rather given up on entering the Cabinet when I appointed him to Transport in 1983.[3] I wish I had brought him in earlier. He would have been a superb Chancellor.

---

[1] Sir Edwin Landseer Lutyens (1869–1944), English architect.
[2] A humorous allusion to Prime Minister John Major's 1996 Party Conference speech, in which he had contrasted his own modest background with the public (i.e. private) school education of Tony Blair.
[3] Nicholas – later Lord – Ridley (1929–93) served in the Thatcher Cabinet as Transport Secretary 1983–85, Environment Secretary 1986–89, and Trade and Industry Secretary 1989–90.

But whether in or out, he had the breadth of insight of the true, Renaissance, universal man. He was as content and proficient painting the sunset, or building his wonderful water-garden, as directing his Department.

All this confirms that Nick was one of a long British line of individualists – a term which is often used disparagingly, but which should be rehabilitated, for it explains much about our country's history, traditions and achievements.

The most persuasive defence of British individualism is contained in John Stuart Mill's little manual for freedom, *On Liberty*. Mill understood how necessary it was in a mass society, with its inherent trend towards the mediocre and the monochrome, to welcome genius, even if to the mob it seemed like eccentricity – indeed, even if it *was* eccentricity. Mill wrote:

The initiation of all wise or noble things comes and must come from individuals; generally at first from some one individual ... In this age, the mere example of nonconformity, the mere refusal to bend the knee to custom, is itself a service.

Nick Ridley never 'bent the knee'.

He could never be intimidated into believing that what was fashionable was sound, or what was accepted was true, or what was mediocre was best. He lived by his principles, trusted his judgement and had the measure of his abilities. He was unconcerned by soundbites, unimpressed by smoothness, unmoved by pleas to fiddle or fudge the facts as he knew them to be. He dressed, smoked, ate and drank as he liked, said what he thought, did what he wanted – or more precisely did what *he* thought best.

As a result, he was often pilloried for what the critics described as his 'gaffes'. But one man's gaffe is another man's home truth. Even pearls begin with grit. And, as in his final interview as a Minister with a certain weekly journal, his blunt language could contain an insight that now seems prophetic.[1] In any case, there was no point in complaining about Nick's undiplomatic openness – and I for one never did. You rarely find

---

[1] An allusion to an interview given by Nicholas Ridley to the *Spectator* in July 1990, in which he criticized moves towards European federalism, describing them as 'a German racket'. He resigned from the Cabinet in the wake of subsequent criticism.

a man of Nicholas Ridley's guts, brains and integrity who is also made to be a political mannequin.

Opposition to Socialism

But though all these character traits – above all his rugged and robust refusal to follow the herd – made Nick Ridley a remarkable man, they would not in themselves be sufficient to constitute greatness. It was, rather, the impact which Nick had on *events* that qualified him for that accolade.

So let us take a step back for a moment, and raise our eyes to the historical horizon.

As we review the experience of this century, we can see that one vast theme encapsulates all the rest: it is that of the struggle between state domination and individual liberty.

The two totalitarian systems which we in Britain had to fight, Nazism and communism – two *socialist* tyrannies, let's remember – represented one single model. The other was represented by *our* Anglo–American liberal political culture – our Parliamentary institutions, our law, our notions of human rights and our free enterprise system based on private property.

The conflict also occurred *within* as well as between our societies. Within the command economy and the controlled society of the Evil Empire, captive nations and courageous dissidents staged their own resistance. Within our open society and free polity, left-wing parties sought – and sometimes obtained – mandates to make our countries more like the socialist model. But in doing this, the left had, of course, one large advantage. For while the rulers of the socialist dictatorships employed the full panoply of repression against their democratic opponents, we in the West had *in free debate* to demonstrate that our system was superior. So, while for the dictators ideas represented a danger, for us they represented hope. It is Nick Ridley's claim to greatness that no one in our times fought this battle of ideas more heroically, persistently and effectively than he.

He began when a very young man. And he quickly grasped that socialism was more than a matter of labels and parties, but rather in essence the extension of state control at the expense of individual freedom. This insight, so obvious to us now, was not at all so to most Conservatives then.

For there was a strong paternalistic streak in the Conservative Party when Nick and I entered politics; and it was something both of us disliked. The Tory paternalists were well-intentioned, of course; but because economics was below them – and philosophy beyond them – the main impact of Tory Governments was to legitimize and consolidate socialism.

Nick never hesitated to oppose the statism of post-war Conservatives as consistently as that of the Labour Party. From the backbenches after 1972 he aimed his barbs of unwelcome – because unanswerable – criticism at those who had fallen away from the verities of Selsdon Man[1] (and Woman). For Nick it must have seemed a thankless, hopeless, sojourn in a wilderness populated by prowling Whips and sharp-toothed Party managers. But had he and others not then stayed true to their beliefs, I am not sure that we could have later turned the Party round.

With Nick's help in the opposition years that followed we set out the philosophy which would direct the Party's policies for all the subsequent years of government – a philosophy which is no less relevant to Britain's circumstances now. Let me draw attention to just three of its features.

Restating Conservative Principles

The first and perhaps the most important insight which we Conservatives have is that government can do little that is good and much that is harmful, and so the scope of government must be kept to a minimum. Contrary to myth, most government intervention at most times in most countries is not the result of wise conclusions by enlightened men pursuing noble objectives. True, the general stated objectives may indeed seem elevated enough. And just recently we have heard proclaimed such spiritually refined objectives that it seems almost bad form to question them. But the actual intervention (or perhaps coercion would be a more accurate description) is generally the result of the ambitions of politicians, the self-interest of bureaucracies and the pressure of vested interests. And these – not the theological virtues or even the deadly sins – are what democracies must keep in mind.

When Dr Johnson remarked that patriotism was the refuge of the

---

[1] The reference is to the programme agreed by the Conservative Shadow Cabinet at Selsdon Park in January 1970, which (not altogether accurately) was believed to be one of radical right-wing, free market policies, and was ridiculed as such by Labour Prime Minister Harold Wilson in the phrase 'Selsdon Man'.

scoundrel, he was not, of course, attacking patriotism, only noting how easily base motives and shoddy arguments could be concealed in the trappings of high-mindedness. So too, though morality and religion are fine things, we should recall – to adapt Adam Smith – that in a democracy it is 'not from the benevolence' of the politician, but from the clash of his views and interests with those of his opponents that the electors are empowered to choose their country's path. As Britain should have learned, the proper reaction to any excesses of professed idealism on the left . . . is to count the spoons.

This is not, of course, an argument for weak government; it is an argument for limited government. But the vital point is that the claims made for government as a force for general improvement always turn out to be bogus.

Yet it is amazing what claims have been made in the past. For instance, after the war, the nationalization of our industries was justified as a means of safeguarding employment. It did nothing of the sort and, in spite of subsidies extracted from successful firms, the dole queues remorselessly lengthened.

Or take another example. The state effectively squeezed out private healthcare, it suppressed educational choice, it introduced welfare from the cradle to the grave and it decanted whole communities into monotonous acres of municipal housing. The planners did all this to build a utopian society of free and fair shares for all. But, on the contrary, a centralized bureaucratic system forced much of the population into a new dependency. It took a Conservative Government, with policies to which Nick Ridley made a vital contribution, to enfranchise those who had been trudging the Road to Serfdom by offering them choice and opportunities for ownership.

Or take employment laws devised to bring 'social justice' to the labour market. Trade unions were strengthened with special privileges. Employers' rights to hire and fire, or indeed to manage, were subject to a tangle of regulations. And, of course, the effect was quite the opposite of that intended – or at least of that proclaimed. Trade union leaders bullied firms into bankruptcy and workers into the closed shop, and insisted on self-defeating restrictive practices. New firms shut down. Large firms wouldn't expand. So again, slowly and painfully and against the outright opposition of those who now, it seems, welcome the reforms we made, we Conservatives withdrew the state from dominating the workplace. In doing so, we set Britain on course for economic success, bringing more firms, more wealth and more jobs.

Time after time, the disasters could have been foreseen. But ideology and vested interests obscured clear thought. So powerful is the temptation of politicians to step in – and so manifold are the excuses offered for their doing so – that fighting big government is the hardest task on earth.

The second principle we promoted in those days of opposition was the fundamental importance of the rule of law. The rule of law, I should add as a barrister, is something other than the rule of lawyers. And, may I say with the greatest of respect, nor is it the rule of judges.[1] Our great judges have certainly at times proved wise and heroic guardians of our rights. But it is for Parliament to make the laws which shape our lives.

What distinguishes *our* understanding of law is that it should be made by the competent, sovereign authority, that it should apply to all, including government, and that it should be administered impartially by an independent judiciary. In the 1970s it was the manipulation of law to appease the unions and left-wing interests that was so shocking. In the eighties it was the contrast with the Soviet and East European totalitarian systems, based on state *diktat* and *nomenklatura* privilege, which made us appreciate anew the importance of a true rule of law. Now, in the nineties, it is the encroachment of an alien system of Community law that gives most cause for anxiety. Authority is being drained away from our national democratic and judicial institutions towards a bureaucratic entity that increasingly speaks in the tones of a new imperial power. This must be halted – indeed reversed.

The third argument we advanced back in the 1970s was about the role of private property. Of all the rights which constitute what we call 'liberty', the right to own property, though one of the more prosaic, is arguably that of greatest practical importance. Owning property gives a man independence against overweening government. Property ownership has also a more mysterious, but no less real, psychological effect: looking after what one owns provides a training in responsible citizenship. The saints of old often renounced their property, so as to break all attachments and rise above the world. But for most of us, the ties of property lock *us* into duties we might otherwise shirk: to continue the metaphor, they stop us dropping out.

So, encouraging people to acquire property and savings was much

---

[1] There had at the time been a good deal of controversy about some judges' public pronouncements which were widely considered to be excessively 'political'.

more than an economic programme. It was a programme to end what I termed a 'one-generation society', and to put in its place a capital-owning democracy.

Britain in the 1980s

What then happened is history – but since history sometimes undergoes a little rewriting, perhaps I'd better remind you of how it turned out.

In the 1980s we cut back the government deficit and we repaid debt. We sharply cut income tax at both the basic and the higher rates. And to do these things, we steadily reduced public spending as a share of the national income. We reformed trade union law, and removed controls and unnecessary regulations. We created a virtuous circle: by reining back government we allowed more room for the private sector, and so the private sector generated more growth, which again allowed sound finances and low taxes.

Productivity increased. New firms started up. New jobs were created. Living standards rose. And with privatized firms making contributions to the Exchequer in place of nationalized ones draining it, there was more available to improve public services. In 1979 nationalized industries were losing £50 million a week; now privatized companies contribute £60 million a week to the Exchequer in Corporation Tax.

Yes, there were mistakes. Inflation started up again in the last years. And interest rates had to rise to beat it – which they did – with all the unpleasant consequences that brought. And the Community Charge – I still call it that, because I like the Poles very much and have never dreamt of taxing them[1] – the Community Charge in its first year led to high bills which discredited an excellent system.

But the important point is that the *overall* strategy we pursued in the 1980s worked precisely as it was meant to. And it transformed the reality and the reputation of Britain. Moreover, it *was* a strategy. It was not a set of policies cobbled together from minute to minute, begged, borrowed or stolen from other people. It was successful because it was based on clear, firmly-held principles which were themselves based on a right understanding of politics, economics and above all human nature.

This strategy has continued in the 1990s. Our Prime Minister has shown persistence, imagination and skill in taking it forward.

[1] A pun on the Poll Tax, as the Community Charge was popularly known.

Facts never do, of course, 'speak for themselves'. We politicians have to perform this service for them. So let me again remind you:

– that unemployment in Britain is lower than in any other major European country;

– that real take-home pay has increased at all levels of earnings since 1979;

– that there are a million more small firms than when we took office;

– that sixteen of the twenty-five most profitable companies in Europe are British;

– and that foreign investment in this country has never been higher.

Don't Let Labour Ruin It

As Prime Minister, I was never much interested in 'feel-good' or even feel-bad factors. I believed that if the reality was sound, the reaction would ultimately be favourable. So we just got on with the job. But if the British people do *not* 'feel good' about the economy today, I can only warn them that they will feel distinctly worse if they wake up after polling day to discover they've put in a Labour Government. Some slogans run and run: so let me repeat – Don't Let Labour Ruin It![1]

Yet, would 'Labour ruin it'? Apparently not, if you believe some people. If you'll forgive the medley of metaphors, the light has dawned, the ground has shifted and whole lexicons of indigestible words – like socialism, equality and public ownership – have been eaten. I warmly welcome the fact that the Labour Party professes, after losing four elections, to have come to terms with the 1980s. If true, that is a good start. And I wouldn't rule out, after four *more* lost elections, the Labour Party coming to terms with the nineties either. Indeed, I hope they gain the opportunity to do so.

It is, of course, flattering to learn that we are all Thatcherites now. In fact, the road to Damascus has never been more congested. But it's not really very important whether New Labour is sincere in seeing the errors of Old Labour. What is important is that they don't – indeed they can't – understand *why* the policies of the 1980s worked. And because they don't understand the philosophy behind them, they could

[1] The Conservative slogan at the 1959 general election – when Margaret Thatcher was first elected as MP for Finchley – was: "Life's better with the Conservatives, don't let Labour ruin it.'

not in the hurly-burly of government put the right policies into practice. They would be blown off course. And the reefs of interventionism are no less dangerous, and the sirens of financial profligacy no less alluring, than they were in the past.

Of course, the *ways* in which this would happen are different now – but happen it surely would. And to understand – and explain – why *that* is so, we have to appreciate the fact that socialism is not dead; it is not even asleep; it is visibly stirring. In fact, we may well be fast approaching one of those rare occasions in our affairs when a small deviation to right or left brings huge rewards or the gravest dangers.

Socialism Now – And Why it is Still a Threat

Communism and socialism were always beset by fundamental, inherent weaknesses, which became more evident as time went by. Their system failed to mobilize talent and create wealth, failed to conform to the basic human impulses to provide for one's family and to express one's nationhood, and so ultimately failed to engage the loyalties of the system's subjects. From quite early on, communism could only be sustained in power by force and by the vested interests of the elite. And when faced with a resurgent capitalist West it crumbled. All that is true. But it is not the whole truth.

Socialism in the broader sense – that is, not as defined by Clause 4 of the old Labour Party Constitution[1] or the dogma of Marx, but as a system of pervasive state control and influence over people's lives – that socialism corresponds to an ever-present weakness in human nature.

Idleness, selfishness, fecklessness, envy and irresponsibility are the vices upon which socialism in any form flourishes and which it in turn encourages. But socialism's devilishly clever tactic is to play up to all these human failings, while making those who practise them feel good about it.

It is still happening. Whenever, as now, Britain enjoys the benefits of a booming economy, the left begins complaining about the social perils

---

[1] Clause 4 of the old (since amended) Labour Party Constitution promised '. . . to secure for the workers by hand or by brain the full fruits of their industry . . . *upon the basis of the common ownership of the means of production, distribution and exchange*'. (Emphasis added.)

of individualism and greed, attributing any number of crimes and moral deficiencies to the same capitalism they ultimately expect to pay for all their social planning.

The Leader of the Labour Party decries (I quote) 'rampant individualism, the atomization and division of society, the narrow self-interest that characterized the 1980s and helped to fracture our society'[1] – and all sorts of empty heads nod in acquiescence.

But if people thought a little more about it, they would become very angry indeed. For the implication is that because someone exercises his talents to improve his position, sends his children to the best school he can afford, provides for his old age from savings and leaves something worthwhile for the next generation, he is a party to 'rampant individualism', and so in some unspecified way responsible for how *someone else* misuses his time or abuses his neighbours. Only, it is implied, a combination of a nanny state and preaching politicians will keep the majority on the straight and narrow paths of the 'decent society'.

This is not just arrogant. It is absurd.

Do these left-wing politicians really live in the same world as the rest of us? Crime and violence are not the result of the great majority of people being free: they are the result of a small minority of wicked men and women abusing their freedom.

Do they seriously believe that it is 'rampant individualism' that led to the growth of the dependency culture, of a class of people who never work, and whose children may never work, who are habituated to a life on welfare, and whose poverty is not material but behavioural? No: welfare dependence is the classic manifestation of a still-too-socialist society.

And do these New Labour politicians understand nothing of the communist system whose legacy continues to blight Eastern Europe and Russia? In that socialist system there was plenty of individualism of a sort; and 'rampant' at that: for people's whole lives were taken up in attempts to cheat the system, and indeed each other. There will always be individualism as long as there are individuals: but in a free society and a free economy individualism works to the general good – in a socialist society and a controlled economy it works against it.

But we Conservatives must never forget that for large numbers of people real freedom is an intimidating prospect. The apparent security

---

[1] Opposition Leader Tony Blair had written an article in *The Times* (4 November 1996) entitled 'Towards a Decent, Responsible Society' in which this passage occurs.

of state provision is particularly attractive for those doubtful of their own abilities. This is not just a material, but a cultural and indeed a moral problem. And it is one that only conservative believers in the system of liberty *for its own sake* are truly able to confront.

Yesterday's socialism, characterized by militant trade unionism and burdensome state-owned industries, has, in our Western countries at least, almost certainly gone for good. But in the form of a continuing tendency to intervene in people's lives for ends which are quite extraneous to the state's proper functions it is very much present.

Socialism and Political Correctness

It has, for example, resurfaced in the language and programmes of 'group rights'. The process has gone furthest in the United States: though I suspect that if Britain were so foolish as to elect a Labour Government we could quickly catch up.

In America, such affirmative action programmes have not only become a heavy burden on employers of all kinds; by increasing the resentment of the majority against minorities they have precisely the opposite effect to that intended.

Closely linked to this approach is the obsessive political correctness that imperils serious scholarship in so many American universities and colleges. Concepts like truth and falsehood, beauty and ugliness, civilization and barbarism have been deconstructed to give way to judgements based on ideology. The results would be funny, if the consequences were not so serious.

Whole shelf-loads of classics written by what they call 'DWEMs' – dead white European males – are nowadays consigned to 'the dustbin of [whatever these people now call] history'.

The great Milton is now, in the words of a Stanford University English Professor, regarded as 'an ass [and] . . . a sexist pig'. Shakespeare is still on the syllabus of Duke University – but only, in the words of a Professor, 'to illuminate the way seventeenth-century society mistreated women, the working class, and minorities'.

All this can be called many things – collectivism, relativism, multiculturalism – or just good old-fashioned stupidity. But it also provides a new ideological basis for socialism. For the upside-down world of political correctness is one in which strategies of social control – the enduring objective of the left – are given free rein. Ordinary, established individual rights – rights of property, or free speech, or the right to choose one's child's education – are crushed by the imposition of collective rights. And the ultimate adjudicator is always the state.

Stakeholding

'It couldn't happen here,' you may say. But if the Labour Party have their way, it could. For it is precisely this assertion of artificial group rights at the expense of individual freedom that lies at the heart of the Labour Leader's idea of 'stakeholding'.[1] Because the politics of overt confiscation and control are out of fashion, left-wing intellectuals, whose verbal facility has always matched their practical ineptitude, have devised this new way of undermining capitalism. Shareholders – those who own a business – and managers – those the owners appoint to run it – would be subject to pressure from an array of politically correct pressure groups and trade unions which would be given a 'stake' in the business. Businesses would thus be transformed from maximizers of profit into agents of socialism.

Labour's stakeholding economy may sound comfortingly similar to the Conservative vision of a property-owning democracy. In fact, the two are diametrically opposed. For those wielding power under Labour's plans would not be individual men and women as owners and customers: they would be all those busybody representatives of left-wing causes and special interests that now enjoy in New-Labour-speak the vague but venerable title of 'the community'.

Shackling British businesses in this way – and imposing a minimum wage to boot – is precisely what our thriving economy does *not* need. And those tycoons who earned their millions in Tory Britain, but are currently attracted to New Labour, may become rapidly less cheerful if they experience stakeholding in practice.

---

[1] Tony Blair first advocated a 'stakeholding economy' in a much-trailed speech in Singapore on 8 January 1996. The concept derives from the work of a number of left-wing intellectuals, like Will Hutton and Charles Handy.

Socialism and Europe

These trends towards more intervention would, of course, rapidly accelerate if Britain were to move closer to the European model of the corporate state. Again, as with socialism, there is a problem of definition: it is not of course fascist corporatism, any more than Marxist socialism, which is the threat. Rather, it is a creeping but persistent, and possibly irreversible, shift towards a planned economy and a controlled society.

The Social Chapter, from which our Prime Minister wisely gained us an exemption, but which the Opposition Leader would accept, is the most obvious example. We know already – not least from the saga of the forty-eight-hour working-week directive[1] – how the European Commission and the European Court regard their mandate of achieving closer European integration by undermining national sovereignty. Accepting the Social Chapter would give them one more major opportunity to tie up our successful businesses with regulation in order to prevent them competing successfully with the over-regulated firms of Continental Europe. And have no doubt: if *they* succeed in imposing *their* higher-cost industrial system here, *we* will experience *their* high unemployment.

Attention has recently focused upon the huge and quite possibly unsustainable burden of pensions which countries like France and Germany face because of past imprudence worsened by present demography – burdens which doubtless under any single currency regime they would generously seek to share with us. But we should really not be surprised as each new day seems to bring with it some new scandal or gross injustice or absurd folly for which Europe is responsible.

Instead of gazing into the crystal ball to learn about the new European politics, we only need consider Belgium – where proportional representation ensures constant coalitions of the same political class, where Parliamentary democracy has been effectively suspended, where confidence in the integrity of honest government and justice has collapsed, and where separate national groups squabble endlessly within a single state that no one respects.

[1] The European Court had recently found against the British Government in the matter of the European Commission's introduction of a directive imposing a forty-eight-hour working week, introduced under cover of European health and safety provisions.

These Continental European countries' ideas, traditions and history are fundamentally different from our own. The kind of liberal individualism which J.S. Mill's *On Liberty* describes, let alone the free economy of Adam Smith's *Wealth of Nations*,[1] never took root there. The battles between the European left and right were essentially between different brands of collectivism, and they largely remain so. Moreover, in many cases there are deep-rooted tendencies toward bureaucracy, authoritarianism and corrupt abuse of power. Indeed, European politicians, dividing their time between courts, jails and debating chambers, have recently managed to give a whole new meaning to the expression 'conviction politics'.

But the European Union is not the only forum in which socialism in new, drab guises is evident. And here again we need to stand back a little and reflect on the significance of that titanic global clash of systems we call the Cold War.

Socialism in the Post-Cold War World

On this subject the revisionists have been much at work. Those who once warned of the dire consequences of daring to stand up to the Soviets can now be found explaining that the Kremlin was never in any case more than a zoo for paper tigers.

The significant worry for us now, however, is that because the revisionists minimize the importance of the struggle between freedom and socialism, they fail to grasp the fact that so much of the defeated system is still in place.

The diplomats and the members of that nebulous but ubiquitous 'international community' never cease to warn against *nationalism* as a threat to peace and security. But one man's nationalism is another man's patriotism. And, oddly, the new internationalists rarely consider that without British patriotism, or French patriotism, or American patriotism, there would be no national armies to enforce international justice in the first place. Far better if the commentators worried instead about what the unstable and dangerous regimes of the world have most in common, which is not nationalism but various guises of *socialism*.

---

[1] Adam Smith's *Inquiry into the Nature and Causes of the Wealth of Nations* (1776) transformed economic thinking, and remains one of the most influential explanations of the beneficial effects of the free market.

Our victory in the Cold War, unlike our victory in the Second World War, was not followed by occupation of enemy territory and the purging of those who had been the ideological opponents of freedom. In fact, only the Czechs practised this process of lustration against senior Party members; and perhaps it is significant that the Czechs have since gone furthest in creating the structures of liberty.

Generally, though, yesterday's communists have crept back into power, or never even left it; and not just political power either – the old *nomenklatura* has exploited its connections to grow rich under the new pseudo-capitalism. As a result, the world is full of seedy regimes and unsettled disputes that the socialist elites have a powerful interest in continuing.

We delude ourselves if we imagine that most of the former communist countries are steadily moving in the direction of our Western system. Rather they are, particularly in the former Soviet Union, locked into conditions that resemble more closely rule by robber barons than liberal democracy. Whether in Russia or in China or in the former Yugoslavia, the one thing that most of the problem states of the world have in common is that they are largely in the hands of ex-, and not always 'ex-', communists.

Thankfully, in recent months there is some movement in the other direction, as the socialist regimes find their failures catching up with them: in the Baltics and Balkans, non-socialist Governments have been or should soon be installed in Lithuania, Romania and Bulgaria. But what a rich and terrible irony that, forty years on from the crushing of Hungary by Russian tanks, the present Prime Minister of that country is a communist who sided with the invader against his own people. And Hungary itself is still excluded from NATO because of Western feebleness in face of Russian threats. There could be no greater symbolic demonstration of how we in the West failed to carry through to its conclusion our crusade for freedom. We now need Western leaders untainted with socialism who will raise the standard for liberty – because they actually believe in it.

The Watershed

Mr Chairman, the beginning of the next millennium may coincide with a real historical watershed – and socialism remains the real obstacle to crossing it successfully. Britain needs, more than ever before, a Government which understands, believes in and practises the politics and economics of liberty.

For three great choices face us.

First, we have to choose whether we in Britain are prepared to go further in reducing public spending and taxation so as to join the most successful world economies – or accept that half or more of our national income be taken by a paternalist state.

Secondly, we have to choose whether we are going to enjoy our freedom to trade as and where our interests demand, maximizing the advantages which the economic reforms of the 1980s have given us – or whether we accept a new model of socialism, imposed by the bureaucratic superstate towards which the core countries of the European Union now seem irrevocably headed.

Thirdly, we have to choose whether we are going to strive for a truly free – which means a socialist-free – international order – or surrender the future of the post-Cold War world to socialist regimes that discredit democracy by battening on the corruption and disorder which communism left behind.

Three choices, but all adding up to one choice – the age-old choice – between the rugged grandeur of liberty and the ignoble ease of dependence. And, yes, that *is* a moral choice.

Let it be said of us – as we with pride and gratitude can say of Nick Ridley – that we too kept faith with freedom.

Index